Windows® Small Business Server 2011

Administrator's Companion

Charlie Russel
Sharon Crawford

Windows® Small Business Server 2011

Administrator's Companion

Charlie Russel
Sharon Crawford

Published with the authorization of Microsoft Corporation by:
O'Reilly Media, Inc.
1005 Gravenstein Highway North
Sebastopol, California 95472

ISBN: 978-0-7356-4911-8

1 2 3 4 5 6 7 8 9 TG 6 5 4 3 2 1

Printed and bound in Canada.

Microsoft Press books are available through booksellers and distributors worldwide.
If you need support related to this book, email Microsoft Press Book Support at
mspinput@microsoft.com. Please tell us what you think of this book at *http://www.
microsoft.com/learning/booksurvey.*

Microsoft and the trademarks listed at *http://www.microsoft.com/about/legal/en/
us/IntellectualProperty/Trademarks/EN-US.aspx* are trademarks of the Microsoft
group of companies. All other marks are property of their respective owners.

The example companies, organizations, products, domain names, email addresses,
logos, people, places, and events depicted herein are fictitious. No association
with any real company, organization, product, domain name, email address, logo,
person, place, or event is intended or should be inferred.

This book expresses the author's views and opinions. The information contained
in this book is provided without any express, statutory, or implied warranties.
Neither the authors, O'Reilly Media, Inc., Microsoft Corporation, nor its resellers,
or distributors will be held liable for any damages caused or alleged to be caused
either directly or indirectly by this book.

Acquisitions Editor: Ken Jones
Developmental Editors: Laura Sackerman and Ken Jones
Production Editor: Teresa Elsey
Proofreader: Nancy Sixsmith
Compositor: Ron Bilodeau
Technical Reviewer: Andrew Edney
Copyeditor: Roger LeBlanc
Indexer: Angela Howard
Cover Design: Twist Creative • Seattle
Cover Composition: Karen Montgomery
Illustrator: Robert Romano

For Dana Epp, always a mensch

Contents at a Glance

Contents

PART VI   **MAINTENANCE AND TROUBLESHOOTING**

Chapter 27   **Performance Monitoring**   **711**

Introduction

If you run a small business, you don't need us to tell you that the highly competitive marketplace, unpredictable economic cycles, time pressures, and technological demands are constantly exerting pressure on your bottom line.

Your business needs the same technologies that large companies do. You need the ability to share information with customers, partners, and employees. You have the same worries about spam, malware, and security. And you have the same need to manage resources and employee access to those resources.

The major difference is you probably don't have the luxury of an in-house IT staff.

Windows Small Business Server (SBS) 2011 allows small businesses to operate at the same technology level as much larger organizations, but without the added costs of maintaining a network administration department.

Windows Small Business Server 2011 Administrator's Companion is a reference, assistant, and coach for the busy network administrator, whether the administrator is on the scene or accessing the network from another location.

Conventions

Even though Windows Small Business Server 2011 has automated many, many of the tasks associated with configuring and securing a network, this book is required when you want to do something slightly out of the ordinary—or when you need additional understanding of what a wizard is doing.

Look for book elements such as these:

 Under the Hood Because wizards are so efficient at what they do, it can be very difficult to know what's going on in the background. Sidebars titled "Under the Hood" describe the technical operations being performed by the wizard. These sidebars also include methodological information to help you understand Windows Small Business Server.

 Real World Everyone can benefit from the experiences of others. "Real World" sidebars contain elaboration on a particular theme or background based on the adventures of other users of Windows Small Business Server.

NOTE Notes include tips as well as alternative ways to perform a task or information that needs to be highlighted.

IMPORTANT Information marked Important shouldn't be skipped. (That's why these elements are called Important.) Here you'll find security notes, cautions, and warnings to keep you and your network out of trouble.

What's in This Book

Windows Small Business Server 2011 Administrator's Companion is divided into seven parts. The first four parts roughly correspond to the developmental phases of a Windows Small Business Server network. Part V deals with Premium Add-on features, and Part VI covers maintenance and troubleshooting. The last part is made up of appendices with helpful information.

Part I, Preparation and Planning   Planning and preparation are the *sine qua non* for any kind of network. It comes down to the old saying, "If you don't have the time to do it right, how will you find the time to do it over?" Chapters 1 through 4 are all about doing it right the first time.

Part II, Installation and Setup   Chapters 5 through 8 take you through the process of installing Windows Small Business Server and performing initial configurations using the Getting Started Tasks. This section includes helpful chapters on configuring Windows SBS virtualization and migrating from Windows SBS 2003.

Part III, Performing the Basic Tasks   Chapters 9 through 16 cover the day-to-day tasks in running a network: configuring disks, setting up user accounts, arranging the sharing of information among users, adding and removing computers and printers, managing software updates, and backing up and restoring data.

Part IV, Performing Advanced Tasks   Chapters 17 through 23 provide insight and information about managing email, connectivity technologies, and using Group Policy. In this part, you'll also find chapters about setting up and managing a SharePoint site.

Part V, Premium Edition Features   Chapters 24 through 26 address features found the in Windows SBS 2008 Premium Add-on. These chapters are about installing a second server, installing Microsoft SQL Server, and adding terminal servers to your network.

Part VI, Maintenance and Troubleshooting   Chapter 27 covers the extensive library of monitoring tools available in Windows Small Business Server, and Chapter 28 is all about how you save your business, your network, and yourself in the face of the many varieties of disaster that can afflict networks.

Part VII, Appendices   The final part consists of appendices with supplemental information. This includes an introduction to networking, instructions for automating installation, and a list of resources for the users of Windows SBS 2011.

About the Companion Web Content

The companion content for this book contains Windows PowerShell scripts for common adminstrative tasks.

These files can be downloaded from the web at:

http://go.microsoft.com/FWLink/?Linkid=217073

Full documentation of the contents and structure of the companion files can be found in the Readme.txt file.

For instructions on accessing the online edition of this book, see "How to Access Your Online Edition Hosted by Safari."

How to Access Your Online Edition
Hosted by Safari

The voucher bound in to the back of this book gives you access to an online edition of the book. (You can also download the online edition of the book to your own computer; see the next section.)

To access your online edition, do the following:

1. Locate your voucher inside the back cover, and scratch off the metallic foil to reveal your access code.

2. Go to *http://microsoftpress.oreilly.com/safarienabled*.

3. Enter your 24-character access code in the Coupon Code field under Step 1.

Step **1**

Coupon Code: | 95QX-TEZQ-MHK2-F8QZ-N1SR |

CONFIRM COUPON

(Please note that the access code in this image is for illustration purposes only.)

4. Click the CONFIRM COUPON button.

   A message will appear to let you know that the code was entered correctly. If the code was not entered correctly, you will be prompted to re-enter the code.

5. In this step, you'll be asked whether you're a new or existing user of Safari Books Online. Proceed either with Step 5A or Step 5B.

   5A. If you already have a Safari account, click the EXISTING USER – SIGN IN button under Step 2.

   5B. If you are a new user, click the NEW USER – FREE ACCOUNT button under Step 2.

   - You'll be taken to the "Register a New Account" page.
   - This will require filling out a registration form and accepting an End User Agreement.
   - When complete, click the CONTINUE button.

6. On the Coupon Confirmation page, click the My Safari button.

7. On the My Safari page, look at the Bookshelf area and click the title of the book you want to access.

How to Download the Online Edition to Your Computer

In addition to reading the online edition of this book, you can also download it to your computer. First, follow the steps in the preceding section. After Step 7, do the following:

1. On the page that appears after Step 7 in the previous section, click the Extras tab.

2. Find "Download the complete PDF of this book," and click the book title.

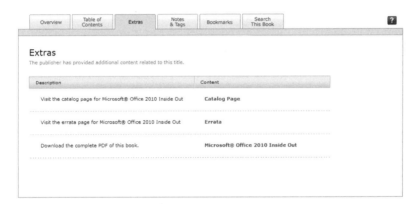

A new browser window or tab will open, followed by the File Download dialog box.

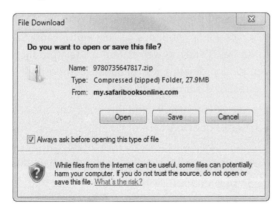

3. Click Save.

4. Choose Desktop and click Save.

5. Locate the .zip file on your desktop. Right-click the file, click Extract All, and then follow the instructions.

NOTE If you have a problem with your voucher or access code, please contact *mspbooksupport@oreilly.com*, or call 800-889-8969, where you'll reach O'Reilly Media, the distributor of Microsoft Press books.

Acknowledgments

As most people know, the creation of a book is a collaborative process. The ink-stained wretches who do the actual writing are only part of a large and multi-talented team.

First, thanks to the numerous people at Microsoft who were of great assistance.

Kevin Beares helped us many times in ways from small to very large.

Thanks to Sean Daniels of the SBS product group for more things than we can remember. Sean was the first call whenever we needed something beyond the ordinary.

Thanks to Jonas Svensson for being responsive and effective when we needed builds and resources.

And much gratitude to the entire SBS Product Group for giving us a great product and for pulling out all the stops to get us what we needed. They really went above and beyond.

Thanks to Greg Starks of Hewlett-Packard for his support of the SMB community, and in particular his support of our HP server when we needed it.

Of course, the people at Microsoft Press are the ones that really made the book possible. In particular senior editor Ken Jones, project editor Laura Sackerman, and technical editor Andrew Edney, as well as Teresa Elsey (production editor), Sumita Mukherji (vendor coordinator), Ron Bilodeau (compositor), Rob Romano (illustrator), and the rest of the production team.

We owe a true debt to Roger LeBlanc, who edited this book with a knowing and careful hand. It's a much better book because of his efforts.

Additional and sincere thanks to Richard Siddaway for his blog post on Windows Server Backup and the PowerShell Snap-in for it. And to Sean Wallbridge, SharePoint MVP, whose help in sorting through the changes in how SharePoint Foundation 2010 behaved with Web Parts was indispensable.

Errata

We have made every effort to ensure the accuracy of this book and its companion content. If you do find an error, please report it on our Microsoft Press site at oreilly.com:

1. Go to *http://microsoftpress.oreilly.com*.
2. In the Search box, enter the book's ISBN or title.
3. Select your book from the search results.
4. On your book's catalog page, under the cover image, you will see a list of links.
5. Click View/Submit Errata.

You will find additional information and services for your book on its catalog page. If you need additional support, please email Microsoft Press Book Support at msinput@microsoft.com.

Please note that product support for Microsoft software is not offered through the addresses above.

We Want to Hear from You

At Microsoft Press, your satisfaction is our top priority and your feedback our most valuable asset. Please tell us what you think of this book at:

http://www.microsoft.com/learning/booksurvey

The survey is short, and we read every one of your comments and ideas. Thanks in advance for your input!

Stay in Touch

Let us keep the conversation going! We are on Twitter:

http://twitter.com/Microsoft

PART I

Preparation and Planning

## CHAPTER 1

Introducing Windows Small Business Server 2011

There's an oft-repeated story that the head of the U.S. Patent Office in 1899 declared that the office should be closed because "Everything that can be invented has been invented." Alas for the legend, Charles H. Duell never said anything of the kind. Duell was, in fact, a great believer in the creativity of inventors. He also knew that evolutionary change was every bit as valuable as revolutionary change.

In our time, the evolution of Microsoft Windows Small Business Server from its inception to the latest version in 2011 has been an orderly progression of improvements both large and small—and the total distance covered is immense.

Windows Small Business Server Editions

Windows Small Business Server is available in two editions: Standard and Essentials. The Standard edition is the version covered in this book. It's the ideal solution for small businesses with up to 75 users.

> **NOTE** Windows Small Business Server Essentials is a new, first-server solution for small businesses (up to 25 users) that can seamlessly integrate into online services such as Microsoft Office 365, cloud backup solutions, and cloud management solutions. It is expected to be released in the first half of 2011.

Also available is the Windows Small Business Server Premium Add-on, which includes a second Windows Server 2008 R2 license and Microsoft SQL Server 2008 R2 technologies.

What's New and Improved

Probably the best new "feature" in Windows SBS 2011 is that it's built on Windows Server 2008 R2. You get all the advantages of Windows Server 2011—high levels of security and control over your network, sophisticated report and management tools, and enhanced access to email, the Internet, and business applications—all in a single, integrated, low-maintenance package. In addition to great hardware and scaling features and easier virtualization, you'll also have

- A straightforward interface designed for small businesses
- An easier installation and migration process
- Remote Access for simple access almost anywhere
- A health-monitoring infrastructure that analyzes both server and client well-being

64-Bit Architecture

The major shift for Windows SBS Server from 2003 to 2008 was from 32-bit architecture to 64-bit. The 64-bit architecture continues in SBS 2011. When Microsoft Exchange Server 2007 was released in a 64-bit version only, the shift was inevitable. It's also a desirable shift. The 32-bit version of Windows was rapidly coming up against its own limitations.

A 32-bit operating system is limited to 4 gigabytes (GB) of RAM (random access memory). A 64-bit operating system can have up to 32 GB of RAM. That, in and of itself, is a significant difference. But the real difference is in the area of address space. Vastly increased amounts of address space help minimize the time spent swapping processes in and out of memory by storing more of those processes in RAM rather than on the hard disk. This, in turn, can increase overall program performance.

A 32-bit computer works very well for most programs, however. For example, spreadsheet programs, web browsers, and word-processing programs will run at about the same speed on either a 32-bit or 64-bit computer. However, when you're running a server and hosting multiple clients, a mail server, and shared applications and files, a 64-bit computer is much preferred.

For more on how 64-bit architecture works, see Chapter 2, "Understanding 64-Bit Windows."

SBS Console

When you install Windows SBS 2011, you'll immediately notice that the interface includes SBS Console (shown in Figure 1-1), a central organizational point from which you can perform many administrative tasks associated with Windows SBS.

FIGURE 1-1 The Windows SBS Standard Console

NOTE A shortcut to the console is automatically placed on the server desktop.

From Users And Groups at the top of the console window, you can add users and groups as well as configure these objects. Similarly, click Network to add or remove computers, manage devices such as printers, and configure your Internet connection and other networking features.

Other areas of the console connect you to the tools for shared folders, backup, report generation, and security. Chapter 17, "Windows SBS Console vs. Server Manager," provides more information on the use of SBS Console.

Remote Web Access

Formerly known as Remote Web Workplace (RWW), the new Remote Web Access (RWA) has many pluses, a few of which are

- The ability to remotely access shared folders
- Secure, anywhere access to your files and documents through any common web browser
- The ability to connect to the PCs in your network and even run applications from virtually any location
- A new interface that administrators can reorganize without programming knowledge
- Full Outlook Web Access (OWA) support

Chapter 20, "Managing Remote Access," covers the new features and uses of Remote Web Access.

Installation and Migration

Whether you're upgrading or installing a new server, SBS 2011 Standard makes it simple. In addition to the familiar Windows interface, you'll also get

- A much simplified setup procedure with complete guidance for configuring the server, and the Internet and domain configuration for each connected PC
- The ability to let users connect their own PC—without requiring an administrator
- Enhanced source server validation tools for better preparation for migration
- Automatic administration of your Internet domain name

Installation details are in Chapter 5, "Installing Small Business Server 2011." The procedures for migration are in Chapter 7, "Migrating to Windows Small Business Server 2011 Standard."

Data Protection

Everyone agrees that the easiest way to protect your data is to back it up at frequent intervals. SBS 2011 makes this chore a good deal easier by conducting automatic, daily backups of every computer and server on the network.

Restoration of individual files, folders, or an entire computer is fairly easily done using uncomplicated disaster recovery tools.

The full story on setting up and using backup is found in Chapter 16, "Configuring Backup."

Exchange Server 2010 SP1

SBS 2011 Standard features the powerful new Microsoft Exchange Server 2010 SP1. With this upgrade from Exchange Server 2007, you'll have

- The enhanced Outlook Web Access (OWA), which mirrors Microsoft Office Outlook more closely than ever
- The improved Exchange Management Console for a single place to manage all your email tasks
- Automatic detection and repair of corrupted mailboxes and databases
- New features that help users organize their inboxes efficiently
- The ability to set retention policies and tags through a straightforward interface, and deployment options for roles and features
- New archiving options, such as defining when email data expires, deployment rules, and how to provision personal archives to a different database
- New transport security rules to protect sensitive business information

"Configuring and Managing Email," Chapter 18, covers Exchange Server 2010 SP1 and all aspects of email.

SharePoint Foundation Services 2010

SBS 2011 Standard features Microsoft SharePoint Foundation Services 2010—the newest version of Microsoft Windows SharePoint Services—with features and capabilities that help you collaborate securely online—from any location. You'll have

- An improved Remote Web Access (formally Remote Web Workplace) that allows you to share internal documents, harmonize calendars, manage issues, and participate in discussions—no matter where you are
- The ability to consolidate intranet sites into a single on-premises location
- Quick methods for producing secure and simple solutions for your specific needs
- Built-in monitoring, alerts, and administrative tools for SharePoint

Using SharePoint is covered in Chapter 23, "Customizing a SharePoint Site."

Small Business Server 2011 Premium Add-on

When you have limited IT resources but still need to run a large number of applications, the Windows Small Business Server 2011 Premium Add-on can save the day. The Premium Add-on contains

- An additional license for Windows Server 2008 R2 Standard, which allows you to deploy another server on your Windows SBS 2011 network.

- Microsoft SQL Server 2008 R2 for Small Business, which includes a range of features that can help organizations make the most of their information with better tools for development, manageability, business intelligence, and data warehousing. SQL Server 2008 R2 for Small Business has the same capabilities as SQL Server 2008 R2 Standard; however, it is available to use only in the SBS 2011 environment.

An additional server adds great flexibility to a Small Business Server network, including the potential for a second domain controller. An additional server can be used for multiple business applications, remote desktop services, or virtualization.

Hardware Requirements

The hardware requirements for Windows SBS Server are detailed in Tables 1-1 and 1-2. Actual requirements can vary based on your system configuration and the applications and features you need to use. Processor performance is dependent on not only the clock frequency of the processor, but also the number of cores and the size of the processor cache.

As always, disk space requirements for the system partition are approximate. Additional available hard-disk space might be required if you are installing over a network.

TABLE 1-1 Hardware requirements for Windows Small Business Server 2011 Standard

HARDWARE	MINIMUM REQUIREMENT
Processor	Quad core 2 GHz 64-bit (x64) or faster; 1 socket (4 sockets maximum)
Physical memory (RAM)	8 GB minimum
	10 GB recommended minimum (32 GB maximum)
Storage capacity	120 GB
DVD ROM drive	DVD ROM drive
Network adapter	One 10/100 Ethernet adapter
Monitor and video adapter	Super VGA (SVGA) monitor and video adapter with 1024 x 768 or higher resolution

HARDWARE	MINIMUM REQUIREMENT
Network devices	A router or firewall device that supports IPv4 NAT
Internet connection	Windows SBS 2011 Standard requires that you connect the server to the Internet.

These minimums are definitely minimal—particularly the minimum 8 GB of physical memory. Even on a small network, 10 GB is the least amount of RAM you'll need if your users are to be reasonably content.

TABLE 1-2 Hardware requirements for Premium Add-On server license

COMPONENT	REQUIREMENT
Processor	Minimum: Single processor with 1.4 GHz (x64 processor) or 1.3 GHz (Dual Core)
Memory	Minimum: 512 MB RAM Maximum: 32 GB
Disk Space Requirements	Minimum: 32 GB or greater
Display	Super VGA (800 × 600) or higher resolution monitor
Other	DVD Drive, Keyboard, and Microsoft Mouse (or compatible pointing device), and Internet access (fees may apply)

Summary

In this chapter we covered some—far from all—of the high points in Windows Small Business Server 2011. In the next chapter, you start the process of developing and maintaining a high-performing network.

## CHAPTER 2

Understanding 64-Bit Windows

If you've been running Microsoft Windows Small Business Server (SBS) 2008, you've already made the change to 64-bit Windows when you migrated to SBS 2008. But for a lot of folks still running SBS 2003, the move to Windows Small Business Server 2011 Standard (SBS 2011) is a leap into a whole new world of 64-bit computing.

SBS 2011 is a complete architectural change from SBS 2003—it is built on the 64-bit version of Windows Server 2008 R2. This is a radical change for those who have been using only 32-bit Windows. Gone are the memory constraints inherent in 32-bit Windows, and with them some of the limitations inherent in SBS.

In this chapter, we'll cover some underlying reasons for the change to 64-bit, how it affects what you can (and can't) do with SBS 2011, and how this change will also affect the clients on your SBS network.

 REAL WORLD Overcoming the Fear Factor

We've been running 64-bit Windows—first as Windows XP Professional x64 Edition and now with Windows 7 and Windows Server 2008 R2—since early in 2005, and we have to admit, it was a bit of a struggle early on. Drivers were the biggest issue because all drivers had to be rewritten for 64-bit. But careful selection of hardware solved that issue, and we were up and running.

What we quickly figured out was that pretty much all our programs worked—just as we expected them to. They were just as fast (in some cases, a bit faster), and the few things that didn't work were predictable and expected. But even more important was that Windows XP Professional x64 Edition looked, felt, and behaved just like our familiar 32-bit Windows XP Professional. Oh, there were a few differences, but they were trivial compared to the similarities. Windows XP x64 just felt "right." And now with Windows 7, the differences between 32-bit and 64-bit are difficult to even find.

On the Windows Server side, the driver issues are pretty much long gone. It would be hard today to buy any server-class computer that doesn't support 64-bit Windows. SBS 2011 will work on virtually any server you buy today, with the obvious exception of one based on Intel's Itanium processor. Those servers are 64-bit, but they have a completely different architecture and are entirely focused on the enterprise side of the server market.

Why the Change?

The first question most users ask about the move to 64-bit for Windows Small Business Server is "Why?" A simple answer is because Microsoft Exchange is available only on 64-bit Windows Server, and now Microsoft no longer supports 32-bit versions for any server operating system. But the real answer is a bit more complex.

Windows Small Business Server 2003, which is 32-bit only, runs adequately on current, 64-bit-capable server hardware. Our main server here is a Hewlett Packard (HP) ML350G5. It is fully 64-bit-capable, but it can also run 32-bit Windows Server, allowing us to install Windows Small Business Server 2003 R2 on it without issue. But if we did that, we'd lose access to most of the 16 gigabytes (GB) of RAM we've installed on the server because Windows Small Business Server 2003 supports only 4 GB of RAM. With 64-bit Windows Small Business Server 2011 Standard, we can see and use all 16 GB of RAM, and SBS 2011 will actually support 32 GB of RAM.

The limitations on RAM are especially important with SBS because we run so much on a single server. Even adding a second server to offload some of the burden still leaves many SBS 2003 servers memory constrained. The move to 64-bit removes those constraints and allows us to use more powerful servers. Tables 2-1 and 2-2 compare the memory limits of 32-bit and 64-bit Windows Server.

TABLE 2-1 General memory limits

GENERAL MEMORY LIMITS	SBS 2003 (32-BIT)	64-BIT WINDOWS SERVER 2008 R2
Total Virtual Address Space	4 GB	16 terabytes
Virtual Address Space per 32-bit process	2 GB (3 GB if system is booted with /3GB switch, which is *not* recommended)	4 GB if compiled with /LARGEADDRESSAWARE (2 GB otherwise)
Virtual Address Space per 64-bit process	Not applicable	8 terabytes
Paged Pool	47 MB	128 GB

GENERAL MEMORY LIMITS	SBS 2003 (32-BIT)	64-BIT WINDOWS SERVER 2008 R2
Non-Paged Pool	256 MB	128 GB
System PTE	660 MB to 900 MB	128 GB

TABLE 2-2 Memory limits for SBS versions

PHYSICAL MEMORY AND CPU LIMITS	SBS 2003 (32-BIT)	SBS 2008 AND SBS 2011 STANDARD (64-BIT)
Physical Memory	4 GB	32 GB
Number of CPU Sockets	2	4
Number of CPU Cores	8	48

NOTE Microsoft counts CPUs according to the number of physical CPU sockets that are present—not according to the number of cores. With current processors that support 12 cores on a single CPU, Windows Small Business Server 2011 Standard supports 48 cores.

Another consideration is that Windows Server 2008 was the final version of Windows Server that supported 32-bit. The limitations of the 32-bit architecture and memory model made the move to 64-bit compelling, and beginning with Windows Server 2008 R2 (the underlying operating system for SBS 2011), there is no longer a 32-bit version of Windows Server.

What Are the Advantages?

Why the big push to 64-bit by Microsoft for its server operating systems? Is it just the memory limitations of 32-bit, or are there other compelling reasons? In our opinion, there are four compelling reasons to use 64-bit for servers: memory, performance, security, and virtualization.

Memory

The 32-bit versions of Windows Server use a flat memory addressing scheme, limiting them to a 232 address space. This means a virtual memory address space of only 4 GB, which is divided into 2 GB of virtual memory address space for the operating system and 2 GB of virtual memory address space for applications.

By contrast, 64-bit versions of Windows Server support 16 terabytes of virtual memory address space, divided equally between that reserved for the operating system and that available to applications.

The actual RAM supported by various versions of Windows Server is related to, but somewhat different from, the actual memory address space. Enterprise and Datacenter editions of 32-bit Windows Server use a technique called *Physical Address Extension* (PAE) to support larger RAM configurations. PAE uses a memory address window within the 4 GB of the 32-bit address space to swap in segments of memory located at addresses beyond 4 GB. This is less efficient than a flat memory address model, obviously, but it is the only solution to supporting RAM configurations of more than 4 GB with 32-bit Windows.

The 64-bit versions of Windows Server support different amounts of RAM, but the differentiation is a marketing difference, not a technology difference. The 64-bit versions of Windows Server 2008 R2 Standard (and Windows Small Business Server 2011 Standard that runs on Standard) support 32 GB of RAM, while the Enterprise and Datacenter versions support 2 terabytes of RAM. But all of them have the same 16 terabytes of virtual memory address space.

Performance

The performance and efficiency of 64-bit Windows also benefits from an improved overall I/O efficiency and throughput. With support for greater physical memory and memory address space, caches can be substantially larger than in 32-bit Windows, enabling SBS 2011 to fully use the improved I/O hardware available, such as PCI Express and PCI-X 266, to improve overall I/O performance. The larger address space allows more I/O to be in progress simultaneously. Even 32-bit applications can benefit from this improvement, especially those that need to use the /3GB switch. When using the /3GB switch, Windows is forced into a constrained address space, limiting the amount of non-paged pool available. This can cause non-paged pool to be exhausted when there are several I/O requests outstanding.

 UNDER THE HOOD   **Registers**

Processors have many ways to store information that applications will need, but each storage location has a cost associated with retrieving that information. The fastest and lowest cost locations are local registers on the processor. These are fast, local slots where applications (and the operating system) can store values that will be needed shortly. Data stored in registers is available for reuse at full processor speeds and is faster than even cached data in an on-chip cache. All 32-bit x86 processors have a mere eight general-purpose registers, making them significantly register-poor compared to Reduced Instruction Set Computing (RISC) processors. Worse, because the x87 floating-point architecture is stack-oriented, floating-point arithmetic instructions require at least one of the operands to be on top of the stack. This requirement leads to further inefficiencies and relatively poor floating-point performance.

The x64 architecture addresses this issue by doubling the number and size of the registers available. Although 32-bit x86 processors are limited to eight 32-bit general-purpose registers, eight floating-point registers, and eight Streaming Single Instruction-Stream, Multiple Data-Stream (SIMD) Extensions (SSE) or SSE2 registers, the 64-bit x64 architecture has sixteen 64-bit wide general-purpose registers and sixteen 128-bit wide SSE/SSE2 registers.

Another improvement in 64-bit Windows Server is a faster I/O subsystem. There are a couple of reasons for this. First, the operating system is no longer constrained by the limited address space available to it in 32-bit Windows. This limitation can become especially important for server functions that create and release many connections, such as an active web server. In 32-bit Windows, this can lead to fragmentation of the address space used by Windows and the eventual slowing down of the server, or an inability of the server to accept additional connections. With 64-bit Windows, this address space is far larger, allowing the web server to function at full speed.

Another way that the I/O subsystem benefits from 64-bit Windows is that it has a wider data path, allowing faster disk reads and writes and faster memory access. Disk-intensive operations are significantly faster in 64-bit Windows.

Security

All 64-bit-capable processors include support for the hardware data execution protection (DEP) bit. DEP controls which areas of memory can be used to execute code, protecting against buffer overflows. This protection helps to prevent the kinds of attacks that led to the Code Red and the SQL Slammer worms, though good coding practices are equally important.

 UNDER THE HOOD **Buffer Overflows**

When an application buffer is stuffed with more data than it is designed to handle, the buffer spills the extra data into unexpected areas of memory, putting data where it wasn't supposed to be. This creates a buffer overflow. *Buffer overflow* is a generic term for exploits that load executable code into areas that are supposed to contain only data, and then jump program execution into that code by overloading heaps, stacks, and other memory pools.

For example, if your email client is designed to handle attachments with a maximum of 255-character file names and you receive a message that has a file name with 256 characters, a buffer overflow can occur. When this happens, memory space adjacent to that file name buffer gets overwritten and malicious code can be executed with the privileges associated with the original program. The infamous MSBlaster worm was this type of exploit. The hardware DEP in x64 processors protects against this type of exploit.

This buffer overflow protection is combined with Microsoft's PatchGuard technology, which prevents non-Microsoft-originated programs from patching the Windows kernel. This technology, available only on 64-bit Windows, prevents kernel-mode drivers from extending or replacing kernel services, including system service dispatch tables, the interrupt descriptor table (IDT), and the global descriptor table (GDT). Third-party software is also prevented from allocating kernel stacks or patching any part of the kernel.

In some ways, however, an even more important security feature of SBS 2011 (and all versions of Windows Server 2008 R2) is the requirement that every driver be signed to assure the authenticity of the driver provider. This won't prevent a badly written driver from causing problems, but it will ensure that when you download and install a driver, you know that it really is written by the company that claims to have written it. This helps to protect against an important and difficult-to-detect security loophole that could allow an unscrupulous virus or root-kit author to provide an imitation of a commonly used driver that contained code that lets the author bypass Windows security.

 SECURITY ALERT Always know the source of any driver you install on any computer in your network. If you need a driver for an HP component, go directly to the HP site or to the Windows Update site to obtain the driver. Do not download from some third-party site. Signed drivers can help ensure that you're getting what you think you're getting, but they aren't required for the 32-bit computers on your network.

Virtualization

One of the most important features that is available only on 64-bit Windows is Hyper-V. Hyper-V is hypervisor-based native virtualization that uses the hardware virtualization capabilities of the latest Intel and AMD processors to provide a robust, fast, and resource-conserving virtual environment.

Because Hyper-V is built in to Windows Server 2008 R2, it runs more efficiently and natively. A server running the Hyper-V role has multiple *partitions*, each running natively on the underlying hardware. The first partition is known as the *parent* (sometimes called *host)* partition, and it acts as the hardware and operating system control partition for all the other partitions where virtualized operating systems (virtual machines) run.

The other partitions are *child* (sometimes called *guest)* partitions, each with its own operating system, running directly on the hypervisor layer. Windows Small Business Server 2011 Standard can run as a child partition, but it can't be used for the parent partition. We'll cover virtualization and SBS 2011 in more detail in Chapter 6, "Configuring SBS in Hyper-V."

What Are the Challenges?

So is moving to 64-bit all good and wonderful? Or do special challenges need to be considered and dealt with to make the transition easier? Not surprisingly, the transition to 64-bit is not without some special concerns, including driver, hardware, and software considerations.

Drivers

Every driver for Windows Small Business Server 2011 Standard must be 64-bit and must be a signed driver. This means that before you buy a server you need to verify that the manufacturer fully supports 64-bit Windows Server 2008 R2. If your environment includes other hardware, such as printers, which are directly controlled by SBS, you need to make sure that there are drivers available for that hardware.

We'll cover how to configure SBS to support both 64-bit and 32-bit clients for your printers in Chapter 13, "Installing and Managing Printers." But if you're buying one or more printers for your SBS network, verify that they have drivers for 64-bit Windows Server 2008 R2 available. And if you've got legacy hardware or printers you need to maintain, verify that there are 64-bit drivers available. If not, consider your options for either replacing them or providing an additional 32-bit Windows computer that can provide access to the legacy hardware.

Hardware and Software Considerations

There are some general hardware considerations you should take into account when moving to Windows Small Business Server 2011, as well as some software considerations that are specific to 64-bit Windows. One consideration you don't have to worry about is whether you're running AMD or Intel processors. There is full binary compatibility between AMD's AMD64 and Intel's EM64T, allowing Windows Small Business Server 2011 to use the same binary whether the underlying processor is an AMD processor or an Intel processor.

Server-Grade Hardware

As we mentioned earlier, you need to make sure that any hardware you use with your SBS 2011 network has the proper signed drivers available that support 64-bit Windows Server 2008 R2. But it's more than just drivers. Avoid choosing lower consumer-grade hardware, especially printers. Because you're sharing that printer across your entire network, having a better printer makes sound financial sense and also makes it easier to support.

Many consumer-grade printers have no actual intelligence built in to the printer; instead, they are entirely dependent on the operating system to work. Server-grade (also referred to as business-grade) printers support a full printer control language in the printer itself, usually either PCL or PostScript. Having a server-grade printer removes many of the compatibility issues associated with printer drivers because even if there isn't a perfect match for your printer, there will be one that is close.

> **NOTE** All-in-one printer/fax/scanner devices present a particular challenge in 64-bit Windows—very few of them have drivers that support all of their functionality. If you absolutely have to have this kind of device, you'll probably have better luck connecting it to a centrally located personal computer.

32-Bit Software Compatibility

SBS 2011 uses the Windows On Windows 64-bit (WOW64) subsystem to support 32-bit applications running on 64-bit Windows. The WOW64 subsystem provides a high-performance, 32-bit Windows environment that supports existing 32-bit Windows applications. Because of the underlying hardware compatibility of the x64 architecture, 32-bit applications are able to run at full speed in the WOW64 subsystem. Because of the larger available memory address space and the greater efficiencies of the x64 processor architecture, many applications actually run faster in WOW64 than they do in 32-bit Windows.

WOW64 isolates 32-bit applications from 64-bit applications, but it provides for interoperability and data exchange across the boundary through the Common Object Model (COM) and remote procedure call (RPC) and through transparent cut and paste. WOW64 runs 32-bit applications seamlessly while preventing file and registry collisions between 32-bit and 64-bit versions of an application.

An important WOW64 limitation is that 32-bit applications cannot load 64-bit DLLs, and 64-bit applications cannot load 32-bit DLLs. This means that 32-bit ActiveX controls, for example, cannot be run in the 64-bit version of Internet Explorer, and this is why 32-bit and 64-bit versions of Internet Explorer are both included with all 64-bit versions of Windows. The 32-bit version is the default.

Another limitation is that 32-bit DLLs that provide context-sensitive menu extensions to Windows Explorer don't work. They must be rewritten to run natively in 64-bit.

Legacy Software in 64-Bit Windows

Running legacy software in 64-bit Windows raises some special concerns. The vast majority of 32-bit software will work without issue in the WOW64 subsystem. The only real exceptions to this are applications that have specialized drivers, such as antivirus software, disk defragmentation utilities, and so on. These generally use special file system drivers. Check with your software vendor—many provide updated versions that work well with 64-bit Windows.

What won't work are 16-bit or MS-DOS applications. There is no support at all in any 64-bit version of Microsoft Windows for 16-bit applications. Nor is there any support for pure DOS applications. (This does not mean that applications written to run from the command line won't work. Just not older MS-DOS applications such as DOS Edit, or one of our favorites, Vern Buerg's List.)

So, what's the best way to handle an application that doesn't run in 64-bit Windows? We find virtualization to be a great solution. Create a virtual machine (VM) that runs a 32-bit version of Windows, and use that VM to run your incompatible application.

If you're running SBS 2011 virtualized already, creating a small VM for this is no problem. If you're running SBS 2011 Standard Edition on a physical host, however, you have to run the VM on another host because SBS 2011 doesn't support enabling the Hyper-V role. If you have the Windows Small Business Server 2011 Premium Add-On, you already have a perfect place to enable Hyper-V. See Chapter 6 for more details on setting up and configuring virtual machines using Hyper-V.

What About Clients?

SBS 2011 provides full support for 64-bit Windows clients. That said, the need for 64-bit at the client level is still far less compelling than it is for servers. 32-bit Windows is quite adequate for the vast majority of desktop and laptop computers used in business today. The exceptions to this are development workstations, drawing and computer-aided design (CAD) workstations, or other specialized workstations used for memory-intensive applications that need to address greater than 4 GB of RAM.

The 64-bit business versions of Windows 7, Windows Vista, and Windows XP support up to 128 GB of RAM and two physical processors. If you have specialized needs for very large RAM workstations, 64-bit is definitely the way to go. But most users will find 32-bit Windows sufficient, though this is definitely changing as the availability of desktop computers with 8 GB and even 12 GB of RAM become more common. Table 2-3 shows the support matrix for processors and RAM in Windows.

NOTE Although you can run Windows XP Professional x64 Edition (XP x64) as a client operating system in an SBS 2011 network, it is not a fully supported scenario. Certain wizards, including the Connectcomputer Wizard, will not work in XP x64.

TABLE 2-3 32-bit vs. 64-bit Windows clients

	MAXIMUM RAM		# OF CPU SOCKETS	
WINDOWS EDITION	32-BIT	64-BIT	32-BIT	64-BIT
XP Professional	4 GB	128 GB	2	2
XP Tablet PC Edition	4 GB	not applicable	2	not applicable
XP Media Center Edition (not supported in SBS network)	4 GB	not applicable	1	not applicable
Windows Vista Business	4 GB	128 GB	2	2
Windows Vista Enterprise (available only with Software Assurance)	4 GB	128 GB	2	2
Windows Vista Ultimate	4 GB	128 GB	2	2
Windows Vista Home Basic (not supported in SBS network)	4GB	8 GB	1	1
Windows Vista Home Premium (not supported in SBS network)	4 GB	16 GB	1	1
Windows 7 Professional	4 GB	128 GB	2	2
Windows 7 Enterprise (available only with Software Assurance)	4 GB	128 GB	2	2
Windows 7 Ultimate	4 GB	128 GB	2	2
Windows 7 Home Premium (not supported in SBS network)	4 GB	16 GB	1	1

Summary

In this chapter, we covered how 64-bit computing is different from the familiar 32-bit approach, as well as how it's really the same. We highlighted some key reasons why Windows Small Business Server 2011 Standard is available only as a 64-bit solution.

The next chapter covers how to design and prepare a network prior to installing Windows Small Business Server. We also cover naming conventions, how to plan for adequate network security, and how to calculate the number and type of licenses you'll need.

CHAPTER 3

Planning Your SBS Network

Before you actually start installing Windows Small Business Server 2011 Standard, you should spend some time and thought planning what your network will look like. Time spent now, *before* you actually start installing anything, will save you time, energy, and complications later. By designing your network infrastructure, naming conventions, and network security before you actually implement them, you'll save costly reconfiguration later.

Planning the Network Infrastructure

The first tasks in designing a network for your company are

- Evaluating the computing needs of the organization
- Choosing an Internet connection method and local network type
- Selecting network devices
- Choosing server hardware
- Choosing client hardware and software

 UNDER THE HOOD **Network Operating Systems**

On an ordinary PC, the role of the operating system is to manage the file system; handle the running of applications; manage the computer's memory; and control the input and output to attached devices such as cameras, printers, and scanners. A network operating system expands that role, managing the following:

- Centralized security
- Remote access
- Remote file systems
- Running shared applications
- Input and output to shared network devices
- CPU scheduling of networked processes

When multiple computers are connected in a *workgroup*, as shown in Figure 3-1, the result is called a *peer-to-peer network*: a network without a central server and with no network operating system.

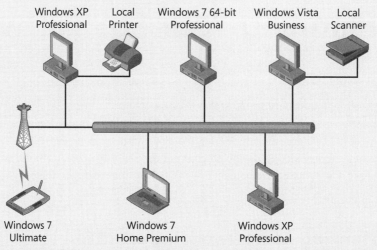

FIGURE 3-1 A peer-to-peer network, which has no central server or management

Adding one or more servers running Windows Server 2008 R2 or a Windows Small Business Server 2011 Standard, as shown in Figure 3-2, is a *client/server-based network*—one or more servers and multiple clients, all sharing a single security policy. The servers provide both the resources and the security policy for the network, and the clients are the computers that use the resources managed by the server.

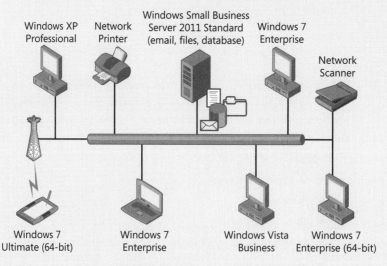

FIGURE 3-2 A client/server network, which has a central management and resource server

Servers Use Network Operating Systems

Because SBS 2011 has to supply services to as many as 75 users, and you're depending on it to run your business, a high-powered, robust operating system and highly reliable hardware are essential. When your users rely on a server to get their work done and keep your business running, you certainly don't want frequent failures—you don't even want to reboot!

In addition to supplying print, file, or other services, the network operating system has to provide network security. Different businesses and organizations have varying security needs, but *all* must have some level of data protection. Therefore, the system must offer a range of configurable security levels, from the relatively nonintrusive to the very stringent.

Clients Use Workstation Operating Systems

Like other computers, client computers on a network need an operating system. However, a client operating system doesn't need to manage the resources for other computers or manage security for the network. Rebooting a workstation can be an annoyance for the user but doesn't usually disrupt anyone else's work.

On a Windows Small Business Server network, clients can run Microsoft Windows XP Professional (including Windows XP Tablet PC Edition and Windows XP Professional x64 Edition) and business editions of Windows Vista or Windows 7. However, for best performance and security, Windows Vista SP1 or Windows 7 should be deployed on clients.

Determining Your Needs

Before designing a network, decide which features of SBS 2011 your business needs; doing so helps ensure that the network design is dictated by business needs rather than by fancy technology. Key needs to consider include

- Centralized user account management
- Centralized update management
- Web and email access for employees
- File sharing and centralized file storage
- Database storage using Microsoft SQL Server
- Printer sharing
- Centralized backup
- Centralized fax server

- Remote access to the internal network via the Internet, including remote access directly to the user's desktop from the web
- Management of remote computers
- Collaboration and document management (SharePoint Foundation 2010)

You also must decide how important the following factors are, as well as what resources are available to support your choices:

- Performance
- Reliability
- Security

> **PLANNING**   Get a thorough idea of what kind of work will be done on the network, when and where it will be done, and by whom. For example, your organization might need to do payroll every other Friday, during which time the file server and printers are under a heavy load.

Choosing an Internet Connection

To choose an Internet connection method, you must balance an organization's bandwidth needs and budget against the available Internet connection methods. The following sections discuss how to do this, as well as how to choose an Internet service provider (ISP).

Determining Bandwidth Needs

First, determine the baseline level of bandwidth you require. You can then balance this against the organization's budget and performance goals. Allow for 100 kilobits per second (Kbps) of download bandwidth and 50 Kbps of upload bandwidth for each simultaneous user of email and the web. If remote access is important, allow for a minimum of 100 Kbps of upload bandwidth for each simultaneous remote access user. Table 3-1 lists various Internet connection speeds and the number of users supported for each speed, assuming that users will be browsing the web and using email. This table does *not* include requirements for remote connections.

> **IMPORTANT**   Running an Internet-accessible web server on your network requires at least 50 Kbps or more of upload bandwidth per simultaneous visitor, depending on the size of images or files. This can quickly swamp your Internet connection, which is one reason most small businesses pay for web hosting.

TABLE 3-1 Bandwidth requirements for web browsing and email

DOWNLOAD/UPLOAD SPEED	NUMBER OF USERS
256/128 Kbps	1–5
512/256 Kbps	1–5
1024/512 Kbps	5–10
3072/768 Kbps	10–20
5120/1024 Kbps	15–30

NOTE These bandwidth numbers are not intended to be definitive—they are a minimum planning baseline. Each organization and its users have different usage patterns and needs, and you should evaluate your needs accordingly. Be prepared to add more bandwidth if necessary. Your users will never complain that the Internet connection is too fast, but they will definitely complain if it's too slow!

 UNDER THE HOOD **Bits and Bytes**

Network speeds are measured in either kilobits per second (Kbps) or megabits per second (Mbps), whereas download speed and hard disks are rated in kilobytes per second (KBps) or megabytes per second (MBps). For example, a 640-Kbps DSL connection might download files at 60 KBps from a fast website, but a 1.5-Mbps cable Internet connection might download at 180 KBps from the same site. (Some of the bandwidth is used up by transmission overhead and inefficiencies.) When you compare network speeds, make sure you're using the same units of measurement.

Types of Internet Connections

To choose an Internet connection method, you need to know which methods are available as well as their performance characteristics. Table 3-2 lists the most common connection methods and their speeds.

TABLE 3-2 Internet connection types

TYPE OF CONNECTION	DOWNLOAD SPEED	UPLOAD SPEED	NOTES
Dial-up	28.8–53 Kbps	28.8–40 Kbps	Analog telephone line. Sometimes referred to as Plain Old Telephone Service (POTS).
ISDN (Integrated Services Digital Network)	64–128 Kbps (one channel or two)	64–128 Kbps (one channel or two)	Must be within 50,000 feet of a telephone company central office (CO). Connection is dial-up (not persistent).
ADSL (Asynchronous Digital Subscriber Line)	256 Kbps– 8 Mbps	128 Kbps– 1 Mbps	Must be within 18,000 feet of a CO.
IDSL (DSL over ISDN)	128–144 Kbps	128–144 Kbps	Works at greater distances from a CO than other DSL variants.
SDSL (Synchronous DSL)	128 Kbps– 2.3 Mbps	128 Kbps– 2.3 Mbps	Must be within 20,000 feet of a CO.
Cable	128 Kbps– 15 Mbps	128 Kbps– 1 Mbps	Must have access to broadband cable service; speed can fluctuate depending on the number of users on a given cable loop.
Microwave wireless	256 Kbps– 10+ Mbps	256 Kbps– 10+ Mbps	Must be in line of sight to the ISP's antenna; maximum distance 10 miles.
Frame relay/T1	56 Kbps– 1.54 Mbps	56 Kbps– 1.54 Mbps	Good availability; very reliable; consistent throughput; expensive.
802.11b (WiFi)	Up to 11 Mbps	Up to 11 Mbps	Speed decreases with increasing distance from access point.
802.11g or 802.11a	Up to 54 Mbps	Up to 54 Mbps	Speed decreases with increasing distance from access point.
802.11n	Up to 540 Mbps	Up to 540 Mbps	Speed decreases with increasing distance from access point.
Geosynchronous satellite	150 Kbps– 3 Mbps	33.6 Kbps– 128 Kbps	Requires line of sight to satellite (southern sky in North America). Unsuitable for real-time multimedia because of high latency.
Ethernet	10 to 1000 Mbps	10 to 1000 Mbps	Limited availability. Backbone connection might be DSL or T1, limiting actual bandwidth.

Choosing ISPs

After determining the preferred connection type and bandwidth, it's time to actually find ISPs. Two websites to check are *http://www.cnet.com/internet-access* and *http://www.dslreports.com*. In addition to speed and cost, look for the following features:

- **Static IP address** To host any kind of Internet-accessible service such as email, Microsoft Outlook Anywhere, remote access, or websites, you need a static IP address or an ISP that supports the Dynamic DNS service, or you need to manage your external DNS with a DNS service that supports dynamic updates, such as *http://www.zoneedit.com*. SBS 2011 includes support for tzo.com dynamic DNS if you use the built-in wizards to register or transfer your domain name.

- **Terms of service and ports** Many ISPs have terms of service (TOS) on consumer-grade accounts that prohibit hosting email servers, or they have a policy that blocks specific ports such as port 25. You need to ask *before* you buy.

- **Transfer limitations** If the ISP has a monthly data transfer limit, make sure the limit isn't lower than your anticipated usage—charges for going beyond the limit can be significant.

- **Web hosting** If you want the ISP to host the organization's Internet website, look for virtual hosting (so that your organization can use its own domain name) with enough disk space on the ISP's web servers.

- **Backup Internet connection** If your business is dependent on always being connected to the Internet, choose a secondary Internet connection with sufficient bandwidth to allow you to maintain minimal service in case the primary Internet connection fails. This second Internet connection should use a different ISP and a different connection technology. You can use a dual WAN router to use both connections simultaneously.

Choosing a Network Type

The next step in designing a network is to choose a network type. (See Table 3-3.) Start by looking at where your computers are physically located. If you can easily run cable between all computers, the choices are simple: Gigabit Ethernet (GigE) or Fast Ethernet (100BaseT). Choose GigE if your wiring supports it; otherwise, stick to Fast Ethernet. If you're installing new cabling, hire a professional cabling expert. Spending money on good wiring now can save you a *lot* of problems in the future.

If the computers are widely scattered or mobile, consider including some wireless *access points* (APs). These are network devices that permit wireless clients access to a wired network. Even Fast Ethernet is virtually as fast as the real-world speeds of the fastest current wireless standard (802.11n), while being far more reliable, more secure, and cheaper as well. For these reasons, use wireless networks to supplement wired networks, not to replace them.

MORE INFO For more information about wireless access points, see the section "Choosing a Wireless Standard: 802.11a/b/g/n" later in this chapter.

SECURITY ALERT All wireless technologies have the potential to introduce security risks. When using wireless networking, always use appropriate security measures, such as Wireless Protected Access (WPA), 802.11i (WPA2), or 802.1x. For more information, see the section "Planning for Security" later in this chapter.

TABLE 3-3 Common network types

TECHNOLOGY	SPEED	SPEED (REAL WORLD)	CABLING	MAXIMUM DISTANCE	OTHER HARDWARE REQUIREMENTS
Fast Ethernet	100 Mbps	94 Mbps	Cat 5, Cat 5e, Cat 6	328 feet from hub or switch	Fast Ethernet hub or switch
Gigabit Ethernet	1000 Mbps	327 Mbps	Cat 5e or Cat 6	328 feet from hub or switch	Gigabit hub or switch
802.11b (WiFi)	11 Mbps	4.5 Mbps	Wireless	1800 feet (60–150 feet typical indoors)	802.11b or 802.11g access point (AP), 32 users per AP
802.11a	54 Mbps	19 Mbps	Wireless	1650 feet (50–100 feet typical indoors)	802.11a AP, 64 users per AP
802.11g	54 Mbps	13 Mbps	Wireless	1800 feet (60–150 feet typical indoors)	802.11g AP, 32 users per AP
802.11n	540 Mbps	130 Mbps	Wireless	7200 feet (100–500 feet typical indoors)	802.11n AP, 32 users per AP

NOTE Wireless speeds vary greatly depending on the distance from the access point, and the number and type of walls, floors, and other interference between the access point and the client device.

Choosing the Right Network Cable

Choosing the right cable for a wired Fast Ethernet (100 Mbps) network is easy—Cat 5 cable. However, there are exceptions to this rule that pertain to existing installations and new construction.

Cables in an existing network might not be usable. 10-megabit Ethernet equipment might be usable for small networks until it can be replaced, but expect to replace it soon—you'll find it slow. Coaxial (thinnet) Ethernet and Cat 3 Unshielded Twisted Pair (UTP) cables are unreliable and slow and should be replaced.

New construction should run several strands of Cat 5e or, ideally, Cat 6. Although Cat 5 cable can be used with Gigabit Ethernet, it is marginal at best. Cat 5e and Cat 6 cables are more reliable and provide headroom for possible 10-Gigabit Ethernet standards. Cables should converge at a reasonably clean, centrally located wiring closet with adequate power, ventilation, and security for all servers and network devices. (Be sure to leave room for future growth.)

Shielded Cat 5, Cat 5e, and Cat 6 cables are available for situations that potentially involve high levels of electromagnetic interference (such as antennas). You should use plenum-grade cable any time wiring is placed in a drop ceiling. (Before running cable in a drop ceiling, talk to the building manager.)

Choosing a Wireless Standard: 802.11a/b/g/n

Currently, you can choose from four wireless standards: 802.11b, 802.11a, 802.11g, and 802.11n. Here's what you need to know about each (also refer to Table 3-3):

- **802.11b** 802.11b was the first widely deployed standard, though the speed was limited (11 Mbps theoretical; 5 Mbps or even less in the real world). 802.11b supports a maximum of 32 users per AP, and a maximum of 3 simultaneous channels in use in the same location. *Channels* separate wireless networks, with each channel providing 11 Mbps of bandwidth. You should not buy new equipment that supports only 802.11b, and if you currently have 802.11b equipment, you should upgrade it to 802.11n. There are serious security considerations with older wireless hardware that preclude it from being deployed in a business environment.

- **802.11g**   802.11g is faster than 802.11b (54 Mbps theoretical; 13 Mbps real-world) and backward-compatible with 802.11b. 802.11g supports a maximum of 32 users per AP, and a maximum of 3 simultaneous channels in use in the same location.

- **802.11a**   802.11a is faster than 802.11g (54 Mbps theoretical; 19 Mbps real-world) and is more tolerant of microwave interference and network congestion because it uses the 5 GHz frequency band. 802.11a supports a maximum of 64 users per AP, and a maximum of 8 channels in use simultaneously in the same location. 802.11a is not compatible with either 802.11b or 802.11g.

  If you decide to use 802.11a network devices, stick with devices from the same vendor and consider a tri-mode 802.11a/b/g device that will allow other devices, such as laptops with built-in 802.11b/g connectivity, to work on the wireless network. (This strategy also permits the highest network density, with 11 channels available simultaneously for wireless networks.)

- **802.11n**   802.11n is faster than 802.11g (up to 540 Mbps theoretical; 100–130 Mbps real-world) and backward-compatible with 802.11g and 802.11b. Most 802.11n equipment is in the same frequency band (2.4 GHz) as 802.11b/g, but the standard supports dual-band equipment that can also use the 5-GHz range of 802.11a. This dual-band equipment provides the greatest flexibility and compatibility and is especially good at avoiding interference from other equipment. Choosing dual-band equipment from a single OEM is the safest choice for compatibility at the highest speeds. If you're buying new wireless equipment, we strongly recommend 802.11n and prefer dual-band 802.11n where possible.

Choosing Network Devices

After selecting a network type and Internet connection method, create a network diagram to visually show which network devices are needed. Then select the necessary devices for the network, such as switches, wireless access points, firewalls, and network adapters.

> **BEST PRACTICES**   Choose a single brand of network hardware if possible. This ensures greater hardware compatibility, simplifies administration, and makes obtaining vendor support easier.

Diagramming the Network

Creating a diagram of the network can quickly show which devices you need and where they should be located, as shown in Figure 3-3.

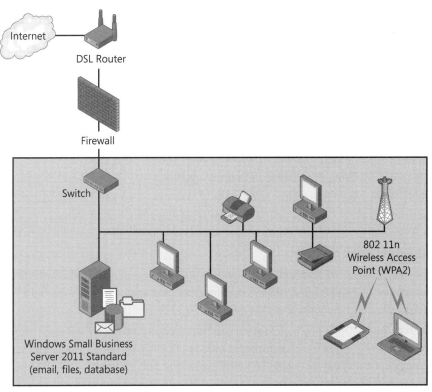

FIGURE 3-3 A network with the Windows Small Business Server computer connected directly to the Internet

Use the following list as a guide when creating the network diagram:

- **Internet connection** The Internet connection usually comes in the form of a telephone or coaxial cable that connects to a DSL or cable router. It is traditionally represented by a cloud at the top of the drawing and a line that connects to the router or firewall.

- **DSL or cable modem** The Internet usually enters the organization in the form of a telephone or cable line that plugs into a DSL or cable modem.

- **Firewall** The DSL or cable modem is then plugged into the firewall, which should be a router or firewall. Some modems are combined with built-in routers that have basic firewall capabilities. Consumer routers or DSL modems are not sufficient protection for a business network.

- **Perimeter network** This is an optional area of the network between the DSL or cable modem and the firewall, where low-security devices such as wireless access points can be placed.

- **Internal network** The internal network includes the SBS computer, the client computers, and any network-connected devices, such as printers.

> **PLANNING** Wireless access points should be on the internal network and use 802.11i (WPA2) encryption. You can also place access points in the perimeter network when you want to provide Internet access to the general public (such as in a coffee shop, conference room, or lobby).

Choosing a Network Switch

Ethernet networks use the *star* network topology (also known as *hub and spoke*), which means that all network devices must be plugged into a central hub or switch. Choosing the right switch requires evaluating the following factors:

- **Switch or hub** Don't buy a hub unless you have a specialized need and understand why you're doing it. Get a switch instead. Switches are inexpensive, provide additional performance, and facilitate mixing 10 Mbps, 100 Mbps, and 1 Gbps devices on the same network segment.

- **Number of ports** Make sure that the switch provides more than enough ports for all computers, access points, network printers, and Network Attached Storage (NAS) devices on the network, along with spare ports for expansion or to use in the event of a port failure.

- **Speed** Fast Ethernet (100/10 Mbps) switches offer basic performance for small businesses, but GigE (1000/100/10 Mbps) switches are hardly different in price and provide extra bandwidth for improved performance of file servers and high-quality streaming video where the network cabling will support it.

- **Management** Managed switches provide the ability to view the status of attached devices from a remote connection, which can be useful for off-site technicians. In general, save the cash and stick with an unmanaged switch unless the cost difference is slight or the organization uses an off-site consultant who wants the ability to remotely administer switches.

Choosing Wireless Access Points

As you learned earlier in the chapter, wireless access points permit clients to wirelessly connect to a wired network. Access points are often integrated into routers, but they are also available as stand-alone devices that must be plugged into a switch like any other network device. Avoid wireless "gateway" or router products for connecting to your internal network—they will complicate your network management and TCP/IP configuration. They're fine for externally connected wireless access points. Some wireless routers can be reconfigured to be simple access points.

NOTE Business-grade access points are more expensive than consumer-oriented access points; however, they are usually more reliable and full-featured.

When choosing an access point, consider the following features:

- Routers with built-in access points are often no more expensive than stand-alone access points and are useful when creating a perimeter network. But be sure they can be used as a pure access point—many can function only as a router, which will complicate your network setup.
- Access points should support 802.11i (WPA2). WEP is simply not acceptable for any wireless device connected to your internal network, and even WPA should not be considered sufficient protection for an internally connected access point.
- Access points should support 802.1x (RADIUS) authentication if you want to provide the highest level of security and ease-of-use to a wireless network.

SECURITY ALERT Two "features" that some suggest to improve wireless security are disabling of SSID broadcasts and Media Access Control (MAC) address filtering. Don't bother. They are a significant and ongoing administrative burden, and a hacker with a port scanner can easily defeat them anyway.

- Some access points have two or more antennas that can be adjusted for better coverage; others support external antennas that can be mounted on a wall for better placement.
- Stand-alone wireless bridges (often referred to as *wireless Ethernet bridges*) and some access points provide the ability to wirelessly bridge (connect) two wired networks that can't be connected via cables. There are a number of different types of bridging modes, including Point-to-Point and AP Client. Point-to-Point uses two wireless bridges to link two wired networks. AP Client uses an AP on the main network (to which wireless clients can connect) and a wireless bridge in AP Client mode on the remote network segment, acting as a wireless client.

Clients on the other side of a wireless bridge will experience slower performance to the main network segment because of the shared wireless link, so use wireless bridges with discretion, and always use bridges and APs made by the same manufacturer.

■ Don't include "turbo" or other high-speed modes offered by some manufacturers in your buying criteria. They provide little performance gain, if any, in the real world and can have a deleterious effect on compatibility.

REAL WORLD **Placing Access Points for the Best Coverage**

Wireless access points have a limited range, especially in the environment of a typical office. The indoor range of 802.11b, 802.11g, and tri-mode 802.11a access points is usually around 60–100 feet at the highest connection speed, and 25–75 feet for first-generation, single-mode 802.11a access points.

That said, 2.4-GHz cordless phones, microwave ovens, and Bluetooth devices can cause serious interference with 802.11b and 802.11g networks (but not with 802.11a networks) when they are turned on. Fluorescent lights, metal walls, computer equipment, furniture, and standing too close to the access point can also reduce the range of wireless networks.

Unfortunately, there is no reliable way to quantify these variables—trial and error is the best way to position access points. With 802.11n, and especially dual-band 802.11n, the effective distance is at least double that of 802.11g, but this still requires full 802.11n deployment and optimal conditions. In our initial tests of 802.11n, it does appear to provide a more stable and reliable signal at a significantly greater distance than our previous 802.11a/g equipment. There are some useful guidelines when selecting access point locations:

■ Place the access point and wireless network card antennas as high as possible to get them above objects that might attenuate the signal.

■ If you place access points in the plenum (the space inside a drop ceiling or raised floor), make sure you obtain access points or enclosures certified for plenum installation.

■ Place the access point in the center of the desired coverage area to provide the best coverage while also reducing the publicly exposed "surface area" of the network.

■ Only use the minimum signal strength (power) required to provide coverage for your office. Most WAPs have multiple levels of signal strength but ship with a default of "maximum."

■ Use multiple access points as necessary to cover multiple floors or large offices, or to service a large number of clients simultaneously. Twenty clients per 802.11g AP is a reasonable maximum, with an average of no more than two to four simultaneously active users per AP yielding the best network performance.

- Use wireless bridges to place another Ethernet network segment (or another wireless access point) in a location unreachable by cables. Wired clients on this segment communicate with other wired devices on this segment at the speed of the wired network (1000/100/10 Mbps); however, communication with the main network segment takes place at the speed of the wireless network (10–100 Mbps real-world bandwidth).

- When selecting channels for access points, *sniff* (search by using a wireless client) for the presence of other networks and then choose an unused channel, preferably one that is four or more channels separated from other channels in use. For example, channels 1, 6, and 11 can be used simultaneously without interference.

Choosing a Firewall Device or Router

SBS 2011 is designed to connect directly to a firewall and does not provide any direct protection for the rest of the SBS network. This is a major change from earlier versions of SBS that acted as the gateway between the Internet and the internal network when SBS was deployed with two network cards (NICs). Windows Small Business Server 2011 Standard includes the new Windows Firewall that is part of Windows Server 2008 R2 to protect the server, but it should be protected by an additional, separate firewall that will also act to protect the computers on the internal network.

You should look for the following features on your network firewall device:

- **Packet filtering**   Firewalls should support inbound packet filtering and Stateful Packet Inspection (SPI).

- **Protection from specific attacks**   Firewalls should support protection from the denial-of-service (DoS) attacks and other common attacks such as Ping of Death, SYN Flood, LAND Attack, and IP Spoofing.

- **Network Address Translation (NAT)**   NAT is the backbone of most firewall devices, providing basic security and Internet connectivity to internal clients.

- **IPv6 Support**   As IPv6 becomes more pervasive, and as our pool of available IPv4 addresses approaches exhaustion, the need to directly support IPv6 for our Internet connection becomes more compelling. Choosing a firewall device that fully supports IPv6 now will save money and time later.

- **VPN pass-through**   To permit properly authenticated Internet users to establish VPN connections with a Windows Small Business Server computer behind a firewall, the firewall must support VPN pass-through of the desired VPN protocol (PPTP, L2TP, and/or IPSec).

- **VPN tunnels**   Some firewall devices provide direct support for establishing VPN connections. If you do choose to use a firewall device to establish VPN connections with clients and servers in remote offices, make sure the firewall supports the necessary number of simultaneous VPN tunnels.

- **UPnP support**   Windows Small Business Server can automatically configure firewalls that support Universal Plug and Play (UPnP) to work with Windows Small Business Server services such as Exchange Server and remote access (by opening the necessary ports on the firewall). UPnP support can be found in most consumer firewall devices as well as in some business firewalls.

> **NOTE**   Enabling UPnP on a dedicated firewall device makes configuring the device to work with Windows Small Business Server easy, but it does have security implications. We suggest using UPnP to do the initial setup of the firewall device, if the device supports it, but then disabling UPnP completely.

- **Dual-WAN support**   Some firewalls come with support for two WAN connections to increase speed and reliability, which is a great solution for networks looking for a reliable Internet connection. Other firewalls provide a serial port so that an external dial-up modem can be used as a backup connection, but this connection is much slower.

- **RADIUS support**   RADIUS support on your firewall will enable additional functionality and security, including easily integrating Two Factor Authentication (TFA) into your remote access configuration.

- **Content filtering**   Most firewalls make blocking certain websites possible, such as websites containing specified keywords. Many businesses use this feature to reduce the employees' ability to visit objectionable websites, although most content filters are largely ineffective.

- **Built-in wireless access point**   Firewalls with built-in access points and switched, GigE, wired ports combine several functions and can be a cost-effective solution. However, their primary function is to protect the network, and that should be the first and most important evaluation criterion.

Choosing Server Hardware

If you have a server that can meet the capacity needs of the network or can be upgraded to do so while allowing for future growth, by all means use this server. But realistically, because there is no in-place upgrade to Windows Small Business Server 2011 Standard, you should plan on buying a new server as part of your migration plan.

> **MORE INFO**   See Chapter 7, "Migrating to Windows Small Business Server 2011 Standard," for more information about migrating to SBS 2011 from an existing SBS domain.

When evaluating server hardware, see Table 3-4, which lists the effective minimum configurations necessary for adequate performance at different load levels.

MORE INFO   The sidebar "Determining Server Load" later in this chapter provides more information about configuration and performance.

TABLE 3-4 Minimum server configurations for different load levels

COMPONENT	LIGHT LOAD	MEDIUM LOAD	HEAVY LOAD
CPU	Quad core Intel or AMD processor	Quad core or greater Xeon or Opteron processor	Dual Xeon or Opteron processors, with at least four cores each
Memory	10–12 GB	12–16 GB	12–32 GB
Storage	Two or more hard drives in hardware mirror (RAID-1) with 200 GB available for Windows Small Business Server 2011 Standard	Four-drive, hardware-based RAID using SATA or SAS drives	Four-drive (or more), hardware-based SCSI or SAS RAID
LAN Network Adapter	100/10 Mbps PCI card	1000/100/10 Mbps PCI card	1000/100/10 Mbps PCI-x or PCIe card
Backup	Two or more external USB hard drives	Two or more external eSATA or USB hard drives	Two or more external eSATA or USB hard drives

MORE INFO   See Chapter 11, "Disk Management," for more information on RAID. See Chapter 12, "Storage Management," for more information about choosing the appropriate storage solution. See Chapter 16, "Configuring Backup," for more information about creating a backup strategy and choosing backup devices.

 UNDER THE HOOD   **Determining Server Load**

The appropriate hardware for an SBS 2011 server depends on the load you place it under. Think of load as equal to the number of requests per unit of time multiplied by the difficulty of fulfilling each request.

The easiest way to determine load is to sample the performance of the existing server over a range of conditions. Of course, this is tricky when you're constructing a new network or restructuring an existing network. Consider the following factors:

- **The usage pattern over time (number of requests per unit of time)** A server that handles an average load can easily become swamped at key times, such as at the beginning and end of a workday, when many users simultaneously log on or log off; during lunch, when users might browse the Internet for personal use; or around deadlines, when many users make heavy use of file, email, or database services.

- **The kinds of user requests (the complexity of each request)** This determines which server subsystems are stressed most heavily. Database serving stresses storage, memory, and possibly CPU; file serving stresses mostly storage and I/O; remote access stresses memory and I/O primarily; Exchange Server stresses storage, memory, and to some extent CPU.

Choosing Client Hardware and Software

When selecting client computers for use on a network, choose systems that are fast enough to perform adequately when running Windows7 Professional. (See Table 3-5 for recommended configurations.) Other operating systems—such as Windows XP, Mac OS X, and Linux—can be made to work on an SBS 2011 network; however, they won't provide full support for many features of SBS.

TABLE 3-5 Recommended client computer configurations

COMPONENT	MINIMUM CONFIGURATION	BETTER CONFIGURATION
Operating System	Windows XP Professional SP3	Windows 7 Professional or Enterprise
CPU	Pentium 4, 2.0 GHz or faster	Dual-core processor, 2.0 GHz or faster
RAM	256 MB	2 GB
Hard drive	30 GB	100 GB
Network Adapter	Fast Ethernet or 802.11g	GigE, 802.11n
Display	15-inch monitor running at 800 x 600 resolution	17-inch monitor running at 1024 x 768 resolution

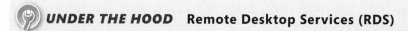

UNDER THE HOOD Remote Desktop Services (RDS)

Computers too slow to adequately run a Windows XP operating system can be put to use as Remote Desktop or Virtual Desktop Infrastructure (VDI) clients. In this configuration, users connect to a separate Windows Server 2008 R2 computer running the RD Session Host or RD Virtualization Host role. This server can provide a full desktop replacement (VDI) or a full desktop session (RD Session Host), or it can be used to supplement the power of the client by running key applications as RemoteApps and displaying them on the client.

This second server *cannot* be the same physical computer as the Windows Small Business Server computer unless virtualization is used to run multiple *virtual machines* (VMs) on a single physical computer. With either RDS or VDI, all processing is done on the server, and the display is sent back to the client computer, which can run any supported RDS client operating system.

This approach can make more efficient use of resources and make central management easier. The new RemoteApps simplifies deploying resource-intensive applications to users without having to upgrade everyone's computer, while the use of VDI allows full-featured Windows 7 desktops to be deployed to less powerful clients. For more information on Remote Desktop Services and VDI, see Chapter 26, "Adding a Terminal Server."

Choosing Naming Conventions

Creating naming conventions makes choosing names for computers, shared folders, and users easier and lends consistency to the network. This consistency results in a more user-friendly network.

> **MORE INFO** For help with naming users, see Chapter 9, "Managing Users and Groups." For help with naming shared folders, see Chapter 10, "Shares and Permissions."

Choosing a Domain Name for the Network

The domain name is the most important and politically sensitive name on the network, and it is one you can't change without starting all over and completely rebuilding your network. Do *not* make this decision without consulting everyone who has a stake in the result. By getting others involved in the process, you'll have a much greater chance of acceptance.

Some questions to ask when choosing a domain name include

- Is the name easy to remember, and does it make sense for the company? This could be the company name in its most common form or an abbreviation.

- Is the name 15 characters or shorter? Use only letters, numbers, the underscore, and a hyphen in the name to ensure DNS and NetBIOS compatibility.

- Is the name available? If the name is already in use as an Internet domain name for another company, you'll have to either choose a different name or have a different internal and external domain name.

- If you already have an Internet website, use the same name, without the extension, for your internal domain name. For example, if the company uses *www.example.com* for its Internet website, use *example* for the domain name. The Windows Small Business Server 2011 Standard Installation Wizard will automatically add a .local extension to the name you choose.

- As soon as you choose a domain name, register it (preferably with .com, .net, or .org) on the Internet so that another company can't purchase it.

> **IMPORTANT** Changing your internal domain name is impossible without a complete re-installation, so picking a name that will last is critical.

 REAL WORLD **Internal Domain Name vs. Internet Domain Name**

There are two domain names you need to worry about when setting up your network: the Internet domain name that the outside world sees for your company and email, and the internal domain name that Windows Small Business Server uses. They are usually related but not identical. The public, Internet domain name needs to be globally unique, officially registered with a Domain Naming Service, and clearly identifiable as your company. The internal, Windows name can be anything at all, though it usually is the same as the external, public one, but with a different top-level domain.

So if your company is Example Widgets and your public Internet domain name is example.com, your internal Windows domain name could be something like example.local. This makes it easy to keep track of, and it gives you complete control over managing the internal DNS of your Windows Small Business Server network while allowing you to have a reliable third party manage your public DNS records.

Although it is technically possible to change your public name, it's neither easy nor painless, and it's virtually impossible to change your internal name without having to completely rebuild your network from scratch. So it's worth spending time up front to make sure you're choosing a name that is appropriate and has the support of all parties.

Another possibility is to choose a completely generic name for your internal domain that has nothing whatsoever to do with your company name. This works great if you change your public name because nothing has to change on your network. But it's not an approach we like. We've always preferred naming based on the company name—it's just easier for everyone to understand and remember.

Naming Computers

It's easy for *you* to keep a map of what the different clients and servers are called and where they are on the network, but if you make life hard on users, you pay in the long run. So naming all the computers after Shakespearean characters or Norse gods might make sense to you, but it isn't going to help users figure out that Puck is the Windows Small Business Server computer and Odin is the desktop used for payroll.

On the other hand, using Srv1 for the SBS server tells everyone immediately which computer it is. When naming computers, use a consistent convention and sensible names, such as the following:

- SRV1 or SBSSRV for the Windows Small Business Server 2011 Standard computer
- FrontDesk for the receptionist's computer

In this book, we'll be using a somewhat more complicated naming convention that identifies the physical host computer, the role of the computer, and the IP address of the computer. Thus our SBS server is hp160-SBS2011, signifying that it's running on the Hewlett-Packard DL 160 G6 server, and that it's running Windows Small Business Server 2011 Standard. There are several virtual machines running on that HP server, so it gets a fair workout.

Our naming convention is more complicated than most small businesses need, but it serves our needs where we are continually building and rebuilding test environments for writing projects. Ultimately, it doesn't matter what you name your computers, as long as everyone understands the convention and can find the resources they need.

Planning for Security

It is far easier to implement effective security measures to protect your SBS network if you plan for security *before* you actually start installing software. In the following sections, we'll cover some of the most common attack vectors and the preliminary steps you can take in this planning stage to prepare your defenses:

- **Careless or disgruntled employees and former employees**   Internal users and former users are the biggest risk factors to data loss and data theft on most computer networks. Whether from laziness, disregard of security policies, or outright malice, the internal user is often the most dangerous on your network. To help reduce risks related to this, refer to the "Ensuring Physical Security" section of this chapter as well as to Chapter 8, "Completing the Getting Started Tasks."

- **Internet hackers**   All computers and devices attached directly to the Internet are subject to random attacks by hackers. According to the Cooperative Association for Internet Data Analysis (CAIDA), during a random three-week time period in 2001 more than 12,000 DoS attacks occurred: 1200–2400 were against home computers and the rest were against businesses. If your organization has a high profile, it might also be subject to targeted attack by hackers who don't like your organization or who are engaging in corporate espionage.

  For more information about securing a network against Internet hackers, see the "Securing Internet Firewalls" section of this chapter.

- **Wireless hackers and theft of service**   Wireless access points are exposed to the general public looking for free Internet access and to mobile hackers. To reduce this risk, refer to the "Securing Wireless Networks" section in this chapter.

- **Viruses and worms**   Networks are subject to virus exposure from email attachments, infected documents, and worms such as CodeRed and Blaster that automatically attack vulnerable servers and clients. Refer to the "Securing Client Computers" section of this chapter for more information.

Ensuring Physical Security

Although security is not something that can be achieved in absolute terms, it should be a clearly defined goal. The most secure operating system and network in the world is defenseless against someone with physical access to a computer. Evaluate your physical environment to decide what additional security measures you should take, including the following:

- Place servers in a locked server room. And control who has keys!
- Use case locks on your servers, and don't leave the keys in them.
- Place network hubs, routers, and switches in a locked cable room or wiring closet.
- Install case locks on client systems or publicly accessible systems.

- Use laptop locks when using laptops in public.
- Use BitLocker to encrypt the data on laptops that contain sensitive data.

Securing Client Computers

Even a highly secure network can be quickly compromised by a poorly secured client computer—for example, a laptop running an older version of Windows with sensitive data stored on the hard drive. To maximize the security of client computers, use the following guidelines (refer to Chapter 8, "Completing the Getting Started Tasks," and Chapter 14, "Managing Computers on the Network," for more security procedures):

- **Use a secure operating system** Use Windows Vista or Windows 7 on all client computers, with a strong preference for Windows 7 on laptops.
- **Use NTFS, file permissions, BitLocker, and EFS** Use NTFS for all hard drives, and apply appropriate file permissions so that only valid users can read sensitive data. Encrypt sensitive files on laptop computers using the Encrypting File System (EFS), and encrypt at least the system drive on laptops using BitLocker. (BitLocker is available only on Enterprise and Ultimate versions of Windows Vista and Windows 7.)
- **Keep clients updated** Use the Automatic Updates feature of Windows to keep systems updated automatically. Ideally, use the Windows Software Update Service (WSUS), integrated into SBS 2011, to centrally control which updates are installed, as described in Chapter 15, "Managing Software Updates."
- **Enable password policies** Password Policies is a feature of SBS 2011 that requires user passwords to meet certain complexity, length, and uniqueness requirements, ensuring that users choose passwords that aren't trivial to crack.

> **NOTE** Remembering passwords has become an increasingly difficult prospect, leading to the resurgence of the yellow-sticky-note method of recalling them. It's important to discourage this practice, and encourage the use of distinctive but easy-to-remember passphrases. See the Under The Hood sidebar "Beyond Passwords—Two-Factor Authentication" for an alternative to annoyingly complex passwords.

- **Install antivirus software** Antivirus software should be installed on the SBS 2011 computer as well as on all clients. The best way to do this is to purchase a small-business antivirus package that supports both clients and the server. There are good third-party solutions specifically designed for the SBS market from several vendors.
- **Install antispyware software** Antispyware software should be installed on all client computers on the network and configured for real-time monitoring and daily full scans.
- **Keep web browsers secure** Unpatched web browsers are a significant security issue. Always keep web browsers updated with the latest security updates.

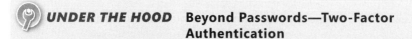

UNDER THE HOOD Beyond Passwords—Two-Factor
Authentication

Password policies are a difficult subject for many small businesses. Serious security using only passwords requires long and complex passwords, changed regularly and never repeated. That's a nice goal, but it's also not something users are going to be all that happy with. If your network contains sensitive information—and whose doesn't these days?—you should consider providing an additional layer of security beyond simple passwords.

Windows Small Business Server 2011 Standard sets reasonable, if somewhat minimal, password policies, but even the best of password policies is a balancing act between making the password difficult to crack and making it easy for users to remember and use so that they aren't tempted to write it down on the back of their keyboards. The four kinds of authentication methods or factors are

- Something you know (password)
- Something you have (token or physical key)
- Something you are (biometric)
- Somewhere you are (location)

Of these, only the first three are realistic and usable in a small business environment, though the fourth—location—is starting to be used by banks as one factor to be sure that the person trying to access your bank account is actually you.

Passwords alone are a single-factor authentication method—in this case, something you know. Two-factor authentication requires two of the main three factors, and it provides a definite improvement in the surety that the person authenticating to your network is really who he claims to be. By enabling a second authentication factor, your need for overly draconian password policies is greatly reduced.

For a second authentication factor, we like the simplicity, moderate cost, and effectiveness of a one-time password (OTP). Generated automatically by a token you carry around with you, the combination of the token, a personal identification number (PIN), and your SBS password provides an additional level of security. Requiring administrators and all remote users to use two-factor authentication is a good way to improve the overall security of the sensitive data on your network.

Third-party providers of OTP tokens include AuthAnvil (*http://www.authanvil.com*), CryptoCard (*http://www.cryptocard.com*), and RSA SecureID (*http://www.rsa.com*). Of these, only AuthAnvil is focused on the small business market, with a suite of products that are fully integrated into SBS. Plus their soft tokens run on our users' phones, greatly simplifying token management and deployment. We use AuthAnvil on our SBS network for all laptops and servers, and for all remote users.

Securing Wireless Networks

Wireless networks using the 802.11b, 802.11a, 802.11g, and 802.11n standards are very convenient but can also introduce significant security vulnerabilities if not properly secured. To properly secure wireless networks, follow these recommendations:

- Change the default password of all access points.

- Change the default SSID. Pick a name that doesn't reveal the identity or location of your network.

- Enable 802.11i (WPA2) encryption on the access points.

- If the access points don't support WPA2-Enterprise, don't use them on your internal network.

> **NOTE** WPA2 provides two methods of authentication: an "Enterprise" method that makes use of a RADIUS server, and a "Personal" method known as WPA2-Personal that uses a Pre-Shared Key (PSK) instead of a RADIUS server.

- Disable the ability to administer access points from across the wireless network.

For more on configuring and protecting wireless networks, see Chapter 19, "Managing Local Connectivity."

Securing Internet Firewalls

Most external firewall devices are secure by default, but you can take some additional steps to maximize the security of a firewall:

- Change the default password for the firewall device! We know this seems obvious, but unfortunately, it is all too often ignored.

- Disable remote administration, or limit it to responding to a single IP address (that of your network consultant).

- Disable the firewall from responding to Internet pings. OK, we admit this is controversial. It's certainly a best practice, but it can also make troubleshooting a connectivity issue remotely a lot harder.

- Enable Stateful Packet Inspection (SPI) and protection from specific attacks, such as the Ping of Death, Smurf, and IP Spoofing.

- Leave all ports on the firewall closed except those needed by the SBS 2011 server.

- Regularly check for open ports using trusted port-scanning sites. We use *http://www.dslreports.com*.

- Require two-factor authentication for all access to the firewall.

- Keep the firewall updated with the latest firmware versions, which are available for download from the manufacturer's website.

Summary

In this chapter, we covered how to design or prepare a network prior to installing Windows Small Business Server 2011 Standard. We also covered basic naming conventions and how to plan for adequate network security.

The next chapter covers planning for fault tolerance and fault avoidance on your SBS network to help you build a reliable SBS network that can support your business.

## CHAPTER 4

Planning Fault Tolerance and Avoidance

E ven the most optimistic system administrator knows that sooner or later she or he will be faced with a major problem. We'll cover preparing for disasters in depth in Chapter 28, "Disaster Planning," and you should refer to that chapter for information on how to prepare for major problems and build a disaster recovery plan to respond quickly and efficiently to major trouble. But as exhilarating as it may be to work through a major problem and successfully recover from it, it's far better to avoid major problems as much as possible.

This chapter focuses on the hardware and software tools that help you to build a highly available and fault-tolerant Microsoft Windows Small Business Server (SBS) environment. Remember, however, that hardware and software are only a small part of the equation—building and deploying for fault tolerance requires time, a clear understanding of the necessary tradeoffs, and—most important—discipline. Yes, you can avoid most computer downtime, but you'll need to be realistic about what your resources are and what you can reasonably afford to spend.

Because SBS does not support clustering (although we'll cover an interesting workaround using virtualization in Chapter 6, "Configuring SBS in Hyper-V"), your options for high availability are somewhat limited. However, you can still take some important steps to improve your availability and fault tolerance. Your primary focus needs to be on building fault tolerance into your server and network infrastructure.

Building fault-tolerant systems doesn't come without costs, in both effort and money. In this chapter, we'll try to help you make informed decisions about where to most cost-effectively build fault tolerance into your SBS environment, while making the best use of your current resources. To use this information, you should have a clear understanding of the business needs you're trying to resolve, and a realistic assessment of the resources available to meet those requirements.

When planning for a highly available and fault-tolerant deployment, you should consider all points of failure and work to eliminate any single point of failure. Redundant power supplies, dual-disk controllers, multiple network interface cards, and fault-tolerant disk arrays such as redundant array of independent disks (RAID) are all strategies you can and should employ.

Mean Time to Failure and Mean Time to Recover

The two most common metrics used to measure fault tolerance and avoidance are the following:

- **Mean time to failure (MTTF)** The mean time until the device will fail
- **Mean time to recover (MTTR)** The mean time it takes to recover after a failure has occurred

Although a great deal of time and energy is often spent trying to lower the MTTF, realize that even if you have a finite failure rate, an MTTR that is zero or near zero might be indistinguishable from a system that hasn't failed. Downtime is generally measured as MTTR divided by MTTF, so increasing the MTTF will reduce the downtime—but at a significant cost.

Trying to increase the MTTF beyond a certain point can be prohibitively expensive. A more cost-effective and realistic strategy, especially in the small business space where resources are finite and customers are very cost-conscious, is to spend both time and resources on managing and reducing the MTTR for your most likely and costly points of failure.

Most modern electronic components have a distinctive "bathtub" curve that represents their failure characteristics, as shown in Figure 4-1. During the early life of the component (referred to as the burn-in phase), it's more likely to fail. When this initial phase is over, a component's overall failure rate remains quite low until it reaches the end of its useful life, when the failure rate increases again.

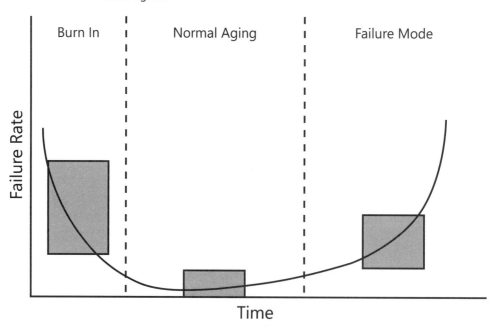

FIGURE 4-1 The normal statistical failure rates for mechanical and electronic components: a characteristic "bathtub" curve

UNDER THE HOOD Hard Disk Reliability

The typical commodity hard disk of 15 years ago had an MTTF on the order of three years. Today, the manufacturer's published MTTF for a typical commodity hard disk is more likely to be 35 to 50 years, with MTTF ratings of server-oriented hard drives hitting 134 years!

At least part of that difference is a direct result of counting only the portion of the curve in the normal aging section, while taking externally caused failure out of the equation. Therefore, a hard disk that fails because of an improperly filtered power spike doesn't count against the MTTF of the disk, nor does a disk that fails in its first week or two. This might be nice for the disk manufacturer's statistics, but it doesn't do much for the system administrator whose system has crashed because of a disk failure.

As you can see, it's important to look at the total picture and carefully evaluate all the factors and failure points on your system. Only by looking at the whole system, including the recovery procedures and methodology, can you build a truly fault-tolerant environment.

Protecting the Power Supply

The single biggest failure point for any network is its power supply. If you don't have power, you can't run your computers. It seems pretty obvious, and most of us slap an uninterruptible power supply (UPS) on the order when we're buying a new server. However, this barely scratches the surface of what you can and should do to protect your network from power problems. You need to protect your network from four basic types of power problems:

- **Local power supply failure** Failure of the internal power supply on a server, router, or other network component
- **Voltage variations** Spikes, surges, sags, and longer-term brownouts
- **Short-term power outages** External power failures lasting from fractions of a second to several minutes
- **Long-term power outages** External power failures lasting from several minutes to several hours or even days

Each type of power problem poses different risks to your network and requires somewhat different protection mechanisms. The level of threat that each poses to your environment varies depending on the area where you are located, the quality of power available to you, and the potential loss to your business if your computers are down.

Local Power Supply Failure

Computer power supplies have made substantial gains in the last 10 years, but they are still one of the greatest risk points. All the power conditioning, uninterruptible power supplies, and external generators in the world won't help much if your server's power supply fails. Most servers these days either come with a redundant power supply or have the option of including one. Take the option! The extra cost associated with adding a redundant power supply to a server or critical piece of network hardware is far less than the cost of downtime if the power supply fails.

We found this out the hard way recently—our main server turned out to have a run of bad power supplies. The manufacturer knew about the problem and replaced them without question. But if it hadn't been for the second power supply in it, we'd have been down and out until the replacement got to us. As it was, they also replaced the second power supply in the server without waiting for it to fail because it was part of the same batch of bad power supplies.

If your server, router, or other piece of network hardware doesn't have the option of a redundant power supply, order a spare power supply for it when you order the original hardware. Don't count on the hardware manufacturer's "four-hour response time," especially when you consider the cost to your business even if they actually repair the equipment in four hours. If you have a spare power supply in a well-marked cabinet where you can easily find it, you can quickly and with minimal disruption replace the failed power supply and return the equipment to full functionality. *Then* you can afford to wait patiently for the manufacturer's service response.

> **NOTE** Most major manufacturers use proprietary components in their servers. This usually means that you can't count on using an off-the-shelf component, such as a power supply, but must use one specifically designed to fit the particular brand and model of server you have.

 REAL WORLD It's Only Useful if You Can Find It!

Having a good supply of critical spares is a great idea, but sometimes reality intrudes. Storage can be the weak link here. Most server rooms are not nearly as spacious as we would like them to be, and in the SBS world a server room might be little more than a lockable closet. If that's the case, make sure the closet has adequate, filtered ventilation and cooling—servers produce a significant amount of heat, and a poorly ventilated environment will greatly shorten the life of your server.

Dust is the enemy of your server—it will impede cooling and can actually short out electrical components. Server rooms should not have carpeting. And remove any printers from the area—printers are dust generators.

All too often, the spare parts end up jammed into a bin or shoved onto an upper shelf with inadequate or nonexistent identification. If your network is down and you need a power supply to get it back up, you don't want to be pawing through a jumble of spare parts looking for the right power supply.

Make every effort to develop a single, central, secure location for all spare parts. At least then you have only a single place to search. Then make sure the manufacturer's part number is visible, and clearly label the computer or computers each part is for. Protect the part from dust and spilled coffee by keeping it in a sealed plastic storage bag.

We like to tape a list of the manufacturer's part numbers, details of the installed hardware, and the list of spare parts we have right inside the case cover of the server itself. It's easy to find and doesn't end up getting lost. It does you no good to have a spare power supply if you can't find it or don't know you have it. And don't forget to include the location of any special tools required. It never ceases to amaze us how many different and apparently unique screwdriver bits we need to get into our various computers! We started our toolkit with an inexpensive computer toolkit, and we add tools to it as needed.

Finally, practice! If you've never replaced a power supply before, and you don't have clear and detailed instructions, it will take you orders of magnitude longer to replace it when the server is down and everyone is yelling and the phone keeps ringing. By practicing the replacement of the power supplies in your critical hardware, you'll save time and reduce the stress involved.

Ideally, document the steps you need to perform, and include well-illustrated and detailed instructions on how to replace the power supplies of your critical hardware as part of your disaster recovery standard operating procedures. If you can swap out a failed power supply in 10 minutes, rather than waiting hours until an outside technician arrives, you've saved more than enough money to pay for the spare part several times over.

Voltage Variations

Even in areas with exceptionally clean power that is always available, the power that is supplied to your network inevitably fluctuates. Minor, short-term variations merely stress your electronic components, but major variations can literally fry them. You should never, ever simply plug a computer into an ordinary wall socket without providing some sort of protection against voltage variations. The following sections describe the types of variations and the best way to protect your equipment against them.

Spikes

Spikes are large but short-lived increases in voltage. They can occur because of external factors, such as lightning striking a power line, or because of internal factors, such as a large motor starting. The most common causes of severe voltage spikes are external and outside your control. The effects can be devastating. A nearby lightning strike can easily cause a spike of 1000 volts or more to be sent into equipment designed to run on 110 to 120 volts. Few, if any, electronic components are designed to withstand large voltage spikes of several thousand volts, and almost all will suffer damage if they're not protected from them.

Protection from spikes comes in many forms, from the $19.95 power strip with built-in surge protection that you can buy at your local hardware store to complicated arrays of transformers and specialized sacrificial transistors that are designed to die so that others may live. Unfortunately, those $19.95 power strips just aren't good enough. They *are* better than nothing, but barely. They have a limited ability to withstand really large spikes.

More specialized (and more expensive, of course) surge protectors that are specifically designed to protect computer networks are available from various companies. They differ in their ability to protect against really large spikes and in their cost. There's a fairly direct correlation between the cost of these products and their rated capacity and speed of action within any company's range of products, but the cost for a given level of protection can differ significantly from company to company. As always, if the price sounds too good to be true, it is.

In general, these surge protectors are designed to work by sensing a large increase in voltage and creating an alternate electrical path for that excessive voltage that doesn't allow it to get through to your server. In the most severe spikes, the surge protectors should destroy themselves before allowing the voltage to get through to your server. The effectiveness of these stand-alone surge protectors depends on the speed of their response to a large voltage increase and the mechanism of failure when their capacity is exceeded. If the surge protector doesn't respond quickly enough to a spike, bad things will happen.

Most UPSs also provide some protection from spikes. They have built-in surge protectors, plus isolation circuitry that tends to buffer the effects of spikes. The effectiveness of the spike protection in a UPS is not directly related to its cost, however—the overall cost of the UPS is more a factor of its effectiveness as an alternative power source. Your responsibility is to read the fine print and understand the limitations of the surge protection a given UPS offers. Also remember that just as with simple surge protectors, large voltage spikes can cause the surge protection to self-destruct rather than allow the voltage through to your server. That's the good news; the bad news is that instead of having to replace just a surge protector, you're likely to have to repair or replace the UPS.

> **NOTE** Online or continuous UPSs are far more effective at protecting downstream electronic equipment than standard reactive UPSs. Even though an online UPS typically costs 1.5 to 2 times the price of a standard reactive UPS of the same capacity, it's money well spent.

Finally, one other spike protection mechanism can be helpful—the constant voltage transformer (CVT). You're not likely to see one unless you're in a large industrial setting, but they are often considered to be a sufficient replacement for other forms of surge protection. Unfortunately, they're not really optimal for spike protection. They do filter some excess voltage, but a large spike is likely to find its way through. However, in combination with either a fully protected UPS or a good stand-alone surge protector, a CVT can be quite effective. They also provide additional protection against other forms of voltage variation that surge protectors alone can't begin to manage.

Surges

Voltage surges and spikes are often discussed interchangeably, but we'd like to make a distinction here. For our purposes, a surge lasts longer than most spikes and isn't nearly as large. Most surges last a few hundred milliseconds and are rarely over 1000 volts. They can be caused by many of the same factors that cause voltage spikes.

Providing protection against surges is somewhat easier than protecting against large spikes. Most of the protection mechanisms just discussed also adequately handle surges. In addition, most CVTs are sufficient to handle surges and might even handle them better if the surge is so prolonged that it threatens to overheat and burn out a simple surge protector.

Sags

Voltage sags are short-term reductions in the voltage delivered. They aren't complete voltage failures or power outages and are shorter than a full-scale brownout. Voltage sags can drop the voltage well below 100 volts on a 110- to 120-volt normal line and cause most servers to reboot if protection isn't provided.

Stand-alone surge protectors provide no defense against sags. You need a UPS or a very good CVT to prevent damage from a voltage sag. Severe sags can overcome the rating of all but the best constant voltage transformers, so you generally shouldn't use a CVT as the sole protection against sags. A UPS, with its battery power supply, is an essential part of your protection from problems caused by voltage sags.

Brownouts

A brownout is a planned, deliberate reduction in voltage from your electric utility company. Brownouts most often occur in the heat of the summer and are designed to protect the utility company from overloading. They are *not* designed to protect the consumer, however.

In general, a brownout reduces the available voltage by 5 to 20 percent from the normal value. A CVT or a UPS provides excellent protection against brownouts, within limits. Prolonged brownouts might exceed your UPS's ability to maintain a charge at the same time that it is providing power at the correct voltage to your equipment. Monitor the health of your UPS carefully during a brownout, especially because the risk of a complete power outage increases if the power company's voltage reduction strategy proves insufficient.

The best protection against extended brownouts is a CVT of sufficient rating to fully support your critical network devices and servers. If you live in an area that is subject to brownouts and your budget can afford it, a good CVT is an excellent investment. This transformer takes the reduced voltage provided by your power company and increases it to the rated output voltage. A good constant voltage transformer can handle most brownouts for an extended time without problems, but you should still supplement the CVT with a quality UPS and surge protection between the transformer and the server or network device. This extra protection is especially important while the power company is attempting to restore power to full voltage, because during this period you run a higher risk of experiencing power and voltage fluctuations.

Short-Term Power Outages

Short-term power outages last from a few milliseconds to a few minutes. They can be caused by either internal or external events, but you can rarely plan for them even if they are internal. A server that is unprotected from a short-term power outage will, at the very least, reboot or, at the worst, fail catastrophically.

The best protection against a short-term power outage is a UPS in combination with high-quality spike protection. Be aware that many momentary interruptions of power are accompanied by large spikes when the power is restored. Further, a series of short-term power outages often occur consecutively, causing additional stress to electronic components.

Long-Term Power Outages

Long-term power outages, lasting from an hour or so to several days, are often accompanied by other, more serious problems unless your server room is in a very remote location. Long-term power outages can be caused by storms, earthquakes, fires, and the incompetence of electric power utilities, among other things. As such, plans for dealing with long-term power outages should be part of an overall disaster recovery plan. (See Chapter 28 for more on disaster planning.)

Protection against long-term power outages really becomes a decision about how long you want or need to function if all power is out. If you need to function long enough to be able to gracefully shut down your network, a simple UPS or a collection of them will be sufficient, assuming that you've sized the UPS correctly. However, if you need to be sure that you can maintain the full functionality of your SBS network during an extended power outage, you're going to need a combination of one or more UPSs and an auxiliary generator. But before you start spending money on generators and failover switches, evaluate the overall infrastructure supplying your power. If you're dependent on Internet connectivity to do business, it does you no good to be up and running in the middle of a two-day power outage if your Internet is also down.

REAL WORLD **Generators Require Serious Expertise and Maintenance**

We've been involved with more than one operation that depended on—and implemented—auxiliary generators to support their operations during extended power outages. Included in this group is our office, thanks to the regular (and often extended) outages that the weather here causes. The results of having an auxiliary generator have been rather mixed, however. The one lesson we've learned the hard way is that simply buying and installing an auxiliary generator will do little, if anything, to keep you up and running when the power goes out. Generators are complex mechanical and electrical machines that require specialized expertise and consistent, conscientious processes and maintenance.

If your situation requires an auxiliary generator to supplement your UPSs, you should carefully plan your power strategy to ensure that your generator has sufficient clean load capacity to provide the power your network will require in the event of a long-term power outage. Portable industrial generators often do not provide clean, sine wave power and are not appropriate for computer networks. Verify with the manufacturer that the generator you are considering is rated for electronics and computers. Generators that produce sine wave output and are rated for electronics are inevitably more expensive than the generators intended for most construction jobs. We had to spend nearly twice as much within the same brand and power rating to get a suitable generator for our office. But it has more than paid for itself since!

Make sure you have a sufficient fuel source to power the generator for as long as you reasonably expect to have power out.

> **IMPORTANT**   For all but the smallest businesses, a generator powered by piped-in natural gas is a far safer and more appropriate solution than a gasoline-powered generator with all the potential issues that storage of gasoline can entail.

To install and set up the generator, you'll need the expertise of a licensed electrician who has experience installing and configuring generator failover switches. Test your solution to make sure you didn't miss anything! Further, you should regularly test the effectiveness of your disaster recovery plans and make sure that all key personnel know how to start the auxiliary generator manually in the event it doesn't start automatically.

Finally, you should have a regular preventive maintenance (PM) program in place that services and tests the generator and ensures that it is ready and functioning when you need it. This PM program should include both static tests and full load tests on a regular basis, and it should also call for periodically replacing the fuel to the generator if it's gasoline powered. One of the best ways to do all of this is to plan and execute a "disaster day" for testing your entire disaster recovery plan in as close to real-world conditions as possible, including running your entire operation from the backup generator.

Disk Arrays

The most common computer hardware malfunction is probably a hard disk failure. Even though hard disks have become more reliable over time, they are still subject to failure, especially during their first month or so of use. They are also vulnerable to both catastrophic and degenerative failures caused by power problems. Fortunately, disk arrays have become the norm for servers, and good fault-tolerant hardware RAID systems are available and supported on SBS. The choice of RAID and the particulars of how you configure your RAID system can significantly affect the cost of your servers. To make an informed choice for your environment and needs, you must understand the tradeoffs and the differences in fault tolerance, speed, configurability, and so on.

Hardware vs. Software

RAID can be implemented at the hardware level, using RAID controllers, or at the software level, either by the operating system or by a third-party add-on. SBS supports both hardware RAID and its own software RAID.

Hardware RAID implementations require dedicated controllers and cost somewhat more than an equivalent level of software RAID. However, for that extra price, you get a faster, more flexible, and more fault-tolerant RAID. When compared to the software RAID provided in SBS 2010, a good hardware RAID controller supports more levels of RAID, on-the-fly reconfiguration of the arrays, hot-swap and hot-spare drives (discussed later in this chapter), and dedicated caching of both reads and writes.

Software RAID requires that you convert your disks to dynamic disks. We don't recommend converting your system disk or boot disks, because dynamic disks can be more difficult to access if a problem occurs, and the SBS setup and installation program provides only limited support. For maximum fault tolerance, we recommend using hardware mirroring (RAID-1) on your system drive. Dynamic disks, and the software RAID they support, are also a problem for virtualization and should not be used when you are virtualizing SBS.

RAID Levels for Fault Tolerance

Except for level 0, RAID is a mechanism for storing sufficient information on a group of hard disks so that even if one hard disk in the group fails, no information is lost. Some RAID arrangements go even further, providing protection in the event of multiple hard disk failures. The more common levels of RAID and their appropriateness in a fault-tolerant environment are shown in Table 4-1.

TABLE 4-1 RAID levels and their fault tolerance

LEVEL	NUMBER OF DISKS*	SPEED	FAULT TOLERANCE	DESCRIPTION
0	N	+++	- - -	Striping alone. Not fault-tolerant—it actually increases your risk of failure—but does provide for the fastest read and write performance.
1	2N	+	++	Mirror or duplex. Slightly faster read than single disk, but no gain during write operations. Failure of any single disk causes no loss in data and minimal performance hit.
3	N+1	++	+	Byte-level parity. Data is striped across multiple drives at the byte level with the parity information written to a single dedicated drive. Reads are much faster than with a single disk, but writes operate slightly slower than a single disk because parity information must be generated and written to a single disk. Failure of any single disk causes no loss of data but can cause a significant loss of performance.
4	N+1	++	+	Block-level parity with a dedicated parity disk. Similar to RAID-3 except that data is striped at the block level.
5	N+1	+	++	Interleaved block-level parity. Parity information is distributed across all drives. Reads are much faster than a single disk, but writes are significantly slower. Failure of any single disk provides no loss of data but results in a major reduction in performance.
6	N+2	+	+++	Replicated interleaved block-level parity. Parity information is distributed across all drives, with two parity blocks on separate drives for every stripe. Reads are much faster than a single disk, but writes are significantly slower. Failure of any two disks provides no loss of data but results in a major reduction in performance.

LEVEL	NUMBER OF DISKS*	SPEED	FAULT TOLERANCE	DESCRIPTION
0+1 and 10	2N	+++	++	Striped mirrored disks or mirrored striped disks. Data is striped across multiple mirrored disks, or multiple striped disks are mirrored. Failure of any one disk causes no data loss and no speed loss. Failure of a second disk could result in data loss. Faster than a single disk for both reads and writes.
Other	Varies	+++	+++	Array of RAID arrays. Different hardware vendors have different proprietary names for this RAID concept. Excellent read and write performance. Failure of any one disk results in no loss of performance and continued redundancy.

In the Number of Disks column, N refers to the number of hard disks required to hold the original copy of the data. The plus and minus symbols show relative improvement or deterioration compared to a system using no version of RAID. The scale peaks at three symbols.

NOTE RAID is an excellent solution for fault tolerance, but it can't protect you against corruption caused by hardware or software failures. Only a good backup of data from before the corruption can protect against that.

When choosing the RAID level to use for a given application or server, consider the following factors:

- **Intended use** Will this application be primarily read-intensive, such as file serving, or will it be predominantly write-intensive, such as a transactional database? SBS servers are heavily write-intensive, at least on the disks that Microsoft Exchange uses. Virtualization is also highly disk-intensive.

- **Fault tolerance** How critical is this data, and how much can you afford to lose?

- **Availability** Does this server or application need to be available at all times, or can you afford to reboot it or otherwise take it offline for brief periods?

- **Performance** Is this application or server heavily used, with large amounts of data being transferred to and from it, or is this server or application less I/O-intensive? If this is your main SBS server, it's heavily used.

- **Cost** Are you on a tight budget for this server or application, or is the cost of data loss or unavailability the primary driving factor?

You need to evaluate each of these factors when you decide which type of RAID to use for a server or portion of a server. No single answer fits all cases, but the final answer requires you to carefully weigh each of these factors and balance them against your situation and your needs. The following sections take a closer look at each factor and how it weighs in the overall decision-making process.

Intended Use

The intended use, and the kind of disk access associated with that use, plays an important role in determining the best RAID level for your application. Think about how write-intensive the application is and whether the manner in which the application uses the data is more sequential or random. Is your application a three-square-meals-a-day kind of application, with relatively large chunks of data being read or written at a time, or is it more of a grazer or nibbler, reading and writing little bits of data from all sorts of different places?

If your application is relatively write-intensive, you'll want to avoid software RAID or RAID-5 and RAID-6 if other considerations don't require them. With RAID-5 and RAID-6, any application that requires more than 50 percent writes to reads is likely to be at least some-what slower, if not much slower, than it would be on a single disk or a RAID-1 mirror. You can mitigate this to some extent by using more but smaller drives in your array and by using a hardware controller with a large cache to offload the parity processing as much as possible. RAID-1, in either a mirror or duplex configuration, provides a high degree of fault tolerance with no significant penalty during write operations—a good choice for the system disk.

If your application is primarily read-intensive and the data is stored and referenced se-quentially, RAID-3 or RAID-4 might be a good choice. Because the data is striped across many drives, you have parallel access to it, improving your throughput. And because the parity information is stored on a single drive rather than dispersed across the array, sequential read operations don't have to skip over the parity information and are therefore faster. However, write operations are substantially slower, and the single parity drive can become an I/O bottleneck during write operations.

> **NOTE** RAID-3 and RAID-4 have been largely supplanted by other RAID technologies, primarily RAID-5 and RAID-10. In an SBS environment, RAID-3 and RAID-4 are unlikely to be an appropriate choice, and you should consider them only for specialized applications.

If your application is primarily read-intensive and not necessarily sequential, RAID-5 and RAID-6 are obvious choices. They provide a good balance of speed and fault tolerance, and the cost is substantially lower than the cost of RAID-1 or RAID-10. Disk accesses are evenly distributed across multiple drives, and no single drive has the potential to be an I/O bottle-neck. However, writes require calculation of the parity information and the extra write of that parity, slowing write operations down significantly. Windows Small Business Server file shares are a good fit for RAID 5 and RAID 6, but avoid them for the volume that holds write-intensive database files.

If your application provides other mechanisms for data recovery or uses large amounts of temporary storage that doesn't require fault tolerance, a simple RAID-0, with no fault tolerance but fast reads and writes, is a possibility. However, we strongly advise against RAID-0 on an SBS server unless you clearly understand that anything on a RAID-0 array is completely unprotected and is actually more likely to fail than a single disk.

Fault Tolerance

Carefully examine the fault tolerance of each of the possible RAID choices for your intended use. All RAID levels except RAID-0 provide some degree of fault tolerance, but the effect of a failure and the ability to recover from subsequent failures are different.

If a drive in a RAID-1 mirror or duplex array fails, a full, complete, exact copy of the data remains. Access to your data or application is unimpeded, and performance degradation is minimal, although you do lose the benefit gained on read operations of being able to read from either disk. Until the failed disk is replaced, however, you have no fault tolerance on the remaining disk. Once you replace the failed disk, overall performance is significantly reduced while the new disk is initialized and the mirror is rebuilt. Modern RAID controllers can vary the speed of data reconstruction when replacing a failed disk, allowing you to balance the speed of regeneration against the performance degradation.

In a RAID-3 or RAID-4 array, if one of the data disks fails, a significant performance degradation occurs because the missing data needs to be reconstructed from the parity information. Also, you'll have no fault tolerance until the failed disk is replaced. If the parity disk fails, you'll have no fault tolerance until it is replaced, but also no performance degradation. Once you replace the failed disk, overall performance is significantly reduced while the new disk is initialized and the parity information or data is rebuilt.

In a RAID-5 array, the loss of any disk results in a significant performance degradation, and your fault tolerance will be gone until you replace the failed disk. Once you replace the disk, you won't return to fault tolerance until the entire array has a chance to rebuild itself, and performance is seriously degraded during the rebuild process.

In a RAID-6 array, the loss of any disk results in a significant performance degradation, but you will still be fault tolerant. The failure of a second disk will not cause data loss, but it will leave you with no fault tolerance. Once you replace a failed disk, you won't return to full fault tolerance until the entire array has a chance to rebuild itself, and performance is seriously degraded during the rebuild process.

If a drive in a RAID 0+1 or RAID-10 array fails, a full, complete, exact copy of the data remains. Access to your data or application is unimpeded, and performance degradation is minimal. Until the failed disk is replaced, however, you have incomplete fault tolerance on the array. A second disk failure, if it occurs on the opposite side of the mirror, will cause data loss. Once you replace the failed disk, overall performance is significantly reduced while the new disk is initialized and the mirror is rebuilt. Modern RAID controllers can vary the speed of data reconstruction when replacing a failed disk, allowing you to balance the speed of regeneration against the performance degradation.

RAID systems that are arrays of arrays can provide for multiple failure tolerance. These arrays provide for multiple levels of redundancy and are appropriate for mission-critical applications that must be able to withstand the failure of more than one drive in an array.

Availability

All levels of RAID, except RAID-0, provide higher availability than a single drive. However, if availability is expanded to also include the overall performance level during failure mode, some RAID levels provide definite advantages over others. Specifically, RAID-1 and its derivatives, RAID-10 and RAID 0+1, provide enhanced availability when compared to RAID levels 3, 4, 5, and 6 during failure mode. The performance degradation is minimal when compared to a single disk if one half of a mirror fails, whereas a RAID-5 or RAID-6 array has substantially compromised performance until the failed disk is replaced and the array is rebuilt.

In addition, RAID systems that are based on an array of arrays can provide higher availability than RAID levels 1 through 6. Running on multiple controllers, these arrays are able to tolerate the failure of more than one disk and the failure of one of the controllers, providing protection against the single point of failure inherent in any single-controller arrangement. RAID 1 that uses duplexed disks running on different controllers—as opposed to RAID-1 that uses mirroring on the same controller—also provides this additional protection and improved availability.

Hot-swap drives and hot-spare drives (discussed later in this chapter) can further improve availability in critical environments, especially hot-spare drives. By providing for automatic failover and rebuilding, they can reduce your exposure to catastrophic failure and provide for maximum availability.

Performance

The relative performance of each RAID level depends on the intended use. The best compromise for many situations is arguably RAID-5 or RAID-6, but you should question the adequacy of that compromise if your application is fairly write-intensive. Especially for relational database data and index files where the database is moderately or highly write-intensive, the performance hit of using RAID-5 or RAID-6 can be substantial. A better alternative is to use RAID 0+1 or RAID-10.

Whatever level of RAID you choose for your particular application, it will benefit from using more small disks rather than a few large disks. The more drives contributing to the stripe of the array, the greater the benefit of parallel reading and writing you'll be able to realize— and your array's overall throughput will improve.

Cost

The delta in cost between RAID configurations is primarily the cost of drives, potentially including the cost of additional array enclosures because more drives are required for a particular level of RAID. RAID-1—either duplexing or mirroring—is the most expensive of the conventional RAID levels because it requires at least 33 percent more raw disk space for a given amount of net storage space than other RAID levels.

Another consideration is that RAID levels that include mirroring or duplexing must use drives in pairs. Therefore, it's more difficult (and more expensive) to add on to an array if you need additional space on the array. A net 144-gigabyte (GB) RAID 0+1 array, comprising four 72-GB drives, requires four more 72-GB drives to double in size—a somewhat daunting prospect if your array cabinet has bays for only six drives, for example. A net 144-GB RAID-5 array of three 72-GB drives, however, can be doubled in size simply by adding two more 72-GB drives, for a total of five drives.

RAID arrays based on 2.5-inch drives are rapidly replacing traditional 3.5-inch drives. The smaller 2.5-inch drives take up less physical space for the same amount of total storage, while consuming substantially less power and generating less heat. The initial cost of the array is essentially similar to that of an equivalent array using 3.5-inch drives, but the ongoing costs are less. Our current preferred array system uses eight 2.5-inch SAS drives configured as RAID 0+1. The entire array fits in the space of a pair of standard CD/DVD drives.

Hot-Swap and Hot-Spare Disk Systems

Hardware RAID systems can provide for both hot-swap and hot-spare capabilities. A hot-swap disk system allows failed hard disks to be removed and a replacement disk to be inserted into the array without powering down the system or rebooting the server. When the new disk is inserted, it is automatically recognized and either will be automatically configured into the array or can be manually configured into it. Additionally, many hot-swap RAID systems allow you to add hard disks into empty slots dynamically and automatically or manually increase the size of the RAID volume on the fly without a reboot.

A hot-spare RAID configuration uses an additional, preconfigured disk or disks to automatically replace a failed disk. These systems can be configured to automatically regenerate the array in the event of a failure, thus maintaining maximal redundancy. When combined with a RAID configuration that can withstand multiple drive failures, such as RAID-6, a hot-spare system provides a very high degree of redundancy and availability.

Even where you don't have a hot-spare drive already configured into your array, it makes sense to always keep a matching spare drive available in your replacement-parts cabinet. Hard drives aren't all that expensive, and having a spare will save you time if you have a drive failure in your array. Plus, with drive sizes and technology changing rapidly, it can be annoying to try to find a matching drive two or three years after you buy the original array.

Redundant Networking

Having a server up and running is fairly useless if the server can't communicate with the rest of your network or the outside world. Building redundancy into your power and disk systems is important, but it does you little good if your networking fails.

Protecting against a network-card failure can be as simple as having a spare network card, ideally of the same type as is in your server. In the event of a failure, replacing the card takes only a few minutes longer than it takes to reboot the server, if you can find the spare. A better option is to leave the spare card plugged in to a spare slot but disabled in Windows.

Finally, if your server supports it, using network card teaming provides redundancy in the event of failure with higher throughput under normal operation. But be sure your application supports teamed networking before implementing it. Unfortunately, SBS doesn't officially support network teaming, and it can play havoc with the SBS wizards. Given that, we don't recommend it.

When your network interface is on the motherboard, as is common these days, it's generally not as easy to provide identical redundant network interfaces unless they are built into the server. Nonetheless, having a server-quality network card available and ready to drop into the server in the event of a failure can make recovery much quicker.

If your business depends on Internet connectivity (and whose business doesn't at least require email these days?), one point of failure that can easily be missed is your Internet connection. Solving this problem, however, is not at all difficult—simply replace your standard router with a dual-WAN router and bring in a second Internet service. We have both cable and DSL available to our office, so we added a Xincom dual-WAN router that does basic load balancing when both connections are working, but still provides acceptable bandwidth when either connection is down.

Finally, under networking, we strongly suggest your server have a low-level network port that can be used to directly connect to the server even if the operating system is unresponsive. If you have a Hewlett-Packard device, this is called an iLO port (short for integrated lights out). For Dell, it's a DRAC (Dell Remote Access Card). Other server manufacturers have similar technologies. This is a network card that is powered up and reachable well before any operating system gets loaded and is managed entirely in firmware.

Other Spare Parts

So you've got a spare power supply, a spare hard drive for your array, and a spare NIC. Is that enough? Well, it puts you way ahead of many businesses, but are there any other parts that you should keep available? Any other peripheral or card that you couldn't run your business without is a good candidate for a spare. Another candidate is a spare video card, though this is less critical. You can, after all, always Remote Desktop into the server if you need to, and replacement video cards are easy and quick to come by.

Any other cards or peripherals that you would have problems doing without for the time it takes to get a new one to replace a failure is a good candidate for your spare-parts cabinet. We like to keep a spare network switch with a few spare network cables available. Another smart choice is to keep a spare of your DSL modem or boundary router.

Summary

Building a highly available and fault-tolerant system requires you to carefully evaluate both your requirements and your resources to eliminate single points of failure within the system. You should evaluate each of the hardware subsystems within the overall system for fault toler-ance, and ensure that recovery procedures are clearly understood and practiced to reduce recovery time in the event of a failure. UPSs, redundant power supplies, redundant network-ing, and RAID systems are all methods for improving overall fault tolerance.

Now that we've covered the planning and preparation of your SBS network, it's time to move on to the actual installation and setup of SBS. In the next part, we'll cover new installa-tions, migrating from an existing SBS or Windows Server network, and some special consid-erations for using virtualization to build your SBS network. The first chapter in this next part covers a typical first-time installation of Windows Small Business Server 2008.

PART II

Installation and Setup

## CHAPTER 5

Installing Small Business Server 2011

This chapter covers performing a clean installation of Microsoft Windows Small Business Server (SBS) 2011. All installations of SBS 2011 are clean installs because there is no direct upgrade path from an existing SBS installation—only a migration. We'll cover migrations in detail in Chapter 7, "Migrating to Windows Small Business Server 2011," so if you're installing in an existing Windows domain environment—either SBS or Windows Server—you'll want to jump ahead to Chapter 7.

If you're installing in a virtual environment, and it's a fresh install, go ahead and read this chapter, but hold off on actually performing any of the steps until you've had a chance to read Chapter 6, "Configuring SBS in Hyper-V."

Planning

Chapters 2 through 4 already covered most of the planning issues associated with installing SBS, but there are a few more items to take care of. You should have the hardware all assembled; now it's time to

- Verify the physical configuration of the network.
- Decide on what IP address range you'll be using.
- Choose network names.

You'll also want to decide how the storage on your SBS server should be apportioned. The installation wizard for Windows Small Business Server 2011 is quite good and asks only a few basic questions about your business and the network names and passwords you want to use. Everything else is saved for the Getting Started task list once the installation completes.

Planning Partitions

One thing that the installation wizard does not explicitly ask is how to partition your hard disk space. The default installation will put everything on a single partition that takes up all the space on your first hard disk. SBS 2011 makes it easy to move data such as user shares and Microsoft Exchange data to new locations whenever you want, so careful planning up front isn't critical, especially if some of your hard disk space won't be visible until the operating system is fully installed and you can install drivers for the space.

Our recommendation is to at least create a partition for the initial installation, and to size it appropriately for the system drive of SBS. We recommend that you create a partition during the initial installation screens for Small Business Server 2011 that is *at least* 120 gigabytes (GB) in size. (200 GB is a more realistic minimum.)

 REAL WORLD **Dividing Storage**

Although you can have a single large partition and put everything on it, there are compelling reasons to divide hard-drive space into at least three different partitions, even if you are using hardware RAID. The three partitions are

- The primary operating system partition.

- A partition for static storage. Use this primarily for read-intensive storage, such as company-wide shared folders, application installations, and installation sources.

- A partition for data, logs, and other volatile information. This will be the most active partition and should have a storage technology optimized accordingly.

Dividing your storage space into logical partitions in this way makes backups and disaster recovery easier and allows you to focus your efforts on the critical data partition.

Planning Location and Networking

The other planning step you should take prior to installing SBS 2011 is to decide your physical layout and networking layout. The main areas of concern for the physical layout are

- **Server security**   Is the server secure from unauthorized physical access?

- **Network device security**   Are the main network devices secure from unauthorized physical access?

- **Ease of access**   Is it easy to get to the server, and the connections to it, for maintenance?

- **Expandability**   Is there room to add servers as the business grows?

Your SBS server should be physically protected, and access to it should be controlled and monitored. Although not every small business has the luxury of an air-conditioned server room with high-security access control, there are still basic security steps you can and should take.

The server (and main networking equipment) should be in a separate room that can be locked. In a pinch, using a lockable cage in a multipurpose room can work, but then choose your servers for their noise level. A keycode lock is a good choice because it can be easily changed if an employee leaves, and most keycode locks allow for separate keys for individuals and for determining who has been in the room. See Chapter 3, "Planning Your SBS Network," for more on planning for security.

Planning the logical networking is another important step to make sure you've done before starting the actual install. We like to use a simple spreadsheet that shows the necessary information we'll need for the installation. Details on the spreadsheet include

- Internet services provider (ISP) information, including account names, IP addresses, support phone number, and so on.
- Internal network details, including IP address range, router IP address, number and names of clients, and number and names of servers.
- DNS and NetBIOS names that will be used for the new network.
- Router configuration, including any updates that are required to the router, what its default settings are if you have to reset it, what settings you've changed on the router to configure it for SBS, and so on. If your router is enabled for Universal Plug and Play (UPnP), SBS can make at least some of the changes for you automatically.

NOTE Many routers default to either 192.168.0.1, 192.168.1.1, or 10.0.0.1 for their IP address. If you have to reset the router, make sure you have a well-documented way to upload a configuration file to return it to the configuration you've chosen for your network. Leaving the router at one of these common defaults can create issues when setting up virtual private networks, so it's not recommended.

Preparing the Server

Finally, there are a few last steps to take before launching the installation:

- Make sure the server is sized appropriately for the load under which you plan to place it. For more information on server sizing, see Chapter 3.
- If you're installing on an existing server, back up all data and record any important settings.
- Remove the uninterruptible power supply (UPS) management cable from the server (even if it's USB).
- Upgrade the system BIOS to the latest version available.

- Set the boot order in the BIOS to boot from the DVD before the hard disk.

- Locate any mass storage drivers necessary for the system.

- Configure the firewall or router as required.

Installation

The actual installation of Windows Small Business Server 2011 is simple compared to earlier versions of SBS. The initial installation of the operating system asks fewer questions, and the installation of the SBS portion also asks far fewer questions. Plus both can be automated or semi-automated using answer files. We'll walk through a basic installation first, and then address customizations, advanced settings, and automation.

Installation Process

The installation process for Windows Small Business Server 2011 is in two stages. The first stage installs 64-bit Windows Server 2008 R2 Standard, and the second stage installs SBS itself. The important thing here is that the underlying operating system is Windows Server 2008 R2 Standard. There are only three limitations placed on Windows Server 2008 R2 by SBS:

- SBS can only be in a single domain environment—no trust relationships are possible.

- The SBS server must hold all of the Flexible Single Master Operation (FSMO) roles. Additional domain controllers can be installed in the SBS network, but none of the FSMO roles can be moved.

- A maximum of 75 users or device Client Access Licenses (CALs) are allowed.

Installing the Base Operating System

Installing the underlying Windows Server 2008 R2 Standard operating system can be done using any of the deployment methods supported by Windows Server 2008 R2, but you will usually do it by booting from the Windows Small Business Server 2011 Standard Disk1 and following these steps:

1. At the initial screen of the Install Windows Wizard, shown in Figure 5-1, set the localization information for this installation of SBS.

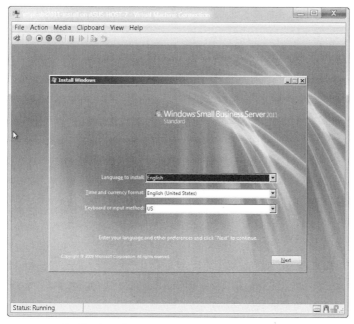

FIGURE 5-1 The first installation window

2. Click Next to open the Install page of the Install Windows Wizard, as shown in Figure 5-2.

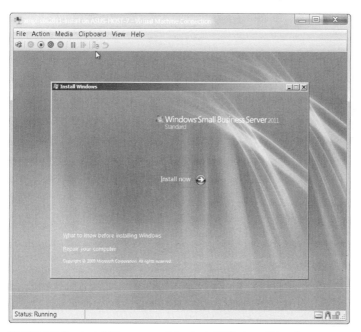

FIGURE 5-2 The Install Now page of the Install Windows Wizard

3. Click Install Now to start Set Up. The next screen presents the licensing terms. Read the terms, select the box to accept the licensing terms, and then click Next.

4. On the next screen, you are asked if you want an Upgrade or a Custom Installation. Select Custom Installation.

NOTE You can choose the Upgrade option, but because upgrades to SBS 2011 aren't possible, this option will lead you in a merry circle, accomplishing nothing.

5. Click Custom (Advanced) to open the Where Do You Want To Install Windows page. You'll see a list of drives and partitions available for installing SBS. If the drive you want to use isn't listed, click Load Driver to open the Load Driver dialog box shown in Figure 5-3. Drivers can be loaded from floppy disk, CD, DVD, or a USB flash drive.

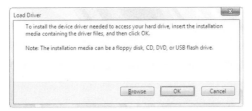

FIGURE 5-3 The Load Driver dialog box during installation

6. Click OK to have Windows search attached removable media and display the results on the Select The Driver To Be Installed page, shown in Figure 5-4. If the driver isn't displayed, click Browse and navigate to the device and folder where the driver is located.

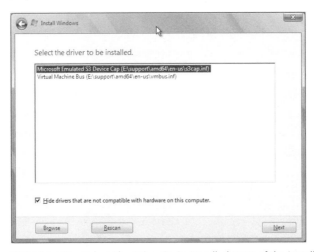

FIGURE 5-4 The Select The Driver To Be Installed page of the Install Windows Wizard

7. Click Next to load the selected driver and return to the Where Do You Want To Install Windows page. Select the partition where you want to install Windows.

8. Click Next to begin the actual installation of Windows Server 2008 R2 Standard. (See Figure 5-5.) No further questions will be asked until the SBS portion of the installation begins.

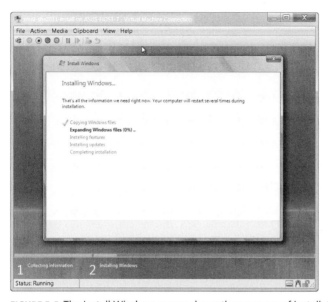

FIGURE 5-5 The Install Windows screen shows the progress of installation

Installing the SBS Portion

After the underlying operating system is installed, Windows will log on and the SBS installation will automatically start. This installation will configure your time zone, your networking, and your server and Windows domain names; configure your business information; and set your administrator account and password for the SBS domain.

Also during this process, you'll have a chance to install any required networking drivers, if Windows doesn't have a built-in driver for your network card, and download the latest updates to protect your server.

> **NOTE** Windows Small Business Server 2011 Standard installation requires that a functioning network card be detected prior to installation. If your network card is not automatically detected by Windows Server 2008 R2, you'll need to download the driver and have it available before the installation of SBS can proceed.

The next screen (see Figure 5-6) asks you to specify a setup mode: a clean install or a migration. Select Clean Install, and click Next to continue the installation.

FIGURE 5-6 Choosing a setup mode

Continue the installation by following these steps:

1. The Verify The Clock And Time Zone Settings page shown in Figure 5-7 opens. Click the Open Date And Time To Verify The Clock And Time Zone Settings link to the standard Windows Date And Time dialog box. Set the time zone and current date and time if they aren't correct, and click OK to return to the Verify The Clock And Time Zone Settings page. Click Next.

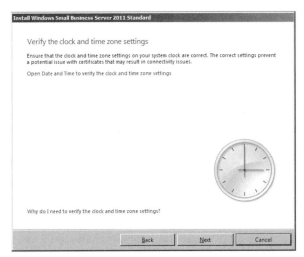

FIGURE 5-7 Use the Open Date And Time link on this page to verify the time and date are correctly set

2. On the Server Network Configuration screen, select how you want the server to detect network settings. Chose Automatic, or you can specify the IP address for your network adapter and server. Click Next.

3. Click Go Online And Get The Most Recent Installation Updates (Recommended). This will download only critical updates that are directly related to installation issues.

4. When the update check is complete, click Next to open the Company Information page shown in Figure 5-8. This information will be used to customize various other areas of SBS. Nothing is required here, but there's no good reason not to enter the information, either—none of it is sent to Microsoft.

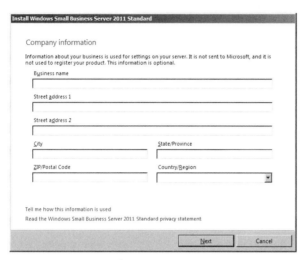

FIGURE 5-8 Company Information screen

5. Click Next to open the Personalize Your Server And Your Network screen, supply a name for your server and the name for your internal network, as shown in Figure 5-9. Click Next.

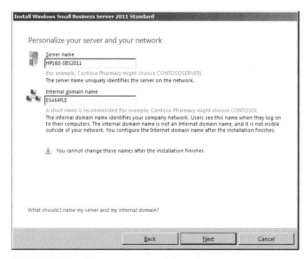

FIGURE 5-9 Providing a server and domain name

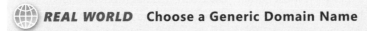

REAL WORLD   Choose a Generic Domain Name

The temptation is to choose a simple domain name that somehow reflects the name of the company that will be using the SBS server. This makes perfect sense, and no one will question it. In fact, this is what we used to do when we set up networks for our customers. And it seemed to work fine. Until the first time one of them merged with another small company and changed their name to reflect the new company. And we had to tell them that there wasn't any way to change the domain name.

The only solution was to rebuild the network from scratch—with all the pain and risk that involved. We learned an important lesson, however. Although it's important to choose a name that makes sense to users—because they'll see it every time they log on to their workstations—make it a generic name that reflects function, not the specific company name.

6. Click Next to add an administrator account, as shown in Figure 5-10. Enter a name for the administrator and an account name (user name) for the account. SBS 2011 does not allow the main administrator account to be named "Administrator". See the "Under The Hood" sidebar for more details on the Administrator account.

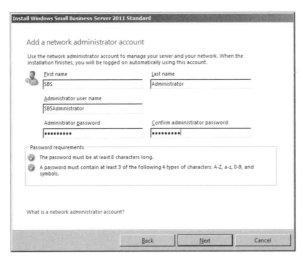

FIGURE 5-10 The Add A Network Administrator Account page of the Install Windows Small Business Server 2008 Wizard

7. Click Next to open the confirmation page shown in Figure 5-11. If everything looks correct, click Next to install SBS.

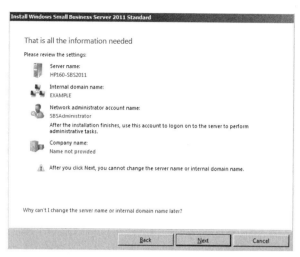

FIGURE 5-11 The confirmation page of the Install Windows Small Business Server 2008 Wizard

---

UNDER THE HOOD **Administrator 500 Account**

SBS requires you to create a new administrator account during a new installation. (We called this account "SBSAdministrator" in the previous examples.) This administrator account is used for all future administration of SBS, and the original *Administrator* account—often referred to as the 500 account from an easily recognizable portion of the account's globally unique identifier (GUID)—is disabled.

The new administrator account password is synchronized with the Directory Service Restore Mode (DSRM) Administrator account password, which is used to recover Active Directory if there's a problem. So far, so good.

But when the password changes for the new administrator account, the underlying DSRM Administrator account is *not* updated. This means that the DSRM Administrator password is tied to that original password and you'll need to keep a permanent record of it in case you need to recover from a problem with Active Directory.

We understand the reasons why Microsoft developers disable the *Administrator* account, but we think it's unfortunate that there isn't a solution in place that would allow the passwords to remain synchronized. However, because SBS 2011 is built on Windows Server 2008 R2, you can use the Restartable AD DS feature, combined with appropriate registry changes, to enable other recovery scenarios. See *http://technet.microsoft.com/en-us/library/cc732714.aspx* for more information on using Restartable AD DS.

Using the SBS Answer File Generator

New in Windows Small Business Server 2008 and still in force in SBS 2011 is the ability to simplify the SBS portion of the installation using an answer file. The answer file is required for doing a migration from an existing domain environment, but it's optional for a clean new installation. It does, however, have some advantages because it allows you to customize some portions of the install that aren't available in the normal install.

Disc1 of Windows Small Business Server 2011 Standard includes a tool called the SBS Answer File Generator (SBSAfg.exe) to create an answer file. SBSAfg.exe is located in the \Tools directory. To use SBSAfg.exe, follow these steps:

1. Copy the file SBSAfg.exe from the SBS 2011 Disc1 to your local hard disk. Where you copy it isn't important as long as you can find it.

2. From Windows Explorer, double-click SBSAfg to start the SBS Answer File Tool, shown in Figure 5-12.

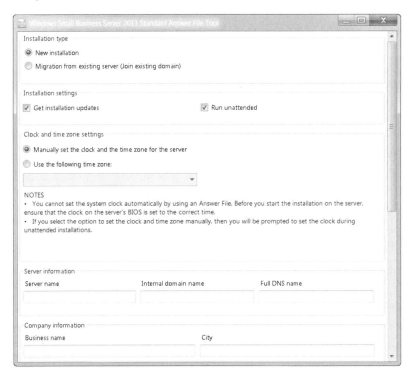

FIGURE 5-12 The SBS Answer File tool

3. Fill in the fields of the Answer File Tool to configure your installation of SBS. If you leave a required field blank, you'll be prompted for that value during the installation.

4. When you've filled in the fields of the Answer File Tool, click Save As to save the answer file. The file name should be SBSAnswerFile.xml.

5. To use the answer file, copy it to removable media such as a USB flash drive or USB hard drive and connect the USB drive to the SBS server *prior* to the initial SBS installation screen (shown earlier in Figure 5-5); SBS will automatically load the answer file and proceed to use it during the installation. You can also copy it to the root of any hard disk attached to the SBS server.

> **NOTE** If you create an empty XML file with the name SBSAnswerFile.xml and make it available to the SBS installation process, as described in step 5, you will have additional options available during the installation process.

> **NOTE** If you're installing on a Hyper-V child partition, where there is no USB available, you can use a virtual floppy drive (VFD) with the SBSAnswerFile.xml on it. Floppy disks work just as well for automating the installation.

Using the answer file is the only way you can specify a different internal root DNS domain name other than ".local". If you use the standard SBS installation, it will automatically add a .local to the internal domain name. But when using an answer file, you can specify any root DNS domain to add.

Summary

This chapter has covered the steps required to prepare for and perform a clean installation of Windows Small Business Server 2011 Standard. After installation, additional configuration specific to your environment is done using the Getting Started task list, which is covered in Chapter 8, "Completing the Getting Started Tasks."

Chapter 6, which follows, discusses Hyper-V in general, and it describes the special considerations for installing SBS in a Hyper-V environment. These considerations, while specific to Hyper-V, are also relevant in a general way for any virtualization environment. Chapter 7 covers migrating an existing Windows Server or Windows Small Business Server environment to Windows Small Business Server 2011 Standard.

## CHAPTER 6

Configuring SBS in Hyper-V

Hyper-V is Microsoft's hypervisor-based, native Windows Server 2008 R2 virtualization solution. Virtualization is one way to simplify and consolidate your Windows Small Business Server (SBS) 2011 server hardware. Using virtualization for your SBS network can be a cost-effective solution that provides an excellent end-user experience while also enabling improved disaster recovery and ease of management. However, virtualization is simply a tool, and one you should choose *when it solves a business problem*.

When we wrote the *Microsoft Windows Small Business Server 2003 Administrator's Companion*, virtualization was a tiny fraction of the market and almost exclusively the province of very large organizations. Microsoft had no virtualization products and provided little or no support for companies and individuals using virtualization. By the time we wrote *Microsoft Windows Small Business Server 2003 R2 Administrator's Companion*, a huge shift had already taken place. Microsoft had bought out a virtualization company and had two products on the market: Virtual PC and Virtual Server. More and more companies were looking to virtualization as a way to consolidate servers, reduce server room footprints, and provide flexible test environments. Virtualization had gone from the "Hey, that's kinda neat" phase to the "Hmmm, you know, that might just make sense" phase. Companies large and small were actively investigating virtualization, planning how to use it, or already deploying it.

Now, fast forward a few years, and virtualization is a way of life for many of us. We couldn't begin to do what we need to do without being able to virtualize, and we're actively deploying virtual solutions in production. Microsoft has gone from having a couple of virtualization products to having a suite of solutions around virtualization, including building it right in to the operating system with the inclusion of Hyper-V in Windows Server 2008.

 **REAL WORLD** **What's Different?**

Why has virtualization suddenly become such a compelling scenario? What has changed? We think that two very important changes are driving the move to virtualize: official support from Microsoft and the move to 64-bit hardware.

Official support means that if you have an issue with Windows or just about any of the Microsoft server applications, and you're running in a virtualized environment, you're still supported, and Microsoft support won't say, "Sorry. Please reproduce that problem on a physical server and we'll be happy to help you." This is an important concern for anyone using virtualization in a production environment.

The wide availability of multicore, 64-bit processors and larger RAM densities is also driving the move to virtualization. The biggest limiting factor for running virtualization on 32-bit Windows is the RAM limitation—you just can't virtualize very many server workloads on a server that is limited to 4 GB of RAM. With Windows Server 2008 R2, which is available *only* in 64-bit, and includes native Hyper-V, running many server workloads on a single physical server is easy. For example, while writing this book, we've been using an HP DL160 G6 server with 24 gigabytes (GB) of RAM and two quad-core processors. That lets us easily run two copies of Windows Small Business Server 2011 in virtual machines, along with a Premium Add-On server and several Windows 7 and Windows Vista virtual machines. And if we need more, the server will easily handle four times that amount of RAM.

In this chapter, we'll cover the specifics of installing and configuring SBS in a Hyper-V environment while we also provide a general overview of Hyper-V and cover basic installation and configuration.

Hyper-V Overview

Windows Server 2008 R2 includes built-in virtualization with the Hyper-V role. Hyper-V is hypervisor-based, native virtualization that uses the hardware virtualization capabilities of the latest Intel and AMD processors to provide a robust, fast, and resource-conserving virtual environment.

Emulation vs. Hypervisor

There are two basic methods of virtualizing operating systems: emulation and hypervisor. *Emulation* builds an execution environment on top of the underlying operating system of the host computer and uses software to simulate the hardware that is made available to the guest operating systems.

A *hypervisor* is software that runs directly on the hardware of the physical server and provides a narrow hardware abstraction layer between the hardware and the base operating system. The hypervisor can use the native hardware support in current Intel and AMD processors to improve the overall performance and security of the hypervisor.

Because Hyper-V is a hypervisor and is built in to Windows Server 2008 R2, it runs more efficiently and natively. A server running Hyper-V has multiple partitions, each running natively on the underlying hardware. The first partition is known as the *parent* partition (or sometimes *host*) and acts as the hardware and operating system control partition for all the other partitions where virtualized operating systems run. The other partitions are *child* partitions (or *guests*), each with their own operating systems, running directly on the hypervisor layer, as shown in Figure 6-1.

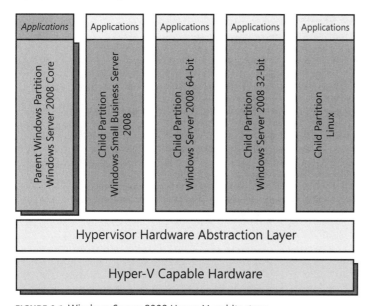

FIGURE 6-1 Windows Server 2008 Hyper-V architecture

Windows Server 2003 supported using Microsoft Virtual Server 2005 R2 as a virtualization solution. Virtual Server is not a hypervisor-based virtualization: it is designed to run on top of an existing operating system—the host operating system—and provide an emulated hardware environment for guest operating systems, as shown in Figure 6-2.

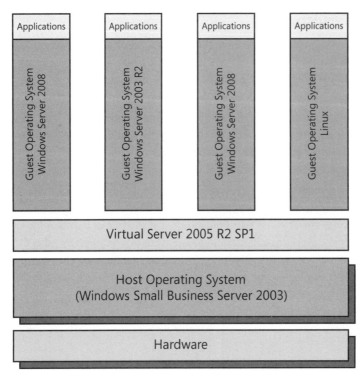

FIGURE 6-2 Microsoft Virtual Server architecture

Hyper-V runs on Windows Server 2008 R2, including Server Core installations, and is also available as a completely free stand-alone server: the Microsoft Hyper-V Server 2008 R2, hereafter known as the Hyper-V Server. In most cases, a Server Core installation or the Hyper-V Server is the preferred parent partition for a server that will be used for virtualization. This limits the resource footprint of the parent partition and also makes it easier to protect because the number of services and attack vectors is fewer. For Windows Small Business Server 2011 Standard, we prefer the stand-alone Hyper-V Server or, for installations using a Premium Add-on, full Windows Server 2008 R2 where a graphical interface is preferred.

Requirements

The requirements for enabling the Hyper-V role on Windows Server 2008 R2 are

- Hardware virtualization support (Intel-VT or AMD-V–enabled CPUs)
- Hardware data execution protection (DEP)–enabled (Intel XD bit or AMD NX bit)

In addition to the requirements for the parent partition of Windows Server 2008 R2, each child partition requires approximately 75 megabytes (MB) of RAM and the hard disk space used by the operating system in the child partition.

Finally, it is important that your server have a minimum of two network interface cards (NICs) installed, exclusive of any special management NICs such as an HP iLO. One of these NICs will be reserved for remote management of the parent server and ensures that you can always connect to the parent partition to manage the child partitions.

REAL WORLD I/O Subsystem

Any virtualization solution puts a lot of stress on the hardware of the I/O subsystem, especially the disk subsystem. Each virtual hard disk is a file, and with multiple operating systems each writing to files independently and concurrently, a lot of I/O traffic is writing to the parent partition's file system. As a result, a weak or slow I/O subsystem will quickly become the bottleneck limiting the overall performance of the virtual machines.

Also, unlike many applications, virtualization tends to be write-intensive, making it essential that you plan your RAID subsystem accordingly. RAID-5 is a much less appealing alternative as a base RAID choice for the parent operating system. You also do not want to run software RAID on the parent Windows Server 2008 R2.

Any RAID subsystem works better the more disks it has. A RAID 0+1 array that has four 1-terabyte disks has 2 terabytes of disk space available, but it is not as fast as a RAID 0+1 array of eight 500-GB disks, which provides the same 2 terabytes of disk space. By adding extra disks, writing to and reading from the array is distributed across more disks, putting less load on each disk.

The same stresses apply to the networking portion of the I/O subsystem that apply to the disk portion. Because many virtual machines can connect through a single physical NIC, you'll want to specify fast and resource-sparing network cards for your Hyper-V server. Here's a clue: a $20 GigE network card is not going to provide the same satisfactory experience as a quality, server-class network card connected to either the PCI-X or PCIe busses. And if you're running more than three or four virtual machines, you're definitely going to want additional NICs to spread the load.

If you're building or specifying a server for Hyper-V (or any virtualization product), don't skimp on the I/O subsystem. A fast RAID controller with a large cache and a wide array with as many disks as you can manage is an important performance choice. And be especially aware of redundancy. If your Hyper-V server fails because you've had two disks in a RAID-5 array fail, not only is the one physical server down, but also your SBS server and every other virtual machine running on that server.

Installation

Installing Hyper-V on Windows Server 2008 R2 uses the native Windows Server 2008 R2 tools—either the graphical Server Manager or, from the command line, ServerManagerCmd. exe or Windows PowerShell's Add-WindowsFeature cmdlet. When installing on Windows Server 2008 R2 Core, use the sconfig utility or the Add-WindowsFeature cmdlet.

REAL WORLD   Choosing a Hyper-V Version

Choosing the source of your Hyper-V virtualization is a balance among convenience, cost, features, and security, and it isn't always an easy choice. The three basic options are

- Windows Server 2008 R2 Full installation
- Windows Server 2008 R2 Core installation
- Microsoft Hyper-V Server 2008 R2

If you bought the Premium Add-on for SBS, you already have a license for Windows Server 2008 R2 Standard. This license gives you the right to install one copy of Windows Server 2008 R2 on the physical server and one copy as a virtual machine, *if you use the copy on the physical server only to support virtualization*. That's an important limitation, and one that is often misunderstood. In practice, if you're using Hyper-V as your virtualization solution, it means you can install *only* the Hyper-V role on the physical server. No additional roles can be installed or you lose the right to install a second copy of Windows Server 2008 R2 Standard as a virtual machine. And here the distinction between a server *role* and a server *feature* is critical. You can't install Active Directory Domain Services or DNS or DHCP or even Fax Server. They're all roles, and by installing them you'd lose your right to install an additional copy of Windows Server. But you *can* install features such as Windows Server Backup, the Windows PowerShell Integrated Scripting Environment (ISE), or the Remote Server Administration Tools (RSAT).

Choosing between the Full installation and the Core installation with the Premium Add-on server is really about your comfort level with the command line for the initial setup. But if you're willing to consider the command line, we think the best bet is the stand-alone Microsoft Hyper-V Server 2008 R2. It's completely free, you don't have any issues with licensing because Hyper-V Server doesn't include any additional roles, and it supports 8 physical processors, 1 terabyte of RAM, and even clustering.

Installing on Microsoft Hyper-V Server R2

To install the Microsoft Hyper-V Server R2, you follow many of the same steps as you would when installing Windows Server, but you don't need to make any choices about which version you're installing because there is only the one version. You'll then perform basic initial configuration of the operating system, including setting the IP addresses, setting the server name, and configuring the Windows Firewall, as detailed in the following section. You will *not* be joining the Hyper-V Server to the domain because the domain will be a child of the parent partition. Scripts to simplify the installation and initial configuration are provided on the companion media that accompanies this book. You will need to enable remote administration as part of the installation because there is no graphical way to directly manage or create virtual machines on the Hyper-V Server—the Hyper-V Manager console won't run on Server Core or Hyper-V Server.

Initial Configuration

The initial configuration steps for a basic Hyper-V Server installation are

- Set a fixed IP address.
- Change the server name to something reasonable.
- Enable remote management through Windows Firewall.
- Enable remote desktop.

Table 6-1 contains the settings we'll be using during this install scenario.

TABLE 6-1 Settings for the initial Hyper-V Server configuration (example)

SETTING	VALUE
IP Address (Management NIC)	192.168.0.4
Gateway	192.168.0.1
DNS Server	192.168.0.2
IP Address (Child Partition NIC)	DHCP
Gateway	192.168.0.1
DNS Server	192.168.0.2
Server Name	Hp160-hyperv
Default Desktop Resolution	1024x768
Remote Management	Enable for All Profiles

> **IMPORTANT** Normally, servers used for SBS 2011 are equipped with only a single network card because SBS 2011 supports only a single NIC configuration. However, if you are using Hyper-V virtualization, you'll want a second NIC to ensure that you maintain management access to the physical computer even if there are problems with the virtualized SBS. That second NIC can be connected to the same subnet (range of IP addresses) as the primary NIC, or it can be on a completely separate network.

To configure the initial settings of a Hyper-V Server installation, follow these steps:

1. Log on to the newly installed Microsoft Hyper-V Server R2 computer. You'll be prompted to change your initial password.

2. After your password change has been accepted, you'll be logged in to the main Hyper-V Server desktop. An uninspiring pair of command windows appears, one running Sconfig.cmd as shown in Figure 6-3.

FIGURE 6-3 The initial Sconfig.cmd screen for a new Hyper-V Server installation

3. Use the Sconfig.cmd menus to configure the initial settings of the Hyper-V Server. Do *not* join it to a domain—leave the server in a workgroup. The settings we used on our test setup are shown in Table 6-1. In addition, you'll likely want to select Download And Install Updates and enable Remote Desktop, at a minimum. The initial configuration will take at least one reboot, and possibly two.

4. After you've finished configuring the Hyper-V Server, you should select option 10 on the main Sconfig menu. This will disable the automatic launching of Sconfig every time you log on to the server. You can always get it back by typing Start Sconfig from the main Cmd window. This will launch Sconfig and also re-enable the automatic launching.

5. Select option 15 to exit Sconfig and return to a simple Cmd window.

Installing on Full Windows Server 2008 R2

To install the Hyper-V role on full Windows Server 2008 R2, first complete the normal installation and configuration of Windows Server 2008 R2, as described in Chapter 24, "Installing the Second Server." When initial configuration has completed, you can install the Hyper-V role using the following steps:

1. Open the Server Manager console if it isn't open already.

2. Select Add Roles from the Action menu to open the Before You Begin page of the Add Roles Wizard.

3. Read the advice on the Before You Begin page. It's actually good advice and a useful reminder. If you've read the page, understand all its implications, and don't ever want to see the page again, select the Skip This Page By Default check box. We leave it unchecked, personally.

> **NOTE** If you've already run the Add Roles Wizard and selected Skip This Page By Default, you won't see the Before You Begin page of the Add Roles Wizard.

4. Click Next to open the Select Server Roles page of the Add Roles Wizard.

5. Select Hyper-V from the list of roles.

6. Click Next to open the Hyper-V page, as shown in Figure 6-4. This page describes the Hyper-V role and includes a Things To Note section that has cautions and advisories specific to the Hyper-V role. The page also has a link to several Additional Information pages with up-to-date information on Hyper-V.

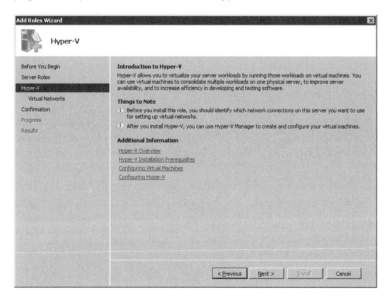

FIGURE 6-4 The Hyper-V page of the Add Roles Wizard

7. After you've read the Things To Note section, click Next to open the Create Virtual Networks page shown in Figure 6-5.

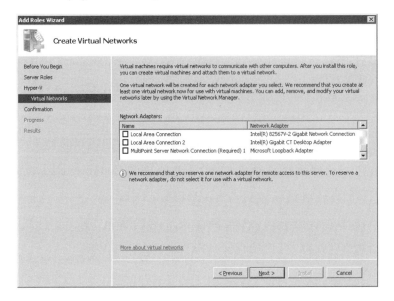

FIGURE 6-5 The Create Virtual Networks page of the Add Roles Wizard

8. Select the ethernet cards you want to create virtual networks for. The general rule is to leave at least one network card not used for virtual networks to ensure that you maintain full remote connectivity to the server.

9. When the Add Roles Wizard has all the information necessary to proceed, it will open the Confirm Installation Selections page. If everything looks correct, click Install to begin the installation.

10. When the installation completes, you'll see the Installation Results page. The Hyper-V installation will require a reboot. Click Close to complete the wizard. Click Yes to reboot right away.

11. After the server reboots, log back on with the same account you used to add the Hyper-V role. The Resume Configuration Wizard will open, and when the configuration is complete, you'll see the final Installation Results page.

12. Click Close to exit the wizard.

Initial Configuration

After you've installed the Hyper-V role, you need to actually configure Hyper-V and then start adding virtual machines. The management tool for Hyper-V is the Hyper-V Manager console. Like other management consoles in Windows Server 2008 R2, it integrates into the Server Manager console. You can use it there or run it as a stand-alone tool. We prefer stand-alone—frankly, it takes up less screen space. Open Administrative Tools, and select Hyper-V Manager from the list to run the stand-alone Hyper-V Manager console.

> **NOTE** You could run the Hyper-V Manager console by starting it from the command line, but unlike other Windows Server 2008 management consoles, it's not put in %windir%\system32. It is actually in %ProgramFiles%\Hyper-V, which isn't on your path. The command line for this is

`"%ProgramFiles%\Hyper-V\virtmgmt.msc"` (quotes required)

> **NOTE** If you're running Hyper-V on Server Core, you need to install the Hyper-V management tools onto a Windows 7 or Windows Server 2008 R2 computer and run them remotely. See Microsoft Knowledge Base article 974877 at *http://support.microsoft.com/kb/974877*. You use the same steps as if you were running the console locally, but you have to connect to the server first.

Configuring Networks

The first step after installing Hyper-V is to configure your networks. The step in the Add Roles Wizard creates the network and attaches it to the network cards you selected. Depending on the selections you made, the networks created during the install might need to be changed to reflect the type of network you need. And, of course, if you installed on Hyper-V Server, no network configuration has been done at all.

Hyper-V supports three kinds of virtual networks:

- **External** An external network is a virtual network switch that binds to the physical network adapter, providing access to resources outside the virtual network. An external network can be assigned to a VLAN.

- **Internal** An internal network is a virtual network switch that allows virtual machines on the server to connect to each other and to the parent partition. An internal network can be assigned to a VLAN.

- **Private** A private network is a virtual network switch that allows virtual machines to connect to each other, but it provides no connection between the virtual machines and the physical computer.

Setting Network Type

To set your networks to be external networks, allowing them to connect through the physical network adapter to outside the physical computer, use the following steps:

1. Open the Hyper-V Manager console if it isn't already open.

2. Select the Hyper-V computer in the left pane, and then click Virtual Network Manager in the Actions pane to open the Virtual Network Manager as shown in Figure 6-6.

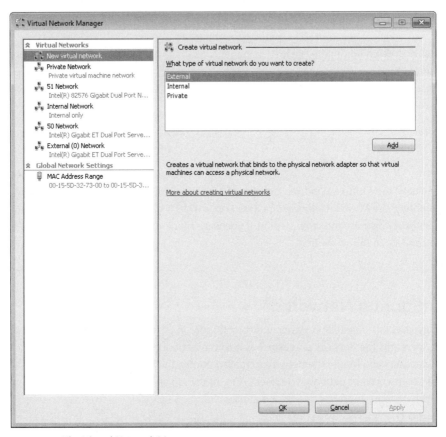

FIGURE 6-6 The Virtual Network Manager

3. Select the Virtual Network you want to make an external network. Edit the name to provide a more meaningful description, and add any notes you want to add.

4. Select External, and select the physical network adapter you want to connect this virtual network to from the drop-down list, as shown in Figure 6-7.

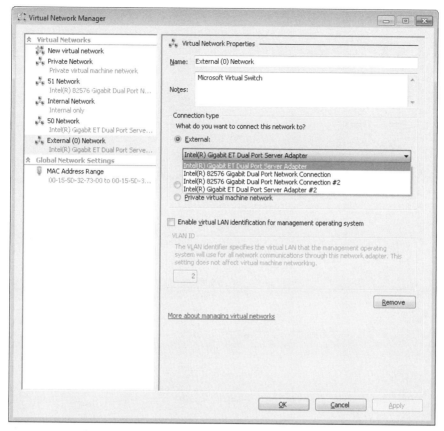

FIGURE 6-7 Attaching a virtual network to a physical adapter to create an external network

5. Click OK to close the Virtual Network Manager, and apply your changes.

Server Settings

The next step in configuring your Hyper-V server is to set the overall server settings and the user-specific settings. General server settings include the default location for hard disks and the default location for virtual machines. User-specific settings include keyboard settings and saved credentials.

To set the server settings for a Hyper-V server, use the following steps:

1. Open the Hyper-V Manager console if it isn't already open.

2. Select the Hyper-V computer in the left pane, and then click Hyper-V Settings in the Actions pane to open the Hyper-V Settings dialog box, shown in Figure 6-8.

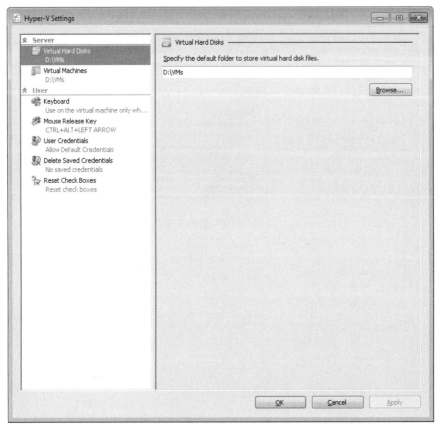

FIGURE 6-8 The Hyper-V Settings dialog box

3. Select Virtual Hard Disks in the left pane, and enter the top of the path to use as a default for storing the virtual hard disk (VHD) files used by virtual machines. You can change the actual path of any specific VHD later. This just sets the default location.

4. Select Virtual Machines in the left pane, and set the default path for storing virtual machine snapshot files.

5. Select Keyboard in the left pane, and specify how special Windows key combinations (such as Alt+Tab and Ctrl+Esc) are used.

6. Select Mouse Release Key, and set the default key combination to release a captured mouse when connecting to a virtual machine that doesn't have integration components installed.

7. Select Delete Saved Credentials or Reset Check Boxes to remove any saved credentials on the server or to reset all the Don't Ask Me Again check boxes on the server.

8. Click OK to change the settings and return to the main Hyper-V Manager.

 REAL WORLD **Default Locations**

The default locations that Microsoft has chosen for VHD files and snapshot files don't make any sense at all. The default location is on the system drive of the parent partition. That's just a really bad idea. Your VHD files could take up hundreds of gigabytes of space, possibly terabytes of space. Do they really think your system drive is the right place for all that? Well, we certainly don't. Frankly, we think they should either ask the question during the install or actually go out and inspect your system and choose an appropriate default based on your system configuration. But they didn't make that choice, so you need to take steps to fix it.

The default for snapshots is also on the system drive of the parent partition, and again these are files that are going to take up a lot of space. Plus, putting these files on the system drive is a bad decision for performance.

We suggest creating one or more disk volumes specifically for storing VHDs and snapshots. This makes backups easier, allows you to store your VHDs on your fastest array, and just makes good sense. Even if you had to completely rebuild the server, by having your VHDs and snapshot files on separate volumes, you greatly simplify the recovery process.

Creating a Virtual Machine

OK—enough of that getting-ready stuff and basic configuration. The real reason you're running Hyper-V is to actually create and use virtual machines (VMs), so let's get down to it. There are several ways you can make a VM, but they all start with the Hyper-V Manager console.

The basic steps for creating a VM are as follows:

- Create a new VM, giving it a name and location.
- Assign RAM to the VM.
- Connect to a network.
- Assign or create a virtual disk.
- Specify where the operating system will be loaded from.

The New Virtual Machine Wizard handles all these basic steps but is pretty limited, and insufficient for creating a VM for SBS. You'll want to actually configure the VM further before installing SBS or the SBS second server on your VM. We'll start by walking through the steps for creating a VM and then show you how to change that basic VM to be a bit more useful and flexible.

Creating a Basic VM

To create a new VM, follow these steps:

1. Open the Hyper-V Manager console if it isn't already open.

2. Select the Hyper-V computer in the left pane, click New, and then click Virtual Machine on the Actions menu to start the New Virtual Machine Wizard.

3. If you haven't disabled the Before You Begin page, you can read the description of what's going to happen, or click the More About Creating Virtual Machines link to open the Help pages for creating a VM. Select the Do Not Show This Page Again check box so that you don't have to see this page again.

4. Click Next to open the Specify Name And Location page, shown in Figure 6-9.

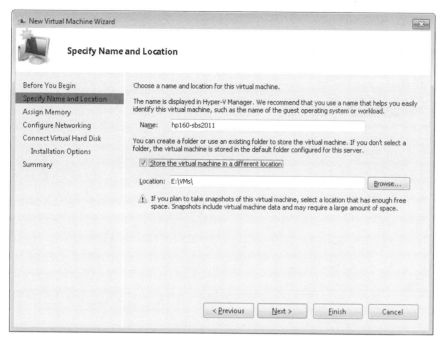

FIGURE 6-9 The Specify Name And Location page of the New Virtual Machine Wizard

5. Enter a name for the VM, and select the Store The Virtual Machine In A Different Location check box. When you select this check box, all the files for this VM will be stored in a directory with the same name as the VM, shown below in the Location field.

> **NOTE** For this first VM, with a name of hp160-sbs2011 and a default location of E:\ VMs\, the result will be a new directory of E:\VMs\hp160-sbs2011, with the files and subdirectories of the VM stored in it.

6. Click Next to open the Assign Memory page, shown in Figure 6-10. Specify the amount of memory that will be assigned to the new VM. You should specify the same amount of memory you would specify for the RAM of a physical SBS computer, but *do not exceed the memory of the host physical computer.*

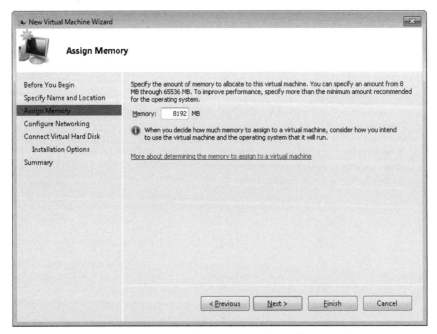

FIGURE 6-10 The Assign Memory page of the New Virtual Machine Wizard

7. Click Next to open the Configure Networking page. Select the network that the VM will be connected to, as shown in Figure 6-11.

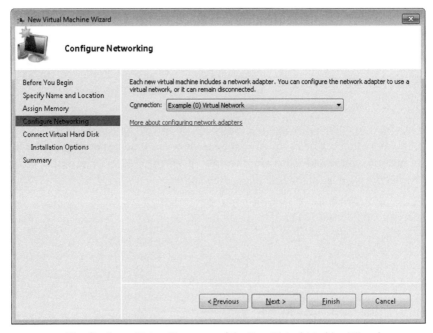

FIGURE 6-11 The Configure Networking page of the New Virtual Machine Wizard

8. Click Next to open the Connect Virtual Hard Disk page, shown in Figure 6-12.

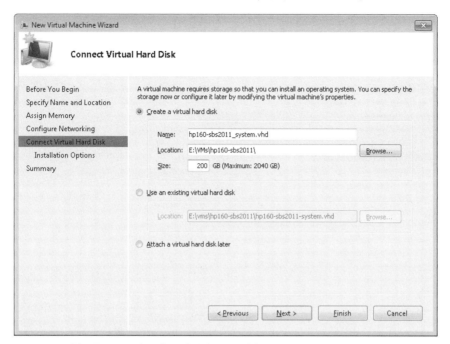

FIGURE 6-12 The Connect Virtual Hard Disk page of the New Virtual Machine Wizard

9. Select Create A Virtual Hard Disk to create a new, automatically expanding, virtual disk with a nominal size of 127 GB. Accept the default location, and name or modify the disk as appropriate for your environment. Even though 127 GB seems like a lot, we suggest you change the Size field to at least 200 GB.

The default is to create a dynamically expanding hard disk. Now that's just great if this isn't a production server, but we think it's a good idea to create a fixed-size VHD for a production system. Even though dynamic VHDs have gotten a lot faster since the original release of Hyper-V, there's still a definite performance advantage to a fixed-size VHD. To use a fixed-size VHD, run the New Virtual Hard Disk Wizard and create the disk first, and then attach it at this stage of the New Virtual Machine Wizard, or skip the Connect Virtual Hard Disk page of the wizard for now and attach a disk later.

> **IMPORTANT** The maximum size of an IDE VHD in Hyper-V is 2 terabytes (2040 GB, actually). But a dynamically expanding virtual hard disk doesn't actually take up any more room on your physical hard disk or array than it needs to. As you expand your use of the VM, the size of the disk will continue to grow, up to the size you set when you create the disk. But if you run out of actual disk space because you overcommitted the total size of dynamic VHDs, ugly things will happen.

10. Click Next to open the Installation Options page, as shown in Figure 6-13.

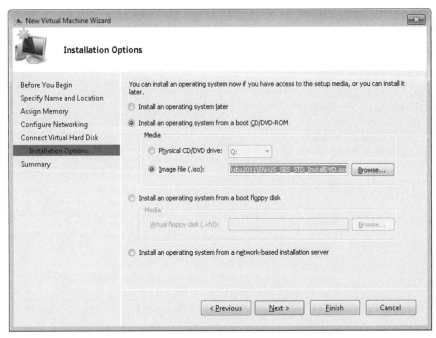

FIGURE 6-13 The Installation Options page of the New Virtual Machine Wizard

The choices are

- **Install An Operating System Later** This option requires you to configure how your operating system will be installed manually before starting the VM.

- **Install An Operating System From A Boot CD/DVD-ROM** This option allows you to connect to the physical computer's CD or DVD drive, or to mount an ISO file stored on the physical computer's hard disk as if it were a physical CD/DVD drive.

- **Install An Operating System From A Boot Floppy Disk** This option allows you to connect to a virtual floppy disk (.vfd) file as if it were a physical floppy drive.

- **Install An Operating System From A Network-Based Installation Server** This option changes the BIOS setting for the VM to enable a network boot from a PXE server, and it also changes the network card for the VM to be an emulated legacy network adapter instead of the default synthetic network adapter.

11. Click Next to open the Completing The New Virtual Machine Wizard summary page, or click Finish to skip the last step. On the last page, you can choose to automatically start the new VM as soon as you close the wizard, but we think that's a bad option. Just skip it—you should probably adjust the settings for the new VM before you start it anyway.

Machine Settings

After you've created the VM for your SBS server, you should make some changes to the machine settings that the New Virtual Machine Wizard has configured. To adjust the settings of a VM, select the VM in the center Virtual Machines pane of Hyper-V Manager, and click Settings on the Action menu to open the Settings dialog box for the VM, as shown in Figure 6-14.

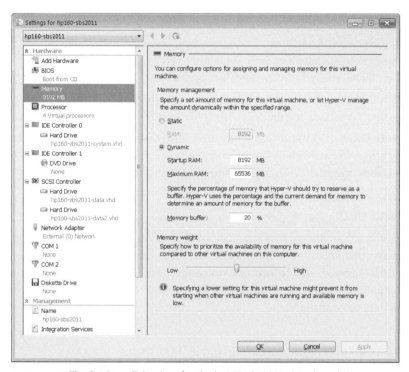

FIGURE 6-14 The Settings dialog box for the hp160-sbs2011 virtual machine

The settings page of a VM allows you to control the virtual hardware available to that VM. The settings that can be changed on a VM include

- **Add Hardware**   Add a SCSI Controller, network adapter, or legacy network adapter.
- **BIOS**   Change the boot order and Numlock state.
- **Memory**   Set the amount of memory assigned to the VM. SBS VMs are limited to 32 GB of RAM, just as they are on physical hardware.
- **Processor**   Set the number of logical processors assigned to the VM. This is limited to the number of logical processors available on the host computer or four logical processors, whichever is less. For SBS 2011, assign at least two logical processors, and four is preferred.
- **IDE Controllers 0, 1**   Set the drives connected to each IDE controller. Both Hard Disk and DVD Drive types are supported on IDE controllers.

- **SCSI Controller(s)** Set the drives connected to the synthetic SCSI controller. Each SCSI controller is assigned to SCSI ID7 and can support up to six virtual SCSI drives. SCSI drives cannot be used as boot drives and are not available until integration components are installed. Even if your physical drives are SCSI or SAS, do *not* choose SCSI here for your boot disk. That must always be IDE.

- **Network Adapters** Set the network, Mac type, and VLAN connections of the synthetic network adapters. SBS 2011 supports only a single network adapter, and you should choose a synthetic network adapter (the default).

- **Legacy Network Adapters** Set the network, Mac type, and VLAN connections of the legacy network adapters. Each VM is limited to a maximum of four legacy network adapters. Avoid these if at all possible—they're slow.

- **COM 1, COM 2** Set the named pipe used to communicate with the physical host computer. This setting is essentially useless for most things in the SBS environment.

- **Diskette Drive** Set the virtual floppy drive (.vfd) that is connected to the virtual floppy drive. No pass-through to the physical floppy drive on the host (parent) computer is supported. Use VFDs for SBS Answer Files to automate deployment.

Memory and CPU

Hyper-V supports a maximum of four processors and 64 GB of RAM per VM. On host computers with fewer than four processors, you'll be limited to the number of logical processors on the host itself. And you need to be careful to not over-specify the RAM for VMs on a physical computer. You need to leave at least 500 Mb of RAM for the host partition, plus a bit (less than 100 Mb) per running VM.

 REAL WORLD **Dynamic Memory Allocation**

Windows Server 2008 R2 Service Pack 1 (SP1) and Microsoft Hyper-V Server 2008 R2 SP1 support dynamic memory for Hyper-V virtual machines. Dynamic memory allows you to allocate a minimum amount of memory to supported virtual machines, but also set a maximum amount of memory. The Hyper-V host can now dynamically assign memory to virtual machines based on the dynamic memory needs of the virtual machines and their overall memory weighting as set by the administrator. This dramatically enhances your ability to effectively use the resources of the Hyper-V host to support the maximum number of virtual machines without performance degradation.

When you configure the settings on a virtual machine, you enable dynamic memory for that machine and you set a *Startup RAM* and a *Maximum RAM*, along with a memory buffer percentage, and the memory weight of the virtual machine, as shown in Figure 6-14. The Hyper-V host first attempts to start all the virtual machines that are scheduled to start by allocating the Startup RAM specified to each VM. Once that RAM has been allocated, it looks at the buffer specified for each virtual machine and, if it can, reserves the full buffer to each virtual machine. If it is unable to assign each virtual machine the full buffer specified, it then uses a combination of the weighting of the memory for the virtual machines and the memory pressure of the virtual machines to allocate the available memory resources as effectively as possible. As the memory pressure from each virtual machine changes dynamically over time, the Hyper-V host will be allocated more or less RAM depending on the settings of the VMs on the host and the available RAM resources.

To use dynamic memory, your Hyper-V host must be running SP1 and your guest operating systems must be supported. For SBS networks, this means you must install Windows Server 2008 R2 SP1 on the Premium Add-on server if you have one, *and* upgrade the integration components on the virtual machine. Dynamic memory allocation is not supported for the main SBS server. Additional virtual machines running Windows Server 2003, Windows Server 2008, Windows Vista (Enterprise or Ultimate), or Windows 7 (Enterprise or Ultimate) are also able to take advantage of dynamic memory if they have been upgraded to the latest service pack.

Disks and Controllers

Hyper-V uses a pair of synthetic IDE controllers for hard disks and DVD drives by default. You must use an IDE for the boot hard disk—the synthetic SCSI controller won't have drivers available in the operating system until after the integration components are installed.

If you're familiar with the IDE controller in Virtual Server 2005, you'll know that it was slow and only supported hard disks up to 127 GB. We quickly learned to use Virtual Server's SCSI controller and floppy disk to load the drivers during installation, greatly speeding up the process. But that workaround is no longer necessary and won't work with the Hyper-V SCSI controller. The new IDE controller in Hyper-V has full LBA-48 support, and it's much faster than the old Virtual Server one.

In Windows Server 2008 R2 Hyper-V, all virtual machines include a SCSI controller by default. You can add additional SCSI controllers if necessary. You should use a SCSI disk type for any additional data disks you assign to the SBS VM. Windows Server 2008 R2 supports hot add and remove of SCSI hard disks to running VMs.

REAL WORLD   Choosing Disk Types

Hyper-V supports three virtual disk types—dynamically expanding disks, fixed-sized disks, and differencing disks.

Dynamically expanding disks are created with a maximum size, and this is the size that the operating system of the VM sees. But the actual .vhd file of the disk takes up only as much space on your physical hard disk or array as absolutely required for the current contents of the VM drive. As the VM requires more storage space, Hyper-V automatically grows the .vhd file. This is very efficient, allowing you to add hard disk space only as absolutely required. But it does result in a slight performance hit every time the disk needs to grow, and more important, the .vhd file tends to become somewhat fragmented over time, also impacting performance. Nonetheless, we almost always use this type of disk for our nonproduction VMs. But *not* for the main SBS VM.

A fixed-size disk is also a .vhd file, but with a fixed-size .vhd file, the .vhd file is created at the full size on disk that it needs to be. It takes a significant amount of time to create the .vhd file, but it will be created as a contiguous file (or as contiguous as the underlying fragmentation of your physical disk or array allows).

A differencing disk is an interesting disk type. It is like a dynamic disk in that it gets only as large as it needs to. But a differencing disk is a great way to combine the disk space requirements of multiple VMs. You create the original "base" VM, and then mark the disks as read-only. You can actually delete the VM that created the base disks. Then you create one or more VMs that have the same operating system, and you create them with one or more differencing disks. The differencing disk points to the original base .vhd file, and the only thing that gets saved to the differencing disk is any change from the base VM. This allows multiple VMs to share the same base, simplifying deployment of different versions of the same base system—very useful for quickly building test networks.

The biggest disadvantage of differencing disks is their impact on speed. As more VMs point back to the original VHD files, the access to that VHD can be slowed. And if anything causes a change to the original VHD, all the VMs that point to it can be lost. Over time, the size advantage of differencing disks is also reduced as updates and service packs are applied to the differenced VMs. But for a test environment? Differencing disks can be a great speed and resource saver.

The final option is a pass-through disk that points directly to the physical partition. This is the fastest option, but it provides the least flexibility. You might choose this option if you are running Microsoft SQL Server on a VM and you have a performance-sensitive application. But even there, we tend to avoid it if at all possible. The difference in performance compared to a fixed-size VHD is small (on the order of 5 percent, we're told). Spend your money on good disk I/O subsystems and avoid pass-through disks.

Network Adapters

When you create a new VM, it will automatically include a single network adapter. Unless you choose to install the operating system from the network, it will add one of the synthetic network adapters that are new to Hyper-V. These work great and are definitely the preferred choice—unless you are running an operating system that doesn't have integration components available for it. If that's the case, you need to change this adapter to a legacy network adapter. You can't directly change the adapter type—you need to delete the existing one and add a legacy adapter.

Because SBS 2011 includes the necessary integration components built in to the base operating system, you should always choose a synthetic network adapter unless you are using PXE to boot from the network.

COM and Floppy

Hyper-V automatically configures a pair of virtual COM ports (COM1 and COM2) and a virtual floppy disk drive for each VM. But it doesn't actually connect them to anything. To connect a COM port to the host computer, you need to use named pipes, which are, unfortunately, useless for faxing or anything else we might be doing with our SBS servers. For floppy disks, you need to create a virtual floppy disk file (.vfd). A VFD file is an image of a floppy disk. There is no way in Hyper-V to connect directly to any existing floppy drive on the server.

Working with a Virtual Machine

Working with a Hyper-V VM is almost identical to working with a physical computer. You should do virtually everything you need to do from the client operating system, just as you would on a physical computer. You can connect to the client operating system using Remote Desktop when that is a supported option, and you can always connect using the Virtual Machine Connection. You can open the Virtual Machine Connection to a particular VM by either double-clicking the VM in the Hyper-V Manager console or selecting it and then clicking Connect on the Action menu. You can connect either locally from the parent partition or remotely if you're running the Hyper-V Remote Management Tools. This connection to the VM is the same as the physical keyboard, mouse, and monitor of a physical computer. However, there are some actions that need to be performed from the parent partition, either from the Hyper-V Manager console or the from the menu bar of the Virtual Machine Connection.

Starting, Stopping, Saving, Snapshotting

To start a VM, you need to either set the VM to automatically start or use the Hyper-V Manager console to start the VM. Right-click the VM in the console, and select Start from the menu. If you have the Virtual Machine Connection for that VM open, you can select Start from the Action menu.

To stop a VM, you should shut down the operating system in the VM. You can initiate this from the Hyper-V Manager console or on the Virtual Machine Connection Action menu, if integration components are installed in the VM. You can also stop a VM by right-clicking the VM in the console and selecting Turn Off, but this can cause corruption issues for the VM's operating system and is not recommended when other alternatives are available. Selecting Turn Off is exactly like pulling the power cord out of the back of a running physical server.

You can save a VM from the Hyper-V Manager console or the Virtual Machine Connection for that VM by selecting Save from the Action menu. This will save the current state of the VM to disk and is similar to hibernating a physical computer. It does release memory and resources back to the parent partition.

Pausing a VM is similar to putting a physical computer into sleep mode. It's not actively doing anything, but it also doesn't release any of the VM's resources back to the parent partition, except that it isn't using a CPU or doing any disk I/O. But the RAM it has allocated to the VM stays unavailable to other VMs.

Snapshots are one of the ways VMs are more useful and flexible than any physical computer. Snapshots allow you to take a "picture" of a running virtual machine at an exact moment in time and save it. You can revert back to that snapshot later, starting up the VM at that exact configuration. This is *extremely* useful for building test computers because it lets you try a new configuration or software application without the risk of having to rebuild the computer if something really bad happens, or just without wasting the time trying to get back to where you were before the change if it didn't work.

Snapshots can be a powerful tool, giving you the ability to try something with the calm assurance that you can recover completely if it doesn't work. And snapshots happen in seconds. Just select the VM in the Hyper-V Manager console, right-click, and select Snapshot. The VM can be running or not—it doesn't matter.

After you create a snapshot, the VM returns to its previous state. You can rename the snapshot, check the settings that applied at the time of the snapshot, delete it, or even delete an entire snapshot subtree. All these actions are available from the Actions pane of the Hyper-V Manager console or from the Action menu of the Virtual Machine Connection. You can also revert a VM to its previous snapshot or select another snapshot in the tree and apply it.

As you can see, it's powerful stuff, and the possibilities are something you'll just have to work with a bit to begin to understand. A caution, however: it's generally a *really bad idea* to use snapshots on production SBS servers. Or on any other domain controller.

Clipboard

The Hyper-V Virtual Machine Connection supports a limited ability to pass the contents of your clipboard between the parent partition and the running VM. Only text can be passed, but this allows you to replay the text as keystrokes into the VM. To use this capability, you need to copy text to your clipboard on the parent partition using Ctrl+C or any other method.

Then, in the child partition, prepare the location you want to type the text into, and select Type Clipboard Text on the Clipboard menu of the Virtual Machine Connection. The text is typed into the child partition at the cursor, one character at a time.

The other feature of the Hyper-V Virtual Machine Connection Clipboard menu is a screen capture utility. A pretty limited one, frankly, but it works if what you need to do is capture the entire screen of the child computer. To capture the screen, just select Capture Screen from the Virtual Machine Connection Clipboard menu. This puts the screen into your clipboard, and from there you can paste it into Microsoft Paint or any other graphics program.

 REAL WORLD **Screen Capture Utilities**

The ability to capture screens is essential for any documentation task, and often important for troubleshooting as well. Having an exact picture of the situation at a specific point in time just makes everything clearer, in our experience. The screen capture utility in Hyper-V only does the full screen. You can't get screen shots of individual windows or buttons because the key strokes are usually captured from the parent partition, not the child. Our solution is to use a small utility that is much smarter at creating screen shots than anything we could do with the built-in facilities of Windows—HyperSnap (*http://www.hyperionics.com*). There are other screen capture utilities out there, but we've been using HyperSnap for more than 16 years now, and it does an excellent job. We can capture exactly what we want and save it in any format we can imagine. Plus, if we do need to manipulate an image for some reason, HyperSnap has the ability to do that, too. We load a copy of Hyper-Snap into every test computer we run, using Group Policy to deploy it. And when we needed screen shots for Server Core? Hyperionics created a custom version for us that worked where nothing else had.

SBS in Hyper-V

Running SBS as a Hyper-V child partition is a solution that we think makes a lot of sense. Microsoft fully supports running Windows Small Business Server 2011 Standard in a Hyper-V child partition. The "Microsoft server software and supported virtualization environments" KnowledgeBase article (*http://support.microsoft.com/?kbid=957006*) has the full details. Additionally, the second server that is part of the Premium Add-on is also supported.

One thing you can't do, isn't supported, won't work, and would be a bad idea even if it *did* work is using the SBS server as the parent partition. If you try to run the Hyper-V role on the main SBS server, you will not be able to get everything to work correctly, especially DNS. You can, however, run the Premium Add-on server as the parent partition and run SBS as a child, along with a copy of the Premium Add-on server as a child.

Hyper-V should always run in a partition where little or nothing else is going on. The parent partition should be just that—strictly a parent. This keeps the attack surface of the entire set of virtual machines smaller, reduces the number of reboots required, and prioritizes the resources for the VMs, which should be the ones doing the heavy lifting.

We can imagine scenarios where the parent partition is also running a couple of key infrastructure roles as well—DNS and DHCP come to mind. We generally prefer not to do this, but it can make life a bit easier in some scenarios. However, once you start running any other roles beyond Hyper-V on your parent partition, you've changed the licensing equation.

Licensing

With Windows Server 2008 R2 Standard, you are entitled to what are called 1+1 licensing rights. This means you can use the same physical license to install Windows Server 2008 R2 on the parent partition and the first child partition, *as long as the only role you install into the parent is Hyper-V.* That's an important limitation. As soon as you start adding in other roles, you lose the right to run a child partition without buying a full license for it. The copy of Windows Server 2008 R2 Standard that is included in the Premium Add-on is a full copy of Windows Server 2008 R2 and can be used with these 1+1 rights. Additionally, there is a specific exclusion that allows the parent partition to *not* have to be joined to the SBS domain. It can run in workgroup mode as long as it's on the same physical network as the SBS domain.

Windows Server 2008 R2 Enterprise gives you the right to install a parent partition and four child partitions as long as that parent partition is used only for the Hyper-V role. As soon as you add in any other roles to the parent, you lose one of your secondary rights.

Windows Server 2008 R2 Datacenter gives you the right to install a parent partition and as many child partitions as you want. Of course, the actual cost of a Datacenter license is just a bit out of the reach of most small businesses.

Configuration

When you configure a child partition for SBS 2011 Standard, you should allocate the same level of hardware resources to the child as you would to a physical server running SBS 2011 Standard. This means a *minimum* of 6 GB of RAM, but we think 10 GB is a more appropriate minimum for any production environment. And assign four processor cores to the SBS server VM. You should always use the synthetic network adapters, which are much faster than the legacy emulation ones. And create the same number of virtual hard disks for your server as you would have arrays with a physical computer. We like to have a minimum of three disks— one for the system, one for user space, and one for Microsoft Exchange data. Even if your circumstances require you to have them sitting on the same RAID array, having three separate virtual disks puts you in a position to add more arrays if you need to and easily move the VHDs over to the new array to balance the load.

The one configuration we see used increasingly as consultants and others begin to understand the power and capabilities of 64-bit servers is the "SBS Premium in a Box" deployment.

This starts with a small Hyper-V parent partition, possibly running the Microsoft Hyper-V Server, and then two child partitions—the first running the main SBS server and the second running the Premium Add-on second server with SQL Server on it. Or, in many deployments, a Windows Server 2008 R2 Standard server running Remote Desktop Services.

This all-in-one solution could easily be supported on a single, well-thought-out, mid-range server, with two quad-core CPUs and 16 to 24 GB of RAM, a good caching RAID controller, and a Serial-Attached SCSI (SAS) disk array.

Summary

Virtualization is a hot topic these days, and with good reason. The new capabilities of 64-bit servers and Microsoft's new Hyper-V technology make it a compelling option in many scenarios. In this chapter, we covered the basics of using Hyper-V to virtualize Windows Small Business Server 2011. In the next chapter, we cover migrating from an existing Windows Small Business Server network to SBS 2011.

## CHAPTER 7

Migrating to Windows Small Business Server 2011 Standard

With Microsoft Windows Small Business Server 2011 Standard (SBS 2011), there is no "upgrade" from *any* other version. The only way to preserve an existing deployment of SBS, including email and Active Directory, is to migrate to SBS 2011. This is true whether you're coming from the 32-bit Windows Small Business Server 2003 (SBS 2003), the 64-bit Windows Small Business Server 2008 (SBS 2008), or another copy of SBS 2011.

Migration is far more complex than a clean install or in-place upgrade, although the SBS team has made a significant effort to simplify the most common cases. However, SBS 2011 requires some significant changes to your network that you need to plan out ahead of time:

- SBS 2011 supports only a single network interface card (NIC). The preferred SBS 2003 configuration is two NICs, so if you're migrating from SBS 2003, you'll need to reconfigure it for a single NIC first.

- SBS 2011 Premium does not include Internet Security and Acceleration (ISA). If you're an SBS 2003 Premium customer running ISA as your firewall, you'll need to replace it with an alternative.

- Your new SBS 2011 server will have a different name than your existing SBS server, and a different IP address. The migration process will configure DNS to correct for this.

- The new Companyweb SharePoint site will replace your existing Companyweb site. You can migrate your existing Companyweb, but the process adds complexity to the migration process.

- After you start the migration, there really is no "undo" button. And you'll have 21 days to complete the process and remove the old server from the network.

These are all significant issues, in our opinion. But if you prepare your existing SBS server properly and plan your migration thoroughly before beginning the process, the migration will succeed.

In this chapter, we'll primarily be covering the migration from SBS 2003 because that will be the largest group of migrations, but much of what we'll cover here is also applicable to migrations from SBS 2008 or SBS 2011. If you're migrating from one of these later versions, we recommend still that you read this chapter thoroughly before you begin, and follow the basic steps here. However, you'll use a slightly different document from Microsoft to refer to during the process.

The Migration Process

Before you start your SBS 2011 migration, you should read and understand this chapter and the appropriate Microsoft migration guide. There are three migration guides, and the one you'll use depends on which version of SBS you are migrating from. The three guides are

- "Migrate to Windows Small Business Server 2011 Standard from Windows Small Business Server 2003" at *http://technet.microsoft.com/en-us/library/gg563801.aspx*

- "Migrate to Windows Small Business Server 2011 Standard from Windows Small Business Server 2008" at *http://technet.microsoft.com/en-us/library/gg615506.aspx*

- "Migrate Windows Small Business Server 2011 Standard to New Hardware" at *http://technet.microsoft.com/en-us/library/gg616008.aspx*

We'll refer to these generically as the *Microsoft migration guides*, and you should always refer to the appropriate one for your specific migration scenario.

The steps in a successful migration are as follows:

1. Prepare your existing SBS server for migration.

2. Create the SBSAnswerFile.xml using the SBS AnswerFile Generator tool.

3. Install SBS 2011, using the Answer File to run in migration mode.

4. Use the Migration Wizard to migrate data and settings from your existing SBS server to your new SBS 2011 server.

5. When migration is complete, demote your existing SBS server to a domain member and then remove it from the domain. You must reformat the server before you can reuse it.

6. If you're using Folder Redirection in SBS 2003, you'll need to delete the old Group Policy object (GPO) for folder redirection.

7. Perform optional post-migration tasks—including mapping users to computers and enabling folder redirection—and Microsoft Exchange tasks such as adding POP3 connectors and updating mailbox quotas.

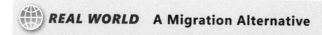

REAL WORLD A Migration Alternative

With SBS 2003, the Microsoft solution for migration caused significant user disruption and was only a viable solution if you needed to change your SBS domain name for some reason. In our *Microsoft Windows Small Business Server 2003 R2 Administrator's Companion* book, we recommended an alternative solution—Swing Migration (see *http://www.sbsmigration.com*). Swing Migration uses a temporary domain controller to capture the Active Directory, DNS, and other information from the existing domain controller (the source SBS server) and transfer that to the new SBS 2003 server, allowing the new SBS server to retain the exact same name and IP address as the original source SBS server. Microsoft Exchange data is generally moved with a simple forklift technique, and SharePoint sites are handled in a similar fashion—overall, an excellent and time-effective way to manage a migration that has several virtues over other methods, including:

- No disruption or change to SBS client computers.

- No disruption in email or other network functions except for the final switchover, which can easily be done during normal downtimes. Most work is done offline and can be done on a flexible schedule.

- Full data and configuration protection.

- The ability to restart the process at any point in time with no risk of data loss if there is a problem.

Unfortunately, Swing Migration as it exists for SBS 2003 will not completely work for SBS 2011, although we can see some definite benefits to using a similar process. It certainly covers the server name and IP address change issue, and we can envision how to work around most of the possible email issues.

We expect Jeff Middleton, Microsoft MVP for SBS and principal of *www.sbsmigration .com*, to have a full version of Swing Migration for SBS 2011 soon, and we expect it to be a very good offering—especially if your migration project is not a perfect fit for the Microsoft assumptions. We've known Jeff for several years now, and even though his final version of Swing isn't yet available, we have enough confidence in him to recommend it fully. Because, ultimately, what you really need for any migration is just that—confidence.

Preparing Your Server

The most important part of any migration to SBS 2011 involves properly preparing your existing SBS server. The time and thought you spend on a full and careful preparation of your existing SBS server has a direct impact on the success of your migration. Don't just start a migration without first preparing. Read this entire chapter carefully, and read Microsoft's migration guide as well. Be sure you understand what will happen and what the requirements are before you start.

The steps for preparing your server are as follows:

1. Do a full and complete backup of the existing SBS server.
2. Install all current service packs and other updates on the server.
3. Configure your network for the migration.
4. Configure Active Directory.
5. Run the Best Practices Analyzer (BPA) to verify the health of the existing SBS network.
6. Clean up and optimize the current Microsoft Exchange mailboxes.
7. Use the Migration Preparation Tool to extend the Active Directory schema, modify the Microsoft Exchange Server mode, and extend the time that both versions of SBS can be running to 21 days.
8. Identify line-of-business applications running on the existing SBS server, and plan for their migration.

Before You Start

You're going to need certain tools during this process, and they may or may not already be on your source server. To simplify things and make sure you have everything ready and available, we suggest you download the following ahead of time:

- Windows PowerShell 2.0 and the Management Framework Core from *http:// go.microsoft.com/fwlink/?LinkId=188528*
- Microsoft Baseline Configuration Analyzer 2.0 (MBCAv2) from *http://go.microsoft.com/ fwlink/?LinkId=188529*
- Microsoft .NET Framework 2.0 SP1 from *http://go.microsoft.com/fwlink/?linkid=153680*
- Microsoft SBS 2003 Best Practices Analyzer from *http://go.microsoft.com/fwlink/ ?LinkId=113752*

Also, collect any other tools you generally like to have available during the build process. If you create an ISO file of these or burn them to a DVD, they'll be available whenever and wherever you need them. For ISO creation, we like the simplicity of ISO Recorder (*http://isorecorder.alexfeinman.com/isorecorder.htm*). It's simple, it does the job really well, and it's free.

Go ahead and install Windows PowerShell 2.0, MBCAv2, and the BPA on your source server. They usually don't trigger a reboot.

Back Up Your Existing SBS Server

The first and most important step in any migration is making sure you have a full and verified backup. We all do backups, and we hope that we never need to use them. But if you aren't taking steps to actually verify that your backup can be restored, you haven't really got a backup you can count on. Before beginning any SBS migration, it's essential that you establish a sound fallback position that will allow you to recover in case something goes wrong. Of course, nothing *should* go wrong, but we're firm believers in Murphy's Laws—after all, we wrote the books on them!

For details on how to back up your existing SBS 2003 server, see *http://go.microsoft.com/ fwlink/?LinkId=27140*, or see Chapter 13, "Backing Up and Restoring Data," in our *Microsoft Windows Small Business Server 2003 R2 Administrator's Companion* book. (For SBS 2008, see Chapter 16, "Configuring Backup," in our *Windows Small Business Server 2008 Administrator's Companion* book or Chapter 16 in this book for SBS 2011.)

In *addition* to doing a conventional backup using SBS Backup, we strongly suggest making an image backup of at least the system volume of your existing SBS server and any other volumes that are used to store core SBS data files, such as Microsoft Exchange data files. This will allow for a faster full recovery in the event that you have to cancel the migration for some reason. Products we've used for this image backup include StorageCraft, Acronis, and Windows Home Server. Currently, we're using, and really liking, Windows Storage Server 2008 R2 Essentials to back up the virtual hard disks (VHDs) of SBS.

Whatever backup methods you use, you should *verify the integrity* of the backup by doing a test restore. For image backups, this means restoring the entire partition image to a disk of equal or greater size and, at a minimum, verifying that files can be read and opened. For an SBS Backup test, you should restore multiple files from different locations to an alternate location and verify that the files can be opened and read.

Install Current Updates

It seems obvious to us, but bears repeating nonetheless—bring your current SBS server up to date, installing all current service packs and security updates. If you're running SBS 2003 R2 or later, with built-in Windows Server Update Service (WSUS), this should be happening automatically. But even if you're sure you are up to date, connect to Microsoft Update to verify.

The migration process expects minimum levels of service packs, and not being fully "patched up" can create issues in the migration. Given that the migration is a one-way process, you really don't want to get well into it and find you have a blocker. We hope the tools in this preparation stage will enable you to catch any blockers before you start, but it's still just a really good idea to get all your updates installed before you start.

Network Configuration

Before you can migrate to SBS 2011, you need to configure your existing SBS server for a single NIC. This means a significant change for most SBS 2003 networks, because the preferred configuration for SBS 2003 calls for two NICs—one connected to the external Internet and one connected to the internal SBS network. All traffic on the internal network actually passes through the SBS server to get to the Internet, as shown in Figure 7-1.

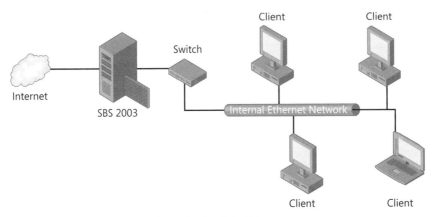

FIGURE 7-1 Default two NIC configuration for SBS 2003

This configuration also uses SBS as the firewall for the SBS network—something it does quite well when running SBS 2003 Premium Edition with ISA 2004. Because SBS 2011 requires a single NIC configuration, you need to change your SBS 2003 configuration before the migration. In a single NIC configuration, as shown in Figure 7-2, you'll need to add a router and firewall to your existing SBS network, along with reconfiguring the default gateway and other settings for your client computer and devices.

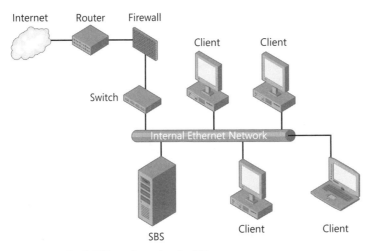

FIGURE 7-2 Single NIC configuration for SBS

Most consumer-grade routers include minimal firewall capabilities, but they really aren't sufficient to properly protect an SBS network. You should either add a firewall appliance in addition or buy a true firewall router, such as one of the TZ series firewalls from SonicWALL (*http://www.sonicwall.com/us/products/TZ_Series.html*). Other possibilities include Watch-Guard firewalls (*http://www.watchguard.com*) and NETGEAR ProSecure firewalls (*http://www.prosecure.netgear.com/products/prosecure-utm-series/models.php*).

The basic process of network reconfiguration uses the following steps:

1. Reconfigure DHCP for shorter license times (optional), and save the DHCP database.

2. Disable or remove the Internet-facing NIC in your existing SBS server.

3. Run the Configure E-Mail And Internet Connectivity Wizard (CEICW) to reconfigure networking.

4. Install a router/firewall, and connect to Internet.

5. Connect the router/firewall to a switch on the internal Ethernet.

6. Run the Remote Access Wizard to disable virtual private networks (VPNs) and reconfigure Routing And Remote Access (RRAS).

7. Reconfigure client computers and devices with fixed IP addresses and verify DHCP configuration.

DHCP Reconfiguration

Although it's not absolutely required, you can simplify DHCP address reconfiguration on your SBS network if you shorten the lease time in advance of beginning the migration. This will allow client computers and devices on your network to get updated network information without a reboot in a reasonable time frame. The default DHCP lease duration is eight days. To change the duration, follow these steps:

1. Log on to your existing SBS server with an account that has administrative privileges.

2. Open the DHCP console (dhcpmgmt.msc).

3. In the left pane, drill down and select the scope you want to change.

4. Select Properties from the Action menu to open the Scope Properties dialog box shown in Figure 7-3.

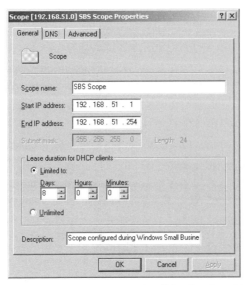

FIGURE 7-3 The Scope Properties dialog box for a DHCP scope

5. Change the Lease Duration For DHCP Clients values to a shorter time. We like to set an 8-hour lease here.

6. Click OK to close the Scope Properties dialog box and return to the DHCP console. Close the DHCP console.

Another useful step to take at this point is to back up the DHCP database. If you are using a standard SBS DHCP with no reservations or other customizations, don't bother—the wizards will take care of it. But if you have done significant configuration, you should probably back up your DHCP database to make it easier to restore that configuration. See the Microsoft Knowledge Base article at *http://support.microsoft.com/kb/962355*.

Disable or Remove the Second NIC

The first essential step in reconfiguring your SBS 2003 network from a two NIC SBS network to a single NIC network is to disconnect the externally facing NIC from your existing Internet connection and disable or remove the network card. You can get away with disabling it, but then you'll have more complaints from the SBS wizards, so we prefer removing it physically from the server. After you've removed the network card, you need to reconfigure your SBS network to the IP address range you'll use for your Internet connection.

NOTE You can skip this entire section if you're migrating from SBS 2008 or SBS 2011, because you're already configured for a single NIC with appropriate settings.

REAL WORLD Address Ranges

Because you're reconfiguring your network anyway, now is a good time to make a decision about the IP address range you want to use. The default range of many routers is 192.168.0.xxx or 192.168.1.xxx. The easy answer is to use whatever the default range of your new router/firewall is. We actually don't much like that solution because it can cause complications down the road if you're ever in a situation where you need to set up a static VPN to another network that has chosen that range. We prefer choosing pretty much any of the other possibilities in the private "C-class" range—anywhere from 192.168.2.xxx to 192.168.254.xxx. The default range for SBS 2003 is actually 192.168.16.xxx, and that's a good choice that doesn't seem to interfere with any other common ones we've seen. On our networks here, we have used 192.168.16.xxx and 192.168.51.xx for our test networks. The one thing you can *not* do is choose an address range in the 10.xxx.yyy.zzz private "A-class" range—the SBS 2011 wizards will not support that range.

After you've decided the range for your new SBS network, you can complete the reconfiguration by following these steps:

1. Shut down the SBS server.

2. Disconnect the Internet-facing network cable from the server, open the server enclosure, and remove the network card.

3. Turn on the server. It will likely take longer than usual to restart—be patient.

4. Log on to the server with the main Administrator account.

5. In the left pane of the Server Management console, click Internet And E-mail to display the Manage Internet And E-mail page as shown in Figure 7-4.

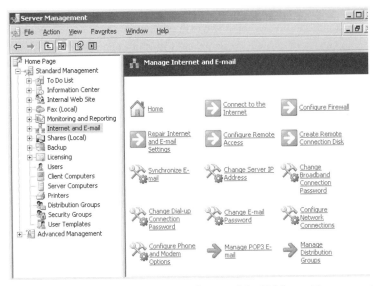

FIGURE 7-4 The Manage Internet And E-Mail page of the SBS Server Management console

6. Click Connect To The Internet to open the CEICW.

7. Click Next to open the Connection Type page of the CEICW, as shown in Figure 7-5.

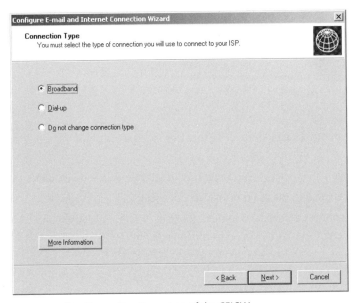

FIGURE 7-5 The Connection Type page of the CEICW

8. Select Broadband, and click Next to open the Broadband Connection page, as shown in Figure 7-6. Select A Local Router Device With An IP Address from the My Server Uses drop-down list.

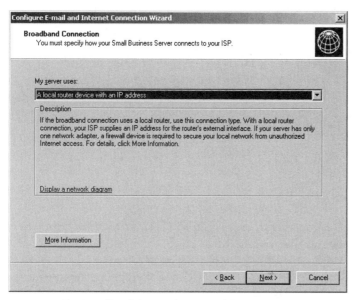

FIGURE 7-6 The Broadband Connection page of the CEICW

9. Click Next to open the Router Connection page shown in Figure 7-7. Type in the IP address you'll be using with your new router/firewall and the IP addresses for your ISP's DNS servers.

> **NOTE** If your router/firewall does DNS forwarding, you can use the IP address of the router/firewall for the Primary DNS Server address and leave the Secondary DNS Server address blank. If you want to always use root hints for DNS, you can leave both addresses blank.

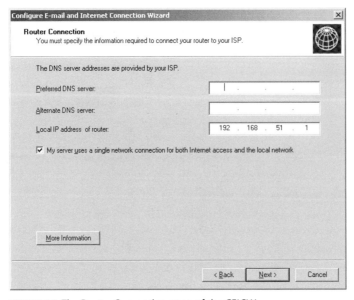

FIGURE 7-7 The Router Connection page of the CEICW

10. Select the My Server Uses A Single Network Connection For Both Internet Access And The Local Network check box.

11. Click Next. If the IP address of the router/firewall is in a different address range from your previous internal address, you'll see the message shown in Figure 7-8.

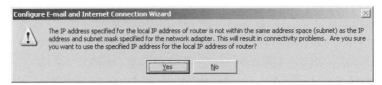

FIGURE 7-8 The warning message generated during network reconfiguration

12. Click Yes to open the information message shown in Figure 7-9. Because we're not connected to anything at this point, click No.

FIGURE 7-9 The firewall informational message of the CEICW

13. On the Web Services Configuration page, select the services that you want to be available when your existing SBS server is back online.

14. Click Next twice more, and then click Finish to complete the wizard.

15. Click Close when the CEICW finishes.

If you've chosen to use a different IP address range for your SBS network than the one you're currently configured to use, now is a good time to change it by following these steps:

1. On the Manage Internet And E-mail page of the Server Management console, click Change Server IP Address to open the Change IP Address Tool dialog box shown in Figure 7-10.

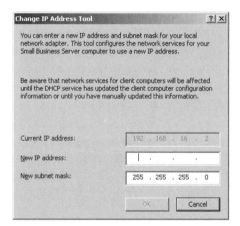

FIGURE 7-10 The Change IP Address Tool

2. Type in the new IP address for the server and click OK. When the tool completes, you'll see the message shown in Figure 7-11.

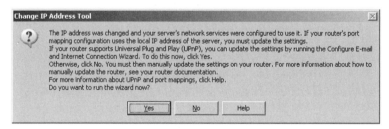

FIGURE 7-11 When you change the server's IP address, it offers to run the CEICW again

3. Click No to complete the process and close the Change IP Address Tool dialog box. As shown in Figure 7-12, the IP address has been reconfigured to point to the new router/firewall that we will install at 192.168.51.1.

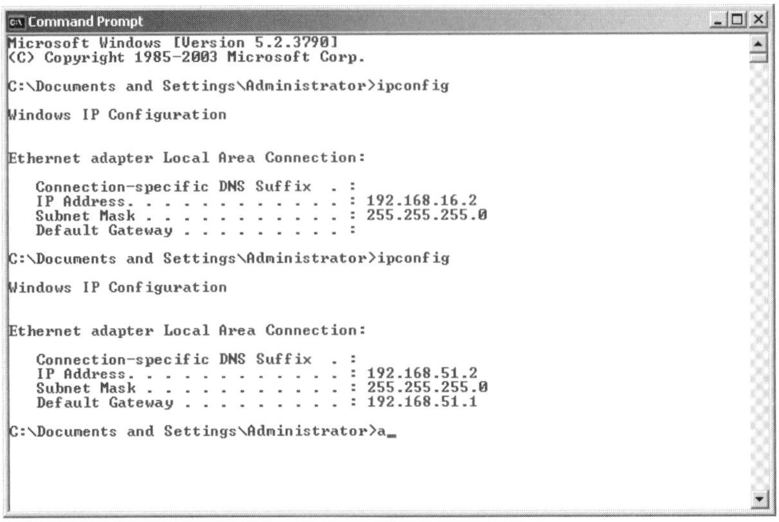

```
Command Prompt                                                    _|□|x|
Microsoft Windows [Version 5.2.3790]
(C) Copyright 1985-2003 Microsoft Corp.

C:\Documents and Settings\Administrator>ipconfig

Windows IP Configuration

Ethernet adapter Local Area Connection:

        Connection-specific DNS Suffix  . :
        IP Address. . . . . . . . . . . : 192.168.16.2
        Subnet Mask . . . . . . . . . . : 255.255.255.0
        Default Gateway . . . . . . . . :
C:\Documents and Settings\Administrator>ipconfig

Windows IP Configuration

Ethernet adapter Local Area Connection:

        Connection-specific DNS Suffix  . :
        IP Address. . . . . . . . . . . : 192.168.51.2
        Subnet Mask . . . . . . . . . . : 255.255.255.0
        Default Gateway . . . . . . . . : 192.168.51.1
C:\Documents and Settings\Administrator>a_
```

FIGURE 7-12 The IP address has changed on the server

NOTE If you have fixed IP devices on your network, you'll need to manually reconfigure their default gateway. This won't matter for devices that don't need to connect to the Internet, such as printers, but if you have additional servers or workstations that use fixed IP addresses, you should reconfigure them now to point to the new router.

Install Router and Firewall

After you've reconfigured your existing SBS to use a single network card, you need to reconnect it to the Internet. You need to insert a router into the network if you don't already have one, and configure it for the network address range that you've chosen for your SBS network.

In many cases, you'll already have a router in place—we did. But that router is likely not a full-fledged firewall. Now is the time to replace it or add an additional firewall appliance. When you do, you'll need to configure the firewall for your SBS network. The port's SBS 2003 uses include

- **25** Simple Mail Transfer Protocol (SMTP). Used by Microsoft Exchange for incoming and outgoing email.

- **80** Hypertext Transfer Protocol (HTTP). Outbound, this port is used to surf the web. Inbound, it can be used to initially connect to the Remote Web Workplace site.

- **443** Hypertext Transfer Protocol Secure (HTTPS). It's used outbound for connecting to secure websites and inbound for connecting to Remote Web Workplace.

- **444** Companyweb. This port is used to connect to the SharePoint Companyweb intranet site. Open this port only if your users connect to Companyweb when working remotely.

- **3389** Remote Desktop Protocol (RDP). This port is used only if you allow direct RDP connections from remote locations to your SBS server. If you do enable this for remote management, you should limit the IP addresses that are allowed to connect to specific, known, IP addresses.

- **4125** Remote Web Workplace (RWW). This port is used by RWW for connecting remote users to their desktops.

Additional ports might be in use for specific applications on your network, but these are the basic incoming ports that are used by SBS.

After you've installed and configured your router, connect it to your SBS network as shown earlier in Figure 7-2. Verify that you have connectivity from the server and from your workstations to a known site. If a workstation doesn't have connectivity, reboot and try again. Verify that the DHCP-assigned IP address is in the correct range.

 UNDER THE HOOD   **ISA Server**

The requirements for migrating SBS 2003 Premium Edition networks that are using ISA Server are somewhat different. The basic premise is the same—you need to reconfigure your network to use a single NIC. But you'll also need to remove the ISA Firewall Client from computers on your network. Microsoft's migration guide says that you can leave ISA in place during the migration as long as you are running at least ISA 2004 SP3, but we think this is a bad idea. You need to install a real firewall on your network to protect it and the new SBS 2011 server, and leaving ISA in place on the source SBS 2003 server just confuses the issue and leaves additional places where there could be problems during the migration.

We started to write up a full set of steps for uninstalling ISA and reconfiguring the workstations on your network, but then we found an excellent resource from Kevin Weilbacher, an SBS MVP. He has posted a step-by-step guide to removing ISA 2004 from SBS 2003, and he is actively maintaining it and updating it to cover issues as they're reported, with input from many of the other SBS MVPs. For full details on how to remove ISA 2004, see *http://msmvps.com/blogs/kwsupport/archive/2008/09/07/uninstalling-isa-2004.aspx*.

Disable VPNs

Before you begin the migration, you need to disable virtual private networking to the SBS server. If you need VPN access, you should choose a router/firewall that can act as a VPN endpoint. Ultimately, however, we think a better overall solution is to use Remote Web Access (RWA) and avoid VPNs whenever possible.

To disable VPNs on the existing SBS server, follow these steps:

1. Log on to the server with the main Administrator account.

2. Open the Server Management console if it doesn't open automatically.

3. In the left pane of the Server Management console, click Internet And E-mail. The Manage Internet And E-mail page opens.

4. Click Configure Remote Access to open the Remote Access Wizard.

5. Click Next on the Welcome page to open the Remote Access Method page as shown in Figure 7-13.

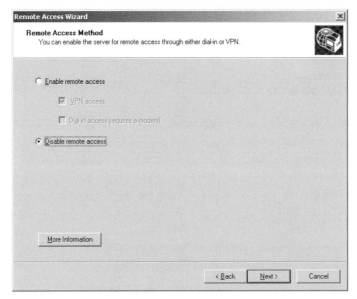

FIGURE 7-13 The Remote Access Method page of the Remote Access Wizard

6. Select Disable Remote Access, click Next, and then click Finish.

7. When the wizard completes, click Close to return to the Server Management console.

This completes the network reconfiguration for your SBS migration. Now is a good time to verify that all the computers and devices on your network are working as you'd expect and can connect properly. Pay particular attention to devices such as printers, wireless access points, and web cams that have a fixed or DHCP reservation address to make sure that they are communicating correctly with the rest of the network.

Configuring Active Directory

Before you can complete the migration to SBS 2011, you need to raise the domain and forest functional levels of your current SBS 2003 Active Directory. The migration requires that the Active Directory forest and domain functional level be Windows Server 2003. The default for SBS 2003 is the Microsoft Windows 2000 functional level.

You can't move to a Windows Server 2003 functional level if there are any Windows 2000 or earlier domain controllers in your SBS domain. If there are, you must first demote them from being domain controllers. For Windows 2000, run Dcpromo.exe as a domain administrator to demote the legacy Windows 2000 domain controller. If you still have Windows NT 4 domain controllers in your network, you'll need to rebuild these servers as non–domain controllers or remove them from the network entirely. Given that Windows NT 4 is no longer supported by Microsoft and won't get any updates or security patches, you need to remove any remaining Windows NT 4 computers.

To raise the domain and forest functional level of your SBS 2003 Active Directory, follow these steps:

1. Log on to the SBS 2003 server with an account that has both Domain Admins and Enterprise Admins privileges. The Administrator account is a good choice for this.

2. Click Start, then click Administrative Tools, and then click Active Directory Domains And Trusts to open the Active Directory Domains And Trusts console shown in Figure 7-14, or you can type domain.msc at the Run menu.

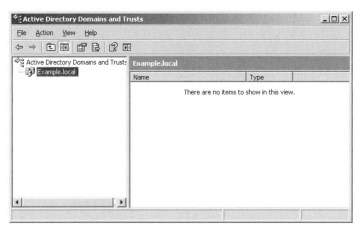

FIGURE 7-14 The Active Directory Domains And Trusts console

> **NOTE** Raising the domain functional level is an irreversible change. You can't later lower the functional level.

3. Click the domain (example.local in Figure 7-14), and select Raise Domain Functional Level from the Action menu to open the dialog box shown in Figure 7-15.

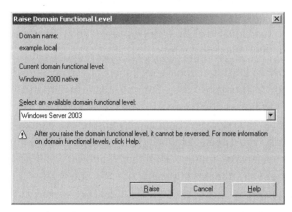

FIGURE 7-15 The Raise Domain Functional Level dialog box

4. Select Windows Server 2003 from the drop-down list (this should be the only choice in most SBS networks) and then click Raise to raise the domain functional level.

> **NOTE** If the Current Domain Functional Level is shown as Windows Server 2003, you won't be able to change the functional level.

5. Click OK at the warning that this change can't be reversed, and click OK again at the success message.
6. Click Active Directory Domains And Trusts in the left pane at the top of the tree.
7. Click Raise Forest Functional Level on the action menu to open the Raise Forest Functional Level dialog box shown in Figure 7-16.

> **NOTE** Raising the forest functional level is an irreversible change. You can't later lower the functional level.

FIGURE 7-16 The Raise Forest Functional Level dialog box

8. Click Raise. You'll see the warning message that this change is irreversible as shown in Figure 7-17.

FIGURE 7-17 Raising the forest functional level is irreversible

9. Click OK. If the raise was successful, you'll see the informational message in Figure 7-18.

FIGURE 7-18 The Raise Forest Functional Level success informational message

10. Click OK to close the message, and then close the Active Directory Domains And Trusts dialog box.

Best Practices Analyzer

The Best Practices Analyzer (BPA) is a useful tool to run against your SBS server regardless of whether you're planning on migrating to SBS 2011 immediately or later on. The BPA can identify all kinds of problems in an SBS environment with over 200 errors, warnings, and informational messages about the health of your SBS network.

You can download the BPA from *http://go.microsoft.com/fwlink/?LinkId=113752* and then install it on your SBS 2003 server. The Knowledge Base article for the BPA is 940439. After you've downloaded the BPA, execute the SBS2003SP1-KB940439-x86-enu.exe file to install it. (The actual file name varies depending on the language.)

You can then run the BPA using the following steps:

1. Click Start, click All Programs, and select SBS Best Practices Analyzer Tool.

2. The first time you run the BPA, you'll be asked if you want to check for new versions every time you start it, and you'll be offered an opportunity to check now. Click Yes to receive automatic updates, and choose to check now—even with a fresh download, we still got a newer version after the check.

3. From the Welcome screen shown in Figure 7-19, you can select the options to use for a scan or view a previous scan.

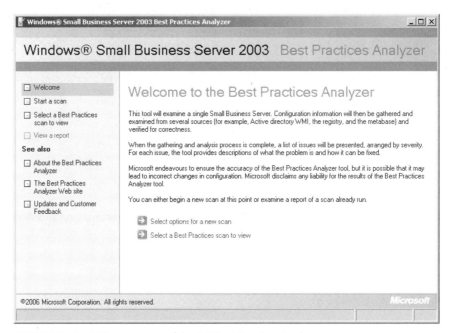

FIGURE 7-19 The Welcome screen of the SBS Best Practices Analyzer

4. Click Select Options For A New Scan to open the Start A Scan page shown in Figure 7-20.

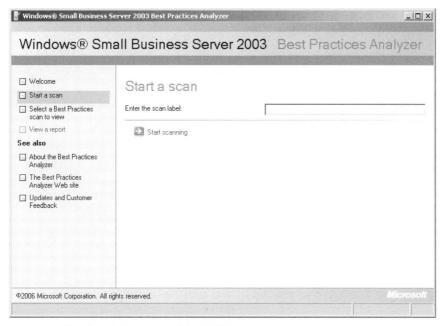

FIGURE 7-20 The Start A Scan page of the SBS BPA

5. Type in a label for the scan, and click Start Scanning. When the scan completes, you'll see a summary of the results as shown in Figure 7-21.

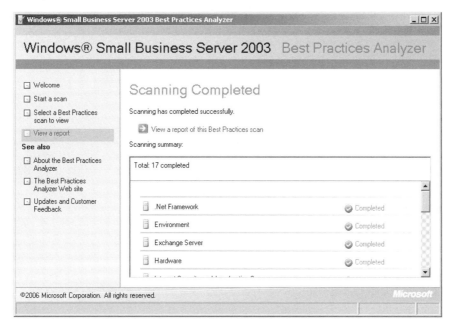

FIGURE 7-21 The Scanning Completed summary page of the SBS BPA

6. To view the results of the scan, click View A Report Of This Best Practices Scan. A typical report is shown in Figure 7-22.

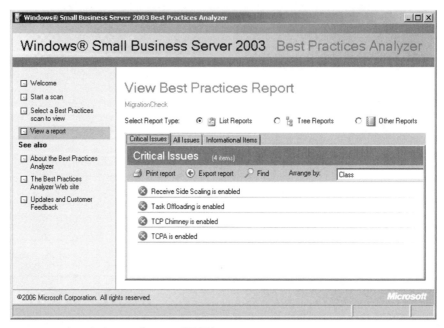

FIGURE 7-22 A typical report from an SBS BPA scan

7. Click any listed issue to see more details on the issue, including links to Knowledge
Base articles on how to correct the issue. The detail screen for the Receive Side Scaling
issue shown in Figure 7-22 is shown in Figure 7-23.

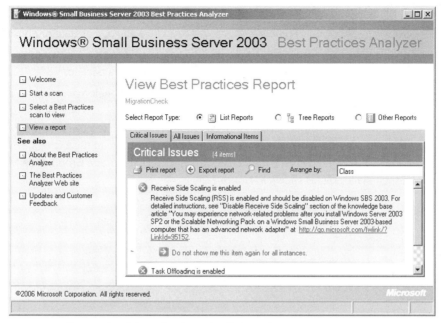

FIGURE 7-23 The Receive Side Scaling issue details from the SBS BPA

8. After you've corrected the issues that could prevent a successful migration, run the BPA again by repeating steps 4 through 7 to verify that all the problems are corrected. At a minimum, you should correct all critical issues, and you should carefully evaluate the issues listed on the All Issues tab and correct any that are possible problems for your migration.

> **IMPORTANT** Do not proceed with your migration until all critical issues identified by the BPA have been resolved. Seriously. The migration will fail if you do. You should also carefully evaluate any additional issues shown on the All Issues tab and resolve as many as possible.

Optimize Exchange Mailboxes

You should have your users optimize their Microsoft Exchange mailboxes to reduce the time it takes to migrate them to Exchange 2010. If you've been enforcing strict mailbox limits, this likely isn't a major issue. However, if you've got a couple of users who are special and have seriously large mailboxes, now is a good time to try to get this under control. Anything that removes excess mail from the mailboxes is a good thing, but the most obvious steps are

- Ask all users to empty their Deleted Items folders.
- Ask all users to empty their Junk E-mail folders.

- Ask all users to archive all mail items older than some reasonable date.
- Carefully inspect Public Folders, and remove or archive any out-of-date or unused contents to reduce the overall size of the Public Folder database.
- Make a separate archive (PST) of all active Public Folders as a backup.

When users have had a reasonable amount of time to clean up their mailboxes, it's usually useful to examine the mailbox store in Exchange to see whether any outstandingly large mailboxes remain. This allows you to have a more direct discussion with the owner of the mailbox to help reduce its size. You can check the size of mailboxes by opening the Exchange System Manager and navigating to Servers, then *servername*, then First Storage Group, then Mailbox Store, and then Mailboxes, as shown in Figure 7-24.

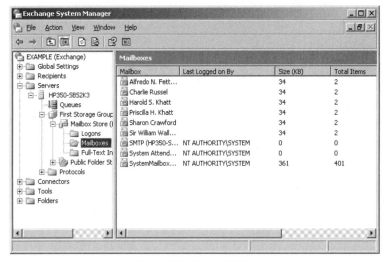

FIGURE 7-24 A very empty Microsoft Exchange Mailbox store

NOTE The mailboxes listed in Figure 7-24 are not typical of a working system but reflect what you would see on a brand-new system.

Running the Migration Preparation Tool

There are several tasks that need to be done on all SBS 2003 networks to prepare for the actual migration, including the following:

- Upgrade the Active Directory schema.
- Set the Microsoft Exchange Server mode.
- Extend the time that two SBS servers can coexist in the same network.

To make life easier, these tasks are automated with the Migration Preparation Tool.

There's one other task we'll cover in this section—synchronizing the time source. On most SBS networks, this should already be OK, but it's critical for the proper migration to the new SBS 2011 server, so make sure it's correct and synched to an external source.

> **IMPORTANT** The changes made by the Migration Preparation Tool are irreversible. You should ensure that you have a fully tested backup of your existing SBS 2003 server before running the Migration Preparation Tool. The only way to return to your original configuration is to restore your backup.

Before you start the migration, you need to upgrade the Active Directory schema to align with the schema used by SBS 2011. To upgrade the schema, you *must* be logged on to the existing SBS server with an account that is a member of the Domain Admins, Enterprise Admins, and Schema Admins groups. The default Administrator account is in all three groups. To verify that the account you are using is in the necessary groups, open Active Directory Users And Computers and double-click the account you are using. Click the Member Of tab to see a list of groups the account belongs to, as shown in Figure 7-25.

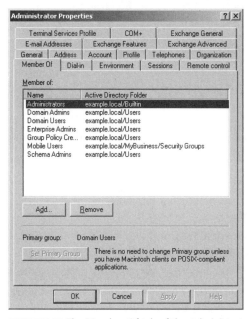

FIGURE 7-25 The Member Of tab of the Administrator account properties

To run the Migration Preparation Tool, use the following steps:

1. Log on to your source server with an account that has Domain Admins, Enterprise Admins, and Schema Admins privileges.

2. Insert the first SBS 2011 DVD into the DVD drive of the source server. If you have autorun enabled on the source server, you'll see the screen shown in Figure 7-26.

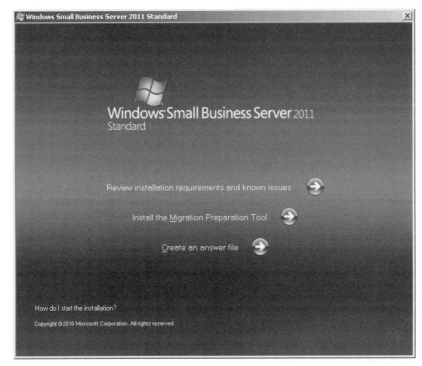

FIGURE 7-26 The Autorun screen for Windows Small Business Server 2011 Standard when run on SBS 2003

NOTE If you don't have a DVD drive on your existing SBS server, insert the DVD in a client workstation and copy the entire tools directory to a location on the server and run SourceTool from there.

3. Click Install The Migration Preparation Tool.

4. Acknowledge the End-User License Agreement (EULA), and click Install and then Finish. (Leave the Run The Migration Preparation Tool option selected.)

5. On the Get Important Updates screen, choose either Download And Install Updates (Recommended) or Do Not Download Updates. Personally, we avoid downloading any additional updates at this point, though the official Microsoft recommendation is to always download updates.

6. On the Prepare Your Source Server For Migration page, select the I Have A Backup And Am Ready To Proceed check box and then click Next. The tool will start updating your schema, extending your coexistence time, and configuring Exchange Server as shown in Figure 7-27. The process takes several minutes, so just be patient. The largest chunk of time is for the schema upgrade.

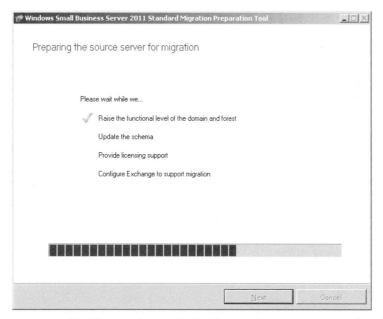

FIGURE 7-27 The Migration Preparation Tool is preparing the source server for migration

7. When the tool completes its tasks, click Next and the source server will be scanned for any additional problems. If any are identified, as shown in Figure 7-28, correct them before continuing.

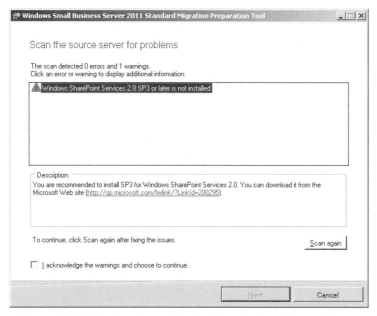

FIGURE 7-28 The Migration Preparation Tool found an issue that must be corrected before continuing

8. Review the Migration Guide, select the check box for it, and then click Create An Answer File. See the steps under Creating A Migration Answer File, later in this chapter. After you've finished creating it and storing it on the USB or other media you'll use, click Finish to close the Windows Small Business Server 2011 Standard Migration Preparation Tool.

9. When you exit the Migration Preparation Tool, you'll be prompted to reboot. You should reboot your server before going any further.

After you reboot, you need to make sure your existing SBS 2003 server is correctly synchronized with an external time source. To set the time synchronization on your SBS server, use the following steps:

1. Log on to your existing SBS server with an account that has Domain Admins privileges.

2. Open a command window (cmd.exe). Type the following commands in the window, as shown in Figure 7-29:

```
w32tm /config /syncfromflags:domhier /reliable:no /update

net stop w32time

net start w32time
```

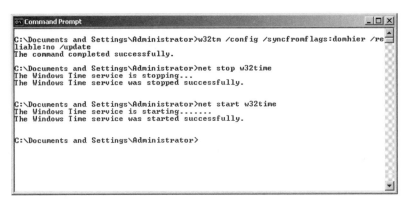

FIGURE 7-29 Configuring Windows Time synchronization

3. Close the command window.

IMPORTANT   If you are running SBS 2003 and SBS 2011 in virtual machines on a Hyper-V server, the parent partition must have the same time zone, date, and time as the child partitions.

Finally, before you can migrate your existing SBS 2003 server, ensure that any line-of-business applications are moved off the main SBS server, or that you have a clear migration path to move them to another server on your SBS network after the migration completes. Remember that once you migrate to SBS 2011, your old SBS server must be completely de-commissioned and removed from the network. Before you can return it to the SBS network, you need to format the system disk and reinstall an operating system. The old and new SBS servers can co-exist on the network for a maximum of only 21 days.

Creating a Migration Answer File

After you have your existing SBS server prepared for migration, you need to create an answer file that can be used to install SBS 2011. You *must use an answer file* for the installation of SBS 2011 if you are migrating. Fortunately, there's an excellent Answer File Generator tool on the SBS 2011 installation DVD. But there is one step you need to take first—creating a new SBS administrator account.

Administrator Account

SBS 2003 creates a default Administrator account during initial installation and setup. This account, often referred to as the 500 account because of a distinctive portion of the GUID for the account, is the master account from which all things spring. This is a legacy from when we were less security-aware and less concerned about having everything installed by and dependent on a well-known account.

Today, that is far from a best practice, and in SBS 2011 the Administrator account is disabled by default. So to ensure that we have an account for both servers that has the necessary privileges to complete the migration, we're going to first create a new administrator account and make that account part of all the groups that the current Administrator account is part of. This new account must have Domain Admins, Enterprise Admins, and Schema Admins privileges, at a minimum. In fact, we're simply going to make a copy of the Administrator account.

To create the new administrator account, follow these steps:

1. Log on to the existing SBS 2003 server with an account with at least Domain Admins privileges.

2. Click Start, and open Active Directory Users And Computers from the Administrative Tools folder.

3. Open the Users folder in the left pane, and select the Administrator account in the right pane.

4. Select Copy from the Action menu, as shown in Figure 7-30.

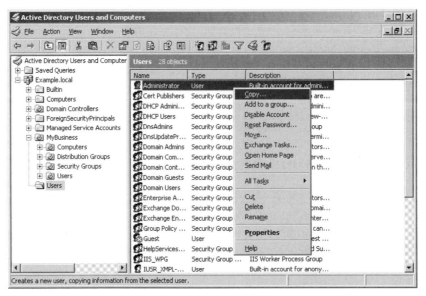

FIGURE 7-30 To ensure that all the necessary permissions are copied to the new account, use Active Directory Users And Computers to copy the Administrator account

5. On the user Copy Object – User dialog box, enter the details for the new account, as shown in Figure 7-31.

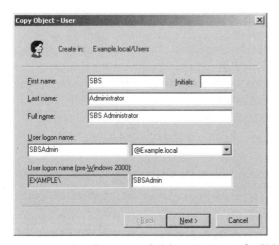

FIGURE 7-31 Creating a new administrator account for SBS 2003

6. After supplying the information for the new administrator account, click Next to fill in password information for the new account. Use a password of at least eight characters that is a mixture of uppercase and lowercase letters, special characters, and numerals to ensure that it meets complexity requirements for SBS 2011.

7. Click Next to open the Exchange mailbox creation step of the Copy Object – User Wizard, as shown in Figure 7-32.

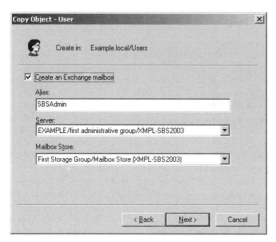

FIGURE 7-32 Creating the Exchange mailbox for the new administrator account

8. Click Next and then click Finish to create the account. The account will be created in the Users container, which isn't where we want it.

9. Expand the MyBusiness organizational unit (OU) container, and then expand the Users OU under it so that you can see the SBSUsers OU as shown in Figure 7-33.

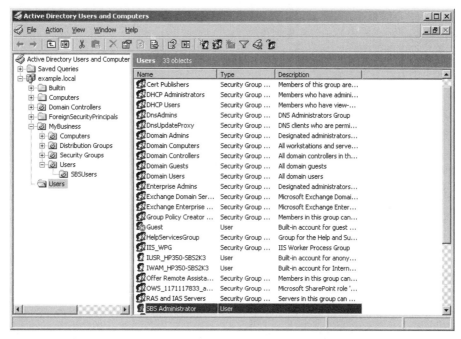

FIGURE 7-33 The MyBusiness OU is expanded so that you can see the SBSUsers OU

10. Select the new user you just created, and drag it into the SBSUsers OU. You'll see the warning shown in Figure 7-34.

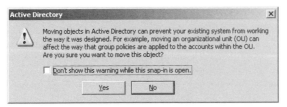

FIGURE 7-34 The warning about moving objects in Active Directory

11. Click Yes to move the user. Figure 7-35 shows the SBSUsers OU with the new administrator account in it.

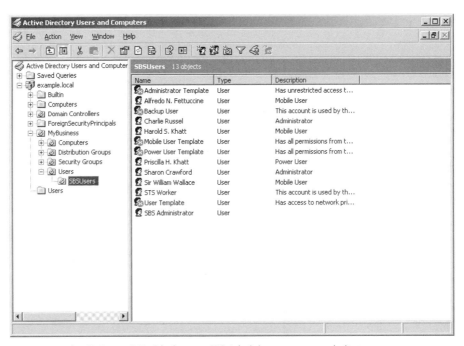

FIGURE 7-35 The SBSUsers OU with the new SBS Administrator account in it

12. Close Active Directory Users And Computers.

Using the SBS Answer File Generator

The SBS Answer File Generator (SBSAfg.exe in the Tools folder of the Installation DVD) can be used to automate a fresh, new install of SBS, and we've covered it in some detail in Chapter 5, "Installing Windows Small Business Server 2011 Standard." But it has a second and more important function—it is used to generate an answer file for enabling a migration installation.

You *must* use an answer file when doing a migration. You do not have the option of doing it purely interactively.

Before you start the answer file generator, you should make sure you have all the information you'll need. Put together a table with all the answers you'll need. This will help ensure you're not missing a vital piece of information before you start. Table 7-1 shows our working table for the migration of our Example.local SBS 2003 network to SBS 2011.

TABLE 7-1 Answer File checklist for SBS 2003 migration

FIELD	ANSWER	REQUIRED
Get Installation Updates	No	No.
Run Unattended	Yes	No.
Use Time Zone	Manually Set The Clock And Time Zone For The Server	No, and we think it's a good idea to do this one manually, because it allows you to verify that the time is correct.
Business Name	SBS Example	Optional. Not sent to Microsoft.
Street Address 1	1 Microsoft Way	Optional. Not sent to Microsoft.
Street Address 2		Optional. Not sent to Microsoft.
City	Redmond	Optional. Not sent to Microsoft.
State	WA	Optional. Not sent to Microsoft.
Zip/Postal Code	98052	Optional. Not sent to Microsoft.
Country/Region	United States	Yes.
Certificate Authority Name		**Leave Blank for Self-Issued Cert. **
Domain Administrator Account Name	SBSAdmin	Yes.
Password	Iforget!	Yes.
Source Server Name	XMPL-SBS2k3	Yes.
Source Domain Name	Example.local	Yes.
Default Gateway	192.168.51.1	Yes.
Source Server IP Address	192.168.51.2	Yes.
DHCP Server Running On Source Server	Yes	Highly recommended. It will allow the migration process to move DHCP to the destination server.
Destination Server Name	HP160-SBSMIG	Yes.
Destination Server IP Address	192.168.51.3	Yes.

After you have all the settings for your migration written down, it's time to run the SBS Answer File Generator using the following steps:

1. Double-click the SBSAfg.exe file in the \Tools directory of the first DVD (the Installation DVD) of the SBS 2011 distribution media.

2. In the Installation Type section of the Windows Small Business Server 2011 Standard Answer File Tool (shown in Figure 7-36), select Migration From Existing Server (Join Existing Domain).

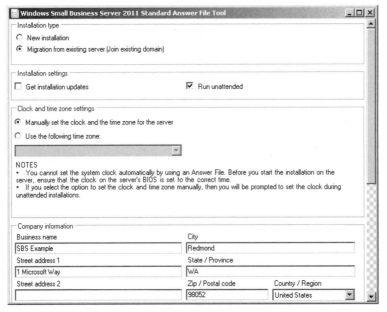

FIGURE 7-36 The Windows Small Business Server 2011 Standard Answer File Tool

3. Fill in the fields according to the table you created, making sure to scroll to the end of the file so that you don't miss any.

4. Click Print to print a copy of the settings to the default printer if you want a hard copy of the settings.

5. Click Save As to save a copy as SBSAnswerFile.xml. You can save the copy to a local hard disk, to a network share, or to removable media.

> **IMPORTANT** The SBSAnswerFile.xml file that is generated has the administrative password in plain text. This will also be the domain recover password. Protect the file until you use it, and delete it when you're done.

6. Click Cancel to close the Answer File Generator.

7. Copy SBSAnswerFile.xml to the root directory of the removable media you'll use during installation of SBS 2011. This can be a USB key disk, a floppy disk, or other removable media that your server can read during the installation.

Installing SBS 2011

OK—we've prepared our server, we've created our answer file, and we're ready to go. Time to install SBS 2011. We're going to follow the normal steps covered in Chapter 5, except that we're using the answer file we created earlier in this chapter. Insert the removable media with the SBSAnswerFile.xml, insert your Installation DVD, and turn on the server.

> **NOTE** You won't actually need the answer file to be available until the Windows Server 2008 R2 portion of the installation completes.

You need to set your BIOS to boot from the DVD drive as the first option to ensure that the server boots from the DVD. Then walk through the normal Windows Server 2008 R2 installation steps as covered in Chapter 5. You'll choose your installation disk, and you can set the size of your system volume for SBS at this time. Do not set it at fewer than 120 GB—we really prefer 200 GB or more. It's a real pain to increase the size later, and there are just too many things that end up going onto your primary system volume.

After you've answered the initial installation questions, the installation of Windows Server 2008 R2 proceeds automatically. When it completes and the system reboots, the installation of SBS will automatically begin if the SBSAnswerFile.xml file is available and you've set the answer file for unattended installation. Even if you've selected the Run Unattended check box in the SBS Answer File Generator, the installation will stop if it is missing a critical piece of information. If you've left the Run Unattended check box cleared, the SBS installation process will use the answers you've provided in the file, but it will expect manual input from you to move from step to step.

The server will reboot several times during the installation, but if you've filled out the answer file fully and you've selected the Run Unattended check box, you should be able to start it, answer the initial questions, and go away for a while. Have lunch. Play a game of racquetball. The whole process might be automated, but it's still slow. When the installation is complete, you'll see the Installation Finished screen shown in Figure 7-37.

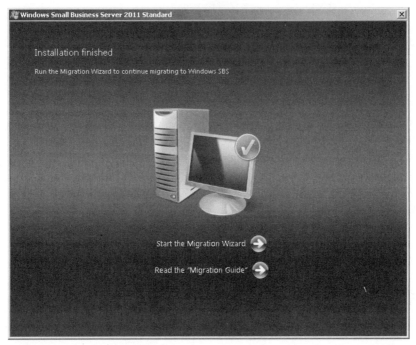

FIGURE 7-37 The Installation Finished screen, ready to start the migration from SBS 2003 to SBS 2011

Migrating Settings and Data

After you've completed the installation of SBS 2011 into your SBS 2003 network, you have 21 days to complete the migration and decommission the original server. There are several steps in the process—some automated, some not.

Using the Migration Wizard

From the time that Windows Small Business Server 2011 Standard is first installed and running on your existing SBS network, you have a maximum of 21 days to complete the migration. Required tasks listed in the Migration Wizard must be completed in the order listed. Optional tasks can be completed later because the other tasks in the task list are not dependent on them. The tasks in the Migration Wizard are listed in Table 7-2.

TABLE 7-2 Tasks in the Migration Wizard

TASK	REQUIRED OR OPTIONAL
Change data storage locations on the new SBS 2011 server.	Optional
Configure networking.	Required
Configure Internet address.	Required
Migrate network settings from old SBS server.	Optional
Migrate Exchange Server mailboxes.	Required if Exchange is used
Clean up legacy Group Policy settings.	Optional
Migrate users' shared data.	Optional (but not if you're the user!)
Migrate Companyweb.	Optional
Migrate fax data.	Optional
Migrate user accounts and groups.	Required
Migrate SQL Server data.	Optional and not in the wizard
Migrate line-of-business applications.	Optional and not in the wizard
Decommission the old SBS 2003 server.	Required

You can start and stop the Migration Wizard as often as necessary. Each time you open it after the initial time, it opens to the Migration Wizard Home page.

> **NOTE** For the steps of this wizard, we've chosen to break the process up in sections that correspond to the individual tasks in the wizard. Each section begins with a heading and includes a series of steps. You can complete each section independently of the other sections, except that each required task in the wizard must be performed in order.

Starting the Migration Wizard

To run the Migration Wizard, follow these steps:

1. Log on to the new SBS 2011 server with the new administrator account you created earlier.

2. Open the Windows SBS Console if it doesn't open automatically. Clicking the Start The Migration Wizard link in the Installation Finished screen shown in Figure 7-37 will automatically launch the Windows SBS Console.

> **NOTE** The Windows Small Business Server 2011 Standard Console is the official name of the Windows SBS Console, but we don't want to type that out every time, and we don't think you want to read that whole long name every time, either. So we've shortened it to Windows SBS Console or even sometimes just SBS Console. But it's still just the same console, and it's the heart of everything you do with SBS.

3. Click Migrate To Windows SBS to open the Migrate To Windows Small Business Server 2011 Standard Wizard. The first time you run the wizard, you'll see a Welcome page.

4. Click Next to open the Migration Wizard Home page, shown in Figure 7-38.

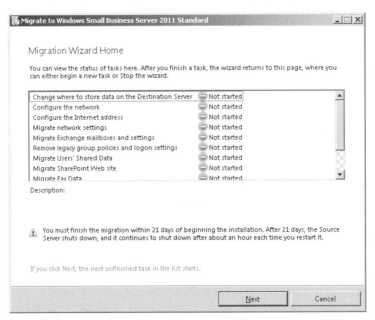

FIGURE 7-38 The Migration Wizard Home page before starting the migration

5. Select Change Where To Store Data On The Destination Server, and click Next to open the page shown in Figure 7-39.

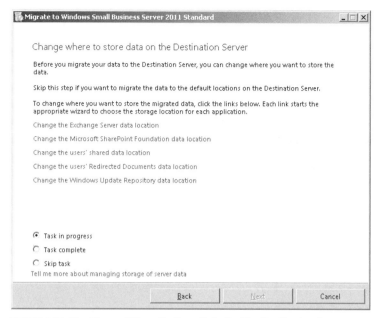

FIGURE 7-39 The Change Where To Store Data On The Destination Server page

6. This is an optional task, so you can choose to skip it. Because the default location for Exchange Server data is on the C drive, we definitely want to change that. So click Change The Exchange Server Data Location to open the Move Exchange Server Data Wizard.

7. Click Next and your server hard drives are examined. When the wizard finishes the examination, it prompts you with the warning Server Backup Is Not Configured, as shown in Figure 7-40. We know that, so click OK.

FIGURE 7-40 Warning that Server Backup isn't configured

8. On the Choose A New Location For The Data page, shown in Figure 7-41, select the location you want to use for the data and click Move.

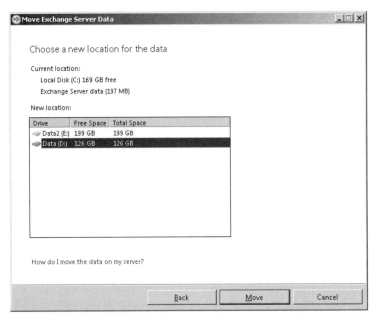

FIGURE 7-41 The Choose A New Location For The Data page of the Move Exchange Server Data Wizard

9. Click Finish when the task completes.

10. Complete the rest of the relocations on this page now, or complete them later. SBS includes wizards that simplify these tasks even after the migration is complete.

11. Click Skip Task when you've completed all the steps you want to do at this time, and then click Next to return to the Migration Wizard Home page.

> **NOTE** You could also click Task Complete and return to the Migration Wizard Home page, but by clicking Skip Task, you will have the option to return to this task later if you want to.

Configure the Network

To configure the network, follow these steps:

1. Click Next to move to the Set Up The Network page shown in Figure 7-42.

2. Click Start The Connect To The Internet Wizard link to open the Before You Begin page of the Connect To The Internet Wizard. Read it carefully to know what you'll need before you start.

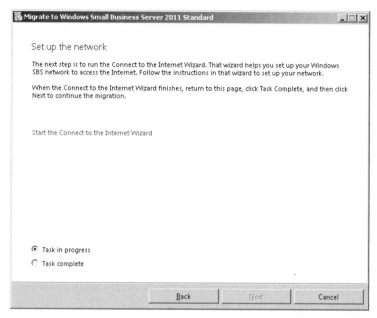

FIGURE 7-42 The Set Up The Network page of the Migrate To Windows Small Business Server 2011 Standard Wizard

3. Click Next and the wizard will start detecting your current network and locating your router. When it completes, you'll see the page shown in Figure 7-43.

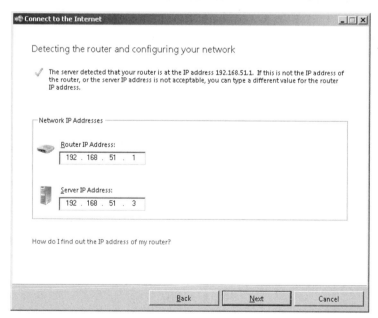

FIGURE 7-43 The Connect To The Internet Wizard has correctly detected the router and server IP addresses

4. Click Next. If you have a UPnP router, the wizard will automatically configure it. If you don't, you'll see a page describing how to manually configure the settings required.

5. Click Finish, and then select Task Complete and click Next to return to the Migration Wizard Home page. The Configure The Network task now shows as Completed.

Configure the Internet Address

To configure the Internet address, follow these steps:

1. Click Next to open the Configure The Internet Address page. Read the warning about certificate distribution to remote users. If you are using self-signed certificates and you don't follow the advice shown now, your users will be locked out of Remote Web Access (RWA) and Outlook Web Access (OWA) until you distribute new certificates to them.

2. Click Start The Internet Address Management Wizard when you're ready to move your RWA and OWA sites to the new SBS 2011 server.

3. Click Next on the Before You Begin page (after reading it) to open the Do You Want To Register A New Domain Name page, shown in Figure 7-44.

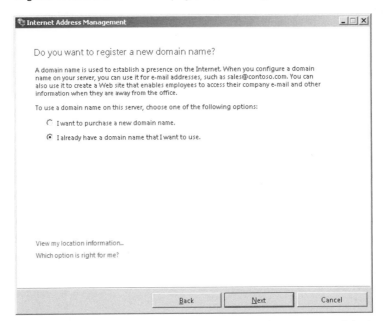

FIGURE 7-44 The Do You Want To Register A New Domain Name page of the Internet Address Management Wizard

4. Select the appropriate choice for your network. If you're not changing your Internet domain name, choose I Already Have A Domain Name That I Want To Use.

5. Click Next to open the How Do You Want To Manage Your Domain Name page, shown in Figure 7-45. If you're already managing your domain name, there's no reason to change.

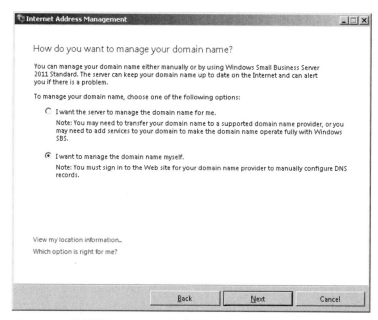

FIGURE 7-45 SBS 2011 can automatically manage DNS records and your domain name

6. Click Next to open the Store Your Domain Name Information page of the wizard, as shown in Figure 7-46.

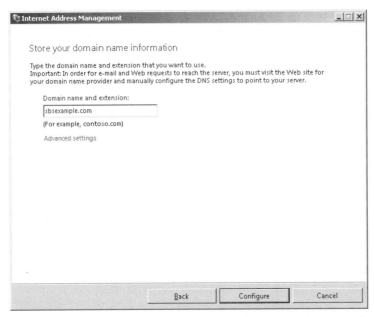

FIGURE 7-46 The Store Your Domain Name Information page of the Internet Address Management Wizard

7. Type your Internet domain name in the Domain Name And Extension field and then click Configure. This will configure your RWA site, your Exchange email address, and your Internet router if it supports UPnP. If it doesn't, you need to manually configure the settings on the router.

   If you need to use a remote access prefix other than remote.*yourdomainname.com* for your RWA site, you can click the Advanced Settings link to open the Advanced Settings dialog box shown in Figure 7-47. But really, stick with the defaults unless there is a compelling reason not to.

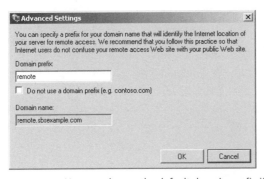

FIGURE 7-47 You can change the default domain prefix if necessary

8. Click Configure to run the Internet Address Management Wizard, as shown in Figure 7-48.

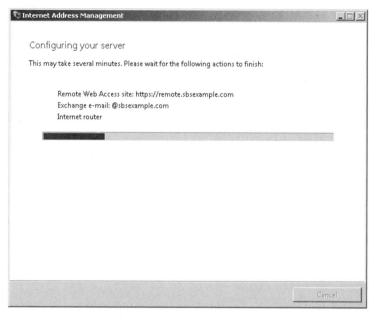

FIGURE 7-48 The Configuring Your Server page of the Internet Address Management Wizard

9. If your router doesn't use UPnP (and we certainly don't run it on ours or recommend that others do), you'll see a warning on the Congratulations! page, as shown in Figure 7-49.

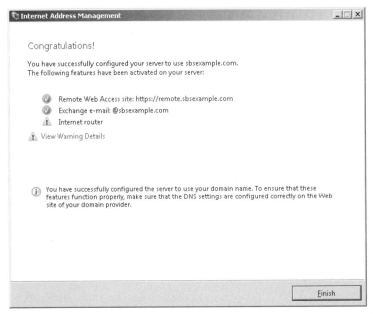

FIGURE 7-49 If your router doesn't have UPnP enabled, you'll see a warning symbol next to Internet Router

10. Click on the View Warning Details link to open the Internet Address Management Warning Details dialog box shown in Figure 7-50. You can safely ignore this warning now, but write down the ports listed. You'll want to go manually configure your router or firewall to forward those ports to your new SBS 2011 server.

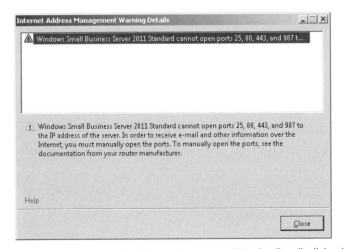

FIGURE 7-50 The Internet Address Management Warning Details dialog box

11. Click Close and then click Finish to return to the Configure The Internet Address page of the Migration Wizard. Select Task Complete and then click Next to return to the Migration Wizard Home page.

Migrate Network Settings

To migrate network settings, follow these steps:

1. Click Next to open the Migrate Network Settings page of the Migration Wizard, shown in Figure 7-51.

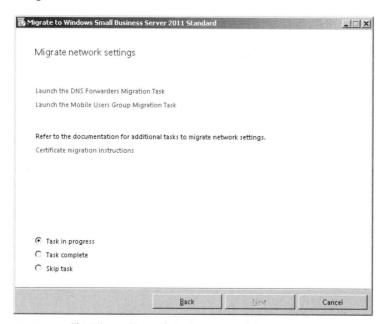

FIGURE 7-51 The Migrate Network Settings page of the Migration Wizard

2. Click Launch The DNS Forwarders Migration Task. When the task completes, you'll see the informational message shown in Figure 7-52.

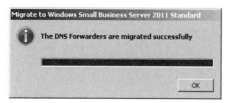

FIGURE 7-52 The DNS Forwarders have been migrated successfully

3. Click OK to return to the Migrate Network Settings page.

4. Click Launch The Mobile Users Group Migration Task to migrate the Mobile Users group. The Mobile Users group is not a default SBS 2011 Security Group.

5. Click OK when the wizard completes to return to the Migrate Network Settings page.

6. Click the Certificate Migration Instructions link for details on how to migrate certificates. Migration of Self-Issued certificates is not supported, but Trusted Third-Party certificates can be migrated to the new SBS 2011 server.

7. Select Task Complete and then click Next to return to the Migration Wizard Home page.

Migrate Exchange Mailboxes and Settings

To migrate Exchange mailboxes and settings, follow these steps:

1. Click Next to open the Migrate Exchange Mailboxes And Settings page of the Migration Wizard.

2. Click the Migrate Exchange Server Mailboxes And Public Folders link to open the TechNet article on migrating Microsoft Exchange. This is a *critical step* if you're running Microsoft Exchange on your existing SBS server. The steps you'll be performing will

   a. Remove the Internet Connectors from the source server.

   b. Move any POP3 connectors from the source server if you're currently using POP3.

   c. Move your Public Folders from the source server to the destination server.

   d. Move the Offline Address book from the source server to the destination server.

   e. Move the users' mailboxes from the source server to the destination server.

3. Carefully read each step of the process. Do not try to skip any steps, but follow them rigorously.

4. Click the Remove Internet Connectors link, and follow the instructions exactly to remove the SmallBusiness SMTP Connector from the SBS 2003 source server, as shown in Figure 7-53.

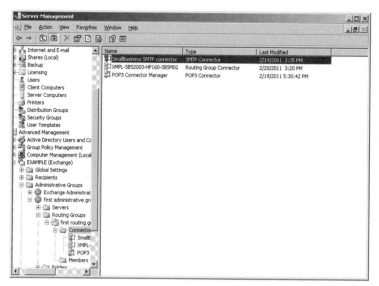

FIGURE 7-53 Removing the SmallBusiness SMTP Connector on the source SBS 2003 server

5. Follow the instructions for moving POP3 connectors if you're using them. This is an optional step.

6. Follow the instructions for moving Public Folders carefully. This is a critical step and can take a substantial amount of time on a large Public Folder store. Do not proceed until the Public Folder Instances folder is empty, as shown in Figure 7-54.

IMPORTANT It takes awhile for the Public Folder Instances container to completely empty, and for a while it seems as if nothing is happening at all. Be patient.

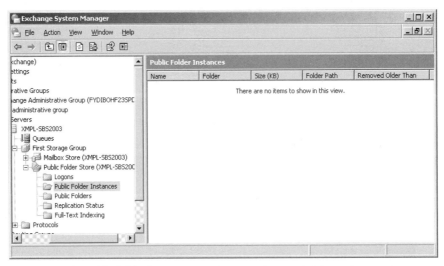

FIGURE 7-54 The Public Folder Instances container must be completely empty

7. Follow the instructions for moving your offline address book (OAB). Unlike the previous steps, this is done on the destination server, as shown in Figure 7-55.

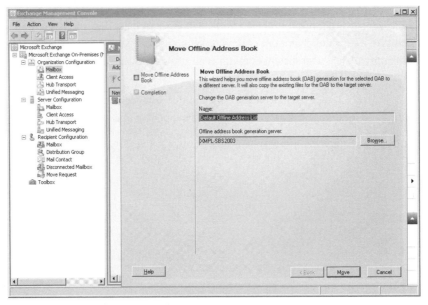

FIGURE 7-55 Moving the Offline Address Book from the source server to the SBS 2011 destination server

8. When the Move Offline Address Book Wizard completes successfully, select the Offline Address Book in the Exchange Management Console. Click Properties from the Action menu to open the Default Offline Address List Properties dialog box.

9. Click on the Distribution tab, and then select the Enable Web-Based Distribution check box, as shown in Figure 7-56.

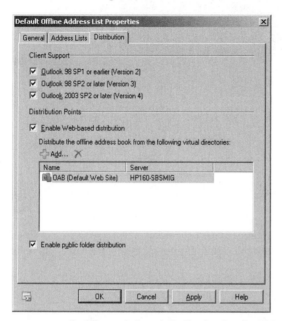

FIGURE 7-56 Enabling web-based distribution for the OAB

10. Click Add, and select OAB (Default Web Site) for the destination server. Click OK, and then click OK again to close the Default Offline Address List Properties dialog box.

11. Continue to follow the instructions to set the offline address book for the Mailbox database. When this task is complete, you can begin to move the users' mailboxes.

12. On the destination server, follow the instructions to move the mailboxes. In the Exchange Management Console, navigate to the Recipient Configuration container.

13. Select Mailbox in the left pane, and then select all the mailboxes in the center pane, as shown in Figure 7-57.

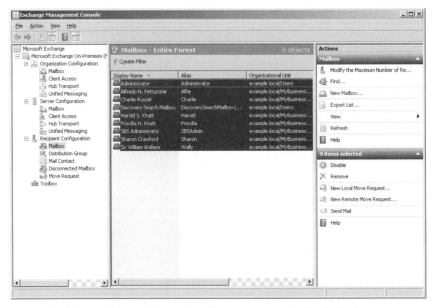

FIGURE 7-57 Moving all the mailboxes from the source server to the destination server

14. Click New Local Move Request in the right pane to open the New Local Move Request Wizard shown in Figure 7-58.

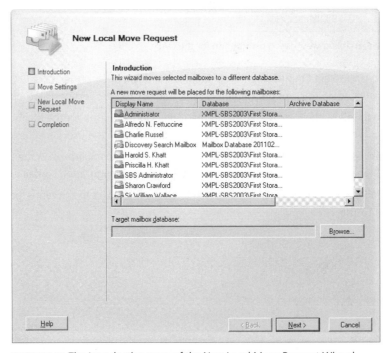

FIGURE 7-58 The Introduction page of the New Local Move Request Wizard

15. Click Browse to open the Select Mailbox Database dialog box, shown in Figure 7-59. Select the destination SBS 2011 server and then click OK to return to the New Local Move Request Wizard.

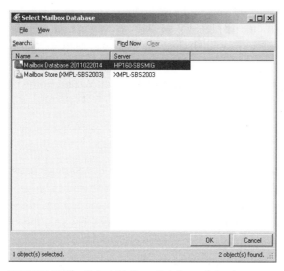

FIGURE 7-59 The Select Mailbox Database dialog box

16. Click Next to open the Move Settings page, shown in Figure 7-60. Set a reasonable number of messages to skip if there is corruption of a mailbox. You might have to do additional cleanup on a problem mailbox to successfully move all the mailboxes.

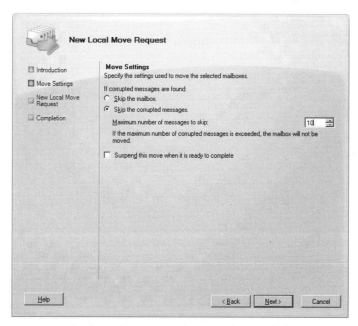

FIGURE 7-60 Configure the Move Settings page for the Local Move Request

17. Click Next, then click New, and then click Finish to close the New Local Move Request Wizard. Any mailboxes that can't be moved will need to be deleted, so be prepared to manually clean up any problem mailboxes.

18. When all the moves have completed, click on Move Request in the Recipient Configuration container and highlight the completed Move Requests item. Click Clear Move Request. Acknowledge the warning and then close the Exchange Management Console, and return to the Migrate Exchange Mailboxes And Settings page.

19. Select Task Complete, and click Next to return to the Migration Wizard Home page.

Remove Legacy Group Policies and Logon Settings

To remove legacy Group Policies and logon settings, follow these steps:

1. Click Next to open the Remove Legacy Group Policies And Logon Settings page. These scripts and Group Policies have already been migrated but now need to be removed because they're not compatible with SBS 2011. If you have customizations in these scripts or Group Policies, you'll need to save them and reapply them after the migration is complete using the new methods in SBS 2011.

2. Log on to the SBS 2003 source server with an administrative account.

3. Click Start and then click Run.

4. Type **\\localhost\sysvol\<*domainname.local*>\scripts** and then press Enter to open Windows Explorer in the replication folder for logon scripts. (Replace <*domainname. local*> with your domain name. In our test network, it's example.local.)

5. Delete or rename the SBS_LOGIN_SCRIPT.bat file, as shown in Figure 7-61.

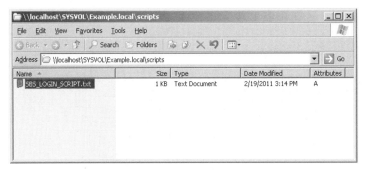

FIGURE 7-61 Renaming the login script file will prevent it from running

6. If any of your users have custom logon scripts, disable or delete them in Active Directory Users And Computers, following the steps in the TechNet article at *http://technet. microsoft.com/en-us/library/gg554043.aspx*.

7. Return to the Migration Wizard, and click Remove Old Group Policy Objects. Follow the instructions in the TechNet article to remove the old GPOs.

8. Be careful to not remove the new SBS GPOs. Most of these start with "Windows SBS." The old GPOs mostly start with "Small Business Server" in the GPO name.

9. Follow the instructions to remove the SBS 2003 WMI Filters, and then close the Group Policy Management Console and return to the Migration Wizard.

10. Select Task Complete, and click Next to return to the Migration Wizard Home page.

Migrate Users' Shared Data

To migrate users' shared data, follow these steps:

1. Click Next to open the Migrate Users' Shared Data page of the Migration Wizard.

2. Click How Do I Migrate Users' Shared Data to open the TechNet article on moving the users' shares.

3. Follow the steps to re-create the shared folders on the new SBS 2011 server and copy the data from the old server.

4. When you've finished, click Task Complete and then click Next to return to the Migration Wizard Home page.

Migrating Companyweb

Migrating the Companyweb site is an imperfect solution at best. Because of the change in versions between SharePoint in SBS 2003 and SharePoint in SBS 2011, the migration of the SharePoint site is not a simple or completely transparent solution. You can easily move the files from your existing Companyweb site by using a USB stick and Windows Explorer. Moving the entire site involves a good deal more work. Unless you have made significant customizations and your users have data stored in the SBS 2003 Companyweb site, you can skip this step. Whether you move files, move the entire site, or simply start over with a new Companyweb site, you need to follow these steps:

1. Click Next to open the Migrate Your Internal Web Site page of the Migration Wizard.

2. If you intend to migrate either files or the entire site, click the Migrate The Internal Web Site link to open the help topic on migrating Companyweb.

3. Follow the steps carefully. When you're finished, click Task Complete and then click Next to return to the Migration Wizard Home page.

4. If you opt to not migrate the site or to migrate the site later, click Skip Task and then click Next to return to the Migration Wizard Home page.

Migrating Fax Data

To migrate fax data, follow these steps:

1. Click Next to open the Migrating Fax Data page of the Migration Wizard.

2. Select where you want to store your fax data on the new SBS 2011 server. You can choose either the default location for the fax service or Companyweb (Internal Web Site). The option to store in Companyweb is a new option in SBS 2011.

3. Click the Click To Start Migrating Your Fax Data link to begin the migration.

4. When the migration completes, click OK to return to the Migrate Fax Data page.

5. Click Task Complete and then click Next to return to the Migration Wizard Home page.

6. If you opt to not migrate the fax data or if you don't use the fax service, click Skip Task and then click Next to return to the Migration Wizard Home page.

Migrating Users and Groups

As a normal part of Active Directory replication when the SBS 2011 server was installed, the users and groups have already been migrated. But they aren't yet visible in the Windows SBS Console. To make them visible in the Windows SBS Console, follow these steps:

1. Click Next to open the Migrate Groups page of the Migration Wizard.

2. Click Display The Security Group Migration Instructions to open the help topic.

3. Now you have a choice. You can go through a fairly complicated step-by-step instruction to migrate each individual group manually, or you can run the GroupConverter application. We think it just makes sense to use the Group Converter, and then do any cleanup afterwards if necessary.

4. Open Windows Explorer on the destination server, and navigate to the C:\Program Files\Windows Small Business Server\Bin directory.

5. Double-click on the GroupConverter application to open the Windows SBS "7" Active Directory Group Converter shown in Figure 7-62.

NOTE In Figures 7-62 through 7-64, we get to see the name SBS 2011 had during its very early days. Oops. Apparently, this file slipped through the cracks. We did file a bug on it, however, so we expect it will get fixed in the next Service Pack.

FIGURE 7-62 The Group Converter automatically converts SBS 2003 groups to work with SBS 2011

6. Click Next to open the Select The Security Groups page shown in Figure 7-63.

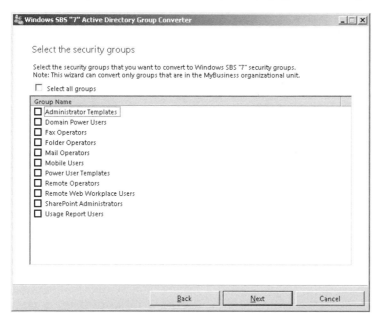

FIGURE 7-63 The Select The Security Groups page of the Group Converter application

7. Don't bother converting standard SBS 2003 groups—SBS 2011 has already created the appropriate groups to match up to the old ones. But if you have created any custom security groups or any distribution groups, you'll probably want to migrate those. Select the security groups you want to convert, and click Next to open the Select The Distribution Groups page, shown in Figure 7-64.

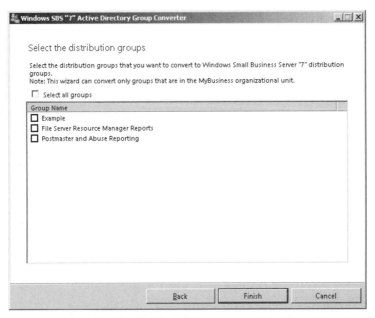

FIGURE 7-64 The Select The Distribution Groups page of the Group Converter application

8. Select any distribution groups you want to continue to use, and then click Finish and then Finish again to close Group Converter and return to the Migrate Groups page of the Migration Wizard.

9. Click Next to open the Migrate User Accounts page of the Migration Wizard.

10. Click the Run The Change A User Role Wizard link to open the Select New User Role page of the Change A User Role Wizard, as shown in Figure 7-65.

11. Select Replace User Permissions Or Settings, and select the role you want to assign to these users.

12. Click Next to open the Select User Account page. This page will probably be blank when you start.

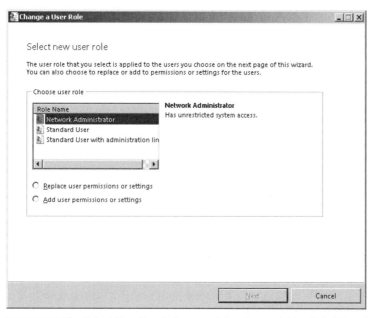

FIGURE 7-65 The Select New User Role page of the Change A User Role Wizard

13. Click Display All User Accounts In The Active Directory to show all the accounts as shown in Figure 7-66.

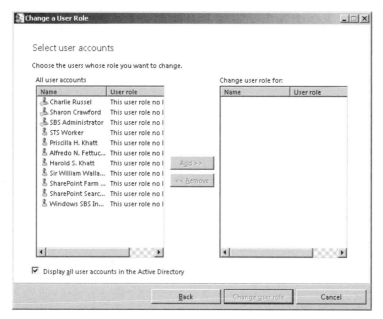

FIGURE 7-66 The Select User Accounts page of the Change A User Role Wizard

14. Select the users you want to change, and click Add to move them to the right pane.

15. Click Change User Role to update the users. Click Finish when the wizard completes to return to the Migrate User Accounts page.

16. Repeat steps 10 through 15 until all the accounts you want to manage in the Windows SBS Console have been migrated. (Don't bother with special accounts such as the STS Worker account or the SharePoint accounts shown in Figure 7-66.)

17. Select Task Complete, and click Next to return to the Migration Wizard Home page.

Finish the Migration

When you finish migrating users and groups, the next step is to finish the migration and de-commission the source server. When you click Next on the Migration Wizard Home page, you get one last chance to complete any steps you marked as skipped, as shown in Figure 7-67.

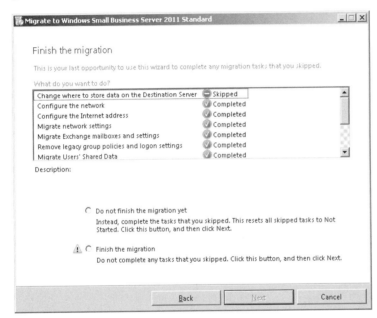

FIGURE 7-67 One last chance to complete skipped tasks before the wizard is done

If there are any optional tasks that you delayed because you weren't ready to complete them, now is the time to complete them. Select Do Not Finish The Migration Yet, and then click Next to reset the Skipped flag and mark them Not Started, as shown in Figure 7-68.

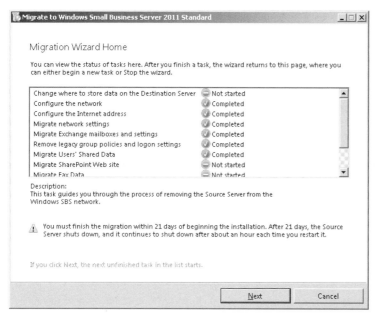

FIGURE 7-68 Restarting the Migration Wizard to do tasks that were skipped the first time

Click Next to begin doing the optional tasks you skipped previously. When you get to the end of the tasks list again, click Next and then select Finish The Migration if you have any skipped tasks that you don't want to do.

Finally, click Next to open the Finish The Migration page. On this page, you are told to demote the old SBS 2003 server to no longer be a domain controller. To demote the SBS 2003 server, follow these steps:

1. Log on to the SBS 2003 server with an administrative account.

2. Open a command window. At the prompt, type **ncpa.cpl** and press Enter to open the Network Connections application as shown in Figure 7-69.

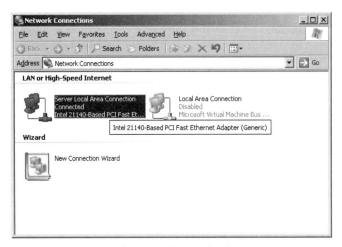

FIGURE 7-69 The Network Connections application

3. Right-click the remaining active network connection and select Properties.

4. Select Internet Protocol (TCP/IP), and click Properties to open the Internet Protocol (TCP/IP) Properties dialog box shown in Figure 7-70.

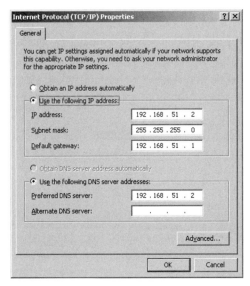

FIGURE 7-70 The Preferred DNS Server address is still pointing to the source server

5. Change the Preferred DNS Server address to the IP address of the destination server, as shown in Figure 7-71. Click OK to close the TCP/IP Properties dialog and then click OK again.

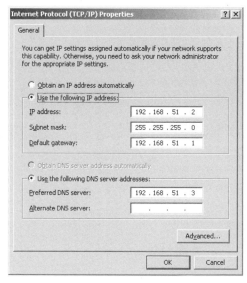

FIGURE 7-71 Change the Preferred DNS Server to point to the destination server

6. Open a command window. At the prompt, type **dcpromo** and press Enter to open the Active Directory Installation Wizard, as shown in Figure 7-72.

FIGURE 7-72 The Welcome page of the Active Directory Installation Wizard

7. Click Next and the Global Catalog server warning shown in Figure 7-73 will be displayed.

FIGURE 7-73 The Global Catalog server warning when demoting your source SBS 2003 server

8. Click OK to open the Remove Active Directory page shown in Figure 7-74.

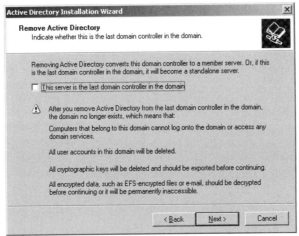

FIGURE 7-74 The Remove Active Directory page of the Active Directory Installation Wizard

9. Leave the check box cleared, and click Next to open the Administrator Password page.

10. Type in a password, type it in again to confirm it, and then click Next to open the Summary page shown in Figure 7-75.

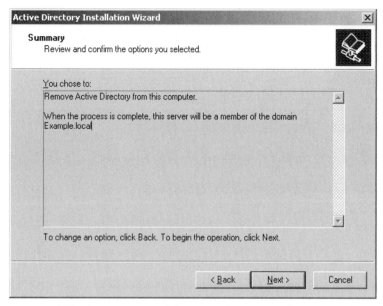

FIGURE 7-75 The Summary page of the Active Directory Installation Wizard

11. Click Next and the wizard will remove Active Directory and demote the original SBS 2003 server to a domain member.

12. When the wizard completes successfully, click Finish and then click Restart Now.

13. On the Finish The Migration page of the Migration Wizard, select The Source Server Is No Longer A Domain Controller and click Next.

14. Disconnect the original SBS 2003 server from the network, and do not reconnect it until you have completely reformatted it and installed a new operating system.

15. On the SBS 2011 server, open the Windows SBS Console if it isn't open.

16. Click Network in the navigation bar and then click on the Computers tab, as shown in Figure 7-76.

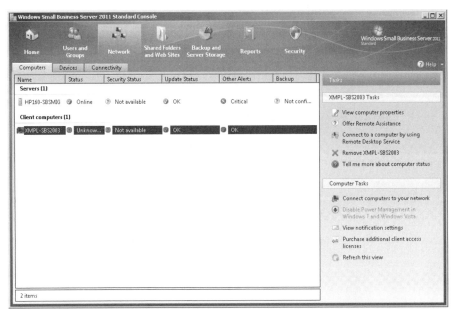

FIGURE 7-76 The Computers tab of the Windows SBS Console

17. Select the former SBS 2003 computer in the Client Computers section and click Remove in the Tasks pane.

18. Click Yes at the prompt and the SBS 2003 computer is removed from the domain.

Re-Enabling Folder Redirection

When the migration tasks are complete, you can re-enable Folder Redirection for user accounts. SBS 2011 allows you to do folder redirection by individual user account instead of requiring you to do it as an all-or-none proposition.

To enable folder redirection, follow these steps:

1. Open the Windows SBS Console if it isn't open.

2. Select Users And Groups in the navigation bar and then click Users.

3. Click Redirect Folders For User Accounts To The Server in the Tasks pane to open the Folder Redirection Properties dialog box shown in Figure 7-77.

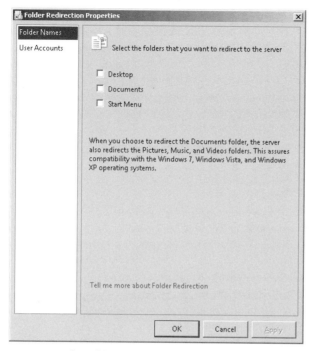

FIGURE 7-77 The Folder Names page of the Folder Redirection Properties dialog box

4. Select the folders that you want to redirect and then click User Accounts in the left pane to open the User Accounts page shown in Figure 7-78.

FIGURE 7-78 The User Accounts page of the Folder Redirection Properties dialog box

5. Select the accounts you want to use folder redirection on and then click OK to redirect the accounts.

6. Click Close at the success message to return to the Windows SBS Console.

Final Thoughts

This completes the basic SBS migration from SBS 2003 to SBS 2011. If you're migrating from SBS 2008 or SBS 2011, your steps are slightly different, but the overall process is essentially similar. The keys to a successful migration are preparation and meticulous attention to detail. Follow the steps completely, accurately, and in order and you will have a successful migration. Deviate from them, skip steps because you think they don't matter, jump ahead because you're bored waiting for Public Folders to migrate, or engage in any other deviation and you've set yourself up for a migration failure. But follow the steps, and you should have success.

If you have a small SBS domain and you carefully clean your Exchange mailboxes and Public Folders before beginning the migration, there's no reason that you can't perform a complete migration in a weekend. But don't even begin until you have thoroughly read all the documentation and are sure you understand the steps involved.

Before you begin a migration, make sure your backups are reliable and that you have a fallback position. Know how long you have to work with a problem before you have to stop and restore your source SBS server from backup. You can't reverse a migration—you can only restore from backup and start again.

Summary

In this chapter, we covered the migration from an SBS 2003 network to an SBS 2011 network. Each migration will be slightly different and will present its own set of challenges. By being fully prepared and understanding all the steps that are involved in a migration, you'll be in the best position to have a successful migration with minimum disruption to your end users. In the next chapter, we cover the Getting Started Tasks that all installations need to complete. Some of these tasks will have been completed as part of the migration, but others remain.

## CHAPTER 8

Completing the Getting Started Tasks

After Microsoft Windows Small Business Server (SBS) 2011 is installed, you have the usual array of chores to complete, configure, and set up before your network is complete. Not all of these chores have to be done at once and some don't need to be done at all, but you do need to review the list.

Start by opening the Windows Small Business Server 2011 Standard Console (SBS Console). When you select Home, you'll see the list displayed in the left pane shown in Figure 8-1. In this chapter, we'll cover the items in the Getting Started Tasks section in order and then look at the items under the Network Essentials Summary, which appears in the pane on the right.

FIGURE 8-1 Select Home to see the items listed under Getting Started Tasks.

The SBS Console is a handy tool you can use from any location—the Windows SBS server computer, a client computer, or remotely—to manage users, groups, network settings, shared resources, backup, and security.

> **IMPORTANT** Advanced administrative tasks are performed using Windows Server 2011 tools available from the Administrative Tools menu. For example, to manage non–Windows SBS users and computers, use Active Directory Users And Computers Management Console.

Finish the Installation

If there are any problems, a View Installation Issues link appears. Click it and correct the problems. Also, click the Using The Windows Small Business Server 2011 Standard Console link to open a help file describing Windows SBS Console functions.

Connect to the Internet

Normally, if the connection is already set up and the router is properly configured, the Internet connection is made during the installation of Windows SBS 2011. Whether or not this connection is set up, you will need to run the Connect To The Internet Wizard if the connection was not made for some reason during installation. If you change your router or Internet provider, you might need to run the wizard again in the future.

To manually connect, click the Connect To The Internet link to get started. The initial page of the Connect To The Internet Wizard advises you on what you need to proceed—namely, the following:

- The IP address for the router you'll be connecting from
- The logon information necessary to connect to the router

After you collect that information, click Next. The Connect To The Internet Wizard attempts to detect existing networks and routers. (See Figure 8-2.)

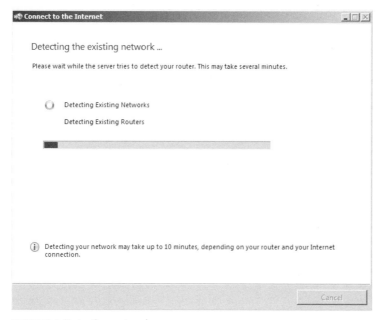

FIGURE 8-2 Detecting networks

After the wizard finishes detecting networks, follow these steps:

1. The next page of the Connect To The Internet Wizard displays the IP address of the router and of the server. (See Figure 8-3.) If either or both of the addresses are incorrect, type in the corrections. Click Next.

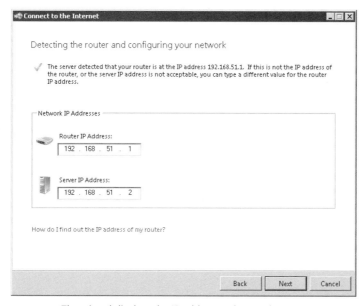

FIGURE 8-3 The wizard displays the IP addresses detected

2. As shown in Figure 8-4, the wizard proceeds to locate and configure the router and the server. When the process is finished, a notification appears announcing that the Internet connection is completed. Click Finish.

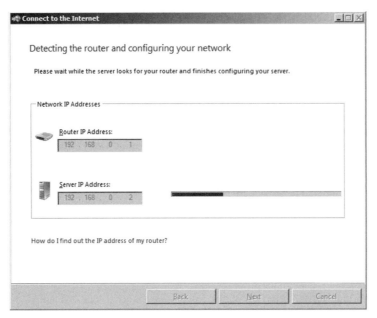

FIGURE 8-4 Detecting the router and completing the Internet connection

Customer Feedback Options

Customer Feedback Options is an area of considerable importance to Microsoft and even to us end users—in the long run. In the short term, you might wonder why you should participate in a program unlikely to be of direct benefit to you.

Well, it's something like paying taxes for schools when you have no children or your children are all adults. We pay those taxes because an educated populace is a greater social good. On a less lofty level, the Customer Experience Improvement Plan should result in better software in the future. And because this is software used by hundreds of millions of people, some considerable social good should therefore emerge.

Click Customer Feedback Options and then click Read More About The Program Online and decide for yourself whether you want to participate.

Set Up Your Internet Address

Before you can set up your Internet presence, you must gather a variety of information:

- You must have an Internet domain name. If you don't have one, you must register one with a domain registration service. You will need a prospective name and several alternatives, and a credit card to pay the registration fee.
- If you already have an Internet domain name, you'll need the name of your Internet providers as well as the logon information for the provider.

Choosing an Internet Domain Name

When choosing an Internet domain name, you want a name that clearly identifies your organization without being too long or too abbreviated—both are difficult to remember.

For example, if your business name is a long one, shorten it in a comprehensible way. A name that's too long tries the patience of people looking for your site.

Names that are too short have their own hazards. Using initials can work, but they must provide *some* information and avoid being inadvertently humorous.

NOTE Don't get hung up on needing to have a .com. You're much more likely to be able to get a name you like with a .net, .biz, or .info extension.

Registering a New Domain Name

Click the Set Up Your Internet Address link to view the list of what you'll need to start the process. Click Next, and then follow these steps:

1. As shown in Figure 8-5, the Internet Address Management Wizard asks you to choose between purchasing a new domain name and using one you already have. Select I Want To Purchase A New Domain Name, and then click Next.

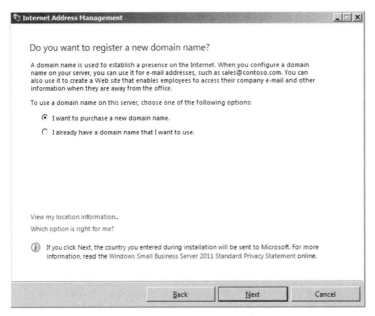

FIGURE 8-5 Getting a new domain name

2. Type the domain name you want to register, and select the extension from the drop-down list. Click Next.

3. Select a domain name provider from the list provided (shown in Figure 8-6) and then click Next.

FIGURE 8-6 Choosing a name provider

NOTE Including your postal address improves the search because some national extensions are available only to residents. For example, you must be in Canada to register a domain name with the .ca extension.

4. If the domain name you choose is not available, possible variations appear in the Available Domain Names list. Accept one of those or search again. If the name is available, you can register it, as shown in Figure 8-7. Click Register Now to be connected to the domain name registry company.

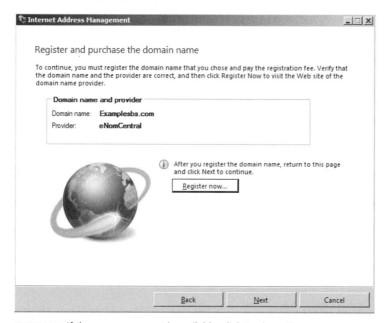

FIGURE 8-7 If the name you want is available, click Register Now

5. After completing the registration, return to the page in Figure 8-7, and then click Next.
6. On the Store Your Domain Name Information page (shown in Figure 8-8), enter the domain name and the user name you registered (if they're not already entered) and the password you used when registering. Click Configure to complete the process.

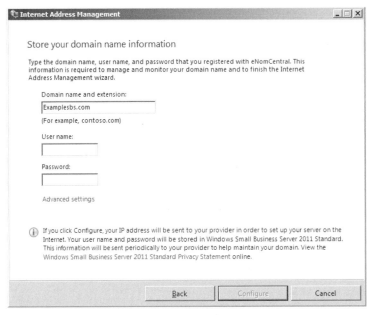

FIGURE 8-8 Storing the domain registration information

Using an Existing Domain Name

If you already have a registered domain name, you can easily set up your presence on the Internet. Before you start, you'll need the domain name and the name and logon information for your domain provider. When you're ready, click the Set Up Your Internet Address link and follow these steps:

1. Read the introductory material, and then click Next.

2. On the Do You Want To Register A New Domain Name page, select I Already Have A Domain Name, and then click Next.

3. You next have to choose whether you want the server to manage the domain name or to manage it yourself. See the sidebar "Who Manages the Domain Name" for more information. Make your selection and click Next. (If you choose self-management, skip to "Managing Your Domain Name" later in this chapter.)

4. On the Type The Domain Name That You Want To Use page, type the domain name you own and select the extension from the drop-down list (shown in Figure 8-9). Click Next.

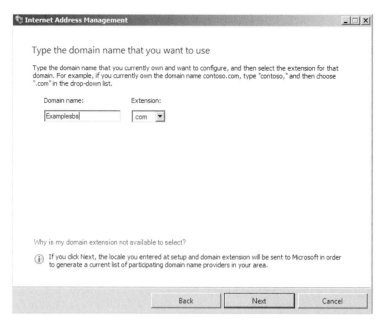

FIGURE 8-9 Entering the existing domain name you want to use

5. Choose a domain name provider from the partner list, and click Next.

6. Click Visit Web Site, and follow the instructions provided. Then return to the Update Domain Name Registration With Your Provider page, and click Next.

7. On the Store Your Domain Name Information page, type the domain name and the user name you registered (if they're not already entered) and the password you used when registering. Click Configure to complete the process.

The Internet Address Management Wizard will proceed to configure your server as shown in Figure 8-10.

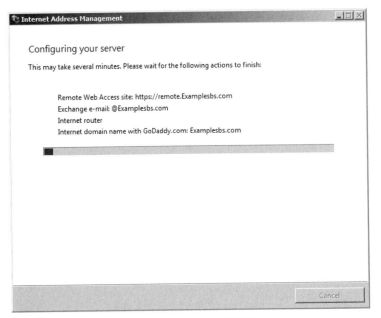

FIGURE 8-10 The wizard configures Windows SBS 2011 to use your domain name

Who Manages the Domain Name?

When you have an existing domain name, you can do the management of the name yourself or let the server do it for you. It's considerably easier to let the server manage the domain name, but the key issues are as follows:

- Is your name registered with one of the domain name providers partnered with Microsoft? If yes, let the server manage the domain name.
- If your name is registered with another domain name provider, are you willing to have the registration transferred to one of the Microsoft partners? If yes, let the server manage the domain name.

However, you might have no choice but to manage the domain yourself if one of the following applies:

- The wizard doesn't list the domain name extension for your existing domain name.
- No partner domain name providers are listed for your country or region.

If the server manages the domain name, the wizard configures the following:

- Domain Name System (DNS)
- Certification Authority
- Internet Information Services (IIS)
- Simple Mail Transfer Protocol (SMTP) mail policies for Exchange Server
- The Universal Plug and Play (UPnP) architecture, if supported by your router

If you manage the domain name yourself, you must add DNS records to your server as shown in Table 8-1.

TABLE 8-1 DNS resource records to add for server self-management

RESOURCE RECORD NAME	RECORD TYPE	SETTING	DESCRIPTION
Remote	A	Static IP address of the WAN side of the router or firewall. Provided by your Internet Service provider.	Maps your domain name to the WAN IP address
MX	Alias	Remote *yourdomainname.ext*	Provides message routing for email to *mailrecipient@ yourdomainname.ext*
SPF	TXT	v=spf1 a mx ~all	Helps to prevent your email from being labeled as spam by receiving mail servers
Autodiscover_tcp	SRV	Service: _autodiscover Protocol: _tcp Priority: 0 Weight: 0 Port: 443 Target host: remote.*your domainname.ext*	Allows Office Outlook 2007 with Service Pack 1 and Windows Mobile 6.1 email clients to automatically identify and set up Outlook Anywhere (RPC over HTTP)

For more information on adding DNS records, see Chapter 18, "Configuring and Managing Email." Or you can simplify things even further by using a DNS management service independent of your domain name registrar or Internet Service Provider. (Type "DNS management" into an Internet search engine for options.)

Managing Your Domain Name

If you already have a registered domain name and want to manage it yourself, you'll need the domain name and the name and logon information for your domain provider. When you're ready, click the Set Up Your Internet Address link and follow these steps:

1. Read the introductory material, and then click Next.

2. On the Do You Want To Register A New Domain Name page, select I Already Have A Domain Name, and then click Next.

3. Type in the domain name and extension (as shown in Figure 8-11), and then click Configure.

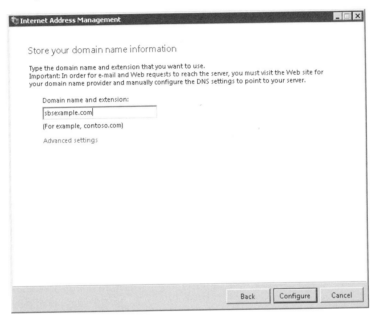

FIGURE 8-11 Domain information for self-management

The Internet Address Management Wizard configures the server to use your domain name. (See Figure 8-12.) To ensure that your Remote Web Workplace, email, and other features work correctly, make sure the DNS settings are correctly configured.

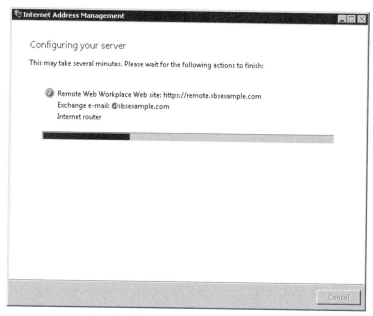

FIGURE 8-12 The wizard configures your server to use your domain name

Configure Email

As soon as you make your Internet connection, you should configure email. Refer to Chapter 18 for information on setting up all forms of email.

Add a Trusted Certificate

Certificates are used to verify the identity of servers on the Internet. Certificates also encrypt data to make a Remote Web Workplace connection secure.

The default installation of Windows SBS 2011 configures what is called a *self-issued* certificate. This certificate lets users securely access your websites if they install it on their remote computer or device. However, if users try to access your websites without installing the certificate on their remote computer, they receive a certificate warning. The warning tells users that the certificate being used to secure the website is not trusted, and as a result the site is not trusted. The user must click through the warning to gain access to the website. And in these times when users are rightfully warned about malicious and deceptive websites, many will be reluctant to take what appears to be a risk.

A trusted certificate verifies the authenticity of your server and the identity of the person or organization applying for a certificate. After you have a trusted certificate, remote users no longer have to install your certificate on their computers. So it is to your advantage to acquire a trusted certificate.

Purchasing a Certificate

Certificates can be purchased from various providers on the Internet. Just type "trusted certificate" in a search engine. Or you can just click the Add A Trusted Certificate link in the Getting Started Tasks list and follow these steps. (If you have an existing certificate you want to use, skip to "Using an Existing Certificate" later in this chapter.)

1. Read the introductory material on the Before You Begin page, and then click Next.

2. Select I Want To Buy A Certificate From A Certificate Provider, and then click Next.

3. Verify the information for the trusted certificate, as shown in Figure 8-13. Click Next.

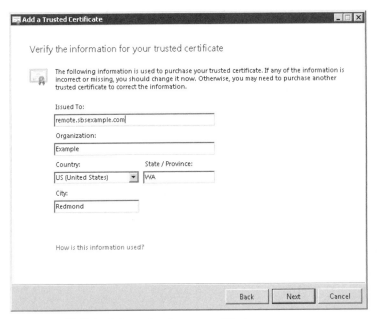

FIGURE 8-13 Verifying information for your certificate

4. The Generate A Certificate Request page displays encoded data from your server that is needed by the certificate provider. (See Figure 8-14.) Click Save To File to save a copy to a location you specify, and then click Copy to copy the data to your clipboard. Click Next.

5. Follow the instructions to purchase and then install a certificate.

FIGURE 8-14 Generating a request for a trusted certificate

Using an Existing Certificate

If you have a certificate and it's available for export, you can move it to Windows SBS 2011.

EXPORTING A TRUSTED CERTIFICATE

To export a trusted certificate, follow these steps:

1. Log on to the server where the certificate currently exists. Click Start and then click Run. Type **mmc** in the Open box, and click OK.

2. Select Add/Remove Snap-in from the File menu.

3. In the Add Or Remove Snap-ins dialog box, select Certificates from the Available Snap-ins list (shown in Figure 8-15), and then click Add.

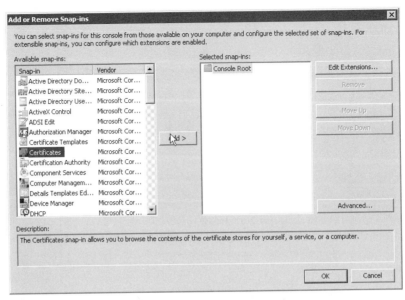

FIGURE 8-15 Constructing a Certificates management console

4. In the pop-up window, click Computer Account. Click Next.

5. In the Select Computer dialog box, select Local Computer. Click Finish and then click OK.

6. Expand Certificates, expand Personal, and then click Certificates.

7. Right-click the certificate to be exported, click All Tasks, and then click Export, as shown in Figure 8-16.

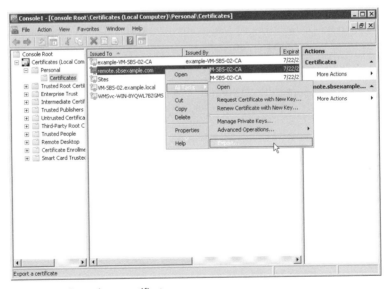

FIGURE 8-16 Exporting a certificate

8. On the Welcome To The Certificate Export Wizard page of the Certificate Export Wizard, click Next.

9. Verify that Yes, Export The Private Key is selected, and then click Next.

10. Select Include All Certificates In The Certificate Path If Possible and Export All Extended Properties, and then click Next. Do not select Delete The Private Key If The Export Is Successful. Enter a strong password to protect the certificate file, and then click Next.

11. Save the .pfx file (giving it an easily identifiable name, such as *trustcertificate.pfx*) to a secure location, and then click Next. Click Finish to complete.

IMPORTANT Several certificates might have the same name. Be sure to choose a certificate that has a valid expiration date and that was issued by the expected trusted authority. If you're not sure which certificate to choose, open Internet Information Services (IIS), establish which certificate IIS is using, and choose that one.

IMPORTING A TRUSTED CERTIFICATE

After the trusted certificate has been exported, you will need to import it to the Windows SBS server and then run the wizard to add a trusted certificate. This process involves quite a few steps, but each one is fairly simple:

1. Move the previously created .pfx file to the Windows SBS server.

2. Log on to the server running Windows SBS 2011. Click Start and then click Run. Type **mmc** in the Open box and click OK.

3. Select Add/Remove Snap-in from the File menu.

4. In the Add Or Remove Snap-ins dialog box, select Certificates from the Available Snap-ins list and then click Add.

5. In the pop-up window, click Computer Account. Click Next.

6. In the Select Computer window, select Local Computer. Click Finish and then click OK.

7. Expand Certificates, expand Personal, and then click Certificates.

8. Right-click Certificates, select All Tasks, and then select Import, as shown in Figure 8-17.

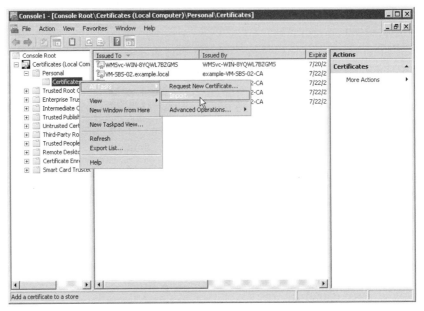

FIGURE 8-17 Importing a certificate

9. The Certificate Import Wizard starts. Click Next on the Welcome To The Certificate Import Wizard page.

10. Type or browse to the location of the saved .pfx file, and then use the drop-down list to change the extension to Personal Information Exchange (.pfx). Click Open, and then click Next.

11. Type the password that you used in the Export procedure, verify that Mark This Key As Exportable and Include All Extended Properties are selected, and then click Next.

12. Be sure that the certificate will be imported to the Personal folder, and then click Next. Click Finish to complete the import.

For applications to be able to use the certificate, after the trusted certificate has been imported you must run the Add A Trusted Certificate Wizard and follow these steps:

1. Click the Add A Trusted Certificate link on the Getting Started Tasks page.

2. Read the introductory material on Before You Begin, and then click Next.

3. On the Get The Certificate page, click I Want To Use A Certificate That Is Already Installed On The Server, and then click Next.

4. On the Choose An Installed Certificate page, click the certificate that you just imported, and then click Next.

Protect Your Data

The best way to protect your data is to configure the server backup. Do this as soon as possible after installation. For all the information on setting up backup, see Chapter 16 "Configuring Backup."

Add Users, Computers, and Devices

For details on the following links, see the chapters listed:

- **How Can Users Access Computers On The Network?** Chapter 9, "Managing Users and Groups"
- **Add A New User Account** Chapter 9, "Managing Users and Groups"
- **Connect Computers To Your Network** Chapter 14, "Managing Computers on the Network"
- **How Can I Add A Shared Printer To The Network?** Chapter 13, "Installing and Managing Printers"

Network Essentials Summary

The Home page of the Windows SBS Console shows a real-time summary of fundamental network health. Click any of the following links to review the nature of any alerts or warnings:

- **Security** The Security Center reports the details of warnings or alerts and directs you to the tools to solve them.
- **Updates** Warns if necessary updates aren't installed. Follow the link to the Update Center to correct the problem.
- **Backup** Alerts you if backups have not been performed. See Chapter 16, for the details on configuring your backup plan.
- **Other Alerts** Warns of other potential problems, such as clients without virus protection or security updates.

Summary

This chapter has addressed the processes necessary to complete the Getting Started Tasks section, including making a connection to the Internet, acquiring an Internet domain name, and handling trusted certificates.

You can always return to the Home page of the Windows SBS Console to perform tasks that you've postponed and rerun the wizards you've already used.

In the next chapter, we move on to the details of creating and configuring individual user accounts as well as the use of groups to refine and simplify the administration of your Windows SBS 2011 network.

CHAPTER 9

Managing Users and Groups

When it comes to a network, the users and administrators all have different sets of needs, and some of those needs can come into conflict. For the most part, users need reliable access to the files, folders, applications, printers, and other devices required to do their jobs. What they don't need are error messages, delays, or any other obstructions. The person in charge of the network has his or her own needs, such as shielding need-to-know material from those who don't need to know and protecting the users from themselves. The key to bringing these needs into balance is the configuration of groups and users—the topic of this chapter.

Understanding Groups

Because Microsoft Windows Server 2008 R2 is the underlying operating system for Windows Small Business Server (SBS) 2011, all the built-in security groups integral to Windows Server 2008 R2 still exist. However, many of these groups are intended for much larger, multidomain networks, so the designers of SBS 2011 created a subset of organizational units to simplify administration.

In practice, a *group* is usually a collection of user, and sometimes computer, accounts. The point of groups is to allow the network administrator to assign rights and permissions to groups rather than to individual users. Groups can be customized and users added or removed in a single step.

SBS allows two group types: security and distribution. Most groups are *security groups* because they're the only groups through which permissions can be assigned. Each security group is also assigned a *group scope*, which defines how permissions are assigned to the group's members, and members of a security group must be *securable objects* in the SBS domain. Securable objects include users, groups, and computers. Contacts are not securable objects and can be added only to distribution groups, not to security groups.

User rights are assigned to security groups to establish what members of the group can or cannot do. Some rights are automatically assigned to some groups—for example, a user who is a member of the Remote Web Workplace Users group has the ability to connect using Remote Web Workplace.

Email distribution groups, on the other hand, are not security-enabled and can be used *only* with email applications to send email to sets of users and contacts.

REAL WORLD: Why Use Groups at All?

Groups are an effective way of simplifying administration. If you have just a few users, it's possible to manage permissions for each user manually, though it's additional work most administrators won't welcome. And with SBS, it could prove to be positively onerous because SBS controls access to many features based on group membership. You can easily use SBS without changing any of the default groups or adding to them at all. Just use the built-in wizards to add users and you'll end up with the correct permissions and rights.

The real strength of groups is that when you change the rights of the group, you change them for everyone in the group, without having to do anything else. This makes it easy to update the rights of users on your network without having to go in and change every single account.

For example, when you have a number of people who travel or telecommute, you don't need to keep track of which users have the right to log on remotely if you add them all to the Virtual Private Network Users group. Changes to that group—granting access to a special share, for example—require only that you assign the right to the group, in just one step.

Email distribution groups don't define rights for users, but they do make it easy to communicate to a defined group of entities. You can create an external email contact for a user and add that contact to an email distribution group to allow a remote user to receive emails at a different location without having to log on to the network, for example.

User rights are assigned to security groups to establish what members of the group can or cannot do.

NOTE Permissions and user rights are different creatures, though easily mistaken for one another. Permissions determine what resources members of a group can access. User rights determine what members of a group can or cannot do. See Chapter 10, "Shares and Permissions," for additional information on rights and permissions.

Creating Groups

Creating new groups is exceedingly easy in Windows SBS 2011—so easy that you should think carefully before you overcomplicate your network with too many groups. Too many distribution groups is merely a nuisance, but too many security groups can have unforeseen consequences such as conflicting permissions that can keep people from getting access to the resources they need.

Setting Up a Distribution Group

To create a new distribution group, follow these steps:

1. Open the Windows SBS Console and select Users And Groups.

2. Click the Groups tab and then select Add A New Group in the Tasks pane. The Add A New Group Wizard launches. Read the Getting Started text and then click Next.

3. In the Add A New Group dialog box, as shown in Figure 9-1, type your information in the Group Name and Description fields. Select Distribution Group in the Group Type box and then click Next.

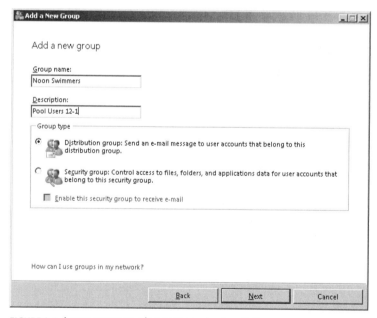

FIGURE 9-1 A new group needs a name and a description

4. On the Create A Group E-Mail Address page, the group name will be automatically entered. You can change the email address for this group, although the default name—linked as it is to the group name—is probably the easiest to remember and use. In the E-Mail Delivery Options box, you can select the check box to allow people external to

your organization to send mail to the address. Leave the check box cleared if you want the address to be completely internal. Click Next.

5. Select the groups or individuals you want to include in this distribution group. When all members have been added to the Group Members list, click Add Group.

> **NOTE** If you're not ready to add members to the group yet, you can simply click Add Group. Even without members, the group will be created and added to the list of groups.

Creating a Security Group

The process of adding a security group is slightly more complicated than creating a distribution group, but it's still simple. Use the following steps to create a new security group:

1. Open the Windows SBS Console, and select Users And Groups.

2. Click the Groups tab and then select Add A New Group in the Tasks pane. The Add A New Group Wizard launches. Read the Getting Started text and then click Next.

3. Enter your information in the Group Name and Description fields. In the Group Type area, select Security Group. If you want to be able to send email to this group, select the Enable This Security Group To Receive E-mail check box, as shown in Figure 9-2. Click Next.

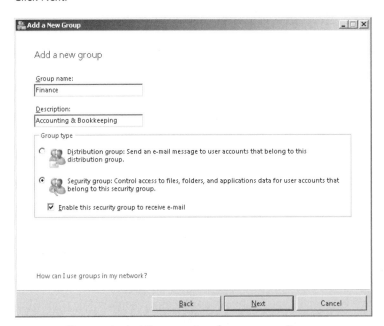

FIGURE 9-2 Name and select the group type for a new security group

4. On the Create A Group E-Mail Address page, the group name will be automatically entered. You can change the email address for this group, although the default name is probably the easiest to remember and use. In the E-Mail Delivery Options box, you can select the check box to allow people external to your organization to send mail to the address. Leave the check box cleared if you want the address to be completely internal. As shown in Figure 9-3, email-enabled security groups have the additional option of allowing messages to be archived on Exchange Public Folders. Click Next.

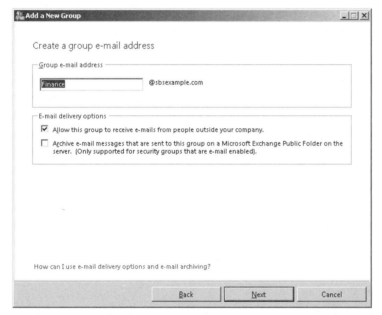

FIGURE 9-3 Security groups that are email-enabled have the option of receiving email from people external to the organization and the option of archiving messages in Exchange Public Folders

5. On the Select Group Members For page, select the groups or individuals you want to include in this security group. When all members have been added to the Group Members list, click Add Group.

The wizard will report that the group has been created. You can view the group in the SBS Console under Users And Groups by clicking the Groups tab.

Working with Groups

If your organization is small or uncomplicated, you might be able to use the built-in groups, add a few of your own, and assign all rights and permissions through shared folders. You can even begin with that expectation. However, your organizational needs will perhaps not align exactly with the groups and tools provided in the Windows SBS Console. In that case, using other built-in groups and customizing them to your needs might be required.

 UNDER THE HOOD **Group Scopes**

All groups have a group scope that defines how permissions are assigned. There are three possible group scopes: global, domain local, and universal. If you're using the Windows SBS Console to create a group, it will be created as a universal group.

Global Scope

A group with a global scope is actually a bit of an anomaly in an SBS domain because it is designed to provide global scope across multiple domains, something that SBS doesn't support. Global groups can be members of universal and domain local groups, and they can have the following members:

- Other global groups
- Individual accounts

Domain Local Scope

A domain local group controls access to specific local resources, and it can have one or more of the following members:

- Other domain local groups
- Global groups
- Universal groups
- Individual accounts

Universal Scope

A universal security group is another concept that is a bit awkward in the single-domain environment of SBS. Universal groups can have the following members:

- Other universal groups
- Global groups
- Individual accounts

All of the groups that are created by SBS and used by the SBS wizards are universal scope. Although there can be valid reasons for using other scopes in large, multi-domain enterprise environments, they don't make much sense in an SBS environment.

Built-In Universal Groups

The built-in groups with universal scope are, with few exceptions, the groups that all users belong to. Table 9-1 lists the security universal groups that are specific to Windows SBS 2011. These are the groups you see when you open the Windows SBS Console, select Users And Groups, and then click the Groups tab.

TABLE 9-1 SBS-specific universal security groups

GROUP NAME	DESCRIPTION
User Roles	Descriptions of user roles.
Windows SBS Admin Tools Group	Members can access and use the Administration tools in Remote Web Workplace.
Windows SBS Fax Administrators	Members can administer the Windows SBS fax service.
Windows SBS Fax Users	Members can make use of the Windows SBS fax service.
Windows SBS Folder Redirection Accounts	Members have folders redirected to the SBS Users folder on the server.
Windows SBS Link Users	Members can access the Link List in Remote Web Workplace.
Windows SBS Remote Web Workplace Users	Members can access Remote Web Workplace.
Windows SBS SharePoint_MembersGroup	Members can perform usual functions on the internal website such as adding, deleting, customizing, and updating material.
Windows SBS SharePoint_OwnersGroup	Members can administer the internal website.
Windows SBS SharePoint_VisitorsGroup	Members have read-only access to the internal website.
Windows SBS Virtual Private Network Users	Members have remote access to the network.

Built-In Domain Local Groups

Built-in domain local groups are created when Windows Small Business Server is installed. These groups can't be members of other groups, and their group scope can't be changed. Table 9-2 shows the built-in local groups.

TABLE 9-2 Built-in domain local groups

GROUP NAME	DESCRIPTION
Account Operators	Members can add, change, or delete user and group accounts.
Administrators	Members can perform all administrative tasks on the computer. The built-in Administrator account that is created when the operating system is installed is a member of the group. When a member server or a client running Windows Vista, Windows XP Professional, or Windows 2000 Professional joins a domain, the Domain Admins group is made part of this group.
Allowed RODC Password Replication Group	Members can have their passwords replicated to all Read-Only Domain Controllers (RODC).
Backup Operators	Members can log on to the computer, back up and restore the computer's data, and shut down the computer. Members cannot change security settings but can override them for purposes of backup and restore.
Cert Publishers	Members are allowed to publish certificates to the directory.
Certificate Service DCOM Access	Members can connect to Certificate Authorities.
Cryptographic Operators	Members can perform cryptographic procedures.
Denied RODC Password Replication Group	Members of this group cannot have their passwords replicated to an RODC. Default members are Cert Publishers, Domain Admins, Domain Controllers, Enterprise Admins, Group Policy Creator Owners, Read-Only Domain Controllers, and Schema Admins.
Distributed COM Users	Members can activate, launch, and use Distributed COM objects on this computer.
DnsAdmins	Members are DNS administrators. No default members.
Event Log Readers	Members can read event logs from local computers.
Guests	Members have the same access as members of the Users group. The Guest account has fewer rights and is a default member of this group.
IIS_IUSRS	Used by Internet Information Services (IIS).
Incoming Forest Trust Builders	Members can create incoming one-way trusts. This group is an anomaly in SBS because SBS doesn't support trusts.

GROUP NAME	DESCRIPTION
Network Configuration Operators	Users can have access to managing some network configurations.
Performance Log Users	Members can schedule some performance counters.
Performance Monitor Users	Provides backward compatibility to allow members access to performance counters locally and remotely.
Pre–Windows 2000 Compatible Access	A backward-compatibility group to allow read access on all users and groups in the domain.
Print Operators	Members can manage printers and print queues on domain printers.
RAS And IAS Servers	Servers in this group can access remote access properties of users.
Remote Desktop Users	Members are allowed to connect remotely. This group does *not* control who has access via Remote Web Workplace.
Replicator	Supports file replication in a domain. Do not add user accounts of actual users to this group. If necessary, you can add a "dummy" user account to this group to permit you to log on to Replicator services on a domain controller and manage replication of files and directories.
Server Operators	Members can administer servers.
Terminal Server License Servers	Members can update user accounts in Active Directory to track and report Terminal Server per user Client Access Licenses usage.
Users	Members can log on to the computer, access the network, save documents, and shut down the computer. Members cannot install programs or make system changes. Authenticated Users and Domain Users are members by default.
Windows Authorization Access Group	Members have access to the computed *tokenGroupsGlobal AndUniversal* attribute on *User* objects.

It takes only a glance at this list of groups to see that many are unlikely to be used in a Small Business Server network. However, look a bit further under the domain name in Active Directory Users And Computers and click the Users node (shown in Figure 9-4) to see more groups.

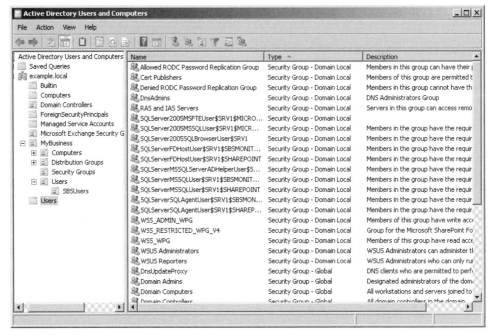

FIGURE 9-4 Additional groups you can use in Windows SBS

The following sections describe some more commonly used groups.

Built-In Global Groups

Default global groups are created to encompass common types of accounts. By default, these groups do not have inherent rights; an administrator must assign all rights to the group. However, some members are added to these groups automatically, and you can add more members based on the rights and permissions you assign to the groups. Rights can be assigned directly to the groups or by adding the default global groups to domain local groups. Table 9-3 lists the commonly used default global groups.

TABLE 9-3 Built-in global groups

GROUP NAME	DESCRIPTION
DnsUpdateProxy (installed with DNS)	Members are DNS clients that can provide dynamic updates to DNS on behalf of other clients. No default members.
Domain Admins	This group is automatically a member of the domain local Administrators group, so members of Domain Admins can perform administrative tasks on any computer in the domain. This group is automatically a member of the Administrators group and the Denied RODC Password Replication group. The Administrator account is a member of this group by default.

GROUP NAME	DESCRIPTION
Domain Computers	All computers in the domain are members.
Domain Controllers	All domain controllers in the domain are members. This group is automatically a member of the Denied RODC Password Replication group.
Domain Guests	The Guest account is a member by default. This group is automatically a member of the domain local Guests group.
Domain Users	The Administrator account and all user accounts are members. The Domain Users group is automatically a member of the domain local Users group.
Group Policy Creator Owners	Members can create and modify group policy for the domain. The Administrator account is a member of this group by default. This group is also a member of the Denied RODC Password Replication group.
Read-Only Domain Controllers	Members are the Read-Only Domain Controllers in the domain.

NOTE Setting rights and permissions for groups and assigning groups to use shared folders are subjects covered in Chapter 10.

Managing User Roles

Gaining access to the resources of the SBS network requires a domain user account, which authenticates the identity of the person making the connection and controls what resources a user has the right to access.

In Windows SBS 2011, by default all user accounts fall into one of three roles, or categories:

- Standard User
- Network Administrator
- Standard User with Administration Links

Each user account you add will be based on one of these user roles (or on another user role that you create). In the interests of sanity (your own), keep the number of user roles to a minimum. It is far easier to control access through group membership rather than creating multiple user roles. You also have the ability to change the specifics of access and resource limits for individual user accounts, but resist the temptation. It can quickly get unmanageable.

The Standard User Role

Most SBS users should be assigned the Standard User role. This role enables access to shared folders, email, the Internet, printers, fax services, Remote Web Workplace, and SharePoint Foundation (Companyweb). All of these access points can be configured within the Standard User Role. To make changes to the Standard User role, start the Windows SBS Console and follow these steps:

1. Click Users And Groups and then click the User Roles tab.

2. Right-click Standard User and select Edit User Role Properties. The Standard User Properties dialog box will open, as shown in Figure 9-5. In the left pane, click a category to see the settings for this role.

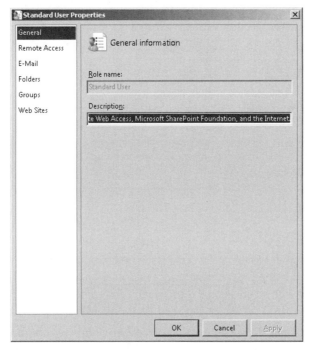

FIGURE 9-5 Settings for a Standard User role

- General displays a description of the role.

- Remote Access shows how the user role can access the network from a remote location. By default, anyone with this user role can access Remote Web Workplace and is automatically a member of the Windows SBS Remote Web Workplace Users. An optional setting is to allow the user role to access the Virtual Private Network. Selecting this check box adds all users assigned to this role to the Windows SBS Virtual Private Network Users group.

- Email allows you to set a maximum mailbox size. Clear the check box if you don't want to impose a limit on the amount of disk space a user can use for storing mail.

- Folders is a page for managing and redirecting folders for the user role. As on the Email page, you can enforce a limit on the size of shared folders. In addition, folder redirection can be set and a folder redirection quota imposed.

- Groups shows the group membership for users assigned this role. You can add a group membership by clicking Add or remove a group membership by highlighting a group and clicking Remove.

- Web Sites allows the choice of sites to be available to this user role.

> **IMPORTANT** All the users assigned the same role will have the same settings. Changes you make to a user role won't just change future user accounts, they will change all accounts assigned to that role. Don't remove any of the standard group memberships from any of the default SBS roles. Doing so will likely have unintended consequences.

3. Click OK when finished. You are asked if you want to apply the customization to all accounts based on the role. Click Yes and the user role changes are applied.

The Standard User with Administration Links

The Standard User with Administration Links role has, as you'd suspect, the Standard User role access plus membership in groups that give users assigned this role the ability to perform administrative tasks. Click the Groups link to view the groups that this role includes.

Network Administrator Role

The Network Administrator Role provides unrestricted system access to any account it is assigned to. The E-mail and Folders settings are the same as for the other default roles. Remote Access and Web Sites are different, however. On the Remote Access page, you can add or remove access to the virtual private network, but not to the Remote Web Workplace (which is on by default). Similarly, the Web Sites page allows Outlook Web Access to be granted or withheld, but all accounts based on the Network Administrator role will have access to Remote Web Workplace and the internal website.

If your network is administered by a third-party provider, access to Outlook Web Access and your virtual private network (if you have one) isn't necessary, but an administrator must be able to log on to the server.

Creating a New User Role

Perhaps you have some users for whom none of the standard user roles is appropriate. In that case, it's simple to create a new user role by following these steps:

1. Open the Windows SBS console, select Users And Groups, and then select User Roles.

2. In the Tasks pane, select Add A New User Role to start the wizard.

3. In the Add A New User Role page, shown in Figure 9-6, enter text in the User Role Name and Description fields.

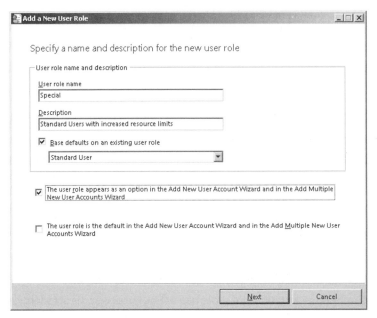

FIGURE 9-6 Creating a new user role

4. By default, the new user role is set to be based on the existing Standard User role. Clear the check box if you want to start from scratch, or choose another user role to base the new role on.

5. Also by default, the new user role will appear as an optional choice when creating new user accounts. Clear the check box if you don't want the role to display in the Add New User Account Wizard or the Add Multiple New User Accounts Wizard.

6. To make the new user role the default choice when adding new user accounts, select the check box labeled The User Role Is The Default In The Add New User Account Wizard And In The Add Multiple New User Accounts Wizard. Click Next.

7. On the Choose User Role Permissions (Group Membership) page, add or remove group memberships. Remember that all user accounts you base on this role will inherit these same memberships. When you've adjusted group memberships, click Next.

8. On the Choose E-mail Settings page, enforce or remove a mailbox size quota for this user role. Outlook Web Access is on by default, but you can remove that as well if you want. Click Next.

9. Choose the remote access settings for this user role, as shown in Figure 9-7. Click Next when you have made these settings.

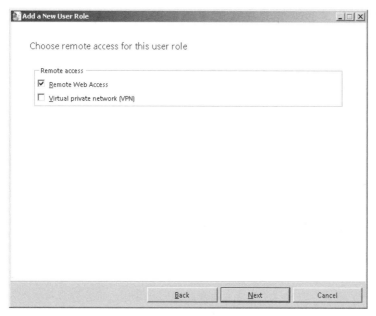

FIGURE 9-7 Choosing remote access settings for a new user role

10. On the Choose Share Folder Access For This User Role page, choose the Shared Folder settings for the user role, including the quota limits that will be applied. Select Back to return to previous pages to change any of your selections. When finished, click Add User Role.

11. The New User Role Was Added Successfully To The Network page announces that the new user role has been added and provides an option to add a user account or multiple user accounts. Click Finish or one of the selection areas to proceed to adding accounts.

Adding a New User Account

User roles are essentially templates that make the adding of user accounts remarkably simple. To add a new user account, open the Windows SBS Console, select Users And Groups, select Users, and then follow these steps:

1. In the Tasks pane, select Add A New User Account to start the wizard. On the Add A New User Account And Assign A User Role page shown in Figure 9-8, enter the full name, user name, email address, and other relevant information. Choose the user role to base the new account on. Click Next.

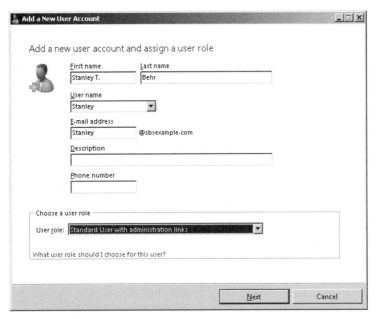

FIGURE 9-8 Adding a new user account

2. Enter and confirm a password for this account. (See the sidebar, "Making Secure Passwords," for more information on creating a strong password.)

3. Click Add User Account to finish the wizard and create the account.

REAL WORLD Making Secure Passwords

By default, SBS requires a password at least eight characters in length. In addition, a password must contain at least three of the following four elements:

- Uppercase letters
- Lowercase letters
- Numbers
- Non-alphanumeric characters

For example, a password such as JuxCLNU1 satisfies the requirement. It has eight characters and among them are uppercase letters, lowercase letters, and a number. Similarly, tuidqx!7*5 is also a valid password, consisting of nine characters including lowercase letters, numbers, and non-alphanumeric characters.

The problem with these passwords is their complete lack of memorability. They're the sort of passwords that get written on sticky notes and left around for anyone to find. A solution is to encourage users to be imaginative when creating a password.

Among the best passwords are alphanumeric acronyms of phrases that have a meaning to the user but are not likely to be known to others. This makes the password easy for the user to remember, while at the same time making it hard for an outsider to guess. For example, a password that meets all requirements is ThinkOT[] (for "Think outside the box"). Or [Thinkit] ("Think inside the box").

Even better are *passphrases*—entire phrases or sentences, complete with spaces (which count as non-alphanumeric characters) and punctuation. "A picture is worth 1000 words" is an example of a passphrase that meets all requirements: length, uppercase and lowercase letters, numbers, and non-alphanumeric characters.

Users should also be advised to avoid catchphrases that they themselves use a lot and certain patterns that would be easy for another person to guess, such as

- A rotation or reuse of the characters in a logon name.
- The user's name or initials, the initials of his or her children or significant other, or any of these items combined with other commonly available personal data such as a birth date, telephone number, or license plate number.

It pays to educate your users about passwords and password privacy, but most of all, it pays to heed your own advice: Make sure the password you select for administration is a good password, and change it frequently. Doing so will help you avoid the consequences of having somebody break into your system and wreak havoc in your very own kingdom.

An even better solution for passwords is to use two-factor authentication. As discussed in the Chapter 3 sidebar "Beyond Passwords—Two-Factor Authentication," we think the use of a secondary authentication factor such as AuthAnvil provides an additional layer of security beyond simple passwords without adding an onerous burden on users.

Adding Multiple User Accounts

Rather than add users one at a time, you can group similar users together and add their accounts simultaneously. To add multiple user accounts, open the Windows SBS Console, select Users And Groups, select Users, and then follow these steps:

1. In the Tasks pane, click Add Multiple User Accounts to launch the wizard.

2. On the first page of the Add Multiple New User Accounts Wizard, choose the user role these accounts will be based on, and then click Add to begin adding new users based on the user role selected, as shown in Figure 9-9.

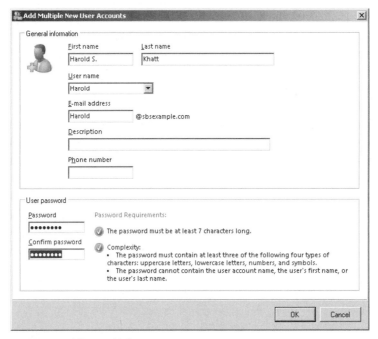

FIGURE 9-9 Adding multiple user accounts

3. Enter the general information about the user and a password, just as you would when adding a single user. Click OK when finished.

4. Click Add again to add another user. When you've completed adding the multiple user accounts, you can highlight a user account to edit or remove it.

5. Click Add User Accounts. The Adding New User Accounts To The Network page opens, as shown in Figure 9-10, and the users are added.

FIGURE 9-10 New accounts are added to the network

Giving Users Access to Computers

To log on to a computer on the network, users need a user account and permission to access the computer. So after you create a user account, the next step is to allow access. From the server, open the Windows SBS console, click Users And Groups, and then follow these steps:

1. Click the Users tab and then double-click the user account.

2. On the Properties page, click Computers.

3. Select the computers that you want to allow this user account to access, and grant the user account the appropriate level of access.

4. If appropriate, select the Can Remotely Access This Computer check box. Click OK when finished.

You can always return to this page to change or update computer access for a user.

Summary

In this chapter, we covered the uses for groups and the simple creation of user accounts. Next, we move on to configuring these users and groups to accomplish the work of your network without getting in each other's way.

## CHAPTER 10

Shares and Permissions

Anyone who has used a computer for any length of time is familiar with the concept of *sharing*. One shares photos and videos and writings with others. This isn't necessarily done on a network—sharing is often done via email or on a website.

On a business network, sharing is the key to getting work done. However, not everything needs to be shared with everyone, which is why the use of shares is always linked with the use of permissions.

Share Permissions vs. File Permissions

There are two kinds of permissions involved in any shared folder—those on the actual share and those imposed by the underlying file system. These permissions are *subtractive*. This means that the most restrictive permission will win. Managing permissions on both the share and the file system at the same time can often be quite confusing, and it's difficult to keep track of the details of both. We generally recommend using the underlying NTFS file permissions to control access and setting the share permissions to Full Control for everyone for most normal shares. The NTFS file permissions give much greater granularity and control over exactly what level of access is granted. However, in some cases using a more restrictive share permission is useful. When you do use a more restrictive share permission, indicate in the share name that the share is restricted.

Whatever your choice, avoid configuring both share permissions *and* NTFS permissions because the result can be unpredictable and hard to troubleshoot.

Share Permissions

Windows SBS provides easy ways to share folders. After a folder is shared, restrictions can be added or removed in the form of *share permissions*. These permissions apply only at the folder level—not at the file level—and are limited to allowing or denying Full Control, Read, and Change. Table 10-1 summarizes the three types of access, from most restrictive to least restrictive.

TABLE 10-1 Types of share permissions

SHARE PERMISSION	TYPE OF ACCESS
Read	Allows viewing of file and subfolder names, viewing data in files, and running programs
Change	Allows the access under Read, plus allows adding files and subdirectories to the shared folder, changing data in files, and deleting files and subdirectories
Full Control	Allows all the access under Change, plus allows changing permissions and taking ownership

Share permissions determine the maximum access allowed over the network. They don't affect a user who logs on locally or a Remote Desktop user of the computer where the shared folders are stored.

File Permissions

File permissions are also called *NTFS permissions*, and the terms are used interchangeably. File permissions, unlike share permissions, control user access regardless of where it originates. Local users, Terminal Services users, and network users are all treated equally.

File permissions can be set on folders and even down to individual files. This means that for any file, you can give individual users different types of access. Although you *can* set such detailed permissions, avoid doing so. Always try to operate with the simplest possible permissions. Set as few restrictions as possible. Assign permissions to groups, not individuals. Simplify, simplify, simplify. Your life will be easier in both the short and long term.

 REAL WORLD **User Account Control**

For many years, various smarty-pants types (including ourselves) have been warning administrators not to do everything using the Administrator account. Save that account for when you need it, we said. Use a standard user account most of the time, we implored. Of course, no one paid the slightest bit of attention, and here's the inevitable result: User Account Control.

User Account Control (UAC) is a security feature introduced in Windows Vista that then became a component of the Windows Server 2008 operating system, and hence, a component of Small Business Server. It's based on the security theory of least privilege. The idea is that users should have the absolute minimum privilege necessary to perform assigned tasks. This might sound as though it contradicts our advice to operate with the simplest possible permissions, but in fact it does not. Shares and permissions remain the best way to allow or restrict access to files and folders.

The goal of UAC is to reduce the exposure of the operating system by requiring users to run in standard user mode, minimizing the ability of users to make changes that could destabilize their computers or expose the network to undetected virus infections on their computers.

Prior to Windows Vista, the Windows usage model has been one of assumed administrative rights. Software developers assumed their programs could access and modify any file, registry key, or operating system setting. Even when Windows NT introduced security and differentiated between granting access to administrative and standard user accounts, users were guided through a setup process that encouraged them to use the built-in Administrator account or one that was a member of the Administrators group. A second problem is that even standard users sometimes need to perform tasks that require administrative rights, such as installing software and opening ports in the firewall.

The UAC solution is to require administrative rights less frequently, enable legacy applications to run with standard user rights, make it easier for standard users to access administrative rights when they need them, and enable administrative users to run as if they were standard users.

NTFS Permissions

The ability to assign enforceable permissions to files and folders is part of the NTFS file system. If you assign NTFS permissions, you need to understand how they work and how they are different for a file and for the folder that contains the file.

What Permissions Mean

NTFS permissions affect access both locally and remotely. Share permissions, on the other hand, apply only to network shares and don't restrict access on the part of any local user (or terminal server user) of the computer on which you've set the share permissions. Windows 2008 Server has a set of standard folder permissions that are combinations of specific kinds of access. The individual permissions are Full Control, Modify, Read & Execute, List Folder Contents, Read, and Write. Each of these permissions consists of a group of special permissions. Table 10-2 shows the special permissions and the standard permissions to which they apply.

TABLE 10-2 Special permissions for folders

SPECIAL PERMISSION	FULL CONTROL	MODIFY	READ & EXECUTE	LIST FOLDER CONTENTS	READ	WRITE
Traverse Folder/ Execute File	Yes	Yes	Yes	Yes	No	No
List Folder/Read Data	Yes	Yes	Yes	Yes	Yes	No
Read Attributes	Yes	Yes	Yes	Yes	Yes	No
Read Extended Attributes	Yes	Yes	Yes	Yes	Yes	No
Create Files/Write Data	Yes	Yes	No	No	No	Yes
Create Folders/ Append Data	Yes	Yes	No	No	No	Yes
Write Attributes	Yes	Yes	No	No	No	Yes
Write Extended Attributes	Yes	Yes	No	No	No	Yes
Delete Subfolders and Files	Yes	No	No	No	No	No
Delete	Yes	No	No	No	No	No
Read Permissions	Yes	Yes	Yes	Yes	Yes	Yes
Change Permissions	Yes	No	No	No	No	No
Take Ownership	Yes	No	No	No	No	No

File permissions include Full Control, Modify, Read & Execute, Read, and Write. As with folders, each of these permissions controls a group of special permissions. Table 10-3 shows the special permissions associated with each standard permission.

TABLE 10-3 Special permissions for files

SPECIAL PERMISSION	FULL CONTROL	MODIFY	READ & EXECUTE	READ	WRITE
Traverse Folder/Execute File	Yes	Yes	Yes	No	No
List Folder/Read Data	Yes	Yes	Yes	Yes	No
Read Attributes	Yes	Yes	Yes	Yes	No
Read Extended Attributes	Yes	Yes	Yes	Yes	No
Create Files/Write Data	Yes	Yes	No	No	Yes

SPECIAL PERMISSION	FULL CONTROL	MODIFY	READ & EXECUTE	READ	WRITE
Create Folders/Append Data	Yes	Yes	No	No	Yes
Write Attributes	Yes	Yes	No	No	Yes
Write Extended Attributes	Yes	Yes	No	No	Yes
Delete Subfolders and Files	Yes	No	No	No	No
Delete	Yes	Yes	No	No	No
Read Permissions	Yes	Yes	Yes	Yes	Yes
Change Permissions	Yes	No	No	No	No
Take Ownership	Yes	No	No	No	No

IMPORTANT Groups or users granted Full Control on a folder can delete any files and subfolders, no matter what the permissions are on the individual files or subfolders. Any user or group assigned Take Ownership can become the owner of the file or folder and then change permissions and delete files or even entire subfolder trees, no matter what the permissions were before that user or group became the owner.

How Permissions Work

If you take no action at all, the files and folders inside a shared folder have the same permissions as the share. Permissions for both directories and files can be assigned to the following:

- Groups and individual users on this domain
- Global groups, universal groups, and individual users from domains that this domain trusts
- Special identities, such as Everyone and Authenticated Users

The important rules for permissions can be summarized as follows:

- By default, a folder inherits permissions from its parent folder. Files inherit their permissions from the folder in which they reside.
- Users can access a folder or file only when they are granted permission to do so or they belong to a group that has been granted permission.
- Permissions are cumulative, but the Deny permission trumps all others. For example, if the Sales group has Read access to a folder and the Finance group has the Modify permission for the same folder, and Wally is a member of both groups, Wally has the

higher level of permission, which is Modify. However, if the Sales group permission is changed to explicitly Deny, Wally is unable to use the folder, despite his membership— and ostensibly higher level of access—in the Finance group.

- Explicit permissions take precedence over inherited permissions. Inherited Deny will not prevent access if an object has an explicit Allow permission.
- The user who creates a file or folder owns the object and can set permissions to control access.
- An administrator can take ownership of any file or folder.

Considering Inheritance

Just to complicate matters a bit more, there are two types of permissions: explicit and inherited. *Explicit* permissions are the ones you set on files or folders you create. *Inherited* permissions are those that flow from a parent object to a child object. By default, when you create a file or a subfolder, it inherits the permissions of the parent folder. If the Allow and Deny boxes are shaded when you view the permissions for an object, the permissions are inherited.

If you don't want the child objects to inherit the permissions of the parent, you can block inheritance at the parent level or child level. *Where* you block inheritance is important. If you block at the parent level, no subfolders will inherit permissions. If you block selectively at the child level, some folders will inherit permissions and others will not.

To make changes to inherited permissions, follow these steps:

1. Right-click the folder and select Properties.
2. Click the Security tab and then click Advanced.
3. On the Permissions tab of the Advanced Security Settings For dialog box, highlight the permission you want to change and click Edit.
4. Clear the check box for Include Inheritable Permissions From This Object's Parent. (See Figure 10-1.)

You'll be given the option to copy existing permissions to the object or to remove all inherited permissions. The object will no longer inherit permissions from the parent object, and you can change permissions or remove users and groups from the Permissions list.

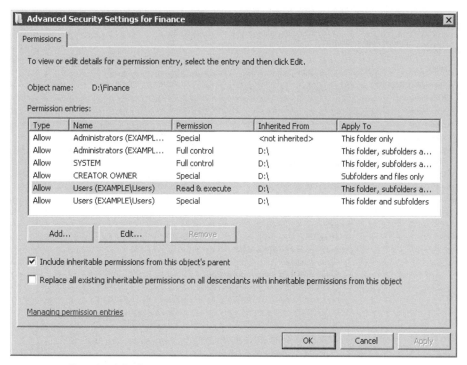

FIGURE 10-1 Changing inheritance

You can also change inherited permissions by changing the permissions of the parent folder or by explicitly selecting the opposite permission—Allow or Deny—to override the inherited permission.

Adding a Shared Folder

Sharing a folder is an easy process in Windows SBS because, as usual, there's a wizard to guide you. Start by opening the Windows SBS Console and then clicking Shared Folders And Web Sites. In the Tasks pane, click Add A New Shared Folder, and follow these steps:

1. Enter the location for the shared folder as shown in Figure 10-2. If you don't know the exact address, click the Browse button. When the location is specified, click Next.

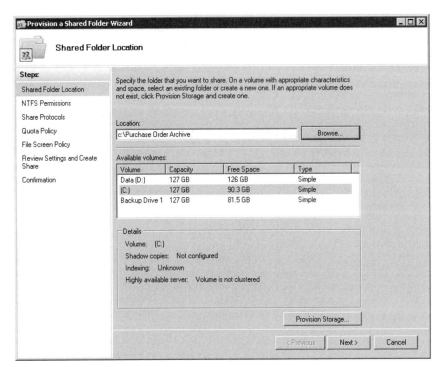

FIGURE 10-2 Specifying the location for a new shared folder

In the lower potion of the dialog box is a button labeled Provision Storage, and though this sounds like a place to store your grain for the coming winter, it is in fact a link to set up storage for the shared folder. Unless you have a storage area network (SAN), you can safely disregard it. If you do have a SAN, click the button to specify a storage subsystem.

2. On the NTFS Permissions page, you can accept the NTFS permissions or change them. If you decide to change the permissions, first read the section "NTFS Permissions" earlier in this chapter. Click Next. On the Share Protocols page (shown in Figure 10-3), choose the protocol that users will use to access the share. Unless you have NFS (Network File System) installed on the computer, the default is SMB (Server Message Block), a native-to-Windows protocol used for shares since Windows NT. Click Next.

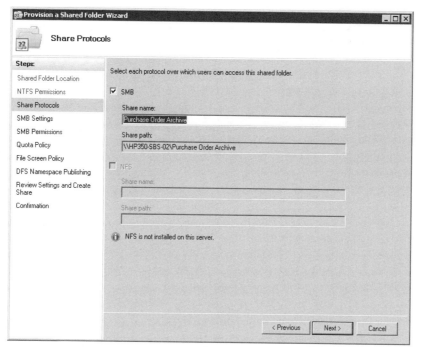

FIGURE 10-3 Specifying a protocol for the share

4. On the SMB Settings page, you can view the User Limit, Access-Based Enumeration, and Offline Settings for the folder. Click Advanced to change any of these. Click Next.

5. On the SMB Permissions page (shown in Figure 10-4), select the share permissions you want and then click Next.

> **NOTE** For details on Share Permissions, see "Share Permissions" earlier in this chapter.

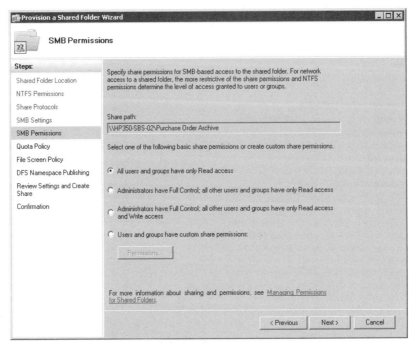

FIGURE 10-4 Setting Share (SMB) permissions

6. On the Quota Policy page, you can set a quota to limit the size of the shared folder. Click Next.

> **NOTE** For more on quotas, see Chapter 12, "Storage Management."

7. On the File Screen Policy page, you can apply a file screen to limit the types of files the shared folder can contain. Choose a template from the drop-down list (as shown in Figure 10-5) and a summary of the file screen properties appears. Click Next.

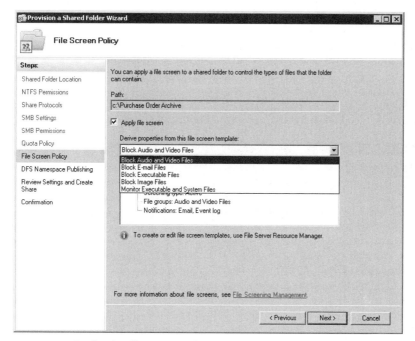

FIGURE 10-5 Configuring file screening for a shared folder

8. On the DFS Namespace Publishing page, you can choose to publish the share to a DFS namespace. (Using and creating a DFS namespace is described in Chapter 12.) Click Next.

9. On the Review Settings And Create Share page, review the settings. Click Previous to change settings. If the settings are correct, click Create.

10. A Confirmation page opens verifying the creation of the share.

Removing a Shared Folder

To stop sharing a folder, open the Windows SBS Console and follow these steps:

1. Click Shared Folders And Web Sites.

2. Select the folder you want to stop sharing.

3. In the Tasks pane, click Stop Sharing This Folder.

4. A warning appears pointing out that if you stop sharing the folder, users will no longer be able to access it over the network. Click Yes to confirm.

IMPORTANT If you remove a share when someone is connected to the folder, it will cause a forced disconnect, which could produce a loss of data. Even if data is not lost, an unexpected and forced disconnect will surely produce user annoyance.

Changing Share Permissions

Changing the permissions on a shared folder is easily done. Open Windows SBS Console, select Shared Folders And Web Sites, and then follow these steps:

1. Select the share. In the Tasks pane, click Change Folder Permissions.

2. To change the permissions for a user or group listed, highlight the name as shown in Figure 10-6 and make the changes in the Permissions area.

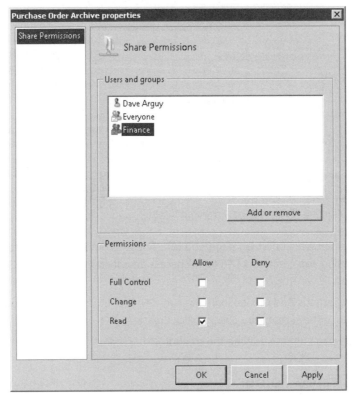

FIGURE 10-6 Changing permissions for users and groups

3. To add or remove users from this share, click Add Or Remove to open the Shared Folders dialog box shown in Figure 10-7. To add users or groups, highlight the name in the All Users And Groups list and then click Add.

4. To remove users and groups, highlight the name in the Selected Users And Groups list and click Remove.

5. Click OK when finished.

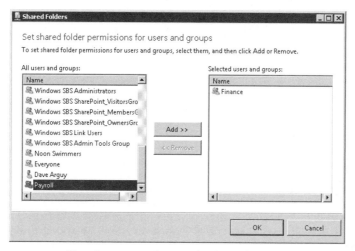

FIGURE 10-7 Changing users and groups for shared folders

Special Shares

In addition to shares created by a user or administrator, the system creates a number of special shares that shouldn't be modified or deleted. These include the administrative shares: the ADMIN$ share and the hidden shares for each hard drive volume (C$, D$, E$, and so on). These shares allow administrators to connect to drives that are otherwise not shared. These shares are not visible by default and can be connected to only by administrators.

Special shares exist as part of the operating system's installation. Depending on the computer's configuration, some or all of the following special shares might be present (and none should be modified or deleted):

- **ADMIN$** Used during the remote administration of a computer. The path is always the location of the folder in which Windows was installed (that is, the system root). Only Administrators can connect to this share.

- **driveletter$** The root folder of the named drive. Only Administrators can connect to these shares on Windows SBS servers or clients.

- **IPC$** Used during remote administration and when viewing shared resources. This share is essential to communication and can't be deleted.

- **NETLOGON** Used while processing domain logon requests. Do not remove.

- **SYSVOL** Required on domain controllers. Do not remove.

- **PRINT$** A resource that supports shared printers.

To connect to an unshared drive on another computer, you need to be logged on using an account with the necessary rights. Use the address bar in any window, and type the address using the following syntax:

*computer_name**[driveletter]*$

To connect to the system root folder (the folder in which Windows SBS is installed) on another computer, use the following syntax:

*computer_name**admin*$

Ownership and How It Works

Every object on an NTFS volume has an owner. By default, the owner is the person who created the file or folder. The owner controls how permissions are set on the object and to whom permissions are granted. Even if the owner is denied access, the owner can always change permissions on an object. The only way to prevent this is for the ownership to change.

Ownership of an object can change in any of the following ways:

- An administrator can take ownership.
- Any user or group with administrative rights on the computer where the object resides can take ownership.
- The owner can transfer ownership to another user if the owner has administrative rights *or* User Account Control is turned off.

Taking Ownership of an Object

To take ownership of an object, you must be logged on as an Administrator or as a remote user with administrative rights, and then follow these steps:

1. Right-click the object and select Properties. Click the Security tab.
2. Click Advanced and then click the Owner tab. Click Edit.

   To change the owner to a user or group that is not listed, click Other Users And Groups. In the Select User, Computer, Or Group dialog box, type the name of the user or group, click Check Names, and then click OK.

   To change the owner to a user or group that is listed, in the Change Owner To box, click the new owner.
3. To change the owner of all subcontainers, select the Replace Owner On Subcontainers And Objects check box.

Transferring Ownership

Users with administrative credentials can transfer ownership of an object by following these steps:

1. Right-click the object and select Properties. Click the Security tab.
2. Click Advanced and then click the Owner tab. Click Edit.
3. If the proposed new owner is in the Change Owner To list, select the name as shown in Figure 10-8 and click OK.

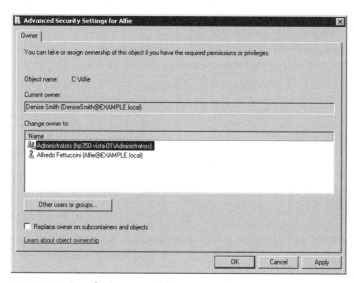

FIGURE 10-8 Transferring ownership

4. If the proposed new owner isn't listed, click Other Users Or Groups to open the Select User, Computer Or Group dialog box.
5. Locate the new owner and click OK.
6. Select the new owner in the Change Owner To list and click OK.

 REAL WORLD Uses for Share Permissions

As stated earlier in this chapter, it's generally best to use NTFS file permissions *instead* of share-level permissions to control access to shared resources over the network. Using share-level permissions alone gives you significantly less control over the specific permissions being granted, and they're less secure than file system permissions because they apply only to users connecting over the network.

However, there are some exceptions to this rule. For example, you might want to permit all authenticated users to access a volume in a certain subfolder but allow only a certain group to access the root directory. In this instance, you can create two file shares: one at the subfolder level with no share-level security (Full Control For Everyone), and one at the root folder level with share-level security to allow only the specified group access.

Somewhat more useful is the ability to hide file shares by adding the dollar sign character ($) to the end of the share name. This notation allows any user to connect to the share—provided that she knows the share name. After users connect, they're still bound by NTFS security permissions, but this approach can be handy for storing advanced tools so that an administrator can access them from a user's system or user account. File security isn't really an issue—you just don't want users messing around with the files.

Effective Permissions

Admittedly, the subject of permissions can be fraught with anxiety—one reason simplicity should be your watchword. However, there will be times when a resource will have acquired a kudzu-like accretion of permissions and it will be your job to wield the machete.

To determine what the effective permissions are on an object—that is, what permissions apply to a given user or group—follow these steps:

1. Right-click the file or folder for which you want to view permissions. Select Properties.

2. Click the Security tab and then click Advanced. Click the Effective Permissions tab.

3. Click the Select button to open the Select User, Computer, Or Group dialog box.

4. Locate the user or group you want and then click OK. The selected check boxes (as shown in Figure 10-9) indicate the effective permissions of the user or group for that file or folder.

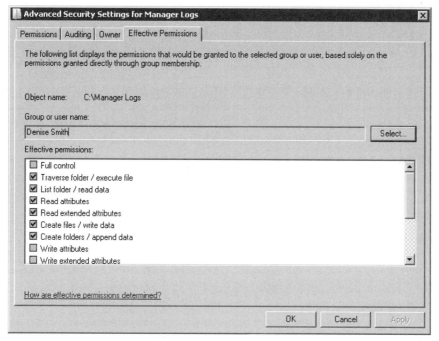

FIGURE 10-9 Viewing effective permissions

NOTE Share permissions are not part of the effective permissions calculation. Access to shared folders can be denied through share permissions even when access is allowed through NTFS file permissions.

Factors Considered in Determining Effective Permissions

The factors that are considered when determining effective permissions are as follows:

- Global group membership
- Local group membership (except when accessing objects remotely)
- Local permissions
- Local privileges (except when accessing objects remotely)
- Universal group membership

Defining User Rights

As if various kinds of permissions weren't enough, we must also address the concept of user rights.

What users can and cannot do depends on the rights and permissions that have been granted to them. Rights generally apply to the system as a whole. The ability to back up files or to log on to a server, for example, is a right that the administrator can grant or withhold. Rights can be assigned individually, but most often they are characteristics of groups, and a user is assigned to a particular group on the basis of the rights that the user needs.

Permissions, as discussed earlier in this chapter, indicate the access that a user (or group) has to specific objects, such as files, directories, and printers. For example, the question of whether a user can read a particular directory or access a network printer is a permission.

Rights, on the other hand, are divided into two types: privileges and logon rights. *Privileges* include such functions as the ability to run security audits or force shutdown from a remote system—obviously not tasks that are done by most users. *Logon rights* are almost self-explanatory: they involve the ability to connect to a computer in specific ways. Rights are automatically assigned to the groups in Windows SBS 2008, although they can be assigned to individual users as well. Assignment by group is usually preferred, so whenever possible, assign rights by group membership to keep administration simple.

When membership in groups defines rights, rights can be removed from a user by simply removing the user from the group. Table 10-4 lists the logon rights and the groups to which they are assigned by default.

TABLE 10-4 Logon rights assigned to groups by default

NAME	DESCRIPTION	GROUPS ASSIGNED THE RIGHT ON THE SBS DOMAIN CONTROLLER	GROUPS ASSIGNED THE RIGHT ON WORKSTATIONS AND SERVERS
Access This Computer From The Network	Permits connection to the computer through the network	Administrators, Authenticated Users, Everyone	Administrators, Backup Operators, Users, Everyone
Allow Logon Locally	Permits logging on to the computer interactively	Administrators, Account Operators, Backup Operators, Print Operators, Server Operators	Administrators, Backup Operators, Users
Allow Logon Through Terminal Services	Allows logging on as a Terminal Services client	Administrators	Administrators, Remote Desktop Users

In Windows SBS, it is much simpler to control logon access through individual user accounts (see the section "Giving Users Access to Computers" in Chapter 9 for more information) unless your network is relatively large and you are using Windows Server 2008 built-in groups in addition to Windows SBS groups.

Managing Default User Rights Assignments

To see the user rights assignment on the Windows SBS server, select Administrative Tools from the Start menu and then select Local Security Policy. Expand Local Policies and then click User Rights Assignment.

To change one of the policies, right-click the name and select Properties. If the Add Users Or Group button is available (as shown in Figure 10-10), you can click it to add additional users who will have the user right.

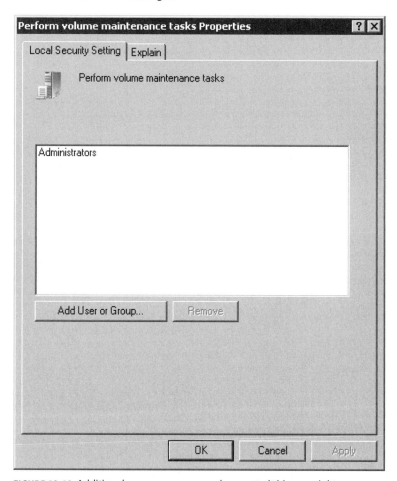

FIGURE 10-10 Additional users or groups can be granted this user right.

If the Add Users Or Group button is unavailable, this user right can be granted only by adding the user or group to the groups already listed.

Summary

This chapter and the previous one have concerned themselves with users, groups, and their abilities and restrictions. In the next chapter, we move to hardware and the management of hard drives, volumes, and storage.

## Chapter 11

Disk Management

Arguably the single most important function that a server provides to the rest of the network is to be a central, secure, managed file storage area. By centralizing file storage on a server, it becomes an order of magnitude easier to ensure the safety, integrity, recoverability, and availability of the core files of your business. Instead of having files spread all across the network on individual users' computers, you have them in a single place—easier to share among collaborators, easier to back up, easier to recover in the event of a disaster, and easier to secure so that only those people who *should* have access to a file, do. The downside to having all your important files in a single location is the potential for a single point of failure. You need to make sure that your files are seriously protected and always available—your business depends on them. This makes it imperative that you carefully manage the underlying disks that support your file storage and that those disks be both redundant and thoroughly backed up.

Storing, securing, backing up, and making available the core files of your business is a bigger topic than we could fit in a single chapter, so we've spread it out and organized it according to the various functions involved. But we can't stress this enough: *All* of the pieces are essential to a safe, secure, and available network. Don't shortchange any of them. In Chapter 4, "Planning Fault Tolerance and Avoidance," we covered some of the planning and preparation steps that will allow you to buy and build a server that is designed to be a safe and secure repository for your files. In this chapter, we'll cover the underlying disk management that makes it possible to store your files and protect against loss, corruption, or disaster. In Chapter 12, "Storage Management," we'll cover the features of Microsoft Windows Small Business Server 2011 that enable you to manage storage, protect critical files, and provide versioning of shared files to protect against corruption or misadventure. Additional backup and recovery details are covered in Chapter 16, "Configuring Backup." Finally, in Chapter 28, "Disaster Planning," we go over the steps to ensure that your data systems and network can be recovered in the event of a serious disaster.

The Search for Disaster Protection

Traditionally, large businesses have used a variety of techniques to ensure that files stored on a server were both secure and safe. These solutions tend to be expensive, but when spread across all the supported workstations and buried in a large MIS budget they are feasible. The same solutions would *not* be feasible or acceptable in most small businesses, but that doesn't change our very real need to protect ourselves from disaster. Fortunately, both hardware and software solutions can provide a very high level of security and safety at a budget more in keeping with the realities of a small business. However, before we talk about those solutions, let's make sure we all understand the terminology of disk management. Let's review some definitions:

- **Physical drive**   The actual hard disk itself, including the case, electronics, platters, and all that stuff. It's not terribly important to the disk administrator.

- **Partition**   A portion of the hard disk. In many cases, this is the entire hard disk space, but it needn't be.

- **Master Boot Record (MBR)**   A technique for partitioning a hard disk. This is the default method for Windows Small Business Server 2011. MBR-partitioned disks are limited to a maximum of four partitions per disk, and a maximum size of 2 terabytes.

- **GUID Partition Table (GPT)**   A technique for partitioning a hard disk, GPT is replacing MBR for larger hard disks and large storage arrays. Windows Small Business Server 2011 supports GPT-partitioned disks for all disks except the boot disk. GPT disks support 128 partitions and are required for disks (or arrays) larger than 2 terabytes.

- **Allocation unit**   The smallest unit of managed disk space on a hard disk or logical volume—also called a cluster.

- **Primary partition**   A portion of the hard disk that's been marked as a potentially bootable logical drive by an operating system. MS-DOS could support only a single primary partition, but Windows Server 2008 can support four primary partitions on an MBR hard disk and 128 primary partitions on a GPT hard disk.

- **Extended partition**   A nonbootable portion of the hard disk that can be subdivided into logical drives. There can be only a single extended partition per hard disk, but this partition can be divided into multiple logical drives. Extended partitions are deprecated in Windows Small Business Server 2011 and can't be directly created from the GUI.

- **Volume**   A unit of disk space composed of one or more sections of one or more dynamic disks.

- **Simple volume**   The dynamic equivalent of a partition. A portion of a single dynamic disk, a simple volume can be assigned either a single drive letter or no drive letter and can be attached (mounted) on zero or more mount points.

- **Extended volume**   Similar to, and sometimes synonymous with, a spanned volume, an extended volume is any dynamic volume that has been extended to make it larger than its original size. When an extended volume uses portions of more than one physical disk, it is more properly referred to as a spanned volume.

- **Logical drive**   A section or partition of a hard disk that acts as a single unit. An extended partition can be divided, for example, into multiple logical drives.

- **Logical volume**   Another name for a logical drive.

- **Basic disk**   A traditional disk drive that is divided into one or more partitions, with a logical drive in each primary partition. Basic disks do not support the more advanced functions of disk management, but they can be converted to dynamic disks in many cases.

- **Dynamic disk**   A managed hard disk that can be used to create various volumes.

- **iSCSI (Internet Small Computer Systems Interface)**   A protocol for using remote, centralized, storage as if it were local. Uses either shared or dedicated TCP/IP networks. Traditionally, they were reserved for storage area networks (SANs) with specialized (and very expensive) hardware, but now they're easily available with software implementations.

- **iSCSI target**   The iSCSI server or provider.

- **iSCSI initiator**   The client or requester for an iSCSI storage device.

- **LUN (Logical Unit Number)**   The "disk" that an iSCSI target presents to an iSCSI initiator. A LUN can be any portion of the available storage on the iSCSI server.

- **RAID (redundant array of independent [formerly "inexpensive"] disks)**   The use of multiple hard disks in an array to provide for larger volume size, fault tolerance, and increased performance. RAID comes in different levels, such as RAID-0, RAID-1, and RAID-5. Higher numbers don't necessarily indicate greater performance or fault tolerance, just different methods of doing the job.

- **Spanned volume**   A collection of portions of hard disks combined into a single addressable unit. A spanned volume is formatted like a single drive and can have a drive letter assigned to it, but it will span multiple physical drives. A spanned volume—occasionally referred to as an *extended volume*—provides no fault tolerance and increases your exposure to failure but does permit you to make more efficient use of the available hard disk space.

- **Striped volume**   Like a spanned volume, a striped volume combines multiple hard disk portions into a single entity. A striped volume uses special formatting to write to each of the portions equally in a stripe to increase performance. A striped volume provides no fault tolerance and actually increases your exposure to failure, but it is faster than either a spanned volume or a single drive. A stripe set is often referred to as RAID-0, although this is a misnomer because plain striping includes no redundancy.

- **Mirror volume**   A pair of dynamic volumes that contain identical data and appear to the world as a single entity. Disk mirroring can use two drives on the same hard disk controller or use separate controllers, in which case it is sometimes referred to as *duplexing*. In case of failure on the part of either drive, the other hard disk can be split off so that it continues to provide complete access to the data stored on the drive, providing a high degree of fault tolerance. This technique is called RAID-1.

- **RAID-5 volume**   Like a striped volume, this combines portions of multiple hard disks into a single entity with data written across all portions equally. However, it also writes parity information for each stripe onto a different portion, providing the ability to recover in the case of a single drive failure. A RAID-5 volume provides excellent throughput for read operations but is substantially slower than all other available options for write operations.

- **SLED (single large expensive disk)**   Now rarely used, this strategy is the opposite of the RAID strategy. Rather than using several inexpensive hard disks and providing fault tolerance through redundancy, you buy the best hard disk you can and bet your entire network on it. If this doesn't sound like a good idea to you, you're right. It's not.

- **JBOD**   Just a bunch of disks. The hardware equivalent of a spanned volume, this has all the failings of any spanning scheme. The failure of any one disk will result in catastrophic data failure.

> **NOTE**   Additional RAID levels are supported by many hardware manufacturers of RAID controllers. These include RAID 0+1, RAID-10, RAID-6, and RAID-50. For more details on various RAID levels, see the manufacturer of your RAID controller or *http://en.wikipedia.org/wiki/RAID#Standard_levels*.

 UNDER THE HOOD   **Disk Access Technologies for the Server**

The first time we wrote a chapter about disk management, there were basically three possible technologies available: Modified Field Modification (MFM), Pulse Frequency Modulation (PFM), and Small Computer System (or Serial) Interface (SCSI). Unless you were a total geek (and had oodles of money), your systems used either MFM or PFM, and RAID wasn't even an option. Over time, SCSI became the only real choice for the vast majority of servers and even became mainstream on high-end workstations. Servers at the high end might use fiber, but SCSI had the vast majority of the server disk market.

Integrated Device Electronics (IDE), later called Advanced Technology Attachment (ATA), became the standard on the personal computer. However, IDE never made serious inroads into the server market because, although it was fast for single tasks, it lacked the inherent multitasking support and bus mastering that a server disk interface technology required, and there were no real hardware RAID solutions that supported it. Largely supplanted by Serial ATA (SATA) even on personal computers, this technology has no place at all on your server.

The introduction of SATA technology has made serious inroads into the lower end of the server marketplace. With SATA RAID controllers built into many motherboards, and stand-alone SATA RAID boards that support eight or more SATA drives and have substantial battery-backed RAM cache onboard, many low-range to mid-range servers are finding SATA RAID solutions to provide a cost-effective alternative to SCSI. While most SATA RAID controllers lack the ability to hot-swap a failed drive, and generally don't have the performance potential of SCSI or Serially Attached SCSI (SAS), they are still quite attractive alternatives where cost is a primary factor. SATA also makes sense as secondary or "near-line" storage for a server.

The new kid on the block, however, is SAS. This is the most interesting addition to the server storage equation in quite a while. Using the same thin cables and connectors as SATA, with none of the configuration nuisance of traditional SCSI, SAS is definitely the way to go. When combined with new 2.5-inch drives, the ability to put a really large amount of very fast storage in a small space has taken a significant step forward. Many SAS controllers fully support SATA drives also, allowing you to combine the two technologies on the same controller.

With the main bottleneck for servers continuing to be I/O in general, and especially disk I/O, there will continue to be pressure to find new and faster methods to access disk-based storage. Using wide arrays of fast, traditional disks—especially using low-power, high-density 2.5" SAS disks—enables fast and flexible storage arrays in remarkably smaller spaces, and with lower energy and cooling requirements.

A new option that directly addresses the limitations of traditional spinning disk technologies is the solid state drive (SSD), a "disk" that is actually a collection of flash memory that connects to a SATA controller. SSDs are currently still quite expensive and not really ideal for large RAID arrays because of performance degradation over time, but the technology is rapidly improving and offers promise for the future.

Choosing the Storage Solution for Your Network

The first decision you need to make when planning your storage solution for SBS is really made when you specify your server. If your budget can afford it, you should definitely consider choosing a hardware RAID solution that lets you add disks on the fly and reconfigure the array without turning off the server or rebooting. This is absolutely the best and most flexible storage solution for protecting your data, and it can take the form of hot-swappable SAS hard drives, or even a SAN. The best choices aren't cheap, and in most cases you need to make at least some portion of the decision as part of the original server purchase.

> **REAL WORLD**   **Network Attached Storage**
>
> Although most hardware storage solutions require you to make decisions very early in the buying process, a growing number of Network Attached Storage (NAS) solutions can provide a cost-effective way to increase the storage flexibility of your SBS network. Many of the available solutions, especially at the lower end of the price range, are designed more for home networks and digital media sharing than for business networks. However, there are also excellent NAS servers available that are based on Microsoft Windows Storage Server. These provide the greatest flexibility and support for an SBS network, and we prefer them when adding a NAS to an SBS network because they also support iSCSI protocols. For more on Windows Storage Server–powered NAS servers, see *http://www.microsoft.com/windowsserver 2008/en/us/wss08.aspx*.
>
> Another interesting option (and one we'll discuss in much greater detail later in Chapter 16) is Windows Storage Server 2008 R2 Essentials (WSSE). Although it's not designed primarily as a NAS, WSSE supports much of the same functionality, while adding in the ability to do client backups very efficiently. If your need for a NAS is primarily to add some near-line storage for occasional-use files, or to store local backups, we think WSSE is a very interesting alternative, and one we're using on our personal SBS network.

After the server is actually in place and is being used, you can't really make a change to the underlying hardware for your existing storage that would allow you to use a hardware RAID solution—at least not easily. But you *can* add a hardware RAID controller and a RAID array when it's time to add more storage to the server, and you can also use the built-in facilities of SBS to make your existing disk subsystem more fault-tolerant by using dynamic disks and the software RAID of SBS, as described in "RAID-5 Volumes" later in the chapter.

Storage Connection Technologies

If you're reading this chapter before you buy your server, congratulations on being a thorough person. If not, some of these decisions have already been made, but you may well find that you will have to add storage. If you do, you'll want to focus on storage solutions designed and optimized for servers—a very different set of needs from the typical workstation. Your choices are

- **Integrated Device Electronics (IDE)**   Strictly a client solution. It's inexpensive, but not appropriate on a server. It's now being replaced even at the client end by SATA.

- **Serial Advanced Technology Attachment (SATA)**   A newer and faster version of IDE. It's still primarily a workstation solution, but it's acceptable when combined with hardware RAID for smaller servers.

- **External Serial Advanced Technology Attachment (eSATA)**   A way to use SATA for external, secondary, or backup storage.

- **Small Computer System Interface (SCSI)**   Perfect for servers and high-end workstations, but significantly more expensive than SATA. It has the ability to have up to 13 drives per SCSI channel.

- **Serially Attached SCSI (SAS)**   Perfect for servers. This is a relatively new technology that is rapidly becoming the mainstream server storage interface. Prices are still more than SATA .

- **Internet SCSI (iSCSI)**   Important for SANs, and can even be used as a boot device for SBS servers. Hardware SANs are generally well outside the budgets of most SBS networks, but software SANs based on Windows Storage Server or third-party iSCSI software are a very viable option for adding storage flexibility to your SBS network.

- **FireWire**   Hot-pluggable. This is a good choice to use as a backup storage device.

- **Universal Serial Bus (USB)**   Only appropriate if you use USB 2.0 or later. It's good for CD and DVD drives, and it's hot-pluggable. It's also a good choice for use as a backup storage device, especially USB 3.0.

- **Fibre Channel**   A great option if you have really large amounts of money to spend.

- **Network Attached Storage (NAS)**   A good way to provide large amounts of storage that can be flexible to meet your needs. Specify Windows Storage Server–based NAS for the greatest flexibility and compatibility.

- **Storage Area Networks (SAN)**   Faster and more flexible than the typical NAS, but also much more expensive and difficult to configure. Hardware SANs are generally not for small business networks, but software-based SANs are becoming a viable option.

- **Solid State Disks (SSD)**   Initially used primarily for notebook computers, these are starting to find their way into servers—especially high-density servers in data centers, where their power savings are a plus. They're still too pricy for most SBS networks.

Managing Disks

There are two kinds of disks in Windows Small Business Server 2011: basic disks and dynamic disks. *Basic disks* are the conventional disks we're used to. *Dynamic disks* were introduced in Windows 2000 Server and support additional management and agglomeration options.

Basic disks support two kinds of partitions: primary and extended. Extended partitions are deprecated in Windows Server 2008, though they can still be created from the command line using Diskpart.exe. And any existing disks you have with extended partitions will be recognized without a problem. If you need to create a disk with many different volumes on it (more than four), create the disk as a GPT disk rather than an MBR type.

Dynamic disks use volumes instead of partitions and support the additional management, redundancy, and agglomeration features of SBS, including Spanned Volumes, Striped Volumes (RAID-0), Mirrored Volumes (RAID-1), and RAID-5.

The primary method for managing disks on an SBS server is the Disk Management console. This can be used as a stand-alone console by running Diskmgmt.msc from the command line, or from Server Manager as shown in Figure 11-1.

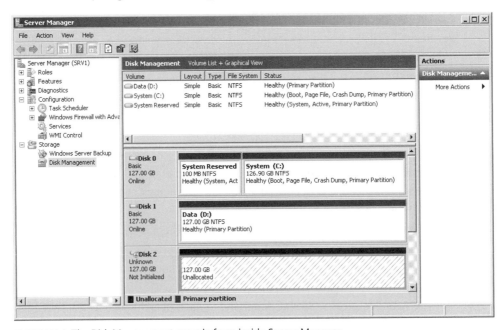

FIGURE 11-1 The Disk Management console from inside Server Manager

The Disk Management console is divided into two panes. The top pane shows the drive letters (volumes) associated with the local disks and gives their properties and status; the bottom pane has a graphical representation organized by physical drive.

NOTE In this chapter, for simplicity, the rest of our screen shots run Disk Management as a stand-alone console, but the exact same functions are available from inside Server Manager as well.

REAL WORLD   Hardware RAID

Although Disk Management provides a software RAID solution, hardware RAID is widely available for a reasonable cost, from either the original server vendor or from third parties, and it provides substantial advantages over software RAID. Hardware RAID solutions range from a simple RAID controller to fully integrated, stand-alone subsystems. Their features vary, as does their cost, but all claim to provide superior flexibility, performance, and reliability over a simple software RAID solution such as that included in Windows Small Business Server 2011. In general, they do. Some of the advantages they can offer include

- Hot-swap and hot-spare drives, allowing for virtually instantaneous replacement of failed drives

- Integrated, battery-protected disk caching for improved disk performance

- A separate, dedicated system that handles all processing, for improved overall performance

- Increased flexibility and additional RAID levels, such as RAID-10 and RAID 0+1, which are a combination of striping (RAID-0) and mirroring (RAID-1) that provide for fast read and write disk access with full redundancy.

Single Server

Although not all hardware RAID systems provide all the possible features, they all have the potential to improve the overall reliability and performance of your hard disk subsystem. With SBS being predominantly a single-server environment, you have your entire business running on that single server. This makes hardware RAID a particularly sound investment for your SBS server.

NAS and SAN

Many NAS systems are built on hardware RAID, providing an easy and cost-effective way to expand your original server storage in a highly fault-tolerant way. However, it pays to look closely at exactly what you are buying—some systems are built on RAID-0, which is *not* fault-tolerant at all and actually increases your risk.

We briefly mentioned storage area networks (SANs) earlier. Although they are excellent, fast, flexible, and highly fault-tolerant, they have traditionally only been for those with really large IT budgets. Plus, they have been rather tricky to implement and configure. With the wide availability of affordable software iSCSI solutions—including third-party software iSCSI targets—and solutions based on Windows Storage Server, this is changing. If you're implanting SBS in a virtualized environment, a SAN solution is a much better choice than a NAS solution.

Windows Storage Server 2008 R2 Essentials

A new player in the stand-alone storage market is Windows Storage Server 2008 R2 Essentials (WSSE). Designed to provide a single storage location and backup solution for the home business and small business markets, WSSE is based on Windows Server 2008 R2 and provides many of the functions of a NAS server. WSSE uses the same code base and technology as Windows Home Server and Windows Small Business Server 2011 Essentials, but it's designed to integrate into existing SBS networks to provide flexible storage and client backup. WSSE provides a flexible secondary storage solution that also does client backups really well. (See Chapter 16.) Now if it only included iSCSI target functionality, it would be perfect.

While limited to backing up 25 client PCs or fewer, WSSE provides a simple interface and flexible storage for extending SBS networks, and it's the clear choice for client backup of key workstations. For SBS networks with more than 25 client PCs, multiple WSSE servers can be used.

Partitions and Volumes

In Windows Server 2008 R2, the distinction between volumes and partitions is somewhat murky. When using Disk Management, a regular partition on a basic disk is called a *simple volume*, even though technically a simple volume requires that the disk be a dynamic disk.

As long as you use only simple volumes or partitions, you can easily convert between a basic disk (and partition) and a dynamic disk (and a volume). After you use a feature that is supported only on dynamic disks, however, changing back to a basic disk will result in data loss.

BEST PRACTICES Recovering or rebuilding a server that has a dynamic disk for the boot disk can be tricky. We suggest keeping your boot disk (C) a basic disk, and that you use hardware mirroring (RAID-1) to safeguard its contents and use dynamic disks only for other disks on your server.

We used to be big fans of dynamic disks. They provided increased flexibility and functionality in a way that was pretty transparent. And they were a huge step forward when they were introduced in Windows 2000. At the time, RAID controllers were both more expensive and less functional, and many servers didn't have hardware RAID on them. That's simply not the case anymore.

If using dynamic disks increases your options, isn't that a good thing? Well, yes. But—and it's a big but—a dynamic disk complicates the disaster recovery process, and we dislike anything that creates potential issues in a disaster recovery scenario. We definitely don't think dynamic disks are appropriate for a system disk. And we just have a hard time seeing the upside, given the functionality that a good RAID controller provides.

Dynamic disks and virtualization don't go well together, and if you're choosing to run SBS virtualized, we strongly suggest that you not use dynamic disks on either the SBS virtual machine or the host storage on which its virtual hard disks reside.

If you do find a need that can't be solved any other way, by all means use dynamic disks. There's no apparent performance cost, and you use the same tools to manage both dynamic disks in SBS and basic disks. But avoid converting your system disk to dynamic. And make sure your disaster recovery procedures are updated appropriately.

Adding a Partition or Volume

Adding a new drive or partition to an SBS server is straightforward. First, obviously, you need to physically install and connect the drive. If you have a hot-swappable backplane and array, you don't even have to shut the system down to accomplish this task. If you're using conventional drives, however, you need to shut down and turn off the system.

After the drive is installed and the system is turned on again, SBS automatically recognizes the new hardware and makes it available. If the disk is a basic disk that is already partitioned and formatted, you can use it immediately. If it's a new disk that has never been partitioned or formatted, you need to prepare it first. If it's a dynamic disk or disks, but from another computer, you can use it as soon as you import it. If the disk is a basic disk that has already been formatted, you aren't prompted to upgrade it to a dynamic disk. If the disk has never been used before, the Initialize And Convert Disk Wizard prompts you to initialize the disk.

Adding a New Disk Using the Initialize Disk Wizard

When you install a new hard drive, the drive is automatically recognized, and the Initialize And Convert Disk Wizard starts when you open Disk Management. To add a new disk, complete the following steps:

1. Open Disk Management.

2. If Disk Management recognizes a new disk, you see the first page of the Initialize Disk Wizard, shown in Figure 11-2. This wizard initializes a disk so that it can be recognized by Windows Small Business Server 2011, and it lets you select whether the disk should be an MBR or GPT disk.

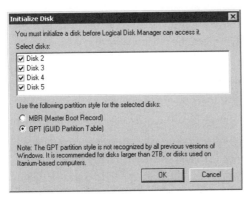

FIGURE 11-2 The Initialize Disk Wizard

3. Clear the check box for any disks you don't want to initialize, and select the partition style for the disks.

When the wizard finishes, you're at the main Disk Management console, shown in Figure 11-3. Notice that the disk is still not formatted or allocated and is highlighted in black (if you haven't changed the default color settings for the Disk Management console).

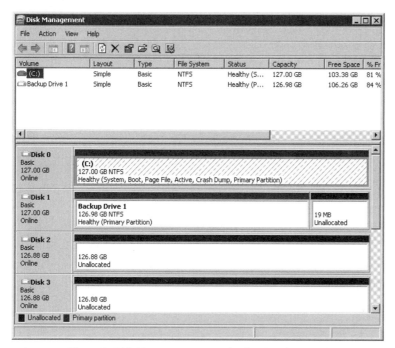

FIGURE 11-3 The main Disk Management console, showing the new disks

Creating a Simple Volume or Partition

To create a new simple volume or partition, complete the following steps:

1. In the Disk Management console, right-click the unallocated disk and choose the type of new volume you want to create. To create a partition, select New Simple Volume, as shown in Figure 11-4.

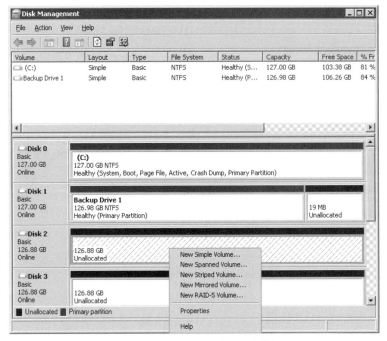

FIGURE 11-4 Creating a new volume on an unallocated disk

2. The New Simple Volume Wizard opens to guide you through the process of creating the new volume on the dynamic disk.

3. Click Next to open the Specify Volume Size page. Specify the size of the volume you'll be creating, as shown in Figure 11-5.

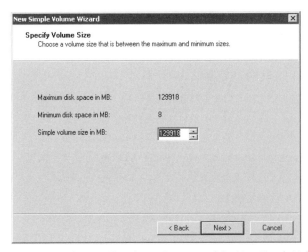

FIGURE 11-5 The Specify Volume Size page of the New Simple Volume Wizard

4. Click Next to open the Assign Drive Letter Or Path page. The next available drive letter will be selected by default. For details on mounted volumes, see "Mounting a Volume" later in this chapter.

5. Click Next to open the Format Partition page shown in Figure 11-6. Specify the format options for the volume, including

- **File System**   The only supported file system for Windows Small Business Server 2011 is NTFS, except for removable devices such as USB key drives.

- **Allocation Unit Size**   The default value is 4 Kb sectors. This is a reasonable balance, but choose a larger size, such as 16 Kb or even 64 Kb if you know that this volume will be used to hold only very large files (such as volume dedicated to virtual hard disks, for example, or large database files).

- **Volume Label**   Specify a meaningful label that identifies the volume.

- **Perform A Quick Format**   Saves waiting for full formatting, but it's not recommended on new disks because no verification pass is performed.

- **Enable File And Folder Compression**   Only an option if the allocation unit size is less than 16 Kb—and it's never recommended.

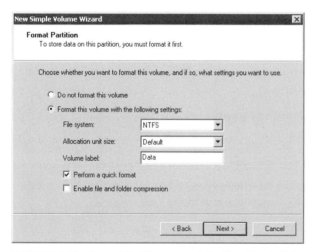

FIGURE 11-6 The Format Partition page of the New Simple Volume Wizard

6. Click Finish to close the wizard and begin provisioning the volume. You return to the Disk Management console, where you see the new volume, as shown in Figure 11-7.

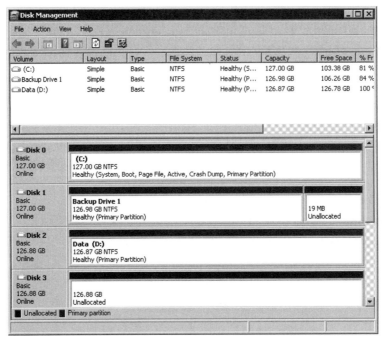

FIGURE 11-7 The new Primary Partition (Data) has been created

S BS adds to the system administrator's toolkit a complete command-line interface for managing disks—Diskpart.exe. This command-line utility is scriptable or
can be used interactively. The following simple script creates a volume on an existing dynamic disk and assigns it to the next available drive letter:

REM Filename: MakeVol.txt
REM
REM This is a DiskPart.exe Script. Run from the command line
REM or from another script, using the syntax:
REM
REM   diskpart /s MakeVol.txt > logfile.log
REM

```
REM to run this script and dump the results out to a log file.
REM
REM This script creates a simple volume of 28 Gb on disk #3, and then
REM assigns a drive letter to it. Note that this does NOT format
REM the volume -- that requires using the format command, not part
REM of diskpart.exe

REM First, list out our disks. Not required for scripting, but useful
REM to show the overall environment if we need to troubleshoot problems
list disk

REM Next, select which disk will have the simple volume created on it.
select disk 3

REM Now, create the volume...
create volume simple size=28672

REM Assign without parameters will choose the next available HD letter.
Assign
```

Creating a RAID-5 or RAID-1 (Mirror) Volume

The process of creating a mirrored (RAID-1) or RAID-5 volume is similar to creating a simple volume, except that the disks will be converted to dynamic disks first, and you'll need to select the disks to add to the volume.

NOTE Creating a mirror or RAID-5 volume will convert the disks used to dynamic disks. This is usually not the best solution for providing redundancy on an SBS server, and we strongly recommend using hardware RAID wherever possible.

To create a new simple volume or partition, complete the following steps:

1. In the Disk Management console, right-click an unallocated disk and choose New RAID-5 Volume or New Mirrored Volume to open the New RAID-5 Volume Wizard (or New Mirrored Volume Wizard).

2. Click Next to open the Select Disks page, as shown in Figure 11-8.

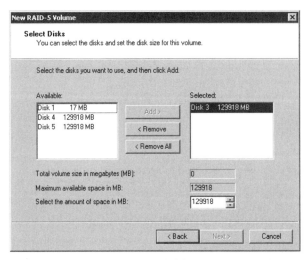

FIGURE 11-8 The Select Disks page of the New RAID-5 Volume Wizard

3. Select the disks to add to the volume, and then specify the amount of space on each disk to use for the volume. The maximum for all disks is the amount of unallocated space on the disk with the least available space.

4. Click Next to open the Assign Drive Letter Or Path page shown in Figure 11-9. See "Mounting a Volume" later in the chapter for more information.

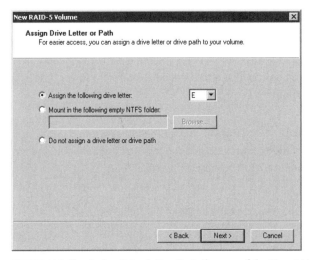

FIGURE 11-9 The Assign Drive Letter Or Path page of the New RAID-5 Volume Wizard

5. Click Next to open the Format Volume page. The formatting options are the same as for a simple volume or partition:

   ▪ **File System** The only supported file system for Windows Small Business Server 2011 is NTFS, except for removable devices such as USB key drives.

- **Allocation Unit Size**   The default value is 4-Kb sectors. This is a reasonable balance, but choose a larger size, such as 16 Kb or even 64 Kb, if you know that this volume will be used to hold only very large files (such as volumes dedicated to virtual hard disks, for example, or large database files).

- **Volume Label**   Specify a meaningful label that identifies the volume.

- **Perform A Quick Format**   Saves you from waiting for full formatting, but is not recommended on new disks because no verification pass is performed.

- **Enable File And Folder Compression**   Only an option if the allocation unit size is less than 16 Kb—and it's never recommended.

6. Click Finish to accept your settings and provision the RAID volume. If the disks are currently basic disks, you'll see the warning message shown in Figure 11-10.

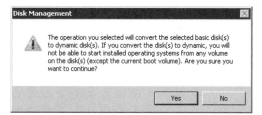

FIGURE 11-10 The Disk Management warning for converting to dynamic disks

7. Click Yes, and the disks will be converted and the provisioning will begin.

 UNDER THE HOOD   **Formatting Options**

Even though SBS can recognize hard drives that are formatted in any of the three file system formats (FAT, FAT32, and NTFS), only NTFS is supported by Windows Small Business Server 2011. Although it is technically possible to format any drive except the system drive as FAT or FAT32, it is neither recommended nor supported.

You can choose to quick-format a drive to make it available more quickly, but this option simply removes the file entries from the disk and does no checking for bad sectors. Choose quick formatting only when recycling a disk that has already been formatted and you are confident it hasn't been damaged.

On an NTFS volume or partition, you can specify the allocation unit size. This option lets you tune the disk for a particular purpose, depending on the disk's size and intended function. A database storage volume that will contain large database files managed by the database program might lend itself to large allocation units (also called *clusters*), whereas a disk that must hold many small files is a candidate for smaller clusters. However, the default sizes are an excellent compromise for most situations—modify them only with caution and with a clear understanding of the consequences for your environment.

You can also choose to enable disk and folder compression on NTFS volumes and partitions. This causes all files and folders on the volume (as opposed to individual files or folders you select) to be compressed. Compression can minimize the amount of hard disk space used by files, but it has a negative impact on performance while making disaster recovery more problematic. Given the cost of hard drive space today, we think this is just a bad idea.

Deleting a Partition or Volume

Deleting a partition and deleting a volume are essentially the same task. When you delete a partition or volume, the entire volume or partition is deleted. However, if you've got an older disk with an extended partition on it that you use with SBS, you won't be able to delete the extended partition until you delete all of the logical drives in the partition. You can directly delete a primary partition or a volume.

In all cases, when you delete a volume, logical drive, or partition, you end up with free or unallocated space and no data on the volume, drive, or partition when you're done, so make sure you have a good backup if there's a chance you might later need any of the data. To delete a partition or volume, follow these steps:

1. Right-click the partition or volume and select Delete Volume.

2. At the Delete Volume warning, shown in Figure 11-11, click Yes to delete the volume.

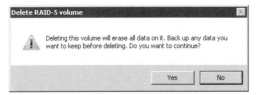

FIGURE 11-11 The Delete RAID-5 Volume warning

When the volume or partition is completely deleted, the space it occupied will be unallocated. Space that is unallocated on dynamic disks can be used to create mirrors, extend an existing volume, create a RAID array, or otherwise manage the storage on your server. Space that is unallocated on basic disks can be partitioned or used to extend a partition.

Extended partitions were a mechanism used by earlier versions of Windows to get around the limitation of MBR disks that allowed a maximum of only four partitions. If you have an extended partition on your disk for some reason, you can create logical drives on the partition using DiskPart.exe. However, you no longer have a graphical way to create an extended partition or a logical drive, nor any real need to do so. With Windows Small Business Server 2011 providing full support for GPT disks, the old limit of a maximum of four partitions on a disk is gone—GPT disks in Windows Server 2008 R2 support 128 partitions. If you have any existing MBR disks that include an extended partition because you moved a disk from another computer to your SBS computer, we suggest you remove the existing extended partition and convert the disk to GPT.

Extending or Shrinking a Volume

Windows Small Business Server 2011 has the ability to extend or shrink a volume, on the fly, without shutting down the server or rebooting. When you shrink a volume, you create unallocated space on the volume. That unallocated space can then be used to extend another volume.

Shrinking a Volume

The ability to shrink a volume is a new feature added to Windows Server 2008, giving you greater flexibility in managing your disks. Before Windows Server 2008, you had to use a third-party application to shrink a volume. And even now third-party applications such as Acronis Disk Director give you greater flexibility and control over resizing partitions and volumes than Disk Management. With Disk Management, you can shrink down the unused space on a volume, recovering some of that empty space to use on other volumes, but the most you can expect to recover is about 50 percent of the free space on the volume. If the file system on the volume is fragmented, you might not get even that much.

To shrink a volume, follow these steps:

1. Open the Disk Management console if it isn't already open.

2. Select the volume you want to shrink and right-click to open the menu shown in Figure 11-12.

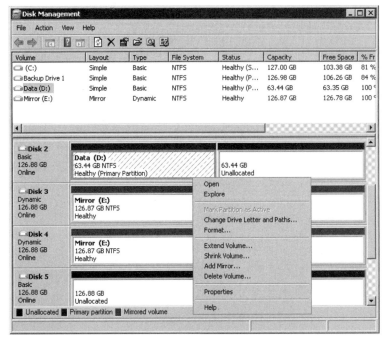

FIGURE 11-12 The Action menu for simple volume

3. Select Shrink Volume from the menu to open the Shrink dialog box shown in Figure 11-13.

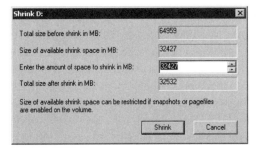

FIGURE 11-13 The Shrink dialog box for the simple volume D

4. Select the amount to shrink the volume and then click Shrink to change the size of the volume.

Extending a Volume

You can add space to a volume without having to back up, reboot, and restore your files if it is a simple volume or a spanned volume. You do this by converting the volume to a spanned or extended volume that incorporates unallocated space on any disk. Unfortunately, you can't increase the size of a mirrored, striped, or RAID-5 volume simply by adding disks to the array.

To extend a volume, complete the following steps:

1. In the Disk Management console, right-click the volume you want to extend. Choose Extend Volume to open the Extend Volume Wizard.

2. Click Next to open the Select Disks page, select one or more disks from the list of disks that are available and have unallocated space. Click Add to add the selected disk or disks, and indicate the amount of space you want to add, as shown in Figure 11-14.

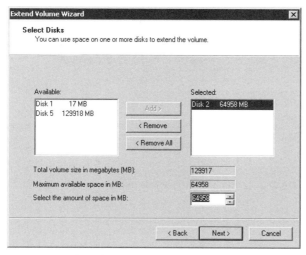

FIGURE 11-14 The Select Disks page of the Extend Volume Wizard

3. Click Next and the Extend Volume Wizard displays a final confirmation page before extending the volume. Click Finish to extend the volume. The extended volume is shown in Figure 11-15.

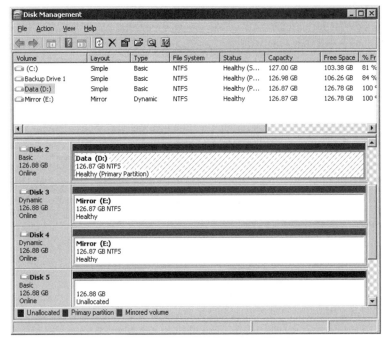

FIGURE 11-15 The Disk Management console, showing the new extended volume D

IMPORTANT A spanned (extended) volume is actually less reliable than a simple disk. Unlike a mirror or RAID-5 volume, which has built-in redundancy, a spanned or striped volume will be broken and all its data lost if any disk in the volume fails.

REAL WORLD Extending—Friend or Foe?

Most people responsible for supporting a busy server have wished at some point that they could simply increase the space of a particular volume or drive on the fly when it got low on space—preferably without having to bring the system offline for several hours while the entire volume is backed up and reformatted to add the additional hard disks, the backup is restored, and the share points are re-created. Fun? Hardly. Risky? Certainly. And definitely a job that means coming in on the weekend or staying late at night—in other words, something to be avoided if at all possible.

All this makes SBS's ability to create additional space on a volume without the need to back up the volume, reformat the disks, and re-create the volume a seductive feature. However, unless you're running hardware RAID, you should think twice before jumping in. Only simple or spanned volumes allow you to add storage on the fly, and because neither is redundant, using them exposes your users to the risks of a failed drive. Yes, you have a backup, but even under the best of circumstances, you'll lose some data if you need to restore a backup. Further, using spanned volumes actually increases your risk of a hard disk failure. If any disk used as part of the spanned volume fails, the entire volume is toast and will need to be restored from backup.

Why, then, would anyone use spanning? Because they have hardware RAID to provide the redundancy. This combination offers the best of both worlds—redundancy provided by the hardware RAID controller and flexibility to expand volumes as needed, using Disk Management. Yet another compelling argument for hardware RAID, as if you needed any more.

NOTE Windows Small Business Server 2011 uses the terms *extended* and *spanned* nearly interchangeably when describing volumes. Technically, however, a spanned volume must include more than one physical disk, whereas an extended volume can also refer to a volume that has had additional space added to the original simple volume on the same disk.

Adding a Mirror

When your data is mission-critical and you want to make sure that the data is protected and always available no matter what happens to one of your hard disks, consider mirroring the data onto a second drive. SBS can mirror a dynamic disk onto a second dynamic disk that is at least the same size as the original so that the failure of either disk does not result in loss of data. To mirror a volume, you can either select a mirrored volume when you create the volume or you can add a mirror to an existing volume. To add a mirror to an existing volume, complete the following steps:

1. In the Disk Management console, right-click the volume you want to mirror. If a potential mirror is available, the shortcut menu lists the Add Mirror command.

2. Choose Add Mirror to display the Add Mirror dialog box, shown in Figure 11-16.

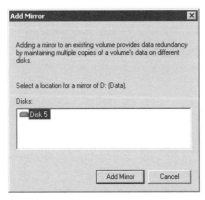

FIGURE 11-16 The Add Mirror dialog box

3. Select the disk to use for the mirror, and click Add Mirror. If either or both of the disks are basic disks, you'll get a warning that the change will convert the disks to dynamic disks. Click Yes to proceed.

4. The mirror is created immediately and starts duplicating the data from the original disk to the second half of the mirror. This process is called *regeneration*, or sometimes *resynching*. (The process of regeneration is also used to distribute data across the disks when a RAID-5 volume is created.)

NOTE Regeneration is both CPU-intensive and disk-intensive. When possible, create mirrors during slack times or during normally scheduled downtime. Balance this goal, however, with the equally important goal of providing redundancy and failure protection as expeditiously as possible.

BEST PRACTICES To improve your overall data security and reliability, mirror your volumes onto disks that use separate controllers whenever possible. This process is known as *duplexing* and eliminates the disk controller as a single point of failure. It can also speed up both reading and writing to the mirror, because the controller and bus are no longer potential bottlenecks.

Drive Failure in a Mirrored Volume

If one of the disks in a mirrored volume fails, you can continue to have full access to all your data without loss. SBS marks the failed disk as missing and takes it offline. It also, however, takes the other half of the mirror and marks it as failed, as shown in Figure 11-17. This doesn't mean your data is lost. But it does mean you can't access it until you break the mirror. The missing disk will then need to be replaced and the mirror re-created to restore redundancy.

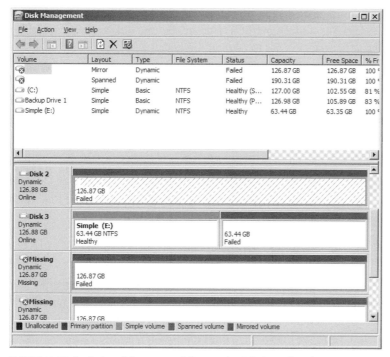

FIGURE 11-17 A missing disk causes a failure on both halves of a mirror

To recover access to the data that was on the failed mirror, you need to remove the mirror and reactivate the good disk by following these steps:

1. Open Disk Management if it isn't already open.

2. Right-click the mirrored disk that shows as online (Disk 2 in Figure 11-17).

3. Select Remove Mirror from the shortcut menu to open the Remove Mirror dialog box shown in Figure 11-18.

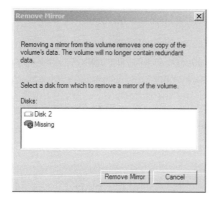

FIGURE 11-18 The Remove Mirror dialog box

4. Select the missing or offline disk, and click Remove Mirror. You'll be prompted to con-firm the removal. Click Yes, and the mirror is removed, but the disk is still not available because the drive letter mapping has to be reestablished.

5. Right-click the now healthy volume, and select Change Drive Letter And Paths to open the dialog box shown in Figure 11-19.

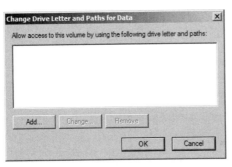

FIGURE 11-19 The Change Drive Letter And Paths dialog box

6. Click Add to open the Add Drive Letter Or Path dialog box, select a drive letter from the drop-down list, and click OK. If you attempt to use the same drive letter as the drive had in the past, you'll see the warning message shown in Figure 11-20.

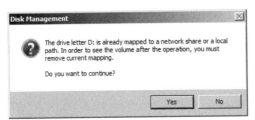

FIGURE 11-20 Disk Management warns when you try to map a drive letter that it has a remem-bered connection to

7. Click Yes, and the drive letter is assigned and the disk is available.

If you need to make additional disk space available on your system and you have no addi-tional disks available, you can remove the mirror from a mirrored volume. When you remove a mirror, the data on one of the disks is untouched, but the other disk becomes unallocated space. Of course, you will have lost all redundancy and protection for the data, so you need to take steps to restore the mirror as soon as possible. Until then, you might want to modify your backup schedule for the remaining disk. To remove a mirror, complete the following steps:

1. In the Disk Management console, right-click either half of the mirror. Choose Remove Mirror from the shortcut menu. The Remove Mirror dialog box opens.

2. Select the disk you want to remove from the mirror. Click Remove Mirror. You get one last chance to change your mind. Click OK, and the disk you highlighted becomes unallocated space.

Breaking a Mirror

If a disk fails and you can't replace it with an identical one, break the mirror until a replacement becomes available. Breaking a mirror severs the connection between the two disks, allowing the remaining disk to continue to function normally until a replacement disk becomes available. When the replacement disk is available, the mirror can be re-created.

You might also find it useful to break a mirror even when both disks are still functioning, because you then end up with two identical copies of the same data. One half of the broken mirror continues to have the same drive letter or mount point, while the second half of the broken mirror is assigned the next available drive letter. To break a mirror, complete the following steps:

1. In the Disk Management console, right-click either disk of the mirrored volume.

2. Choose Break Mirrored Volume from the shortcut menu. You're asked to confirm that you really want to break it.

3. Click Yes, and the mirror is broken. You'll have two volumes. One retains the drive letter or mount point of the original mirror, and the other is assigned the next available drive letter. They will both contain exact duplicates of the data at the instant of the break but will immediately start to diverge as they are modified.

RAID-5 Volumes

Windows Small Business Server 2011 supports a software implementation of RAID-5 that allows you to have a redundant file system without the 50-percent capacity overhead of using mirrored volumes. The overhead on a RAID-5 volume decreases for each additional disk you add to the volume, making this the most space-efficient method of providing redundancy in SBS.

Unfortunately, this efficiency doesn't come without some costs. RAID-5 arrays are inherently slower at write operations than even a plain old stand-alone drive. You also don't have the flexibility that you have with mirrored volumes in SBS. You can't simply remove a drive from a RAID-5 volume, nor can you break a failed drive out of the volume, allowing the remaining drives to regenerate. Further, when a disk fails on a RAID-5 volume, not only is the volume no longer redundant, but it also gets a lot slower because both read and write operations must calculate the correct value for every byte read or written.

Some of the tasks you do with a mirror also apply to a RAID-5 volume. You can

- Create the RAID-5 volume.
- Assign a mount point or drive letter to the RAID-5 volume.
- Format the RAID-5 volume.
- Continue to use the RAID-5 volume after the failure of one of the disks in the volume.

What you can't do with the software RAID in SBS is add or remove disks from the RAID-5 volume after you have created it, except for replacing a failed disk. To be able to dynamically add and remove disks from a RAID-5 array, the solution is to choose a hardware RAID array that supports dynamic reconfiguration.

 REAL WORLD Assigning Volume Names

The name you assign to a volume, partition, or drive should tell you something about it rather than simply mimicking the drive letter. A volume name like "Big140SAS" tells you pretty conclusively that it's that big new SAS drive you just bought—unless, of course, you already have a half-dozen of them on your server, in which case you're going to need to come up with a more effective name. On the other hand, a volume name of "C_DRIVE" is just about useless, because the drive letter is available from anywhere that the volume name is. A common scheme is to assign volume names based on the primary use of the volume, so "UserHome" or "DB_STORE" makes it pretty clear which volume it is from a logical (but not necessarily physical) view. We've moved to preferring this logical view of volume names—in an era of widely available hardware RAID solutions, combined with virtualized servers and virtual hard drives, the particular physical characteristics of a drive are less important than the logical ones. On our server, it's all part of a large SAS array underneath anyway.

Mounting a Virtual Hard Disk

If you're running SBS 2011 on a physical server, as opposed to a virtual machine, you can still take advantage of the flexibility and disaster recovery features of virtual hard disks. With SBS, you can both create and directly mount (*attach*) a virtual hard disk (VHD) file and then treat it just like any other hard disk. To attach a VHD, complete the following steps:

1. Open the Disk Management console if it isn't already open.
2. Select Attach VHD from the Action menu, as shown in Figure 11-21.

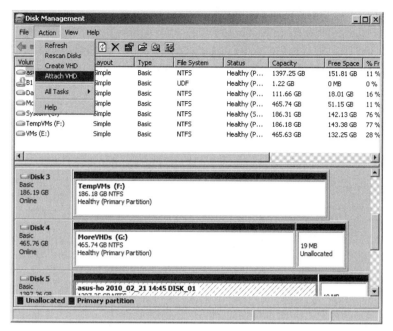

FIGURE 11-21 SBS 2011 can use VHDs just like regular hard disks

3. Specify the location and name of the VHD file, and click OK to attach the VHD. If this is a new VHD, you'll need to initialize it just as you would a new physical hard disk.

Mounting a Volume

SBS borrows a concept from the UNIX world by adding the ability to mount a volume or partition on a subfolder of an existing drive letter. A mounted volume can also have a drive letter associated with it, although it does not need to, and it can be mounted at more than one point, giving multiple entry points into the same storage.

A volume must be mounted on an empty subfolder of an existing NTFS volume or drive. FAT and FAT32 drives do not support mounted volumes. You can mount only a single volume at a given mount point, but you can then mount further volumes on top of an existing mounted volume, with the same rules and restrictions as any other mount. An important caution, however: the properties of a drive do not show all the available disk space for that drive, because they do not reflect any volumes mounted on the drive. Further, mounted volumes are not supported with Windows Services for UNIX on shared Network File System (NFS) exports.

Mounted volumes can be used to provide a mix of redundant and nonredundant storage in a logical structure that meets the business needs of the business while hiding the complexities of the physical structure from the users, but this approach does pose potential issues during disaster recovery and for some kinds of file access.

The volume being mounted appears to users as a simple directory. This feature makes it possible to create larger file systems that use multiple hard disks without the inherent risks of using spanned volumes, because the failure of any one of the mounted volumes affects only the directories that were part of that volume. To mount a volume, complete the following steps:

1. From the Disk Management console, right-click a volume or partition. Choose Change Drive Letter And Paths from the shortcut menu. The Change Drive Letter And Paths dialog box opens.

2. Click Add to open the Add Drive Letter Or Path dialog box shown in Figure 11-22.

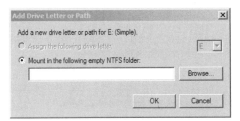

FIGURE 11-22 The Add Drive Letter Or Path dialog box used to mount a volume

3. You can type the mount point or click Browse to select or create a mount point. Any empty directory that resides on a nonremovable NTFS volume can be the mount point.

4. After you select or type the mount point, click OK, and the volume or partition is mounted.

> **IMPORTANT** It's actually easy to get yourself into trouble with this new feature. Disk Management lets you make multiple levels of mounted volumes, including ones that are recursive. You're well advised to mount volumes only at the root level of a drive. Trying to mount below that point can lead to confusion and make management and documentation difficult. Also, verify with your backup vendor that mount points are fully supported by their application.

Summary

In this chapter, we covered the details of how to manage the hard disks on your Windows Small Business Server 2011 computer, and how to configure them for data integrity and redundancy. In the next chapter, we'll cover the configuration and management of file storage on your SBS server.

CHAPTER 12

Storage Management

Even relatively small networks need a lot of storage, and as time passes and the network grows, the need for storage grows exponentially, not merely arithmetically. Fortunately, hard drives have become cheaper even as their storage capacity increases. Unfortunately, that circumstance often leads to attempts to manage storage requirements by simply buying more disks. Like many quick fixes, this can work for a while but leads to backup and archival complications, and it can end up making it even more difficult to manage the storage of your network.

With a bit of planning and a bit more implementation, you can keep your storage *manageable*.

> **NOTE** In this chapter, we cover file system storage management. However, another option for managed shared storage is Microsoft SharePoint Foundation Server 2010, which is the basis for the Companyweb in Microsoft Windows Small Business Server (SBS) 2011 Standard. For more information, see Chapter 23, "Customizing a SharePoint Site."

Distributed File System

Distributed File System (DFS) allows you to group shared folders located on different servers and present them to users as a virtual tree of folders known as a *namespace*. A namespace has many benefits, including increased availability of data, load sharing, and simplified data migration. DFS Replication allows administrators to replicate folders in a bandwidth-efficient manner using the remote differential compression (RDC) algorithm that replicates only the changed blocks within a file.

DFS namespaces and DFS Replication are useful for the following purposes:

- Organizing a large number of file shares scattered across multiple servers into a contiguous namespace so that users can find the files they need

- Improving the availability and performance of file shares, especially in network environments with multiple sites, where DFS namespaces can redirect users to the closest available server

- "Caching" data at a branch office so that users can access files at a local file server, which then efficiently replicates with a central file server across a wide area network (WAN) connection
- Centralizing backup from branch offices by replicating all data from the branch office to a central server that is backed up regularly
- Keeping two or more file shares in sync over local area network (LAN) or WAN links

> **NOTE** You can use DFS to create a loosely coupled collaboration environment where DFS Replication replicates data between multiple servers. However, DFS Replication does not include the ability to check out files (as you'd check out books from a library) or replicate files that are in use, such as multiuser databases. Therefore, use Windows SharePoint Services in environments where users regularly attempt to edit the same file at the same time from different locations.

DFS Terminology

Much of the terminology in DFS is very specific to the DFS environment. Acquainting yourself with these terms will save a lot of confusion later:

- **Namespace**   A namespace is a virtual view of shared folders. The folders can be in a variety of locations but appear to the user as a single tree.
- **Namespace server**   A namespace server hosts a namespace. The namespace server can be a member server or a domain controller.
- **Namespace root**   The namespace root is the shared folder that serves as the root for a particular namespace. Because DFS is a virtual file system, the namespace root can be any shared folder on an NTFS partition.
- **Folders**   Folders in a DFS namespace can provide structural depth to a hierarchy or contain folder targets that map to shares.
- **Folder target**   A folder target is the Universal Naming Convention (UNC) path of a shared folder or another namespace that is associated with a folder in a namespace. The folder target is where data and content are stored.

> **NOTE** Folders can contain folder targets or other folders, but not both at the same level in the hierarchy.

DFS clients automatically choose a folder target in their site, if available, reducing intersite network utilization. If more than one target is available on the client's site, each client randomly selects a target, spreading the load evenly across all available servers. If a target goes down, the client automatically picks a different target. (This process is called *client failover.*) When the original target comes back online, the client automatically switches back to the preferred target if the namespace server and the client support client fail back. In this way, targets provide fault tolerance, load balancing, and site awareness. You can use DFS Replication to keep folder targets synchronized.

Namespace Type

There are two types of DFS Namespaces: stand-alone and domain-based. A stand-alone namespace (for example, *srv1\public*) stores all namespace information on the registry of the namespace server instead of in Active Directory. Any server running Windows 2000 Server or later can host a stand-alone namespace, regardless of whether the server belongs to a domain (though servers running Windows Server 2003 and Windows 2000 Server do not support all features of DFS Namespaces).

Stand-alone namespaces can host more folders (up to 50,000 folders with targets) than domain-based namespaces (which can hold up to 5,000 folders with targets), but the only way to provide redundancy for a stand-alone namespace root is to use a server cluster. You cannot use multiple namespace servers to host a stand-alone namespace as you can with a domain-based namespace.

However, you can replicate folders in a stand-alone namespace as long as all replication members belong to the same Active Directory forest as in a Windows SBS domain. Domain-based namespace roots (for example, *example.local\public*) differ from stand-alone namespace roots in two ways. First, you must host domain-based namespace roots on a member server or domain controller of an Active Directory domain. Second, domain-based namespace roots automatically publish the DFS topology in Active Directory. This arrangement provides fault tolerance and network performance optimization by directing clients to the nearest target.

Choose a stand-alone namespace if the network does not use Active Directory or if the namespace contains more than 5,000 folders with targets. Otherwise, choose a domain-based namespace to use multiple namespace servers for redundancy and to take advantage of Active Directory for site-aware client referrals.

You can also combine the two. For example, you can create a domain-based namespace that includes a stand-alone root as a folder. Before creating namespaces, design the namespace hierarchy in a similar manner to the way you designed the domain structure for the organization.

Create a namespace structure that is logical, easy to use (for end users!), and matches the organization design, and then get the key stakeholders in the project to sign off on the design. Enlist some representative users from the organization to review the namespace design and provide feedback.

Namespace Server Requirements

The following servers can host multiple namespaces:

- Windows Server 2008 R2 Enterprise
- Windows Server 2008 R2 Datacenter
- Windows Server 2008 Enterprise
- Windows Server 2008 Datacenter
- Windows Server 2003 R2, Enterprise Edition
- Windows Server 2003 R2, Datacenter Edition
- Windows Server 2003, Enterprise Edition
- Windows Server 2003, Datacenter Edition

Servers running the following operating systems can host only a single namespace:

- Windows Server 2008 R2 Standard
- Windows Server 2008, Standard
- Windows Server 2003 R2, Standard Edition with Service Pack 2 or later
- Windows Server 2003, Standard Edition with Service Pack 2 or later

> **NOTE** Windows Server 2003, Web Edition cannot host any namespaces. It can act as a folder target. Up to ten concurrent incoming Server Message Block (SMB) connections are permitted.

Namespace Client Requirements

To access the DFS folder structure, you need a DFS client. Users can access file shares that are part of a DFS namespace without a DFS client; however, the user does not benefit from any of the DFS features, such as hierarchical namespaces, multiple folder targets, and site-aware client referrals.

The following operating systems include full support for DFS Namespaces, including support for client failback to the preferred folder target:

- Windows 7
- Windows Server 2008
- Windows Server 2008 R2
- Windows Vista Business, Windows Vista Enterprise, Windows Vista Ultimate
- Windows Server 2003 R2
- Windows Storage Server 2003 R2
- Windows Server 2003 with SP2, or SP1 and the Windows Server 2003 client failback hotfix
- Windows XP Professional with SP3, or SP2 and the Windows XP client failback hotfix

The client failback hotfixes are described in Microsoft Knowledge Base article 898900 at http://support.microsoft.com/kb/898900.

Users running the following operating systems can access namespaces, but if a folder target becomes unavailable and then later comes back online, the computer will not fail back (return) to the preferred folder target:

- Windows Storage Server 2003

- Windows XP Professional

- Windows Preinstallation Environment (Windows PE)

   Windows PE can access stand-alone namespaces, but it can't access domain-based namespaces.

- Windows 2000 Server

- Windows 2000 Professional

For optimal use of DFS, clients that can fail back are preferred.

DFS Replication

Before deploying DFS Replication, verify that all the following tasks have been done:

- Extend (or update) the Active Directory Domain Services (AD DS) schema to include Windows Server 2003 R2 or Windows Server 2008 schema additions.

> **NOTE**   For information about extending the AD DS schema, see *http://technet .microsoft.com/en-us/magazine/cc462798.aspx?pr=blog.*

- Install the File Services role with the DFS Replication role service on all servers that will act as members of a replication group.

- Ensure that all members of the replication group are running Windows Server 2008 or Windows Server 2003 R2.

- Install DFS Management on a server to manage replication.

- Store replicated folders on NTFS volumes.

- Verify that your antivirus software is compatible with DFS Replication.

File Replication Service

File Replication Service (FRS), introduced in Windows Server 2000, replicates files and folders that are stored in DFS folders or in the SYSVOL folder on domain controllers. FRS in Windows Server 2008 is an optional role service of the File Services server role that allows replication of content with other servers that use FRS instead of DFS Replication.

DFS Replication replaces FRS for replication of DFS folders on servers running Windows Server 2003 R2 or Windows Server 2008. In domains that use the Windows Server 2008 domain functional level, DFS Replication replaces FRS for the SYSVOL folder as well.

Neither DFS Replication nor FRS supports file support checkout or merging. If two or more users modify the same file simultaneously on different servers, DFS Replication uses a conflict-resolution method of "last writer wins" for files that are in conflict (that is, a file that is updated at multiple servers simultaneously) and "earliest creator wins" for name conflicts. DFS Replication moves the other copies to a conflict folder on the losing server but does not replicate this folder by default, unlike FRS, so the folder remains on the local server. To avoid conflicts, use Windows SharePoint Services when users in multiple locations need to collaborate on the same files at the same time. (Windows SharePoint Services allows users to check out files.)

DFS Replication, like FRS, is a multimaster replication engine that detects changes in a file by monitoring the update sequence number (USN) journal and replicating the changed file after the file is closed. Unlike FRS, DFS Replication uses a version vector exchange protocol to determine what parts of the file are different, and then uses the RDC protocol to replicate only changed blocks of files larger than 64 KB. This makes DFS Replication much more efficient at replication than FRS, which is particularly important when replicating with servers across a WAN link. DFS Replication does not replicate files that make use of Encrypting File System (EFS) encryption.

Replication Topologies

DFS Replication can make use of several topologies: hub and spoke, full mesh, and custom. These topologies are familiar to most network administrators, but here is a quick review:

- **Hub and spoke**   This topology is also known as a star topology. Each server replicates with a central server, minimizing the use of WAN links. This topology is similar to an Ethernet network, which uses a hub or switch as the center of the network. Choose this topology to reduce network usage when the replication group has more than 10 members, or when members of the replication group are in a site connected via a WAN connection.

- **Full mesh**   All servers replicate with all other servers. Choose this topology when the replication group has fewer than 10 servers and all links have low enough costs (performance or monetary) to allow each server to replicate with every other server. The full-mesh topology minimizes the time it takes to propagate changes to all members of the replication group and increases reliability by replicating with all members of the replication group, but it also increases network traffic from replication.

- **Custom** This topology allows you to manually specify replication connections.

Installing DFS Management

To manage a DFS namespace and DFS Replication, you must first install DFS Management.

Select Server Manager from the Administrative Tools menu, and install the File Services role on the server. Then follow these steps:

1. In Server Manager, expand the Roles node; then right-click File Services and select Add Role Services. (See Figure 12-1.)

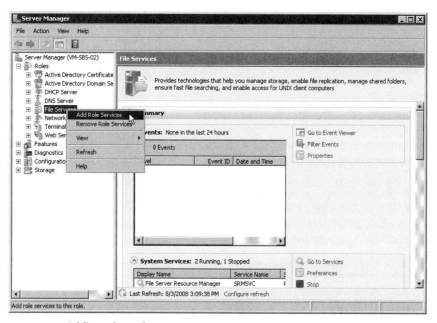

FIGURE 12-1 Adding role services

2. Select Distributed File System, as shown in Figure 12-2, and then click Next.

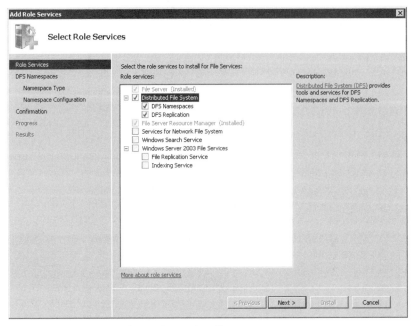

FIGURE 12-2 Selecting the file services to install

3. On the Create A DFS Namespace page, select Create A Namespace Now and provide a name. Alternatively, you can choose to create the namespace later. Click Next.

4. On the Select Namespace Type page, select Domain-Based Namespace and click Next.

5. On the Configure Namespace page, click Add to add folders to the namespace. In this process, shown in Figure 12-3, you can browse for folder targets and place the targets in the folders you choose. Click OK.

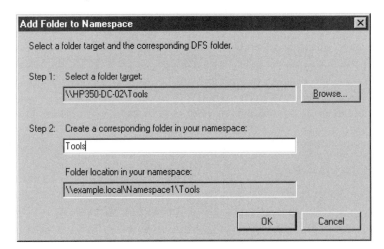

FIGURE 12-3 Adding a folder to the namespace

6. When you finish adding folders to the namespace, click Next.

7. Review the selections and click Install.

Creating or Opening a Namespace Root

The first step in working with DFS Namespaces is to create a namespace or open an existing namespace root. If you created a namespace root when installing DFS Management, you can use this procedure to open it; otherwise, follow these steps to create one:

1. Launch DFS Management from the Administrative Tools folder. Navigate to DFS Management and then to the Namespaces node.

2. To open an existing namespace root, right-click Namespaces and choose Add Namespace To Display. To create a new namespace root, right-click Namespaces and choose New Namespace. The New Namespace Wizard appears.

3. On the Namespace Server page, type the name of the server that you want to host the namespace root and then click Next. If the DFS service is disabled, click Yes in the Warning dialog box to start the DFS service and set its start-up setting to Automatic.

4. On the Namespace Name And Settings page, type the name to use for the namespace root. This name appears as the share name to users—for example, *example.local*\ *public*. The New Namespace Wizard creates the namespace root in the *%SYSTEM-DRIVE%*:\DFSRoots\name folder and gives all users read-only permissions. To change these settings, click Edit Settings. Click Next.

5. On the Namespace Type page (shown in Figure 12-4), choose whether to create a domain-based namespace or a stand-alone namespace, and then click Next.

   - Select Domain-Based Namespace to store the namespace on multiple servers in Active Directory. An example of a domain-based namespace is *example.local**public*.

   - Select Stand-Alone Namespace to create the namespace on a single server or server cluster. An example of a stand-alone namespace is *srv1**public*.

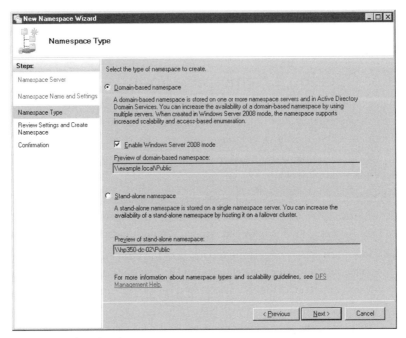

FIGURE 12-4 Choosing the namespace type

6. On the Review Settings And Create Namespace page, click Create. The New Namespace Wizard creates the namespace root. Correct any errors using the Previous button and then click Close.

Creating a Namespace from a Command Prompt

To create a namespace from a command prompt, use the Dfsutil /Addftroot or Dfsutil /Addstdroot commands. For example, to create the same namespace shown in Figure 12-4, follow these steps:

1. Open the Command Prompt window. Start the DFS service, and set the start-up type to Automatic if it is not already by typing the following commands:

```
Sc Start Dfs

Sc Config Dfs Start= Auto
```

2. Create a folder and file share for the namespace root by typing the following commands:

```
Md E:\Public

Net Share Public=E:\Public
```

3. Create the domain-based namespace root by typing the following command:

```
Dfsutil /Addftroot /Server:Srv1 /Share:Public
```

Adding Namespace Servers

The namespace root is the most important part of the namespace. Without it, clients cannot access any DFS folders. Because of this, the first step in creating a more fault-tolerant namespace is to add namespace servers to the namespace root. If possible, add at least one namespace server on each site where users need access to the DFS namespace by following these steps:

1. In the DFS Management console, navigate to Namespaces, right-click the domain-based namespace root you want to replicate, and then choose Add Namespace Server.

2. In the Add Namespace Server dialog box, type the path to the namespace server and then click OK. Windows creates the namespace root on the target server in the *%SYSTEMDRIVE%*:\DFSRoots*name* folder and gives all users read-only permissions. To change these settings, click Edit Settings.

3. If the DFS service is disabled, click Yes in the Warning dialog box to start the DFS service and set its start-up setting to Automatic.

4. To add a namespace server to a namespace from a command prompt, create the appropriate shared folder, verify that the DFS service is started and the start-up type is set to Automatic, and then use the Dfsutil /Addftroot command. For example, open a command prompt window and then type **Dfsutil /Addftroot /Server:Srv2/ Share:Public**.

Adding DFS Folders

DFS folders allow users to navigate from the namespace root to other file shares on the network without leaving the DFS namespace structure. To create a DFS folder, follow these steps:

1. Right-click the namespace root to which you want to add a folder, and then choose New Folder. This displays the New Folder dialog box, shown in Figure 12-5.

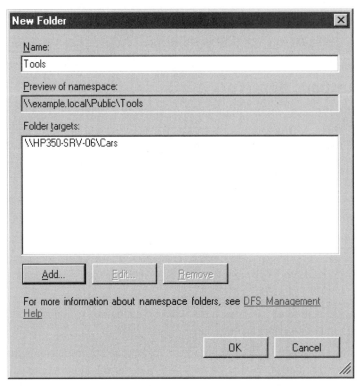

FIGURE 12-5 Creating a new folder

2. Type a name for the folder in the Name box. To create a folder that contains other DFS folders, click OK without adding any target folders. This creates a layer of structure to the namespace.

3. To add target folders, click Add and then type the shared folder's UNC or DNS path, or click Browse to browse to the shared folder.

4. Add any additional folder targets, and then click OK.

If you added multiple folder targets, click Yes in the Replication dialog box to create a replication group for the folder targets or click No to set up a replication group later (or not at all). If you click Yes, the Replicate Folder Wizard appears with some settings already entered. For more information, see "Creating a Replication Group" later in this chapter.

To create a DFS folder from a command prompt, create the appropriate file shares, and then use the Dfscmd /Map command. (You cannot add DFS folders without folder targets from a command prompt.) For example, open the Command Prompt window and then type the following commands:

```
Dfscmd /Map \\Example.local\Public\Software \\Dc1\Software
Dfscmd /Add \\Example.local\Public\Software \\Srv2\Software
```

Changing Advanced Settings

The default settings for DFS Management are appropriate for most installations, but if you need to change advanced namespace settings such as the referral order, change how namespace servers poll domain controllers for DFS metadata, or delegate DFS Management permissions, use the information in the following sections.

Changing Namespace Referral Settings

To change the cache duration, the order in which domain controllers or namespace servers refer clients to namespace servers and folder targets, or the failback settings for an entire namespace, right-click a namespace root or folder, choose Properties, and click the Referrals tab. (See Figure 12-6.)

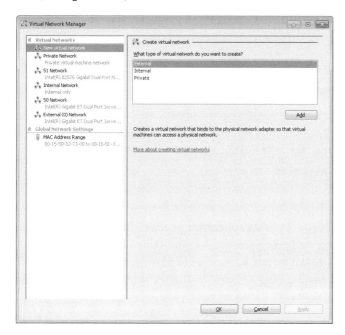

FIGURE 12-6 The Referrals tab of a namespace Properties dialog box

Use the following list to complete the process:

- In the Cache Duration box, specify how long clients should cache referrals before polling the domain controller or namespace server for a new referral.
- In the Ordering Method drop-down box, choose how domain controllers and namespace servers should refer clients to folder targets and namespace servers.
- Select the Clients Fail Back To Preferred Targets option to force a client to switch back to using its preferred server when it comes back online.

The preferred server is based on site and any custom referral ordering settings you specify on folder targets. This setting is supported by clients running Windows XP with Service Pack 2 (SP2) and the post-SP2 Windows XP client failback hotfix, Windows Server 2003 with Service Pack 1 and the Windows Server 2003 client failback hotfix, and Windows Server 2003 R2. See Knowledge Base article 898900 at *http://support.microsoft.com/kb/898900* for information on how to obtain this hotfix.

Overriding Referral Settings on Individual Folders

DFS folders inherit referral settings from the namespace root unless you specifically override them. To override the referral settings for a folder, right-click the appropriate folder, choose Properties, click the Referrals tab, and then specify the settings you want to override.

To explicitly set a single folder target as the preferred target or set the folder target as a target of last resort, right-click the folder target, choose Properties, click the Advanced tab, select the Override Referral Ordering check box, and then specify the priority for the target folder.

Delegating Management Permissions

DFS Management sets the permissions on the namespace object in Active Directory or in the registry of the namespace server (when using a stand-alone namespace). To change the ability of users to perform common management tasks, use the following list:

- **Create and manage namespaces**   To view, add, or remove groups that can manage namespaces, right-click the Namespaces node, choose Delegate Management Permissions, and then use the Delegate Management Permissions dialog box.
- **Manage individual namespaces and replication groups**   To view groups that can manage a namespace or replication group, select the namespace or replication group, and then click the Delegation tab. To remove management permissions for a group, right-click the group and choose Remove. To give management permissions for the namespace to a group, right-click the namespace, choose Delegate Management Permission, type the name of the group in the Select Users Or Groups dialog box, and then click OK.

- **Create and manage replication groups** To view, add, or remove groups that can manage replication, right-click the Replication node, choose Delegate Management Permissions, and then use the Delegate Management Permissions dialog box.

Changing Namespace Polling Settings

To change how namespace servers poll domain controllers for the latest namespace metadata in a domain-based namespace, right-click the appropriate namespace, choose Properties, click the Advanced tab, and then choose one of the following polling methods:

- **Optimize For Consistency** Polls the primary domain controller (PDC) emulator for new namespace polls data every hour and after each change to the namespace. Use this setting when the network contains 16 or fewer namespace servers to minimize the time it takes to propagate namespace changes to all namespace servers. This is the default setting.

- **Optimize For Scalability** Polls the nearest domain controller every hour for changes to the namespace. Use this setting when the network contains more than 16 namespace servers to reduce the load on the PDC emulator. However, choosing this setting increases the amount of time it takes to propagate namespace changes to all namespace servers. Servers running Windows 2000 Server do not support this setting and continue to use the Optimize For Consistency polling method.

To enable the Optimize For Scalability polling method from a command prompt, use the Dfsutil /Rootscalability command. For example, open the Command Prompt window, change to the directory in which you placed the Dfsutil.exe file, and then type **Dfsutil /Root:Example.local\Public /Rootscalability /Enable**.

Backing Up and Restoring the DFS Folder Targets

The DFS Namespaces database for domain-based DFS is stored in Active Directory, and you can back it up and restore it using Active Directory–aware backup methods. To back up the listing of folder targets for a stand-alone namespace root, type the following text at a command prompt (replacing *ServerName* and *Namespace* with the name of the appropriate server name and namespace root):

DFScmd /View \\ServerName\Namespace /Batch >DFS_backup.bat

To restore this DFS structure, re-create the DFS namespace and then run the batch file you created.

> **NOTE** In addition to backing up the DFS topology, back up the contents of the actual file shares routinely. Always test the backup before relying on it. You can use the Dfsradmin Replicationgroup command to export DFS Replication settings such as replication group members and connections.

Using DFS Replication

An easy-to-use, fault-tolerant, and high-performance file system is not worth much if the data you want to access is unavailable or out of date. To ensure that files are available to users even if a server goes down, create additional folder targets (as described earlier in the "Adding DFS Folders" section) and use DFS Replication to keep the folder targets in sync. You can also use DFS Replication to synchronize folders that are not part of a DFS namespace—for example, to replicate data from a branch office to a server in the main office that you back up regularly and reliably.

Creating a Replication Group

A *replication group* is defined as two or more servers that participate in replication. Replication groups define the replication topology used by members for replication. To create a replication group, follow these steps:

1. Click Start, point to Administrative Tools, and then click DFS Management.

2. In the console tree, right-click the Replication node, and then click New Replication Group.

3. Follow the instructions in the New Replication Group Wizard.

Conflict Resolution During the Initial Replication

If other members of the replication group have data in the replicated folders, Windows takes the following actions during the initial replication:

- If an identical file already exists on the target server (any server other than the primary member), the primary member does not replicate the file.

- If a file already exists on a target server but the file is not identical to the version on the primary member, Windows moves the file on the target server to the local conflict folder and then replicates the primary member's version of the file, even if this file is older than the version on the target server.

- If a file exists on a target server that is not present on the primary member, Windows does not replicate it during the initial replication but does replicate it during subsequent replications to other members, including the primary member.

After the initial replication, the primary member role goes away and replication is multiple-master-based. Do not delete, rename, or move files on the primary member or any member that has already replicated until the first replication is complete. (Look for Event 4104 in the DFS Replication log.) Deleting, renaming, or moving files before the first replication is complete can cause the files to reappear if they existed on a target that had not yet replicated.

Replicating a DFS Folder

To create a replicated folder in a new replication group that replicates a DFS folder, use the following steps:

1. Right-click the appropriate folder under the Namespaces node of DFS Management, and choose Replicate Folder. The Replicate Folder Wizard appears.

2. On the Replication Group And Replicated Folder Name page, confirm the name for the replication group and for the replicated folder. (The name for the replication group must be unique on the domain. To add to an existing replication group, use the instructions in the following sections.)

3. On the Replication Eligibility page, review the target folders that will be replicated. Click Next.

4. On the Primary Member page, select the server that holds the data that you want to use as the seed for the initial replication.

5. On the Topology Selection page, select one of the following replication topologies:

   - **Hub And Spoke** Spoke servers replicate with one or two central hub servers. Hub servers replicate with all other hub servers by using the full-mesh topology, as well as with designated spoke servers. Choose this topology in large network environments and environments with multiple branch offices. This topology requires a minimum of three members.

   - **Full Mesh** All servers replicate with all other servers. Choose this topology when there are fewer than 10 servers in the replication group and all links have low enough costs (performance or monetary) to allow each server to replicate with every other server instead of a central hub server.

   - **No Topology** This option does not specify a topology and postpones replication until you specify a replication topology manually. To specify a replication topology after creating the replication group, right-click the replication group in the DFS Management snap-in and then choose New Topology.

6. On the Hub Members page that appears if you chose the Hub And Spoke topology, specify the hub servers.

7. On the Hub And Spoke Connections page that appears if you chose the Hub And Spoke topology, verify that the wizard lists the proper spoke servers. To change the required hub server with which a spoke member replicates preferentially, or the optional hub member with which a spoke member replicates if the required hub member is unavailable, select the spoke server, click Edit, and then specify the required hub and the optional hub.

8. On the Replication Group Schedule And Bandwidth page, choose when to replicate and the maximum amount of bandwidth you want DFS Replication to use.

9. To create a custom schedule, choose Replicate During The Specified Days And Times and then click Edit Schedule. You can create a custom schedule that uses Coordinated Universal Time (UTC) or the local time of the receiving server.

10. On the Review Settings And Create Replication Group page, review the settings and then click Create. Review any errors and then click Close. Windows then replicates topology and replication settings to all domain controllers. A replication group member polls its nearest domain controller regularly. (By default, replication group members perform a lightweight poll every five minutes for Subscription objects under the local computer container and a full poll every hour.) It receives the settings after Windows updates the domain controller. To change the replication polling interval, use the Dfsrdiag command.

Creating a Branch Office Replication Group

To create a replication group that replicates a single branch server with a single hub server, use the following steps:

1. In the DFS Management snap-in, right-click Replication and choose New Replication Group. The New Replication Group Wizard appears.

> **NOTE** Creating replicated folders within an existing replication group is faster than creating a new replication group for each replicated folder because the replication group automatically applies its schedule, topology, and bandwidth-throttling settings to the new replicated folder.

2. On the Replication Group Type page, choose Replication Group For Data Collection.

3. On the Name And Domain page, type a name for the replication group that is unique on the domain, specify in which domain to host the replication group, and optionally type a description of the replication group.

4. On the Branch Server page, type the name of the branch server that holds the data that you want to replicate with the hub server.

5. On the Replicated Folders page, click Add, and then use the Add Folder To Replicate dialog box to specify the local folder on the branch server to replicate with the hub server. Click OK when you are finished.

6. On the Hub Server page that appears if you chose Replication Group For Data Collection on the Replication Group Type page, type the name of the hub server that serves as a replication target for the replicated folders.

7. On the Target Folder On Hub Server page, specify the local folder on the hub server in which you want to place replicated data from the branch server. This folder is usually located in a folder or volume that you back up regularly.

8. On the Replication Group Schedule And Bandwidth page, choose when to replicate and the maximum amount of bandwidth you want to allow DFS Replication to use. To create a custom schedule, choose Replicate During The Specified Days And Times and then click Edit Schedule. You can create a custom schedule that uses Coordinated Universal Time (UTC) or the local time of the receiving server.

9. On the Review Settings And Create Replication Group page, review the settings and then click Create. Review for errors and then click Close.

Windows then replicates the topology and replication settings to all domain controllers. A replication group member polls its nearest domain controller regularly. (By default, replication group members perform a lightweight poll every five minutes for Subscription objects under the local computer container and a full poll every hour.) It receives the settings after Windows updates the domain controller. To change the replication polling interval, use the Dfsrdiag command.

Creating a Multipurpose Replication Group

To create a replication group that replicates any number of servers with any number of other servers, use the following steps:

1. In the DFS Management snap-in, right-click Replication and choose New Replication Group. The New Replication Group Wizard starts.

2. On the Replication Group Type page, choose Multipurpose Replication Group.

3. On the Name And Domain page, type a name for the replication group that is unique on the domain, specify in which domain to host the replication group, and optionally type a description of the replication group.

4. On the Replication Group Members page, add the servers on which you want to replicate content.

5. On the Topology Selection page, choose a replication technology.

6. On the Hub Members page that appears if you chose the Hub And Spoke topology, specify the hub servers.

7. On the Hub And Spoke Connections page that appears if you chose the Hub And Spoke topology, verify that the wizard lists the proper spoke servers. To change the required hub server with which a spoke member replicates preferentially, or the optional hub member with which a spoke member replicates if the required hub member is unavailable, select the spoke server, click Edit, and then specify the required hub and the optional hub.

8. On the Replication Group Schedule And Bandwidth page, choose when to replicate and the maximum amount of bandwidth you want to allow DFS Replication to use. To create a custom schedule, choose Replicate During The Specified Days And Times and then click Edit Schedule. You can create a custom schedule that uses Coordinated Universal Time (UTC) or the local time of the receiving server.

9. On the Primary Member page, select the server that holds the data that you want to use as the seed for the initial replication.

10. On the Folders To Replicate page, click Add, and then use the Add Folder To Replicate dialog box to specify the folder to replicate. Click OK when you are finished.

11. On the Local Path Of *Folder* On Other Members page, select a replication member that you want to participate in the replication of the specified folder, click Edit, and then use the Edit Local Path dialog box to enable replication and specify the local folder on the target server in which to place replicated data from the hub server. Repeat this step for every replicated folder you specify in the Replicated Folders page.

12. On the Review Settings And Create Replication Group page, review the settings and then click Create. Review any errors and then click Close.

Windows then replicates the topology and replication settings to all domain controllers. A replication group member polls its nearest domain controller regularly. (By default, replication group members perform a lightweight poll every five minutes for Subscription objects under the local computer container and a full poll every hour.) It receives the settings after Windows updates the domain controller. To change the replication polling interval, use the Dfsrdiag command.

Managing Replication Groups

Select a replication group, and then use the Memberships, Connections, Replicated Folders, and Delegation tabs of the DFS Management console to manage the replication group, as discussed in the following list.

> **NOTE** Click a column heading to change how Windows groups items in the view. To add or remove columns, right-click the column heading and choose Add/Remove Columns.

Use the following options on the Memberships tab to view and manage the member servers for each replicated folder:

- To disable a member of the replication group, right-click the member and then choose Disable. Disable members that do not need to replicate a specific replicated folder. Do not disable members temporarily and then enable them—doing so causes roughly one kilobyte of replication traffic per file in the replicated folder and overwrites all changes on the disabled member. (See the "Conflict Resolution During the Initial Replication" sidebar earlier in the chapter for more information.)

- To delete a member of the replication group, right-click it and then choose Delete.

- To add a member server that participates in replication, right-click the replication group in the DFS Management console, choose New Member, and then use the New Member Wizard to specify the local path of the replicated folders, connections, and schedule.

- To change the size of the conflict or staging folders or to disable the retention of deleted files, right-click the member, choose Properties, click the Advanced tab, and then use the Quota boxes. The conflict folder stores the "losing" files that Windows deletes when it encounters two versions of the same file during replication as well as the most recently deleted files in the replicated folder, and the staging folder queues replication data.

> **NOTE** The default size of the staging folder is 4096 MB, but by increasing the size of the staging folder, you can increase the performance of replication group members that replicate with a large number of replication partners or that contain large files that change often. Look for event ID 4208 in the DFS Replication event log; if this event appears multiple times in an hour, increase the staging folder size 20 percent until the event no longer appears frequently.

- To create a report showing the replication health as well as RDC efficiency, right-click the replication group, choose Create Diagnostic Report, and then use the Diagnostic Report Wizard to create the report.
- To verify the replication topology, right-click the replication group and then choose Verify Topology.
- On the Connections tab, view and manage all replication connections. To add a new replication connection between two members of a replication group, right-click the replication group and choose New Connection. Then use the New Connection dialog box to specify the sending member, the receiving member, the schedule, and whether to create a one-way replication connection or a two-way connection.
- Use the following options on the Replicated Folders tab to view and manage all replicated folders:
  - To add a new replicated folder to the replication group, right-click the replication group in the DFS Management console, choose New Replicated Folder, and then use the New Replicated Folder Wizard to specify the primary member and the local folders to replicate.
  - To omit certain file types or subfolders from replication, click the Replicated Folders tab, right-click the replicated folder, choose Properties, and then use the File Filter and Subfolder Filter boxes on the General tab.
  - To share a replicated folder on the network and optionally add the folder to a DFS namespace, right-click the replicated folder, choose Share And Publish In Namespace, and then use the Share Or Publish Replicated Folder Wizard.

NOTE RDC increases processor utilization on the server, so you might want to disable it on servers with slow processors or high-speed links, and in environments that replicate only new content or files smaller than 64 KB. To disable RDC on a connection, click the Connections tab, right-click the member, choose Properties, and then clear the Use Remote Differential Compression (RDC) check box. You can also change the minimum file size that RDC engages from the 64 KB default size by using the Dfsradmin ConnectionSet command. Monitor RDC statistics and CPU utilization before and after disabling RDC to verify that you reduce processor utilization enough to warrant the increased network traffic.

- On the Delegation tab, view and manage administrative permissions. See "Delegating Management Permissions" in this chapter for information about the Delegation tab.

NOTE To change the replication polling interval, which controls how often a server checks for updated files, use the Dfsrdiag command.

Using File Server Resource Manager

The File Server Resource Manager (FSRM) is installed as a role service of the File Services Role and is made up of three tools:

- Storage Reports Management
- Quota Management
- File Screening Management

These tools allow administrators of Windows Server 2008 file servers to keep track of storage growth and usage, as well as create hard or soft policies limiting the amount and type of files that users can save in specific folders.

NOTE In the SBS Console, you can set the size of individual users' shared folders. Other quotas you might want to set would be on public folders or central company resource folders.

Scheduling Storage Reports

FSRM supports reporting in Dynamic Hypertext Markup Language (DHTML), HTML, Extended Markup Language (XML), Comma-Separated Values (CSV) text, or plain text, making it easy to view reports or process them using scripts, Microsoft Office Excel, or other applications.

FSRM can search and report on the following files and events. Additional reports can be defined and included in the list.

- Duplicate files
- File-screening audit
- Files by file group
- Files by owner
- Large files
- Least-recently accessed files
- Most-recently accessed files
- Quota usage

File Server Resource Manager is automatically installed when you install Windows SBS 2011. To use it, you need only open Server Manager from the Administrative Tools menu and then follow these steps:

1. In the left pane, expand Roles, then File Services, then Share And Storage Management, and then File Server Resource Manager.

2. Right-click Storage Reports Management and select Schedule A New Report Task (shown in Figure 12-7).

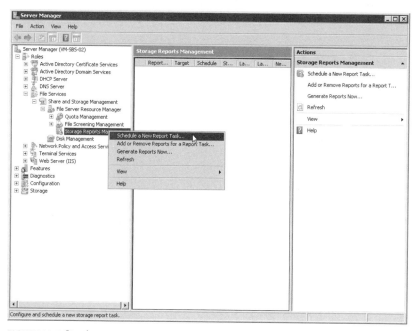

FIGURE 12-7 Starting a new report

3. The Storage Reports Task Properties dialog box opens (shown in Figure 12-8).

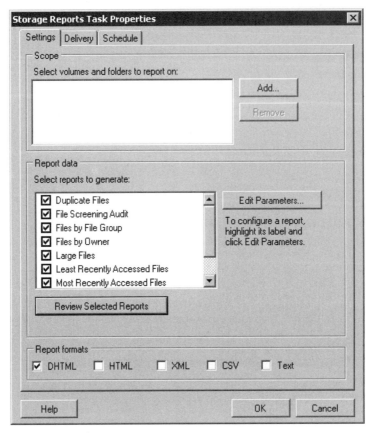

FIGURE 12-8 Configuring a storage report

4. In the Scope section of the dialog box, click Add to select the local folders that you want to monitor.

5. In the Report Data section of the dialog box, select the reports that you want to generate. To view the settings for all selected reports, click Review Selected Reports. To adjust the settings for a report, select the report and then click Edit Parameters.

6. In the Report Formats section of the dialog box, select the formats in which you want to generate the reports.

7. Click the Delivery tab, select the Send Reports To The Following Administrators check box, and type the email addresses of the administrators who should receive the storage reports, using a semicolon to separate addresses.

8. Click the Schedule tab and then click Create Schedule. In the Schedule dialog box (shown in Figure 12-9), set the date and time for the report to be generated.

FIGURE 12-9 Setting a report schedule

9. When all three tab selections are made, click OK. The new scheduled report task appears in the File Server Resource Manager console.

To run the scheduled report immediately, right-click it and choose Run Report Task Now. The Generate Storage Reports dialog box appears, asking whether you want to view the reports immediately or whether File Server Resource Manager should generate the reports in the background for viewing later from the report storage folder.

 UNDER THE HOOD   Storage Reports and Performance

To create a storage report, Windows creates a scheduled task in the Task Scheduler library that uses the Volume Shadow Copy Service to take a snapshot of the specified storage volumes, and then creates the storage report from this snapshot using XML style sheets stored in the %*WINDIR*%\system32\srm\xslt folder. This process minimizes the performance impact on the server, but does degrade file server performance temporarily.

Schedule your storage reports during slack times to minimize the impact on users, and combine reports whenever possible. Because all storage reports in a storage report task use the same snapshot, you can minimize the performance impact on a server by consolidating your reports to minimize the number of snapshots required.

Using Directory Quotas

One way to slow the growth of storage on a network is to limit the amount of disk space each user can use on a server. SBS 2011 provides two ways of doing this: disk quotas and directory quotas. Directory quotas allow you to manage storage at a folder level. You can create quota templates and auto quotas that Windows automatically applies to subfolders and newly created folders. Directory quotas, unlike disk quotas, look at the actual amount of disk space used by a file and provide powerful notification capabilities.

Directory quotas apply to all users as a group; disk quotas apply to individual users. Both directory quotas and disk quotas apply to a single server. Quotas can use either hard limits, which prevent users from exceeding their quotas, or soft limits, which provide only a warning and notification.

NOTE Directory quotas are preferred in Windows SBS 2011. If you choose to use disk quotas, you can set them by opening a disk's Properties dialog box and clicking the Quota tab.

Directory Quota Types

Directory quotas come in three varieties:

- **Quotas** Sets the total amount of disk space that a folder *and all subfolders* can consume. For example, if you create a quota that limits the \Users folder to 10 GB, the total contents of this folder and all subfolders cannot exceed 10 GB in size. If one user uses 9 GB of file space, all the other users combined are limited to 1 GB.

- **Auto Quotas** Sets the amount of disk space that the first-level subfolders (child folders) of a folder can consume. For example, if you create an auto quota for the \Users folder and set the limit at 2 GB, each first level of subfolder (for example, \Users\ Charlie; \Users\Wally) is limited to 2 GB in size. An auto quota does not set a limit on the contents of the parent folder, only the subfolders (child folders).

- **Quota Templates** Standardizes and centralizes quota and auto quota settings. When you change the settings of a quota template, you can automatically apply the changes to all quotas that use the quota template you change.

Creating Quotas and Auto Quotas

To create a quota or auto quotas, follow these steps. To create a quota template, see the "Creating and Editing Quota Templates" section later in this chapter.

1. In the File Server Resource Manager, expand Quota Management.

2. Right-click Quotas in the console tree and choose Create Quota.

3. The Create Quota dialog box opens, as shown in Figure 12-10.

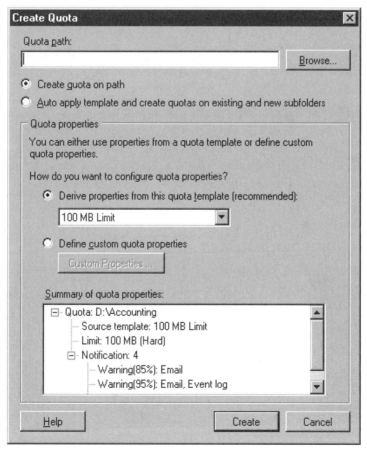

FIGURE 12-10 Creating a quota

4. Click Browse, select the folder to which you want to apply a quota, and then click OK.

5. To create a quota that limits the size of a folder, including all subfolders, select the Create Quota On Path option. To create an auto quota, which limits the size of subfolders individually (useful for setting quotas on the \Users folder), select the Auto Apply Template And Create Quotas On Existing And New Subfolders option.

6. Select the quota template you want to apply, or choose Define Custom Quota Properties and click Custom Properties to create a custom quota. (You cannot create custom quotas for auto quotas.) Click Create when you are finished.

7. If you chose to create a custom quota, the Save Custom Properties As A Template dialog box appears. Use this dialog box to save the custom quota as a quota template, or choose Save The Custom Quota Without Creating A Template.

8. To create a directory auto quota from a command prompt, use the Dirquota Quota Add command. For example, open a command prompt window and then type the following command:

```
Dirquota AutoQuota Add /Path:E:\Users /SourceTemplate:"200 MB Limit Reports
To User" /Remote:Srv1
```

> **NOTE** Use quota templates instead of custom quotas whenever possible. A quota template allows you to make changes to the template that apply to all quotas derived from the template. For example, to change the administrator email address for all quotas on a server, edit the appropriate quota templates and then apply these changes to all quotas. This eliminates the need to manually update each quota.

Viewing and Managing Quotas

To view the particulars of a quota, highlight it in the File Server Resource Manager and view the details in the lower pane as shown in Figure 12-11.

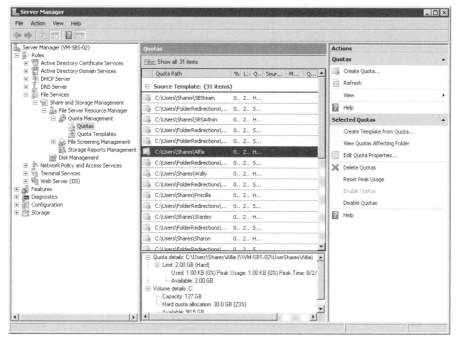

FIGURE 12-11 Viewing the details of an individual quota

Use the following sections for additional quota management.

- To filter the display by quota type or path, click the Filter hyperlink and then use the Quota Filter dialog box.

- To disable a quota, right-click the quota and select Disable Quotas. To enable a quota, right-click the quota and select Enable Quotas.

- To reset the peak-usage data, select the quota, right-click, and select Reset Peak Usage.

Creating and Editing Quota Templates

Quota templates enable you to quickly apply standardized quota settings, as well as simultaneously update all quotas that make use of a template—when you edit a quota template, Windows gives you the option to update all quotas based on the template. To create or edit a quota template, follow these steps:

1. In the File Server Resource Manager console, right-click Quota Templates and choose Create Quota Template, or right-click an existing quota template and choose Edit Template Properties. To create a quota template based on an existing quota, right-click the quota and choose Create Quota From Template.

2. To base the template on an existing template, in the Create Quota Template dialog box choose a template from the Copy Properties From Quota Template box and then click Copy, as shown in Figure 12-12.

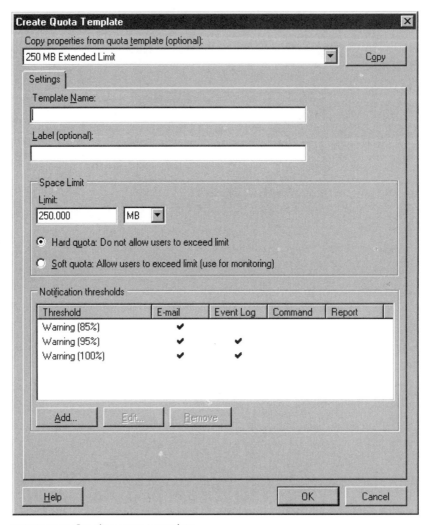

FIGURE 12-12 Creating a quota template

3. Type a name and label for the template in the Template Name and Label boxes.

4. In the Limit box, type the maximum amount of disk space each user can utilize in the specified folder.

5. Choose Hard Quota to prevent users from exceeding the limit you specify, or Soft Quota to use the quota only for monitoring.

6. In the Notification Thresholds section of the dialog box, click Add to create a new notification, or select an existing notification, and then click Edit to open the properties for the threshold, as shown in Figure 12-13.

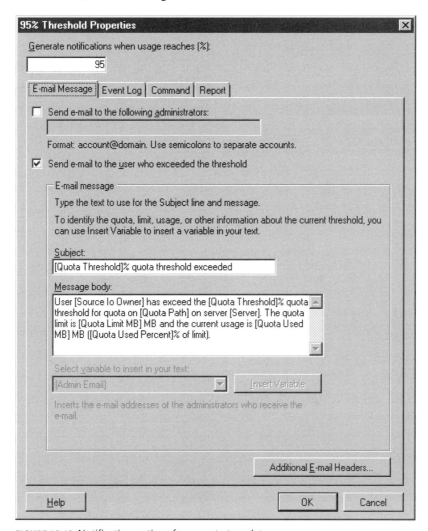

FIGURE 12-13 Notification options for a quota template

7. In the Generate Notifications When Usage Reaches box, specify when to notify users. A typical configuration is to use three notification thresholds, which are often set at 85 percent, 95 percent, and 100 percent.

8. Specify what actions to take when a user exceeds the threshold you specify, and click OK when you are finished:

- Use the E-Mail Message tab to send an email notification to users who exceed the threshold. (You can also choose to send the notification to an administrator.) Use the E-Mail Message section of the tab to customize the message that Windows generates.

- Use the Event Log tab to record a log entry on the server when a user exceeds the threshold.

- Use the Command tab to run a command or script when a user exceeds the threshold.

- Use the Report tab to generate a storage report when a user exceeds the threshold.

> **MORE INFO** See the "Scheduling Storage Reports" section earlier in this chapter for more information about storage reports.

9. Click OK when you're finished. If you're editing an existing template, the Update Quotas Derived From Template dialog box opens. Choose one of the following options and then click OK:

- **Apply Template Only To Derived Quotas That Match The Original Template** Updates quotas based on the quota template only if you have not customized them.

- **Apply Template To All Derived Quotas** Updates all quotas based on the quota template.

- **Do Not Apply Template To Derived Quotas** Does not update any quotas based on the template.

Screening Files

Administrators who use storage reports for the first time are often surprised, and occasionally dismayed, at how many audio and video files they find on file servers. In addition to the massive amounts of disk space that audio and video files consume, organizations can be exposed to legal liability if these files are obtained or shared illegally.

To help administrators control what type of files users can save on a file share, File Screening Management is part of the File Server Resource Manager console. With File Screening Management, administrators can block users from saving files with certain file extensions to a specific file share, as discussed in the following sections.

 REAL WORLD **Controlling Audio and Video Files on Servers**

I f you are serious about blocking personal audio and video files on public file shares, you need two things:

- **An acceptable use policy that clearly states what users can and cannot place on file shares** This policy should state that users cannot save illegally obtained files of any type on company file servers, including audio and video files for which the users have not purchased a license. You might also want to state that users can save only *legally* obtained audio and video files to their home directory (on which you create a directory quota, limiting users to a reasonable amount of disk space).

- **A file screen that implements this policy** The best way to get people to follow a company policy is to make it hard for them to violate the policy. A file screen makes it difficult for an average user to violate an acceptable-use policy concerning audio and video files, and it reduces legal liability by demonstrating that the organization is taking active steps to prevent its employees from violating its written policy.

Because file screens use a file-name mask and not a content mask to block files, users can still save MP3 files by changing the file extension of the file to something that isn't blocked. However, if you have a clear and unambiguous acceptable-use policy and a file screen for that policy in place, this requires a willful violation on the part of the user and a conscious attempt to cover up the violation—something that most employees are unlikely to risk.

Creating File Screens

To create a file screen, open the File Server Resource Manager console and follow these steps:

1. Click the File Screening Management node.

2. Click the File Screens container, right-click File Screens in the console tree, and choose Create File Screen. The Create File Screen dialog box opens, as shown in Figure 12-14.

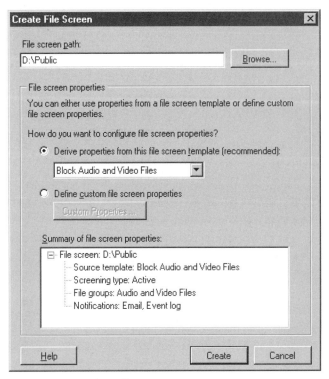

FIGURE 12-14 Creating a file screen

3. Click Browse, select the folder to which you want to apply the file screen, and then click OK.

4. Select the file screen template you want to apply, or choose Define Custom File Screen Properties and then click Custom Properties to create a custom file screen. Click OK when you are finished.

5. If you chose to create a custom file screen, the Save Custom Properties As A Template dialog box appears. Use this dialog box to save the custom file screen as a file screen template, or choose Save The Custom File Screen Without Creating A Template.

Creating Exceptions

To create an exception to a file screen, follow these steps:

1. Click the File Screens container, right-click File Screens in the console tree, and choose Create File Screen Exception. The Create File Screen Exception dialog box appears, as shown in Figure 12-15.

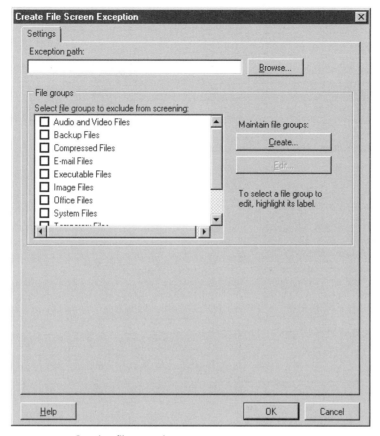

FIGURE 12-15 Creating file exceptions

2. Click Browse, select the folder to which you want to apply the file screen exception, and then click OK. The folder you select cannot already contain a file screen, but it can be a subfolder of a folder that contains a file screen.

3. Select the groups that you want to allow, excluding them from any file screens applied to parent folders. Click OK when you are finished to return to the File Server Resource Manager console.

Creating and Editing File Screen Templates

To create or edit a file screen template, follow these steps:

1. In the File Server Resource Manager console, right-click File Screen Templates and choose Create File Screen Template, or right-click an existing template and choose Edit Template Properties. To create a file screen template based on an existing file screen, right-click the file screen and choose Create A Template From File Screen.

2. To base the template on an existing template, in the Create File Screen Template dialog box, choose a template from the Copy Properties From Template box, as shown in Figure 12-16. Click Copy.

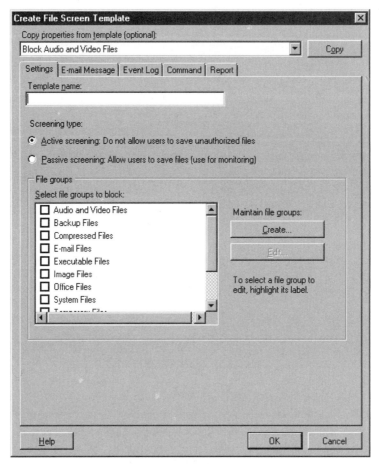

FIGURE 12-16 Working with a file screen template

3. Type a name and label for the template in the Template Name box.

4. Choose Active Screening to prevent users from saving files of the type you specify, or choose Passive Screening to use the file screen only for monitoring.

5. Select the file group or groups that you want to block. To create a new file group, click Create; to edit an existing file group, select the group and then click Edit.

6. Specify what actions to take when a user saves a screened file type, and then click OK:

   ■ Use the E-Mail Message tab to send an email notification to the user who saved a screened file type. (You can also choose to send the notification to an administrator.) Use the E-Mail Message section of the tab to customize the message that Windows generates.

   ■ Use the Event Log tab to record a log entry on the server when a user saves a screened file type.

   ■ Use the Command tab to run a command or script when a user saves a screened file type.

   ■ Use the Report tab to generate a storage report when a user saves a screened file type. See the "Scheduling Storage Reports" section of this chapter for more information about storage reports.

7. If you are editing an existing template, the Update File Screens Derived From Template dialog box appears. Choose one of the following options and then click OK:

   ■ **Apply Template Only To Derived File Screens That Match The Original Template**   Updates file screens based on the quota template only if you have not customized them

   ■ **Apply Template To All Derived File Screens**   Updates all file screens based on the quota template

   ■ **Do Not Apply Template to Derived File Screens**   Does not update any file screens based on the template

Working with File Groups

A file group is a group of files with a common set of characteristics in their file names. For example, the Audio and Video file group includes audio files (with .mp3, .wma, and .aac file extensions), and video files (with .wmv, .mpeg, and .mov file extensions). Storage reports use file groups when reporting on the types of files present on a file share, while file screening uses file groups to control which files to block. To create or edit a file group, follow these steps:

1. In the File Server Resource Manager console, select File Screening Management.

2. Right-click the File Groups container and choose Create File Group. The Create File Group Properties dialog box opens, as shown in Figure 12-17.

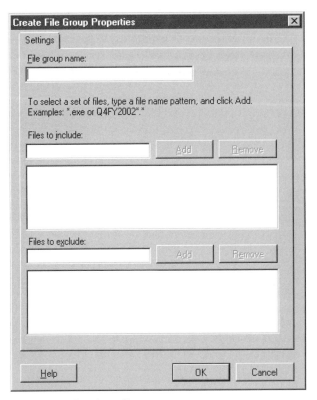

FIGURE 12-17 Creating a file group

3. Type a name for the file group in the File Group Name box.

4. In the Files To Include box, type the file-name criteria to include in the group. Use asterisks (*) as wildcards and then click Add.

5. To exclude files from the file group, type the file-name criteria to exclude from the file group in the Files To Exclude box. Click OK.

REAL WORLD Creative Use of File Groups

File screening isn't just for file extensions. It's actually based on pattern matching against the entire file name to define the file group. This means you can have a file group that matches all MP3 files by creating a file group that matches "*.mp3". But you could also have a file group that matched all Company Policy files by matching "pol*.pdf" if all your company policies are stored in files that start with "pol" and are Adobe PDF files. Or, if monthly financial reports are consistently stored as MMYYYY.XLS, you could create a file group that matched all 2010 financials by using *??2010.XLS* as your pattern.

The usual tendency with file groups is to think of selecting files solely by extension. But by using the entire file name in the pattern match, you can use file groups more creatively and also do enhanced reporting based on the file groups.

Summary

In this chapter, you saw the details of some very sophisticated ways to manage file storage, including Distributed File System incorporating DFS namespaces and DFS Replication, as well as the storage reports, quotas, and file screens of File Server Resource Manager.

In the next chapter, we move on to installing, sharing, and configuring printers on the network.

## CHAPTER 13

Installing and Managing Printers

As much as everyone would like to have a paperless office, it appears we'll all be much grayer (or balder, or both) before that completely comes to pass. Office paper consumption peaked in 1999, and since then the quantities of waste in the office paper-recycling bin have leveled off and in some places they have actually begun to shrink—slightly. However, even if few are printing out their emails before reading them, paper remains at the center of many business operations.

The cost of basic printers has declined dramatically, and companies are investing in sophisticated high-speed printers that allow users to handle jobs that once required an outside print shop. These printers are expensive both to buy and to use. Therefore, printer sharing remains an important function of enterprise networks. Setting up multiple users to share printers reduces cost and can improve printing output. You can direct routine work to low-cost-per-page printers, schedule long print jobs for off-hours, and limit access to high-end printers.

In other words, there's not much you can do to keep people from printing out the occasional grocery list or soccer schedule, but you can prevent them from doing it on the full-color laser printer with toner cartridges that cost as much as a new printer.

Understanding Print Servers

Print servers are computers (or sometimes network appliances) that manage the communications between printers and the client computers generating the print jobs.

Generally, there are two approaches to print servers. The Microsoft approach is to use a Windows computer as an "intelligent" print server that handles communication between the printers and the client computers (reducing strain on the clients), and maintains a common print queue for all clients. Microsoft print servers also make it easy to find printers on the network by name (NetBIOS, DNS, or Active Directory) and install the appropriate printer drivers.

In contrast, other operating systems, such as Linux, and printers with built-in network interfaces use a relatively "dumb" print server called the Line Printer Daemon (LPD), which acts strictly as an interface between the network and the printer. Each client maintains its own printer queue and performs all preprint processing, increasing the amount of time the computer is partially or completely unavailable for other tasks.

These two approaches aren't in opposition to each other and, in fact, the best way to connect a printer to a Windows print server is via a network connection to a printer, which usually runs the LPD service. The Windows print server connects to the printer using the traditional Line Printer Remote (LPR) service (the client-side equivalent of LPD) or via the higher-performance standard TCP/IP printer port, and shares the printer on the network. The Windows print server holds the printer queue and sends each print job to LPD, which passes the job to the printer.

 UNDER THE HOOD **Printer Terminology**

Although the term *printer* is usually used to refer to both the physical device and its software interface, strictly speaking, a printer is a device that does the actual printing, and a logical printer is the software interface (printer driver) for the printer. You can have one logical printer associated with a single printer, or you can have several logical printers associated with a single printer. In the latter arrangement, the logical printers can be configured at different priority levels so that one logical printer handles normal printing and another handles print jobs that should be printed during off-peak hours. For a printer that supports both PostScript (PS) and Printer Control Language (PCL), two logical printers allow users to choose which type of printing to do.

A single logical printer can also be associated with multiple physical printers in a printer pool, as long as all the printers work with the same driver. Printer pools distribute the printing load more evenly, increasing performance. Because the physical printers in the pools are interchangeable, printer pools also make it possible for an administrator to add or remove physical printers without affecting the users' configurations.

Selecting Printers

Choosing the right printers for an organization is a lot like choosing the right car. There are certain practical matters to look at such as up-front cost, cost of consumables (gas, ink, or toner), and suitability to the task at hand (for example, hauling lumber or printing brochures).

Color laser printers have become affordable for most businesses, but the cost of color toner remains very high. However, if you have a property sales office and need to print hundreds of high-quality color photos daily, a color laser printer is not an extravagance. A printer that will produce beautiful color at a rate of 20 or more pages per minute can be had for well under $1,000.

On the other hand, if you need lots of black-and-white pages and only occasional color, a black-and-white laser printer plus a color inkjet printer might be the most economical option. Color ink cartridges for inkjet printers are expensive, but they last a long time if used infrequently. And inkjet printers themselves are so low in cost they're practically disposable (as reprehensible as that is from an environmental point of view).

Look for printers with built-in network interfaces because they print faster, require less processing power on the print server, and can be flexibly located anywhere there's a network cable. Printers with a USB connection can be used if print volumes are low (or for backup printers), but steer clear of printers using parallel port connections—they can drastically slow a print server.

 REAL WORLD **Other Ways That Printers Are Like Cars**

In our office, we have three printers:

- A standard, small-business-size, black-and-white laser printer (the sensible sedan)
- A multifunction color inkjet copier/scanner/printer/fax (the efficient hybrid)
- A very fast color laser printer the size of a small file cabinet (the impractical but cool sports car)

Printers are undoubtedly essential to your business, but there's no reason you can't have some fun at the same time.

Planning Printer Placement

In a very small office, there's no need to spend time planning printer deployment. The printers go wherever there's room for them. However, in a larger organization you'll need to establish printer-naming and location-naming conventions, evaluate whether to upgrade or migrate existing print servers, and prepare for print server failures.

Naming Printers

An effective printer-naming convention is important to ensure that users can easily identify printers on the network. When creating a printer-naming convention, consider the following:

- The *printer name* can be any length up to 220 characters, which is plenty of room for any scheme you devise. Of course, the name should also be as short as possible without sacrificing clarity.

- The *share name* is the name that all clients see when they browse for a printer, use the Add Printer Wizard, or use the Net Use command. The share name can be up to 80 characters long, but again it should be shorter for readability. Some older applications cannot print to printers with fully qualified printer share names (the computer name and printer share name combined) that exceed 31 characters, or to print servers where the default printer's share name exceeds 31 characters. Clients using other operating systems might also have trouble with names longer than 31 characters or names containing spaces or other special characters. But whether you have to deal with such applications or not, shorter is generally better.

Naming Printer Locations

In small organizations, finding printers is easy—just stand up and look around or ask the person sitting next to you. This doesn't work as well in larger organizations where printers have varying capabilities and might be widely scattered. Under these circumstances, users need to be able to browse or search for printers based on the criteria they want, including printer features and printer location.

Location names are similar in form to domain names and use the *name/name/name...* syntax. They start with the most general location name and become progressively more specific. Each part name can have a maximum of 32 characters and can contain any characters except the forward slash (/), which Windows reserves as a delimiter.

Keep the naming convention simple and easy to understand. End users are usually interested in the answer to only one question: "Where's my printout?"

Design/ArtStudio/HPOfficeJetE809 is one example of a clear location name, as is Marketing/DirectMail/RicohProofing.

Installing Printers

Before a Windows print server can share a printer on the network, it must first connect to the printer and install the necessary drivers. The following sections walk you through adding printers that are attached directly to the print server via a USB or parallel port interface, as well as connecting to printers with built-in network adapters.

REAL WORLD   Local vs. Network Printers

In the consumer world, most printers are directly connected to a computer with a parallel port, USB port, or IEEE 1394 port. This solution—simple to use and to understand—is perfectly adequate and appropriate for individual users, or even most very small offices. But it has some significant disadvantages over a network-attached printer. It limits where the printer can be physically located because it must be within a few feet of the computer that supports it. And it can seriously slow the work of the individual whose computer acts as the print server. Printer input/output is not very efficient, especially when using the traditional parallel printer port.

A network-attached printer, on the other hand, can be located virtually anywhere. If you're using standard Ethernet to connect to the printer, you'll need a network port nearby, but if you use a wireless print server, even that requirement is eliminated. As a bonus, network printing doesn't have an adverse effect on the server that supports it—you can manage all your print queues directly from the SBS server, thereby simplifying management.

If your printers don't have a network interface, you can use one of the widely available stand-alone print server appliances, either wireless or Ethernet. SBS treats these as if they were a standard network printer, but you don't have to buy a printer with a network card included—the print server appliance has a port or ports to connect to the printer as well as a network interface.

An exception to the "all printers are network printers" rule is for the user who has a privacy (or other) need for a locally attached printer. Human resources and hiring managers are two classes of users that this might apply to.

Adding and Sharing a Network Printer

To add a network printer to your Windows SBS 2011 network, follow the instructions provided by the manufacturer of the printer. If the specific instructions are long gone, make sure you have the drivers you need (you can download them from the manufacturer's website, if necessary) and follow these steps:

1. Make the physical connection between the printer and a network jack using a network cable.

2. Turn the printer on. (If the printer is already on, turn it off and then on again.)

3. From the computer running Windows SBS 2011, select DHCP from the Administrative Tools menu.

4. In the DHCP task pane, expand IPv4, expand Scope, and then expand Address Leases under your domain name. Locate the DHCP address assigned to the new printer (shown in Figure 13-1), and make a note of it.

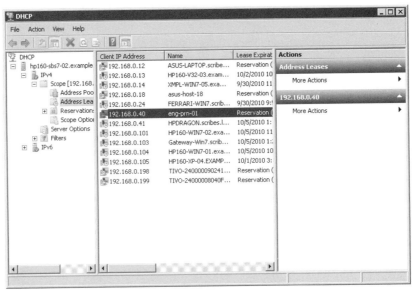

FIGURE 13-1 Locating the assigned TCP/IP address for a network printer

5. Select Control Panel from the Start menu. Under the Hardware heading, click View Devices And Printers.

6. In the Printers window, select Add A Printer.

7. In the Add Printer dialog box, select Add A Local Or Network Printer As An Administrator (shown in Figure 13-2).

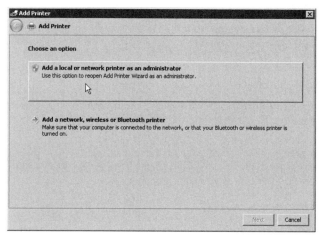

FIGURE 13-2 Choosing the Add Printer option

8. In the next dialog box, under What Kind Of Printer Do You Want To Install, select Add A Local Printer.

9. In the Choose A Printer Port dialog box, select Create A New Port and select Standard TCP/IP Port from the drop-down list. Click Next.

10. In the Type A Printer Hostname Or IP Address dialog box, type in the IP address you noted in step 4. The Port Name is automatically filled in. (See Figure 13-3.) Click Next.

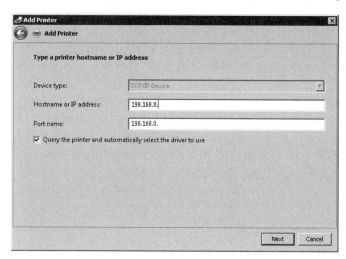

FIGURE 13-3 Entering the printer IP address

NOTE To query the printer and automatically select the driver to use, leave the check box selected. If Windows SBS 2011 already has built-in drivers for the printer, you won't need to provide additional ones.

11. Windows SBS 2011 contacts the printer and displays the Install The Printer Driver dialog box. Choose the manufacturer name from the list on the left and the printer model from the list on the right. Click Next.

> **NOTE** A designation (MS) next to the printer name indicates that the driver is part of Windows SBS 2011. If your printer needs multiple drivers (such as Postscript in addition to PCL), click Have Disk and point to the location of the drivers.

12. In the Type A Printer Name dialog box, accept or revise the printer name. The printer will be set as the default printer unless you clear the check box. Click Next.

13. In the Printer Sharing dialog box, accept or revise the share name. Add a location and comments if wanted. Click Next.

14. The successful installation is announced (as shown in Figure 13-4). Print a test page to confirm that all is well. Click Finish.

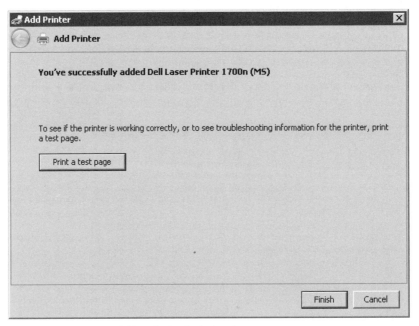

FIGURE 13-4 The successful installation is declared

Showing a Shared Printer in Windows SBS Console

Even after a network printer is successfully installed and shared, it still might not appear in the Devices list under the Network tab of Windows SBS Console. If that's the case, follow these steps:

1. Open Windows SBS Console, click Network and then click Devices.

2. In the Tasks Pane, click Refresh This View. If the printer is still not listed, click List A Shared Printer In This Console.

3. In the Show Shared Printer In The Console dialog box, provide the network path for the shared printer or click Browse to locate the printer.

4. When the \\computer\share path is displayed as shown in Figure 13-5, click OK.

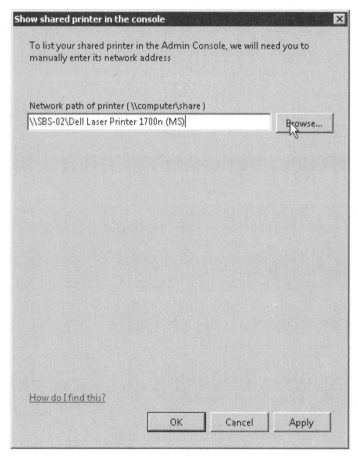

FIGURE 13-5 Entering a shared printer's network address

5. In the Windows SBS Console, click Refresh This View in the Tasks list. The printer appears in the list of printers.

Now you can manage this printer from the Windows SBS Console. Right-click the printer name to view printer jobs. Or select Printer Properties to view and modify printer settings.

Sharing Locally Connected Printers

If you're using a USB or IEEE 1394 (FireWire) connection to the printer, as soon as you plug the printer into the server, Windows automatically detects, installs, and shares the printer on the network, and also publishes it in Active Directory (although you might be prompted for drivers).

Sharing a Printer Connected to a Windows Vista Computer

From the computer running Windows Vista, click Start and then follow these steps:

1. Select Control Panel and then click Printers or Hardware And Sound\Printers.

2. Right-click the printer you want to share and select Properties.

3. On the Sharing tab, click Change Sharing Options.

4. Click Share This Printer as shown in Figure 13-6, and select the check boxes for Render Print Jobs On Client Computers and List In The Directory.

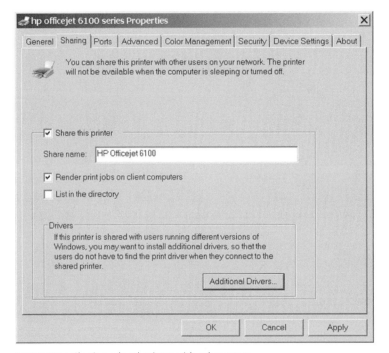

FIGURE 13-6 Sharing a local printer with other users

5. Click the General tab. In the Location text box, enter a description of the printer's location. Add any notes in the Comment section. Click Apply.

6. Click Print Test Page to verify that the printer is correctly attached.

On the Windows SBS Console, click Network and then Devices. The printer appears in the Printers list.

Sharing a Printer Connected to a Windows XP Computer

From the computer running Windows XP, click Start and then follow these steps:

1. Select Control Panel and then click Printers And Faxes.

2. In the task pane, click Add A Printer to start the Add A Printer Wizard. Follow the instructions to complete the wizard.

3. In the details pane, right-click the printer and select Properties.

4. On the Sharing tab, click Share This Printer, and then click List In The Directory. Verify that Render Print Jobs On Client Computers is selected.

5. Click the General tab. In the Location area, type the physical location of the printer.

6. Click Apply.

On the server, open the SBS Console. Click Network and then click Devices. Confirm that the printer is included in the Printers list.

Sharing a Printer Connected to a Windows 7 Computer

From the computer running Windows 7, click Start and then follow these steps:

1. Click Control Panel and then click Devices And Printers.

2. Right-click the printer you want to share and select Properties.

3. On the Sharing tab, click Change Sharing Options.

4. Click Share This Printer, and select the check boxes for Render Print Jobs On Client Computers.

5. Click the General tab. In the Location text box, enter a description of the printer's location. Add any notes in the Comment section. Click Apply.

6. On the Windows SBS Console navigation bar, click Network and then click Devices. The printer will appear in the Printers list.

Adding Client Drivers for Shared Printers

Before a shared printer can be used by clients of a different architecture, such as x64 editions of Windows, you need to add the drivers for the printer to SBS. This isn't automatic when initially sharing a printer, so you'll need to add the necessary client drivers after the shared printer is created.

To install drivers for clients of different architectures, follow these steps:

1. Open the Windows SBS Console, click Network and then click Devices. Right-click the printer and select Printer Properties.

2. Click the Sharing tab and then click the Additional Drivers button.

3. In the Additional Drivers dialog box, shown in Figure 13-7, select the check box next to any client drivers to be installed and then click OK. To install additional client drivers,

you need access to the installation files for the appropriate driver version either locally or across the network.

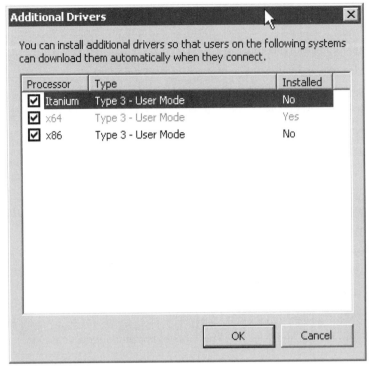

FIGURE 13-7 Selecting additional printer drivers to install

4. SBS will prompt you for the location of the appropriate drivers for the printer.

5. Click OK through the next dialog boxes to install the drivers.

Managing Printers from Windows SBS

To manage print jobs, open Windows SBS Console. Click Network and then click Devices. Right-click the printer you want to manage and select Printer Jobs from the shortcut menu. From there, you can choose to do any of the following tasks:

- To temporarily stop a *single* document from printing, right-click the selected document and choose Pause from the shortcut menu. To resume printing, right-click the document and choose Resume.

- To temporarily stop *all* documents from printing, choose Pause Printing from the Printer menu. To resume printing all documents, select Pause Printing a second time from the Printer menu.

- To cancel one or more print jobs, select the documents, right-click, and choose Cancel from the shortcut menu. (You can also cancel print jobs by selecting them and pressing the Delete key.)

- To cancel *all* print jobs in the print queue, choose Cancel All Documents from the Printer menu.

- To restart a print job (force the document to print from the beginning again), right-click the document and choose Restart from the shortcut menu.

- To change the priority of a print job, right-click the print job, choose Properties from the shortcut menu, and then use the Priority slider to adjust the priority of the document, with 1 being the lowest priority and 99 being the highest priority.

- To specify that a print job should be printed only during a certain period, right-click the print job, choose Properties from the shortcut menu, select the Only From option, and choose the time range to allow the document to print. This feature is useful when you want to set a large document to print only during a time when you anticipate the printer to be free.

Managing Printers from the Command Line

Windows SBS 2011 makes command-line administration almost practical for those who are so inclined. You can perform almost all administration tasks from a command line—printer tasks included. Use the following list of commands and scripts to get started:

- **Print**   Prints the specified text file to the specified printer.

- **Lpr**   Prints the specified text file to the specified LPD print queue.

- **Net print**   Displays information about the specified print queue or print job. It can also hold, release, or delete print jobs.

- **Lpq**   Displays information about the specified LPD print queue.

- **Net start**   Starts the specified service. You can use the Net start spooler and Net stop spooler commands to start or stop the spooler service.

- **Cscript %*Windir*%\System32\Printing_Admin_Scripts\en-US\Prrnmngr.vbs**
  Adds, deletes, or lists printers on a Windows print server.

- **Cscript %*Windir*%\System32\ Printing_Admin_Scripts\en-US\Prrnjobs.vbs**
  Lets you view and manage the print jobs of printer shares on a Windows print server.

- **Cscript %*Windir*%\System32\ Printing_Admin_Scripts\en-US\Prrncfg.vbs**
  Allows you to view and change the settings of printers on a Windows print server.

- **Cscript %*Windir*%\System32\ Printing_Admin_Scripts\en-US\Prrnqctl.vbs**
  Pauses or resumes printing, clears the print queue, or prints test pages.

- **Cscript %*Windir*%\System32\ Printing_Admin_Scripts\en-US\Prrnport.vbs**
  Administers all things related to printer ports.

- **Cscript %*Windir*%\System32\ Printing_Admin_Scripts\en-US\Prrndrvr.vbs**
  Adds, deletes, or lists printer drivers on a Windows print server.

> **NOTE** To view a list of parameters, type the command followed by /? at a command prompt.

Setting Security Options

Security options come into play when you have a range of printers that are separate but not at all equal. For example, you might not want everyone to print to the five-dollar-per-page, dye-sublimation printer purchased for the art staff. At a more down-to-earth level, security settings can preserve printer properties or printing priorities from unauthorized changes.

To set permissions on a printer, right-click the printer, choose Printer Properties, and then use the Security tab to assign permissions to groups of users. Click Advanced to exert finer control over permissions or to enable auditing. You can view the results of the audit settings in the security log.

A printer has three levels of permissions: Print, Manage Documents, and Manage Printers. These are defined as follows:

- **Print** Users or groups with Print permission can connect to the printer; print documents; and pause, restart, or delete their own documents from the print queue. Windows, by default, grants members of the Everyone group the Print permission.
- **Manage Documents** Users or groups with Manage Documents permission have the Print permission along with the ability to change the settings for all documents in the print queue and to pause, restart, and delete any user's documents from the print queue. Windows grants the Creator/Owner group the Manage Documents permission level by default.
- **Manage Printers** Users or groups with Manage Printers permission have the Manage Documents and Print permissions along with the ability to modify printer properties, delete printers, change printer permissions, and take ownership of printers.

Determining Printer Availability

To set up a printer to be available only during certain times—perhaps to discourage after-hours printing—complete the following steps:

1. In the SBS Console, right-click the printer you want to modify and select Printer Properties from the shortcut menu.
2. Click the Advanced tab, and then click Available From.
3. Select the earliest and latest times the printer is to be available to users, and then click OK.

Group Priorities and Printer Availability

Changing printer availability as just described changes the printer use times for everyone and makes no further restrictions. With a few additional steps, you can set up a printer so that print jobs submitted by some users print before jobs submitted by other users; for example, you can give priority to managers or groups with tight deadlines. You can also reserve a printer for exclusive use by certain groups during certain times; for example, you can reserve a printer outside of normal business hours so that the groups you specify can print large, high-priority print jobs.

To control availability or group priority, create two or more logical printers for a single physical printer, give each logical printer a different priority and/or make it available at different times, and give different sets of users or groups permission to print to each logical printer.

Creating a Logical Printer

To create a logical printer, follow these steps:

1. Select Control Panel from the Start menu. Under Hardware, click View Devices And Printers.

2. From the File menu, select Add A Printer.

> **NOTE** If the menu bar isn't visible in the Printers window, press Alt to display it.

3. In the Add Printer dialog box, select Add A Local Or Network Printer As An Administrator.

4. In the next Add Printer dialog box, select Add A Local Printer.

5. In the Choose A Printer Port dialog box, click Use An Existing Port, select the port that the physical printer is on, and then click Next.

6. In the Install The Printer Driver dialog box, choose the manufacturer name from the list on the left and the printer model from the list on the right. Click Next.

7. Choose the version of the driver you want to use and click Next.

8. Give the printer a name that describes its function or who uses it. Click Next.

9. In the Printer Sharing dialog box, provide the location and additional comments if wanted. Click Next.

Configuring Usage of the Logical Printer

When the logical printer exists, you next configure how it is used and by whom. Open Control Panel and follow these steps:

1. Under Hardware, select View Printers And Devices.

2. Right-click the logical printer and select Printer Properties.

3. Click the Security tab, and assign permissions to the users or groups that will have special access to this printer.

4. Click the Advanced tab (shown in Figure 13-8). If the logical printer is to be available only at certain times, select Available From and set the times.

5. To change the priority of the users and groups that use this logical printer, type a number in the Priority list box. The priority range goes from 1, which is the lowest priority, to 99, which is the highest priority.

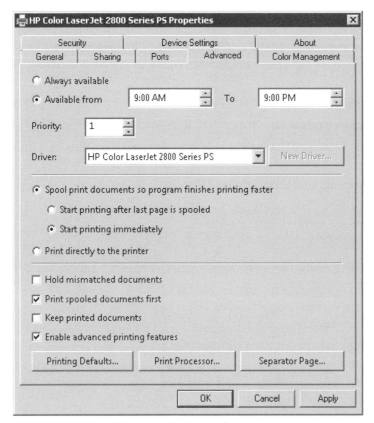

FIGURE 13-8 Advanced printer settings

6. Click OK, and repeat the process for all other logical printers you created for the printer.

Viewing the Logical Printer in the SBS Console

As when installing a new printer, the logical printer might not automatically appear in the list of network devices in the Windows SBS Console. If this is the case when you view the Printers list, first click Refresh This View in the Tasks pane. If the printer still doesn't appear, follow these steps:

1. Click List A Shared Printer In This Console, and browse to the printer as shown in Figure 13-9.

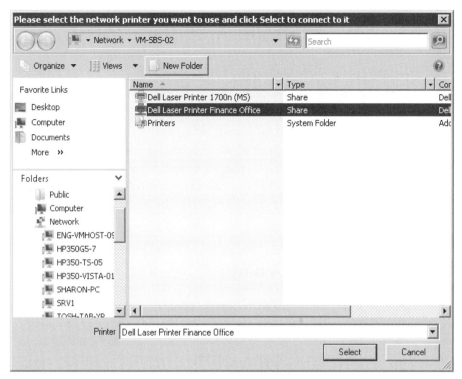

FIGURE 13-9 Selecting a printer to show in the Console

2. Click Select and then click OK.

3. In the Windows SBS Console, click Refresh This View in the Tasks list. The printer appears in the list of printers.

Setting Up a Printer Pool

A printer pool consists of multiple printers sharing a single driver and appears as a single printer to users. The advantage of using a printer pool is that clients don't need to look for an available printer; they simply print to the single logical printer on the print server, which then sends the print job to the first available printer. Administration of the printers is also simplified because all printers in the printer pool are consolidated under one driver. If you modify the properties for the single logical printer, all physical printers in the printer pool use the same settings.

To set up a printer pool, complete the following steps:

1. Select Control Panel from the Start menu. Under Hardware, select View Printers And Devices.

2. Right-click the first printer to be part of the pool and select Printer Properties.

3. Click the Ports tab.

4. Select the Enable Printer Pooling check box.

5. To add printers to the printer pool, select the ports to which the additional printers are connected.

> **IMPORTANT** All printers in a printer pool must be able to use the same printer driver. If they are not identical printer models, you can sometimes achieve this by careful selection of a printer driver that will support an acceptable level of functionality for several different but related printers.

Configuring Print Spooling

Print spooling, or storing a print job on disk before printing, affects the actual printing speed as well as how clients perceive printing performance. You can change the way print spooling works to correct printing problems or to hold printed documents in the printer queue for repeated printing. To change the spool settings for a printer, right-click the printer you want to modify and select Printer Properties.

Click the Advanced tab to modify the spool settings. The following list describes the print spool settings on the Advanced tab:

- **Spool Print Documents So Program Finishes Printing Faster**   Spools the print documents to the print server, freeing the client to perform other tasks more quickly.

- **Start Printing After Last Page Is Spooled**   Ensures that the entire document is available to the printer when printing begins. This step might correct some printing problems, and it also helps high-priority documents print before low-priority documents.

- **Start Printing Immediately**   Select this option to reduce the time it takes to print a document.

- **Print Directly To The Printer**   Turns off spooling, causing a performance hit on the server (though it might fix some printing problems).

- **Hold Mismatched Documents**   Holds documents in the queue that don't match the current printer settings (for example, documents that require legal-size paper when letter paper is currently in the printer). Other documents in the print queue are unaffected by held documents.

- **Print Spooled Documents First** Prints the highest-priority document that is already spooled first, ahead of higher-priority documents that are still spooling. This step speeds overall printer throughput by keeping the printer from waiting for documents.

- **Keep Printed Documents** Keeps a copy of print jobs in the printer queue in case users need to print the document again. In this circumstance, the user can resubmit the document directly from the queue rather than printing from her application a second time.

- **Enable Advanced Printing Features** Enables metafile spooling and printer options such as page order, booklet printing, and pages per sheet (if available on the printer). Disable this when you're experiencing printer problems.

Using the Fax Service

As long as you have an email address and a scanner, you have no need for a fax machine or a fax modem. Ninety percent of faxes are documents generated by your computer and can therefore be sent by email. Other types of documents can be easily scanned, saved as a file and...sent by email.

If you must send faxes to recipients with fax numbers but no email, you can use an Internet-based fax service for a few dollars per month.

If you *do* need to send and receive faxes, Windows 2011 offers a way to send, receive, and manage them. This section describes how to use the fax tools.

Adding a Fax Modem

To start and configure the fax service, you must first install a fax modem. Attach the fax modem to the computer and to the phone line and then follow these steps:

1. Open Control Panel, and select Phone And Modem Options.

> **NOTE** If Phone And Modem Options is not visible, click View By and select Large Icons.

2. In the Phone And Modem Options dialog box, click the Modems tab and then click Add to start the Add Hardware Wizard.

3. Follow the instructions on the Install New Modem page. Windows will automatically detect the modem you have attached unless you select the Don't Detect My Modem check box. Click Next.

4. If Windows does not detect your modem, select the type of modem from the Install New Modem dialog box (shown in Figure 13-10). Click Next.

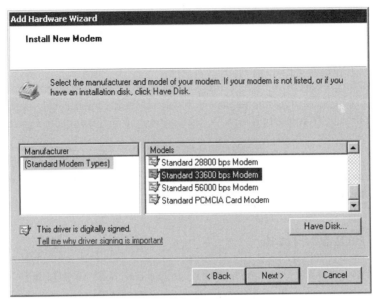

FIGURE 13-10 Designating the type of modem to install

5. Select the port(s) for the modem. Click Next.

6. Windows installs the modem and notifies you of the successful installation. Click Finish.

Starting and Configuring the Fax Service

When a fax modem has been installed, you can start and configure the fax service. Open the Windows SBS Console, click Network, click Devices, and then follow these steps:

1. In the Tasks pane, click Start The Fax Service.

2. In the next dialog box (shown in Figure 13-11), you're advised that the fax service is started but not configured. Click Yes to start the configuration process.

FIGURE 13-11 Click Yes to run the Configure Fax Service Wizard

3. Enter your Organization's Name, Phone Number, Fax Number, and Address for the fax cover page. Click Next.

4. Enter the Fax Header Text that will print on faxes you send. (See Figure 13-12.) Click Next.

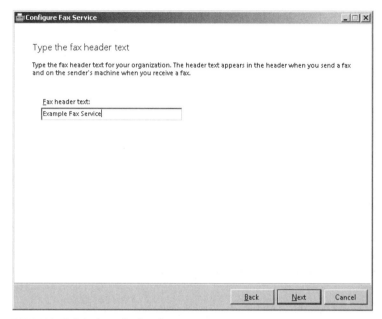

FIGURE 13-12 Entering a fax header

5. Select the modem to use for sending faxes. (If you install multiple modems, you can dedicate some to sending and others to receiving, if needed.) Click Next.

6. Select the modem to use for receiving faxes. In the case of multiple modems, you can configure different delivery options for different modems. Click Next.

7. The following four options are available for routing incoming faxes. (See Figure 13-13.) You can use any or all of them.

- **Route Through E-mail** Deliver faxes to the email address or addresses specified.
- **Store In A Document Library** Deliver faxes to a document storage area of your internal website.
- **Print** Route all faxes to a specified printer.
- **Store In A Folder** Deliver all faxes to a specified folder.

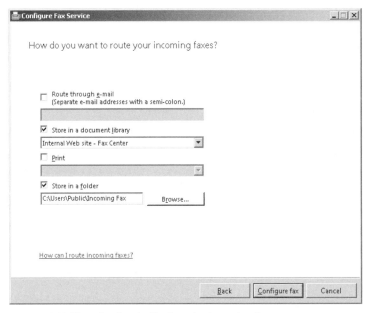

FIGURE 13-13 Choosing the destinations for incoming faxes

8. Click Configure Fax when you've made your selections.

Managing Fax Users and Administrators

By default, all users are added to the Windows SBS Fax users group. To change membership in this group, open the Windows SBS Console, select Network, and then select Devices. In the Tasks pane, select Configure The Windows SBS Fax Users Group.

Select Add Or Remove to change the membership. Click E-mail to add an email address specifically for this group.

Similarly, you can click Configure The Windows SBS Fax Administrator Group. By default, all administrators are members of this group. Click Add or Remove to change the membership of this group. Click E-mail to add an email address specifically for this group.

Summary

Printing is an essential service on any network. Aside from actual network failure, few things will generate as much unrest as the inability to print documents. In this chapter, we've covered the fundamentals of printer and fax administration, along with sufficient information on planning to keep your printing operations viable into the future. Next we move on to the equally critical subject of managing computers—and their users—on the network.

## CHAPTER 14

Managing Computers on the Network

Microsoft Windows Small Business Server (SBS) 2011 streamlines the client management process, making it easy to connect computers to the network and manage them from a single console.

When you connect a client computer to the SBS network, SBS automatically configures the computer for optimal operation in an SBS environment. Existing accounts on the computer are migrated to the users assigned to that computer, the Windows Firewall configuration is set to work properly on an SBS network, and the Internet Explorer home page is set to the internal website.

Connecting Computers to the Network

SBS supports the 32-bit and 64-bit versions of Windows XP Professional; the Business, Enterprise, and Ultimate editions of Windows Vista; and the Professional, Enterprise, and Ultimate editions of Windows 7. Windows Server 2003 and Windows Server 2008 are also supported, either as member servers or secondary domain controllers, but they can't be joined to the domain using the SBS wizards.

 REAL WORLD Domain Controllers

There has been a longstanding misunderstanding about additional domain controllers on an SBS network: many people believe that the main SBS server is the *only* domain controller allowed on an SBS network. This simply isn't true. You can have additional domain controllers on an SBS network. The only requirement is that these secondary domain controllers must not hold any of the Flexible Single Master Operations (FSMO, pronounced *fizmo*) roles. Those FSMO roles must all remain on the original SBS server.

With SBS 2011, this requirement becomes even clearer because the Premium Add-on of SBS 2011 includes a second copy of Windows Server 2008 R2 and the right to install it on the SBS network. You can use this second server to support Microsoft SQL Server (the default behavior) or to support Remote Desktop Services, including RemoteApps—or you can use it as a secondary domain controller.

Having a secondary domain controller *sounds* like a really good idea, but it can lead to complications when trying to recover from a catastrophic event. The primary reasons for having more than one domain controller (load balancing and geographic redundancy) make a lot of sense for a large organization, but really don't make much sense for most small businesses.

However, if you're supporting a remote site, such as a branch office, using a secondary domain controller is a very good idea. We like to take advantage of the new Read-Only Domain Controller (RODC), introduced in Windows Server 2008, for that branch office.

Creating Computer Accounts

Unlike previous versions of SBS, with SBS 2011 you don't need to create a computer account ahead of time. Instead, you (or the user of the computer) plug the computer into the SBS network, you're assigned an IP address from the DHCP server, and you're then joined to the SBS domain when you use the *http://connect* page to connect the client. Or you can manually run the Launcher.exe application from a USB key.

Before you try to connect a new computer to the network, first create the user account(s) that will have access to the computer. This simplifies the setup process for the computer account, and ensures that the correct user accounts are given permission to log on to the new computer.

Establishing Basic Network Connectivity

The first step in connecting a computer to an SBS network is to connect to the network and obtain a valid IP address. This process is pretty simple: plug the computer into an Ethernet switch on the network, and configure the system for Dynamic Host Control Protocol (DHCP). Wireless clients must first associate with an access point and provide a WPA key.

Configuring Windows 7, Windows Vista, and Windows Server 2008 to Use DHCP

By default, Windows 7, Windows Vista, and Windows Server 2008 will use DHCP to configure TCP/IP, and you shouldn't have to change anything. However, if the client has been set to use a fixed IP address, you can change it back to using DHCP by completing the following steps:

1. Open the Network Connections folder shown in Figure 14-1. The easiest way to get to this in Windows 7 and Windows Vista is to type ncpa.cpl in a command window or in the Search field on the Start menu.

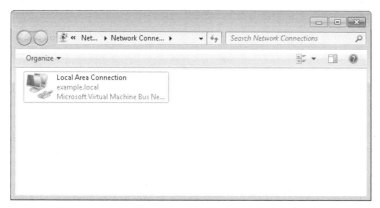

FIGURE 14-1 The Network Connections folder in Windows 7

2. Select the network card, and right-click to open the Action menu shown in Figure 14-2.

FIGURE 14-2 The Action menu for a network card

3. Select Properties to open the properties of the Local Area Connection, as shown in Figure 14-3.

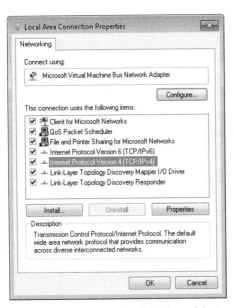

FIGURE 14-3 The Properties dialog box of the Local Area Connection

4. Select Internet Protocol Version 4 (TCP/IPv4), and click Properties to open the Internet Protocol Version 4 (TCP/IPv4) Properties page. Select Obtain An IP Address Automatically and Obtain DNS Server Address Automatically, as shown in Figure 14-4.

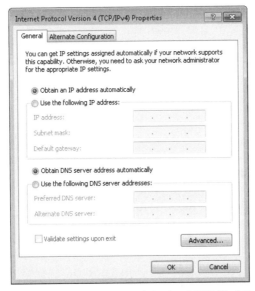

FIGURE 14-4 Internet Protocol Version 4 (TCP/IPv4) Properties page

5. Click OK and then click Close to configure the network connection to use DHCP.

For Windows Server 2008, the steps are much the same. If your server needs to have a fixed IP address, either provide a reservation in DHCP (preferred) or assign a static IP address that is within the same subnet range as your SBS server and that is excluded from the DHCP address range offered by SBS.

Configuring Windows XP and Windows Server 2003 to Use DHCP

By default, Windows XP (including x64 Edition) and Windows Server 2003 use DHCP to configure TCP/IP, and you shouldn't have to change anything. However, if the computer has been set to use a fixed IP address, you can change it back to using DHCP by completing the following steps:

1. In the Network Connections folder (available in Control Panel), right-click the appropriate network adapter (usually Local Area Connection) and choose Properties.

2. In the Local Area Connection Properties dialog box, select the Internet Protocol (TCP/IP) component, and click Properties to open the Internet Protocol (TCP/IP) Properties dialog box, shown in Figure 14-5.

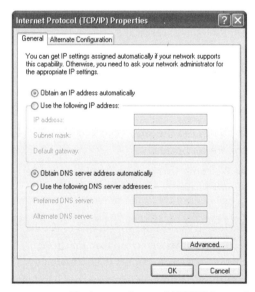

FIGURE 14-5 The Internet Protocol (TCP/IP) Properties dialog box in Windows XP

3. Verify that the Obtain An IP Address Automatically and Obtain DNS Server Address Automatically options are selected, and then click OK.

NOTE If your SBS environment includes more than one server, the secondary servers are good candidates for static IP addresses. If you use a static IP address, configure the server with an IP address in the excluded IP address range of 192.168.yyy.3 through 192.168.yyy.9 (where yyy is the subnet used by your SBS network), or add an appropriate exclusion in DHCP.

Using the Small Business Server Connect Computer Wizard

After you establish network connectivity and you've created the appropriate user accounts, the next steps in connecting a computer to an SBS network are to log on to the computer, open Internet Explorer or Firefox, and launch the Small Business Server Connect Computer Wizard by connecting to *http://connect*. This wizard configures the computer to run on the network by performing the following actions:

- Verifies that the computer meets minimum requirements to run on an SBS 2011 network
- Changes the computer's workgroup or domain membership to be a member of the SBS domain
- Configures the computer to automatically get updates from the SBS server
- Assigns users to the computer
- Optionally migrates existing local user profiles stored on the computer to new domain user profiles, preserving the data and settings of local user accounts
- Sets the browser home page to *http://companyweb*
- Enables Remote Web Access connections
- Configures the Windows Firewall
- Installs (but doesn't enable) the SBS Gadget if it's a Windows Vista or Windows 7 client
- Configures Group Policies on the client computer to align with SBS 2011

To use the Connect Computer Wizard from Internet Explorer or Firefox, follow these steps:

1. Log on to the computer you want to connect to the SBS network, and open your browser. Internet Explorer and Firefox are supported.

2. Browse to *http://connect* to open the Welcome To Windows Small Business Server 2011 Standard home page, as shown in Figure 14-6.

> **NOTE** If the computer you're trying to join to the SBS network doesn't meet the minimum requirements for joining, you'll see a different screen than that in Figure 14-6, with a description of the problem and possibly a link to correct it. One example is a Windows XP computer that doesn't have the Microsoft .NET Framework 2.0 installed. After you've corrected the deficiency, you can restart your browser and connect to the *http://connect* site to continue.

FIGURE 14-6 The Welcome To Windows Small Business Server 2011 Standard home page

3. Click Start Connect Computer Program to open the Launcher.exe application. You'll see a security warning as shown in Figure 14-7.

FIGURE 14-7 The File Download Security Warning for Launcher.exe

4. Click Run (and click Continue if you get a User Account Control prompt) to start the Connect Computer Wizard at the Choose How To Set Up This Computer page shown in Figure 14-8.

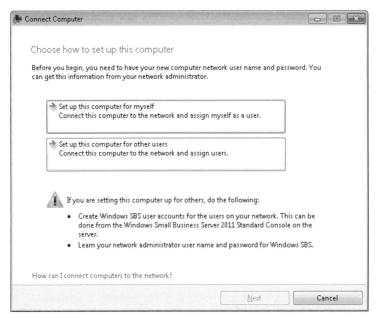

FIGURE 14-8 The Choose How To Set Up This Computer page of the Connect Computer Wizard

5. Select Set Up This Computer For Myself if you'll be the only user using this computer. Select Set Up This Computer For Other Users if this will be a shared computer, or if you're setting up another user's computer.

6. The Connect Computer Wizard verifies that the computer being connected meets minimum requirements and reports the success, as shown in Figure 14-9.

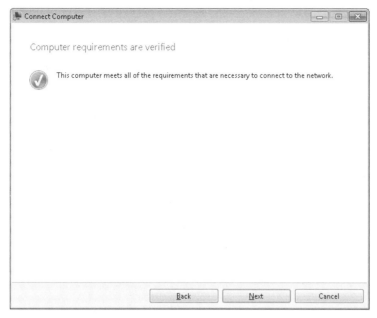

FIGURE 14-9 The Computer Requirements Are Verified page of the Connect Computer Wizard

7. Click Next to open the Type Your Network Administrator User Name And Password page of the Connect Computer Wizard. Enter the credentials for a Network Administrator account.

> **NOTE** This page will be slightly different if you've selected to set the computer up only for yourself. You'll need to type in your user name and your password.

8. Click Next to open the Verify The Name And Description Of This Computer page of the Connect Computer Wizard. Modify the name if required, and enter an optional description for the computer, as shown in Figure 14-10.

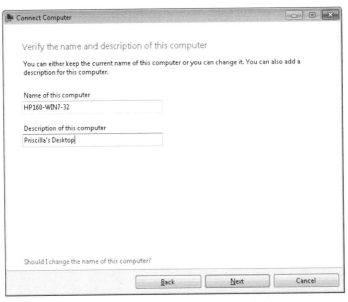

FIGURE 14-10 The Verify The Name And Description Of This Computer page of the Connect Computer Wizard

9. Click Next to open the Assign Users To This Computer page, as shown in Figure 14-11. Any Network Administrator accounts will already be assigned to the computer, automatically. Select additional users in the left pane, and click Add to assign them to the computer.

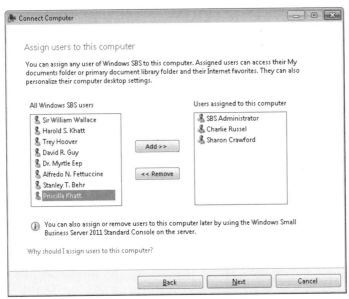

FIGURE 14-11 The Assign Users To This Computer page of the Connect Computer Wizard

10. Click Next to open the Move Existing User Data And Settings page, shown in Figure 14-12. Here you'll see a list of SBS user accounts that are assigned to the computer, with matching drop-down lists of accounts that can have their user data migrated to the new SBS account.

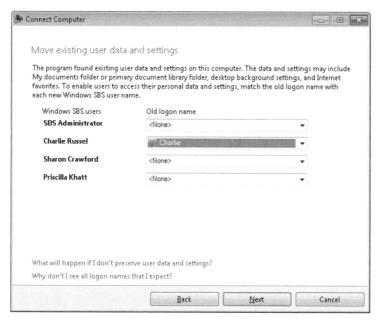

FIGURE 14-12 The Move Existing User Data And Settings page of the Connect Computer Wizard

11. Select the accounts to migrate, as shown in Figure 14-12, and click Next to open the Assign Level Of Computer Access For Users Of Windows SBS page shown in Figure 14-13. Here you assign the permission level *on the local computer* for the SBS domain account. By default, SBS Standard Users are assigned Standard User on their local computers as well, though in some scenarios you might choose to assign them Local Administrator privilege.

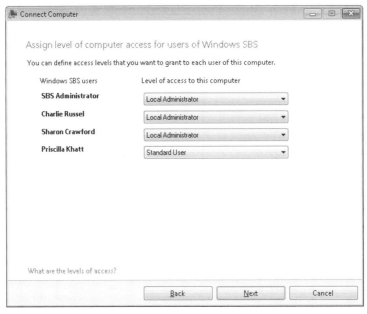

FIGURE 14-13 The Assign Level Of Computer Access For Users Of Windows SBS page of the Connect Computer Wizard

12. Click Next to open the Confirm User Data And Settings Selections page, and if everything is as you expected, click Next and then click Restart to begin the account migration and domain join. This process might require more than one reboot, but should proceed automatically.

13. When the Connect Computer Wizard is finished, log on and click Finish.

REAL WORLD Local Administrator Accounts

The SBS default is to create SBS standard users as only standard users on their local computers, and we think this is a very good idea. Most local users have no need to run with elevated privileges, and the security of your network is significantly improved if they don't. However, this can be a nuisance for some users who have a legitimate but only occasional need to do something that requires elevation. You could create those users as local administrators, but then that privilege is always available to them.

Another solution is to create all PCs with a generic local administrative account that the user can use. But this becomes either unwieldy to keep track of and administer, or too generic, giving users the ability to use that same password to log on to computers that aren't their own.

We think a better solution is to create one or more (depending on departmental needs and concerns) Standard User SBS domain accounts that can be assigned to individual PCs as local administrator.

These SBS Standard User accounts should be assigned only to PCs that have an actual need to occasionally elevate, and they should also be allowed to log on only during normal business hours, and only locally—no RWA access for these accounts. Passwords should be changed regularly.

Now when a user needs to elevate privilege to do something, you don't need to give the user access to an account that has domain administrator privileges. The user can elevate to this special account that is a local administrator, but only a domain user.

Connecting Alternate Clients

Windows Vista and Windows 7 business-class clients provide the best experience when running on a Windows Small Business Server 2011 network, especially Windows 7. Windows XP Professional can also be joined to the SBS network automatically using the *http://connect* wizard, but you should be aware that Windows XP is now on extended support and this will limit the availability of updates to only critical updates. Computers running Windows 2000 Professional, Mac OS/X, or even Linux can also connect to your SBS network. They won't have all the functionality of Windows 7 or Windows Vista, but they can be managed and used.

Connecting computers that don't meet the minimum requirements for using the Connect Computer Wizard is possible, but doing so requires you to manually configure and add the computers to the SBS domain and then manually assign users to the computer.

Manually Connecting Clients

To connect Windows 2000 or non-Windows clients to an SBS network, you need to manually join the domain and set the permissions and properties of the client. In the case of Windows 2000, we strongly recommend that you upgrade the computer to a newer version of Windows, at least Windows XP Professional SP3, or replace it entirely. Windows 2000 is no longer supported or available and will not receive even critical updates.

The process of connecting a nonsupported client to an SBS network varies depending on the operating system involved, but for Windows 2000 Professional, you need to manually join the domain and then configure accounts on the computer by following these steps:

1. Log on to the Windows 2000 client with a local administrative account.
2. Open System Properties by right-clicking My Computer and selecting Properties.

3. Click the Network Identification tab, and then click Properties to open the Identification Changes page shown in Figure 14-14.

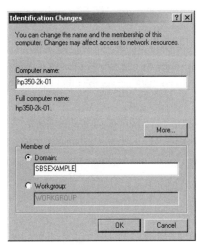

FIGURE 14-14 The Identification Changes page of the System Properties dialog box

4. Type the SBS domain name into the Domain field, and click OK.

5. In the Domain Username And Password dialog box, provide the user name and password of an SBS Network Administrator account and click OK.

6. Click OK three more times to acknowledge the welcome message and the reboot warning, and to close the System Properties dialog box. Click Yes to reboot the Windows 2000 computer.

7. When the computer restarts, log on to the computer with an SBS account to ensure that everything went as expected.

Older and non-Windows clients, with the exception of Windows 2000 Server, are not accessible from Remote Web Access because they don't support Remote Desktop.

Connecting Mac OS X Clients

Mac OS/X clients can function reasonably well on an SBS network. Mac OS/X 10.4 and later versions can connect correctly to an SBS 2011 network, and versions 10.2 and 10.3 can be made to connect, though you should upgrade your version of OS/X to 10.4 or later if at all possible.

Microsoft Office 2004 and newer versions work well with Microsoft Office documents from Windows clients, and the Mail client component of Office for Mac also works well with Microsoft Exchange. Plus the Outlook Web App that is part of Windows Small Business Server 2011 works well with Safari or Firefox on a Mac.

To connect to a Windows file share, follow these steps:

1. Configure the computer to obtain its IP address using DHCP, if it doesn't already do so.

2. Select Connect To Server from the Go menu of Finder.

3. In the Connect To Server window, browse to the computer or type the address of the Windows file share, using one of the following formats:

   smb://fullyqualifieddomainname/sharename

   smb://domain.name;servername/sharename

   For example, to connect to the Data share on the hp160-sbs-srv computer, type in

   smb://hp160-sbs-srv.example.local/Data

4. In the SMB/CIFS FilesystemAuthentication dialog box, verify the domain name, type in a Windows user name and password, and click OK.

Using Remote Desktop

The current version of the Remote Desktop Connection Client for Mac is 2.1, which is available as a free download from the Microsoft website at *http://www.microsoft.com/mac/remote-desktop-client*. This version supports multiple connections to Windows computers, including Windows 7 and Windows Server 2008 R2. Network Level Authentication and printing from Windows applications to Mac-connected printers are supported. But RemoteApps and RD Gateway are not, unfortunately.

Using Remote Web Access

Windows Small Business Server 2011 includes an updated version of Remote Web Access (RWA). This website gives the remote user access to email, her desktop at work, the internal website, and any RemoteApps–enabled remote applications that have been configured for RWA.

Connecting to RWA

Connecting to Remote Web Access doesn't require any special settings except that you need to be running Internet Explorer 6 or later for full functionality. The default location for RWA is *https://remote*.domainname.com, where *domainname.com* is replaced by your public Internet domain name.

When you connect to RWA, you're presented with a logon page like that shown in Figure 14-15.

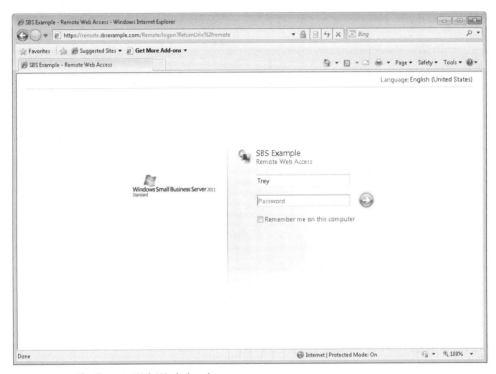

FIGURE 14-15 The Remote Web Workplace logon page

 UNDER THE HOOD **Two-Factor Authentication**

I f your network contains sensitive information—and whose doesn't these days—you should consider providing an additional layer of security beyond simple passwords. Windows Small Business Server 2011 sets reasonable password policies, but even the best of password policies is a balancing act between making the password difficult to crack and making it easy for users to remember and use so that they aren't tempted to write it down on the back of their keyboards. The four kinds of authentication methods or factors are

- Something you know (password)
- Something you have (token, or physical key)
- Something you are (biometric)
- Somewhere you are (location)

Of these, only the first three are realistic and usable in a small business environment, though the fourth—location—is starting to be used by banks as one factor to be sure that the person trying to access your bank account is actually you.

Passwords alone are a single-factor authentication method—in this case, something you know. Two-factor authentication requires two of the main three factors, and provides a definite improvement in the surety that the person authenticating to your network is really who he claims to be.

For a second authentication factor, we like the simplicity, moderate cost, and effectiveness of a one-time password (OTP). Generated automatically by a token you carry around with you, the combination of the token, a personal identification number (PIN), and your SBS password provides an additional level of security. Requiring at least users with administrative privilege (and we think *all* remote users) to use two-factor authentication is a good way to improve the overall security of the sensitive data on your network.

Third-party providers of OTP tokens include AuthAnvil (*http://www.authanvil.com*), CRYPTOCard (*http://www.cryptocard.com*), and RSA SecurID (*http://www.rsa.com*). Of these, only AuthAnvil is focused on the small business market, with a suite of products that are fully integrated into SBS, including RWWGuard, which replaces the logon page shown in Figure 14-15 with a new page that includes an additional field to directly enter your OTP. We use RWWGuard and AuthAnvil on our SBS network.

After you've logged on to RWA, you'll see the main RWA page shown in Figure 14-16. From here, you can connect to a computer on your SBS network, access shared folders on the network, log on to Outlook Web Access (by clicking Check Email), go to your internal home page, change your password, or, if you're logged on as an administrator, connect to a server to perform system maintenance.

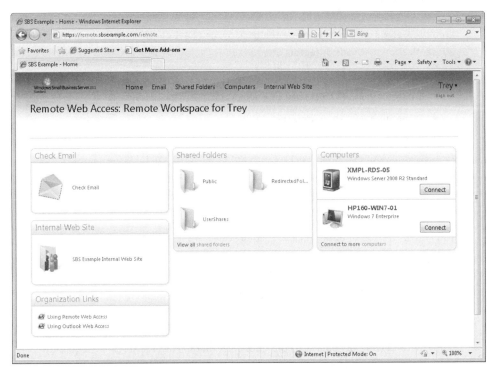

FIGURE 14-16 The main RWA landing page

You can customize this RWA landing page, even adding links to applications on your network using RemoteApps. We'll cover customization of this site in Chapter 20, "Managing Remote Access," and RemoteApps is covered in Chapter 26, "Adding a Terminal Server."

Managing Computers

You can manage the clients that are available on your network, along with many of the settings that control their availability and behavior, from the Windows SBS Console. To see a list of computers joined to your SBS domain, open the Windows SBS Console and click the Network button to open the Computers page, as shown in Figure 14-17.

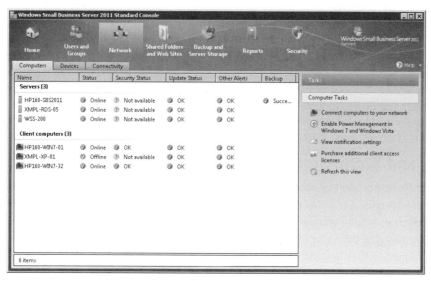

FIGURE 14-17 The Windows SBS Console Computers page

From the Computers page, you can see a quick status for the computers on your network: which are online, which need updates, and which have other problems or warnings. When you click a computer in the list, a new section of the Tasks pane opens showing you tasks you can perform that are specific to the computer selected, as shown in Figure 14-18 where we've selected computer HP160-WIN7-01.

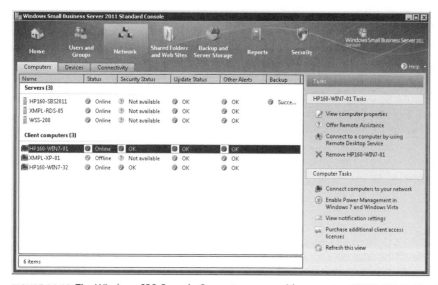

FIGURE 14-18 The Windows SBS Console Computers page with computer HP160-WIN7-01 selected

From here, you can offer remote assistance, connect directly to the computer using Remote Desktop (if the computer supports Remote Desktop), view the properties of the computer, check on update and other security-related status, and even remove the computer from the domain.

If there are problems with a client computer, you can select the computer and then click the Go To Security or Go To Updates links in the Tasks pane to navigate to the appropriate page of the Windows SBS Console.

Viewing and Modifying Client Computer Settings

To view or modify the properties and settings of a client computer in SBS, select the computer in the Windows SBS Console Computers page, as shown in Figure 14-18, and click View Computer Properties in the Tasks pane to open the Properties dialog box for the computer. From here, you can view the name of the computer, set the description of it, view the status of updates assigned to the computer, and control who has remote access to the computer.

To set the remote access to the computer, follow these steps:

1. Open the Windows SBS Console Computers page, and click the computer you want to change the remote access for in the left pane.
2. Click View Computer Properties in the Tasks pane.
3. Click User Access in the left pane of the Properties page, as shown in Figure 14-19.

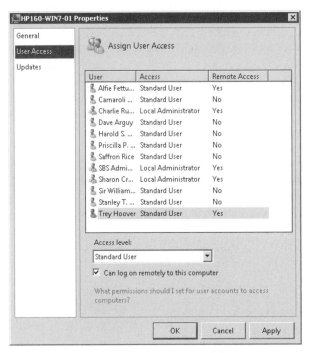

FIGURE 14-19 The Assign User Access page of the Computer Properties dialog box

4. Select the user you want to assign, modify, or remove access from, and then choose the level of access the user will have on the computer from the Access Level drop-down list.

5. Select the Can Log On Remotely To This Computer check box if the user should be allowed to log on over RWA or from a local Remote Desktop session.

6. Click OK to close the wizard.

 UNDER THE HOOD **Controlling Local Access to a Computer**

The SBS wizards allow you to control only remote access to a computer. Any SBS user with physical access to the computer can log on locally with at least Standard User privilege. This is not restricted by SBS in any way, despite what the help files appear to indicate. We think this is a mistake, and one that we frankly don't understand—especially because the fix to directly control who has access to a computer is fairly easy. So we wrote a little script to do it. This script uses Windows PowerShell to directly edit the ADSI properties for a user account, enabling access to specific computers. If a computer isn't explicitly granted access, it is denied after this script is run.

```
# Script Name: set-comprestrict.ps1
# ModHist: 12/07/08 - Initial
#              : 02/08/10 - Updated for SBS 2011
#
#  Script to restrict a user to one or more computers on an SBS 2011
network
#     Expects: two parameters--
#         logon name (sAMAccountName)
#         client computer names (in a quoted, comma separated list)
#
#  With Thanks to Richard Siddaway (Microsoft MVP) for his help.


# Copyright 2011 by Charlie Russel and Sharon Crawford. All rights
reserved.
#   You may freely use this script in your own environment, modifying it
to meet
#   your needs. But you may not re-publish it without permission.
#


param($UserName, $comp)
$_OU="ou=SBSUsers,ou=Users,ou=MyBusiness,dc=Example,dc=local"
$searchOU=[ADSI]"LDAP://$_OU"
$searcher= New-Object System.DirectoryServices.DirectorySearcher
$searchOU
```

```
$searcher.filter = "(&(objectClass=User)(sAMAccountName=$UserName))"

$userResult = $searcher.FindOne()
$user = $userResult.GetDirectoryEntry()

$user.userWorkstations = $comp
"Restricting user account: $UserName to clients: $comp"

$user.SetInfo()
"Computer access for $user has been updated."
```

You'll need to run this script, which is on the companion CD, from an elevated Pow-erShell console.

Another solution is to use the native Active Directory Users And Computer console. For more on using the native tools, including when you should and should not use them, see Chapter 17, "Windows SBS Console vs. Server Manager." But the short answer is always use the Windows SBS Console if at all possible. Only use the native Server Manager consoles when you're really sure there's no other way to achieve the desired end result.

Remotely Managing Computers

Network Administrators can remotely manage a computer from the Windows SBS Console, either offering remote assistance to the currently logged-on user or directly connecting to the computer over Remote Desktop.

Offering Remote Assistance

One way of managing computers remotely is by directly helping users to perform their tasks. Remote Assistance gives the Network Administrator a way to share the session of a user on a Windows XP or Windows Vista computer. It is not available on down-level Windows computers such as Windows 2000 Professional, or on non-Windows computers.

When you share a session using Remote Assistance, both the user and the Network Administrator see the same thing and both can interact with the session using both keyboard and mouse.

To offer Remote Assistance, follow these steps:

1. Open the Windows SBS Console if it isn't already open.

2. Click the Network button, and then select the computer you want to offer Remote Assistance to.

3. Click Offer Remote Assistance from the Tasks pane. If you haven't disabled the warning, you'll see a reminder that you need to make sure the user you want to help is logged on, as shown in Figure 14-20.

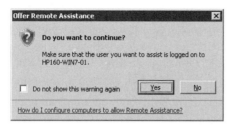

FIGURE 14-20 Warning before remote assistance is offered

4. Click Yes. The user logged on to the computer you're offering assistance to is prompted to let you share her session, as shown in Figure 14-21.

FIGURE 14-21 Windows Remote Assistance offer

5. If the user accepts the offer by clicking Yes, her desktop will be shared back to the SBS server console, and both screens will have the Remote Assistance toolbar displayed, as shown in Figure 14-22.

FIGURE 14-22 The Remote Assistance toolbar is displayed on both screens on top of the user's desktop

6. When the Remote Assistance session has accomplished its task, either user can click the Disconnect button in the Remote Assistance toolbar to end the session.

Connect Remotely

Remote management tasks that can't be easily accomplished in a Remote Assistance session, or that need to be performed when no user is logged on to the remote computer, often needed to be performed by physically going to the computer and logging on with the administrator's account. A major nuisance, certainly. With the inclusion of Remote Desktop in business-focused editions of Windows, administrators have an alternative—a Remote Desktop session. When you join a computer to the SBS domain using *http://connect*, one of the settings that is propagated to the new client is to enable Remote Desktop on the computer.

Although it's easy enough to directly connect to a remote computer using either the Remote Desktop link in the All programs, Accessories folder of the Start Menu or from the command line using mstsc.exe, the Windows SBS Console gives you direct access from the console. Just highlight the computer in the Computers page of the Windows SBS Console and click Connect To A Computer Using Terminal Services in the Tasks pane. You'll see a prompt for the connection credentials to use, as shown in Figure 14-23, and then a full-screen Remote Desktop session opens.

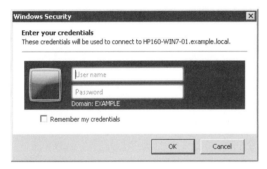

FIGURE 14-23 Remote Desktop credentials prompt

If there is an active session on the remote computer, you'll get a warning that the other user will be disconnected from the session. Unlike with Remote Assistance, you can't share a Remote Desktop session to a client computer. (The exception to this is that Remote Desktop connections to Terminal Server sessions can be shared, if necessary.)

The only real problem with using the Windows SBS Console to initiate a Remote Desktop session is that it will always be a full-screen session. That's fine for some things, but it can be a nuisance if you're trying to do the same task on multiple client computers. In that event, we like to use the command line:

```
mstsc /v:<computername> /h:<height> /w:<width>
```

So, to open three Remote Desktop sessions, each with a resolution of 1024x768, to the computers hp160-win7-01, xmpl-vista64-01, and hp160-v32-03, a simple PowerShell command line will get the job done:

```
PSH> $RDP_Array = "hp160-win7-01", "xmpl-vista64-01", "hp160-v32-03"

PSH> foreach ($computer in $RDP_Array) {mstsc /v:$computer /h:768 /w:1024}
```

NOTE You can easily use a combination of hard file links and the PowerShell code just shown to create a smart script that lets you log in to a machine simply by entering its name from the PowerShell command line. My current version has two dozen hard links to the same PowerShell script.

Removing Computers from the Network

You should remove computers from the network only if the computers are being decommissioned. When you remove a computer from the network, you make any SBS user accounts on the computer unavailable, and even if you later rejoin the computer to your SBS domain, new user profiles will be created and the old ones will be unavailable. If you do have to temporarily have a user use a computer without being part of the domain, you can usually just create a local user account on the computer and have the user log on to that account.

If circumstances require you to remove a computer from the domain and you want to save some of the settings for an existing account, use the Windows Easy Transfer (WET) Wizard, or with Windows XP, the Files And Settings Transfer Wizard. This won't save everything, but it will save many of the current user's settings.

To remove a computer from the SBS domain, follow these steps:

1. Open the Windows SBS Console if it isn't already open.

2. Click the Network button, and then select the computer you want to remove from the SBS domain.

3. Click Remove *Computername* in the Tasks pane.

4. When prompted, as shown in Figure 14-24, click Yes to remove the computer.

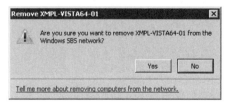

FIGURE 14-24 The Remove Computer warning message

Summary

In this chapter, we covered the basic management tasks available for individual computers on the network. Windows Small Business Server 2011 simplifies many of them by automating tasks and ensuring that computers meet the necessary requirements before they join the SBS network. In addition, by making both Remote Assistance and Remote Desktop directly available from the Windows SBS Console, the Network Administrator has direct access to computers for management and assistance.

In the next chapter, we'll cover the details of setting up and managing software updates to your Windows computers on your SBS network.

CHAPTER 15

Managing Software Updates

Software updates, or patches in the common parlance, are something that everyone hates, but they have become a basic part of life in the modern computing world. We hated them and complained about them when we were UNIX system administrators some 20 years ago, and we still hate them, even though the overall process of obtaining, testing, and applying them has improved greatly. We doubt that anything we can say will make you like patches any better than we do, but in this chapter we'll try to cover the basics to make the patch-management process as straightforward and manageable as possible. We'll cover how Microsoft Windows Small Business Server (SBS) 2011 uses Windows Server Update Services (WSUS) to enable a fully integrated software update management solution for SBS networks.

 REAL WORLD **Terminology**

The first rule of *patches* is that Microsoft doesn't like that word. Microsoft uses several different terms, each with a slightly different meaning, but the reality is that to the rest of the world, they're still called patches. We call them patches, the magazines and newspapers call them patches, even most Microsoft employees call them patches, unless they're giving a formal presentation. So throughout this chapter, that's what we'll call them. But Microsoft does have official terminology, and we should all be clear on what it is:

- **Critical update**   A generally available fix for a critical but non-security-related bug. A critical update has an accompanying Knowledge Base article.

- **Security update**   A generally available fix for a security vulnerability. Security updates have an accompanying Knowledge Base article and a Security Bulletin.

- **Software update**   A broad term that covers service packs, hotfixes, update rollups, security updates, feature packs, and so on. A software update has an accompanying Knowledge Base article.

- **Service pack**   A generally available collection of fixes and feature enhancements. Service packs are cumulative and contain all currently available updates, update rollups, security updates, critical updates, and hotfixes, and they might contain fixes for problems that were found internally and have not been otherwise released. Service packs also sometimes add new features (Microsoft Windows XP SP2, for example).
- **Hotfix**   A narrowly available fix for a specific issue. Hotfixes are generally available only through Microsoft Product Support Services and cannot be redistributed. Hotfixes are not tested as thoroughly as updates, update rollups, or service packs.
- **Update**   A generally available fix for a specific, non-security-related, noncritical problem. An update has an accompanying Knowledge Base article.
- **Update rollup**   A generally available and tested collection of hotfixes, security updates, critical updates, and updates that are packaged together. An update rollup has an accompanying Knowledge Base article.

See? All sorts of terms and terminology and not one of them includes the word "patch." For complete, up-to-date details on Microsoft update terminology, see *http://support.microsoft.com/kb/824684*.

Why Patching Is Important

In the old days, when your network wasn't connected to the Internet, system administrators were the only people who installed software, and users had only a green screen terminal, deciding when to apply a patch was a fairly straightforward decision. If you were having a specific problem and you wanted a bit of overtime on the weekend, you came in and applied a patch. If no one was complaining and you didn't want to work on the weekend, you threw the tape (patches always came on tapes in those days) in the drawer and waited until you had to come in on the weekend for some other maintenance, or users started complaining about a problem that seemed related. Or you simply never got around to it at all.

Even in the more recent past it was possible to have a more considered and gradual approach to applying patches. When a vulnerability was identified, it often took months before there was any real risk to your network.

Today that approach simply won't work, as Code Red, Nimda, Slammer, and others have all too clearly demonstrated. Within hours or (at most) days of the release of a critical security update, there will almost certainly be sample exploit code posted on the Internet, telling anyone and everyone how to exploit the vulnerability. If you ignore critical security updates, you place your entire SBS network—and the data stored on it—at risk.

Applying software updates is only one part of a defense-in-depth strategy to protect your network, but it's a critical part. Don't neglect it.

In the old days, patches—especially security updates,—were released whenever a new vulnerability was identified and corrected. When that happened a few times a year, it wasn't a big problem, and the system administrator dealt with each patch as it came out. In most cases, you could just wait until the Service Pack came out and deal with a whole bunch of them at once. But as more and more security updates and critical updates were released on an almost daily basis, it became increasingly difficult to properly test and identify all the patches that were necessary for your system. The whole process became a serious impediment to productivity and security.

In direct response to many, many complaints, Microsoft moved to a monthly update release process. Unless there is a compelling and immediate need for a critical security update to be released off-cycle, all security updates are released once a month, on the second Tuesday of the month. This change has greatly simplified the planning and deployment of patches.

The Patching Cycle

There are (or there should be) four basic phases in the ongoing cycle of maintaining a well-patched, up-to-date network:

- Assess
- Identify
- Evaluate and plan
- Deploy

Each of these phases is essential to the successful management of updates on your network. And in a typical well-run enterprise network, each of these phases is quite formal and carefully delineated.

Given the relative simplicity of SBS networks, and the more realistic IT budgets and resources we have, you're going to have to combine and simplify the overall process a bit, and you'll probably even bypass phases on occasion. However, it's good to have an understanding of the phases and to think through the steps involved in each one, even if you're combining them. In the following sections, we'll cover each of the phases of the full patching cycle, and then provide an "SBS Version" subsection that provides a realistic description of the phase for an SBS network. Obviously, there is no single SBS version—the resources and requirements of an SBS network of 50 users are a good deal different from those of 5 users.

Assess

The *assess* phase of patch management is all about understanding what your environment is, where and how it is vulnerable and can be attacked, and what resources and procedures are in place to reduce those vulnerabilities.

When a patch is released, you can't make an informed decision about whether you need to install that patch unless you first know what software is present in your environment and what your critical business assets are that absolutely, positively must be protected. So the first step to an overall patch management process is to figure out what software you're running in your environment. All of it, we hope. Whether you build a spreadsheet, have a Microsoft Office Access database, or just a keep it all in a chart in Microsoft Office Word, you need to get your software environment audited and documented.

Identify your critical business assets. Is there confidential data that you couldn't function without? Are there critical systems that must be available at all times? Are there individuals whose productivity is mission-critical? All of these are business assets that you should factor into your overall patch management strategy.

The next part of the assessment phase is to understand what security threats and vulnerabilities you currently have. Do you have legacy Windows systems that are no longer supported? Are there non-Windows systems that aren't being fully monitored and updated automatically?

Are you running old versions of software programs that can't be easily updated or replaced? Do you have public-facing web servers that are not behind your firewall? What are your security policies and how are they enforced? These and many, many more questions need to be asked—and answered.

Finally, you need to assess your patching infrastructure and resources. How do you deploy software and patches now? Who is responsible for identifying, testing, and deploying patches? What resources are available to help with that? How rapidly can you respond to a critical vulnerability that affects your systems? What steps can you take to improve your response time?

SBS Version

If all that seems a bit much, it's really just a lot of somewhat formal words to say that you need to know what software is running on your network and how it is updated. It's also good to have a record of what kinds of patches have caused trouble for you in the past—when you see new patches that affect these areas, you'll probably want to do some additional testing before you send the patch out.

Identify

The *identify* phase is about finding out what software updates or patches are available, and how critical it is that they be deployed in your environment. You need to take the following actions:

- Discover the patch.
- Decide whether it's relevant to your environment.
- Download the patch.
- Identify the patch's criticality.

There are many ways to discover patches, but for Microsoft products one of the best ways is to sign up for email alerts. If you do this, Microsoft will send you notifications of security updates before they are actually released. The signup page is at *http://www.microsoft.com/ technet/security/bulletin/notify.mspx*. You can tailor the notification method and detail level to suit your environment.

> **NOTE** This link provides alerts only for security-related patches.

Whatever method you use to discover patches, it's important that you have a way to trust the source of the patch information. All Microsoft security update alerts are signed with a publicly available PGP key, for example. And it shouldn't be necessary to say this, but just in case: Microsoft will never send a security update as an attachment to an email! Never.

> **IMPORTANT** Wait, maybe you missed that. Again, for emphasis: Microsoft will *never send a security update as an attachment to an email! Never.*

Once you know about a patch, you need to decide whether it's relevant to your environment. If all your client computers are running Windows 7 (and they should be!), a patch that applies only to Windows XP isn't really relevant to your environment. However, if the patch is a critical security update for Microsoft Office 2010 and you run that in your environment, you'll need to apply it.

When you determine that a patch is relevant to your environment, you need to obtain the patch from a known and trusted source. For a Microsoft patch, this generally means downloading it directly from Microsoft. With SBS, this means letting WSUS download the patch by synchronizing, but we'll get to the gory details of WSUS later. Find the relevant Knowledge Base article for the patch, and then cut and paste the link to the download page directly into your browser. Do not click the link in an email to get your patch. Even when you have verified that the email is really from Microsoft and is a legitimate email, you shouldn't click the links. Get into the habit of always using cut and paste. When you use cut and paste to put a link into your browser, you greatly reduce the likelihood of a phishing attack—being unknowingly redirected to a site that looks exactly like the site you expected to go to, but is actually a site designed to steal information from you or download unwanted spyware onto your computer.

After you've downloaded the patch and read the associated Knowledge Base article, you are in a position to determine just how critical the patch is in your environment. Is this a patch that needs to be deployed immediately, with limited testing—or even with no testing? Or are there ameliorating factors that allow the patch to be deployed as part of a regular patching schedule after full testing?

SBS Version

Again, if that seemed a bit much, you're probably right. But it's actually what we had to go through before the R2 version of SBS 2003 if we didn't have some method—usually third-party—to automatically download and identify patches for our environment. With the R2 release of SBS 2003, we were able to let WSUS take care of the downloads and the initial analysis. SBS 2011 extends that to fully support WSUS version 3, but you'll still want to do some thinking before you let it fire off an automatic update to every client in the network.

Evaluate and Plan

The *evaluate and plan* phase of patch management flows naturally out of the identify phase, and in many ways is an extension of it. In this phase, you determine how to respond to the software update you've downloaded. Is it critical, or even necessary? How should it be deployed? And to whom? Should interim countermeasures be employed that will minimize your exposure to the vulnerability? What priority does the patch have?

The initial determination of need, suitability, and priority is made during the identify phase, but in the evaluate and plan phase, you should take a closer look at the patch. What priority is the patch? If it affects a critical business asset and there's no easy or appropriate countermeasure except the patch, it will have a higher priority for testing and deployment than if there's a simple countermeasure that you can implement until the patch can be deployed. If it targets critical business assets, it's going to have a higher priority than if the only computers that are affected are several old Windows 2000 computers that aren't running any critical business applications. (But you got rid of those old Windows 2000 computers, right?)

After you've identified the priority of the patch, you need to plan the actual deployment. Which computers need to have the patch deployed to them? Are there any constraints or issues that interfere with the deployment? Who needs to be notified, and what steps need to be taken so that the deployment minimizes the disruption to the environment? If this is an emergency release, will it go through a staged deployment, or is every affected computer going to have the patch deployed as soon as possible?

SBS Version

In any SBS network larger than a few clients, you should have a couple of clients that are designated canaries. In all but emergency-patch situations, these computers will have the new patches deployed to them first. If they survive the patch without major issues, you can OK the deployment onto the rest of your clients.

Unfortunately, WSUS—as included with SBS 2011—doesn't support having a special group of client computers that are treated differently from other clients. The workaround we've found is to have one (or two) users who go directly to Microsoft Update every Patch Tuesday and update their computers. This gets the update onto their computers quicker than any other method and allows some testing time before any automatic deployment can happen. If you go this route, choose a user who has a fairly typical computer and, most important, who is willing to take on this role. Also, make sure that you carefully review the "Caveats" section of the Security Bulletin. This section details known issues and interactions that you should be aware of.

Deploy

The *deployment* phase of patch management is in many ways the easiest phase. You've done all your preparatory work; now all you need to do is the actual deployment.

First and foremost, communicate. Let everyone who will be affected know that you will be deploying a patch, and what application or area of the operating system it affects. If you know that the deployment will cause changes in behavior, tell your users before the deployment. You'll have far fewer support calls if you've warned people that a certain behavior is expected than if you surprise them.

SBS Version

With SBS, we have WSUS to do the deployment and track its progress. If your canary user has survived, you should proceed with the deployment. But the same rule applies as for a really large enterprise—communicate. If users have open files and SBS automatically deploys an update that requires a reboot, they could potentially lose work. Sending a reminder email to your users on Patch Tuesday is a good idea.

Repeat

After you've deployed a patch, the process starts over again. It really is a continuous process—or it should be. At a minimum, verify that the patch has been successfully deployed to the affected computers. Update your software map and database so that you know which computers have had the patch applied. Because our assumption is that every patch is on every computer, we only keep track of the exceptions. When a patch cycle is complete, we make a note of any issues, confirm that deployment has been successful, and get ready for the next round.

Using SBS Software Updates

SBS includes a customized and configured version of Windows Server Update Services (WSUS). The SBS team has already done the heavy lifting to get WSUS configured and working optimally for SBS networks. When the SBS install is finished, updates are already being managed and deployed, but you can do additional customization from the Updates page of the Windows SBS Console.

Configuring Software Update Settings

The default software update settings for SBS 2011 are adequate for most small businesses, but there are additional settings you can use to customize how updates are handled on your network. You can

- Change the update level for servers and clients.
- Change the update schedule.
- Change which computers are managed by WSUS.

> **NOTE** For those familiar with SBS 2003 R2, these settings are very similar, though the interface is different.

Changing the Update Level

SBS uses the following four *update levels* to control which updates for SBS and your SBS client and server computers are automatically deployed:

- **High** Automatically approves all security, critical, and definition updates, and also approves all service packs. This is the default for client computers.

IMPORTANT This setting will automatically approve service packs. This is a change in behavior from SBS 2003 R2, and you should allow this only if you understand the repercussions in the event of issues with a service pack, such as those experienced with Windows 7 SP1.

- **Medium** Automatically approves all security, critical, and definition updates. This is the default for server computers.

- **Low** Automatically approves all security and definition updates. Critical updates that are not security-related will not be automatically approved.

- **None** No updates are automatically approved. Each update must be manually approved or rejected—not a good idea.

To change the level for a class of computers, follow these steps:

1. Open the Windows SBS Console if it isn't already open.

2. Click Security on the navigation bar.

3. Click on the Updates tab, if it isn't on top, to display the Updates page, as shown in Figure 15-1.

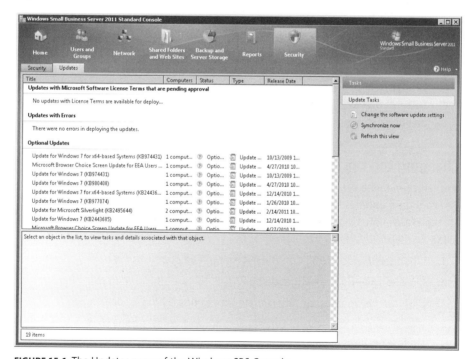

FIGURE 15-1 The Updates page of the Windows SBS Console

4. Click Change The Software Update Settings in the Tasks pane to open the Software Update Settings dialog box shown Figure 15-2.

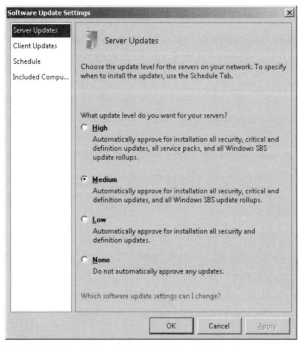

FIGURE 15-2 The Software Update Settings dialog box

5. In the left pane, click Server Updates to change the settings for servers, or click Client Updates to change settings for client PCs.

6. Select the level to use for this class of computers, and then click OK to close the dialog box and change the level.

Changing the Update Schedule

You can change the day of the week and the time of day that automatic updates happen, and also configure updates to download automatically to computers but wait for the user to initiate the installation, by changing the update schedule. To change the update schedule, use the following steps:

1. Open the Windows SBS Console if it isn't already open.

2. Click Security on the navigation bar.

3. Click on the Updates tab, if it isn't on top, to display the Updates page.

4. Click Change The Software Update Settings in the Tasks pane to open the Software Update Settings dialog box.

5. Click Schedule in the left pane to open the Schedule page of the Software Update Settings dialog box as shown in Figure 15-3.

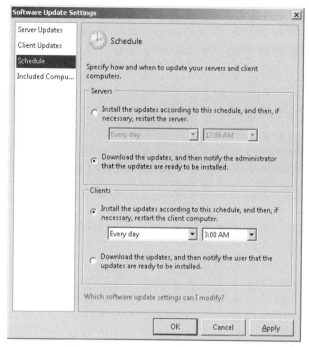

FIGURE 15-3 The Schedule page of the Software Update Settings dialog box

6. To configure automatic downloads to client computers, select that option in the Clients section.

> **NOTE** Configuring client computers for automatic downloads requires that an administrator initiate the install on the client.

7. To configure servers to automatically update, including automatically rebooting, change that option in the Servers section.

> **NOTE** Configuring servers to automatically install updates is a really bad idea. This will cause the server to automatically reboot if the update requires a reboot, and you run a significant risk of lost work or unexpected downtime. This option should be chosen only if you've carefully considered all the alternatives and have a clear understanding of the need for automatic update installation. And even then we think that server updates should be a manual process.

8. To change the day of the week or the time of day that an automatic update is installed, select the day of the week from the drop-down list. You can have updates always be installed on a specific day, or on any day that they're available. The default is Every Day.

The default time of day for updates is 3:00 A.M. If you have automatic backups of client computers, you should adjust this time to *not* interfere with the backup window.

9. After you've completed any changes to the update schedule, click OK to close the dialog box and implement the changes.

Excluding Computers from Automatic Updates

By default, Software Updates in SBS includes all computers on your SBS network and automatically assigns updates to either server or client computers. You can use the exclusion to prevent any updates from being offered to a particular computer, while also excluding it from error reporting on update status.

 REAL WORLD **Permanently Excluding Remote Users**

A reasonable question to ask is why you might want to exclude a computer from the automatic updates of SBS. One type of computer that it makes sense to exclude is the computer that never, or only rarely, connects to the network. This includes the laptops used by external employees, for example, or by salespeople who spend most of their time on the road. If you include them in the normal SBS software updates list, you'll never get a nice green check that all is well because they are rarely available to verify their status. Nor should they primarily be using the SBS network for updates. Instead, these computers should be configured to go directly to the Microsoft Update site for updates. And we think they should be configured to automatically update from there, just as client computers on your SBS network are configured to automatically update. If anything, these computers are at greater risk because they routinely connect to unsecured networks, and thus should be maintained at a fully patched level. Even if you're running DirectAccess for your remote computers, it might still make sense to have them configured to automatically download and install updates directly from Microsoft Update.

To exclude a computer from automatic updates, follow these steps:

1. Open the Windows SBS Console if it isn't already open.
2. Click Security on the navigation bar.
3. Click on the Updates tab, if it isn't on top, to display the Updates page.
4. Click Change The Software Update Settings in the Tasks pane to open the Software Update Settings dialog box.
5. Click Included Computers in the left pane to open the Included Computers page of the Software Update Settings dialog box as shown in Figure 15-4.

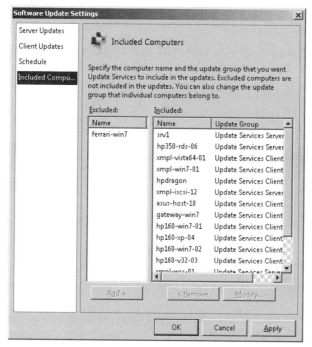

FIGURE 15-4 The Included Computers page of the Software Update Settings dialog box

6. Select the computer you want to exclude from the list of included computers, and click Remove to move it to the Excluded list.

7. After you've completed your changes to the Included Computers page, click OK to close the dialog box and apply the changes.

Modifying the Update Group

Generally, SBS correctly identifies whether a computer is a server or a client and includes it in the appropriate group for update purposes. You wouldn't normally change that setting. But if you want to force a particular computer that is a server to automatically be updated, for example, or to ensure that a particularly critical workstation isn't automatically rebooted at 3:00 A.M. the Wednesday morning after Patch Tuesday, you can modify the group the computer is in to match the behavior you need.

To modify the update group of a computer, follow these steps:

1. Open the Windows SBS Console if it isn't already open.

2. Click Security on the navigation bar.

3. Click on the Updates tab, if it isn't on top, to display the Updates page.

4. Click Change The Software Update Settings in the Tasks pane to open the Software Update Settings dialog box.

5. Click Included Computers in the left pane to open the Included Computers page of the Software Update Settings dialog box.

6. Select the computer you want to change, and click Modify to open the Change The Members Of An Update Group dialog box, as shown in Figure 15-5.

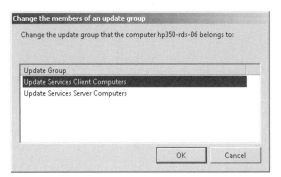

FIGURE 15-5 The Change The Members Of An Update Group dialog box

7. Select the group to move the computer to, and click OK.

8. After you've completed your changes to the Included Computers page, click OK to close the dialog box and apply the changes.

Deploying Updates

Most updates are automatically accepted and deployed by the built-in rules of SBS Software Updates, but some updates are considered optional or require explicit acceptance of a separate End User License Agreement (EULA), and these will require intervention by an SBS administrator to either deploy or decline the update.

The main Updates page, shown in Figure 15-6, includes the overall status of updates on your SBS network and also the specific details of any selected update. In the details pane of the Updates page, you can find more information on the specifics of the update, what applications or versions of Windows it applies to, and whether it will require a reboot. The details also include a link to the appropriate Knowledge Base article or download page for the update.

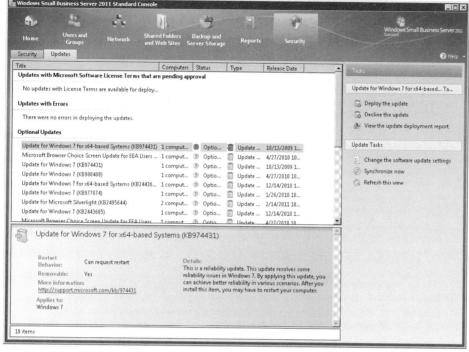

FIGURE 15-6 The Updates page, showing details for an optional update

To deploy or decline an update, follow these steps:

1. Open the Windows SBS Console if it isn't already open.

2. Click Security on the navigation bar.

3. Click on the Updates tab, if it isn't on top, to display the Updates page.

4. Select the update you want to deploy or decline in the main pane of the Updates page, and read the description of the update in the details pane.

5. Click Deploy (or Decline) in the Tasks pane to open the Software Updates dialog box shown in Figure 15-7. (The Decline dialog box is essentially the same, except that it says Declining instead of Deploying.)

FIGURE 15-7 The Software Updates Deploying Updates dialog box

6. Click OK to deploy (or decline) the update. If the update requires a separate EULA acknowledgment, you'll be prompted to accept the Software License Terms, as shown in Figure 15-8.

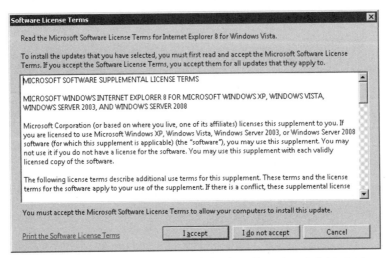

FIGURE 15-8 The Software License Terms dialog box allows the administrator to accept the agreement for all computers affected by the update.

7. Click I Accept and the update is deployed. You'll see a final acknowledgment message that the update is scheduled for deployment in the next 4 to 24 hours.

8. Click OK and the update will be added to the Updates In Progress section.

 UNDER THE HOOD   **Changing Your Mind**

When you decline an update, it disappears from the SBS Updates page completely. There's really no way to change your mind and decide to deploy it from within the Windows SBS Console. To approve an update that has been previously declined, you'll need to use the native WSUS console. Use the following steps to approve an update that has either been automatically declined by SBS Software Updates or that you've manually declined:

1. Open the Update Services console by selecting Microsoft Windows Server Update Services in the Administrative Tools folder of the Start menu.

2. In the left pane of the Update Services console, navigate to Updates and then to All Updates. Then select Declined from the Approval drop-down list in the All Updates center pane. Click Refresh to update the view.

3. Select the update you want to approve from the list of declined updates, and click Approve on the Actions pane.

4. In the Approve Updates dialog box, select the groups of computers to approve the update for and select Approved from the drop-down list of options.

5. Click OK to approve the update, and click Close to close the progress dialog box.

6. Close the Update Services console.

Using the native Update Services console is not something you should ordinarily do because it can interfere with the normal operation of the SBS Software Updates. But sometimes it's just the only way to do something, as in this case.

Viewing Update Deployment Reports

When updates are showing in the Updates In Progress section of the Updates page, it often means that some computers have had the update deployed but others are still pending for one reason or another (usually because the affected computer has been offline). To see what the status is for all the computers affected, follow these steps:

1. Open the Windows SBS Console if it isn't already open.

2. Click Security on the navigation bar.

3. Click on the Updates tab, if it isn't on top, to display the Updates page.

4. Select the update you want to see the deployment report for, and click View The Update Deployment Report on the Tasks menu to open the Deployment Report for the update, as shown in Figure 15-9.

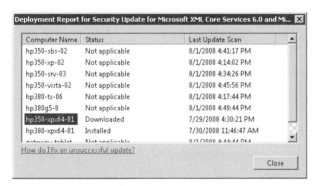

FIGURE 15-9 The Deployment Report for a security update

5. After you've identified which computers are causing the update to not complete, you can take the appropriate steps to correct the situation.

Synchronization

SBS synchronizes with the Microsoft servers once a day, at 10:00 P.M. local time. Normally, this is a sufficiently frequent and timely synchronization that you shouldn't need to do anything special to synchronize. In the event of an active outbreak of a critical exploit that affects your network, however, or for any other reason you need to manually synchronize the SBS Software Updates, you can manually trigger an update at any point in time. To initiate an update, follow these steps:

1. Open the Windows SBS Console if it isn't already open.

2. Click Security on the navigation bar.

3. Click on the Updates tab, if it isn't on top, to display the Updates page.

4. Click Synchronize Now on the Tasks pane to open the Software Updates Synchronize Now confirmation dialog box, shown in Figure 15-10.

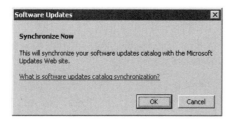

FIGURE 15-10 The Synchronize Now confirmation dialog box

5. Click OK and the synchronization will begin, and the Software Updates dialog box will change to a progress dialog box. When the synchronization completes, you'll see the dialog box shown in Figure 15-11.

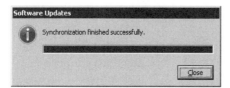

FIGURE 15-11 The Software Updates synchronization has completed

6. Click Close to return to the Windows SBS Console.

Third-Party Solutions

SBS Software Updates does a good job of managing the various patches for Microsoft products on your SBS network. It has a single, integrated, and consistent method for patch management that will meet the basic needs of the majority of SBS environments. And it's certainly easier to get set up and working correctly than using the regular Windows Server Update Services download from Microsoft.com. But having said all that, there are limitations.

The WSUS on which SBS Software Updates depends will only manage updates of Microsoft products, and it doesn't give you the fine-grained control that some SBS networks might need. If your needs go beyond the basics of SBS Software Updates, you need to go either to a product such as Microsoft's Windows Intune or to a third-party product. Windows Intune is a good product and well-suited to larger SBS networks, but it does move your update management and deployment from your own network to a managed, fee-based, cloud subscription service. Windows Intune includes software licensing for updating your client computers to Windows 7 Enterprise.

An alternative to the Microsoft patch-management solutions that we've used and like a lot is Shavlik's NetChk Protect (*http://www.shavlik.com/netchk-protect.aspx*). This is a full-featured, powerful product that gives you the ability to create multiple patch groups, control the download and deployment actions and schedules for each group differently, and even patch computers that aren't part of your SBS domain but are connected to your network. It supports patching of popular non-Microsoft products that you're likely to have on your SBS network, such as WinZip, Firefox, Apple QuickTime, and Adobe Acrobat.

Other alternatives that we've not used but that have come recommended by fellow SBS administrators include Lumension Endpoint Management and Security Suite (*http://www.lumension.com*) and BigFix (*http://www.bigfix.com*). For a comprehensive solution that includes far more than simple patch management, Kaseya (*http://www.kaseya.com*) is getting good reviews from SBS administrators and consultants alike. One part of Kaseya that appeals to us is its integration with AuthAnvil, our preferred authentication solution.

Summary

In this chapter, we covered both the process of patch management and the mechanics of using Windows Small Business Server 2011 Software Updates. In the next chapter, we'll cover another critical security process—backing up and restoring your SBS network.

## CHAPTER 16

Configuring Backup

B ackup is one of those chores that everyone knows is necessary but everyone hates to deal with. In Microsoft Windows Small Business Server (SBS) 2011 Standard, the solution can be simple if you only need to do disaster recovery backups of the server. Setting up a more robust backup of your entire network, including the clients on the network, requires more than just SBS 2011 by itself. You'll need either a third-party product or our preferred solution—Windows Storage Server 2008 R2 Essentials. After you've done the initial setup and configuration of backups, they should happen automatically and without intervention. Which does *not* mean you can ignore them. As we'll discuss in this chapter, backups aren't very important. It's *restores* that are important. If you can't restore from a backup, the backup is useless.

The backup function in the Windows Small Business Server 2011 Standard Console (SBS Console) provides a simple interface for scheduling and configuring your backups. It's still Windows Server Backup underneath, however, and some functions are available only through the native Windows Server Backup application (located on the Administrative Tools menu), including all of the advanced functionality introduced in Windows Server 2008 R2.

In this chapter, we'll look at both the SBS wizards and the native Windows Server wizards for doing backups, along with showing you how to integrate Windows Storage Server 2008 R2 Essentials into your network to protect your client computers. And, of course, we'll also cover how to recover files or your entire server when necessary.

Configuring the Backup Service

SBS 2011 uses the Windows Server Backup that is included in Windows Server 2008 R2, but before you can use the backup, you need to configure it. You can use the SBS Configure Server Backup Wizard to do this, and if you intend to back up to an external USB, FireWire, or eSATA drive, that's exactly what we'd recommend. But if you need to use some of the additional capabilities included in the R2 release of Windows Server 2008, you'll need to use the native tools to configure your backups.

In this section, we'll walk you through both scenarios—first the SBS Configure Server Backup Wizard, and then the native Backup Schedule Wizard. The SBS Configure Server Backup Wizard has the following requirements:

- Backups are performed to dedicated disks, either external or internal.
- Backups must be of the entire server or of entire volumes—no file-by-file backups.

With the native Windows Server 2008 R2 tool, the Backup Schedule Wizard, you can configure more backup options:

- Full server backups
- Custom backups, including file-level backups
- Dedicated external or internal disks
- Internal volumes that are not dedicated to backups
- Network shares

As you can see, the native tools give you a great deal more flexibility, but for the majority of cases you should use the SBS Configure Server Backup Wizard. It's fully integrated into and supported by SBS 2011, and it uses the best backup mechanism for recovering a failed server.

 UNDER THE HOOD **Ntbackup Users**

Current users of Ntbackup.exe who switch to the Windows SBS 2011 Backup should consider the following:

- Settings for creating backups aren't upgraded when you migrate to Windows SBS 2011, so you'll need to reconfigure your settings.
- You need a separate, dedicated disk for running scheduled backups if you use the SBS Configure Server Backup Wizard.
- Only NTFS-formatted volumes on a locally attached disk can be backed up.
- Windows Server Backup supports backing up to external and internal disks. You can no longer back up to tape.

You can't recover backups created with Ntbackup.exe by using Windows SBS Backup. However, a version of Ntbackup.exe is available as a download for users who want to recover data from backups created using Ntbackup.exe. The downloadable version of Ntbackup.exe is only for recovering backups for older versions of Windows and can't be used to create new backups. To download Ntbackup.exe, see *http://go.microsoft.com/fwlink/?LinkId=82917*.

Windows Server Backup Using SBS Wizards

To start the configuration, open Windows SBS Console, click Backup And Server Storage, and then follow these steps:

1. In the Tasks pane, click Configure Server Backup to start the Configure Server Backup Wizard, as shown in Figure 16-1.

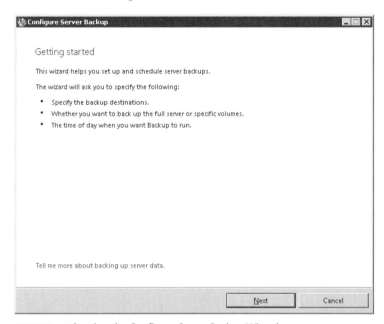

FIGURE 16-1 Starting the Configure Server Backup Wizard

2. Click Next to open the Specify The Backup Destination page, and select one or more drives as destinations for your backup. If your drive isn't listed, select the Show All Valid Internal And External Backup Destinations check box, as shown in Figure 16-2.

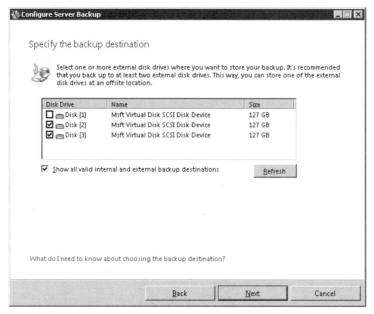

FIGURE 16-2 By default, only removable USB disks are shown as backup destinations

As detailed in Table 16-1, the location you choose for storing the backups also has consequences in terms of what can be restored.

> **IMPORTANT** The drives you select will be reformatted when backup is configured. Make sure the drives are empty or have nothing on them that needs to be saved.

TABLE 16-1 Backup locations for SBS backup

STORAGE LOCATION	WHAT CAN BE RECOVERED	WHAT CANNOT BE RECOVERED	DETAILS
Local hard disk	Files, folders, applications, and volumes. System state and operating system if the backup contains all the critical volumes.	Operating system if the backup is on the same physical disk as one or more critical volumes.	The local disk you choose will be dedicated for storing your scheduled backups and will not be visible in Windows Explorer.
External hard disk	Files, folders, applications, and volumes. System state and operating system if the backup used contains all the critical volumes.		Backups can be easily moved offsite for disaster protection.

3. Click Next to open the Label The Destination Drives page. Type in label information for each backup disk.

4. Click Next to open the Select Drives To Back Up page. Select the individual drives, or click Back Up All to include all drives. If there are critical system or application files on a volume, you cannot deselect that volume.

5. Click Next to specify the backup schedule, as shown in Figure 16-3. Select the frequency and the times of day. By default, Configure Server Backup schedules a backup to run daily at Noon and 11:00 P.M. To adjust the backup schedule, select Custom and you can schedule multiple backups at times you choose.

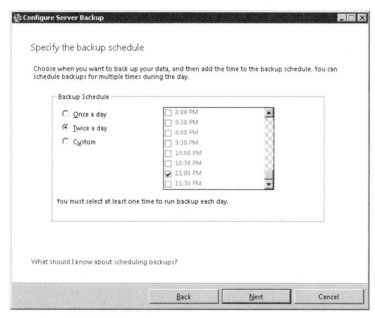

FIGURE 16-3 Setting backup times

6. Click Next to confirm the selections you've made and then click Configure. You'll be warned that the disks being used for backup will be formatted.

7. Click Yes to confirm the formatting, and the backup configuration will complete.

8. Click Finish when the configuration is complete.

Changing the Backup Configuration

You can change your backup settings in the SBS Console. Click Backup And Server Storage and then click the Backup tab. When you select the currently configured backup, the Tasks pane updates to show the changes you can make as well as providing details about the current backup configuration, as shown in Figure 16-4. You can

- Add or remove backup destinations
- Add or remove backup items (entire volumes only)
- Change the backup schedule
- Temporarily pause backups (without changing other settings)
- Disable the backups (deletes the current configuration entirely)

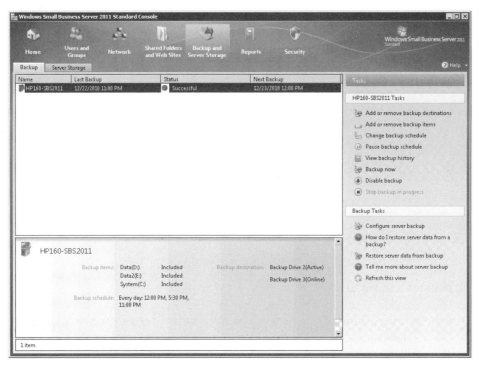

FIGURE 16-4 The server backup is configured

MODIFYING BACKUP DESTINATIONS

In the SBS Console, click Backup And Server Storage, highlight the server, and click Add Or Remove Backup Destinations to open the Server Backup Properties dialog box, as shown in Figure 16-5.

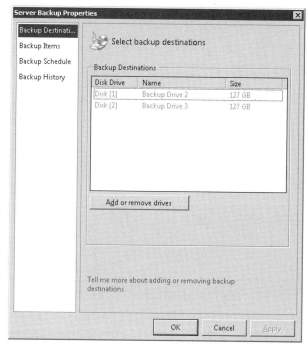

FIGURE 16-5 The Server Backup Properties dialog box

From the Server Backup Properties box, you can change the configuration of your existing backup without destroying already created backups. To change the backup destinations, follow these steps:

1. Click Backup Destination in the left pane.

2. Click Add Or Remove Drives to open the Add Or Remove Backup Destination Drives page.

3. The currently configured backup drives will be shown, along with any other available removable drives. Select the drives you want to add, and clear the drives you want to no longer use as backup destinations. If your drive isn't listed, select the Show All Valid Internal And External Backup Destinations check box.

4. Click Next. If you've added a drive, you are asked to provide a label for it as shown in Figure 16-6.

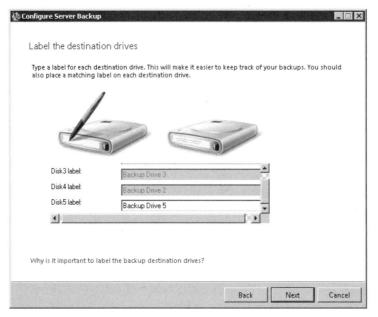

FIGURE 16-6 Labeling a new backup destination drive

5. On the confirmation page, review your selections and click Configure.

CHANGING ITEMS TO BE BACKED UP

You can change what is backed up in the SBS Server Backup from that same Server Backup Properties dialog box shown in Figure 16-5. To change what is backed up, select Backup Items in the left pane of the Server Backup Properties dialog box. Select the drives to include, or clear the check box for any drives you want to exclude from the backup. Although SBS should not allow you to clear drives where critical application files, such as Exchange databases, are stored, this isn't reliably detected from this dialog box, so use caution. In general, you should back up all available drives (volumes) with SBS Server Backup unless you know that the drive contains only transient or easily replaceable files.

MODIFYING THE BACKUP SCHEDULE

You can change when backups begin from the Server Backup Properties dialog box shown earlier in Figure 16-5. To change the backup times and frequency, select Backup Schedule in the left pane, and then select one of the options for the backup schedule. The options are

- Choose Once A Day and a backup will be performed every day at 11:00 P.M. local time.
- Choose Twice A Day and backups will be performed daily at noon and 11:00 P.M. local time.
- Choose Custom and you can select a backup schedule of your own devising, so long as it's at least once a day.

> **IMPORTANT** Store your external storage drives offsite and regularly rotate them to protect your data against disaster.

VIEW BACKUP HISTORY

You can view your backup history from the Server Backup Properties dialog box shown earlier in Figure 16-5. Just highlight the server to view in the SBS Console and choose View Backup History to open the Server Backup Properties dialog box.

Windows Server Backup Using Native Tools

The alternative to using the Configure Server Backup Wizard in the Windows SBS Console is to run the native Windows Server Backup console, shown in Figure 16-7. By configuring your SBS server's backup using the Windows Server Backup console, you have additional configuration choices while still fully protecting your SBS server.

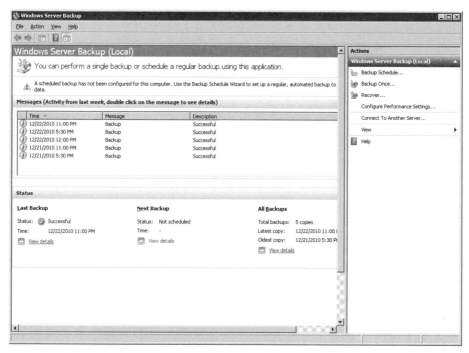

FIGURE 16-7 The native Windows Server Backup console

Create a Backup Schedule

The native tools equivalent of the Configure Server Backup Wizard is the Backup Schedule Wizard, which is launched by selecting the Backup Schedule task on the Actions menu. This wizard configures the backup type, file selection, backup destination, and the backup frequency.

To create a new backup schedule that backs up the entire server, open the Windows Server Backup application and then use the following steps:

1. Select Backup Schedule from the Actions menu to open the Backup Schedule Wizard, shown in Figure 16-8.

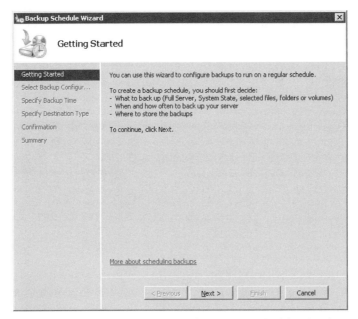

FIGURE 16-8 The Getting Started page of the Backup Schedule Wizard

2. Click Next to open the Select Backup Configuration page of the Backup Schedule Wizard as shown in Figure 16-9. Select Full Server (Recommended).

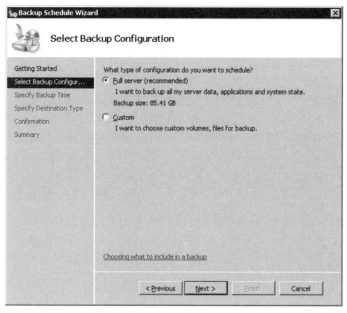

FIGURE 16-9 The Select Backup Configuration page of the Backup Schedule Wizard

3. Click Next to open the Specify Backup Time page. The default is once a day, but you can choose to have backups happen more frequently.

4. Click Next to open the Specify Destination Type page, shown in Figure 16-10. The choices are

   - **Back Up To A Hard Disk That Is Dedicated For Backups (Recommended)** This option behaves essentially the same as running the SBS Configure Server Backup. You must have a separate, dedicated hard disk, preferably external, that will be used only for Windows Server Backup. The disk is formatted before initial use and does not get assigned a drive letter.

   - **Back Up To A Volume** This option allows the backup files to share an existing volume on the SBS server. This significantly impacts the performance of the volume and should be selected only if there is no other viable option.

   - **Back Up To A Shared Network Folder** This option allows you to back up to another computer on the network that has shared disk space, such as a Windows Storage Server 2008 R2 Essentials (WSSE) server. However, this option only keeps a single backup file, so you won't have multiple generations of backups. If you choose this, you should do a secondary backup of the backup file to another location to provide a way to recover older generations of backups.

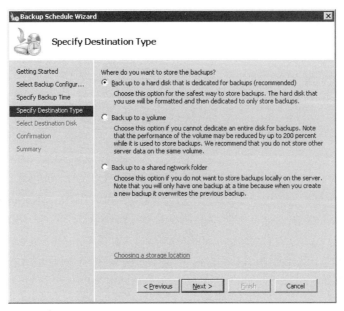

FIGURE 16-10 The Specify Destination Type page of the Backup Schedule Wizard

5. Specify the destination type and then click Next to open the Select Destination Disk, Select Destination Volume, or Specify Remote Shared Folder page. The options on this page will vary slightly depending on which type you choose. For this step, we'll choose a shared folder on the WSSE server, as shown in Figure 16-11.

FIGURE 16-11 The Specify Remote Shared Folder page of the Backup Schedule Wizard

6. Click Next and you'll be prompted for credentials to connect to the remote shared folder. Provide the credentials, click OK, and then click Finish to complete the Backup Schedule Wizard.

> **NOTE** If the computer hosting the shared volume is in a workgroup and is not a member of the SBS domain, you'll need to provide credentials for the remote computer that won't cause issues. The trick is to have a local user on the remote computer that has the same user name (and password) as an administrator for the SBS network. When asked to specify the credentials for the share, use the user name alone, not the *DOMAIN\Username* format. So, for example, I used *Charlie* as the user name, not *EXAMPLE\Charlie* or *WSS-200\Charlie*.

7. Click Close to close the wizard and return to the Windows Server Backup console.

Changing the Backup Configuration

Even when you use the native Windows Server Backup console to configure backups, you can still use the Windows SBS Console to modify some of the settings. Click Backup And Server Storage and then click on the Backup tab. When you select the currently configured backup, the Tasks pane updates to show the changes you can make as well as providing details about the current backup configuration. You can

- Add or remove backup items (entire volumes only)
- Change the backup schedule
- Temporarily pause backups (without changing other settings)
- Disable the backups (deletes the current configuration entirely)

What you can't do from the Windows SBS Console is change the backup destination, or change what items on a particular volume are backed up. To make these changes, you need to open the Windows Server Backup console and select Configure Backup Schedule.

Using the Backup Once Wizard

The Backup Once Wizard is intended as a supplement to regularly scheduled backups, not as a substitution for them. For example, you can use the Backup Once Wizard for the following situations:

- Volumes or folders that are not included in regular backups
- Volumes or folders that are part of the regular backup but that contain important items that should be backed up immediately before making changes that will affect them
- Backups of regularly scheduled items to a location other than where scheduled backups are stored

If you are using a local disk, be sure the disk supports either USB 2.0 or IEEE 1394 (if external) or is attached to the server. If using DVDs, make sure that a DVD writer is connected to the server and online, and that you have enough blank DVDs to store the contents of all the volumes you want to back up. Backups to DVDs can span multiple DVDs if the backup is too large for a single DVD.

> **NOTE** Using Backup Once is not the same as the Backup Now link in Windows SBS Console. Backup Now performs a full backup using the settings you've already configured. Backup Once allows configuring as you go.

To create a manual backup on a local disk, DVD, or removable media, open the Windows Server Backup application and then follow these steps:

1. In the Actions pane, under Windows Server Backup, click Backup Once to start the Backup Once Wizard.

2. On the Backup Options page, select either Scheduled Backup Options to use the same settings as your regular backups or Different Options to change what is being backed up or where it is being backed up to.

3. If you select Scheduled Backup Options, the next page will be a Confirmation page. Click Backup and the backup will proceed.

4. If you selected Different Options, on the Select Backup Configuration page, select Full Server to back up everything, or select Custom to specify the volumes and folders to back up.

5. If you selected Full Server, the backup will proceed, but if you selected Custom, the Select Items For Backup page, shown in Figure 16-12, opens.

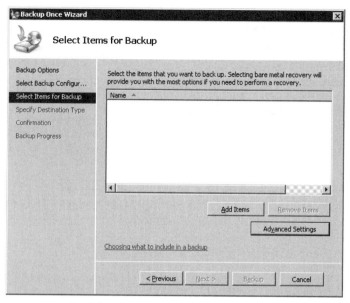

FIGURE 16-12 The Select Items For Backup page of the Backup Once Wizard

6. Click Add Items to open the Select Items dialog box, shown in Figure 16-13. You can specify whole volumes or individual files and folders. When you finish selecting items, click OK to return to the Select Items For Backup page.

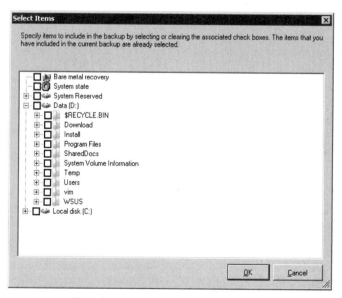

FIGURE 16-13 The Select Items dialog box allows you to specify individual files and folders

7. Click Advanced Settings to open the Advanced Settings dialog box. On the Exclusions tab, you can exclude files and folders from the backup. On the VSS Settings tab, shown in Figure 16-14, you can specify either VSS Full Backup or VSS Copy Backup. In general, on an SBS server, you should specify VSS Full Backup unless you are using a third-party backup program as your primary backup.

FIGURE 16-14 The Advanced Settings dialog box allows you to set the VSS backup type

8. Click Next to open the Specify Destination Type page. Select Local Drives to back up to a drive connected to the server, including a DVD drive, or select Remote Shared Folder to save to a network share. Click Next.

9. On the Confirmation page, review the details and then click Backup.

10. On the Backup Progress page, shown in Figure 16-15, you can view the status of the backup. If you are backing up to a DVD, you are notified to insert the first DVD in the drive and then, if the backup is too large for a single DVD, you will be prompted for subsequent DVDs as the backup progresses.

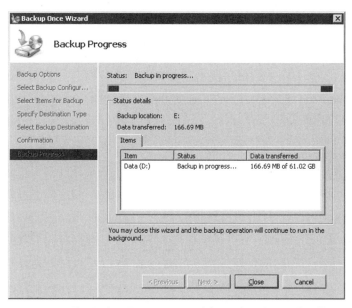

FIGURE 16-15 The Backup Progress page of the Backup Once Wizard

11. Click Close to close the Backup Once Wizard. The backup will continue.

The Backup Once Wizard allows you to perform a custom backup without disturbing your existing backup schedule, or deleting any existing backups. It's a useful tool, and one you should use before making any major change to your SBS server.

Recovering Backups

There's not much point to doing regular backups unless you can recover what you need when you need it. After your first full backup and periodically thereafter, you should test that your backups can be restored. We've said it before, in a wide variety of places, but it bears repeating: *If you haven't tested your backup by restoring from it, you should assume you don't have a backup at all.*

Recovering Your Server

The backups you've created with Windows Server Backup can be used to recover your operating system, system state, volumes, application data, backup catalog, and local files and folders. Different tools are used to recover different objects. For example:

- The Recovery Wizard in Windows Server Backup can recover the system state, files and folders, applications, and volumes.

- Windows Setup disc or a separate installation of the Windows Recovery Environment can recover the operating system and the full server (all volumes).

- The Catalog Recovery Wizard can recover the backup catalog. This wizard is available only when the backup catalog is corrupted.

NOTE You can perform all of these recovery procedures using the Wbadmin command described in the section "Using the Wbadmin Command" later in the chapter.

Recovering Volumes

When you restore a full volume using the Recovery Wizard, all contents of the volume are restored—you can't select individual files or folders to recover. To recover just certain files or folders and not a full volume, see "Recovering Files and Folders from the Local Server" and "Recovering Files and Folders from Another Server" later in this chapter.

To recover selected volumes, follow these steps:

1. Open the Administrative Tools menu, and click Windows Server Backup.

2. In the Actions pane, under Windows Server Backup, click Recover to start the Recovery Wizard.

   - On the Getting Started page, specify whether the volumes will be recovered from backups stored on this computer or another computer. If you're recovering files from the local backup, select This Server (SERVERNAME).

   - If you are recovering volumes from backups of another computer, specify where the files are located. The choices are a local drive or a remote shared folder. The local drive option supports only DVD full volume backups or backups stored on drives that are recognized as removable. Many eSATA drives will not be recognized as removable.

3. If you are recovering from this computer, on the Select Backup Location page, select the location of the backup from the drop-down list. If you are recovering from DVD or removable media, you are prompted to insert the device or first DVD in the series. Click Next.

4. For a recovery either from the local computer or another computer, on the Select Backup Date page, select the date from the calendar and the time from the drop-down list of backups you want to restore from. Click Next.

5. On the Select Recovery Type page, click Volumes and then click Next.

6. On the Select Volumes page, select the check boxes associated with the volumes in the Source Volume column that you want to recover. Then, from the associated drop-down list in the Destination Volume column, select the location that you want to recover the volume to. Click Next.

> **IMPORTANT** A message informs you that any data on the destination volume will be lost when you perform the recovery. Be sure the destination volume is either empty or doesn't contain information that could be needed later.

7. On the Confirmation page, review the details and then click Recover to restore the specified volumes.

8. On the Recovery Progress page, you can view the status of the recovery operation and determine whether it was completed successfully.

Recovering Files and Folders from the Local Server

Occasionally, files will be corrupted or overwritten and it's necessary to recover them from a recent backup. To recover individual files and folders, follow these steps:

1. Open the Administrative Tools menu, and click Windows Server Backup.

2. In the Actions pane, under Windows Server Backup, click Recover to start the Recovery Wizard.

3. On the Getting Started page, select This Server and click Next.

4. On the Select Backup Date page, select the date and time of the backup you want to recover from. Click Next.

5. On the Select Recovery Type page, select Files And Folders as the type of recovery. Click Next.

6. On the Select Items To Recover page, under Available Items, expand the list until the folder you want is visible as shown in Figure 16-16. Click a drive to see a list of folders in it, or select a folder to see a list of files and subfolders in it. Select the files and folders you want to restore in the Items To Recover pane.

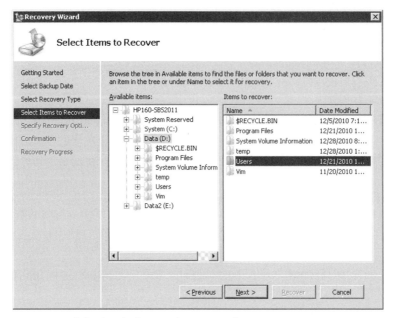

FIGURE 16-16 Selecting the items to be recovered

7. On the Specify Recovery Options page, under Recovery Destination, select one of the following:

    ■ Original Location

    ■ Another Location (Type the path to the location or click Browse to select it.)

> **IMPORTANT** We strongly recommend that you always recover to a different location whenever possible. This allows the greatest flexibility and safety in recovery and can protect you from inadvertently overwriting files.

8. On the same page, in the When This Wizard Finds Items In The Backup That Are Already In The Recovery Destination section, choose one of the following options and then click Next:

    ■ Create Copies So I Have Both Versions Of The File Or Folder

    ■ Overwrite Existing Files With Recovered Files

    ■ Don't Recover Those Files And Folders

9. On the same page, select whether to restore access permissions or not and then click Next.

10. On the Confirmation page, review the details and then click Recover to restore the specified items.

11. The Recovery Progress page displays the status of the recovery operation. Click Close when the process is finished.

Recovering Files and Folders from Another Server

To recover files and folders from a backup on another server, follow these steps:

1. Open the Administrative Tools menu, and click Windows Server Backup.

2. In the Actions pane, under Windows Server Backup, click Recover to start the Recovery Wizard.

3. On the Getting Started page, select Another Server and click Next.

4. On the Specify Location Type page, select one of the following and then click Next:

   - Local Drives

   - Remote Shared Folder

5. If you are recovering from a local drive, on the Select Backup Location page, select the location of the backup from the drop-down list.

6. If you are recovering from a remote shared folder, specify the path to the remote shared folder. Click Next.

7. On the Select Backup Date page, select the date from the calendar and the time from the drop-down list of backups you want to restore from. Click Next.

8. On the Select Recovery Type page, select Files And Folders and then click Next.

9. On the Select Items To Recover page, expand the list under Available Items until the folder you want is visible. Click a folder to display the contents in the adjacent pane, select each item that you want to restore, and then click Next.

10. On the Specify Recovery Options page, under Recovery Destination, click one of the following and then click Next:

    - Original location (For some scenarios, this option may be unavailable.)

    - Another location (Type the path to the location or click Browse to select it.)

> **IMPORTANT** We strongly recommend that you always recover to a different location whenever possible. This allows the greatest flexibility and safety in recovery and can protect you from inadvertently overwriting files.

11. On the same page, in the When This Wizard Finds Items In The Backup That Are Already In The Recovery Destination section, choose one of the following options and then click Next:

   - Create Copies So I Have Both Versions Of The File Or Folder
   - Overwrite Existing Files With Recovered Files
   - Don't Recover Those Files And Folders

12. On the same page, select whether to restore access permissions or not and then click Next.

13. On the Confirmation page, review the details and then click Recover to restore the files and folders.

14. On the Recovery Progress page, view the status of the recovery operation to determine whether it was completed successfully. Click Close when the recovery is completed.

Recovering Applications and Data

The Recovery Wizard in Windows Server Backup can be used to recover applications and data from a backup, provided that the application in question uses Volume Shadow Copy Service (VSS) technology so that it is compatible with Windows Server Backup. Also, the VSS writer for the application must have been enabled before you created the backup being used for recovery. Most applications do not enable the VSS writer by default. You will have to explicitly enable it. If the VSS writer was not enabled for the backup, you will not be able to recover applications from it.

To recover an application, follow these steps:

1. Open the Administrative Tools menu, and click Windows Server Backup.

2. In the Actions pane, under Windows Server Backup, click Recover to start the Recovery Wizard.

3. On the Getting Started page, specify whether the application will be recovered from backups run on this computer or another computer and then click Next.

4. If you're recovering local applications, the location of the backup is already known. If you're recovering an application for a different server, you'll be prompted for the location of the backup files. Click Next.

5. On the Select Backup Date page, select the date and time of the backup to restore from and click Next.

6. On the Select Recovery Type page, choose Applications and then click Next.

7. On the Select Application page, under Applications, select the application to recover, as shown in Figure 16-17.

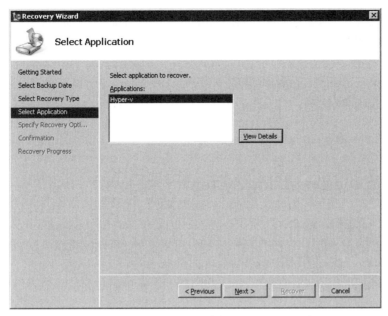

FIGURE 16-17 The Select Application page of the Recovery Wizard

If the backup that you are using is the most recent and the application you are recovering supports a roll-forward of the application database, you will see a check box labeled Do Not Perform A Roll-Forward Recovery Of The Application Databases. Select this check box if you want to prevent Windows Server Backup from rolling forward the application database that is currently on your server. Click Next.

> **IMPORTANT**   Roll-forward recovery uses information stored in transaction log files to return a database to the state it was in at an exact point in time. To perform a roll-forward recovery, archival logging must be enabled and a full backup image of the database must be available, as well as access to all archived log files created since the last successful backup image.
>
> If a roll-forward recovery isn't possible, a version recovery will be performed. Version recovery is the process used to return a database to the state it was in at the time a particular backup image was made.

8. On the Specify Recovery Options page, select How Do You Want To Recover The Application Data and then select one of the following options:

   - Recover To Original Location
   - Recover To Another Location (Type the path to the location or click Browse to select it.)

> **NOTE** If you recover to a different location, only the application data will be recovered. The application itself will not be recovered.

9. Click Next to open the Confirmation page, review the details, and then click Recover to restore the listed items.

10. On the Recovery progress page, view the status of the recovery operation to determine whether it was completed successfully.

Recovering the Operating System

You can recover your server operating system or full server by using a Windows SBS Installation DVD and a backup created with Windows Server Backup. The Windows Installation disc allows access to the System Recovery Options page in the Windows Recovery Environment.

Before you start, you need to determine the following:

- Where you will recover to
- What backup you will use
- Whether you will perform an operating system–only or full-server recovery
- Whether you will reformat and repartition your disks

> **IMPORTANT** When recovering to a new hard disk, the new disk must be at least as large as the disk that contained the volumes that were backed up—no matter what size those volumes were. For example, if you backed up only one 50 GB volume on a 1-terabyte disk, you have to use a 1-terabyte or larger disk when restoring.

To recover the operating system or the full server to a new server or hard disk, using the Windows SBS Installation disk, follow these steps:

1. Insert the Windows SBS Setup disc into the DVD drive, and turn on the computer. The Install Windows Wizard appears.

2. Select the language options and then click Next.

3. On Install Now page, shown in Figure 16-18, select Repair Your Computer.

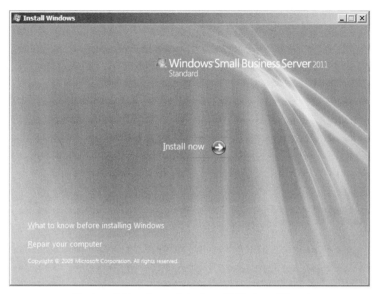

FIGURE 16-18 The Install Now Page of the Install Windows Wizard

4. Setup searches the hard disk drives for an existing Windows installation and then displays the results in System Recovery Options, as shown in Figure 16-19.

FIGURE 16-19 The System Recovery Options dialog box

5. Click Next and Windows will attempt to locate an image to recover. If you are recovering from a removable hard disk or DVD image, it should locate it. But if you are recovering from an internal disk or from a network share, it will fail and you'll see the error message shown in Figure 16-20.

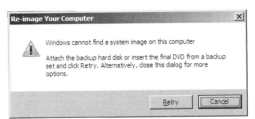

FIGURE 16-20 The recovery can't find a Windows image backup

6. Click Cancel to open the Select A System Image Backup page, shown in Figure 16-21.

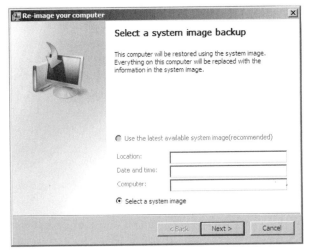

FIGURE 16-21 The Select A System Image Backup page of the Re-image Your Computer Wizard

7. Click Next to open the Select The Location Of The Backup For The Computer You Want To Restore page shown in Figure 16-22.

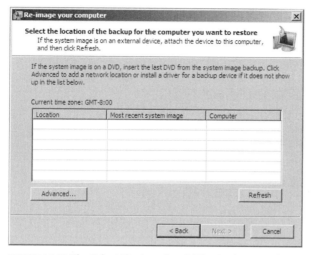

FIGURE 16-22 The Select The Location Of The Backup For The Computer You Want To Restore page

8. Attach a hard disk with the image on it and click Refresh, or click Advanced to open the dialog box shown in Figure 16-23.

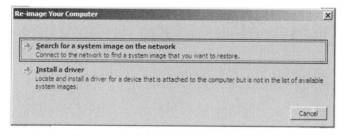

FIGURE 16-23 You can search for an image on the network

9. Click Search For A System Image On The Network. You'll be warned that this should only be done on a trusted network. Security updates are not installed at this point, and the Windows Firewall is not enabled.

10. Click Yes in the warning dialog box, and then specify the location of the network folder to connect to, as shown in Figure 16-24.

FIGURE 16-24 Specify the network folder share where your SBS backups are located

11. Click OK and then specify the user name and password to connect to the network share as shown in Figure 16-25. On most SBS networks, this will have to be a *local* computer account on the remote computer because there will not be a domain controller to authenticate you.

FIGURE 16-25 You'll need to specify local credentials to connect to the network share

12. Select the computer that you want to restore, as shown in Figure 16-26.

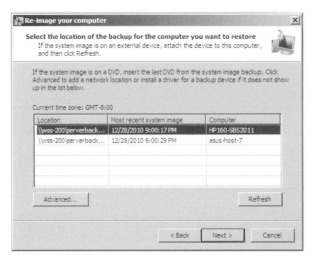

FIGURE 16-26 Select the computer image to restore

13. Click Next to open The Select The Date And Time Of System Image To Restore page, shown in Figure 16-27.

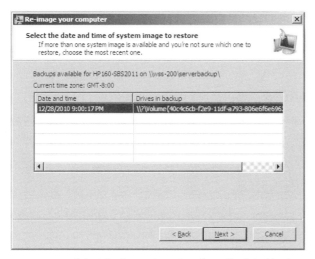

FIGURE 16-27 Select the image to restore from the list of backups available

14. Click Next to open the Choose Additional Restore Options page. On this page, you can select to format and partition disks if the wizard sees sufficient disks available, or select Only Restore System Drives if you want to just restore the drives required to run Windows. You can restore data drives after SBS is restored.

15. On the confirmation page, verify that the actions are correct and click Finish.

16. You'll be warned that all disks used for the restore will be formatted. Click Yes and the restore will start.

Restoring a Backup Catalog

The details of your backups are stored in a file called a *backup catalog*. This file contains information about what volumes are backed up and where they're located. Windows Server Backup stores the catalog in the same place that you store your backups. If the catalog file is corrupted, Windows Server Backup sends you an alert and an event is added to the event log (Event 514). Before you can perform additional backups, the catalog must be restored or deleted.

If you have no backups that you can use to recover the catalog, the corrupted file must be deleted. This means information about previous backups is lost and the backups can't be accessed using Windows Server Backup. Therefore, it's important to create a new backup immediately after deleting the catalog file.

NOTE The Catalog Recovery Wizard is available only when Windows Backup Server detects that the catalog file is corrupted.

To recover a backup catalog, follow these steps:

1. Open the Administrative Tools menu, and click Windows Server Backup.
2. In the Actions pane, under Windows Server Backup, click Recover to start the Catalog Recovery Wizard.
3. On the Specify Storage Type page, select one of the following:
   - If you don't have a backup to use to recover the catalog and you just want to delete the catalog, click I Don't Have Any Usable Backups, click Next, and then click Finish.
   - If you do have a backup that you can use, specify whether the backup is on a local drive or remote shared folder and then click Next.
4. Do one of the following:
   - On the Select Backup Location page, if the backup is on a local drive (including DVDs), select the drive that contains the backup that you want to use from the drop-down list. If you are using DVDs, make sure the *last* DVD of the series is in the drive. Click Next.
   - If the backup is on a remote shared folder, on the Specify Remote Folder page, type the path to the folder that contains the backup that you want to use and then click Next.

   A message informs you that backups taken after the backup that you are using for the recovery will not be accessible. Click Yes.
5. On the Confirmation page, review the details and then click Finish to recover the catalog.
6. On the Summary page, click Close.

After the catalog recovery is completed or you have deleted the catalog, you must close and then reopen Windows Server Backup to refresh the view.

Using the Command Line to Manage Backups

There are two ways to do backups from the command line—using Windows PowerShell or using the Wbadmin command. Personally, we much prefer using Windows PowerShell for everything we can, but there are limitations here. The PowerShell interface to backups is done through a PowerShell snap-in, and this snap-in does not provide any interface to doing restores, only backups. This isn't a huge problem because in the vast majority of cases you don't need to automate restores, but you can and should be automating backups.

The other significant limitation of Windows PowerShell support for managing backups is that it isn't available on the Microsoft Hyper-V Server. This means that you can't use Windows PowerShell to manage your backups on the Microsoft Hyper-V Server if you're using that as your virtualization solution. You'll need to use the Wbadmin command.

Using the Windows.Serverbackup PowerShell Snap-in

Windows Server Backup includes the Windows.Serverbackup PowerShell snap-in. This snap-in includes the cmdlets necessary to configure and manage backups on the SBS server. Table 16-2 includes a list of the cmdlets included in the snap-in.

TABLE 16-2 The cmdlets in the Window.Serverbackup snap-in

NAME	SYNOPSIS
Get-WBDisk	Returns a list of internal and external disks that are attached to the local computer.
Get-WBVolume	Returns a list of volumes that are included in the current backup policy.
Add-WBVolume	Adds volumes to the current backup policy.
Remove-WBVolume	Removes volumes from the current backup policy.
New-WBPolicy	Creates a new backup policy (WBPolicy object).
Get-WBPolicy	Returns the current backup policy for the computer.
Set-WBPolicy	Sets a WBPolicy object as the current backup policy for scheduled backups.
Remove-WBPolicy	Deletes the current backup policy.
Get-WBSummary	Returns a history of backup operations.
New-WBBackupTarget	Creates a new backup location.
Get-WBBackupTarget	Returns the current backup target locations.
Add-WBBackupTarget	Adds a backup target location to the backup policy.
Remove-WBBackupTarget	Removes the backup target locations from the backup policy.
Get-WBSchedule	Returns the current backup schedule for backups.
Set-WBSchedule	Sets the times for daily backups.
Get-WBBackupSet	Returns the list of backups.
Start-WBBackup	Initiates a one-time backup.
Get-WBJob	Returns the currently running backup job.
New-WBFileSpec	Creates a new WBFileSpec object. FileSpec objects describe files, folders, and volumes that are included or excluded from the backup.
Add-WBFileSpec	Adds the WBFileSpec object to the backup policy.
Remove-WBFileSpec	Removes the WBFileSpec object (and the files, folders, and volumes that it includes or excludes) from the backup policy.

NAME	SYNOPSIS
Get-WBFileSpec	Returns a list of WBFileSpec objects associated with the backup policy.
Add-WBSystemState	Adds the necessary items to the backup policy to allow for system state recovery.
Get-WBSystemState	Returns *$true* if system state is part of the backup policy.
Remove-WBSystemState	Removes system state from the backup policy.
Add-WBBareMetalRecovery	Adds the necessary items to the backup policy to ensure a full bare-metal recovery.
Get-WBBareMetalRecovery	Returns *$true* if the backup policy includes the necessary items to ensure a full bare-metal recovery.
Remove-WBBareMetal-Recovery	Removes the necessary items from the backup policy that ensure a bare-metal recovery.
Set-WBVssBackupOptions	Sets the VSS backup type for the backup policy.
Get-WBVssBackupOptions	Returns the VSS backup type for the backup policy.

The process of defining and using Windows PowerShell to manage backups requires first creating the Windows Backup policy object and then configuring it with one or more file specification objects (WBFileSpec), a schedule object (WBSchedule), system state and bare-metal recovery options, and a Volume Shadow Service (VSS) backup type. So, to define a full-server backup to the network share \\wss-200\serverbackup that included all the files on volumes C and D except those in \temp, and included the necessary files for bare-metal and system state recovery, using a VSS backup type of VSS Full Backup, the PowerShell script would be:

```
# Script to set a Windows Server Backup policy for SBS
# Created 27/12/2010
# Assumes: Volumes C:, D: and E: to backup.
#          : Target - \\wss-200\serverbackup
#          : Exclusions - D:\temp, E:\temp
#          : VSS Mode - Full Backup
#          : System State - True
#          : Bare Metal Recovery - True
#          : Schedule - 12:30 PM, 9:00 PM
# ModHist: 27/12/10 - initial
#          : 28/12/10 - Final
#
# Copyright 2010, 2011 by Charlie Russel. All rights reserved.
#
# With profound thanks to Richard Siddaway, Windows PowerShell MVP
#
```

```
# You may copy and modify this script for your own internal use.
# If you publish this script or a derivative of it in any form you must
# provide full attribution to the authors of this script,
# Charlie Russel and Sharon Crawford, and to their book:
# "Windows Small Business Server 2011 Standard Administrator's Companion"
# (MSPress, 2011) for which this script was written.

# The following will error if already loaded, but continue, so ignore
Add-PSSnapin Windows.ServerBackup

# First, create a new empty policy
$BackupPolicy = New-WBPolicy


# Now, define the parts of it.
# First, let's do the volumes. This requires us to first get a list of them,
# and then parse that list to add the ones we want (C:, D: and E:)
# We don't actually need C:, since we'll get that as part of Bare Metal Restore,
# but we include it anyway for completeness

$volC = Get-WBVolume -AllVolumes | Where {$_.MountPath -eq "C:"}
$volD = Get-WBVolume -AllVolumes | Where {$_.MountPath -eq "D:"}
$volE = Get-WBVolume -AllVolumes | Where {$_.MountPath -eq "E:"}
$Volumes = $volC,$volD,$volE

# now, add that to the blank policy
Add-WBVolume -policy $BackupPolicy -volume $Volumes

#Define the Exclusions.
$excD = New-WBFileSpec -Filespec D:\Temp -exclude
$excE = New-WBFileSpec -Filespec E:\Temp -exclude
$FileExclusions = $excE,$excD


# and then add that to the policy we're building
Add-WBFileSpec -policy $BackupPolicy -filespec $FileExclusions

# Define the backup target
# First, you need to create a credential to connect to the remote share
# You can specify the username here (DOMAIN\User) but will be
# prompted for the password
$Cred = Get-Credential example\Charlie


# Now, define the target
$Target = New-WBBackupTarget -NetworkPath \\WSS-200\ServerBackup -Credential $Cred
```

```
# Add the target to the policy
Add-WBBackupTarget -policy $BackupPolicy -target $Target


# Define the schedule
$sch1 = [datetime]"12/27/2010 12:30:00"
$sch2 = [datetime]"12/27/2010 21:00:00"
Set-WBSchedule -policy $BackupPolicy -schedule $sch1,$sch2


# Set for system state and for bare metal recovery
Add-WBSystemState -policy $BackupPolicy
Add-WBBareMetalRecovery -policy $BackupPolicy


# Finally, set for full VSS Backup
Set-WBVssBackupOptions -policy $BackupPolicy -VssFullBackup


# Finally, we need to SET the policy before it actually takes control
Set-WBPolicy -force -policy $BackupPolicy


# This completes the configuration of the SBS server backup policy
$SBSname = (hostname).tolower()


" The SBS Server $SBSname now has the following backup configuration: "
" "
Get-WBPolicy
```

Using the Wbadmin Command

The Wbadmin command allows you to back up and restore volumes and files from the command line. Wbadmin replaces the Ntbackup command that was part of SBS 2003. You can't use Wbadmin to recover backups created with Ntbackup. However, if you need to recover backups made with Ntbackup, you can download a version of Ntbackup usable with Windows Server 2008 R2. This downloadable version of Ntbackup allows you to perform recoveries of legacy backups, but you cannot use it on Windows Server 2008 R2 to create new backups. To download this version of Ntbackup, see *http://go.microsoft.com/fwlink/?LinkId=82917*.

The next sections list Wbadmin commands and syntax. Table 16-3 lists and describes the parameters used with Wbadmin. For additional assistance, type **Wbadmin /?** at a command prompt.

TABLE 16-3 Wbadmin parameters

PARAMETER	DESCRIPTION
-addtarget	Storage location for backup. Disk is formatted before use and any existing data on it is permanently erased.
-allCritical	Automatically includes all critical volumes (volumes that contain system state data). Can be used along with the *-include* option.
-backupTarget	Storage location for this backup. Requires a hard disk drive letter (f:) or a Universal Naming Convention (UNC) path to a shared network folder (*servername**sharename*). If a shared network folder is specified, this backup will overwrite any existing backup in that location.
-dfsAuth	Marks the restore as authoritative. Can be used only when the server being recovered is hosting folders that are being replicated by Distributed File System Replication (DFSR). This parameter makes the recovered version of the replicated folders the authoritative copy, thereby overwriting the version stored on other members of the replication group. If this parameter is not used, the data is restored as a nonauthoritative copy.
-excludeDisks	Can be used only with the *-recreateDisks* parameter. Must be input as a comma-delimited list of disk identifiers (as listed in the output of wbadmin get disks). Excluded disks are not partitioned or formatted. This parameter helps preserve data on disks that you do not want modified during the recovery.
-include	Comma-delimited list of volume drive letters, volume mount points, or GUID-based volume names to include in the backup.
-noInheritAcl	If specified, the computer-name folder applies ACLs for the user whose credentials were given when running the backup and grants access to the Administrators group and Backup Operators group on the computer with the shared network folder. If *-noInheritAcl* is not used, the ACL permissions from the remote shared folder are applied to the <ComputerBackedUp> folder by default so that anyone with access to the remote shared folder can access the backup.

PARAMETER	DESCRIPTION
-items	Comma-delimited list of volumes, applications, and files to recover.
	If *-itemtype* is Volume, it can be only a single volume that is specified by providing the volume drive letter, volume mount point, or GUID-based volume name.
	If *-itemtype* is App, it can be only a single application. Applications that can be recovered include SQL Server and Windows SharePoint Services. You can also use the value *ADExtended* to recover an installation of Active Directory.
	If *-itemtype* is File, it can be files or directories, but it should be part of the same volume and it should be under the same parent.
-itemtype	Type of items to recover. Must be Volume, App, or File.
-machine	Specifies the name of the computer for which you want to recover the backup. Should be used when *-backupTarget* is specified.
-notrestoreacl	Can be used only when recovering files. Specifies to not restore the security ACLs of the files being recovered from backup.
	By default, the security ACLs are restored. (The default value is *true*.) If this parameter is used, the default ACLs for the location that the files are being restored to are applied.
-noVerify	If specified, backups written to removable media (such as a DVD) are not verified for errors. If not specified, backups written to such media are verified for errors.
-overwrite	Valid only when recovering files. Specifies the action to take when a file that is being recovered already exists in the same location.
	Overwrite causes the recovery to overwrite the existing file with the file from the backup.
	CreateCopy causes the recovery to create a copy of the existing file so that the existing file is not modified.
	Skip causes the recovery to skip the existing file and continue with recovery of the next file.
-password	Password for the user name that is specified by the parameter *-user*.
-recoveryTarget	Specifies the drive to restore to. Use if this drive is different than the one that was previously backed up. Can also be used for restorations of volumes, files, or applications. If you are restoring a volume, you can specify the volume drive letter of the alternate volume. If you are restoring a file or application, you can specify an alternate backup path.
-recreateDisks	Restores a disk configuration to the state that existed when the backup was created.

PARAMETER	DESCRIPTION
-recursive	Can be used only when recovering files. Recovers the files in the folders and all files subordinate to the specified folders. By default, only files that reside directly under the specified folders are recovered.
-removetarget	Storage location specified in the existing backup schedule.
-restoreAll-Volumes	Restores all volumes from the selected backup. If this parameter is not specified, only critical volumes (volumes that contain system state data) are restored from the selected backup. Useful when you need to restore noncritical volumes during system recovery.
-schedule	Comma-delimited times of day specified as HH:MM.
-showsummary	Can be used only with Wbadmin start sysstaterecovery. Reports the summary of the last run of this command. This parameter cannot be accompanied by any other parameters.
-skipBadCluster-Check	Can be used only when recovering volumes. This skips checking your recovery destination disks for bad cluster information. If you are restoring to an alternate server or hardware, this switch should not be used. You can manually run the command chkdsk /b on your recovery disks at any time to check them for bad clusters, and then update the file system information accordingly
-user	Specifies the user name with write access to the backup destination (if it is a shared network folder). The user needs to be a member of the Administrators or Backup Operators group on this computer.
-quiet	Runs the command with no prompts to the user.
-version	Specifies the version of the backup in MM/DD/YYYY-HH:MM format, as listed by wbadmin get versions.
-vssFull	If specified, performs a full backup using Volume Shadow Copy Service (VSS). Each file's history is updated to reflect that it was backed up. If this parameter is not specified, Start Backup makes a copy backup, but the history of files being backed up is not updated. Caution: Do not use this parameter when using a non-Microsoft program to back up applications.

Wbadmin Enable Backup

The following subcommand enables or configures scheduled daily backup:

```
Wbadmin enable backup
[-addtarget:{backuptargetdisk | backuptargetnetworkshare}]
[-removetarget:{backuptargetdisk | backuptargetnetworkshare}]
[-schedule:timetorunbackup]
[-include:volumestoinclude]
```

```
[-allcritical]
[-user:username]
[-password:password]
[-inheritacl:inheritacl]
[-quiet]
```

Wbadmin disable backup

The following subcommand disables running scheduled daily backups:

```
wbadmin disable backup
[-quiet]
```

Wbadmin start backup

The following subcommand runs a backup job:

```
wbadmin start backup
[-backupTarget:{TargetVolume | TargetNetworkShare}]
[-include:VolumesToInclude]
[-allCritical]
[-vssFull]
[-noVerify]
[-user:UserName]
[-password:Password]
[-noinheritAcl]
 [-quiet]
```

Wbadmin stop job

The following subcommand stops a running backup or recovery job:

```
Wbadmin stop job
[-quiet]
```

Wbadmin start recovery

The following subcommand runs a recovery based on the specified parameters:

```
wbadmin start recovery
-version:VersionIdentifier
-items:VolumesToRecover | AppsToRecover | FilesOrFoldersToRecover}
-itemtype:{Volume | App | File}
[-backupTarget:{VolumeHostingBackup | NetworkShareHostingBackup}]
[-machine:BackupMachineName]
[-recoveryTarget:{TargetVolumeForRecovery | TargetPathForRecovery}]
[-recursive]
[-overwrite:{Overwrite | CreateCopy | Skip}]
```

```
[-notRestoreAcl]
[-skipBadClusterCheck]
[-noRollForward]
[-quiet]
```

Wbadmin start systemstatebackup

The following subcommand creates a backup of the system state of a computer. A backup of the system state can be saved only to a locally attached disk (either internal or external). It cannot be saved to a DVD or to a remote shared folder. In addition, only the system state and system applications can be recovered from this backup—volumes and files cannot be recovered from this backup.

```
wbadmin start systemstatebackup
-backupTarget:<VolumeName>
[-quiet]
```

Wbadmin start systemstaterecovery

The following subcommand runs a system state recovery based on the supplied parameters:

```
wbadmin start systemstaterecovery
-version:VersionIdentifier
-showsummary
[-backupTarget:{VolumeName | NetworkSharePath}]
[-machine:BackupMachineName]
[-recoveryTarget:TargetPathForRecovery]
[-excludeSystemFiles]
[-authsysvol]
[-quiet]
```

Wbadmin start sysrecovery

The following subcommand runs a system recovery based on specified parameters. This command can be run only from the Windows Recovery Environment, and it is not listed by default in the usage text of Wbadmin. (You can access the Windows Recovery Environment from a Windows Server 2008 R2 installation DVD by inserting the DVD and following the steps in the wizard until you see the option Repair Your Computer. Click this link to open the System Recovery Options dialog box.)

```
wbadmin start sysrecovery
-version:VersionIdentifier
-backupTarget:{VolumeHostingBackup | NetworkShareHostingBackup}
[-machine:BackupMachineName]
[-restoreAllVolumes]
[-recreateDisks]
[-excludeDisks]
```

```
[-dfsAuth]
[-skipBadClusterCheck]
[-quiet]
```

Windows Recovery Environment

Windows Recovery Environment (Windows RE) is a recovery platform designed to automatically repair common causes of unbootable operating system installations. When the computer fails to start, Windows automatically fails over into this environment, and the Startup Repair tool in Windows RE automates diagnosis and repair. In addition, Windows RE is a starting point for various tools for manual system recovery.

Windows RE is a partial version of the operating system plus a set of tools you can use to carry out operating system or full server recoveries, using a backup that you created earlier using Windows Server Backup.

Wbadmin get versions

The following subcommand reports on the available backups:

```
wbadmin get versions
[-backupTarget:{VolumeName | NetworkSharePath}]
[-machine:BackupMachineName]
```

Wbadmin get status

The following subcommand reports the status of the current backup or recovery:

```
wbadmin get status
```

Windows Storage Server 2008 R2 Essentials

If Windows Server Backup works perfectly fine, why invest in another backup product? Good question. And a good answer is *client backup*. If you need more than disaster recovery for servers, Windows Storage Server 2008 R2 Essentials (WSSE) is the ideal complement to SBS. WSSE includes a client computer backup that is easy to configure and set up, and it requires no intervention to keep all your SBS network's client computers backed up.

> **NOTE** WSSE is limited to 25 users and computers. However, you can have multiple WSSE servers as members of your SBS network, so even with a large SBS network you can ensure that all client computers are backed up.

When you buy Windows Storage Server 2008 R2 Essentials, you buy the hardware and software combined. You merely plug it in to your network, turn it on, and configure it. We won't cover the initial configuration of your WSSE server here, because each Original Equipment Manufacturer (OEM) will have a slightly different setup experience. But when you have the WSSE server up and running, the experience will be essentially similar, though each OEM might have special additional applications and customizations for their solution.

Configuring Windows Storage Server 2008 R2 Essentials for an SBS Network

Unlike Windows Home Server, WSSE can be a member server in an SBS domain. This allows you to easily manage users and computers assigned to a WSSE server, and also makes it easy to have multiple WSSE servers on your network if you need to support more than 25 users and computers.

Connecting Windows Storage Server Essentials to the SBS Domain

The first requirement for adding a WSSE server to your SBS network, after you get it up and running, is to configure WSSE to be a domain member. Before you can do this, however, you should create a special security group of SBS users who are allowed to connect to the WSSE server.

To configure your WSSE server to be a member of your SBS domain, you first need to create a security group to control which SBS users are allowed to connect to the WSSE server. To create the security group for WSSE users and assign them an email address, use the following steps:

1. Open the Windows Small Business Server Console, and select the Users And Groups tab.

2. Click the Groups tab, and then click the Add A New Group task to open the Add A New Group Wizard.

3. Click Next to open the Add A New Group page, shown in Figure 16-28.

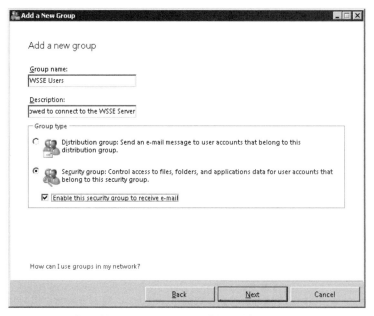

FIGURE 16-28 The Add A New Group page of the Add A New Group Wizard

4. Enter a name for the group, and then select Security Group. If you want to be able to send emails to this group of users, select the Enable This Security Group To Receive E-Mail check box.

> **NOTE** E-mail enabling this security group allows you to send maintenance downtime notifications and other information of interest to the users of the WSSE server. But you should generally not enable outside email for this group.

5. Click Next to open the Create A Group E-mail Address page, as shown in Figure 16-29.

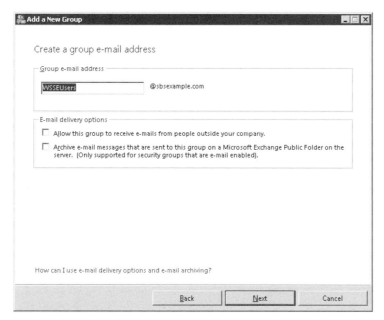

FIGURE 16-29 The Create A Group E-Mail Address page of the Add A New Group Wizard

6. Click Next to open the Select Group Members For WSSE Users page shown in Figure 16-30. (The name on this page will be different if you've chosen a different name for your security group.)

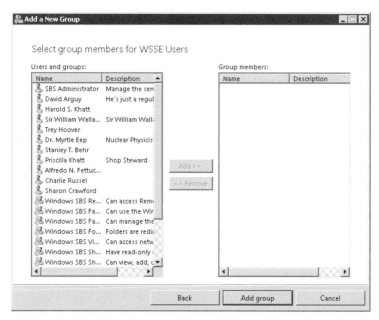

FIGURE 16-30 The Select Group Members For WSSE Users page of the Add A New Group Wizard

7. Select the users that you want to add to this group in the left Users And Groups pane, and click Add to move them to the Group Members pane.

8. Click Add Group to create the new security group, and then Finish when the wizard is done.

After you've created the security group to control which users have access to the WSSE server, you can join the server to the SBS domain and begin connecting computers to the WSSE server for backup. To join the WSSE server to the SBS domain, use the following steps:

1. Open the Windows Storage Server 2008 R2 Dashboard shown in Figure 16-31.

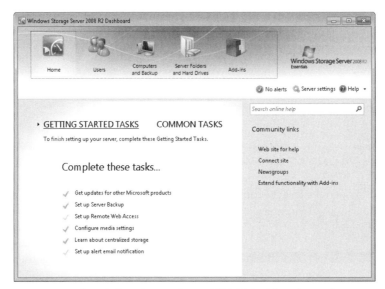

FIGURE 16-31 The Windows Storage Server 2008 R2 Dashboard console

2. Click Server Settings to open the Server Settings dialog box. Click Domain in the left pane, as shown in Figure 16-32, and enter the name of the SBS domain in the Domain To Join field.

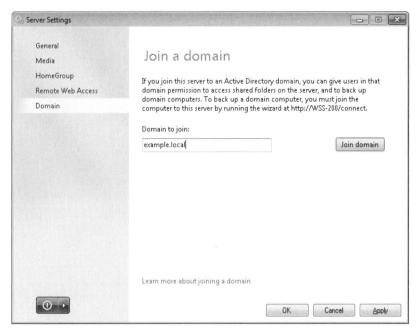

FIGURE 16-32 The Join A Domain page of the Server Settings dialog box

3. Click Join Domain, and enter the credentials for a Network Administrator of the SBS domain.

4. Click OK and then click Yes on the Assign Access To Domain Group dialog box, shown in Figure 16-33.

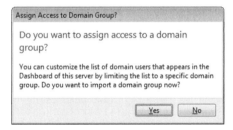

FIGURE 16-33 The Assign Access To Domain Group dialog box

5. In the Select A Group dialog box, shown in Figure 16-34, select the security group you just created and click OK.

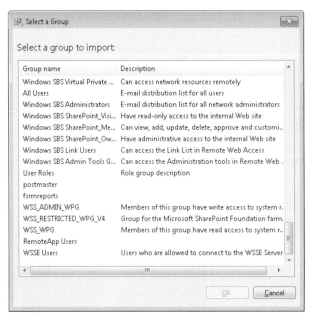

FIGURE 16-34 The Select A Group dialog box

6. Click OK when prompted to reboot the WSSE server.

7. On the Windows SBS server, open Active Directory Users And Computers from the Administrative Tools menu.

8. Navigate to the SBSComputers Organizational Unit (OU) as shown in Figure 16-35.

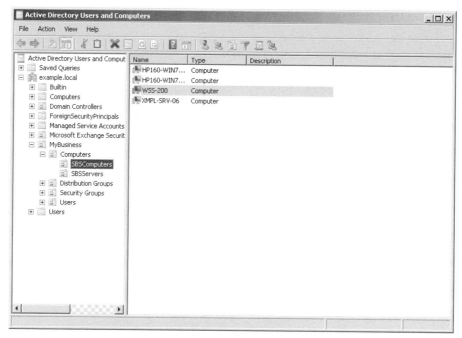

FIGURE 16-35 The WSSE server is in the SBSComputers OU

9. Select the WSSE server in the list of computers in the SBSComputers OU. Drag the computer to the SBSServers OU. You'll be warned about moving objects in Active Directory. Click Yes to confirm you want to do it.

10. Close Active Directory Users And Computers. Your Windows Storage Server 2008 R2 Essentials server is now a member of the SBS domain and ready for client computers to connect to it.

Connecting to Windows Storage Server 2008 R2 Essentials

You must run the Windows Storage Server 2008 R2 Essentials Connector on each client computer that will use WSSE for backup. This connector configures the client computer backup settings and also installs a Launchpad application on the client computer. To connect your computer to the WSSE server, follow these steps (all on the client computer):

1. Open Internet Explorer, and navigate to *http://<WSSEServerName>/Connect*, as shown in Figure 16-36.

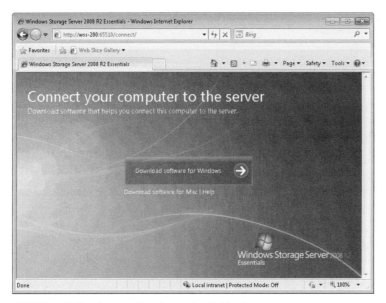

FIGURE 16-36 The Connect Your Computer To The Server page

2. Click Download Software For Windows and then click Run in the File Download – Security Warning dialog box shown in Figure 16-37. Acknowledge the User Account Control (UAC) warning by clicking Yes.

FIGURE 16-37 Always know why you're choosing to run a file over the network

3. Click Next on each of the first two pages of the Connect A Computer To The Server Wizard.

4. On the Log On To Your Windows Storage Server 2008 R2 page, shown in Figure 16-38, enter the password for the WSSE server.

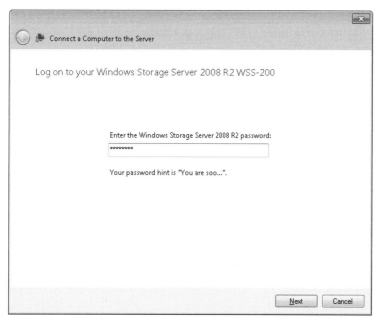

FIGURE 16-38 You'll need to know the password for your Windows Storage Server 2008 R2 server

NOTE The exact steps in this sequence might vary if you don't have all the prerequisites for connecting to the Windows Storage Server 2008 R2 server, including the Microsoft .NET Framework 4.0.

5. Click Next to open the Review And Modify The Description Of This Computer If Needed page. Enter a description for the computer that you're joining to the WSSE server.

6. Click Next to open the Do You Want To Automatically Wake Up This Computer To Back It Up? page, shown in Figure 16-39, and choose whether you want to automatically wake up the computer to run backups or not. We strongly recommend that you enable this feature to ensure that computers are regularly backed up.

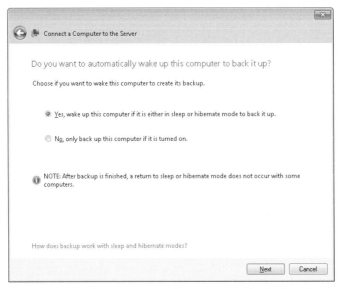

FIGURE 16-39 Enabling automatic wakeup to ensure that backups happen regularly.

7. Click Next to open the Do You Want To Participate In The Windows Customer Experience Improvement Program? page and make a selection.

8. Click Next to begin downloading the software to your computer and configuring it.

9. When the client computer has finished connecting and configuring, you'll see the This Computer Is Now Connected To The Server page, shown in Figure 16-40.

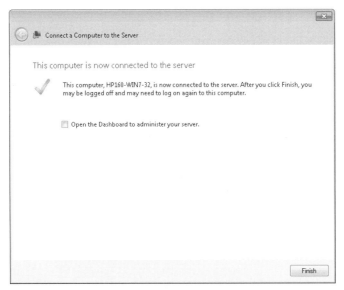

FIGURE 16-40 Your computer is now connected to the WSSE server and configured for automatic backups

10. Clear the Open The Dashboard To Administer Your Server check box, and click Finish to close the wizard.

The Windows Storage Server 2008 R2 Essentials Launchpad

After your computer is connected to the WSSE server, you'll also have a new application added to your desktop, the Launchpad shown in Figure 16-41. This application gives you quick access to your backups for this computer, as well as any Shared Folders that have been provisioned for the SBS network. The Remote Web Access link, however, will attempt to connect to the WSSE version of Remote Web Access, which should not be configured when you're running WSSE in an SBS environment.

FIGURE 16-41 The Launchpad

You can click Backup on the Launchpad to bring up the Backup Properties dialog box shown in Figure 16-42. From here, you can view previous backups, start a new backup, or change the Power Management settings.

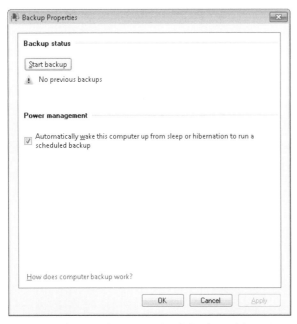

FIGURE 16-42 The Backup Properties dialog box of the WSSE Launchpad

From the Launchpad, you can also connect to the Dashboard for the WSSE server. Click Dashboard on the Launchpad to open the Dashboard window shown in Figure 16-43.

FIGURE 16-43 The Dashboard window of the Launchpad

From the Dashboard, you can configure your Windows Storage Server 2008 R2 Essentials server without having to have a keyboard, mouse, or monitor connected to it. The best place for this server is locked away in the server room or closet, or wherever you have your servers.

Summary

Windows Server Backup provides a basic but configurable backup and recovery tool, making scheduling backups and restoring backed-up information easier and faster. However, if you need to back up client computers, you'll need another solution. We think that Windows Storage Server 2008 R2 Essentials is a perfect solution for an SBS network and provides a high level of recoverability with a very easy to use interface.

In the next chapter, we move on to an analysis of the Windows SBS Console and Server Manager.

#### PART IV

Performing
Advanced Tasks

## CHAPTER 17

Windows SBS Console vs. Server Manager

The Windows Small Business Server (SBS) Console is the heart of the Microsoft Windows Small Business Server 2011 experience and is *the* preferred tool for managing SBS. Whenever possible, use the Windows SBS Console. The wizards and features built into the console are designed to work correctly with SBS and to simplify the tasks you need to perform.

That being said, Windows Server 2008 R2 includes a completely new Server Manager console that is a huge improvement on earlier management consoles. There will be some tasks that you'll likely need to use Server Manager for, so it's useful to familiarize yourself with it and to understand when to use it or the native stand-alone management consoles for Windows Server 2008 R2.

The native Windows Server 2008 R2 Server Manager is the tool you'll use to add a role, role service, or feature to SBS, and it is also a good gateway into native Windows Server 2008 R2 management tasks. There are some tasks, however, that without a doubt are best left to the Windows SBS Console, and we cover those as well, pointing out where using the native tools of Windows Server 2008 R2 is not an optimal choice.

Adding (and Removing) Roles and Features

Adding and removing roles from Windows Server 2008 R2 (and thus Windows Small Business Server 2011) can be done from either the Server Manager console or the Windows PowerShell command line. Both methods perform the same tasks and follow the same logic for which services get installed. But this is definitely a place where it's a whole lot easier to use the GUI. So unless you're deploying dozens of identical servers, just use Server Manager. (I can't believe we said that—we're the quintessential command-line types for almost everything. But this is one time where graphical just makes sense.)

UNDER THE HOOD   Server Manager—A New Way to Do Old Tasks

Previous versions of Windows Server used a freeform method for adding and removing the various features and abilities of Windows Server. This method could easily allow unnecessary services to be enabled, exposing the server to risk. Equally, it was possible to disable a critical feature or ability of Windows Server, causing other services or features not to work correctly. Troubleshooting these issues was time-consuming and frustrating, and the overall security of the server could be compromised. The Configure Your Server Wizard and the Manage Your Server Wizard of Windows Server 2003 were an attempt to resolve some of these issues by providing a simple interface that allowed for a single place to add or remove roles and manage those that were already on the server.

Windows Server 2008 R2 takes these old wizards and completely replaces them with the new Server Manager. The goal of Server Manager is to be the one place where you can add, manage, or remove roles, role services, and features on the server—your "one-stop shop" for all management tasks on Windows Server 2008 R2. For SBS, we've already got our primary interface—the Windows SBS Console. Most management tasks can be handled directly there. But you can't add roles from there, you can't add features, and some management tasks just don't lend themselves to highly standardized wizards, frankly. For all those things, you need Server Manager, the Windows SBS Native Tools Management console, or the individual stand-alone consoles. Plus, if you're running SBS Premium, you'll need Server Manager to manage the included copy of Windows Server 2008 R2 Standard.

What's different about Server Manager (and its PowerShell equivalent) is that it's a *requirement* for adding roles, role services, or features. When we first ran across this requirement to always use Server Manager for these tasks, we weren't very happy about it. In fact, we complained loudly and with a good deal of enthusiasm to more than one set of ears inside Microsoft. We saw it as an unnecessary and unproductive dumbing-down of Windows Server.

Everyone we said this to kept telling us to be patient and work with it. Well, we hate to admit it, but they were right. This is just a whole lot better and smarter way to install roles. Not only do you get the right *minimum* level of dependent services, but you also have the right configuration and exceptions for Windows Firewall—automatically.

Roles, Role Services, and Features

Windows Server 2008 R2 makes a distinction between a server *role*, a *role service*, and a *feature*. *Server roles* are broad groupings of common functionality that help define what a server is used for. Thus, a file server would have the File Services role installed, and a Remote Desktop server would have the Remote Desktop Services role installed.

Each of these broadly defined roles has available one or more role services. A *role service* is a particular functionality that is available only for the role for which it is a role service. Thus, for a file server with the File Services role installed, the following role services are available: File Server, Distributed File System (and its subsidiary services, DFS Namespaces and DFS Replication), File Server Resource Manager, Services for Network File System, Windows Search Service, and Windows Server 2003 File Services (including its subsidiary service, the Indexing Service). For the Remote Desktop Services role, the following role services are available: Remote Desktop (RD) Session Host, RD Virtualization Host, RD Licensing, RD Connection Broker, RD Gateway, and RD Web Access.

Features are Windows Server 2008 R2 functionality that doesn't require a specific role to be installed. Features are useful across a wide variety of server role configurations. Features include broad, general-purpose functionality, such as Group Policy Management, as well as narrow but non-role-specific functionality such as BitLocker Drive Encryption and Message Queuing.

Adding and Removing Roles

Roles reflect the tasks and services we expect of our servers. The File Services role includes various aspects of using SBS as a file server, one of the most basic tasks of our SBS servers. Generally, the roles that should be installed on the main SBS server are installed automatically as part of the installation of Windows Small Business Server 2011. And you should be very cautious about installing any additional roles on the main SBS server. SBS is a complicated and busy server already, and adding additional roles or functionality is not usually recommended. Instead, add a second server to your SBS network to add additional roles whenever possible, or use the second server that is part of the Premium Add-on for SBS.

Add a Role

Using the Server Manager console, you can add a role using the following steps:

> **NOTE** In these steps, we'll add the Remote Desktop Session Host role to our SBS 2011 Premium Edition second server. The steps are essentially similar for any role, though the exact screens and choices will be slightly different.

1. Open the Server Manager console if it isn't open already.

2. Select Add Roles from the Action menu to open the Before You Begin page of the Add Roles Wizard, as shown in Figure 17-1.

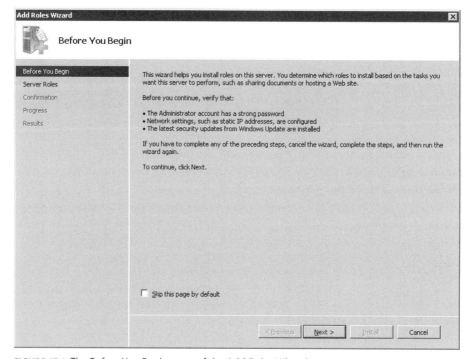

FIGURE 17-1 The Before You Begin page of the Add Roles Wizard

3. Read the advice on the Before You Begin page. It's actually good advice and a useful reminder. If you've read the page, understand all its implications, and don't ever want to see the page again, select the Skip This Page By Default check box.

4. Click Next to open the Select Server Roles page, as shown in Figure 17-2.

5. Select the server role(s) you want to add. You can select more than one, but doing so makes it much more likely that you'll have to reboot before the installation completes.

6. Click Next to open the page for the first role that will be installed, as shown in Figure 17-3 (if you selected Remote Desktop Services in the previous step). This page describes the role that is being installed, and it includes a Things To Note section that contains cautions or advisories specific to the role being installed. There is also a link to an Additional Information page with up-to-date information on the role being installed.

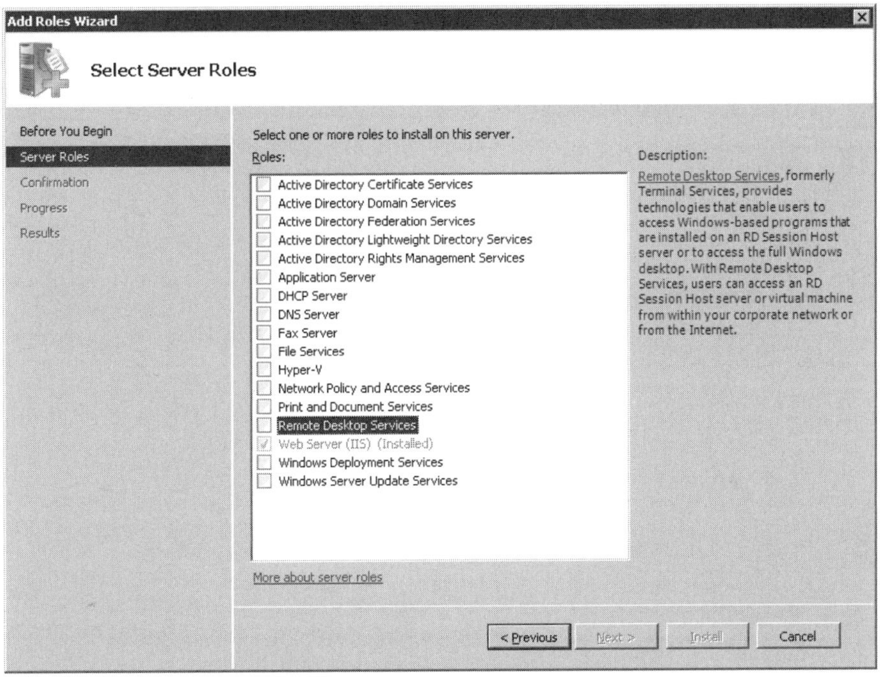

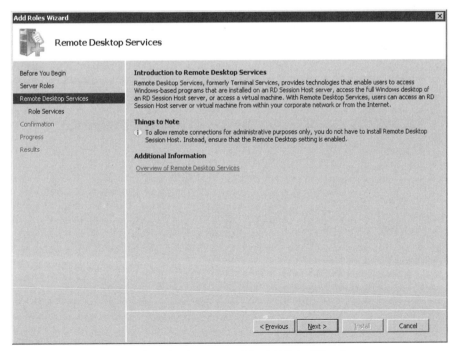

FIGURE 17-2 The Select Server Roles page of the Add Roles Wizard

FIGURE 17-3 The Remote Desktop Services page of the Add Roles Wizard

7. After you've read any Things To Note, click Next to open the Select Role Services page shown in Figure 17-4.

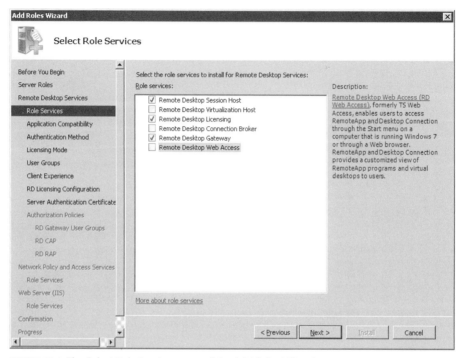

FIGURE 17-4 The Select Role Services page of the Add Roles Wizard

8. Select the role services you want to add at this time. If you select a role service that has a dependency on another role, role service, or feature, you'll see a pop-up dialog box describing the additional functionality that will be installed, as shown in Figure 17-5.

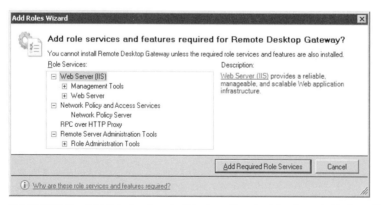

FIGURE 17-5 The Add Role Services And Features Required For Remote Desktop Gateway page of the Add Roles Wizard

9. Click Add Required Role Services to continue and return to the Select Role Services page, or click Cancel if you want to change your role services selection.

10. Click Next to open the next page in the Add Roles Wizard. From here to the end of the wizard, the specific pages will vary depending on what roles and role services you've selected.

> **NOTE** For Remote Desktop Services in an SBS environment, when you get to the Select User Groups Allowed Access To This RD Session Host Server page, it's useful to add the Windows SBS Remote Web Access Users group, as shown in Figure 17-6.

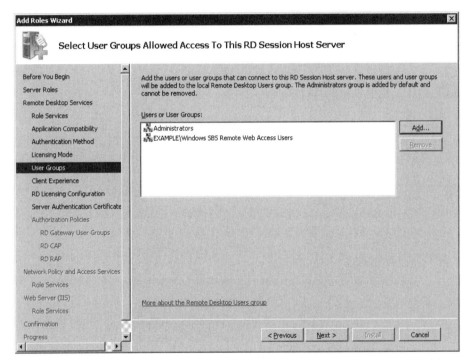

FIGURE 17-6 The Select User Groups Allowed Access To This RD Session Host Server page of the Add Roles Wizard

11. After the Add Roles Wizard has all the information necessary to proceed, it will open the Confirm Installation Selections page. This is your last chance to make sure you've selected the roles and role services you expected, and configured any necessary settings appropriate for your environment. If everything looks correct, click Install to begin the installation.

12. After the installation completes, you'll see the Installation Results page, shown in Figure 17-7. This page indicates whether the installation requires a restart or any other warnings or errors. Click Close to complete the wizard.

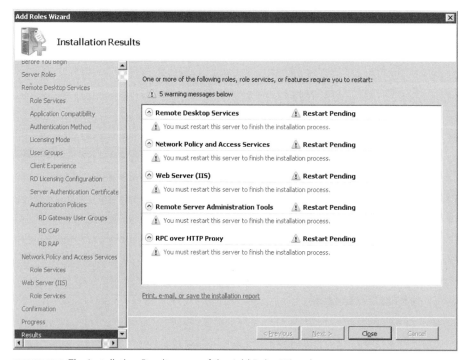

FIGURE 17-7 The Installation Results page of the Add Roles Wizard

13. If your installation requires a restart, you'll be prompted to restart the server. You might as well do it now because you can't install anything else while a restart is pending.

14. If your installation requires a restart, be sure to log back on with the same account you used to add the role. The installation can't complete until you log back on with that account. The Resume Configuration Wizard will open and complete the installation of the roles and role services you selected. Click Close when the installation is complete.

Removing a Role

You can use either the graphical Server Manager console to remove a role, or you can use the deprecated but still available command-line utility ServerManagerCmd.exe. Or you can use the Windows PowerShell Remove-WindowsFeature cmdlet. All have the same functionality: they remove only the explicit role selected. They will not usually remove any roles or role services that were added during the initial role installation to support the role being removed—unless the role, role service, or feature requires the role that is being removed. That's a bit confusing, isn't it? Okay, how about a specific example that makes it a bit clearer: Let's say you installed the Remote Desktop Services role with all its role services. You'll also have Network Policy And Access Services installed, along with Web Server (IIS). You can uninstall the entire Remote Desktop Services role, and neither the Network Policy And Access Services nor Web Server (IIS) roles will removed. But if you remove the Network Policy And Access Services role, it will also remove the Remote Desktop Gateway feature, as shown in Figure 17-8.

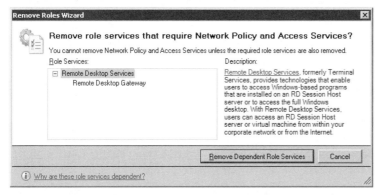

FIGURE 17-8 Removing the Network Policy And Access Services role forces removal of the Remote Desktop Gateway feature.

To remove a role using the Server Manager console, follow these steps:

1. Open the Server Manager console if it isn't already open.

2. Select Remove Roles from the Action menu to open the Before You Begin page of the Remove Roles Wizard.

3. Read the advice on the Before You Begin page. It's good advice and a useful reminder. If you've read the page, understand all its implications, and don't ever want to see the page again, select the Skip This Page By Default check box. Personally, we leave it cleared.

4. Click Next to open the Remove Server Roles page, as shown in Figure 17-9. Clear the roles you want to remove.

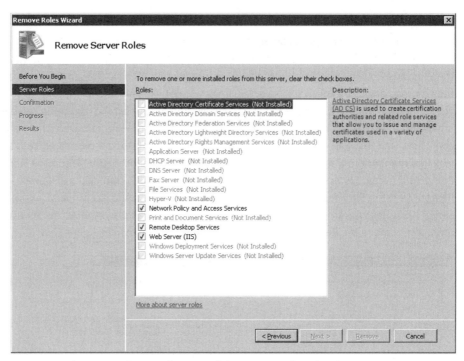

FIGURE 17-9 The Remove Server Roles page of the Remove Roles Wizard

5. If there are any dependent features, you'll be prompted to remove them also, as shown earlier in Figure 17-8.

6. When you've cleared the check boxes for any roles you want to remove, click Next to open the Confirm Removal Selections page, as shown in Figure 17-10. This page will often include one or more informational messages. Be sure you understand all implications of removing the role or roles.

> **NOTE** You can print, email, or save the information in the Confirm Removal Selections page by clicking below the informational window.

7. Click Remove to actually begin the removal.

8. When the removal has completed, you'll see the Removal Results page, as shown in Figure 17-11. If any of the roles or features require a restart, you'll see a message warning you that a restart is pending. In our experience, removing just about anything requires a restart.

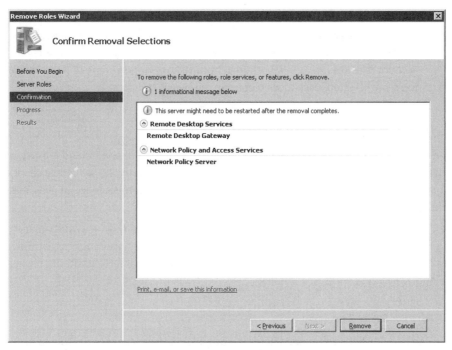

FIGURE 17-10 The Confirm Removal Selections page of the Remove Roles Wizard

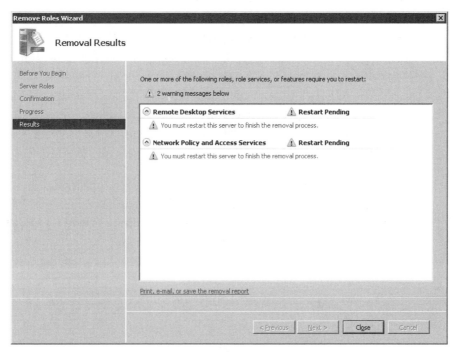

FIGURE 17-11 The Removal Results page of the Remove Roles Wizard

9. Click Close, and then click Yes if prompted for a restart.

10. If your removal requires a restart, be sure to log back on with the same account you used to remove the role. The removal can't complete until you log back on with that account. The Resume Configuration Wizard will open and complete the removal of the roles you selected. Click Close when the removal is complete.

Adding and Removing Role Services

In most situations, you'll add or remove role services as a part of adding and removing the roles they are services for. But often enough, you'll start out with one set of role services for a particular role and at some point discover the need to add a role service or even remove a role service for something that's no longer needed.

The process of adding and removing role services is much the same as adding and removing roles, and follows many of the same steps. Adding a role service requires that the role for that service be installed. You can't add the RD Licensing role service without having the Remote Desktop Services role installed.

Adding a Role Service

You can use either the command line or the graphical Server Manager console to add a role service. For our example, we'll assume you have already installed Remote Desktop Services to your second server, and you want to add the RD Licensing role service to the server. Follow these steps:

1. Open the Server Manager console if it isn't already open.

2. Click Remote Desktop Services in the left pane, and select Add Role Services from the Action menu to open the Add Role Services Wizard, as shown in Figure 17-12.

3. Select the role service you want to add, and click Next. If this role service has configuration choices, you'll have one or more pages of wizard to address. With the RD Licensing role service, you'll have the Configure Discovery Scope For RD Licensing page shown in Figure 17-13.

NOTE You generally should *not* set a discovery scope for RD Licensing on an SBS network. Instead, use the Remote Desktop Session Host Configuration console to explicitly set the RD Licensing server that your RD Session Host should use. In most scenarios, this will be the RD Session Host itself in an SBS environment.

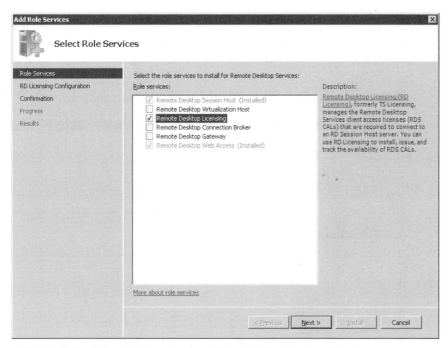

FIGURE 17-12 The Select Role Services page of the Add Role Services Wizard

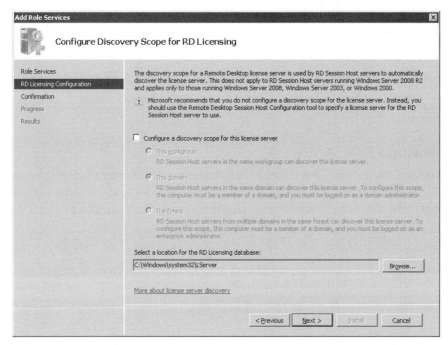

FIGURE 17-13 The Configure Discovery Scope For RD Licensing page of the Add Role Services Wizard

4. Do not select the Configure A Discovery Scope For This License Server check box.

5. Click Next to open the Confirm Installation Selections page.

6. Click Install to begin the installation.

7. After the installation is complete, the Installation Results page will open, as shown in Figure 17-14. If no restart is required, click Close to complete the installation.

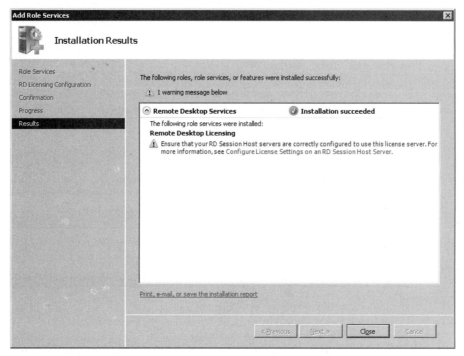

FIGURE 17-14 The Installation Results page of the Add Role Services Wizard

Removing a Role Service

Removing a role service doesn't necessarily remove the role. For example, you can remove the RD Licensing role service without affecting other role services of the Remote Desktop Services role.

As always, you can use either the command line or the graphical Server Manager console to remove role services. As with removing roles, we have a hard time understanding why anyone would use the command line to remove a role service in an SBS environment, but there's no particular reason not to. To remove the RD Licensing role service of the Remote Desktop Services role, follow these steps:

1. Open the Server Manager console if it isn't already open.

2. Click the Remote Desktop Services role in the left pane of the Server Manager console.

3. Select Remove Role Services from the Action menu to open the Select Role Services page of the Remove Role Services Wizard, as shown in Figure 17-15.

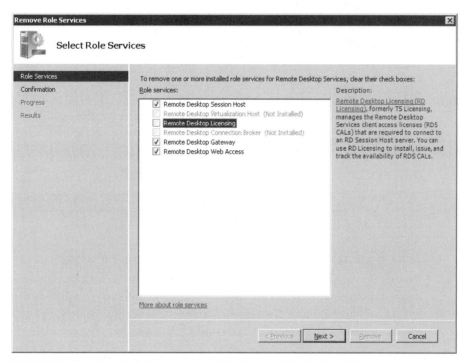

FIGURE 17-15 The Select Role Services page of the Remove Role Services Wizard

4. Clear the Remote Desktop Licensing check box, and click Next to open the Confirm Removal Selections page.

5. Click Remove to begin the removal process. When the process completes, you'll see the Removal Results page, as shown in Figure 17-16.

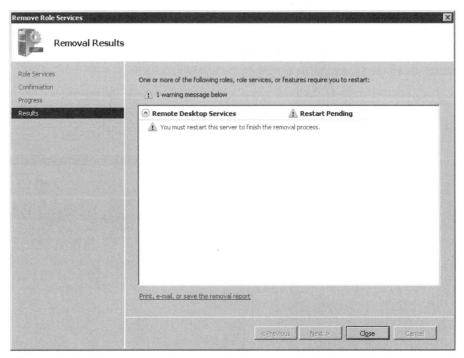

FIGURE 17-16 The Removal Results page of the Remove Role Services Wizard

6. Click Close to exit the wizard. Click Yes to restart the server if prompted.

7. If removing the role services requires a restart, be sure to log back on with the same account you used to remove the role service. The removal can't complete until you log back on with that account. The Resume Configuration Wizard will open and complete the removal of the role service you selected. Click Close when the removal is complete.

> **NOTE** Many roles and role services that can be added without a restart are not so well behaved when being removed. Expect to have to reboot when removing a role or role service.

Adding and Removing Features

Adding or removing a feature in SBS 2011 is a very similar process to adding or removing a role. The difference is that features are independent of the roles on a server—a feature can be added regardless of the roles that are already on the computer. Again, as with adding a role, if there's a dependency, the Add Features Wizard will automatically prompt you to add the required additional roles or features. You can also add features to a Windows Server 2008 R2 server that has the Hyper-V role installed without changing the licensing. For more information on licensing and Hyper-V, see Chapter 6, "Configuring SBS in Hyper-V."

Adding Features

Adding a feature to Windows Server 2008 R2 usually doesn't require other features or roles, though there are exceptions.

To install the two basic features we have on every server, follow these steps:

1. Open the Server Manager console if it isn't already open.

2. Click Features in the left pane of the Server Manager console.

3. Select Add Features from the Action menu to open the Select Features page of the Add Features Wizard, as shown in Figure 17-17.

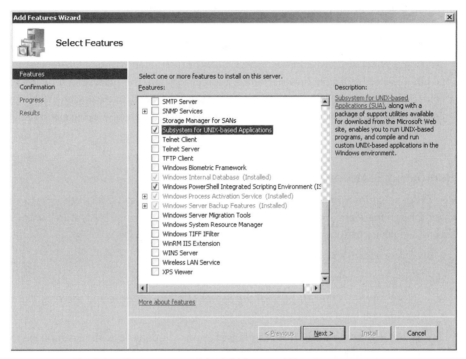

FIGURE 17-17 The Select Features page of the Add Features Wizard

4. Select the features you want to install, and click Next to begin the installation process.

5. When the process completes, you'll see the Installation Results page. If this page shows that one or more of your features has a pending restart, you'll need to restart the server before continuing.

6. Click Close to exit the wizard. Click Yes to restart the server if prompted.

7. If your installation requires a restart, be sure to log back on with the same account you used to add the features. The installation isn't complete until you log back on with that account. The Resume Configuration Wizard will open and complete the installation of the features you selected. Click Close when the installation is complete.

To install the same two features using the command line, use the following command:

servermanagercmd -install PowerShell-ISE Subsystem-UNIX-Apps

To install the same two features using Windows PowerShell, use the following commands:

Import-Module ServerManager

Add-WindowsFeature PowerShell-ISE,Subsystem-UNIX-Apps

In our experience, these two features can be installed together without requiring a server restart. We've added the preceding Windows PowerShell to our standard build configuration, ensuring that the tools we need and expect are available on all servers.

> **NOTE** Windows PowerShell is installed by default on all Windows Server 2008 R2 servers, including Windows Small Business Server 2011. The Integrated Scripting Environment (ISE) is not installed by default, however, and is a useful addition. The Subsystem for UNIX Applications is not installed by default and is probably useful only to those who must support mixed environments where UNIX and Linux are part of the SBS networking environment.

Removing Features

Removing a feature from Windows Server 2008 R2 usually doesn't affect other features or roles, though there are exceptions, including the .NET Framework 3.5.1 feature, which has several subsidiary features.

To remove a feature, follow these steps:

1. Open the Server Manager console if it isn't already open.
2. Click Features in the left pane of the Server Manager console and then highlight the feature you want to remove.
3. Select Remove Features from the Action menu to open the Select Features page of the Remove Features Wizard.
4. Clear the check box of the feature you want to remove and click Next, and then click Remove to begin the removal process.
5. When the process completes, you'll see the Removal Results page. If this page shows a pending restart, you'll need to restart the server before continuing.

6. Click Close to exit the wizard. Click Yes to restart the server if prompted.

7. If your removal requires a restart, be sure to log back on with the same account you used to remove the features. The removal isn't complete until you log back on with that account. The Resume Configuration Wizard will open and complete the removal of the features you selected. Click Close when the wizard is finished.

Using the Native Consoles

For many tasks, even most tasks, you should use the Windows SBS Console. There's even an Advanced Mode version that has links to the native consoles for the most commonly required tasks that don't have special SBS wizards. And for all your native consoles in a single place, use the Windows SBS Native Tools Management console, shown in Figure 17-18. It doesn't matter whether you get to native consoles from the Windows SBS Native Tools Management console, start them directly, or use Server Manager, the behavior is the same.

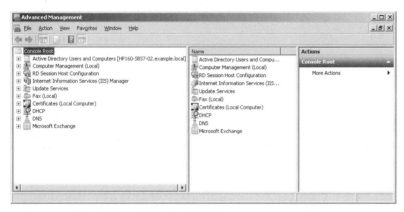

FIGURE 17-18 The Windows SBS Native Tools Management console

NOTE The title bar of this console says it's the Advanced Management console, but you open it from the Windows SBS Native Tools Management link in the Windows Small Business Server section of the Windows Start menu.

Using the Advanced Mode of the Windows SBS Console

The simplest way to work with the most commonly used native consoles is to open them from the Advanced Mode of the Windows SBS Console, shown in Figure 17-19.

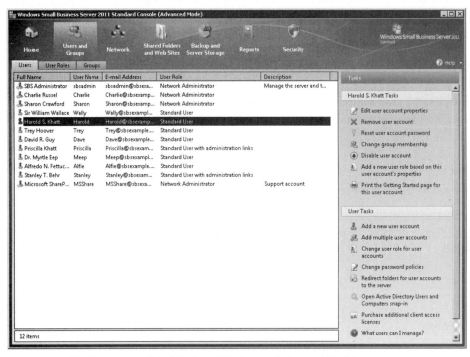

FIGURE 17-19 The Users page of the Windows SBS Console (Advanced Mode)

As you can see in the figure, there is an additional option in the Tasks pane of the Users page—a link to open the Active Directory Users And Computers snap-in. The Active Directory Users And Computers (ADUC) console is the native mechanism for managing users and computers in Windows Server 2008 R2. And there are definitely tasks that can only be performed easily from the ADUC console, not from the Windows SBS Console. For example, you can't add a contact from the Windows SBS Console—you need to use ADUC for that.

To use the Advanced Mode of Windows SBS Console to create a contact, follow these steps:

1. Click Start, All Programs, Windows Small Business Server, and then click Windows SBS Console (Advanced Mode) to open the console. (Be smart—put a link to this on your desktop, or pin it to the Start menu.)

2. Click Users And Groups and then click Users if it isn't in front.

3. In the Tasks pane, on the right, click Open Active Directory Users And Computers Snap-in to open ADUC as shown in Figure 17-20.

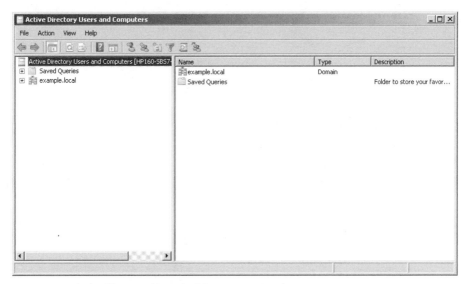

FIGURE 17-20 Active Directory Users And Computers console

4. Expand the domain name in the left pane, and navigate to the MyBusiness organizational unit (OU).

5. Click MyBusiness, select New, and then select Organizational Unit from the shortcut menu to open the New Object – Organizational Unit dialog box shown in Figure 17-21.

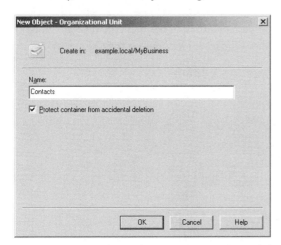

FIGURE 17-21 The New Object – Organizational Unit dialog box

6. Type in a name for the container, and click OK to create the OU.

7. Right-click the OU you just created, select New, and then select Contact as shown in Figure 17-22.

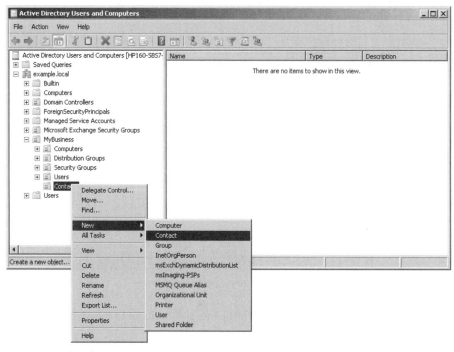

FIGURE 17-22 Creating a new contact

8. In the New Object – Contact dialog box, shown in Figure 17-23, fill in the fields for the new contact. We find it useful to add (external) to the name field when adding secondary email addresses for users who will have an account on the SBS server.

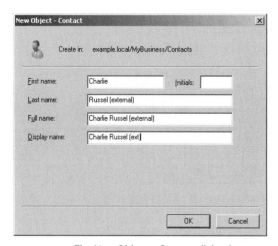

FIGURE 17-23 The New Object – Contact dialog box

9. Click OK to create the contact.

10. Click Properties on the Action menu to open the Properties dialog box for the new contact, and enter an email address as shown in Figure 17-24.

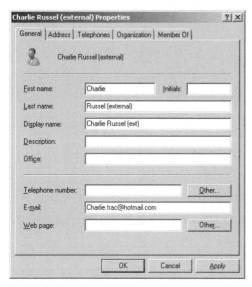

FIGURE 17-24 The Properties dialog box for a contact

11. Click OK to save the changes.

Using Server Manager

A good way to see the entire management interface for any server, regardless of the number of roles installed, is to use the Windows Server 2008 R2 Server Manager. This combines administrative, management, and monitoring functionality into a single console, giving you a single place to manage and monitor all the functionality of your SBS server that isn't managed and monitored from the SBS Console.

The most important part of the Server Manager console, shown in Figure 17-25, is the Roles section. Here you have not only a summary of the events, messages, and general health of the roles that are installed on your server, but also direct access to the individual management consoles for each role.

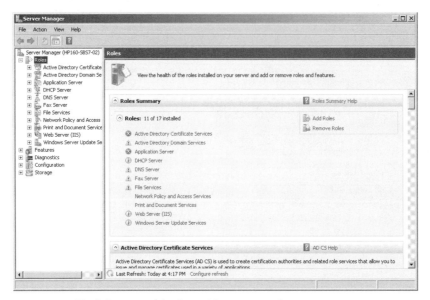

FIGURE 17-25 The Roles page of the Server Manager console

We'll use the Server Manager console to take care of a bit of configuration we need to do on our hp350-sbs-02.sbsexample.local server—configuring the printer and a couple of key workstations for DHCP reservations. This is something that simply can't be done directly from the SBS Console. And we *could* manually configure each of them with static IP addresses, but we prefer to use DHCP whenever possible. So the best solution is a DHCP reservation. It ensures that key workstations are always at the address we expect, but if we need to make a major change to the network addressing, it's all handled at one location, saving us from having to go around and manually configure individual devices or workstations.

To open the DHCP console in Server Manager and add a DHCP reservation, follow these steps:

1. Open the Server Manager if it isn't already open, and click Roles in the left pane.

2. Expand the Roles section and then expand the DHCP Server section by clicking the little plus sign to the left of the section you want to expand.

3. Drill down to the IPv4 Address Leases for your SBS server, as shown in Figure 17-26.

4. Right-click the device that you want to give a DHCP reservation to—in our case, the HP 3505 Color LaserPrinter that is in the Engineering office (ENG-PRN-01)—and select Add To Reservation from the menu, as shown in Figure 17-27.

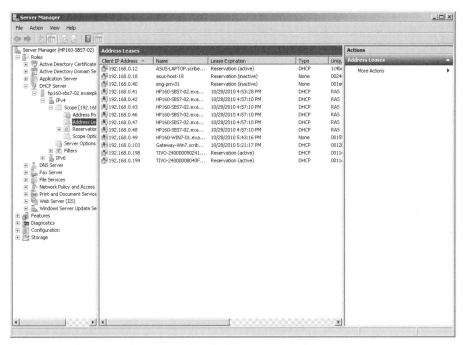

FIGURE 17-26 The IPv4 Address Leases for our EXAMPLE network

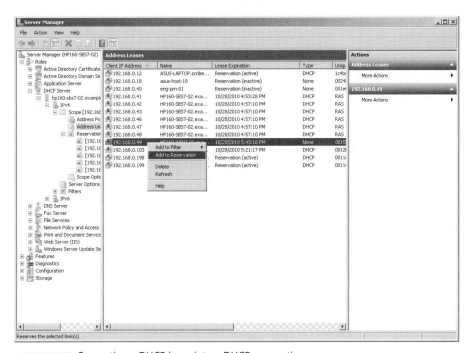

FIGURE 17-27 Converting a DHCP lease into a DHCP reservation

5. If the DHCP lease is successfully converted to a reservation, you'll see the message shown in Figure 17-28. Click OK.

FIGURE 17-28 The DHCP lease conversion message

Directly Opening Native Consoles

Although using the Server Manager console to access the management consoles for the roles and features on your server is a simple way to get at all of them from one location, we often find that it is awkward to navigate when a lot of roles are installed, and we also hate giving up any of our screen real estate for that left pane. So our solution is to simply open up the native management consoles directly. The GUI way is to open the Start menu and click Administrative Tools. This gives you a list of the available Administrative consoles, as shown in Figure 17-29.

The other way is to open them directly, either from the Run menu or using a Cmd or Windows PowerShell window. Our preference is to keep a Windows PowerShell window open on the desktop, and use that. Table 17-1 has a list of the management consoles, along with a couple of keyboard shortcuts for Control Panel applications that are easier to get at from the command line.

FIGURE 17-29 The available Administrative consoles on a Windows Small Business Server 2011 server

TABLE 17-1 Command-line shortcuts

COMMAND LINE	CONSOLE OR APPLICATION
Adsiedit.msc	Active Directory Services Interface (ADSI) Editor *
Azman.msc	Authorization Manager
Certmgr.msc	Certificates Manager
Certsrv.msc	Certificate Authority Manager
Certtmpl.msc	Certification Templates Console
Comexp.msc	Component Services Console
Compmgmt.msc	Computer Management Console *
Devmgmt.msc	Device Manager *
Dhcpmgmt.msc	DHCP Console *
Diskmgmt.msc	Disk Management Console *
Dnsmgmt.msc	DNS Manager Console *
Domain.msc	Active Directory Domains and Trusts
Dsa.msc	Active Directory Users and Computers *
Dssite.msc	Active Directory Sites and Services
Eventvwr.msc	Event Viewer *
Fsmgmt.msc	Shared Folders (File Services Manager)
Fsrm.msc	File Server Resource Manager
Gpedit.msc	Group Policy Editor
Gpmc.msc	Group Policy Management Console *
Gpme.msc	Group Policy Management Editor *
Gptedit.msc	Group Policy Starter GPO Editor
Lusrmgr.msc	Local Users and Groups Manager (Not for use on a domain controller)
Napclcfg.msc	Network Access Protection (NAP) Client Configuration Console
Nps.msc	Network Policy Server Console
Perfmon.msc	Performance Monitor *
Pkiview.msc	Private Key Infrastructure (PKI) Viewer
Rrasmgmt.msc	Routing and Remote Access Manager
Remoteprograms.msc	TS RemoteApp Manager *
Rsop.msc	Resulting Set of Policies Console
Secpol.msc	Local Security Policy Console

COMMAND LINE	CONSOLE OR APPLICATION
Servermanager.msc	Server Manager Console *
Services.msc	Services *
Storagemgmt.msc	Share and Storage Management Console *
Storexpl.msc	Storage Explorer Console
Tapimgmt.msc	Telephony Console
Taskschd.msc	Task Scheduler *
Tpm.msc	Trusted Platform Module (TPM) Management
Tsadmin.msc	Terminal Services Manager *
Tsconfig.msc	Terminal Services Configuration *
Tsgateway.msc	Terminal Services Gateway Manager
Tsmmc.msc	Remote Desktops Console
Virtmgmt.msc	Hyper-V Manager * (Note: this manager is not on your default path, but is installed in C:\Program Files\Hyper-V if present.)
Wbadmin.msc	Windows Server Backup Console *
WF.msc	Windows Firewall with Advanced Security Console *
Wmimgmt.msc	Windows Management Instrumentation (WMI) Manager
Appwiz.cpl	Control Panel: Programs and Features *
Desk.cpl	Control Panel: Display Settings *
Firewall.cpl	Control Panel: Windows Firewall
Hdwwiz.cpl	Control Panel: Add Hardware Wizard
Inetcpl.cpl	Control Panel: Internet Properties (Internet Explorer)
Intl.cpl	Control Panel: Regional and Language Options
Main.cpl	Control Panel: Mouse Properties *
Mmsys.cpl	Control Panel: Sound
Ncpa.cpl	Control Panel: Network Connections *
Powercfg.cpl	Control Panel: Power Options
Sysdm.cpl	Control Panel: System Properties *
Telephon.cpl	Control Panel: Phone and Modem Options
Timedate.cpl	Control Panel: Date and Time

These are the items we use regularly and that we think are worth learning. Also, .MSC is part of the environment variable PATHEXT, allowing you to skip typing the .msc part of the program name when you want to open one of the management consoles.

Summary

The majority of all your daily management tasks in Windows Small Business Server 2011 can be, and should be, performed using the Windows SBS Console or the Windows SBS Console Advanced Mode. But there will inevitably be some tasks that either can't be performed from there or that are more easily performed using the native Windows Server 2008 R2 management interface. Especially for managing the Premium Add-on second server. Before you use the native tools, always verify that you're not doing something that has a built-in SBS wizard. Whenever an SBS wizard is available, you should use it. The wizards almost always do several tasks in an integrated way that would be difficult to do directly using the native management tools, and you'll have a better-behaved and easier-to-manage SBS environment if you stick to the wizards whenever you can.

In the next chapter, we'll cover configuring and managing email, including the initial setup and configuration of Microsoft Exchange Server 2010.

## CHAPTER 18

Configuring and Managing Email

O ne of the central pillars of Microsoft Windows Small Business Server 2011 Standard (SBS 2011) is Microsoft Exchange Server 2010. Exchange Server is installed as part SBS 2011 Standard and provides a robust, full-featured, and flexible email and collaboration infrastructure.

Managing the Exchange infrastructure in a large organization is the task of one or more full-time Exchange administrators, but with Windows Small Business Server, most of the heavy lifting has been done by the SBS team. The initial installation and configuration of Exchange are handled automatically as part of the SBS install and the Getting Started Tasks list.

Basic Email Configuration

The default Exchange Server configuration is set up when you run the initial pass of the Set Up Your Internet Address Wizard and the Configure A Smart Host For Internet E-Mail Wizard. If you haven't completed these tasks, as described in Chapter 8, "Completing the Getting Started Tasks," you need to do that first.

Before you can run the Set Up Your Internet Address Wizard, shown in Figure 18-1, you need to either have your Internet domain name registered or have a good idea of the one you want to register, along with a couple of alternatives in case the one you want isn't available. If you already have a domain, you'll need to know whether you want to manage the DNS settings for it yourself or have SBS manage it for you. Personally, we prefer managing it ourselves, using a service such as ZoneEdit.com as our DNS provider, but for many small businesses it's just as easy to have SBS manage the domain for you.

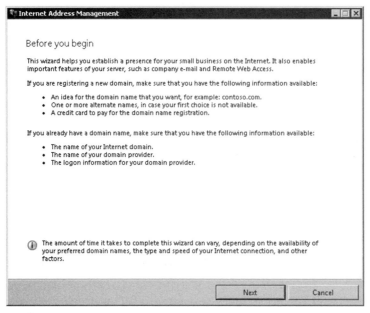

FIGURE 18-1 You need some basic information about your Internet domain name before you can configure email and your Internet address

Configuring Internet Mail

There are two basic methods for sending email from SBS: direct delivery and forwarding. Direct delivery uses DNS to route email directly to the server that the DNS records point to for the recipient's email domain. Email doesn't "pass through" any other Simple Mail Transfer Protocol (SMTP) servers along the way, and is shown as being directly sent from your SBS Internet domain.

The second method forwards all your mail to another SMTP server that is configured to both accept incoming email for forwarding and to understand how to find the correct destination for the email. Most Internet service providers (ISPs) provide this kind of forwarding server, known as a Smart Host, as do a variety of email filtering and protection services that you can use, such as ExchangeDefender (*http://www.exchangedefender.com*), our preferred spam-filtering service.

Choosing forwarding (Smart Host) as your email delivery mechanism has some drawbacks, not the least of which is that all email from your Windows Small Business Server will show that it has been forwarded from your ISP. This used to be a significant problem, but as the attempts to control unsolicited commercial email (UCE, or more commonly, spam) have matured, many ISPs don't give you a choice. If you're on their network, you have to use their SMTP server or they simply block your outgoing email. This is especially true if you have a dynamic IP address, because home computers that have malware installed on them are a common source of spam. In an attempt to prevent propagation of that spam, many ISPs are deliberately blocking TCP port 25 (the default port used by SMTP).

Unfortunately, some very fussy email domains refuse to accept mail that has passed through a mail forwarder, and even those who are not that absolute can end up blocking your email when your ISP gets on their blacklist—something you have no control over.

The solution is to have a fixed IP address on a business-class account with your ISP. This ensures that your IP address is a block of addresses that your ISP won't block and that other servers on the Internet will recognize as fixed addresses. This kind of account is usually a good deal more expensive than a basic floating IP address account designed for a home user. But you're *not* a home user, and you'll have far fewer problems if you use a business-class account.

The default configuration for Exchange Server is to deliver email to recipients directly, not through a Smart Host. Use that configuration by preference, and use a Smart Host only if you experience problems sending email or if you're using a service such as ExchangeDefender that acts as both an inbound filter and an outbound verifier.

Enabling a Smart Host

If you need to use a Smart Host, SBS has a wizard to help configure it for you. Hardly a surprise—SBS has a lot of wizards. Usually, you will have configured this by running the Configure A Smart Host For Internet E-Mail Wizard when you did the initial setup of SBS, but circumstances can change, so you can always run this later as well.

To configure SBS to use a Smart Host for Internet E-mail, follow these steps:

1. Open the Windows SBS Console if it isn't already open.

2. Click Network on the top navigation bar, and then click the Connectivity tab to open the Connectivity page, shown in Figure 18-2.

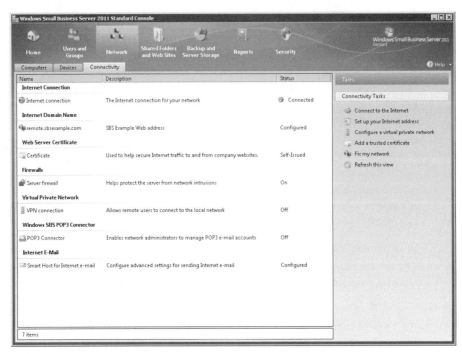

FIGURE 18-2 The Connectivity page of the Windows SBS Console

3. Click Smart Host For Internet E-mail, and then click View Outbound Internet E-mail Properties in the Tasks pane to open the Configure Internet Mail Wizard shown in Figure 18-3.

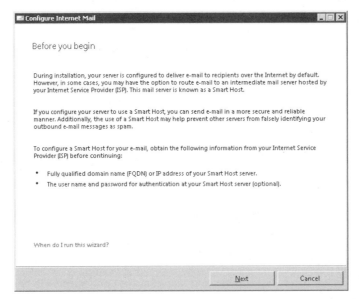

FIGURE 18-3 The Before You Begin page of the Configure Internet Mail Wizard

4. Click Next to open the Specify Settings For Outbound Internet Mail page shown in Figure 18-4.

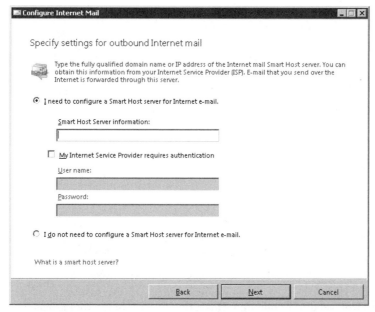

FIGURE 18-4 The Specify Settings For Outbound Internet Mail page of the Configure Internet Mail Wizard

5. Enter the information provided by your ISP for connecting to their Smart Host. Some ISPs require you to provide authentication to connect. This information is usually available on the support pages of your ISP.

6. Click Next to begin the configuration, and then click Finish to close the wizard.

Enabling DNS Email Sending

By default, Exchange Server in SBS uses DNS to determine where to send an email. If you haven't configured a Smart Host, you don't need to do anything at all to use DNS email sending. But if you've configured for Smart Host and need to change back to using DNS, you run the same wizard as when you configured for Smart Host. Follow these steps:

1. Open the Windows SBS Console if it isn't already open.

2. Click Network on the top navigation bar, and then click the Connectivity tab to open the Connectivity page shown earlier in Figure 18-2.

3. Click Smart Host For Internet E-mail, and then click View Outbound Internet E-mail Properties in the Tasks pane to open the Configure Internet Mail Wizard.

4. Click Next to open the Specify Settings For Outbound Internet Mail page shown in Figure 18-5.

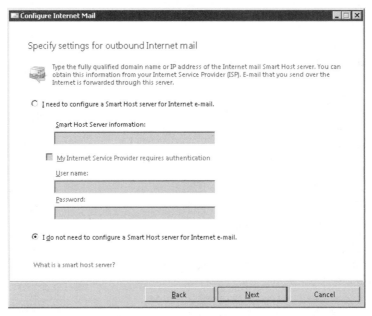

FIGURE 18-5 Removing the Smart Host to return to DNS email delivery

5. Select I Do Not Need To Configure A Smart Host Server For Internet E-Mail.

6. Click Next to begin the configuration, and then click Finish to close the wizard.

POP3 Email

Some small businesses still rely on external email accounts, and these accounts can be useful during the transition to a new SBS installation. We think using Microsoft Exchange is a far better solution overall, but SBS does support using external, Post Office Protocol v3 (POP3) email accounts. The Window SBS POP3 Connector has changed in SBS 2011 from the version in SBS 2003 in three important ways:

- POP3 email is brought to the SBS server using SMTP, allowing for full scanning and filtering, and direct integration into Exchange.
- POP3 email can be scheduled for retrieval every five minutes.
- The POP3 connector no longer supports generic email boxes. Each email box must be explicitly configured and assigned.

Configuring POP3 email requires you to know the email account properties—including the mail server, account name, and password—for each POP3 email account you want to add.

Setting up a POP3 email account requires providing some details about the account and about the settings used by the account provider. These settings usually can be found on the support pages of the ISP or mail account provider. The settings you'll need to know before you can set up an account are

- **POP3 Server**   The DNS name or IP address of the POP3 server—often *pop.ispname.com* or similar.

- **Port**   The TCP port to connect to the server. The default for regular POP3 is 110, and for Secure Sockets Layer (SSL) encrypted POP3 is 995.

- **Secure Sockets Layer**   Used to encrypt traffic to and from the POP3 server. Select this only if your ISP or POP3 mail provider supports SSL encryption.

- **Logon Type**   A drop-down list of supported types—Basic, Secure Password Authentication (SPA), or Authenticated POP (APOP). If your ISP doesn't support SSL and supports only Basic authentication, your account name and password are transmitted in plain text. If you must use a provider that supports only plain text, do *not* connect from a public wireless hotspot and *do not use the same password you use for anything important*.

You'll also need to know the full account name and password for the account. You should warn users not to change their passwords for the account without notifying whoever is responsible for maintaining the POP3 Connector.

Adding a POP3 Account

The process for adding POP3 accounts is simple, but tedious if you have more than a few to add. There's no way we know of to add them with a script.

To add a POP3 email account, follow these steps:

1. Open the Windows SBS Console if it isn't already open.

2. Click Network on the top navigation bar, and then click the Connectivity tab to open the Connectivity page shown earlier in Figure 18-2.

3. Click POP3 Connector in the main pane, and then click View POP3 Connector Properties in the Tasks pane to open the Windows SBS POP3 Connector dialog box, shown in Figure 18-6.

FIGURE 18-6 The Windows SBS POP3 Connector dialog box

4. Click Add to open the POP3 Mailbox Accounts page of the Windows SBS POP3 Connector dialog box, as shown in Figure 18-7. Enter the information to connect to the account. For details on the various settings, see the Under The Hood sidebar "POP3 Account Settings," earlier in this chapter.

FIGURE 18-7 The POP3 Mailbox Accounts page of the Windows SBS POP3 Connector dialog box

5. Click OK to return to the Manage POP3 Mailboxes page. From here, you can add additional mailboxes, edit an existing mailbox, or remove a mailbox.

6. When you've finished adding mailboxes, click OK to close the dialog box and implement the change.

Setting POP3 Retrieval Frequency

SBS allows you to control how often the POP3 connector retrieves messages from POP3 accounts. This control is limited to a single setting for any and all POP3 accounts—you can't set a different frequency on a per-account basis, unfortunately. The default retrieval frequency is every 15 minutes, but you can configure the POP3 connector to retrieve POP3 mail as often as every five minutes if you need to or scale back to only once every few hours, if that's more appropriate.

REAL WORLD   POP3 Frequency

One of the common complaints raised by users of SBS 2003 was the inability to set the POP3 frequency to more often than every 15 minutes. Microsoft has addressed this by allowing retrieval of POP3 mail every five minutes in SBS 2011. But just because you *can* do something doesn't necessarily mean you should.

Setting the POP3 retrieval interval too short can create a situation where the connector never actually completes. When large documents are attached to email and the network is busy, a five-minute interval can be too short a time to retrieve all the email for a site. This leads to churning and a generally unsatisfactory experience for users. If your email is so time-sensitive that you need to retrieve it more often than every 15 minutes, we strongly suggest moving your primary email to Microsoft Exchange. Well, actually, we recommend that anyway, but it's especially true for organizations that expect instant email.

To set the POP3 retrieval frequency, use the following steps:

1. Open the Windows SBS Console if it isn't already open.

2. Click Network on the top navigation bar, and then click the Connectivity tab to open the Connectivity page shown earlier in Figure 18-2.

3. Click POP3 Connector in the main pane, and then click View POP3 Connector Properties in the Tasks pane to open the Windows SBS POP3 Connector dialog box.

4. Click Scheduling in the left pane to open the Set POP3 Connector Schedule page, shown in Figure 18-8.

FIGURE 18-8 The Set POP3 Connector Schedule page

5. Change the Schedule section to automatically retrieve email at the interval desired. If you need to manually initiate a POP3 email retrieval, click Retrieve Now.

6. Click OK to initiate the schedule and return to the Connectivity page.

Advanced Email Configuration

While most things that you'll need to do for email configuration are easily handled from the Windows SBS Console, there are a few things that require running the Exchange Management Console, shown in Figure 18-9, or using Windows PowerShell scripts. Anything that can be done in the Exchange Management Console can also be done using Windows PowerShell in the Exchange Management Shell.

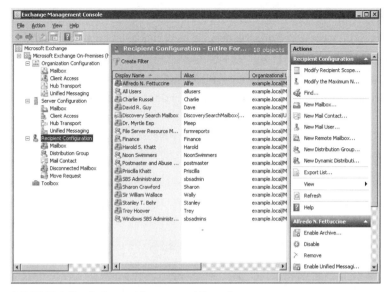

FIGURE 18-9 The Exchange Management Console

Trying to cover everything that can be done to configure Microsoft Exchange Server 2010 is an entire book, and not something we'll even try to do in this chapter. What we'll do is use a couple of examples to give you an idea of what kinds of things can be configured, and how to find them and use the Exchange Management Console to accomplish them. For additional details, we strongly suggest a bit of exploration through the graphical console or, when you need more help, we suggest reading *Microsoft Exchange Server 2010 Administration* (Sybex, 2010).

Using Contacts

In Microsoft Exchange terms, a *contact* is someone who doesn't need an Active Directory user account and doesn't have mail stored in Exchange. But a contact does need to be both a contact in Active Directory and mail-enabled in Microsoft Exchange. If you've created someone as a contact in Active Directory, he or she still needs to be mail-enabled in Exchange. If you're creating the contact directly in Exchange, you will also be adding him or her to Active Directory at the same time, so it's usually more efficient to add contacts directly from within the Exchange Management Console, or using the New-MailContact PowerShell cmdlet.

Mail-Enabling Existing Contacts

You can mail-enable existing Active Directory contacts. To mail-enable an existing contact, follow these steps:

1. Open the Exchange Management Console if it isn't open.

2. Navigate to Recipient Configuration and then click Mail Contact in the left pane of the console.

3. Click New Mail Contact in the Actions pane to open the New Mail Contact Wizard shown in Figure 18-10.

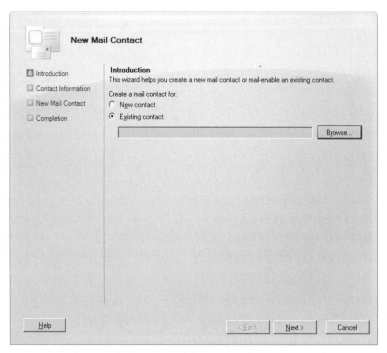

FIGURE 18-10 The Introduction page of the New Mail Contact Wizard

4. Select Existing Contact and click Browse to open the Select Contact dialog box shown in Figure 18-11. You'll see a list of all Active Directory contacts that are not currently mail-enabled.

5. Select the contact you want to mail-enable and click OK to return to the Introduction page of the New Mail Contact Wizard.

6. Click Next to open the Contact Information page of the New Mail Contact Wizard, as shown in Figure 18-12. Most of the fields will already be filled in because this is an existing contact.

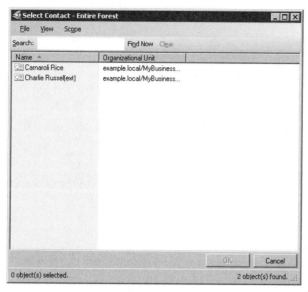

FIGURE 18-11 Browsing to find an Active Directory contact that needs to be mail-enabled

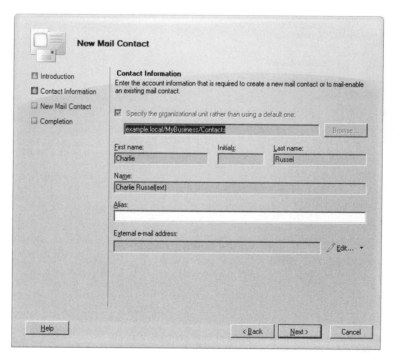

FIGURE 18-12 The Contact Information page for an existing Active Directory contact who is being mail-enabled

7. Click Edit to open the SMTP Address dialog box shown in Figure 18-13.

FIGURE 18-13 Adding an SMTP address to mail-enable a contact

8. Type in the email address for the contact and click OK to return to the Contact Information page of the New Mail Contact Wizard.

9. Enter an alias for the contact, as shown in Figure 18-14.

NOTE It's a good idea to use a standard way to identify contacts so that they don't get confused with internal users.

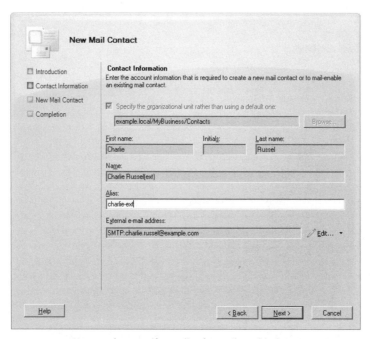

FIGURE 18-14 You need to specify an alias for mail-enabled contacts

10. Click Next to open the New Mail Contact page shown in Figure 18-15. This summarizes the actions that are about to be taken and is your last chance to cancel or to correct the information.

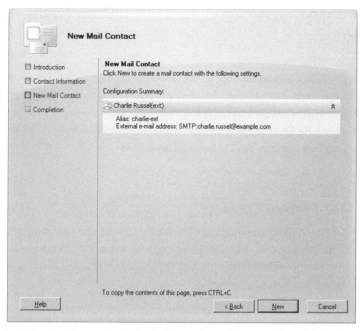

FIGURE 18-15 The New Mail Contact page shows the new mail-enabled contact that will be created

11. Click New to create the contact and open the Completion page shown in Figure 18-16.

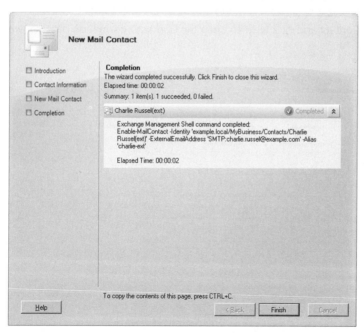

FIGURE 18-16 The Completion page shows the actual Windows PowerShell script that was executed

12. Click Finish to close the New Mail Contact Wizard and return to the Exchange Management Console.

> **NOTE** Press Ctrl+C on the Completion page of the New Mail Contact Wizard (or any other wizard in Microsoft Exchange 2010) to copy the contents of the page to the clipboard. This will include the Windows PowerShell script that was executed to complete the task. You can then paste this into your favorite editor (we use gvim, http://www.vim.org, but even Notepad will work), and use it as the basis to build future scripts.

Adding a New Mail-Enabled Contact

The steps for creating a new mail-enabled contact are similar to those for updating an existing Active Directory contact to be mail-enabled. However, when you're creating a new contact, you'll need to have additional information about the contact and know which organizational unit (OU) you want the contact to reside in.

Use the following steps to create a new mail-enabled contact:

1. Open the Exchange Management Console if it isn't already open.

2. Navigate to Recipient Configuration and then click Mail Contact in the left pane of the console.

3. Click New Mail Contact in the Actions pane to open the New Mail Contact Wizard.

4. Select New Contact and click Next to open the Contact Information page shown in Figure 18-17.

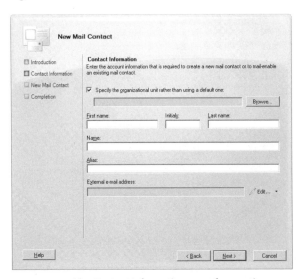

FIGURE 18-17 The Contact Information page for creating a new mail-enabled contact

5. Click Browse to open the Select Organizational Unit dialog box shown in Figure 18-18.

FIGURE 18-18 The Select Organizational Unit dialog box

6. Select the OU to use for this contact, and click OK to return to the Contact Information page.

7. Fill in the rest of the information for the contact, including an alias. We think it's a good idea to have a way to make it clear that this is an external contact in the alias because you'll be sending email to this contact outside your organization.

8. Click Edit to open the SMTP Address dialog box, and enter the SMTP address for the contact.

9. Click OK to return to the Contact Information page, and then Click Next to open the New Mail Contact page. This summarizes the actions that are about to be taken and is your last chance to cancel or to correct the information.

10. Click New to create the contact and open the Completion page.

11. Click Finish to close the New Mail Contact Wizard and return to the Exchange Management Console.

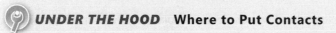

UNDER THE HOOD Where to Put Contacts

The default location used by the Exchange Management Console for new contacts is the SBSUsers OU. This is probably not ideal because by the naming alone, plus the hierarchy, it should have users, not contacts, as its members. We think it's a good idea to create an OU just to hold your contacts, making it clear what they are and helping to keep things organized.

Where to put the Contacts OU? And what to call it? Well, as for what to call it, *Contacts* seems like a perfectly good name, and it has the virtues of being both descriptive and simple. For where, we like to put it: under the MyBusiness OU because that's where everything for SBS tends to go, and then leaving it at the first level below that, as shown in Figure 18-18. But, ultimately, it doesn't really matter—just choose a place that works for you and then stick to it.

Adding an Additional Email Domain Name

One request we see regularly in the SBS forum is how to add an additional email domain that SBS can receive email for. Often a small-business owner combines several businesses under a single office and a single SBS network, but still needs to be able to receive email for each of those business names. Exchange Server makes that easy to implement. You can add additional domains that Exchange accepts mail for, and automatically update the email addresses of your users to include the additional domains.

Before you can accept email for another domain, however, you need to make sure that the outside world knows about that domain and how to reach it. You need to register your second domain name with one of the Internet registrars, and you need to set up DNS records for the domain. Those records need to include an MX record that sends mail to your SBS server. This record should point to the public IP address of your router.

Accepting email for an additional domain, however, is only part of the equation. You also need to change the recipient policies so that the new domain will propagate to your users.

When you're ready to have Exchange Server receive email for an additional domain, use the following steps to add the domain:

1. Open the Exchange Management Console if it isn't already open.

2. Navigate to Hub Transport in the Organization Configuration container in the left pane and then click the Accepted Domains tab in the center pane, as shown in Figure 18-19.

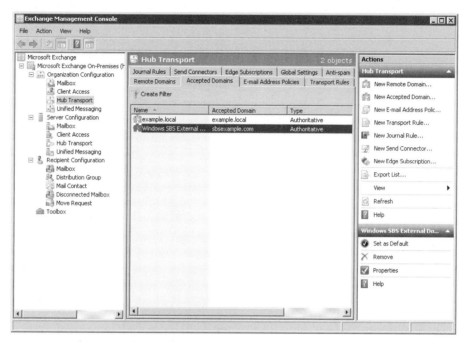

FIGURE 18-19 The accepted domains for our test SBS network

3. Click New Accepted Domain in the Actions pane to open the New Accepted Domain Wizard shown in Figure 18-20.

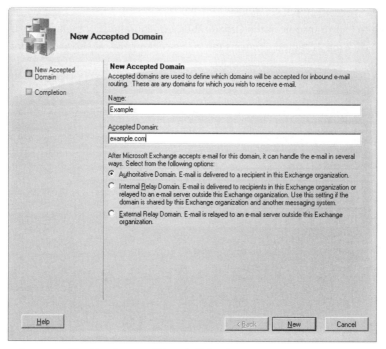

FIGURE 18-20 The New Accepted Domain Wizard

4. Enter a name for the domain you want to receive email for, and then enter the DNS domain name in the Accepted Domain field.

5. Click New and then click Finish when the task has completed. As with all other commands in the Exchange Management Console, you can save the Windows PowerShell script that was executed to complete the command on the Completion page before you close the wizard.

6. Click New E-Mail Address Policy in the Actions pane to open the New E-Mail Address Policy Wizard shown in Figure 18-21.

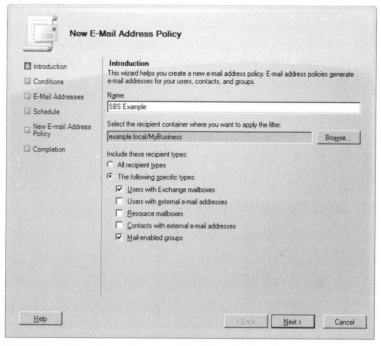

FIGURE 18-21 The Introduction page of the New E-Mail Address Policy Wizard

7. Type in a name for the new policy, and then click the Browse button to set the OU to the MyBusiness OU, as shown in Figure 18-22.

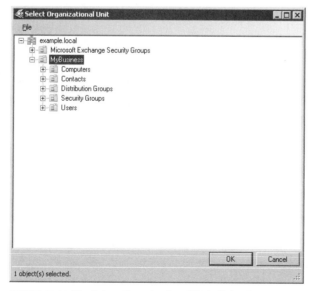

FIGURE 18-22 The Select Organizational Unit dialog box

8. Click OK to return to the Introduction page, and select Users With Exchange Mailboxes and Mail-Enabled Groups as shown in Figure 18-21. This should be a good starting point for most SBS networks, though if you're heavy users of Resource mailboxes (such as for scheduling conference rooms), you might want to add them as well.

9. Click Next to open the Conditions page of the New E-Mail Address Policy Wizard. You can use these conditions to filter which recipients the policy applies to. Click Preview to see a list of the accounts that will be affected by the current set of conditions. In most cases, you should leave the conditions blank on this page.

10. Click Next to open the E-Mail Addresses page.

11. Click Add to open the SMTP E-Mail Address dialog box shown in Figure 18-23.

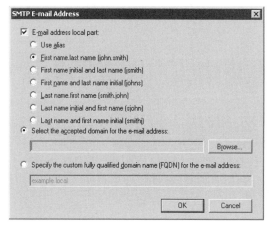

FIGURE 18-23 The SMTP E-mail Address dialog box of the New E-Mail Address Policy Wizard

12. Select the format of the email address to use, and then choose Select Accepted Domain For The E-Mail Address.

13. Click Browse to select the new accepted domain you added earlier.

14. Click OK to return to the E-Mail Addresses page, which will now show the address policy that will be applied, and click OK.

15. Click Next twice to open the Configuration Summary.

16. Click New to apply the policy, and then click Finish on the Completion page to close the wizard.

17. Select the original Windows SBS Email Address Policy and click Change Priority in the Actions pane to open the Change E-mail Address Policy Priority dialog box shown in Figure 18-24.

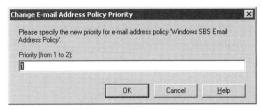

FIGURE 18-24 Set the address policy you want to control the Reply address for to a priority of 1

18. Click OK, and then click Apply in the Actions pane to open the Apply E-mail Address Policy Wizard shown in Figure 18-25. Select Immediately, click Next, and then click Apply to apply the change.

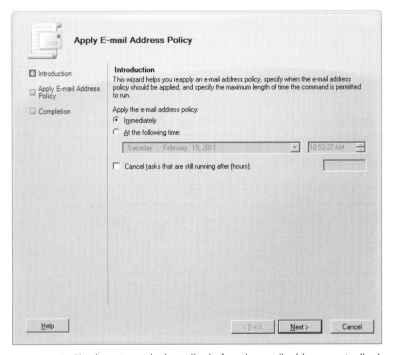

FIGURE 18-25 You have to apply the policy before the email addresses actually change

19. Click Finish to close the wizard and return to the Exchange Management Console. You're now receiving emails for the new domain.

 **UNDER THE HOOD**   Using Windows PowerShell for Exchange Management

The Microsoft Exchange Server 2010 Management Console is built entirely on Microsoft Windows PowerShell. All the commands and functionality that can be performed in the console can also be done from the Exchange Management Shell. Although most things are easily done from the Exchange Management Console, doing repetitive tasks from a graphical console can be a pain and is also far more prone to errors. Using the Windows PowerShell command line that the Exchange Management Shell provides gives you the ability to automate routine tasks.

For those not very familiar with Windows PowerShell, using the Exchange Management Console and then saving the Windows PowerShell script that was actually performed on the Completion page of the wizard gives you a great starting point for building your own scripts to perform similar tasks. A useful resource is the Exchange Team Blog at *http://msexchangeteam.com*.

Another good resource is Windows PowerShell itself, which is an extremely self-discoverable language. You can start by getting a list of all the Exchange-specific Windows PowerShell commands:

> *Get-Excommand > ExchangeCommands.txt*

This creates a file that has a list of all the Exchange-specific Windows PowerShell commands. If you see a command that looks like it might do what you want, such as creating a new distribution list, get some help with that command:

> *Help New-DistributionGroup*

You can get additional help, including examples of using the command, by adding the *–detailed* switch to the help command:

> *Help New-DistributionGroup –detailed*

To get some more general help with Windows PowerShell, try the following:

> *Help about**

This will give you a list of available general help topics and is a great way to start your Windows PowerShell Discovery Tour.

Changing the Maximum Message Size

The default maximum size of email messages, both incoming and outgoing, is set to 10 MB in SBS. Now for most organizations, this is probably adequate, but if you need to support larger messages, you can change the maximum size. But it turns out it's not all that easy, and there are lots of places you need to change it. Yes, you could do this from the Exchange Management Console, but heck, this is a perfect place to use a simple Windows PowerShell script to get the job done quickly and easily. So here's a simple script that accepts a single command-line parameter, the maximum size in megabytes that you want to set for your Exchange messages, and then changes the setting where it needs to. If you forget to include the size, it will prompt you for what size to set.

```
# Change-ExchSize.ps1

# Script to change the size of the maximum send and receive for
# a Windows SBS 2011 Standard installation with Exchange 2010
#
# Expects: maximum size parameter in MB or prompts
#
# Created: 19/2/2011
# ModHist:




param($MaxSize)
if (! $MaxSize ) {
$MaxSize = Read-Host "What's the max size(in MB) you want for all mailboxes? "
}
$stMaxSize = "$MaxSize" + "MB"


"Setting Maximum Send and Receive Transport Size to: $stMaxSize"
Set-TransportConfig -MaxSendSize $stMaxSize -MaxReceiveSize $stMaxSize
Get-TransportConfig | ft -maxsendsize,maxreceivesize


"Setting Maximum Send and Receive Connectors to: $stMaxSize"
$ReceiveConnectors = Get-ReceiveConnector
$SendConnectors = Get-SendConnector

ForEach ($Connector in $ReceiveConnectors ) {
    Set-ReceiveConnector -Identity $Connector.name -MaxMessageSize $stMaxSize
}
ForEach ($Connector in $SendConnectors ) {
    Set-SendConnector -Identity $Connector.name -MaxMessageSize $stMaxSize
}
```

```
"The Maximum Receive Connector size has been set to: "
Get-ReceiveConnector | ft Name, MaxMessageSize

"The Maximum Send Connector size has been set to: "
Get-SendConnector | ft Name, MaxMessageSize
```

NOTE This script must be run from the Exchange Management Shell on the SBS server, from an account in the Network Administrator role.

Summary

In this chapter, we covered the basics of setting up and configuring Microsoft Exchange Server 2010, which is a core component of Windows Small Business Server 2011 Standard. We included how to configure the new POP3 E-mail Connector for SBS. We covered three more advanced topics: mail-enabling contacts, adding an additional email domain name, and changing the maximum size of email messages as a window into the rich additional feature set that is possible with the Exchange Management Console or by using the Exchange Management Shell and Windows PowerShell. All the commands that are performed from the Exchange Management Console can be saved as Windows PowerShell scripts and executed directly from Windows PowerShell as scripts or interactive commands.

In the next chapter, we'll cover local connectivity, including TCP/IP, wireless connectivity, and the Windows Firewall.

## CHAPTER 19

Managing Local Connectivity

onnectivity is a huge topic, so we've decided to split it up this time into two chapters. In this chapter, we'll cover "local" connectivity, which we're arbitrarily defining as everything on the local area network (LAN) and everything you configure on your Microsoft Windows Small Business Server (SBS) 2011 server to allow you to safely connect to the outside world. In Chapter 20, "Managing Remote Access," we'll cover everything you need to connect *to* your SBS network when you're not in the office and physically connected to the LAN.

SBS includes well-designed wizards for many of the connectivity tasks we face in configuring and managing an SBS network. Some of these wizards have already been covered in other chapters:

- The Connect to the Internet Wizard to configure your Internet connection (Chapter 8)
- The Internet Address Management Wizard to set up and manage your Internet domain name (Chapter 8)
- The Add A Trusted Certificate Wizard to obtain and deploy a trusted certificate for your Internet domain (Chapter 8)
- The Configure Internet Mail Wizard to configure Microsoft Exchange to use a Smart Host for mail delivery (Chapter 18)

That's an important list of wizards and covers some of the biggest areas of network connectivity, but it does still leave quite a bit for this chapter, including

- DHCP and DNS
- Wireless connectivity
- Firewall configuration
- Fixing network problems

This last topic focuses on the Fix My Network Wizard, which replaces the Configure E-Mail and Internet Connectivity Wizard (CEICW) of SBS 2003.

Finally, in Chapter 20, we'll cover Remote Web Access and virtual private networks.

DHCP and DNS

SBS manages DHCP and DNS with no user intervention required in most cases. SBS configures itself to be the only DHCP server on the network, and the primary DNS server as well. You should normally not have to change any of the DNS or DHCP settings on your network for basic operation, but there can be specialized needs that require additional configuration. For example, on our network we prefer to have a larger excluded range of IP addresses that the DHCP server can't use because of how we configure key workstations and printers.

> **NOTE** The tools you need for DHCP and DNS are the DHCP console (dhcpmgmt.msc) and the DNS Manager console (dnsmgmt.msc), respectively. You can open these consoles from the Administrative Tools menu, from the SBS Native Tools Management console, from the Windows SBS Console (Advanced Mode), or directly from the command line. We use the command line.

Managing DHCP

DHCP automatically provides computers on the local network segment with valid IP addresses and important additional configuration settings, including the addresses of DNS servers and the default gateway, along with other configuration settings if needed. SBS manages the core DHCP settings automatically, but you can add additional settings as appropriate for your environment, as well as view and manage the current address leases and exclusions. If your network includes printers or other devices that require unchanging IP addresses, you can either exclude the address from use by DHCP and manually set the device or configure DHCP for an address reservation to ensure that the device will always get the same address. On our network, we also assign DHCP reservations to key workstations so that they're at predictable IP addresses to simplify troubleshooting.

> **NOTE** Although it isn't required to exclude a DHCP address that you assign a reservation to, we prefer to exclude an entire range of addresses and then use DHCP reservations within that range for computers and devices we want predictable addresses for. Not the normal way, but it works for us and our admittedly specialized needs.

UNDER THE HOOD   DHCP Options Scope

In SBS, you can set DHCP options at three different levels: server, scope, and reservation. Options that are set at the server level apply to all DHCP address leases on the server, and therefore on your SBS network. Normally, SBS has only a single DHCP scope, so options you set at the scope level are also applied to all DHCP address leases. Options that are set at the DHCP scope level override any options that are set at the server level.

When you create a DHCP reservation, you commit a specific network card to a specific IP address on your SBS network. You can also, as part of the DHCP reservation, configure additional options for that DHCP client. Any options set at the DHCP reservation level will override those set at the scope or server level.

SBS expects to be the only DHCP server on your network, and if it senses another DHCP server, it will stop the DHCP Server service to prevent handing out duplicate IP addresses. During initial installation of SBS, if there are other DHCP servers on your network (such as your router), the setup process will either disable the other DHCP server if it responds to a UPnP request, or will prompt you to disable the server manually. While it's technically possible to use some other DHCP server rather than the SBS server, the SBS wizards are designed to function best if SBS controls the DHCP server functionality.

Viewing Current DHCP Address Leases

To view the addresses currently leased to clients, complete the following steps:

1. Open the DHCP console if it isn't already open.

2. In the left pane, expand the containers until you can select Address Leases in the IPv4 container, as shown in Figure 19-1, to view a list of currently assigned IP addresses and their corresponding host names.

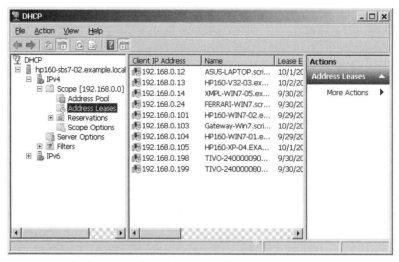

FIGURE 19-1 Viewing assigned IP addresses

Creating Exclusions in DHCP

The pool of addresses that a DHCP server can lease to clients is called a *scope*. For any device on the network that has a static IP address within the scope, you need to create an exclusion to prevent the DHCP server from handing out that address to a client.

 REAL WORLD **DHCP Exclusions**

The default configuration of DHCP in SBS creates an exclusion for IP addresses from .1 to .10 in your SBS network subnet (192.168.0 in our screen shots here). This leaves more than 240 addresses in the subnet that can be handed out by the DHCP server. We prefer to have a larger exclusion on our network to allow for additional fixed IP addresses for key workstations and devices on the network. These are usually configured as DHCP reservations, but can also be configured as fixed IP addresses. We add an additional exclusion from .11 to .40 to allow plenty of room for those fixed IP addresses—which still leaves more than 200 DHCP addresses for computers and devices on the network.

To create an exclusion, complete the following steps:

1. Open the DHCP console if it isn't already open.

2. In the left pane, expand the containers until you can select Address Pool.

3. Select New Exclusion Range from the Action menu.

4. In the Add Exclusion dialog box, shown in Figure 19-2, use the Start IP Address and End IP Address boxes to specify the range of IP addresses you want to exclude. To exclude a single IP address, type it in the Start IP Address box and leave the End IP Address box blank.

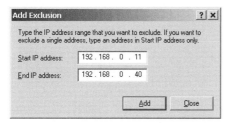

FIGURE 19-2 The Add Exclusion dialog box

5. Click Add to create the exclusion. Create any additional exclusions, and then click Close when you're finished.

Adding a DHCP Reservation

As an alternative to manually setting and managing IP addresses for fixed IP devices, such as printers, you can use DHCP to assign an address and configuration settings to the device, and then use a DHCP reservation to ensure that the device always gets that address and that no other device or client is assigned that address. Because reservations inherit the scope options and can be easily modified from a single point, it's much better to use a reservation instead of manually setting or managing IP addresses for devices that support DHCP.

 UNDER THE HOOD **Finding the MAC Address**

If the device you want to create a reservation for is already connected to the network and has been assigned a DHCP address, you don't need to hunt around to find the Media Access Control (MAC) address for it. But if you want to create a reservation for a device that doesn't yet have an IP address, you need its MAC address to make a reservation. Although you could read the MAC address off the network device (there's a sticker *somewhere* on the device with the address), that's hardly easy in most cases. So, how to easily get the MAC address? Well, two ways we know are using the getmac command, and the ipconfig command.

To obtain the MAC address using the ipconfig command, go to the client computer (or make a remote desktop connection) and type ipconfig /all at the command prompt. The MAC address is listed as the physical address. Using ipconfig /all doesn't require elevation.

To obtain the MAC address using the getmac command, from a command prompt, type

```
getmac /s computer /v
```

where *computer* is the IP address, host name, or DNS name of the remote computer you want the MAC address for.

Finally, you can obtain the MAC address of any current DHCP client by looking at the current DHCP lease for the client—the MAC address is shown in the Unique ID column.

To create a DHCP reservation for an existing DHCP client, complete the following steps:

1. Open the DHCP console if it isn't already open.

2. In the left pane, expand the containers until you can select Address Leases in the IPv4 section.

3. Right-click the device you want to create a reservation for, as shown in Figure 19-3, and select Add To Reservation.

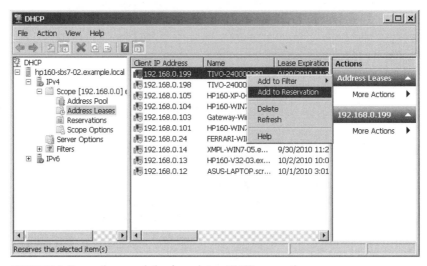

FIGURE 19-3 Converting an existing lease into a DHCP reservation

4. Click OK. The existing DHCP lease will be converted into a DHCP reservation.

To create a DHCP reservation for a device that doesn't currently have a DHCP address, complete the following steps:

1. Open the DHCP console if it isn't already open.

2. In the left pane, expand the containers until you can select Reservations.

3. Select New Reservation from the Action menu to open the New Reservation dialog box shown in Figure 19-4.

- **Reservation Name**   Usually the DNS name for the device or client. Choose a name that conforms to DNS naming requirements for best compatibility.

- **IP Address**   The IP address that you are reserving for this device or client.

- **MAC Address**   The Media Access Control or hardware address of the network card for the device or client. This is a hexadecimal number that is globally unique and is generally printed directly on the device.

- **Description**   A descriptive phrase that will make it easier to identify the specific device the reservation is assigned to.

- **Supported Types**   The choices are Both, DHCP only, or BOOTP only. BOOTP is an older protocol for automatically assigning IP addresses and configuration details that is no longer commonly used, but selecting the Both option is the best choice unless you have a specific reason not to.

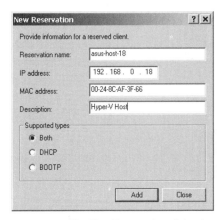

FIGURE 19-4 The New Reservation dialog box

4. Click Add, and the reservation is added. The reservation will inherit the configuration options that have been set for the DHCP scope, and you can add specific options for each reservation.

Setting DHCP Options

The process for setting DHCP options is essentially the same regardless of the level you set the option at. As described in the "DHCP Options Scope" Under The Hood sidebar earlier in the chapter, each level of DHCP inherits options from the higher level but can override them. As an example of setting DHCP options, we'll set the Host Name option for the DHCP reservation for our printer. (The printer is assigned a DHCP reservation at 192.168.0.40.)

To set the host name for the printer using a DHCP option, use the following steps:

1. Open the DHCP console if it isn't already open.

2. In the left pane, expand the containers until you can select Reservations.

3. Select the DHCP reservation for the printer in the left pane, and select Configure Options from the Action menu to open the Reservation Options dialog box.

4. Scroll down in the Available Options list to 012 Host Name, and select the check box next to it as shown in Figure 19-5.

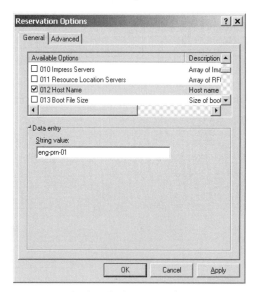

FIGURE 19-5 Setting the host name for a DHCP reservation

5. Enter the host name for the printer in the String Value field, and click OK to return to the DHCP console.

Enabling DNS Updates

On an SBS server, the DHCP server is by default not configured to automatically update the DNS server when it assigns an IP address to a client. This is not a problem for Windows clients because they will update their own records. But if you have other types of DHCP clients, you can configure DHCP to handle the DNS update automatically.

To enable DHCP to automatically update the DNS records, follow these steps:

1. Open the DHCP console if it isn't already open.

2. Right-click IPv4, select Properties, and then click the DNS tab to bring up the IPv4 Properties dialog box, shown in Figure 19-6.

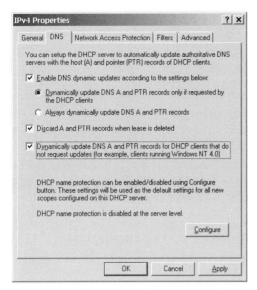

FIGURE 19-6 The DNS tab of the IPv4 Properties dialog box

3. Select the Enable DNS Dynamic Updates According To The Settings Below check box. If you have dumb devices, such as printers, also select the Dynamically Update DNS A And PTR Records For DHCP Clients That Do Not Request Updates check box.

4. Click OK when you've made your changes to return to the DHCP console.

Managing DNS

SBS uses the DNS server service for local name resolution only. SBS automatically creates three DNS zones: two forward lookup zones and a reverse lookup zone. It creates a forward lookup zone for the internal domain (example.local), which allows you to use a DNS name to resolve an IP address with computers and devices on the internal network. It also creates a "split DNS" for resolution of your public DNS name by creating a local version for use by internal clients so that they can reach the "public" resources such as Remote Web Access (RWA) and Outlook Anywhere without actually leaving the internal network. External clients can't reach that internal server, so their DNS queries for these resources point to the public IP address of your SBS network. It also creates a reverse lookup zone (0.168.192.in-addr.arpa in the screen shots in this chapter), which enables you to resolve the DNS name associated with a particular IP address (a useful trick for troubleshooting). All three zones use secure dynamic updates so that Windows clients can automatically and securely update their own DNS records.

SBS manages DNS automatically for Windows clients. Non-Windows clients and devices, however, will not have DNS records automatically created and maintained. In most situations, this is perfectly OK, but if you need to ensure that client IP addresses are fully resolvable on the SBS network, you'll need to either manually create and maintain the records or configure

DHCP to automatically update them as described earlier in the "Enabling DNS Updates" section.

Adding a DNS Record

You can manually configure DNS records for fixed IP address clients or clients that use a DHCP reservation. By adding the records, you ensure that their IP address can be resolved from their names, simplifying management and troubleshooting. However, it does require that you maintain the records and ensure their accuracy, and manual editing and maintenance of DNS records is something to avoid if at all possible. However, for special devices that you need to assign a fixed IP address to and that don't handle DHCP well, manually adding the records to the DNS server is the only solution. To add A and PTR (Address and Pointer) records to the SBS DNS server, follow these steps:

1. Open the DNS Manager console (Dnsmgmt.msc) if it isn't already open.

2. Select the internal DNS domain in the left pane as shown in Figure 19-7 (example.local in the screen shot).

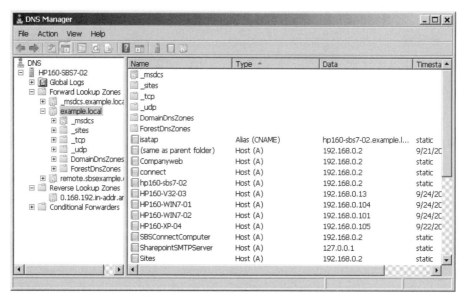

FIGURE 19-7 The DNS Forward Lookup Zone for the internal network

3. Select New Host (A Or AAAA) from the Action menu to open the New Host dialog box shown in Figure 19-8.

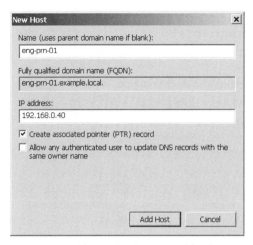

FIGURE 19-8 Adding a new host record for the printer

4. Fill in the host name and IP address for the new DNS record, and select the Create Associated Pointer (PTR) Record check box to also create a reverse lookup record for the device.

5. Click Add Host, and then click OK on the DNS message dialog box to create the record.

6. Click Done to return to the DNS Manager console.

DNS Forwarding

When a client makes a DNS query of a DNS server and it doesn't have the information either in its own records or in its cache of known IP addresses from previous queries, there are three possible options for the server:

- Return a Record Not Found message.
- Forward the query to a nearby server that might have the information.
- Forward the query to one of the Internet's root DNS servers.

Obviously, the first option isn't terribly useful, unless you're creating a very private test network and you don't want any queries going outside it.

The second option, DNS Forwarding, was the default behavior for SBS 2003. In SBS 2003, the DNS server was configured to automatically forward DNS requests that it didn't have the answer for to the DNS server of your Internet service provider (ISP). This was efficient, because the ISP's DNS servers were usually no more than a hop or two away, and the answer was quickly returned. A good idea if you trust your ISP to have accurate and safe DNS servers.

The third option is for the server to forward any DNS query for which it doesn't have the answer to the Internet's DNS root servers. This option, which uses root hints, is somewhat slower than querying the ISP's servers, which are a lot closer, but it does ensure an accurate answer.

REAL WORLD DNS Poisoning Attacks

The standard setup for most internal DNS servers, including SBS 2003, is to set up your DNS server as a primary zone and then configure it to forward all other requests to your ISP's designated DNS servers. This results in fast and private support for internal name resolution, while providing the fastest resolution of names outside your private network and reducing overall traffic for your ISP and the Internet as a whole. Unfortunately, this exposes your network to DNS poisoning attacks such as the widespread cache-corruption attack that affects all versions of BIND before version 9. If some malicious program manages to subvert the DNS servers maintained by your ISP because your ISP hasn't gotten around to updating them, your DNS server will pass that problem on to your internal clients.

The problem is especially a concern if your ISP is somewhat slow to apply patches to its DNS servers, as seems to be the case for many ISPs, both large and small. BIND is the most common DNS server software used by ISPs, and several vulnerabilities have been identified for BIND, especially versions before BIND 9. Patches to correct these vulnerabilities are available, but if your ISP is slow to apply the patch, you could be exposed.

If you don't specify a server to forward to, your DNS server will use root hints to directly resolve the address. This might be somewhat slower, and it certainly increases the overall traffic on the Internet, but if the root servers are poisoned, we're all in trouble. If you trust your ISP to maintain its servers adequately, go ahead and forward to their servers. Personally, we've stopped doing so, and we're really glad that SBS 2011 doesn't, either. If you do trust your ISP and you want to configure SBS 2011 for DNS Forwarding, use the following steps:

1. Open the DNS Manager console if it isn't already open
2. Right-click on IPv4 in the left pane and select Properties from the shortcut menu.
3. Click on the Forwarders tab, as shown in Figure 19-9.
4. Click Edit to open the Edit Forwarders page shown in Figure 19-10.
5. Click in the Click Here To Add An IP Address Or DNS Name field, and enter either the IP address or DNS name of the DNS server you want to forward queries to.
6. Click OK to close the Edit Forwarders dialog box, or add additional entries as desired.

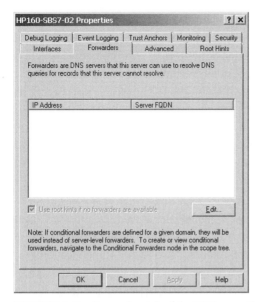

FIGURE 19-9 The Forwarders tab of the DNS server Properties dialog box

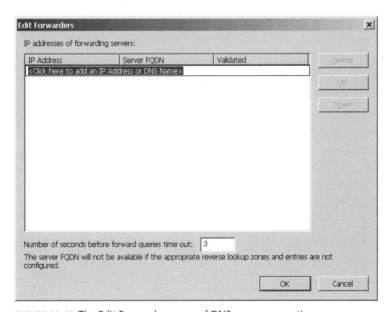

FIGURE 19-10 The Edit Forwarders page of DNS server properties

7. Leave the Use Root Hints If No Forwarders Are Available check box selected unless you want the failure or unavailability of your ISP's DNS server to cause DNS queries to fail on your network.

8. Click OK to close the DNS server Properties dialog box and return to the DNS Manager console.

Wireless Connectivity

Wireless connectivity has become an essential business tool. We expect to be able to connect wirelessly wherever we go and, increasingly, our expectations are met. But providing wireless access inside your SBS network is a bit different. You still generally need to do it, but you need to take serious precautions to ensure that you don't compromise security.

We've heard arguments on all sides of the wireless security question, from those who appear to think that simply hiding your wireless network is all that's required, to those who claim there is no such thing as a secure wireless network and we shouldn't ever use or allow it. Well, as with most such arguments, the answer is somewhere in the middle.

Exactly where in the middle is really about your own comfort level and perception of risk. There are ways to implement full Two Factor Authentication (TFA) for wireless connectivity, and they can be done even on a small network if you want and need to spend the resources to do it. (For more on TFA, see the Real World sidebar "Two Factor Authentication and RWA" in Chapter 20.)

Wireless security has come a long way from the early days of wireless networking. Initially, there was Wired Equivalent Privacy (WEP) that came in two levels: 64-bit and 128-bit. Unfortunately, the algorithm for WEP was seriously flawed, and by 2001 there were widely available decryption programs that let virtually anyone who wanted to compromise WEP security. We now believe that WEP is actually worse than no security at all. It is so easy to compromise that it should be considered no security at all, but it gives users a false sense of security.

WEP was replaced with Wi-Fi Protected Access (WPA), and finally by WPA2. WPA2—also known by its Institute of Electrical And Electronics Engineers (IEEE) standard designation of 802.11i—has two levels of security: WPA2-Enterprise and WPA2-Personal.

WPA2-Enterprise uses an 802.1X or RADIUS server to distribute different initial keys to every user. This 802.1X server can use Two Factor Authentication to further increase security. Realistically, implementing WPA2-Enterprise is more than most SBS networks can do, but if you want to try it, a good starting place is this document on TechNet: *http://technet.microsoft.com/en-us/library/bb457068.aspx*.

> **NOTE** For a full list of available wireless documentation on TechNet, see *http://technet.microsoft.com/en-us/network/bb530679.aspx*.

WPA2-Personal uses a Pre-Shared Key (PSK) of 8 to 63 characters in length, and it can use either Advanced Encryption Standard (AES) or Temporal Key Integrity Protocol (TKIP) encryption. TKIP provides backward compatibility with devices designed for the original WPA standard, but it has been compromised and we don't recommend it. When WPA2-Personal is used with AES and has a minimum 16-character PSK, it provides acceptable security for most small businesses and can be easily implemented. Another important requirement is to choose a wireless network name (SSID) that is not the default on your wireless access point (WAP).

The basic requirements for secure wireless access to your SBS network are

- Use one or more wireless access points (*not* routers).
- Use a static (or DHCP reservation) for the WAP IP address.
- Disable the DHCP server on the WAP.
- Change the SSID of the WAP to one that is appropriate for the network but isn't either the default or something that too clearly identifies your company.
- Change the password of the WAP to a password of at least 12 characters.
- Enable AES as the only encryption method.
- Choose a PSK of at least 16 characters. Longer is better. Alternately, use a USB key and Windows Connect Now (WCN) if your WAP supports it. WCN will generate a random 64-character key.

 REAL WORLD **Wireless Security Strategies**

A variety of security strategies for wireless networking have been suggested and used over the years—some useful and some not. The following list details our evaluation of several of these strategies:

- **MAC Address Filtering**   This strategy allows only a statically managed list of MAC addresses to access the wireless network. It's a nice idea, but this strategy is easy to defeat with a sniffer because MAC addresses can be easily spoofed. Plus, a static list of "allowed" MAC addresses is a hopeless mess to manually maintain. All in all, it's a complete waste of time.

- **SSID Hiding**   This strategy requires that the client know the name of the wireless network to be able to connect to it. And even if the network is known and configured into the Windows client, that client must continually probe to make sure that the network is present. This requirement causes all sorts of problems and limits the ability of Microsoft Windows to manage connections. The strategy is totally useless because anyone with access to the packets in the air can read the SSID from the commonly sent 802.11 management frames in a matter of seconds—whereas broadcasting the SSID, when combined with appropriate security, makes the network easier to manage and easier for users as well. Hiding the SSID is another complete waste of time.

- **WEP Encryption**   The original encryption standard for wireless, this standard uses either a 40-bit or 104-bit key (along with a fixed 24-bit initialization vector). It is easily hacked by anyone with bad intentions and will keep only the most casually curious out of your network. WEP keys are static keys and must be manually maintained. Every time a user who has wireless access leaves the organization, the WEP keys need to be changed. A network protected with WEP alone should be considered completely unsecured.

- **WPA** The original WPA encryption standard is based on RC4, which can be compromised. However, because it changes keys with sufficient frequency and derives the new keys in an improved way as compared to WEP, it was a significant improvement over WEP, and it could generally be implemented without buying new hardware. With 802.1X authentication and the appropriate authentication method, the initial encryption keys are automatically generated.

- **WPA2** The WPA2 encryption is based on AES and is much more secure than RC4, while the WPA2 standard incorporates additional security measures beyond just encryption. Both Pre-Shared Key (WPA-Personal) and RADIUS/802.1X authentication (WPA2-Enterprise) scenarios are supported. This is the minimum wireless security standard you should allow on your SBS network.

- **IEEE 802.11i** This is the underlying standard for WPA2, which is described in the preceding bullet point.

- **VPNs** One solution to setting up secure wireless networks is to place the wireless network outside your main network and use a VPN connection to the main network. This approach has the advantage of getting around the insecurities of older equipment, but it has inherent problems. If the external access point is open and unsecured, it leaves the client exposed to any other computer in range. It also imposes a performance hit and requires a VPN connection for every client. Machine group policies are not applied, and the overall reliability of the connection and the administrative overhead are significant issues as well. For more on the good and bad of VPNs, see Chapter 20.

- **IEEE 802.1X** Using 802.1X as the authentication mechanism for WPA2 encryption is an excellent solution, but implementing it on most SBS networks isn't realistic.

We know some of these points are a bit controversial, but we also think that it's possible to allow wireless clients on your internal SBS network. But only if you set realistic minimum standards and don't use ineffective "security" measures that provide a false sense of security while actually doing little, if anything, to protect you from an attack.

Windows Firewall

The Windows Firewall in Windows Server 2008 R2 is the same basic firewall included in Windows 7 and adds many new features and capabilities compared to the Windows Firewall included in previous versions. These new features include outbound filtering; filtering based on SIDs; a better management UI; configuration for local, remote, local port, remote port, and protocol; and tight integration with IPsec. The other big change is location-specific policies. There are three separate firewall profiles: a domain profile, a private profile for computers that aren't domain members but are on secured networks, and a public profile for computers that reside on publicly accessible networks. And, finally, per-user rules are now supported. Although these profiles aren't terribly useful for the SBS server itself, which uses only the Domain Profile, the same profiles are used by Windows 7 and Windows Vista computers and can be enforced with Group Policy.

In SBS, the Windows Firewall is on by default. All of the wizards in SBS and Windows Server 2008 R2 that are used to add roles and features will automatically set the necessary Windows Firewall rule or rules to ensure proper functionality while still securing the server.

SBS 2003 R2 had a built-in firewall, but most of the wizards used to configure the server were not designed to configure the firewall, and most environments had the Windows Firewall disabled on servers, relying on an external firewall, or ISA 2004 on SBS Premium servers, to protect the network. In SBS 2011, the expectation is that the Windows Firewall remains enabled.

The Windows Server 2008 R2 Windows Firewall allows more granular control over the configuration and settings than previous versions. To open the Windows Firewall With Advanced Security console, shown in Figure 19-11, type **wf.msc** at the command prompt, click Windows Firewall With Advanced Security in the Administrative Tools folder, or open the Firewall Settings in the Security page of the Windows SBS Console.

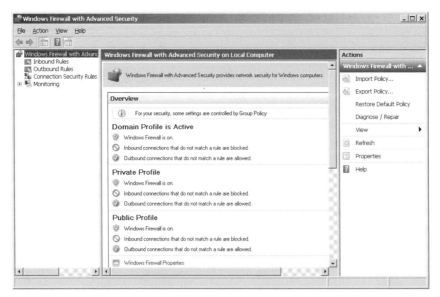

FIGURE 19-11 The Windows Firewall With Advanced Security console

IMPORTANT SBS configures the firewall automatically as part of the normal SBS wizards. You should only make changes directly with extreme caution. Know not only what problem you're trying to solve, but why it isn't automatically handled by the SBS wizards. And be sure you understand the security implications whenever you make a change.

Windows Firewall has three profiles: a Domain Profile, a Private Profile, and a Public Profile. Each profile can have different inbound and outbound rules as needed. To build a specific rule, click Inbound Rules or Outbound Rules and then click New Rule. Custom rules can be set for programs or for ports. The SBS server uses only the Domain Profile.

Setting Firewall Policies Using Group Policy

Use Group Policy to ensure a consistent application of Windows Firewall policies across the domain. Using normal Group Policy rules as discussed in Chapter 21, "Using Group Policy," you can set up a Group Policy to manage a group of systems. Use the built-in Windows Management Instrumentation (WMI) filters of SBS Group Policy to set specific policies for different types of clients and servers.

Firewall Rule Basics

When building Windows Firewall rules, there are three possible actions for a connection that matches the rule:

- Allow the connection.
- Only allow a connection that is secured through the use of IPsec (authenticated bypass).
- Explicitly block the connection.

The order of precedence for Windows Firewall rules is as follows:

- Authenticated bypass
- Block connection
- Allow connection
- Default profile behavior

This means that if you have a Block rule and an Allow rule, and your connection meets both criteria, *the block rule will always win*. By being as specific as possible with your rules, you have less likelihood of conflict and more direct control. Port rules are much more general than application rules and should be avoided whenever possible.

Rule Definitions

Building rule definitions is the process of building a combination of conditions and specific access types into a rule that either allows or disallows a connection.

Rules can be defined for

- **Programs**   Specific applications that are either allowed or disallowed by the rule
- **Ports**   General allow or disallow of a protocol through a port
- **Predefined**   Preconfigured and well-known services and programs
- **Custom**   Can combine programs, ports, and specific interfaces into a custom rule

Rules can allow or disallow traffic to or from programs, system services, computers, or users.

Rules can use protocol values of

- Any
- Internet Assigned Numbers Authority (IANA) IP protocol numbers
- TCP
- UDP
- ICMPv4
- ICMPv6
- Others including IGMP, HOPOPT, GRE, IPv6-NoNxt, IPV6-Opts, VRRP, PGM, L2TP, IPv6-Route, IPv6-Frag

Rules for local ports (UDP or TCP) can include

- All Ports
- Specific Ports (comma-separated list)
- Dynamic RPC
- RPC Endpoint Mapper
- Edge Traversal

Rules for Remote Ports (TCP and UDP) can include

- All Ports
- Specific Ports (comma-separated list)

Rules for ICMP traffic (ICMPv4 and ICMPv6) can be

- All ICMP types
- Specific types of ICMP traffic

Rules can be for a Local IP address scope of

- Specific IPv4 or v6 address or list of addresses
- Range of IPv4 or v6 addresses or list of ranges
- Entire IPv4 or v6 subnet or list of subnets

Rules can be for a remote IP address scope of

- Specific IPv4 or v6 address or list of addresses
- Range of IPv4 or v6 addresses or list of ranges
- Entire IPv4 or v6 subnet or list of subnets
- Predefined set of computers (local subnet, default gateway, DNS servers, WINS servers, DNS servers or a list of such items)

Rules can specify an interface type of

- All interface types
- Local area network
- Remote access
- Wireless

Rules can include program types of

- All programs
- System (a special keyword that restricts traffic to the system process)
- Specific path and .exe name to an executable

Rules for services can

- Apply to all programs and services
- Apply to services only
- Apply to a specified service

There are three predefined special local ports

- Dynamic RPC is used by applications and services that receive dynamic RPC traffic over TCP. (Does not include traffic over named pipes.)
- RPC Endpoint Mapper is used only with the RPCSS service and allows traffic to the endpoint mapper.
- Edge Traversal is used only with the iphlpsvc (Teredo) service and allows the traffic to be decapsulated by the Teredo service on a dynamic port.

Additional rules can be set to allow only secure connections. For secure connections you can specify that the connection

- Require encryption
- Allow connections only from specified computers in Active Directory
- Allow connections only from specified users or security groups in Active Directory

IMPORTANT Whenever possible, resist the temptation to create specific Windows Firewall rules for specific computers or users. Although it is technically possible, it can quickly become a management and documentation nightmare. Use the SBS security groups and OUs to control firewalls. This is flexible and easy to maintain, and can be easily documented.

Creating a Firewall Policy

You create Firewall Policies by combining rules and assigning them to groups of users or computers either through a WMI filter or an organizational unit (OU). As an example, use the following steps to create a rule that blocks Live Messenger from a server computer:

1. Open the Group Policy Management Console.
2. Navigate to the SBSServers OU as shown in Figure 19-12.

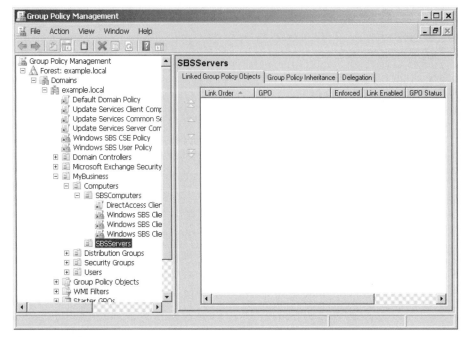

FIGURE 19-12 The SBSServers OU in the Group Policy Management Console

3. Right-click SBSServers and select Create A GPO In This Domain, And Link It Here from the shortcut menu to open the New GPO dialog box shown in Figure 19-13.

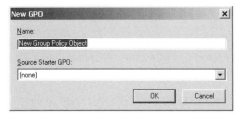

FIGURE 19-13 The New GPO dialog box

4. Give the GPO a name and click OK.

5. Highlight the new policy in the Linked Group Policy Objects pane and right-click. Select Edit from the shortcut menu to open the Group Policy Management Editor, shown in Figure 19-14.

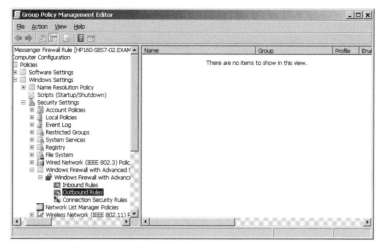

FIGURE 19-14 The Group Policy Management Editor

6. Navigate to the Outbound Rules container of Windows Firewall With Advanced Security, as shown in Figure 19-14.

7. Right-click Outbound Rules and select New Rule from the shortcut menu to open the New Outbound Rule Wizard shown in Figure 19-15.

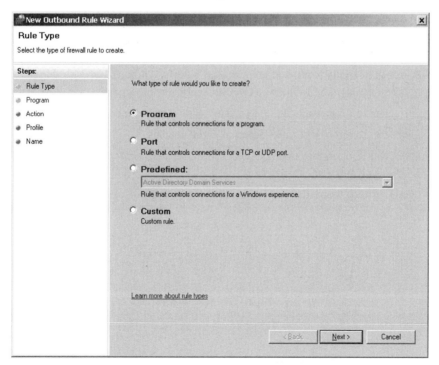

FIGURE 19-15 The Rule Type page of the New Outbound Rule Wizard

8. Select Program and click Next to open the Program page, as shown in Figure 19-16.

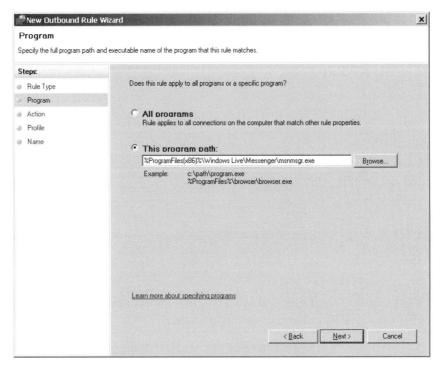

FIGURE 19-16 The Program page of the New Outbound Rule Wizard

9. Select This Program Path and enter the full path to Windows Live Messenger.
   (%ProgramFiles(x86)%\Windows Live\Messenger\msnmsgr.exe).

10. Click Next to open the Action page. Select Block The Connection.

11. Click Next to open the Profile. Select all three profiles.

12. Click Next to open the Name page. In the Name field, enter **Windows Live Messenger**, and add a description.

13. Click Finish to create the rule. The result is shown in Figure 19-17.

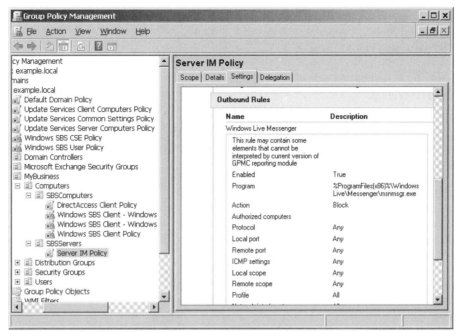

FIGURE 19-17 The Group Policy Management Console, showing the new Outbound Rule

> **NOTE** This block rule is hardly sufficient to block all instances or types of instant messaging from the servers on an SBS network, but it's presented to show how the Firewall Policy rules work and are configured.

Fixing Network Problems

In a perfect world, networks would never fail, no one would ever have to change a network card, IP addresses would be automatically assigned and never change, and no one would ever have to try to troubleshoot a network connectivity problem. Well, IPv6 helps with some of this, but we're afraid that there's still a long way to go until we reach network nirvana. Until we do, however, there's the Fix My Network Wizard (FMNW) in SBS.

The FMNW is the replacement for the Configure E-Mail And Internet Connectivity Wizard (CEICW) of SBS 2003. With the advent of IPv6 as an essential networking protocol, the job of repairing your network and configuring it to an expected state has gotten much bigger, and the FMNW is the result. The role of the FMNW is the same for both local and remote connectivity—identify variances from the networking state that SBS expects, and change everything it can to that expected state. Where it can't make the change, such as the router configuration on a router that doesn't have Universal Plug and Play enabled, it identifies the problem and suggests the changes you need to make manually. Because the FMNW addresses both local and remote connectivity issues, we've chosen to wait and cover it at the end of Chapter 20, "Managing Remote Access."

Summary

Local connectivity is a huge topic, and this chapter has tried to cover the most important areas for SBS networks. We covered DHCP and DNS, wireless connectivity, and firewall configuration.

In the next chapter, we'll cover remote connectivity and network troubleshooting.

## CHAPTER 20

Managing Remote Access

I n the days before computers, workers went to work and then went home. At home, they might be reachable, but anything they needed to do required going back in to work. Then computers and pagers and finally cell phones came along, and workers were expected to be reachable virtually any where and any time. But that electronic leash didn't come with an equal ability to access the resources to resolve the problem or deal with the issue. All too often, responding to that electronic leash meant going in to work. Windows Small Business Server 2011 Standard (SBS), however, gives you new and im-proved tools to enable access to critical resources from wherever you are, without having to come in to the office.

The two central pillars of SBS that give you access to the network's resources are Remote Web Access (RWA) and virtual private networks (VPN). RWA is the replacement for the Remote Web Workplace (RWW) of previous versions of SBS, and it adds impor-tant new functionality. A third remote access solution, Remote Desktop Services (RDS) and RemoteApps, is an excellent solution for SBS sites that have the Premium Add-on and are running a second Windows server. RDS and RemoteApps is covered in detail in Chapter 26, "Adding a Terminal Server," including how to integrate RemoteApps into RWA.

Remote Web Access

When RWW was introduced in SBS 2003, it was a revolutionary new way to enable remote access to network resources in a secure and convenient manner that was the source of not a little envy from enterprise networks that had nothing equivalent.

In SBS 2011, RWW has been replaced by RWA, shown in Figure 20-1, which has im-proved functionality as compared to RWW, and is shared with other products, such as Windows Small Business Server 2011 Essentials, and Windows Home Server 2011.

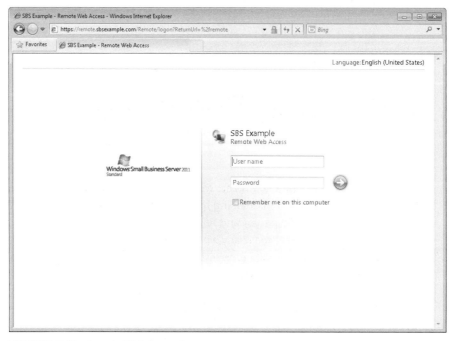

FIGURE 20-1 The Remote Web Access logon page

The basic premise of RWA is to provide a secure way for remote users to access the resources of the SBS network. Users connect to the RWA landing page, shown in Figure 20-2, and from there they can

- Connect to their desktop in the office
- Upload and download files to the folder shares on the SBS server
- Connect to the company's internal website (Companyweb)
- Read their email using Microsoft Outlook Anywhere
- Change their password
- Connect to additional help or features as available

Administrative users have additional options available, including the ability to connect to the SBS server or other servers on the network.

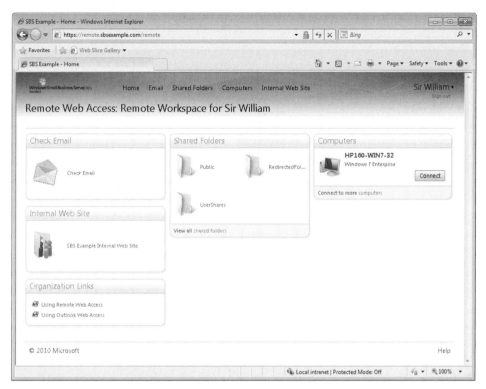

FIGURE 20-2 The Remote Web Access landing page for standard users

Configuring the RWA Computer List

A major change in SBS 2011 RWA is the ability to limit the list of computers that a user sees when he logs in to RWA. In SBS 2003, the list of computers showed all the available workstations in the domain—not a big deal in an SBS domain of 5 users, but a bit of a pain in an SBS network of 50 users.

In SBS 2011, each user sees only the list of computers that he's allowed to connect to. The list is created initially when you join the computer to the SBS network, as shown in Figure 20-3.

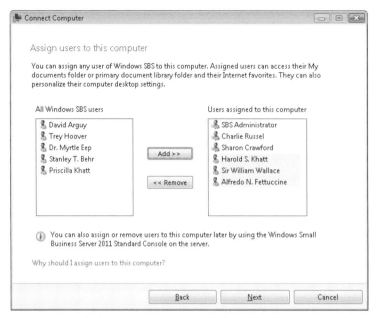

FIGURE 20-3 Assigning users to a computer during initial deployment of the computer

After computers are set up, however, you can easily change this list. We tend to think from a user perspective, rather than a computer perspective, so we change it by configuring the computers that a user account is assigned to. To change the list of computers that a user can connect to from RWA, open the Windows Small Business Server 2011 Standard Console (Windows SBS Console) and then use the following steps:

1. Click on Users And Groups in the navigation bar, and then on the Users tab.

2. Select the user you want to modify, and then click Edit User Account Properties in the Tasks pane to open the Properties dialog box for the user, as shown in Figure 20-4.

3. Click Computers in the left pane to open the Set Network Computer Access page, shown in Figure 20-5.

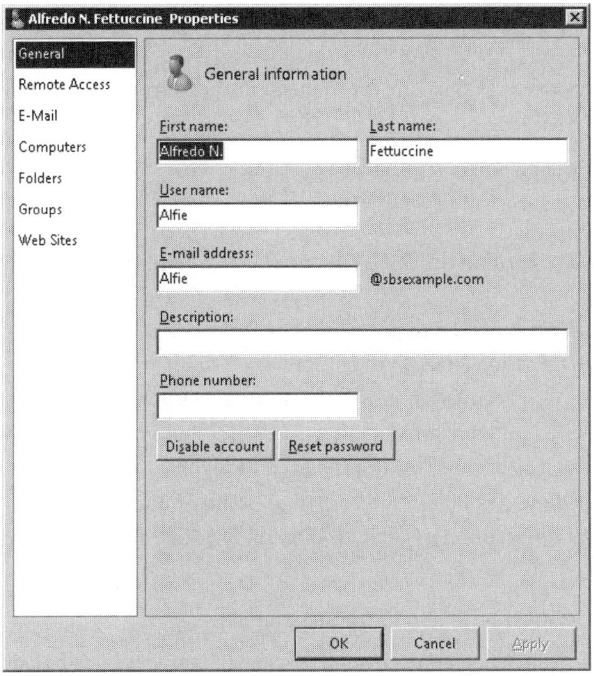

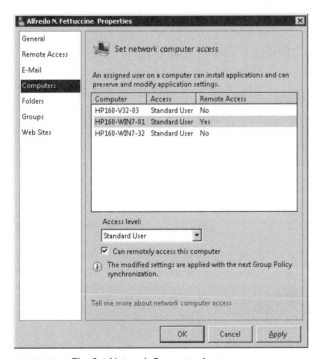

FIGURE 20-4 The Properties dialog box for user Alfredo Fettuccine

FIGURE 20-5 The Set Network Computer Access page

4. Select the computer you want to grant access to, and select the Can Remotely Access This Computer box.

5. Click OK to close the Properties dialog box for the user and return to the Windows SBS Console.

Removing access for a user follows essentially the same steps.

UNDER THE HOOD **Enabling RWA Access to a Terminal Server**

One of the things that we expected to just work, but that doesn't, is having a Remote Desktop (RD) Session Host (terminal server) show up in Remote Web Access as a computer that users can log in to. When we added a Windows Server 2008 R2 computer to our SBS network and enabled the RD Session Host role service on the server, we expected it to automatically get added to the RWA list, but it didn't happen. So we did some poking around and asked some of our SBS MVP friends, and came up with the solution. (Thanks, Handy Andy!) First, there are some minimum requirements:

- The RD Session Host must be joined to the SBS domain.

- RD Licensing must be installed and activated on the SBS network. (It's not strictly required to get things working, but you *must* assign an RD Licensing server within 120 days of initial installation.)

- Users must be added to the Remote Desktop Users local group on the RD Session Host, as shown in Figure 20-6. (Here we've used a global SBS group, RemoteApp Users, and added it to the local Remote Desktop Users Group to simplify and central-ize management.)

FIGURE 20-6 The local Remote Desktop Users group controls access to the RD Session Host

- The RD Licensing mode (per user or per device) for the server must be assigned.

After you've got these minimum requirements met, use the following steps to enable the terminal server for RWA.

> **IMPORTANT** The following steps include editing the registry. Editing the registry is deceptively simple but can have disastrous results, up to and including making your computer unable to boot. Be careful and don't make any changes without knowing exactly why you're making them and what the consequences are. There—you've been warned.

1. Log on to the SBS server with an account that has Network Administrator privileges.

2. Open Active Directory Users And Computers from the Administrative Tools menu.

3. Navigate to the SBSComputers organizational unit (OU), as shown in Figure 20-7.

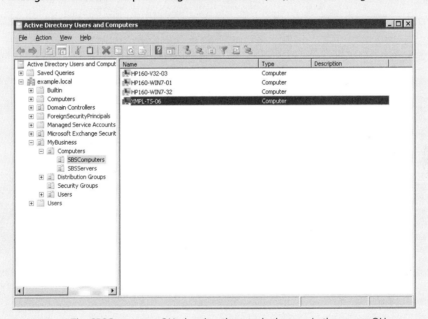

FIGURE 20-7 The SBSComputers OU, showing the terminal server in the wrong OU

4. Select the RD Session Host and drag it into the SBSServers OU.

5. Click Yes on the warning message shown in Figure 20-8.

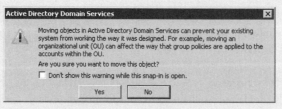

FIGURE 20-8 The Active Directory Domain Services warning message about moving objects

6. Close the Active Directory Users And Computers console.

7. Open the registry editor (*regedit.exe*).

8. Navigate to HKEY_LOCAL_MACHINE\SOFTWARE\Microsoft\SmallBusinessServer.

9. If there is a RemoteUserPortal key, open it. If it doesn't exist, create it.

10. Create a new multistring value (REG_MULTI_SZ) called *TsServerNames*, as shown in Figure 20-9.

FIGURE 20-9 Creating a new multistring value

11. Edit the Multi-String value, adding the exact server names of your terminal servers, each on their own line, as shown in Figure 20-10.

12. Click OK to close the Edit Multi-String dialog box, and then close the registry editor.

13. Open the Windows SBS Console if it isn't already open.

14. Click Shared Folders And Web Sites in the navigation bar, and then click the Web Sites tab.

15. Select the Remote Web Access Web site in the main pane, and click Disable This Site in the Tasks pane.

FIGURE 20-10 The RD Session Host name has been added

16. Click Enable This Site in the Tasks pane.

17. Now, when user Alfie logs in to RWA, he sees the RD Session Host as a computer he can log on to, as shown in Figure 20-11.

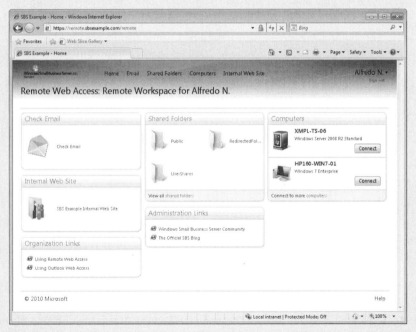

FIGURE 20-11 User Alfredo Fettuccine now has access to the RD Session Host, xmpl-ts-06

Whew. That was a bit more work than we really expected. The SBS team has done a really good job of making SBS just work as we'd hoped and expected. But this one they missed.

Enabling or Disabling a User for RWA

You can enable or disable the access of individual users to RWA. Normally, all users are enabled for RWA, but if you want only a subset of your users to have the privilege to log in to RWA you can disable the access of those you want to exclude.

Follow these steps to enable or disable a user from Remote Web Workplace:

1. Open the Windows SBS Console if it isn't already open.
2. Click on Users And Groups in the navigation bar and then click on the Groups tab.
3. Select the Windows SBS Remote Web Access Users security group in the main pane, and click Edit Group Properties in the Tasks pane to open the Properties dialog box for the group, as shown in Figure 20-12.

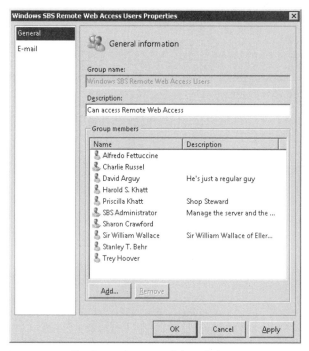

FIGURE 20-12 The Properties page of the Windows SBS Remote Web Access Users security group

4. Select a user account in the Group Members pane, and click Remove to remove the user.
5. To add a user account, click Add to open the Change Group Membership dialog box shown in Figure 20-13.

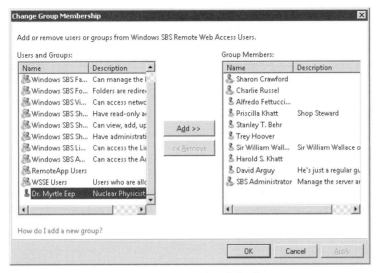

FIGURE 20-13 The Change Group Membership dialog box

6. Select one or more users or groups in the left pane, and click Add to add them to the group. To remove users from the group, select them in the right pane and click Remove.

7. Click OK and then OK again to exit the dialog box and return to the Windows SBS Console.

> **NOTE** If your environment includes multiple users who should not have permission to use Remote Web Access, consider creating a User Role for them that excludes membership in the Windows SBS Remote Web Access Users security group. This is a better way to manage the rights and privileges of multiple users in a consistent way.

REAL WORLD Two Factor Authentication and RWA

Remote Web Access is a secure way to connect to your SBS network. It uses IPSec tunneling, and it uses the authentication of Microsoft's Active Directory (your user name and password) to grant access to the resources of your SBS network. That being said, if your SBS network contains sensitive information and you're subject to regulatory requirements for data protection, you should consider Two Factor Authentication (TFA) on RWA, especially for any accounts that are either Network Administrators or have special access to sensitive data.

Authentication is the process of ensuring that the individual who requests access to a resource is, in fact, the individual she is claiming to be. There are four basic kinds of authentication: "what-you-know," "who-you-are," "what-you-have," and "where-you-are." TFA requires that any user requesting remote access to the resources of your SBS network use two methods to uniquely identify herself. The first method is the providing the user name and password of the user, and the second is some other factor. The real beauty of TFA is that even if one of your factors is compromised, it's useless without the second factor.

The basic user name and password is a what-you-know factor, and it's the most commonly used form of authentication. When combined with a sort of loose where-you-are factor—that is, at the console of your own PC—and when passwords or passphrases are sufficiently complex, it's a good method of authentication.

Who-you-are authentication is usually some form of biometric analysis—fingerprint readers, retina scanners, and even visual recognition software all are forms of who-you-are authentication. We're not big fans of the most common of these, fingerprint readers. They're rather easily defeated from what we've seen to date.

What-you-have authentication is usually something like a smart card or a one-time password generator. Microsoft's corporate network uses smart cards for its TFA, but we think one-time passwords are a lot easier to deal with and deploy in a small business. You don't require deploying smart card readers for everyone, and the overall costs are significantly less as a result.

Finally, where-you-are authentication uses your physical location as a proof of who you are. An example is the variable authentication process that some banks are implementing. It starts with the IP address and machine name from which you're connecting to your bank. The bank knows that the IP address is typical for you and only asks a standard set of verification questions. But if you were to connect from a public wireless access point while you're on vacation, the bank would immediately be more cautious about who you are claiming to be, and the secondary verification process is more detailed. This kind of variable authentication process is expensive to implement and outside the scope of most small businesses.

We use TFA for remote access to our SBS network. We've implemented Scorpion Software's AuthAnvil (*http://www.scorpionsoft.com*). The AuthAnvil RWA agent (formerly known as RWWGuard) extends the standard RWA logon page to require a one-time password, as shown in Figure 20-14.

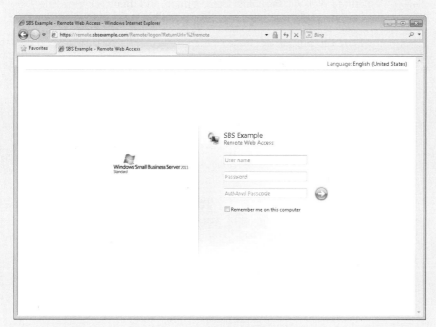

FIGURE 20-14 RWA logon page running the AuthAnvil agent

What we really like about AuthAnvil is that it's almost completely transparent. It looks and feels just like SBS, except for the one additional field for our one-time password. And with the AuthAnvil Soft Token running on our phone, we no longer even have to carry around an AuthAnvil key fob passcode generator.

RWA Links List

There are two separate lists of links that are visible below the main buttons of the RWA home page: Organization Links, and Administration Links. By default, all users are able to see the Organization Links list, but only users with the Network Administrator role or the Standard User With Administration Links role are able to see the Administration Links list.

You can customize these links, adding or removing them as appropriate for your network, and you can also configure which users have the links visible. To change which links are visible in RWA, follow these steps:

1. Open the Windows SBS Console if it isn't already open.

2. Click on Shared Folders And Web Sites in the navigation bar, and then click on the Web Sites tab.

3. Select the Remote Web Access link in the left pane, and then click View Site Properties in the Tasks pane to open the Properties dialog box for RWA.

4. Click Home Page Links in the left pane of the Properties dialog box to open the Home Page Links For Remote Web Access page shown in Figure 20-15.

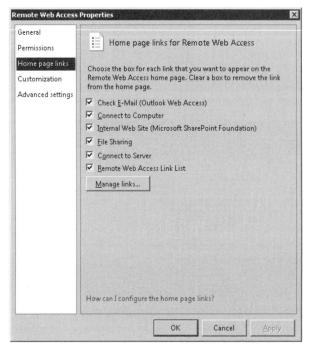

FIGURE 20-15 The Home Page Links For Remote Web Access page

5. Deselect any links you don't want to have visible on RWA. This will affect all users.

6. Click Manage Links to open the Remote Web Access Link List Properties dialog box, shown in Figure 20-16.

7. To disable either Organization Links or Administration Links, deselect them on the General page of the Remote Web Access Link List Properties dialog box.

8. Click Permissions in the left pane to open the Manage Gadget Permissions page, shown in Figure 20-17.

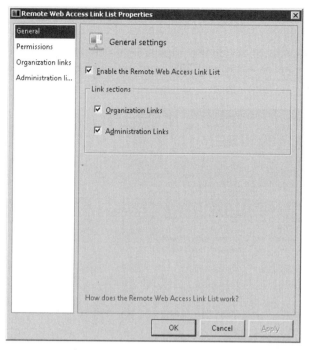

FIGURE 20-16 The General page of the Remote Web Access Link List Properties dialog box

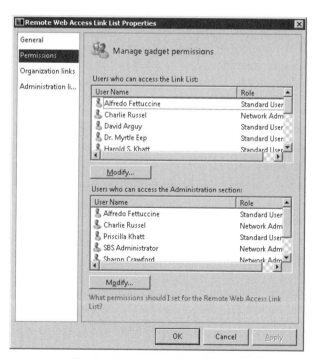

FIGURE 20-17 The Permissions page of the Remote Web Access Link List Properties dialog box

9. Click Modify beneath the list you want to change permissions for to open the Change Group Membership dialog box for the security group.

10. Click Organization Links to open the Manage Organization Links page shown in Figure 20-18. Links added here will be visible to all SBS users who have permission to log on to RWA. (See Chapter 26 for details on adding links here for RemoteApps.)

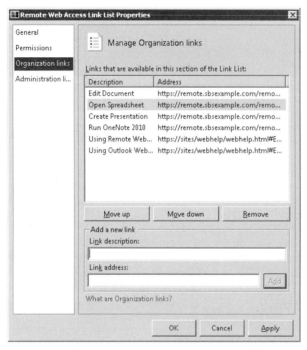

FIGURE 20-18 The Manage Organization Links page of the Remote Web Access Link List Properties dialog box showing several added RemoteApps links

11. Click Administration Links to open the Manage Administration Links page. Links added here will be visible only to users with either Network Administration or Standard User With Administration Links roles.

12. Click OK to return to the main Remote Web Access Properties page.

13. Click Customization in the left pane to open the Customize Remote Web Access page, shown in Figure 20-19. Here you can change the organization name (that appears on RWA logon page), as well as add your company's logo and a custom background image to the logon page.

14. When you've completed your changes to the RWA website properties, click OK to exit and apply the changes. Just to give you an idea of what is easily possible, I added a background image from a photo taken from the office window, and a picture of our health and safety officer to our example domain's RWA logon page, as shown in Figure 20-20.

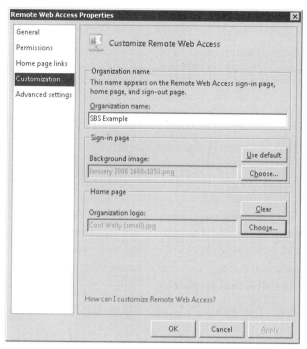

FIGURE 20-19 Customizing the logon page of Remote Web Access

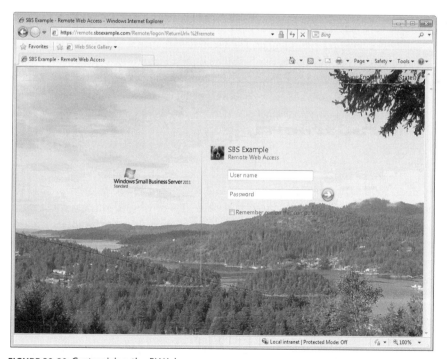

FIGURE 20-20 Customizing the RWA logon page

Virtual Private Networks

Most operations that users and administrators need to do from remote locations can, and should, be performed using Remote Web Access. RWA gives your users a secure portal to connect to the resources of the SBS network, and it's the preferred way to access the network from a remote location.

REAL WORLD When RWA Just Isn't Optimal

Even though we generally try to avoid VPNs whenever possible and use RWA for all our remote access needs, there is still one operation we regularly perform that still works better over a VPN—applying the monthly round of updates to the server. Applying patches remotely is always something that has the potential to cause disruption, but it's also something that's a part of just about every SBS administrator's life. With VPNs, there is less likelihood of the connection being disrupted and not reinstated than with RWA, in our experience.

The problem, of course, is that to enable VPNs for patching, you have to enable a whole additional role on the server and start up more services. And we're firm believers in keeping the running services to as small a number as possible.

So what are the alternatives if RWA is out for patching? One is to use a firewall or router that is a VPN endpoint, offloading this from the SBS server entirely. This didn't work well in a two-NIC SBS 2003 environment, but it works quite well in a single-NIC SBS 2011 environment. The second alternative is to enable RDP directly to the SBS server. This works, but has some significant security implications. If you do this, we strongly suggest that you configure your firewall or router to accept the RDP request only from a specific IP address or set of addresses, and we also strongly suggest implementing AuthAnvil or another form of TFA on the SBS server. Which isn't a bad idea in any case.

If you do have a compelling need to implement VPN onto your SBS network, we strongly suggest that you carefully limit the users that have VPN privileges and that you ensure their machines are fully patched and protected at all times. VPNs significantly increase your security risk from an unpatched and compromised computer causing problems on your SBS network. Because VPNs allow a remote computer to directly connect to your network, any malware on the remote computer has full access to your SBS network.

Enabling VPNs

Enabling VPNs to your SBS network is a simple process. You run the Set Up Virtual Private Networking Wizard from the Windows SBS Console, and you configure your router or firewall for VPN passthrough. If you have Universal Plug and Play (UPnP) enabled, SBS will make the change on the router for you. But we don't enable UPnP on our network, and we don't recommend that you do so, either. Just manually configure the router—it takes only a few minutes, and we think it's safer than leaving UPnP enabled.

To enable VPN access to your SBS network, use the following steps:

1. Open the Windows SBS Console if it isn't already open.

2. Click on Network in the navigation bar, and then click on the Connectivity tab.

3. Select VPN Connection in the main pane, and then click Configure A Virtual Private Network in the Tasks pane to open the Set Up Virtual Private Networking Wizard shown in Figure 20-21.

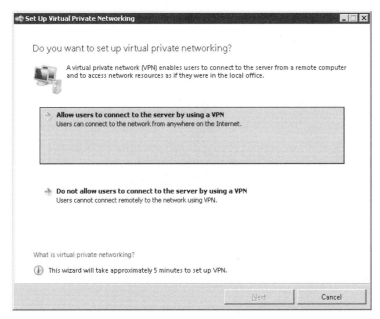

FIGURE 20-21 The Set Up Virtual Private Networking Wizard

4. Click on Allow Users To Connect To The Server By Using A VPN. When the wizard completes, you'll see a status page that tells you the wizard completed successfully, and with any warnings, as shown in Figure 20-22.

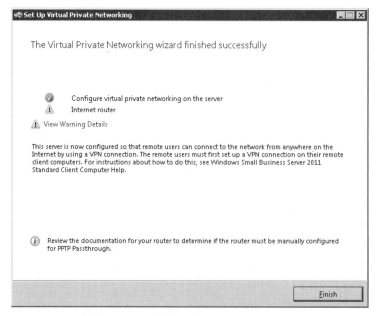

FIGURE 20-22 With UPnP turned off, you'll get a warning that the router wasn't configured

5. If you get a warning, click on View Warning Details to see what the warning is about. If you have UPnP turned off on your router, you'll see the warning details shown in Figure 20-23.

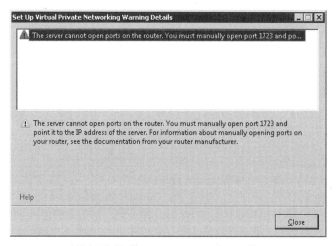

FIGURE 20-23 With UPnP off, you must manually configure ports on your router

6. Click Close to close the Set Up Virtual Private Networking Warning Details page and then Finish to close the wizard.

7. If you don't have UPnP enabled on your router, open Internet Explorer and log on to the router.

8. The details for each router are different, but you need to configure the router to forward port 1723 to the IP address of the SBS server. You might also need to configure PPTP Passthrough. Most routers have an automatic method (often called "Virtual Servers") for configuring port forwarding. Consult your router documentation.

9. After the router is configured, you'll probably need to restart the router. When you do, VPNs will be enabled on your SBS network.

Configure VPN Permissions

By default, only users with the Network Administrator role are enabled for VPN access. To add users, you need to add them to the Windows SBS Virtual Private Network Users security group. As with most things in SBS, there's more than one way to get there, but we use the following steps:

1. Open the Windows SBS Console if it isn't already open.

2. Click Network on the navigation bar, and then click the Connectivity tab.

3. Select VPN Connection in the left pane, and then click View Virtual Private Network Properties in the Tasks pane to open the Virtual Private Networking General Properties page, shown in Figure 20-24.

FIGURE 20-24 The Virtual Private Networking General Properties page

4. Click Modify to open the Change Group Membership dialog box for the Windows SBS Virtual Private Network Users security group, shown in Figure 20-25.

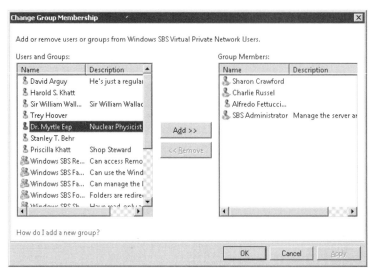

FIGURE 20-25 The Change Group Membership dialog box for the Windows SBS Virtual Private Network Users security group

5. Select users or groups of users in the User And Groups pane on the left, and click Add to add them to the Windows SBS Virtual Private Network Users security group.

6. Select users or groups of users in the Group Members pane on the right, and click Remove to remove them from the Windows SBS Virtual Private Network Users security group. Only members of the Windows SBS Virtual Private Network Users security group have permission to use a VPN to connect to the SBS network.

7. When you finish making your changes, click OK to save the changes and return to the Windows SBS Console.

Fixing Network Problems

In a perfect world, networks would never fail, no one would ever have to change a network card, IP addresses would be automatically assigned and never change, and no one would ever have to try to troubleshoot a network connectivity problem. Well, IPv6 helps with some of this, but we're afraid that there's still a long way to go until we reach network nirvana. Until we do, however, there's the Fix My Network Wizard (FMNW) in SBS.

Now, we have to say right up front that when we heard the name for this new wizard, we were more than a little concerned. It sounded a lot like something you might run on a home PC, with usually less than optimal results. But then we remembered that for SBS 2003, the SBS team had already created one of the best network configuration wizards we've ever used—the Configure E-mail and Internet Connectivity Wizard. Affectionately known as the CEICW (say that fast three times), the CEICW was a sort of one-stop shop for resetting all your network settings back to where they belonged. The CEICW was really good at what it did, but it did have some limits. It couldn't tell that your IP address had changed, it didn't recognize that your router wasn't responding, and it neglected to do a few other things that we'd sort of wished it did. There were also times when you needed to run a different wizard or actually resort to using the native Windows Server tools.

With the FMNW in SBS 2011, the SBS team has taken the concept of the CEICW and extended and improved it significantly. The actual initial configuration of Internet domain name and email, along with public DNS names, have been separated out as discrete tasks with their own wizards, which makes a lot of sense. After you've done those, they really aren't likely to change all that much. But it's all the other things that seem to go wrong with networking.

The FMNW, shown in Figure 20-26, is located on the Connectivity page of the Network section of the Windows SBS Console. The FMNW can identify, and in most cases fix, problems with DHCP, DNS, logons, network access (both local and remote), Internet connectivity, RWA, email, and VPNs. In some cases, you might need to run the wizard multiple times, and if you have UPnP disabled on your router, you'll need to make any router changes that it identifies yourself, manually.

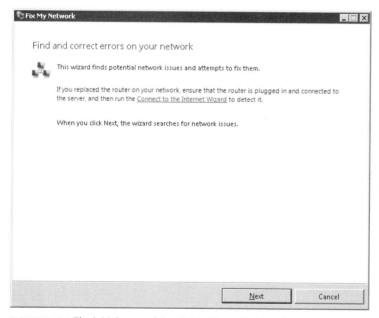

FIGURE 20-26 The initial page of the Fix My Network Wizard

When we ran it on our network, which had IPv6 disabled, we got the Potential Network Issues page shown in Figure 20-27.

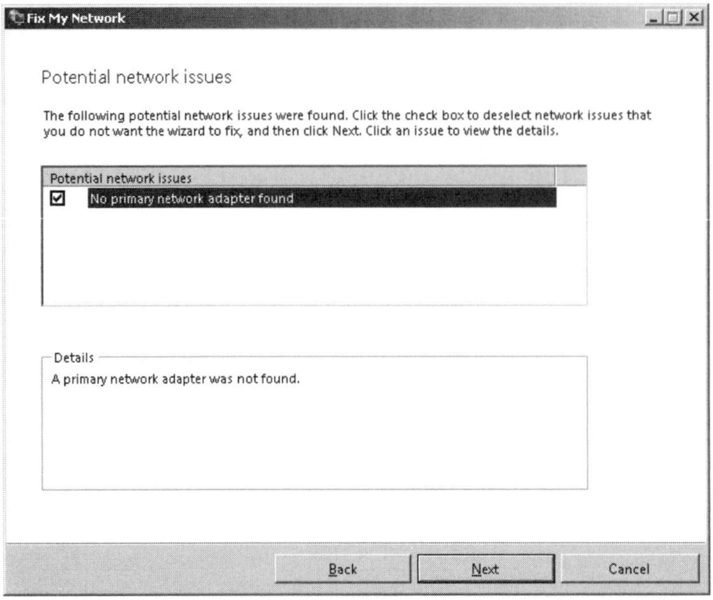

FIGURE 20-27 This is what a disabled IPv6 looks like

Now we expected this, because we deliberately disabled IPv6, knowing that a missing or misconfigured IPv6 is the number one source of the trouble calls to Microsoft Customer Support when Windows Small Business Server 2008 has problems. The Wizard worked away for 10 to 15 seconds, and then gave us the results page shown in Figure 20-28.

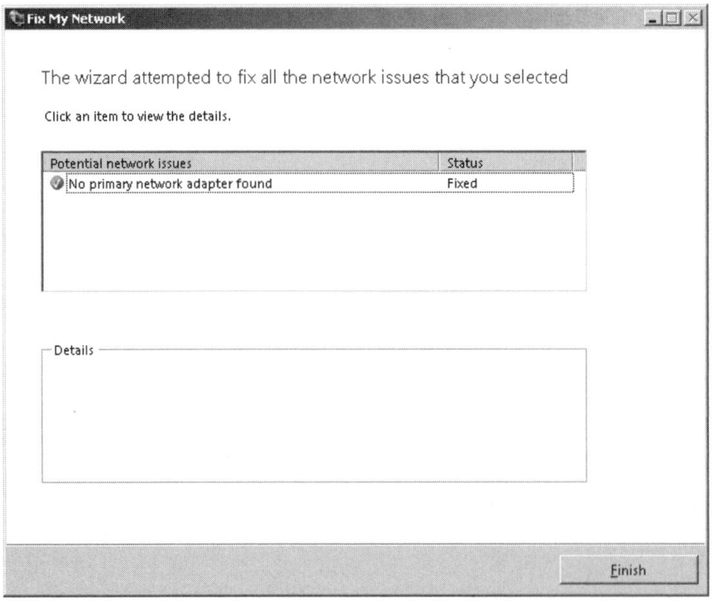

FIGURE 20-28 The Fix My Network Wizard has successfully fixed the first problem

This *looks* like all is well. But you should *always* run the wizard a second time whenever you find an issue. Because sometimes it takes two or more tries to fix all the problems, and it often can't even see a problem until it fixes something else that is blocking. So, even though all looked well, we ran the FMNW again, and result is shown in Figure 20-29.

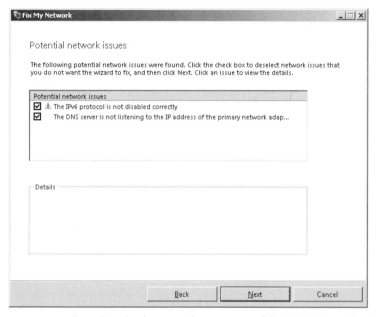

FIGURE 20-29 Sometimes it takes more than one pass of the Fix My Network Wizard to fix everything

Oops. OK, let's run it again. Now it says that there's some stuff we're going to have to do ourselves, as shown in Figure 20-30.

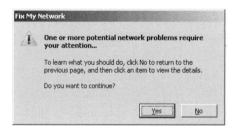

FIGURE 20-30 When the FMNW needs help, it will tell you

So we click Yes and return to the Potential Network Issues page. The first item is highlighted, and we're directed in the Details section to a Microsoft article with details on how to fix it, as shown in Figure 20-31.

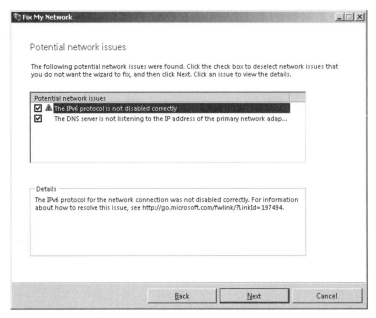

FIGURE 20-31 We didn't disable IPv6 properly

So, we go to the page, where it tells us we shouldn't really ever need to disable IPv6, but if we absolutely insist on disabling it, here's the proper way to do it. All in all, just better to not disable it in the first place. Fix the IPv6 issue, and re-run the FMNW. You should run it until you get either a completely green check on issues, or the only issues left are issues you've already decided you don't want the wizard to fix (such as configuring the router or firewall).

The one limitation of the FMNW is that it won't run successfully if you have more than a single network card enabled on your SBS server. Because that's not a supported configuration, the wizard reports the issue and offers to disable the extra NIC—not a great idea, because it could well disable the wrong one. Our solution is to simply disable the NIC prior to running the Fix My Network Wizard on our production network, which does have more than one network card in the server because of the unusual networking requirements here with all of our test networks.

Summary

Connectivity is a huge topic, but in this chapter we focused on remote connectivity and troubleshooting. The Remote Web Access portal and Virtual Private Networks are the two supported methods of remote access, and the Fix My Network Wizard is a great trouble-shooting tool. In the next chapter, we'll cover Group Policy and how you can use it to help manage your SBS network.

CHAPTER 21

Using Group Policy

In one form or another, Group Policy is all about security. The policies in place after installation include rules about logons, software installation, passwords, and other settings that have an effect on how safe your network will be. You might not need to change most of these settings. However, you do need to know how the policies work, how to make changes, and how to configure new policies for your particular circumstances.

The configuration of intelligent security policies has the serendipitous effect of potentially increasing productivity by providing a barrier against those great time-wasters: the accidental loss of vital folders, the deletion of files, and the inadvertent introduction of viruses and other malicious software to the network. Group Policy also helps the cause of productivity by making it easier for users to find what they need to work efficiently.

 REAL WORLD What's the Use of All This?

While it's true that Microsoft Windows Small Business Server (SBS) does most of the Group Policy work for you, and the underlying Windows 2008 Group Policy is aimed mainly at very large networks, there are still some Group Policy settings that can be very useful in a Windows SBS setting. For example, you can configure the mapped drives for all the client computers (discussed in "Drive Maps" later in the chapter) or create a Group Policy Object that will control software distribution (covered in "Deploying Applications with Group Policy" later in the chapter).

So even if you don't want to get into all the complexities that Group Policy can present, you can make use of some aspects and actually simplify your life.

Components of Group Policy

Group Policy consists of the following configurable components:

- **Security Settings** Configures security for users, computers, and domains
- **Scripts** Specifies scripts for computer startup and shutdown, as well as for user logon and logoff events
- **Preference Items** Configures unenforced settings for users and computers
- **Folder Redirection** Places special folders such as Documents or specified application folders on the network
- **Software Settings** Assigns applications to users

Group Policy Objects

A collection of policy settings is called a Group Policy object (GPO). A GPO contains policies that affect computers and policies that affect users. Computer-related policies include computer security settings, application settings, and computer startup and shutdown scripts. User-related policies define application settings, folder redirection, assigned and published applications, user logon and logoff scripts, and user security settings. In cases of conflicting policies, the convention is that computer-related settings override user-related settings.

In a GPO, most settings have three possible states: enabled, disabled, and not configured. Group policies are inherited and cumulative. When you associate a GPO with an Active Directory container, the Group Policy is applied to all computer and user accounts in the container.

 UNDER THE HOOD **Components of Group Policy**

Group Policy is an abstraction consisting of two parts, a Group Policy Container (GPC) and a Group Policy Template (GPT). Both parts are contained in a Group Policy object (GPO). The GPO is what we work with directly. The GPO contains all the settings that can apply to users and computers. When those settings are changed, the changes are made to the GPO. The two components of the GPO exist in different places.

The GPC is the Active Directory component of the GPO and includes subcontainers with version information, status information, and a list of which Group Policy extensions are employed in the GPO. It also contains some information used by clients, such as the software installation policy.

The GPT is a set of files in the SYSVOL folder on the server. When you create a GPO, the corresponding GPT folder structure is created automatically. The actual name of the folder for the GPT is the *globally unique identifier* (GUID) for the GPO—a number that is useful to the computer but is otherwise incomprehensible. To see the policy folder, look in %SystemRoot%\SYSVOL\sysvol\domain_name\policies. But *do not* change this folder in any way. Work on Group Policy through the Group Policy Management Console (GPMC).

Managing Group Policies

The Group Policy Management Console (GPMC) provides a comprehensive overview of Group Policy in a single console. All Group Policy management tasks can be performed in the GPMC except configuring individual policies in GPOs.

When you want to configure individual policies, the GPMC will launch the Group Policy Object Editor with the policy loaded.

To see the group policies specifically defined for Windows SBS, select Administrative Tools from the Start menu and then select Group Policy Management. Expand Forest and then Domains until you get to MyBusiness as shown in Figure 21-1.

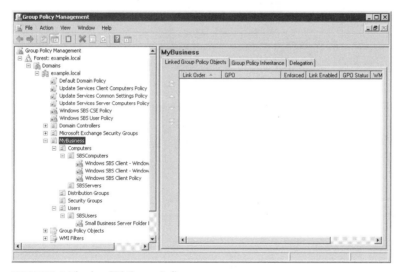

FIGURE 21-1 Viewing SBS Group Policy

To view or modify an existing GPO, right-click the GPO and select Edit as shown in Figure 21-2.

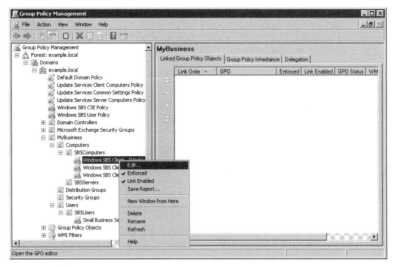

FIGURE 21-2 Choosing to edit a GPO

This action opens the Group Policy Management Editor (shown in Figure 21-3), wherein you can expand various items in the console to view existing settings.

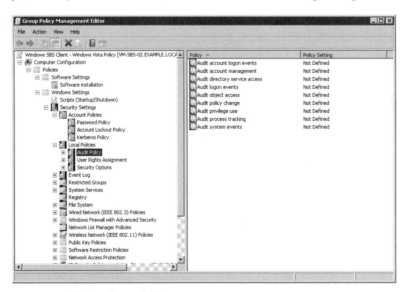

FIGURE 21-3 Viewing Group Policies

Order of Inheritance

As a rule, Group Policy settings are passed from parent containers down to child containers. This means that a policy that is applied to a parent container applies to all the containers— including users and computers—that are below the parent container in the Active Directory tree hierarchy. However, if you specifically assign a Group Policy for a child container that contradicts the parent container policy, the child container's policy overrides the parent Group Policy.

If policies are not contradictory, both can be implemented. For example, if a parent container policy calls for an application shortcut to be on a user's desktop and the child container policy calls for another application shortcut, both appear. Policy settings that are disabled are inherited as disabled. Policy settings that are not configured in the parent container remain unconfigured.

Overriding Inheritance

Several options are available for changing how inheritance is processed. One option, called enforcing a GPO link, prevents child containers from overriding any policy setting set in a higher level GPO. This option is not set by default on all GPOs.

Enforcing a GPO Link in the GPMC

To enforce a link, open the Group Policy Management Console, right-click the Group Policy object link in the console tree, and select Enforced, as shown in Figure 21-4.

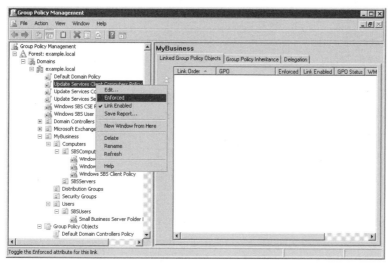

FIGURE 21-4 Enforcing a GPO link

A second option is Block Inheritance. When you select this option, the child container does not inherit any policies from parent containers. In the event of a conflict between these two options, the Enforced option always takes precedence. Simply stated, Enforced is a link property, Block Inheritance is a container property, and Enforced takes precedence over Block Inheritance.

Setting Block Inheritance

To enable Block Inheritance, open the Group Policy Management Console and right-click the domain or organizational unit (OU) for which you want to block inheritance. Select Block Inheritance, as shown in Figure 21-5.

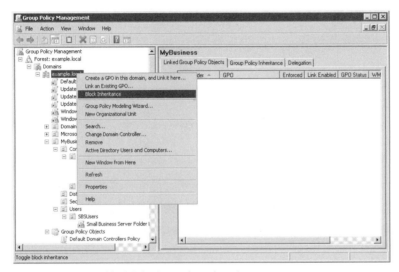

FIGURE 21-5 Setting block inheritance for a domain

Order of Implementation

Group policies are processed in the following order:

1. Local GPO
2. GPOs linked to the site in the order specified by the administrator
3. Domain GPOs, as specified by the administrator
4. OU GPOs, from largest to smallest OU (parent to child OU)

The GPO with the lowest link order is processed last, and therefore has the highest precedence. If multiple GPOs attempt contradictory settings, the GPO with highest precedence wins.

Exceptions to this order are GPOs with enforced or disabled links, GPOs with disabled user or computer settings, and OUs (or the whole domain) set to block inheritance. To see the order of precedence for GPOs for a domain or OU, open the Group Policy Management Console and, in the console tree, select the domain name or the OU. In the details pane, click the Group Policy Inheritance tab, as shown in Figure 21-6.

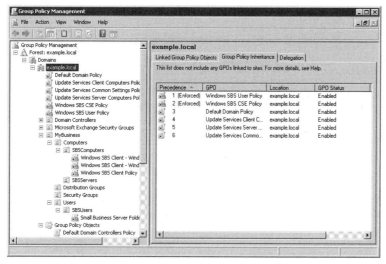

FIGURE 21-6 Viewing a domain's Group Policy order of inheritance

Creating a Group Policy Object

The installation of Windows SBS creates an Active Directory domain that includes a default domain policy, a default Domain Controllers policy, and several policies specifically for Small Business Server. When you need to set up a GPO of your own, follow these steps:

1. Select Group Policy Management from the Administrative Tools menu, and navigate to the container to which you want the new GPO to apply.

2. Right-click the domain, site, or OU; and select Create A GPO In This Domain, And Link It Here.

3. In the New GPO dialog box, type in a name for the Group Policy Object and click OK.

4. Right-click the new GPO and select Edit to launch the Group Policy Object Editor.

5. Specify settings for the GPO. When you're finished, close the Group Policy Object Editor.

6. In the Group Policy Management Console, right-click the domain name or the OU this GPO is to be associated with and select Link An Existing GPO.

7. In the Select GPO dialog box, select the GPO to link and click OK.

To shorten the process by one step, you can also right-click the domain or OU; and select Create A GPO In This Domain, And Link It Here.

> **NOTE** Try to keep the total number of GPOs as low as possible. The processing of each GPO takes time, and too many objects can slow logons and logoffs. The number of settings within a GPO doesn't matter—it's the total number of GPOs.

 UNDER THE HOOD **Inside the Group Policy Object Editor**

When you create a new GPO or edit an existing one, the Group Policy Object Editor is automatically launched. In the console tree, two nodes—Computer Configuration and User Configuration—display. Under each node are extensions for Software Settings, Windows Settings, and Administrative Templates.

Use the Computer Configuration folders to customize policies for computers on the network. These policies go into effect when the computer is turned on and the operating system starts. Settings in these folders apply to any user who logs on to the computer. For example, if you have computers in a training room for which you want to enforce a strict environment, the Computer Configuration node is where you configure those settings.

The User Configuration node contains settings for customizing environments or setting policies for users on the network. User Configuration policies come into play when a specific user logs on to the network.

Deleting a Group Policy Object

To delete a GPO, right-click it in the Group Policy Management Console and select Delete. When you delete a GPO, all links to the GPO will also be deleted. Be sure that you are logged on with an account that has sufficient permissions.

Neither the Default Domain Policy nor the Default Domain Controllers Policy can be deleted.

Managing Group Policy Links

With numerous GPOs on a network, it's important to keep track of GPO links within the domain. To find out what links exist for a particular GPO, follow these steps:

1. Select Group Policy Management from the Administrative Tools menu.
2. Right-click the domain name in the console tree and select Search.
3. In the Search Item drop-down list, select GPO-links.
4. Click Add and then click Search.
5. In the Search Results box shown in Figure 21-7, double-click a GPO to view its links and other settings.

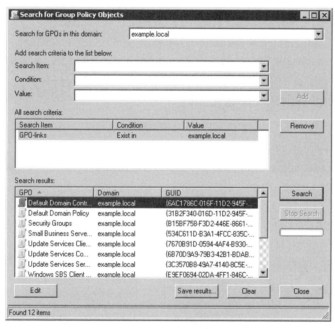

FIGURE 21-7 Finding GPO links

Setting the Scope of the GPO

A GPO applies to all the users and computers in the container with which the GPO is associated. Most GPOs default to applying to Authenticated Users—namely, everyone who can log on to the network. Inevitably, there are GPOs that should apply only to some. To filter the application of a GPO, follow these steps:

1. Select Group Policy Management from the Administrative Tools menu.
2. Select the Group Policy Object you want to filter, and click the Scope tab.

3. On the Scope tab in the Security Filtering section, click Add and locate the groups or users that should have the policy applied to them. In the Select User, Computer, Or Group dialog box, shown in Figure 21-8, make your selection and click OK.

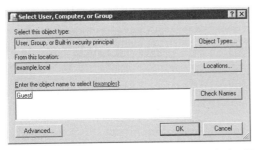

FIGURE 21-8 Selecting groups or users to which the GPO applies

If Authenticated Users appears in the Security Filtering list on the Scope page, select it and click Remove. This ensures that the GPO is applied only to the groups or users you added.

Enabling and Disabling GPO Links

To check or change the status of a GPO link, follow these steps:

1. Select Group Policy Management from the Administrative Tools menu.
2. In the console tree, navigate to the Group Policy Objects under your domain name and select the GPO.
3. On the Scope tab, links are listed and the status of the link is shown under Link Enabled. To change the status, right-click the link and select Link Enabled from the shortcut menu, as shown in Figure 21-9.

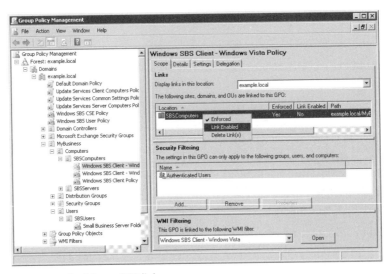

FIGURE 21-9 Enabling a GPO link

Disabling a Branch of a GPO

If a GPO has an entire node under User Configuration or Computer Configuration that's not configured, disable the node to avoid processing those settings. This speeds startup and logon for all users subject to that GPO. To disable a node, open the Group Policy Management Console and follow these steps:

1. In the console tree, expand Group Policy Objects.

2. Right-click the GPO that contains the User or Computer settings you want to disable, point to GPO Status, and then choose one of the following options shown in Figure 21-10:

   - Click User Configuration Settings Disabled to disable user settings for the GPO.

   - Click Computer Configuration Settings Disabled to disable computer settings for the GPO.

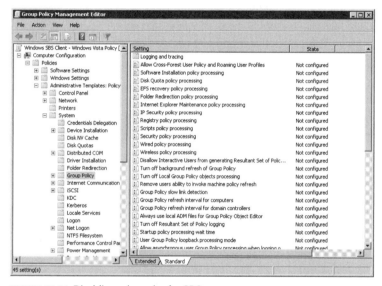

FIGURE 21-10 Disabling a branch of a GPO

A check mark next to User Configuration Settings Disabled or Computer Configuration Settings Disabled indicates that the option is currently selected.

Refreshing Group Policy

Policy changes are immediate, but they are not instantly propagated to clients. Client computers request policy only when one of the following occurs:

- The computer starts.

- A user logs on.

- An application requests a refresh.
- A user requests a refresh.
- A Group Policy refresh interval is enabled, and the interval has elapsed.

By default, Group Policy refreshes in the background every 90 minutes with a random offset of 0 through 30 minutes added so that not all computers request a refresh at the same time.

If you find the default refresh too long or too short, you can change the refresh interval by following these steps:

1. Select Group Policy Management from the Administrative Tools menu.

2. To add the setting to an existing GPO, right-click the GPO and select Edit. To create a new GPO, right-click the domain name or OU; and select Create A GPO In This Domain, And Link It Here. Supply a name for the new GPO, right-click it in the Group Policy Management Console, and select Edit.

3. In the console tree, expand Computer Configuration, expand Policies, expand Administrative Templates, expand System, and then select Group Policy as shown in Figure 21-11.

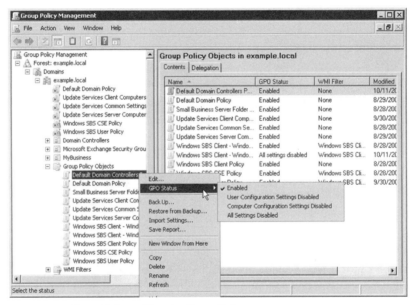

FIGURE 21-11 Group Policy settings for Group Policy

4. In the details pane, double-click Group Policy Refresh Interval For Computers.

5. On the Settings tab, select Enabled, and then supply the new settings. Click OK when finished.

> **NOTE** Don't make the interval very short because a large amount of network traffic is generated by each refresh.

Because policy can be set at several levels, when you look at a policy object, what you see is both local policy and the policy in effect on the system. Local policy and actual policy in effect might not be synonymous if the computer is inheriting settings from domain-level policies. If you make a policy setting and it isn't reflected in effective policy, a policy from the domain is overriding your setting.

It's also possible that the policy change hasn't been refreshed since the change was made. To force a policy refresh for the local computer, open a Command Prompt window and type the following:

```
gpupdate [/target:{computer | user}] /force
```

Backing Up a Group Policy Object

A valuable feature, new in the Group Policy Management Console, is the ability to back up and restore GPOs. Include regular backup of all GPOs as part of your overall planning-for-disaster strategy. To back up a GPO, follow these steps:

1. Open the Group Policy Management Console. In the console tree, navigate to Group Policy Objects in the domain that contains the GPO to be backed up.

   - To back up a single GPO, right-click the GPO and select Back Up.
   - To back up all GPOs in the domain, right-click Group Policy Objects and select Back Up All. (See Figure 21-12.)

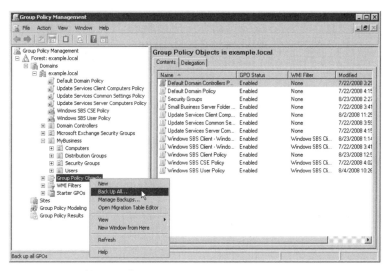

FIGURE 21-12 Backing up all GPOs

2. In the Back Up Group Policy Object dialog box, type the path to the backup location and then click Back Up.

3. After the operation completes, click OK.

> **NOTE** Because the only reason to back up GPOs—or anything else, for that matter—is to protect data that might have to be restored one day, be sure that the backup folder is secure and can be accessed only by authorized administrators.

Restoring a Group Policy Object

You can easily restore GPOs that have been backed up. If you back up all the GPOs in a container, you can restore all of them, some of them, or one at a time.

To restore backed-up GPOs, complete these steps:

1. Select Group Policy from the Administrative Tools menu.

2. In the console tree, navigate to Group Policy Objects.

3. To restore a previous version of an existing GPO or to restore a deleted GPO, right-click Group Policy Objects and select Manage Backups.

4. In the Manage Backups dialog box, select the GPO to restore and click Restore.

When you have a lot of GPOs to sort through, select the check box that allows you to display only the latest versions of the backed-up GPOs. If you're unsure of which GPO to restore, highlight them one at a time and click View Settings.

Deploying Applications with Group Policy

Managing software on client computers can be a tedious task, but you can use Group Policy to deploy applications automatically. The Group Policy Software Installation extension enables you to deploy applications to computers in the domain or forest using Group Policy and includes the capability to do the following:

- Publish applications so that users can view and install programs from the network.

- Assign applications to users or computers so that the applications are installed automatically when users need them or on the next restart or logon.

- Target applications to different groups using Group Policy.

- View the installation status using Group Policy Results.

Publish or Assign Applications

To deploy an application, create or edit the appropriate GPO and add the application's Windows Installer package to either the user or computer policy, depending on whether you want it to apply to users or computers. The next time the user logs on or the computer restarts, Active Directory applies the relevant policy to the user or computer depending on the package settings you specify in the GPO. Table 21-1 lists the GPO settings for installation actions.

TABLE 21-1 GPO settings needed for specific actions

ACTION	SETTING REQUIRED
Automatically install the application	Install This Application At Logon
Add the application to a list of installable programs in Programs And Features	Publish
Add a shortcut to the application in the Start menu, and install it on first use	Assign The Application (Don't use the Install This Application at Logon setting.)

An application published in Active Directory becomes available from Programs And Features for the users to whom the GPO applies. An assigned application, on the other hand, can be assigned to either users or computers and is installed without any action on the user's part. Assigned applications appear on the Start menu and are installed on first use, unless you specify that they should be fully installed at the next logon.

Assign essential applications to users or computers so that these applications are always available, and publish optional programs to make it easy for users to find applications when they need them. Do not assign or publish an application to both computers and users. Table 21-2 summarizes the differences between publishing and assigning applications.

TABLE 21-2 Outcomes when publishing vs. assigning applications

	PUBLISHED APPLICATIONS	APPLICATIONS ASSIGNED TO USERS	APPLICATIONS ASSIGNED TO COMPUTERS
After deployment, when is the software available for installation?	Immediately	After the second logon*	After the second reboot*
How is the software installed?	Through Programs And Features in Control Panel	Automatically on first use or after the next logon event (icons are on the Start menu or desktop)	Automatically installed on reboot*

	PUBLISHED APPLICATIONS	APPLICATIONS ASSIGNED TO USERS	APPLICATIONS ASSIGNED TO COMPUTERS
Is the software installed when an associated file is opened?	Yes	Yes	Already installed
Can a user remove the software?	Yes, using Programs And Features	Yes, but the software is available again after the next logon	No, but software repairs are allowed; local administrators can uninstall
Package types supported	Windows Installer and .zap files	Windows Installer	Windows installer

Windows XP, Windows Vista, and Windows 7 clients process Group Policy asynchronously as a background refresh during startup and logon, which shortens startup times but requires two restarts to install assigned software to computers and users at logon.

Creating a Software Distribution Point

To deploy applications using Group Policy, first create a software distribution point on the network that contains the setup files for the applications. (Make sure you have appropriate licenses for the applications.)

To create a software distribution point, use the following steps:

1. Design and create a DFS or shared folder structure for software.

2. Set the following NTFS permissions on the software distribution folder. (Set the share permissions to Everyone = Full Control to prevent conflicting file and share permissions.)

   - Authenticated Users = Read and Execute
   - Domain Computers = Read and Execute
   - Administrators = Full Control

> **IMPORTANT** Incorrectly set permissions are a common cause of problems when deploying software with Group Policy, so verify that file and share permissions are set properly on the software distribution folder.

3. Copy the application setup files to the folder created in step 1, or use an administrative setup command to install the setup files to the folder.

Consult the software manufacturer for specific instructions and recommendations.

> **NOTE** To publish the software distribution folder in Active Directory so that users can find the folder when searching Active Directory for shared folders, right-click the appropriate container in the Active Directory Users And Computers console, choose New, select Shared Folder, and then type the path of the DFS folder or shared folder in the Network Path box.

Creating a GPO for Software Deployment

Create a new GPO for deployed applications by following these steps:

1. Open Group Policy Management from the Administrative Tools folder on the Start menu.

2. Right-click the domain or OU where you want to create the GPO; and select Create A GPO In This Domain, And Link It Here, as shown in Figure 21-13.

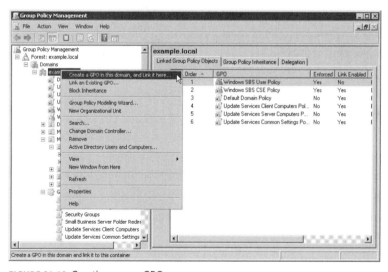

FIGURE 21-13 Creating a new GPO

3. In the New GPO dialog box, type in a name for the GPO as shown in Figure 21-14 and click OK.

FIGURE 21-14 Providing a name for the new GPO

4. Navigate to the new GPO in the left pane, and under Security Filtering click Add to assign this GPO to specific users or computers.

Configuring the Group Policy Software Installation Extension

A number of options control how Group Policy deploys and manages software packages. These options determine how packages are added to the GPO, the amount of control users have over an installation, and the default application for a given file extension, as well as which categories you can use for grouping applications. The following sections cover these options.

> **NOTE** Software installation settings for applications deployed to users are not shared with applications that are deployed to computers. Each type of deployment maintains its own set of applications and settings.

Setting Software Installation Options

To change the default settings for the Group Policy Software Installation extension, first open the Software Installation Properties dialog box by performing the following steps:

1. Open the Group Policy Management Console from the Administrative Tools menu.
2. Right-click the GPO you created for application deployment and select Edit.
3. Under Computer Configuration or User Configuration, expand Policies and then expand Software Settings.
4. Right-click Software Installation and select Properties, as shown in Figure 21-15, to open the Software Installation Properties dialog box.

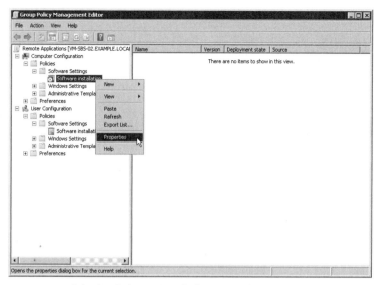

FIGURE 21-15 Selecting Software Installation properties

NOTE Software Installation settings for applications deployed to users are not shared with applications that are deployed to computers. Each type of deployment maintains its own set of applications and settings.

5. On the General tab (shown in Figure 21-16), specify the location of the software distribution point.

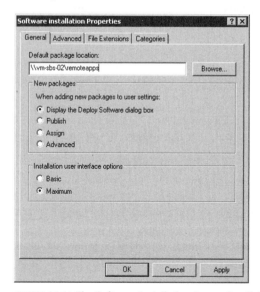

FIGURE 21-16 The Software Installation Properties dialog box

6. In the New Packages area, specify the default behavior for new software packages. Table 21-3 shows the choices.

7. In the Installation User Interface Options area, choose Basic for limited visibility to the user of the installation process; choose Maximum for full visibility during installation.

TABLE 21-3 Default behavior options when adding new packages

OPTION	WHAT IT DOES
Display The Deploy Software Dialog Box	Displays a dialog box asking whether to publish (User Configuration only) or assign the application, or whether to customize the configuration
Publish (User Configuration Only)	Automatically publishes the application using default settings
Assign	Automatically assigns the application using default settings
Advanced	Displays the application's advanced properties, allowing a customized installation

8. Click the Advanced tab to set additional options for the software packages under this GPO:

   ■ To uninstall applications automatically when the GPO no longer applies to the user or computer, select Uninstall The Applications When They Fall Out Of The Scope Of Management.

   ■ To add OLE information as part of the application deployment, select Include OLE Information When Deploying Applications.

   ■ To allow standard .MSI applications to be deployed to 64-bit computers, select Make 32-Bit X86 Windows Installer Applications Available To Win64 Machines. (This is the default behavior.)

   ■ To allow legacy 32-bit applications (ZAP files) to be deployed to 64-bit computers, select Make 32-Bit X86 Down-level (ZAP) Applications Available To Win64 Machines.

9. To set up a list of software categories, thereby making it easier for users to find the applications they want, click the Categories tab, click Add, and type the category name. Categories apply to the entire domain, not just the current GPO. Click OK when finished.

> **NOTE** The File Extensions tab will be empty when you first create a new GPO because Windows lists only file extensions associated with packages already present in the GPO. Later you can return to this tab to select the order in which file extensions should be recognized.

Adding a Software Package to a Group Policy

Before Group Policy can assign or publish applications that you copy to the software distribution point discussed earlier in this chapter, you must add the installation packages to the GPO. To add a package to a GPO, follow these steps:

1. Install the application to the software distribution point using an administrative setup command or by manually copying the setup files, as discussed in "Creating a Software Distribution Point" earlier in this chapter.

2. Open the Group Policy Management Console from the Administrative Tools menu.

3. Right-click the GPO you created for application deployment and select Edit to open the Group Policy Management Editor.

4. Select either User Configuration or Computer Configuration, expand Policies, and then expand Software Settings.

5. Right-click Software Installation, choose New, and then choose Package as shown in Figure 21-17.

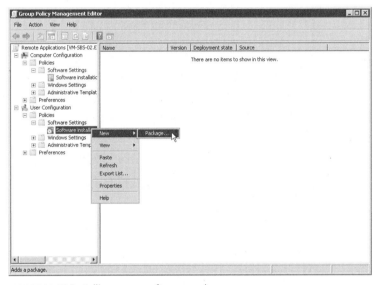

FIGURE 21-17 Installing a new software package

6. Select either Windows Installer Package(*.msi) or make a selection from the drop-down list of file types, depending on the type of application you want to deploy. (Note that you can deploy .zap files only to users, not computers.)

7. Navigate to the software distribution point you created and select the package, as shown in Figure 21-18. Do not use a local file path.

8. Click Open to open the Deploy Software dialog box, and choose from the following options for how to deploy the package. When you have made your selections, click OK.

- Select Published to publish the application in Active Directory with the default settings (available only with User Configuration).

- Select Assigned to assign the application with the default properties.

- Select Advanced to modify how Windows deploys the application.

NOTE Windows deploys packages after the second logon or restart for Windows XP clients, after the first logon or restart for Windows 2000 clients, and after the first logon or restart if you enable the Always Wait For The Network At Computer Startup And Logon policy.

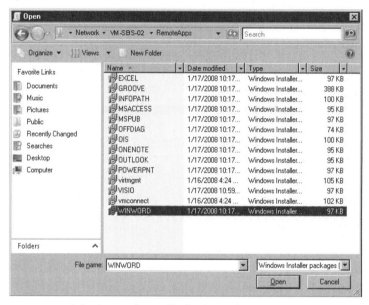

FIGURE 21-18 Selecting a software distribution package

Group Policy Preferences

Group Policy Preferences help you configure, deploy, and manage operating system and application settings that you cannot manage by using Group Policy. Examples include mapped drives, scheduled tasks, and Start menu settings. Using Group Policy Preferences is often a better alternative than logon scripts for configuring these settings. Group Policy Preferences are built into the Group Policy Management Console.

Networks customarily have two types of settings: enforced settings (Group Policy) and optional settings (preferences). Enforced settings can't be changed by users. Preferences, on the other hand, can be changed by users. By specifically deploying preferences, you can create configurations that are more suitable for your organization than the operating system's default settings. Deploying preferences is usually done through logon scripts or default user profiles.

So what are the differences between Group Policy Preferences and Group Policy? The primary difference is that Group Policy is enforced and Group Policy Preferences are not. Table 21-4 shows the other key differences.

TABLE 21-4 Group Policy vs. Group Policy preferences

GROUP POLICY SETTINGS	GROUP POLICY PREFERENCES
Settings are enforced.	Preferences are not enforced.
User interface is disabled.	User interface is not disabled.
Adding policy settings requires application support and constructing administrative templates.	Preference items for files and registry settings are easily created.
Requires Group Policy–aware applications.	Supports non-Group Policy–aware applications.
Filtering is based on Windows Management Instrumentation (WMI) and requires writing WMI queries.	Supports item-level targeting.
Alternative user interface is provided for most policy settings.	Uses a familiar, easy-to-use interface for configuring most settings.

Figure 21-19 shows a decision tree for choosing between Group Policy settings and Group Policy Preferences.

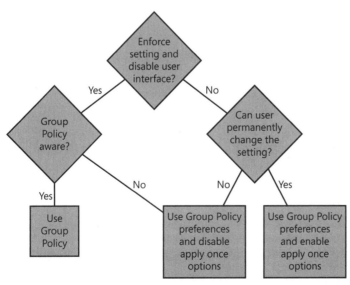

FIGURE 21-19 Deciding between Group Policy and Group Policy Preferences

To view Group Policy Preferences, start Group Policy Management from the Administrative Tools menu and follow these steps:

1. Navigate to Group Policy Objects. Right-click Default Domain Controllers Policy and select Edit.

2. Under Computer Configuration, expand Preferences, expand Windows Settings, and then expand Control Panel Settings.

3. Under User Configuration, expand Preferences, expand Windows Settings, and then expand Control Panel Settings.

As you can see in Figure 21-20, the Computer Configuration and User Configuration lists are very similar. However, even when the names are identical, the properties might differ. The following preferences do not overlap: Applications, Drive Maps, Internet Settings, Regional Options, and Start Menu under User Configuration; and Network Shares and Network Options under Computer Configuration.

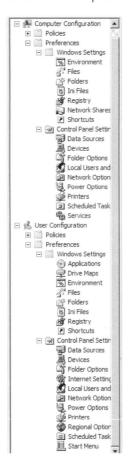

FIGURE 21-20 Group Policy Preferences extensions

Using Group Policy Preferences for Windows

Like Group Policy settings, preferences are almost infinitely configurable. In the next sections, we'll discuss a sample of these extensions, beginning with the Windows settings.

Drive Maps

The Drive Maps setting allows you to create, update, and delete mapped drives and their properties. To create a mapped-drive preference item, follow these steps:

1. Start Group Policy Management from the Administrative Tools menu.

2. Right-click the GPO that will contain the new preference item, and then click Edit.

3. In the console tree, navigate to User Configuration, expand the Preferences folder, and then expand the Windows Settings folder. Right-click the Drive Maps node, point to New, and select Mapped Drive.

4. In the New Drive Properties dialog box, select one of the following actions for Group Policy to perform:

   - **Create**   Creates a new mapped drive
   - **Replace**   Deletes an existing mapped drive, and creates a new one
   - **Update**   Changes specific settings of an existing mapped drive
   - **Delete**   Removes a mapped drive

5. Enter drive-map settings, which are described in Table 21-5.

6. Click the Common tab, and select the options you want. For more information, see "Configuring Common Options" later in this chapter.

7. Click OK. The new preference item displays in the details pane.

The new mapped drive will display when a user logs on. (See Figure 21-21.)

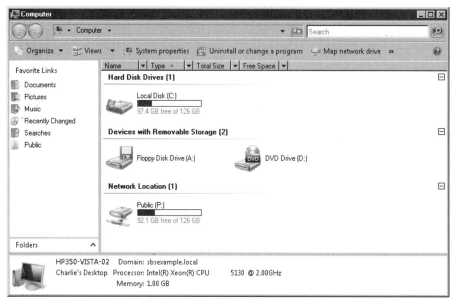

FIGURE 21-21 A drive mapped by Group Policy Preferences

TABLE 21-5 Drive-map settings

SETTING NAME	ACTION	DESCRIPTION
Location	Create, Replace, or Update	To create a mapped drive or replace an existing one, type in a fully qualified UNC path. To modify an existing drive mapping, leave this field empty. Note: This field also accepts processing variables. Press F3 for a list of acceptable variables.
Reconnect	Create, Replace, or Update	Select this box to save the mapped drive in the user's settings and reconnect to it at subsequent logons.
Label As	Create, Replace, or Update	Provide a descriptive label. This field also accepts preference processing variables. Press F5 for a list.
Drive Letter	Create, Replace, or Update	To assign the first available drive letter, select Use First Available Starting At and choose a drive letter. To assign a specific drive letter, select Use and then select a drive letter.
Drive Letter	Update	To change an existing drive mapping, select Existing and then select the drive letter.
Drive Letter	Delete	To delete all drive mappings, select Delete All, Starting At and then select the beginning drive letter. To delete a specific mapping, select Delete and then select the drive letter.

SETTING NAME	ACTION	DESCRIPTION
Connect As	Create, Replace, or Update	To map a drive using credentials other than those of the currently logged-on user, type the name and password to be used.
Hide/Show This Drive	Create, Replace, or Update	To prevent the drive from being displayed in Windows Explorer, select Hide This Drive. To allow it to display, select Show This Drive. These settings take priority over the Hide/Show All Drives setting.

Files

With the Files preference extension, you can copy, modify the attributes of, replace, or delete files. The extension supports wildcards in file paths and environment variables.

Before configuring a file preference item, review the behavior of each type of action and setting shown in Table 21-6.

To create a new file preference item, follow these steps:

1. Start Group Policy Management from the Administrative Tools menu.

2. Right-click the GPO that will contain the new preference item, and then click Edit.

3. In the console tree under Computer Configuration or User Configuration, expand the Preferences folder, and then expand the Windows Settings folder.

4. Right-click Files, point to New, and select File.

5. In the New File Properties dialog box, select one of the following actions from the drop-down list:

   - **Create**   Copies a file or multiple files from a source to a destination, and then configures the file attributes for computers or users.

   - **Delete**   Removes a file or multiple files.

   - **Replace**   Overwrites files at the destination location with replacement files. If the file does not exist at the destination, the Replace action copies the file from the source location to the destination.

   - **Update**   Modifies attributes of an existing file.

6. Enter the file settings, which are described in Table 21-6.

7. Click the Common tab, and select the options you want. (For more information, see "Configuring Common Options" later in this chapter.)

8. Click OK. The new preference item appears in the details pane.

TABLE 21-6 File settings

SETTING	ACTION	DESCRIPTION
Source File(s)	Create, Replace, or Update	Enter the location from which to copy the source file. The field can include variables. You can use a local or mapped drive or a fully qualified UNC path.
Destination File	Create, Replace, or Update *and* the Source File(s) field includes wildcards	Enter the location to which to copy files or the location of the files to be changed. You can use a local or mapped drive (from the perspective of the client) or a fully qualified UNC path.
Delete File(s)	Delete	Type the path to the file or files from the perspective of the client. The field can include wildcards.
Suppress Errors On Individual File Actions	Replace, Update, or Delete	Select this check box to allow multiple files to transfer during the replace, delete, or update operation even if one or more files fail to transfer.
Attributes	Create, Replace, or Update	Select attributes for the file or files being transferred. If necessary to complete an operation, the Read Only attribute will be reset.

Configuring Common Options

All Group Policy preference items have a Common tab, and many items share common options, including the following:

- **Stop Processing Items In This Extension If An Error Occurs**   More than one item can be configured in each extension. If this option is selected, a failed preference item will stop the remaining preference items from processing.

> **NOTE**   Preference items are processed from the bottom of the list, moving toward the top. If you select this option, items processed before the failing item will still be processed successfully. This option only stops preference items that follow the failed item.

- **Run In Logged-On User's Security Context (User Policy Option)**   By default, user preferences are processed using the security context of the SYSTEM account. Select this option and the preference items are processed in the security context of the logged-on user. This lets the preference extension access resources as the user and not as the computer. This can make a difference when using mapped drives and other network resources.

- **Remove This Item When It Is No Longer Applied**   By default, Group Policy doesn't remove preferences when the GPO is removed from the user or computer. Select this option and the preference item is removed when the GPO is removed.
- **Apply Once And Do Not Reapply**   The results of preference items are rewritten each time Group Policy refreshes, which is every 90 minutes by default. Select this option and preferences will apply once for the computer, no matter how many users share the computer. Select this option in User Configuration and the item will be applied once on each computer the user logs in to.
- **Item-Level Targeting**   You can use item-level targeting to apply preference items to individual users and computers. You can include multiple preference items, each tailored for selected users or computers and each targeted to apply settings only to the relevant users or computers.

Using Group Policy Preferences for Control Panel

In addition to the Windows category, you can make preference settings under Control Panel.

Devices

Use the Devices preference item to centralize the enabling or disabling of specific types of hardware for users or computers. You can configure an entire class of devices, such as Ports (COM & LPT), or narrow the selection to a particular type of device, such as Communications Port (COM2). To configure a Device preference item, follow these steps:

1. Start the Group Policy Management Console.
2. Right-click the GPO that will contain the new preference item and then click Edit.
3. In the console tree under Computer Configuration or User Configuration, expand the Preferences folder, and then expand the Control Panel Settings folder.
4. Right-click Devices, point to New, and select Device.
5. In the New Device Properties dialog box, select Use This Device (Enable) or Do Not Use This Device (Disable) from the Action drop-down list.
6. Enter the Device settings. (See Table 21-7 for descriptions.)
7. Click the Common tab, and select the desired options. (For more information, see "Configuring Common Options" earlier in this chapter.)
8. Click OK. The new preference item appears in the details pane.

TABLE 21-7 Device settings

SETTING	ACTION	DESCRIPTION
Device Class	Enable or Disable	Click the Browse button to select the enabled or disabled device class plus the device type, if required.
Device Type	Enable or Disable	If a device type is selected, it will appear in this field.

Using Group Policy Results

The Group Policy Results tool gathers information on all existing policies to determine the policies in effect and the order in which they are applied. To use Group Policy Results, follow these steps:

1. Select Group Policy Management from the Administrative Tools menu.

2. Right-click Group Policy Results and select Group Policy Results Wizard. Click Next.

3. On the Computer Selection page, accept the default setting of This Computer or select Another Computer. Click Next.

4. On the User Selection page (shown in Figure 21-22), select the user for whom you want to view policy settings. Click Next.

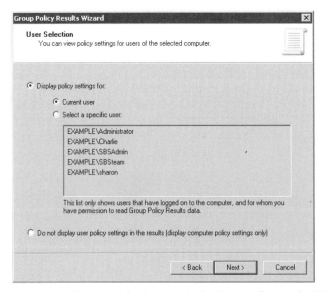

FIGURE 21-22 The User Selection page in the Group Policy Results Wizard

5. Review your selection on the Summary Of Selections page. Click Back to change the selections. Click Next to accept them. Click Finish.

Review the Group Policy Results. You can also right-click the report name and select Advanced View. (See Figure 21-23.) This will open a Resultant Set of Policy window (as shown in Figure 21-24) that details every aspect of policy for the selected user or computer.

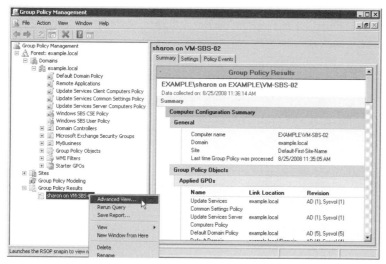

FIGURE 21-23 Group Policy Results

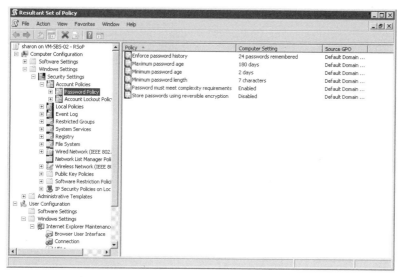

FIGURE 21-24 Advanced view of Group Policy Results

Summary

In this chapter, we described some common uses of Group Policy and Group Policy Preferences, all in pursuit of organizing and centralizing security and other settings. In the next chapter, we move on to configuring and gathering reports on your Windows SBS network's operations.

## CHAPTER 22

Managing Reports

Monitoring and analyzing network reports is frequently far down on an administrator's to-do list. Reports get attention only when something goes wrong or there's a strong suspicion that something is about to go horribly wrong. The purpose of this chapter is to encourage you to schedule reports and alerts *before* that oh-no moment arrives.

Microsoft Windows Small Business Server (SBS) comes with detailed reports built in. These reports are already configured and scheduled, though you can modify all settings. In addition, you can create your own reports for specific circumstances. First, we'll review the two built-in reports, the Summary Network Report and the Detailed Network Report.

Network Reports

To view the default Summary Network Report (also referred to as "the Summary report" in this chapter), open the SBS Console, click Reports, and then highlight Summary Network Report as shown in Figure 22-1.

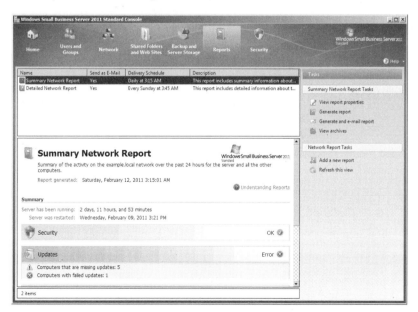

FIGURE 22-1 Viewing the Summary Network Report

This report is run once a day by default. The Detailed Network Report (or "Detailed report"), which is shown in Figure 22-2, runs once a week by default. Both times and frequencies can be reconfigured.

The summary and detailed reports have exactly the same options, just configured differently. Both have the same content and schedule options, and you can configure email options in the same way.

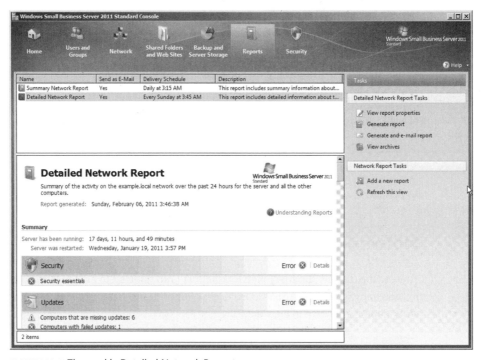

FIGURE 22-2 The weekly Detailed Network Report

Customizing the Summary Report

The default Summary Network Report really doesn't tell you much more than you can see on the Home page of the Windows SBS Console. However, you can easily customize it to display selected reports on network health. To customize the Summary Network Report, follow these steps:

1. Click Reports in the Windows SBS Console.

2. Right-click the Summary Network Report and select View Report Properties.

3. The Summary Network Report Properties dialog box opens on the General page. You can change both the report name and description by typing in new ones. Click Content.

4. On the Content page, shown in Figure 22-3, select the areas you want to include on the report.

FIGURE 22-3 Selecting the content to include in the Summary Network Report

5. Click E-Mail Options. Select the user accounts that should receive the report when it's generated. Enter the email addresses for additional recipients in the Other E-Mail Addresses box. When you enter multiple email addresses, separate each address with a semicolon.

6. Click Schedule to specify the frequency with which the report will be generated and the time it will be generated.

7. Click Archives to view a list of past reports. To see a report, select the report and click View Report. The report will display in an Internet Explorer window. (See Figure 22-4.) Click OK when finished.

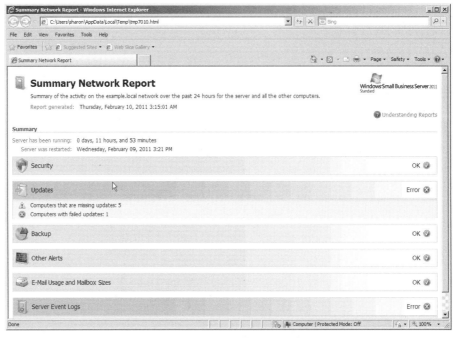

FIGURE 22-4 Viewing an archived Summary Network Report

> **NOTE** When editing report properties, you don't need to go through the pages in order. Select only the ones you need to modify, and click OK when you're finished.

Customizing the Detailed Network Report

To customize the Detailed Network Report, follow these steps:

1. Click Reports in the Windows SBS Console.

2. Right-click Detailed Network Report and select View Report Properties.

3. The Report Properties dialog box opens on the General page. You can change both the report name and description by typing in new ones. Click Content.

4. On the Content page, select the areas you want to include on the report.

5. Click E-Mail Options. Select the user accounts that should receive the report when it's generated, as shown in Figure 22-5. Enter the email addresses for additional recipients in the Other E-Mail Addresses box. When you enter multiple email addresses, separate each address with a semicolon.

FIGURE 22-5 Selecting email accounts that will receive the report

6. Click Schedule to specify the frequency with which the report will be generated and the time it will be generated. The day of the week and time can be changed for weekly reports, or you can choose a daily report and specify the time of day to generate the report. (See Figure 22-6.)

FIGURE 22-6 Changing the report schedule

7. Click Archives to view a list of past reports. To see a report, select it and click View Report. The report will display in an Internet Explorer window. Click OK when finished.

Creating a New Report

Using the same format as the Summary and Detailed reports, you can build a new report to suit your specific needs. For example, let's say you outsource certain administrative tasks and want to send a regular security report to the person who handles it. You'd follow these steps to create that report:

1. Click Reports in the Windows SBS Console.

2. In the Tasks pane, click Add A New Report.

3. On the General page, type in a name and description for the report.

4. Click Content. Select the subject or subjects you want included in the report, as shown in Figure 22-7.

FIGURE 22-7 Selecting content for the report

5. Click E-Mail Options. Select the addresses to email the report to and add the addresses of any others not already listed. (See Figure 22-8.) When you enter multiple email addresses, separate each address with a semicolon.

FIGURE 22-8 Selecting email addresses that will receive the report

6. Click Schedule to specify the frequency with which the report will be generated and the time it will be generated. The day of the week and time can be changed for weekly reports. Or you can choose a daily report and specify the time of day to generate the report.

7. Click OK when you're finished to save the new report and add it to the list in the Windows SBS console.

NOTE The Archives page isn't available until a report has been saved.

Configuring Alerts

Windows SBS includes a large set of alerts. To view the alerts, click Network in the Windows SBS Console and then select Computers. In the Tasks pane, click View Notification Settings.

In the Notification Settings dialog box, there are three pages of notifications to choose from.

Alerts for Services

On the Services page, shown in Figure 22-9, you'll find a list of services with their startup type.

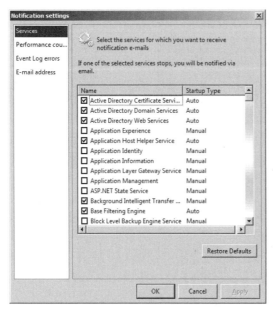

FIGURE 22-9 Setting notifications for services

As you can see, many of the services are already marked for notification if the service stops. Select additional services for notification, or remove the ones you don't care about. When a selected service stops, an alert is sent to the Home page of Windows SBS Console and will also appear on any subsequently generated Summary or Detailed report that includes other alerts, as shown in Figure 22-10.

> **NOTE** Click E-Mail Address in the Notification Settings dialog box, and specify an email address to receive notifications. To send to multiple email addresses, separate them using a semicolon.

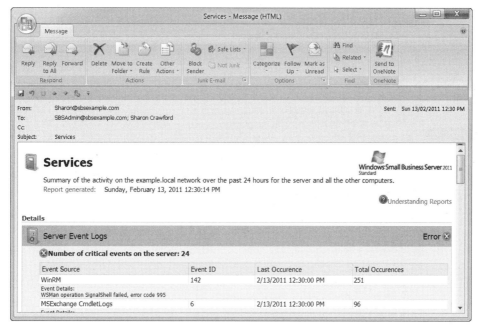

FIGURE 22-10 An email alert indicating that services have stopped

Performance Counter Alert

All the other alerts in this section are interesting and occasionally very useful, but the alert you'll be grateful for on a regular basis is the one for low disk space.

On the Performance Counter page of the Notification Settings dialog box, Percent Free Disk Space is selected by default with a threshold set to five percent. (You can clear the check box to remove the notification, though we'd be hard-pressed to understand why anyone would do so.)

To change the threshold for the notification, highlight Percent Free Disk Space and then click Edit. In the Edit box, shown in Figure 22-11, enter a threshold for notification. Click OK when finished.

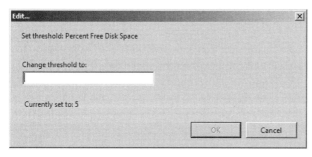

FIGURE 22-11 Changing the notification threshold

Event Log Error Alerts

On the Event Log Errors page shown in Figure 22-12, a large number of potential event log errors are listed.

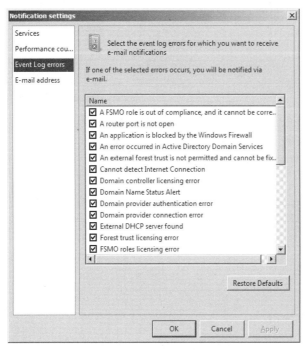

FIGURE 22-12 Selecting event log error notifications

Select or clear errors according to your needs. Click OK when finished.

> **NOTE** Click E-Mail Address, and specify an email address to receive notifications. To send to multiple email addresses, use a semicolon to separate addresses.

Creating Custom Alerts

Of course, one size never fits all. You can create a custom alert that adds alert information to reports and enables users to receive email notifications when the specified event occurs. The custom alert provides information about a specific event that has occurred, which will enable a system administrator to quickly correct a problem.

Creating an Alert for a Stopped Service

Creating an alert is a multistep process but not at all difficult. In this example, we'll configure an alert to appear if the Remote Desktop Gateway service stops or fails to start.

Acquire a GUID

To create a custom alert, you need to first acquire a GUID (globally unique identifier) that will be assigned to the alert. By far the easiest way to get a GUID is to go to *http://www.guidgen.com*, where a GUID is generated the moment you connect. (See Figure 22-13.) The GUID is easily copied and pasted into the Notepad file you're about to create.

FIGURE 22-13 The easy way to get GUIDs

To generate a GUID locally, complete these steps:

1. Select All Programs from the Start menu and then click Windows PowerShell.
2. At the command prompt, type the following command:

   ```
   [System.Guid]::NewGuid().ToString()
   ```

3. Record the GUID that's returned, as shown in Figure 22-14.

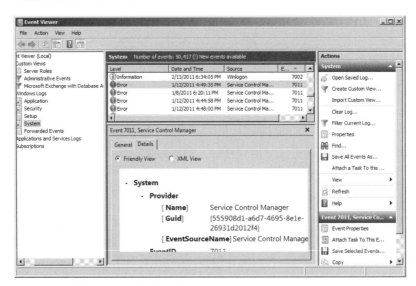

FIGURE 22-14 Acquiring a GUID

Find Event Information

Next, you must obtain information about the event that will be associated with the custom alert. To acquire the information you need, follow these steps:

1. Select Event Viewer from the Administrative Tools menu.

2. Locate the event log where the event is recorded. In this example, we're creating an alert that will appear when a particular service fails to start.

3. In the events pane, shown in Figure 22-15, select the event to associate with the custom alert. For this example, we're using an event with the ID of 7036. The event ID will be used later in this document, so make note of the number.

4. Click the Details tab, and select Friendly View. Then expand System.

5. Make note of the Provider Name and Channel.

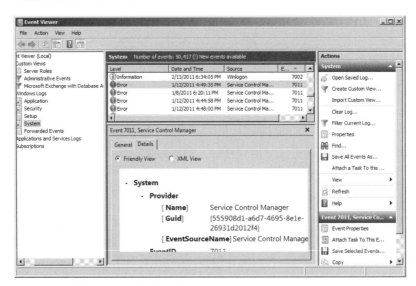

FIGURE 22-15 Viewing event information

Create and Save an .xml File

Next, to create an .xml file that contains the elements and attributes to generate the custom alert, follow these steps:

1. Open NotePad.

2. Add the following data to the NotePad file:

```xml
<?xml version="1.0" encoding="utf-8" ?>
<AlertDefinitions>
  <AlertDefinition ID="GUID"
                   Default="1"
                   Title="Exchange Transport Service"
                   Source="Service Control Manager">
  </AlertDefinition>
</AlertDefinitions>
<Parameters>
  <Path>System</Path>
  <Provider>Service Control Manager</Provider>
  <SetEventID>7011</SetEventID>
  <ClearEventID>7036</ClearEventID>
</Parameters>
```

Table 22-1 lists the attributes and parameters for the alert definition.

TABLE 22-1 Attributes and parameters for a custom alert

PARAMETER	DESCRIPTION
ID	GUID that uniquely identifies the custom alert. Use the GUID that you obtained earlier.
Default	Defines that the alert is enabled and will be preserved when defaults are restored.
Title	Name for the alert when displayed in the Windows SBS Console.
Source	Application that the alert is monitoring. In this example, it's the Service Control Manager.
Path	Name of the event log where the alert is recorded. Use the Channel value you recorded.
Provider	Use the Provider name you acquired.
SetEventID	ID number of the event that triggers the alert.
ClearEventID	Optional element that specifies the ID number of the event that clears the alert. If this element is not defined, the alert will be cleared after 30 minutes. If this element is defined, the alert will only be cleared if the specified event occurs.

3. Save the file as *filename*.xml.

4. Copy the .xml file to the %programfiles%\Windows Small Business Server\Data\Monitoring\External Alerts directory on the computer that is running the Windows SBS 2011 operating system. (You will have to create the External Alerts directory.)

5. Select Services from the Administrative Tools menu.

6. Right-click Windows SBS Manager Service and select Restart as shown in Figure 22-16.

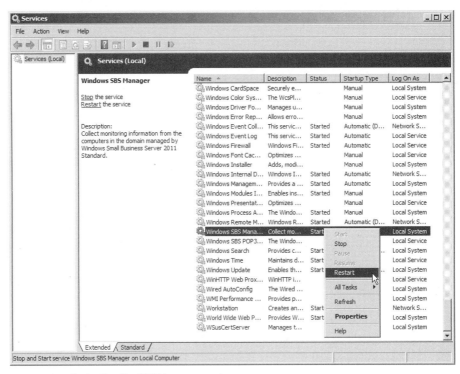

FIGURE 22-16 Restarting the SBS Manager service

Depending on the source for the alert, you might not see the notification for some time. Windows SBS Console polls for changes every 30 minutes, so if you want to check sooner than that, go to the Reports tab, right-click a report that includes Other Alerts (such as the Detailed Network Report), and select Generate Report.

The resultant report will show whether the custom alert has been activated, as shown in Figure 22-17.

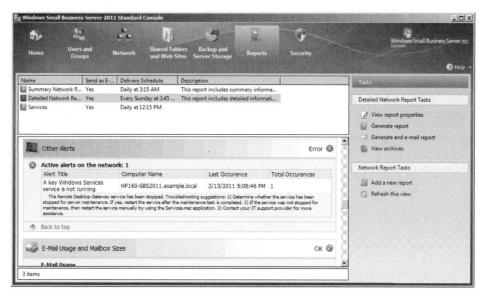

FIGURE 22-17 Report showing an activated custom alert

You can also view the new alert by clicking the Network tab at the top of the SBS Console pane, selecting the server, and then clicking the View Computer Alerts task. (See Figure 22-18.)

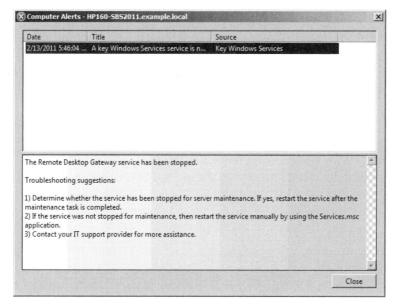

FIGURE 22-18 Viewing a custom alert

Custom Alert for Backup Failure

Backups are so crucial to the security of your network that when one fails you want to know about it sooner rather than later. This section explains what you need to create an .xml file that will generate an alert.

Create a New GUID

Acquire a GUID as described in the earlier "Acquire a GUID" section. Make note of the GUID, and follow these steps:

1. Open NotePad, and add the following data to the NotePad file, substituting the GUID you acquired for *GUID*:

```
<?xml version="1.0" encoding="utf-8" ?>

<AlertDefinitions>

<AlertDefinition ID="GUID" Default="1"

Title="Backup Failure" Source="Server">

    <Parameters>

     <Path>Application</Path>

     <Provider>Microsoft-Windows-Backup</Provider>

     <SetEventID>546</SetEventID>

    </Parameters>

</AlertDefinition>

</AlertDefinitions>
```

2. Save the file with the .xml extension, shown in Figure 22-19, and copy it into the %programfiles%\Windows Small Business Server\Data\Monitoring\ExternalAlerts directory on the computer that is running the Windows SBS 2011 operating system.

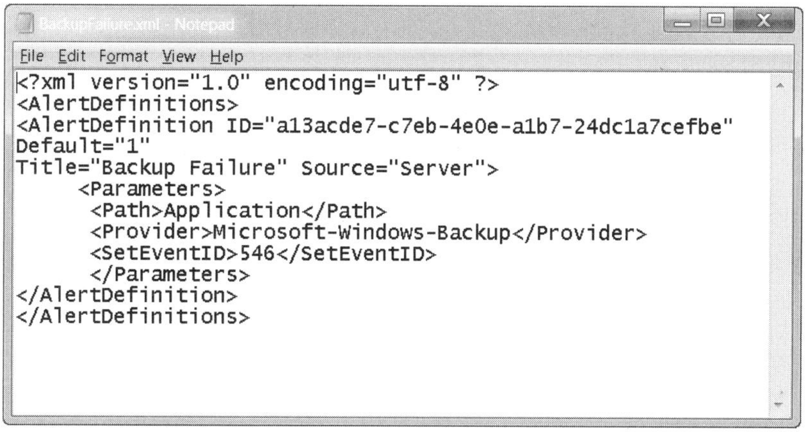

FIGURE 22-19 Backup Failure .xml file

3. Select Services from the Administrative Tools menu. Right-click the Windows SBS Manager Service, and then click Restart.

> **NOTE** For more on building your own alerts as well as security add-ins, visit http://msdn.microsoft.com/en-us/library/cc721702.aspx. Additional custom alerts can be downloaded free at http://sbs.codeplex.com.

Summary

In this chapter, we covered the Reports component of the Windows SBS Console. Fortunately, more detailed notifications can be had through View Notification Settings and particularly through devising custom alerts.

Next, we move on to creating and customizing a useful Windows SharePoint site on the network.

## CHAPTER 23

Customizing a SharePoint Site

M icrosoft Windows Small Business Server (SBS) 2011 Standard includes SharePoint Foundation 2010, and the SBS installation automatically creates an internal website called Companyweb, which is a custom SharePoint site designed for small businesses. This default site meets the needs of most small businesses with little customization required, but you can easily add features to Companyweb to make it even more useful for your environment and needs without being a developer or web designer.

SharePoint keeps getting better with each version, and whole books have been written about how to create, manage, and develop for SharePoint sites. We won't pretend to try to cover everything, but in this chapter we'll cover some of the features and configuration of Companyweb and SharePoint in general, and show you how to add a useful set of links to RemoteApps.

Introducing SharePoint Foundation 2010

SharePoint Foundation is a web-based collaboration and document-management system that is easily and quickly deployed to provide an effective intranet solution for businesses of all sizes. In SBS, SharePoint is installed automatically, and an internal website (*http:// companyweb*), shown in Figure 23-1, is created and configured with a range of features that make sense for small businesses.

> **NOTE** In this chapter, we shorten SharePoint Foundation 2010 to simply *SharePoint*. Microsoft SharePoint 2010, which is designed for hosting multiple, independent SharePoint portals, is a separate product.

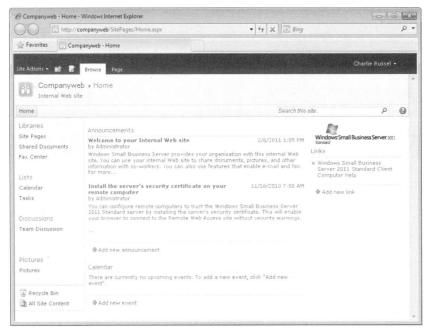

FIGURE 23-1 The default internal website for SBS 2011 Standard

The main center pane of Companyweb has a section for announcements and a calendar section. On the left pane are links into other main areas of the website, including document libraries, the Fax Center, calendar and tasks lists, a team discussion area, and a photo library. These items are generally available from other pages of the website, giving you quick access without having to navigate back to the home page. On the right side of the page is the Links pane, a place to put links to important external resources or applications that users can run.

The starting Companyweb site is a good starting point, but there are plenty of ways you can extend it and add additional features and sections without having to be a web developer. Of course, if you *are* a web developer, you can use myriad options to create additional features and functionality. SharePoint is easily extensible, and there are good books available for both professional developers and interested users.

Understanding SharePoint Items

Let's start by looking at the pieces that can make up a SharePoint site:

- **Libraries**   Libraries come in various formats, including
  - Document libraries for storing and collaborating on documents, including basic versioning features
  - Picture libraries for storing photos and graphics

- Form libraries for storing InfoPath form templates

- Wiki page libraries that let you build interactive, basic wiki sites

- **Lists** Lists come in various formats for presenting and storing list-based information, including

  - Communications lists such as announcements and contacts

  - Tracking lists such as links, calendar, and tasks

  - Custom lists, including a datasheet view

- **Web pages** Web pages include a basic web page, sites, and workplaces or a web parts page.

- **Discussions** A list type used to build a basic forum for ongoing collaborative discussions.

- **Tasks** Tasks come in both basic tasks lists and project tasks that include Gantt chart functionality to graphically track project status.

Understanding SharePoint Roles

SharePoint has five basic permission levels on a site: Full Control, Design, Contribute, Read, and Limited Access. In SBS 2011 Standard, there are three security groups defined for SharePoint permissions: Windows SBS SharePoint_VisitorsGroup, Windows SBS SharePoint_MembersGroup, and Windows SBS SharePoint_OwnersGroup. These correspond to three SharePoint site roles for the default Companyweb site: CompanyWeb Visitors, CompanyWeb Members, and CompanyWeb Owners.

The CompanyWeb Visitors group has only the Windows SBS SharePoint_VisitorsGroup as a member. This group can read but can't edit the site or its contents, nor can members of the group add discussion items. By default, no SBS users are in the Windows SBS SharePoint_VisitorsGroup, though you can move users into it.

The CompanyWeb Members group has only the Windows SBS SharePoint_MembersGroup as a member. This group has Design permissions and can read, write to, and contribute to the Companyweb site, including posting to discussions and customizing the site. By default, all user accounts with the Standard User role and Standard User With Administrative Links role are part of this group.

The CompanyWeb Owners group has only the Windows SBS SharePoint_OwnersGroup as a member. This group has full administrative rights on the Companyweb site and can create new workspaces, change user and site permissions, and create new user roles and permissions. By default, all Network Administrators are part of this group.

The CompanyWeb Members group is a powerful group that has the ability to change the look and feel of your Companyweb site; can add or delete sections, documents, or articles; and generally has very nearly the full power of the Owners, with the sole exception of not being able to control the permissions of other users. As shown in Figure 23-2, there is a lesser level of permissions called Contribute—which still allows users to view, add, and update content but doesn't give them full design capabilities. We think this is a more appropriate role for most users, and you should consider changing the default permissions for CompanyWeb Members to Contribute instead of Design.

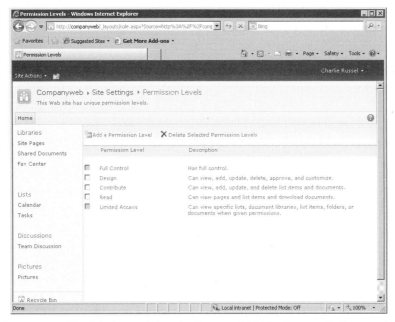

FIGURE 23-2 The default permissions for CompanyWeb Members are Design permissions

To change the permissions for all of CompanyWeb Members, follow these steps:

1. Log on to the Companyweb site with an account that has Owners permissions.

2. On the main Companyweb page, select Site Permissions from the Site Actions drop-down list to open the Permissions page shown in Figure 23-3.

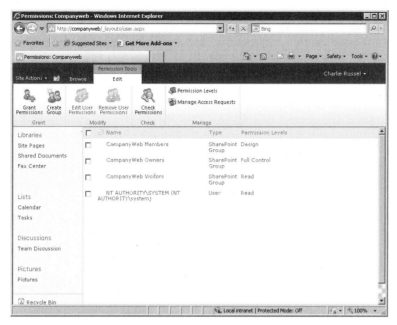

FIGURE 23-3 The Permissions: Companyweb page of the Companyweb site

3. Select the CompanyWeb Members check box, and then click Edit User Permissions on the ribbon to open the Edit Permissions page shown in Figure 23-4.

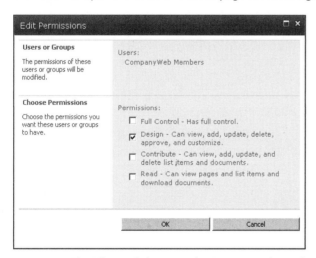

FIGURE 23-4 The Edit Permissions page for CompanyWeb Members

4. Clear the Design – Can View, Add, Update, Delete, Approve, And Customize check box; and select the Contribute – Can View, Add, Update, And Delete List Items And Documents check box.

5. Click OK to return to the Permissions: Companyweb page.

From the Permissions: Companyweb page, you can also create a new group and assign permissions and users to it, or directly add users and assign them permissions. These permissions are carried throughout the site. We strongly recommend that you not start assigning permissions to individual users but stick to the three roles. If there are users who need Design permissions but who should not be full site Owners, you should create an additional group named CompanyWeb Designers specifically for them.

To edit the permissions for a particular section of the Companyweb site, open that section of the site and then select Settings from the Settings drop-down list. Here you can customize the particular section and edit the permissions for the section. As an example, let's modify the permissions of the default Shared Documents library to allow our user "Alfie" to have full control of the library, using these steps:

1. Open *http://Companyweb* if it isn't already open.

2. Click Shared Documents in the left pane to open the Shared Documents page, shown in Figure 23-5.

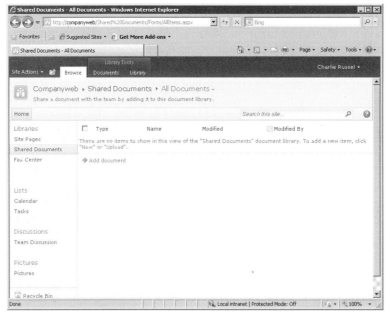

FIGURE 23-5 The Shared Documents library of the default Companyweb site

Edit Permissions

3. Click Library on the ribbon, and then click the Edit Permissions button to open the Permission Tools tab shown in Figure 23-6.

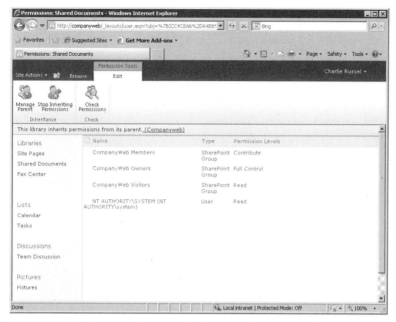

FIGURE 23-6 The Permission Tools tab for the Shared Documents library

4. Click Stop Inheriting Permissions to enable setting unique permissions for this library, which inherits permissions by default from the parent site. You'll be warned that this will disable inheritance, as shown in Figure 23-7.

FIGURE 23-7 Disabling permission inheritance for a document library

IMPORTANT This is a good time to emphasize that when you change permissions on a portion of a site, you lose the inheritance that makes it easy to keep track of what permissions are granted. If you do need to change permissions as we are in this example, be sure to clearly document the changes. Or resist the temptation and find another way to manage things. It is possible, however, to revert to inherited permissions.

5. Select the group that you want to set permissions for, as shown in Figure 23-8.

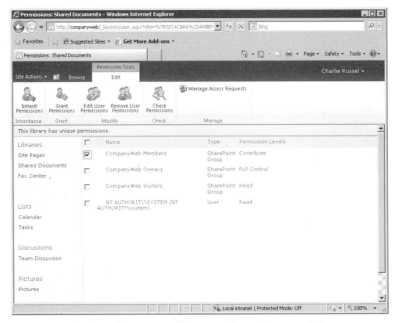

FIGURE 23-8 The Shared Documents library now has unique permissions

6. Click the button that corresponds to the permission change you want to make. You can re-enable inherited permissions, grant specific permissions to individuals or groups, edit the existing permissions, deny permissions, or check the permissions settings for a role.

7. Click Edit to open the Edit Permissions dialog box to change the permissions for this library for the role you have selected, as shown in Figure 23-9.

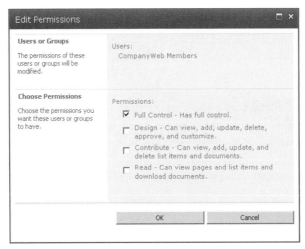

FIGURE 23-9 Setting the Shared Documents library to allow Full Control permissions for CompanyWeb Members

8. Click Grant Permissions on the ribbon to open the Grant Permissions dialog box shown in Figure 23-10. From here you can add individual users or groups, bypassing the default roles in SBS 2011.

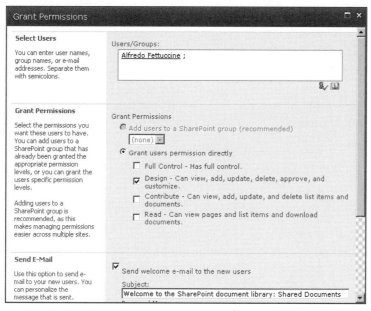

FIGURE 23-10 The Add Users: Shared Documents page

9. Type **Alfie** in the Users/Groups box, and click the Check Names button in the lower right of the box. SharePoint verifies the user and substitutes his full name, Alfredo Fettuccine.

10. Select Full Control – Has Full Control from the Grant Users Permission Directly section.

11. If you want to send Alfie an email message telling him that he's in charge now, select the Send Welcome E-mail To The New Users check box and edit the message as appropriate.

12. Click OK to make the change and return to the Permissions: Shared Documents page shown in Figure 23-11, where Alfie now has full control.

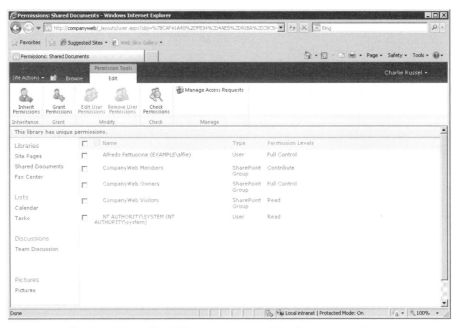

FIGURE 23-11 The Permissions: Shared Documents page of the Companyweb site

Customizing Companyweb

You can customize Companyweb to add additional lists, links, and libraries. Working with a SharePoint site to customize it is pretty straightforward and follows a similar logic wherever you are. We'll start by adding a regular IT team meeting and creating a workspace for it that allows IT team members to file their reports ahead of time and add comments to others' reports.

Adding a Workspace

Adding a workspace creates an area where a group of users can directly interact and share documents and discussions, separate from the overall document libraries. For our example, let's first create a recurring meeting and assign users to the meeting, following these steps:

1. From the main Companyweb page, click Add New Event in the Calendar section of the center pane to open the Calendar – New Item page.

2. Type in a title and location for this meeting, set the time and date to next Monday at 9 AM, finishing at 10 AM, and add a description as shown in Figure 23-12.

FIGURE 23-12 Adding a new Calendar item

3. Select the Make This A Repeating Event check box. The Recurrence section will expand as shown in Figure 23-13.

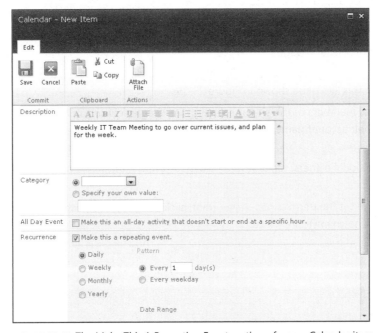

FIGURE 23-13 The Make This A Repeating Event section of a new Calendar item

4. Set the meeting for Weekly, and set it to end after 10 occurrences.

5. Select the Use A Meeting Workspace check box, and click Save to open the New Meeting Workspace page shown in Figure 23-14.

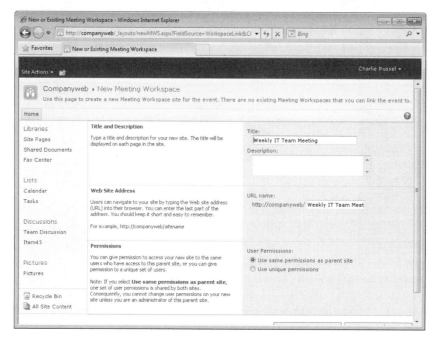

FIGURE 23-14 Creating a new workspace for the IT team meeting

6. Select Use Unique Permissions in the User Permissions section, and click OK to open the Template Selection page.

7. Select Basic Meeting Workspace for this meeting, and click OK to open the Set Up Groups For This Site page shown in Figure 23-15.

8. Add users as members of this site by selecting the Create A New Group option and typing in their account names, separated by semicolons. Click the Check Names icon to verify the names.

9. To add additional owners, repeat the previous step with names for the owners of this site.

10. When you've set the permissions as you want, click OK to open the workspace you've created, as shown in Figure 23-16.

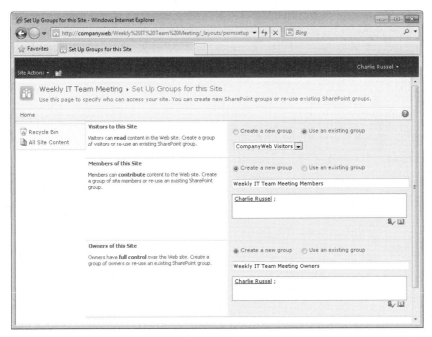

FIGURE 23-15 The Set Up Groups For This Site page

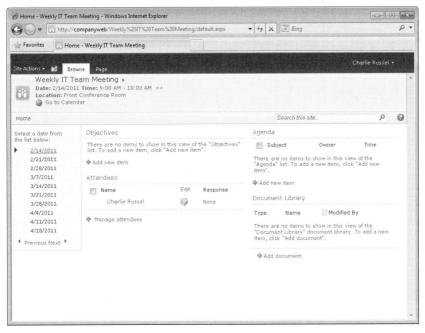

FIGURE 23-16 The new Weekly IT Team Meeting workspace

11. Click Manage Attendees to open the Attendees page, and click the Items tab. Then click New Item to open the Attendees – New Item page shown in Figure 23-17. Type in the name for the attendee and click Save.

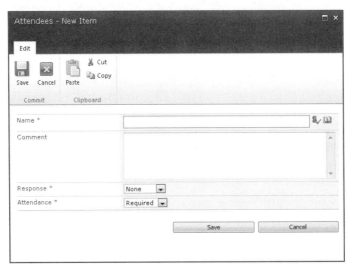

FIGURE 23-17 The Attendees – New Item page

12. Repeat the previous step until you've added all the attendees to the list, as shown in Figure 23-18.

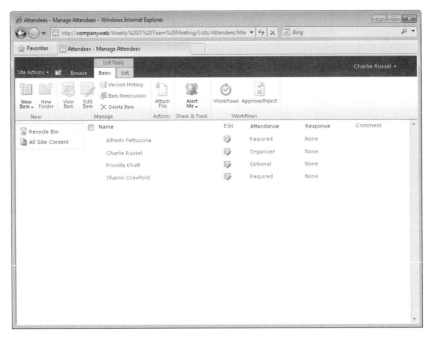

FIGURE 23-18 Attendees have been added to our team meeting.

13. Click Navigate Up next to the Site Actions button to return to the main page for this workspace.

Navigate Up

14. Click Add New Item in the Agenda section to create an agenda for the current meeting, as shown in Figure 23-19.

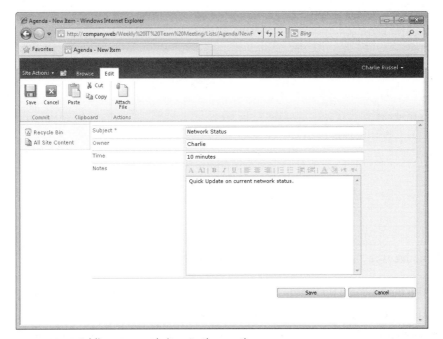

FIGURE 23-19 Adding an agenda item to the meeting

15. Repeat the previous step as required to add items to the agenda, as shown in Figure 23-20.

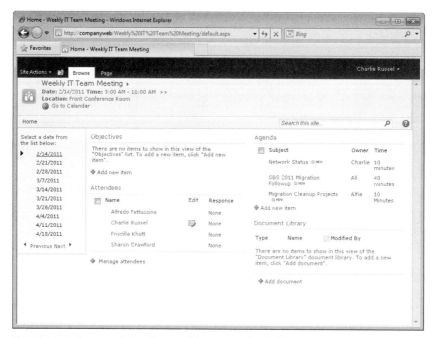

FIGURE 23-20 The agenda for the next IT team meeting is filled out

16. Use the Navigate Up button to navigate back to the main Companyweb page.

SharePoint Foundation 2010 supports additional types of sites and libraries beyond work-spaces, as shown in Figure 23-21. One really useful library type is the Wiki Page Library. Add-ing any of these is an essentially similar process to adding the workspace we've just added, though the particular steps and options will be different for different types.

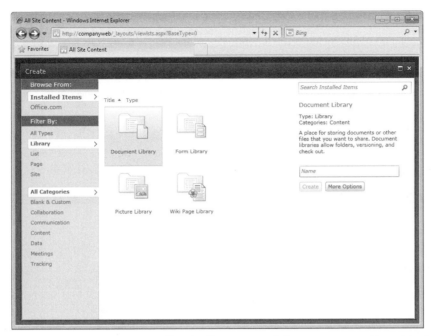

FIGURE 23-21 You can create new libraries, lists, pages and sites to support a wide variety of collaboration

Adding RemoteApps Links

If you have an RD Session Host on your network and you're using RemoteApp programs, you can extend your Companyweb site to add links to those RemoteApp programs directly on your users' home page. The process has four basic steps:

1. Add the RD Web Access role service on the SBS 2011 Standard server.
2. Register the Web Part as a safe control.
3. Create a folder to store the Web Part.
4. Add the Web Part to Companyweb.

The first two steps involve the native Windows 2008 R2 Server Manager. If you need a refresher on Server Manager, see Chapter 17, "Windows SBS Console vs. Server Manager."

Add the RD Web Access Role Service

The default installation of SBS includes the functionality of the RD Gateway role service of Remote Desktop Services, but it doesn't actually include any of the Remote Desktop Services role and doesn't include the RD Web Access role service. So the first thing you need to do is add the Remote Desktop Services role and the RD Web Access role service, using the following steps:

1. Open Windows Server 2008 R2 Server Manager from the Start menu.

2. Click Roles, and then click Add Roles from the Action menu to open the Select Server Roles page shown in Figure 23-22.

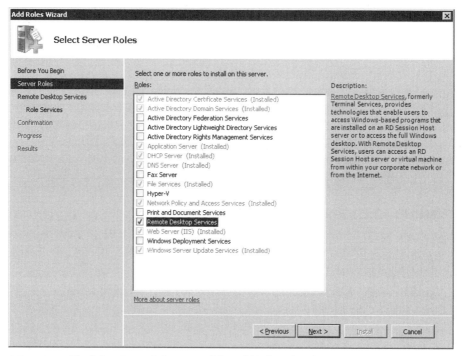

FIGURE 23-22 The Select Server Roles page of the Add Roles Wizard

3. Select Remote Desktop Services and click Next to open the Remote Desktop Services page that includes an introduction to Remote Desktop Services.

4. Click Next to open the Select Role Services page shown in Figure 23-23.

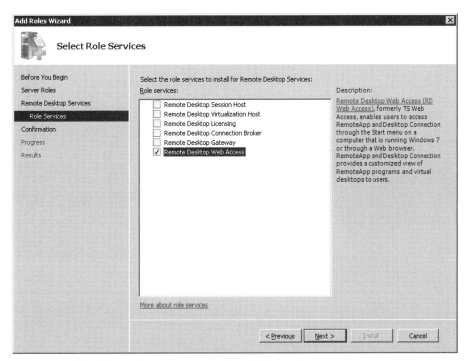

FIGURE 23-23 The Select Role Services page of the Add Roles Wizard

5. Click Next and then click Install to add the RD Web Access role service to the SBS server. When the installation completes, you'll see the Installation Results page shown in Figure 23-24, warning you that you'll need to do some additional configuration to RD Web Access.

> **NOTE** In most cases, you won't need to restart the SBS server when you add this role service, but you might need to add additional updates the next time the server checks for updates.

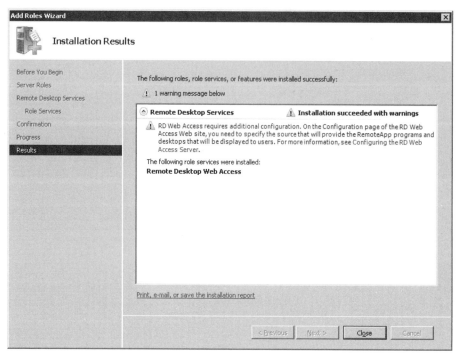

FIGURE 23-24 The Installation Results page of the Add Roles Wizard

6. Click Close to return to Server Manager. You can close the Server Manager console; we're done with it for now.

Configure RD Web Access

You need to do some basic configuration of RD Web Access and of your RD Session Host server to enable the Web Part to work. First, log on to your RD Session Host and follow these steps to add the SBS server to the list of RD Web Access computers allowed to connect to Remote Desktop Services:

1. Open a command prompt as an Administrator.

2. At the command prompt, type **lusrmgr.msc** and press Enter to open the Local Users And Groups console.

3. Select Groups in the left pane, and then open the TS Web Access Computers group in the center pane to open the TS Web Access Computers Properties page shown in Figure 23-25.

FIGURE 23-25 The TS Web Access Computers local group properties on the RD Session Host server

4. Click Add, and then click Object Types and select Computers as shown in Figure 23-26.

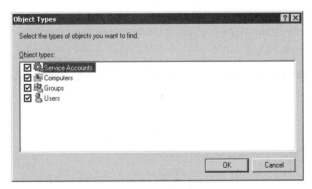

FIGURE 23-26 The Object Types dialog box

5. Click OK, and then type the name of your SBS server in the Enter The Object Names To Select field and click Check Names. Then click OK to return to the Properties dialog box.

6. Click OK to return to Local Users And Groups. You can close the console and then close your session on the RD Session Host.

Next, you need to configure RD Web Access to use your RD Session Host. Open Internet Explorer and follow these steps:

1. Connect to *https://remote.<yourdomain.com>/RDWeb*. For our domain, that is _*https:// remote.sbsexample.com/RDWeb*, as shown in Figure 23-27.

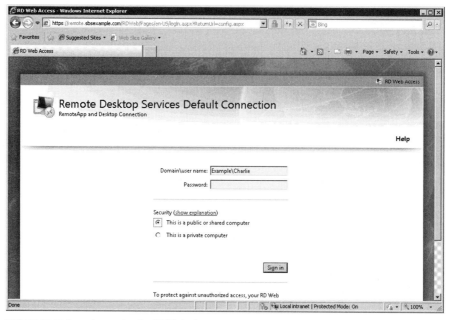

FIGURE 23-27 Logging on to the RDWeb site

2. Log on to the site with an account in the Network Administrator role to open the Configuration page of Remote Desktop Services Default Connection, as shown in Figure 23-28.

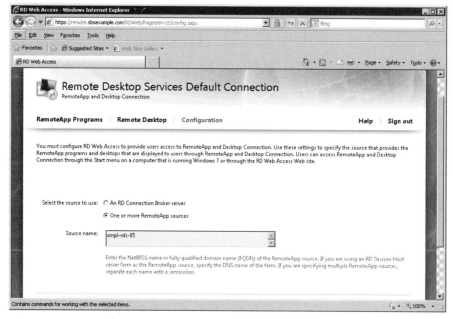

FIGURE 23-28 The Configuration page of the Remote Desktop Services Default Connection site

3. Enter the NetBIOS name of your RD Session Host server in the Source Name field, and then click OK to close the Configuration page and open the RemoteApp Programs page shown in Figure 23-29.

FIGURE 23-29 The RemoteApp Programs page of the Remote Desktop Services Default Connection site

Register the Web Part as Safe

Next you need to register the Web Part you're going to use as a *safe control*. This allows it to run without needing an elevated prompt. To register the Web Part, follow these steps:

1. Open an elevated Cmd or PowerShell command prompt using Run As Administrator.
2. Change to the directory where the configuration file for Companyweb is, and open web.config in Notepad or your favorite plain-text editor as shown in Figure 23-30 by entering the following commands:

```
cd "C:\inetpub\wwwroot\wss\VirtualDirectories\Companyweb80"

notepad web.config
```

FIGURE 23-30 Editing the web.config file for Companyweb

3. In the web.config file, locate the <SafeControls> section of the file. At the end of the section of SafeControl Assembly entries, add the following line:

```
<SafeControl Assembly="TSPortalWebPart, Version=6.1.0.0, Culture=neutral,PublicKe
yToken=31bf3856ad364e35" Namespace="Microsoft.TerminalServices.Publishing.Portal"
TypeName="*" Safe="True" AllowRemoteDesigner="True" />
```

> **NOTE** Add this as a single line, with no line breaks.

4. Save the change and exit Notepad. Keep the elevated command prompt open. You'll need it in the next section.

> **IMPORTANT** Always make a copy of important files before editing them—just in case.

Create a Folder to Store the Web Part

Next you need to create a folder to hold the Web Part and its images, and to give the Network Services account full control on the folder. Use the following steps:

1. In the elevated command prompt from the previous section, type the following commands:

```
mkdir "C:\Program Files\Common Files\Microsoft Shared\Web Server Extensions\
wpresources\TSPortalWebPart\6.1.0.0__31bf3856ad364e35\images"
```

```
mkdir "C:\Program Files\Common Files\Microsoft Shared\Web Server Extensions\
wpresources\TSPortalWebPart\6.1.0.0__31bf3856ad364e35\rdp"
```

> **NOTE** Notice the two underscores after 6.1.0.0 in the preceding command lines.

2. Change the directory to the parent folder of the two folders you just created:

cd "C:\Program Files\Common Files\Microsoft Shared\Web Server Extensions\
wpresources\TSPortalWebPart\6.1.0.0__31bf3856ad364e35"

3. Give the Network Service account and the spwebapp account full control over the two folders you created in step 1:

cmd /c icacls images /grant NetworkService:F

cmd /c icacls images /grant spwebapp:F

cmd /c icacls rdp /grant NetworkService:F

cmd /c icacls rdp /grant spwebapp:F

4. Close the Command Prompt window if you see a success message.

Add the Web Part to Companyweb

Finally, the reason you're doing all this—to add the Web Part to Companyweb, follow these steps:

1. Open Companyweb with an account that has SharePoint Owners privileges.

2. Select Site Settings from the Site Actions menu to open the Site Settings page shown in Figure 23-31.

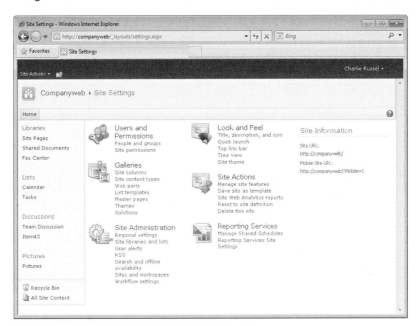

FIGURE 23-31 The Site Settings page for the Companyweb site

3. Click Web Parts under the Galleries section to open the Web Part Gallery page, as shown in Figure 23-32.

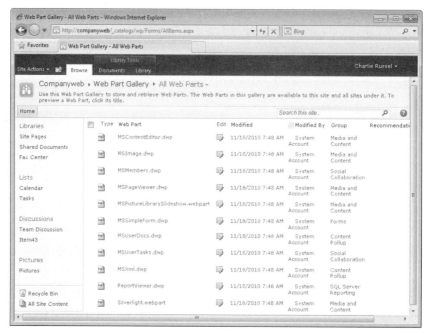

FIGURE 23-32 The Web Part Gallery page

4. Click the Documents tab and then click New Document to open the New Web Parts page. Scroll down to the bottom, and select the Microsoft.TerminalServices.Publishing. Portal.TSPortalWebPart check box as shown in Figure 23-33.

5. Click Populate Gallery (back at the top of the page) to add the Web Part, and return to the Web Part Gallery.

6. Click the Navigate Up button to return to the main Companyweb page.

7. Select Edit Page from the Site Actions menu to open Companyweb in edit mode, as shown in Figure 23-34.

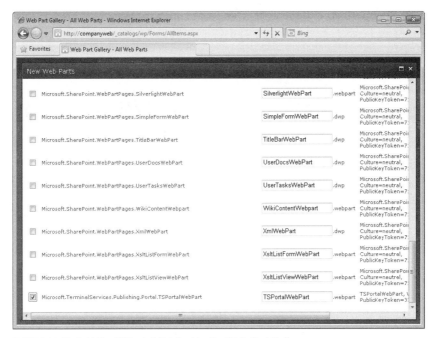

FIGURE 23-33 Add the TSPortalWebPart to the Web Part Gallery

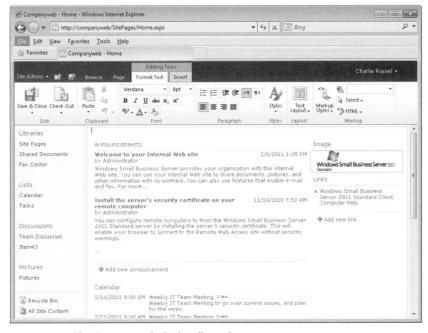

FIGURE 23-34 The Companyweb site in edit mode

8. Click the Insert tab, and then click Web Part to open the Web Parts dialog box shown in Figure 23-35.

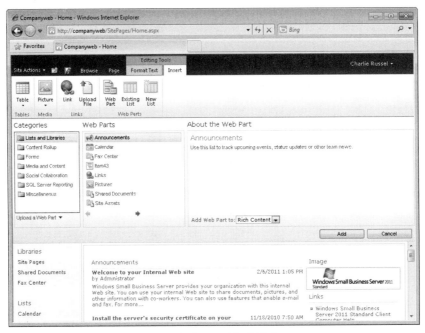

FIGURE 23-35 Editing the Companyweb site to add a Web Part

9. Click Miscellaneous in the Categories pane, select TSPortalWebPart, and then click Add to add the Web Part to your Companyweb page.

10. The new Web Part will be automatically populated with the RemoteApps available on your RD Session Host.

This just begins to scratch the surface of what you can do with SharePoint and the Companyweb site, but we think the new features that are enabled with SharePoint Foundation 2010 are exciting. And having our RemoteApps on the Companyweb page is a great addition.

Summary

In this chapter, we covered customizing the default SharePoint site, Companyweb. We've shown how to modify permissions, add a workspace, and modify the site to use Companyweb as an RD Web Access portal for running remote applications directly from Companyweb.

In the next part, we move on to installing and using the Premium Add-on features, including installing the second server, installing Microsoft SQL Server 2008 R2, and configuring Remote Desktop Services on the second server.

#### PART V

Premium Edition Features

## CHAPTER 24

Installing the Second Server

Microsoft Windows Small Business Server 2011 Standard (Windows SBS 2011) with Premium Add-on includes a full copy of Windows Server 2008 R2 Standard that can be used for any purpose desired, as long as it's installed on the SBS network. Because Windows Server 2008 R2 is available only in a 64-bit version, the Premium Add-on includes downgrade rights to Windows Server 2008 Standard, which has both 32-bit and 64-bit versions. This allows you to support line-of-business (LOB) applications that don't yet support a 64-bit operating system.

Because the second server is full Windows Server 2008 R2 Standard, you can install any of the normal roles and features on the server as you would any other copy of Windows Server 2008 R2 Standard, including Hyper-V and Remote Desktop Services (the new name for Terminal Services). Windows Server 2008 R2 Standard includes "1+1" virtualization licensing, allowing for virtualization of a single instance of Windows Server as a child partition—but only if the parent partition is used solely for the Hyper-V role. We think a very interesting scenario is to install the second server as a Hyper-V parent, and then install the second server again, virtualized to support any additional roles and features, including Microsoft SQL Server (covered in Chapter 25, "Installing Microsoft SQL Server 2008 R2 Standard Edition for Small Business") and the Remote Desktop Session Host role (covered in Chapter 26, "Adding a Terminal Server").

Another choice for some environments will be to install the second server as an additional domain controller. This can make a lot of sense if the second server is going to be used to support a remote site—for example, where a local infrastructure server, with Active Directory Domain Services, DNS, DHCP, File Server, and Print Server roles would likely be installed.

Minimum System Requirements

There are no special requirements for installing the second server that make it different from installing any other version of Windows Server 2008 R2. Your minimum requirements and steps remain the same. The official minimum requirements are shown in Table 24-1, along with our commentary on those requirements and suggested real-world minimums.

TABLE 24-1 Minimum system requirements for second server

HARDWARE	REQUIREMENTS	COMMENTS
Processor	1.4 GHz, single core	2 GHz or greater is more realistic, and at least two cores.
RAM	512 Mb	1 gigabyte (GB) of RAM is a more realistic minimum; 2 GB is recommended. For Server Core, 1 GB of RAM is normally sufficient for typical infrastructure workloads.
Disk	32 GB	No less than 60 GB of hard disk space on the system drive, please. And if your server has more than 16 GB of RAM, increase the minimum to at least 50 GB.
Optical Drive	DVD-ROM	If no optical drive is available, a bootable USB flash drive can be used for installation. For details on creating a bootable USB drive, see *http://msmvps.com/blogs/russel/archive/2010/03/03/making-a-bootable-usb-disk-stickdrive-pendrive-flashdrive.aspx*.
Video	800 × 600	1024 × 768 is a more realistic minimum. Some screens will be difficult to use at a resolution below 1024 × 768.
Other	Keyboard and mouse	
Network	Not required	Who are they kidding? A supported network card is required for joining a domain or almost anything you'll want to do with Windows Server 2008 R2.

Notice what is not on the list of required hardware—a floppy drive! Beginning with Windows Server 2008, we can get rid of the floppy requirement, even if we need to load drivers for our hard disk controller. Drivers can now be loaded from CD or DVD, from a USB flash drive, or from floppy disk.

 REAL WORLD **64-Bit and Signed Drivers**

As you've seen for installing the main SBS server, signed 64-bit drivers are required for Windows Server 2008 R2. This requirement means that you must do your homework and make sure that your vendors provide full support for their hardware in Windows Server 2008 R2. Although the initial response from even major vendors to the need for signed 64-bit drivers was slower than we'd have hoped, there is no issue with current server hardware and 64-bit. If you need to use legacy hardware cards or peripherals that aren't part of the server you ordered from your server vendor, be sure to verify the availability of a supported, signed driver for that hardware card or peripheral before installing Windows Server 2008 R2. Remember, you have the option of downgrading to the 32-bit version of Windows Server 2008 if it is more appropriate for your environment.

Of course, if a driver isn't available, choose a vendor that does have a driver to retain all the advantages that 64-bit provides. Personally, we chose to change hardware vendors when we found deficiencies in 64-bit driver support. And we told our old hardware vendors exactly why we dropped them, too.

Installation and Initial Configuration

Installation and configuration of Windows Server 2008 R2 has changed significantly from the process we're all more or less familiar with from Windows Server 2003. There are far fewer steps required to actually begin the installation, with hardly any input required from the user. You don't even need to enter a Product ID (PID)—see the "PID-less Installs" sidebar. Eventually, you'll have to enter the PID before you can activate the server, but a lot of steps that used to be required before the installation process would begin have now been moved to the initial configuration stage.

 UNDER THE HOOD **PID-less Installs**

Windows Server 2008 R2 normally requires you to enter a PID for installation. But you can simply skip entering the PID and then you'll have to select exactly which version of Windows Server 2008 R2 you're installing. You'll get a couple of extra prompts and warnings, but if you only want to run a demonstration or evaluation environment for 30 days or fewer, just skip entering the PID. You'll have a fully functional Windows Server 2008 R2 installation for those 30 days.

If you decide to convert a server installed without a PID to a fully activated Windows Server 2008 R2 server, you need to enter a PID for the exact same version of Windows Server 2008 R2 that you said you were installing when you initially installed. That means if you used retail media to install the server, you must provide a retail key. If you used the SBS 2008 media, you use the key provided with SBS 2008. You can't change which version is installed without completely reinstalling Windows Server 2008 R2.

To enter a product key for a server installed without a PID, use the slmgr.vbs -ipk command.

Installation

Installing Windows Server 2008 R2 from standard distribution media onto a clean server with no operating system on it requires just seven screens at the very beginning, and the entire rest of the installation will complete without further interruption. You don't need to enter any network information, computer name, domain name, or other information except the actual PID associated with the installation and the language to install.

Use the following steps to install Windows Server 2008 R2 onto a bare server using standard DVD media:

1. Turn on the server, and immediately insert the Windows Server 2008 R2 DVD for the Windows Server 2008 architecture you want to install. If the primary hard disk hasn't got a bootable operating system on it, you'll go directly into the Windows Server 2008 R2 installation process. If the disk has a bootable operating system on it, you might be prompted with Press Any Key To Boot From CD Or DVD. If you are, press a key.

2. When the initial Install Windows page appears, shown in Figure 24-1, select the language and other regional settings to use for this installation.

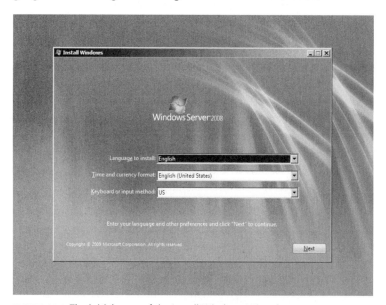

FIGURE 24-1 The initial page of the Install Windows Wizard

3. Click Next to open the page shown in Figure 24-2. From here, you can choose to repair a corrupted Windows Server 2008 R2 installation, or get additional information before installing.

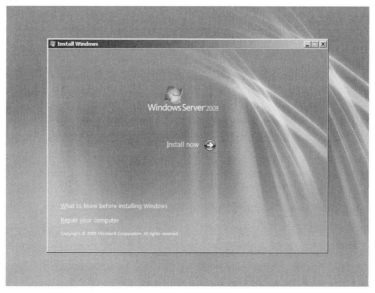

FIGURE 24-2 The Install Now page of the Install Windows Wizard

4. Click Install Now to open the Type Your Product Key For Activation page of the Install
   Windows Wizard as shown in Figure 24-3. (If you're installing a volume license version
   of Windows Server 2008 R2, you won't see this screen.)

FIGURE 24-3 The Type Your Product Key For Activation page of the Install Windows Wizard

5. Type in a product key for this installation of Windows Server 2008 R2. (See the Under The Hood sidebar "PID-less Installs" earlier in this chapter for information on installing without entering a product key for those versions that still have this screen.)

6. Leave the Automatically Activate Windows When I'm Online check box selected unless you need to control when activation occurs.

7. Click Next to open the Select The Operating System You Want To Install page of the Install Windows Wizard as shown in Figure 24-4. If you're installing a version that allows you to enter a product key, you'll only see a list of versions that match the product key you entered.

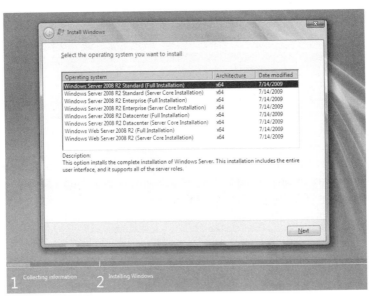

FIGURE 24-4 The Select The Operating System You Want To Install page of the Install Windows Wizard

8. Select either a Full Installation or a Server Core Installation. This selection is irrevocable—you can't change an installation at a later time from Full to Server Core, or from Server Core to Full. (For details on installing and configuring Windows Server 2008 R2 Server Core or the free Microsoft Hyper-V Server R2, see Chapter 6, "Configuring SBS in Hyper-V," where we provide some scripts to simplify the process.)

9. Click Next to open the Please Read The License Terms page. Select I Accept The License Terms. You don't have a choice—either accept them or the installation terminates.

10. Click Next to open the Which Type Of Installation Do You Want page, and select Custom (Advanced) to open the Where Do You Want To Install Windows page shown in Figure 24-5.

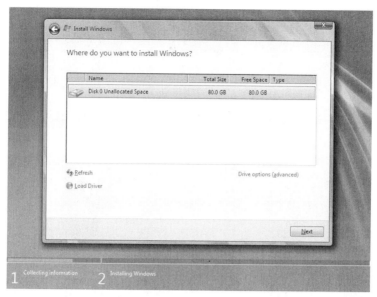

FIGURE 24-5 The Where Do You Want To Install Windows? page of the Install Windows Wizard

11. The first disk on your computer will be highlighted. You can select any disk shown, or if the disk you want to install on isn't displayed, you can load any required driver at this point by clicking Load Driver. Clicking Drive Options (Advanced) will give you additional options to repartition or format the selected drive.

12. When you've selected the drive to install on, click Next and the installation will begin. You won't be prompted again until the installation completes and you're prompted for a password for the Administrator account.

 UNDER THE HOOD   **Drive Options**

The default selected drive when you're installing an SBS second server is the first drive as enumerated by the BIOS. You can change the selection if the drive you want isn't selected, or add drivers for additional controllers if the drive you want isn't visible. For those familiar with earlier versions of Windows, you'll be glad to know that Windows Server 2008 R2 finally adds support for something besides a floppy drive for loading storage drivers during installation! As shown in Figure 24-6, you can load drivers from floppy, from CD or DVD, or from a USB flash drive.

FIGURE 24-6 Windows Server 2008 R2 supports loading storage drivers from floppy disk, optical drive, or USB drive

If you need to change partitions on a drive, format it, or even extend it to add additional space, just click Drive Options (Advanced) to display additional options for managing and configuring your disks during installation, as shown in Figure 24-7.

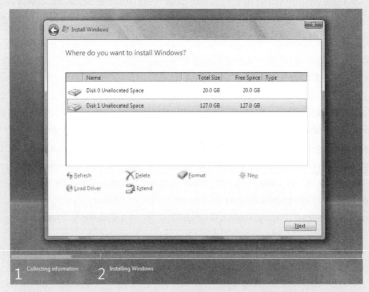

FIGURE 24-7 Advanced drive options are available during installation of Windows Server 2008 R2

New in SBS 2008 and Windows Server 2008 R2 is the ability to extend existing partitions, even during the installation process. Although this isn't a feature that matters in completely new installations, it can be a useful feature when you're recycling a computer. You can extend a partition onto available unallocated space on the same disk.

NOTE If you need to open a command window during the installation process, just press Shift+F10. Now you can manually run Diskpart.exe or any other tool available at this point in the process to manually load a driver or fine-tune partitioning.

When the installation completes, Windows Server 2008 R2 will restart and proceed to the logon screen. You'll need to enter a new password for the Administrator account, as shown in Figure 24-8, and then log on to the new server.

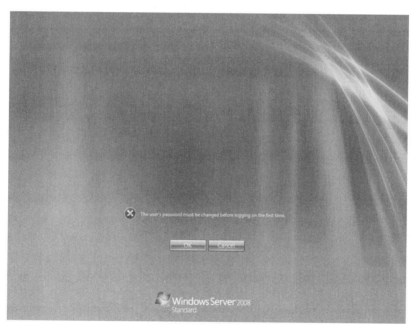

FIGURE 24-8 Setting the initial password for the Administrator account

When you log on, you'll see the Initial Configuration Tasks (ICT) Wizard, shown in Figure 24-9, which makes the initial setup of your new server easy.

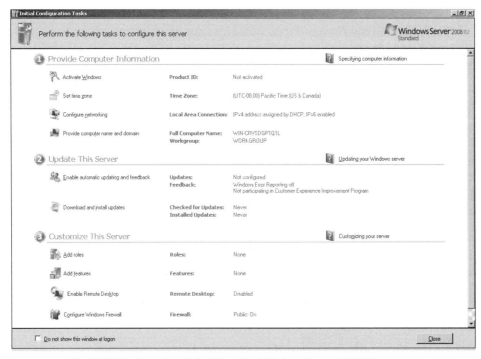

FIGURE 24-9 The Initial Configuration Tasks Wizard for Windows Server 2008 R2

Initial Configuration

After the SBS Premium second server installation completes, there are still quite a few tasks to perform. The basic requirements haven't changed—they've just been shifted to after, instead of during, the install. At minimum, you'll need to perform the following tasks on a fresh server installation:

- Assign the initial Administrator account password.
- Install any hardware drivers required.
- Set the time zone.
- Configure the networking.
- Assign a name to the server.
- Join the server to the SBS domain.
- Configure automatic updates and automatic feedback settings.
- Check for updates and install them.

The first of those tasks, assigning the Administrator account password, is required before you can log on for the first time, so we've already covered that.

There are additional tasks on the Initial Configuration Tasks (ICT) Wizard that you probably want to perform as part of your initial setup:

- Activate Windows.
- Add server roles.
- Add server features.
- Enable Remote Desktop.
- Configure Windows Firewall.
- Exactly which roles and features you'll need to install varies depending on what the server will be used for. We'll cover the basics of adding a feature here, by adding the Windows Backup feature. And in Chapter 26, we'll cover adding roles in more detail. We'll enable Remote Desktop because the SBS 2011 Group Policy that enables Remote Desktop doesn't apply to servers, though it might get automatically enabled initially until the new server is moved to the correct organizational unit (OU). Windows Firewall should be configured automatically by the role and feature wizards and Group Policy.

Install Hardware Drivers

There's a missing piece in the ICT Wizard—no direct way to add hardware drivers for any hardware on the server that isn't recognized. Microsoft makes every effort to get as many drivers as possible on the installation DVD, but the reality is that new hardware will continue to be released, and the drivers are limited to what was available when Windows Server 2008 R2 shipped. So some hardware might require drivers that aren't on the DVD. If these are drivers for hard disk controllers, you always have the option of adding them during the installation, but for other hardware you need to wait until Windows Server 2008 R2 is installed.

After the installation completes and you've logged on, you can install additional drivers as required. We think it's a good idea to do this as the first step before configuring any settings in the ICT. This is especially important if your network card isn't recognized, because you'll need connectivity to the SBS network to complete the rest of the ICT.

Setting the Time Zone

During the initial installation, Windows will pick a time zone (probably not the one you're in unless you live on the west coast of North America) and will also set the current date and time based on your computer's BIOS. To set the date and time, as well as the current time zone, click the link on the ICT Wizard to open the Date And Time dialog box shown in Figure 24-10. After you've set your server's clock and time zone, click Apply and then click OK to return to the ICT Wizard.

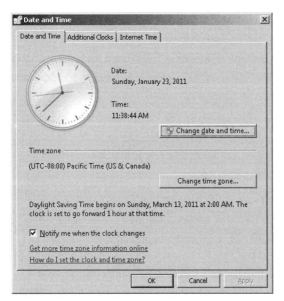

FIGURE 24-10 The Date And Time dialog box

 REAL WORLD Additional Clocks

Windows Server 2008 R2 lets you configure two additional clocks as part of the Date And Time dialog box. If you configure additional clocks, the times in those time zones will be visible when you pause the mouse cursor on the clock.

If you regularly work with folks in another time zone, you eventually get used to the time difference and don't need additional clocks on your server. And, after all, you shouldn't be sitting at the server console in most cases anyway. But we still find it handy, and because we work with folks in Europe and Australia fairly often, we turn on two additional clocks: one set to Greenwich Mean Time (GMT), and the other set to GMT+10 hours, for Sydney, Australia. This ensures that when we call at a totally unreasonable hour, we have absolutely no excuse.

Configuring Networking

Next on the list is configuring your networking. By default, your new server has enabled both IPv4 and IPv6, and with the DHCP server running on the main SBS 2011 server, you should have automatically assigned IP addresses. For servers, we highly recommend that at least the IPv4 address be a fixed address. In most scenarios, the IPv6 address can be a stateless auto-configuration address.

> **NOTE** If no DHCP server is available, the server will have a link-local address—an auto-configuration IP address that is unique on the network but won't be forwarded by routers to another network. These IP addresses begin with 169.254. If your second server has an IP address in this range, check for problems with the physical network connecting the second server to the SBS server, or for problems with the DHCP Server service on the main SBS 2011 server.

To configure the networking and set a fixed IP address for the server, follow these steps:

1. Click Configure Networking in the Initial Configuration Tasks window to open the Network Connections Control Panel application shown in Figure 24-11.

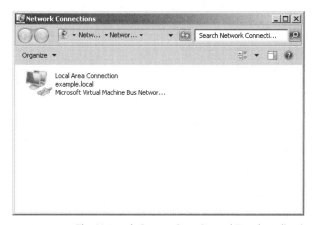

FIGURE 24-11 The Network Connections Control Panel application

2. Right-click the connection you want to configure and select Properties from the short-cut menu to open the Local Area Connection Properties dialog box, shown in Figure 24-12.

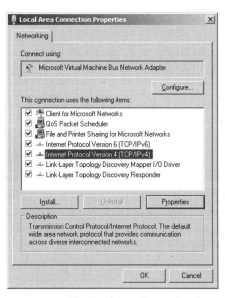

FIGURE 24-12 The Local Area Connection Properties dialog box

3. Select Internet Protocol Version 4 (TCP/IPv4), and click Properties.

4. Select Use The Following IP Address, as shown in Figure 24-13.

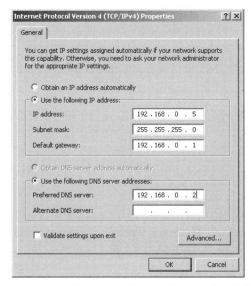

FIGURE 24-13 The Internet Protocol Version 4 (TCP/IP) Properties dialog box

5. Enter an IP address, a subnet mask, and a default gateway appropriate to your network. This should be in the range excluded from the SBS 2011 DHCP server range.

NOTE By default, the SBS server will be at 192.168.nnn.2, where *nnn* is the subnet used by your Internet router. On our network this is 0, so we've assigned 192.168.0.5 as the IP address for our second server. Your subnet will likely be different.

6. Specify the Preferred DNS Server for your network. This will be the IP address of the primary SBS 2011 server.

7. Click OK to close the Internet Protocol Version 4 (TCP/IP) Properties dialog box, and then click Close to complete the configuration of the connection.

8. Close the Network Connections window by clicking in the upper right corner of the window to return to the ICT Wizard page.

Setting the Computer Name and Domain

After you have your networking configured, you're ready to give the computer a name and join it to the SBS domain. The Windows Server 2008 R2 setup process automatically assigns a random and meaningless name to a new server. Although this name is certainly unique on the network, it's not a useful final name, so you'll want to change it.

 REAL WORLD **Naming Computers**

It's a good idea to use a computer name that is both DNS-compatible and NetBIOS-compatible so that all types of clients see the same name for your computer. (And yes, we're going to have to live with NetBIOS for a while still—too many applications, including Microsoft applications, simply don't work properly without it.) To do this, keep the name to 15 characters or fewer and don't use asterisks or periods. To obtain the best application compatibility, use dashes instead of spaces and underscores.

Beyond that, you should use a naming convention that has some internal consistency. We've seen all sorts of naming conventions, from the literary obscurities of naming them after romantic poets or science-fiction characters, to Norse or Greek gods, to colors (with the server fronts all painted to match the color name of the server). But honestly, we like names that actually help identify functionality, location, address, hardware, domain, or some combination of these. So our EXAMPLE network here includes computers with the following names:

- *hp160-sbs2011* (The computer is running as a virtual machine on a Hewlett-Packard DL160SE G6, and it's the main SBS 2011 server.)
- *xmpl-rds-05* (It's running as a virtual machine in our Example network, its primary role is Remote Desktop Services, and its IP address is 192.168.0.5.)

- *hp160-win7-01* (It's running on that same Hewlett-Packard DL160SE G6, it's a Windows 7 VM, and it's the first one we created.)

- hp160-v32-*03* (It's running on that same Hewlett-Packard DL160SE G6, it's a 32-bit Windows Vista VM, and it's the third one we created.)

We know it's a boring way to name things, but we think it's a lot easier to understand than trying to remember that Zeus is the main SBS server and Athena is the second server running SQL Server.

You can save a reboot if you change the computer name and domain at the same time. Both require a reboot that will prevent other tasks from being completed, but fortunately they can be paired. To set the name and domain, follow these steps:

1. Click Provide Computer Name And Domain in the ICT Wizard to open the System Properties dialog box shown in Figure 24-14.

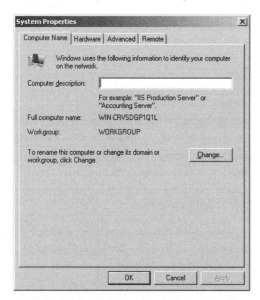

FIGURE 24-14 The System Properties dialog box

2. You can enter a description for this computer if you want, but it's hardly ever visible and thus not terribly useful.

3. Click Change to open the Computer Name/Domain Changes dialog box shown in Figure 24-15.

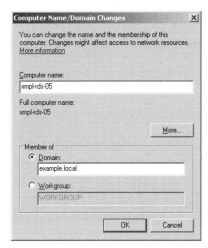

FIGURE 24-15 The Computer Name/Domain Changes dialog box

4. Type in a computer name consistent with your naming convention, and then click Domain to type in the SBS domain name.

> **NOTE** You can use either the NetBIOS version of the domain name (EXAMPLE, here) or the DNS version (example.local).

5. Click OK. You are prompted for credentials to perform the change, as shown in Figure 24-16. This should be the administrator account you chose for the SBS domain.

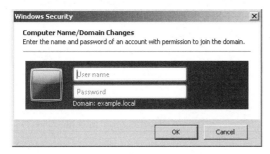

FIGURE 24-16 You must provide administrative credentials for the SBS domain

6. Click OK. If there aren't any problems, you'll get a Welcome message like that shown in Figure 24-17.

FIGURE 24-17 The Welcome message lets you know you're now joined to the domain

7. Click OK to acknowledge the Welcome message. You'll be warned that you need to restart the server before the changes take full effect. Click OK, and then click Close. Then click Restart Now.

> **IMPORTANT** It's tempting at this point to try to delay the reboot to see if you can squeeze a few more things in before having to wait for the server to shut down and restart. And we understand the temptation—we're big fans of minimizing the number of reboots required and doing as many things as we can when we know we're going to have to reboot. But this is the one time we think you shouldn't do it. You need to get that new name and security in place before anything else happens.

8. After the server has rebooted, log on with an SBS account—not the local administrator account—to complete the configuration of the server.

Enable Updates and Feedback

The next group of settings on the ICT Wizard is used to set how updates are handled and what feedback is sent to Microsoft. The first setting in this section of the ICT Wizard is to actually configure what settings are used for updates and feedback. You can make three basic choices when you click Enable Automatic Updating And Feedback on the ICT Wizard:

- Windows and Microsoft Update settings
- Windows Error Reporting settings
- Customer Experience Improvement Program settings

To configure these settings, follow these steps:

1. On the Initial Configuration Tasks Wizard, click Enable Automatic Updating And Feedback to open the dialog box shown in Figure 24-18.

2. Unless you really want your server to be automatically downloading and installing updates with no warning, and with automatic reboots (again without warning), do not select Enable Windows Automatic Updating And Feedback.

3. Click Manually Configure Settings to open the dialog box shown in Figure 24-19.

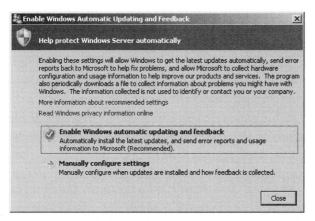

FIGURE 24-18 The Enable Windows Automatic Updating And Feedback dialog box

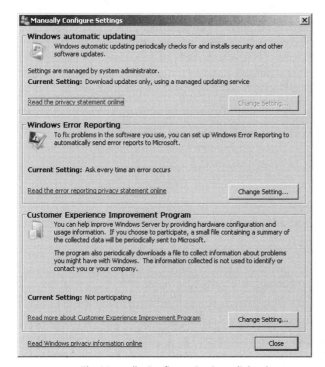

FIGURE 24-19 The Manually Configure Settings dialog box

4. You can't change the settings for Windows Automatic Updating—these are controlled by Group Policy and are set in the SBS Console, as described in Chapter 15, "Managing Software Updates."

5. Click Change Setting in the Windows Error Reporting section to open the Windows Error Reporting Configuration dialog box shown in Figure 24-20.

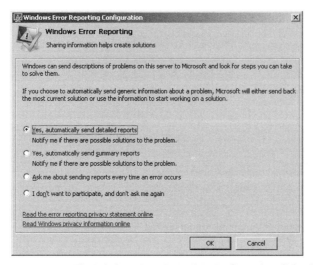

FIGURE 24-20 The Windows Error Reporting Configuration dialog box

6. Select how you want error reports handled. We think that automatically sending at least summary reports, and preferably detailed reports, is good for all of us. See the Under the Hood sidebar "Windows Error Reporting" for more information on what is sent and why we care. After you've made your selection, click OK to return to the Manually Configure Settings dialog box, shown earlier in Figure 24-19.

7. Click Change Setting in the Customer Experience Improvement Program section to open the Customer Experience Improvement Program Configuration dialog box shown in Figure 24-21.

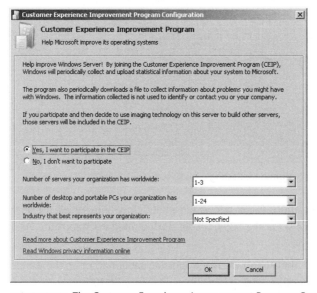

FIGURE 24-21 The Customer Experience Improvement Program Configuration dialog box

8. The default is to not automatically participate in the Customer Experience Improvement Program (CEIP). When you choose to participate, no personal or organizationally identifiable information is sent to Microsoft. None. But they do gather information about your hardware and the Server roles installed on the server, and if you include details about your organization's servers, workstations, and industry, that information is linked to the collected data. Personally, we choose to send it, but we can understand those who would rather not.

9. Make your selections, click OK, and then click Close to return to the ICT Wizard.

 UNDER THE HOOD **Windows Error Reporting**

Windows Error Reporting dates back to the old Dr. Watson errors that we all learned to hate in the earlier days of Windows. But it's come a long way since then. One of the major changes, introduced in Windows XP, was the sending of the crash dumps back to Microsoft when a program crashed or stopped responding. (This is called Online Crash Analysis, or OCA, and it found a lot of bugs!) You were asked each time if you wanted to send the crash dump, and fortunately a lot of people did because the result has been a far more stable and solid Windows, along with much better drivers. Microsoft CEO Steve Ballmer is reliably reported to have observed that "about 20 percent of the bugs cause 80 percent of all errors, and—this is stunning to me—one percent of bugs cause half of all errors." By identifying those 20 percent of the bugs, and focusing efforts on them, we all benefit from more stable, crash-free software.

It is important to note, however, that crash dumps can contain personally identifiable information. If you're in the middle of entering your credit card number when the program you're working in crashes, chances are that the credit card number, or some portion of it, is likely to be inside that crash dump. Microsoft has made repeated—and we think credible—assurances that they will not use any personal information in those crash dumps in any way. You can read their Privacy Statement at *http://oca.microsoft.com/en/dcp20.asp*. In fact, we urge you to read it. It's clear and we think as unambiguous as is possible when lawyers are involved. And we found it reassuring. We've all benefited from the errors that have been reported in the past to help make the software we use better and more reliable.

Getting Updates

The final option in the middle section of the ICT Wizard is to go online and download updates right now. Just click Download And Install Updates. The Windows Update dialog box shown in Figure 24-22 opens.

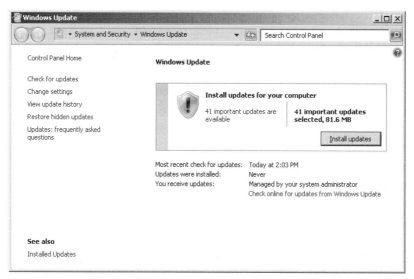

FIGURE 24-22 The Windows Update dialog box

If updates are available, they'll be displayed and you can choose to install them immediately. The default is to connect to Windows Server Update Services (WSUS) running on the main SBS server. Install the updates, and get the reboot out of the way.

Customizing the Server

The final section of the ICT Wizard is used to add roles and features to the server, enable remote access, and configure Windows Firewall. We can finally get down to actually setting the server up to do some real work. All the rest has just been getting ready.

We'll cover adding roles to the server when we talk about Remote Desktop Session Host (Terminal Server) in Chapter 26. Roles are a new way that Windows Server 2008 R2 groups similar functionality together for installation and configuration. A role is a specific set of functionality that the server needs for a particular set of uses. Roles can also have role services, which are subsets of the functionality in the role and can be installed only as part of the role.

Features can be installed on any server, without being specific to a particular function of how the server will be used. We think that at least one feature, the Windows Server Backup Features (including the command-line tools), should be installed on every server that isn't backed up by some other tool, so we'll cover that installation here.

The other two settings in this last section of the ICT Wizard are enabling Remote Desktop and configuring Windows Firewall.

Adding the Windows Server Backup Features

Windows Server Backup is the new backup utility introduced in Windows Server 2008 and significantly enhanced in Windows Server 2008 R2. It includes a graphical user interface (GUI) by default, but also has command-line tools (including Windows PowerShell cmdlets) available. Whenever you add the Windows Server Backup features, you should include the command-line tools to ensure that you can script backups.

You can't back up your new server until you install the Windows Server Backup features. To add the features from the ICT Wizard, follow these steps:

1. Click Add Features in the Initial Configuration Tasks Wizard to open the Add Features Wizard, shown in Figure 24-23.

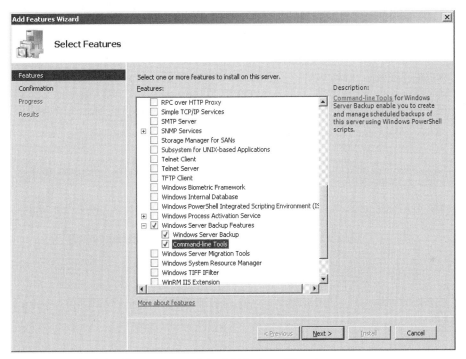

FIGURE 24-23 The Select Features page of the Add Features Wizard

2. Scroll down to near the bottom of the Features list, and select Windows Server Backup Features, including all subfeatures, as shown in Figure 24-23.

3. Click Next to open the confirmation page. You'll see a list of features that are going to be installed and a warning that this might require a reboot. Don't worry, the server will not reboot as long as this is the only feature you're installing.

4. Click Install to begin the actual installation. When the installation completes, you'll see the Installation Results page. Any problems will be highlighted here, or it will simply report that the installation was successful. Click Close to exit the Add Features Wizard.

Remote Desktop

Next on the ICT Wizard list is a link to enable Remote Desktop. Remote Desktop allows administrators to connect directly to the server without having to sit down at the console in the server room. Windows Server 2008 R2 introduces version 7 of the Remote Desktop Protocol (RDP). The Remote Desktop Client version 7 is included in Windows 7 and Windows Server 2008 R2, and version 7 clients for Windows XP SP3 and Windows Vista SP1 and SP2 are downloadable from Microsoft Knowledge Base Article 969084 at *http://support.microsoft.com/kb/969084*.

Version 7 of RDP includes many improvements over earlier versions, including 32-bit color, server authentication, Windows Media Player redirection, Aero glass support, and Remote-Apps support. For remote administration of a server, the most important improvement is server authentication, which ensures that you are actually connecting to the computer you think you are.

At this point, with a freshly installed Windows Server, you'll see that Remote Desktop has been automatically enabled. But it won't last. After you move the server to the correct organizational unit (OU), it will lose that Group Policy setting and you'll need to redo it. So the best thing to do is first move the server to the correct OU now, using the following steps:

1. On the Windows SBS 2011 server, log in with an account that is in the Network Administrator role.

2. Open the Active Directory Users And Computers console by typing **dsa.msc** in the Search field of the Start menu.

3. Navigate to the MyBusiness, Computers, SBSComputers OU as shown in Figure 24-24.

FIGURE 24-24 The Active Directory Users And Computers console

4. Click the server you just added to the domain (xmpl-rds-05 in our case), and drag the server to the SBSServers OU.

5. You'll get a warning about moving objects in Active Directory Domain Services, as shown in Figure 24-25. In this case, you can ignore the warning, so click Yes.

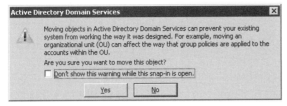

FIGURE 24-25 Never move objects in Active Directory Domain Services without a clear idea of why you're doing it

6. Close Active Directory Users And Computers, and log in to the server you just moved. Use an account in the Network Administrator role.

7. Open a command window (Cmd.exe), using Run As Administrator, and run *gpupdate /force*.

8. The ICT Wizard will now show that the Remote Desktop is disabled, as shown in Figure 24-26.

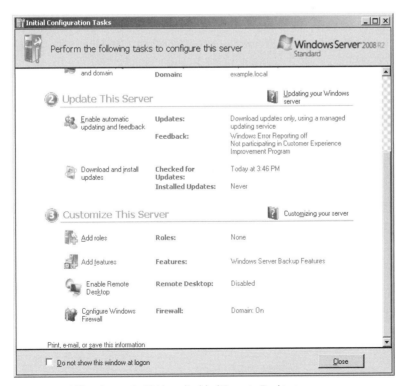

FIGURE 24-26 The change in OU has disabled Remote Desktop

9. Click Enable Remote Desktop to open the System Properties dialog box shown in Figure 24-27. Select Allow Connections From Computers Running Any Version Of Remote Desktop (Less Secure), and click OK to return to the ICT Wizard.

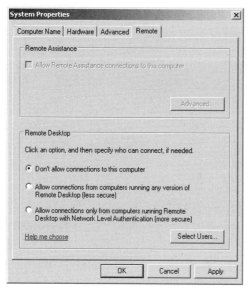

FIGURE 24-27 The System Properties dialog box

10. Select the Do Not Show This Window At Logon check box, and then click Close to close the ICT Wizard. (You can always get it back by running *oobe.exe*.)

11. Finally, there's one more little bit of customization we do on every server. When you closed the ICT Wizard, the Server Manager console opened, as shown in Figure 24-28.

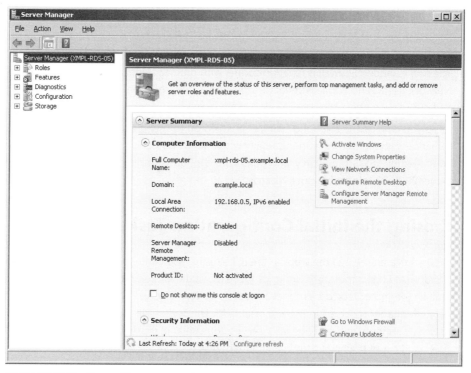

FIGURE 24-28 The Server Manager console

12. In the Server Summary section, click Configure Server Manager Remote Management to open the dialog box shown in Figure 24-29.

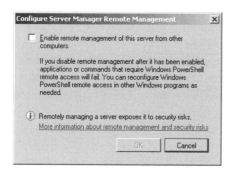

FIGURE 24-29 Enabling Server Manager remote management

13. Select the Enable Remote Management Of This Server From Other Computers check box, and click OK to return to the Server Manager console.

Configure Windows Firewall

By default, Windows Firewall is enabled on all new servers. This is a very different version of Windows Firewall than the one that came with the first release of Windows Server 2003. The new Windows Firewall is location-aware, with different rules for Domain traffic, Private Network traffic, and Public Network traffic. And it's bidirectional, controlling both incoming and outgoing traffic.

As you change the roles and features enabled on the server, Windows Firewall will be automatically configured to work optimally within your SBS network. Some settings are directly controlled by SBS Group Policy, and others are configured automatically by the Windows Server 2008 R2 role and feature wizards.

Closing the Initial Configuration Tasks Wizard

After you've finished all the steps in the ICT Wizard, you can select the Do Not Show This Window At Logon check box and click Close as we did earlier in the list of instructions for enabling Remote Desktop. Whenever you log on to the server, you'll automatically see the Server Manager console (unless you disable it). The Server Manager console gives you a single place to configure and manage your server. You can add, modify, or remove roles and features, and do all the basic daily management tasks from a single console.

> **NOTE** Adding roles and role services is very much like adding features, which we've covered in this chapter, but there are usually additional settings involved during the enabling process. We'll cover adding roles to the Premium Add-on server in Chapter 26.

All the functions on the ICT Wizard are available elsewhere, but we think it's a useful and well-designed feature that pulls together all the initial steps you're likely to need to do on a new server into a single, logical place. If you close the ICT Wizard, turn it off, and then realize you need to configure something that was on the ICT Wizard, but can't easily locate it on the Server Manager, you can open the ICT Wizard again by running oobe from the command line.

> **REAL WORLD** Windows MultiPoint Server 2011
>
> If your reason for buying the Premium Add-on is to use your second server as an RD Session Host and you have no particular need for SQL Server, there's a better option for that second server—Windows MultiPoint Server 2011 (WMS 2011). WMS 2011 combines a dedicated RD Session Host with support for both Ethernet and USB connected stations in a package that has an easy-to-use management console, shown in Figure 24-30.

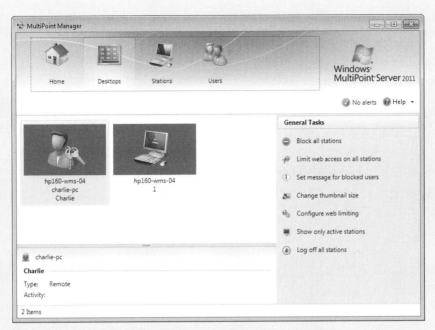

FIGURE 24-30 The Windows MultiPoint Server 2011 Manager console

The WMS 2011 Premium edition is required in an SBS domain, but the pricing—including the costs of client access licenses (CALs)—is usually better than the Premium Add-on, and the additional functionality of WMS 2011 for managing connected users makes this a compelling alternative—one we're implementing on our own SBS network.

Summary

In this chapter, we covered the basic installation and initial configuration tasks you need to do to get your SBS 2011 Premium Add-on second server up and running. SBS does preconfigure some settings for you, but quite a few still need to be done manually.

In the next chapter, we'll cover installing and configuring Microsoft SQL Server 2008 R2 as we continue covering the features of Windows Small Business Server 2011 Standard with the Premium Add-on.

## CHAPTER 25

Installing Microsoft SQL Server 2008 R2 Standard Edition for Small Business

If you purchased the Microsoft Windows Small Business Server 2011 Premium Add-on (SBS 2011 Premium Add-on), you have an additional Windows Server 2008 R2 Standard license for an additional server and a license for Microsoft SQL Server 2008 R2. Before you install SQL Server, you should review both hardware and other requirements.

This chapter can't come close to telling you everything you might need to know about SQL Server—there are many books available on every aspect. However, we can give you an overview of the features and a brief introduction to installing SQL Server.

> **NOTE** SQL Server 2008 R2 includes all service packs for SQL Server 2008 and Power-Pivot technology for sophisticated data analysis working with Microsoft Office.

Installation Options

You have choices when it comes to installing SQL Server 2008 R2, although if you use it to support a particular line-of-business application, the decision might already be made for you. SBS 2011 Premium Add-on consists of licenses for the 64-bit versions of Windows Server 2008 R2 and SQL Server 2008 R2. If you want, you can downgrade to 32-bit versions of Windows Server 2008 and SQL Server 2008.

SQL Server 64-bit can be installed on your Windows SBS 2011 Server or, preferably, on a second server running Windows Server 2008 R2 64-bit.

The downgraded SQL Server 2008 32-bit can be installed on a second server running Windows Server 2008 32-bit.

Installation Restrictions

Before you begin the process of installing and deploying SQL Server, you should be aware of the following restrictions.

The version of SQL Server included in SBS 2011 Premium Add-on is licensed for installation only in your Windows SBS 2011 network. You cannot install SQL Server on a server that is not in the Windows SBS 2011 domain.

The Windows SBS 2011 CAL Suite for Premium Users or Devices is required for users who, or devices that, access SQL Server.

You can install SQL Server on the server running Windows SBS 2011 or on the second server that you set up for your Windows SBS 2011 domain. However, for security reasons, it's a bad idea to install the SQL Server on a domain controller. Use the second server in the Windows SBS 2011 domain.

You can move the Windows SharePoint Services content database to SQL Server Standard Edition, but it's not a sensible idea because then you'll need a SQL Server CAL for everyone who accesses SharePoint.

Installing SQL Server (Part One)

To install SQL Server, insert the DVD in the drive on the server and follow these steps:

1. If the startup sequence doesn't start automatically, select Computer from the Start menu and double-click the DVD drive.

2. The first dialog box that appears, shown in Figure 25-1, advises that Microsoft .NET Framework and an updated Windows Installer will be installed as part of the SQL Server installation. Click OK.

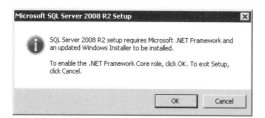

FIGURE 25-1 The first setup dialog box

3. The SQL Server Installation Center, shown in Figure 25-2, opens. The following sections describe the links on each page.

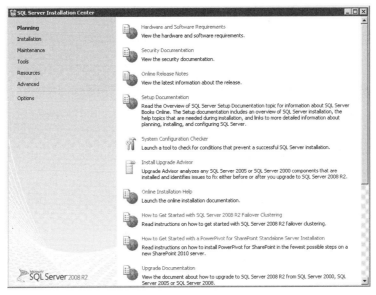

FIGURE 25-2 The SQL Server Installation Center

Planning

The SQL Server Installation Center provides a wealth of information. All that reading might be daunting at first, but at least 90 percent of a successful installation is in the planning. So the planning page is where we'll start.

Hardware and Software Requirements

Click the Hardware And Software Requirements link to see the minimum hardware and software requirements to install and run SQL Server 2008 R2. The link is to the MSDN SQL Server Developer Center.

Security Documentation

Click the Security Documentation link for advice on security measures. Click the links under the heading Before Installing SQL Server, shown in Figure 25-3, for best practices.

FIGURE 25-3 Online SQL Server security documentation

Online Release Notes

The Online Release Notes link takes you to the latest updates about the SQL Server installation. The Release Notes document is available only online and is not on the installation media.

System Configuration Checker

The System Configuration Checker examines the computer for possible installation problems. After it runs, select Show Details to see the rules and results as shown in Figure 25-4. Problems detected by the System Configuration Checkers must be corrected before installation can continue. For even more details, click the View Detailed Report link.

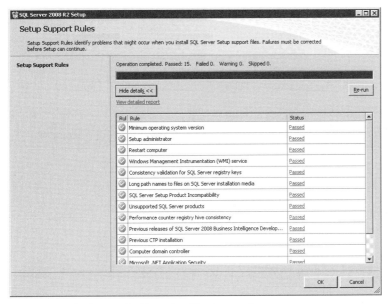

FIGURE 25-4 The System Configuration Checker results

Install Upgrade Advisor

Click Install Upgrade Advisor if you already have either SQL Server 2005 or SQL Server 2008 installed. Upgrade Advisor will check for any issues that need to be addressed before installing SQL Server 2008 R2.

Online Installation Help

The Online Installation Help link connects to the MSDN Library, specifically to the Installation How-To section for SQL Server 2008 R2.

How to Get Started with SQL Server 2008 R2 Failover Clustering

Click the SQL Server 2008 R2 Failover Clustering link to view information on building a SQL Server cluster. A two-node cluster can be built but will require additional licensed copies of SQL Server and Windows Server 2008.

How to Get Started with a PowerPivot for SharePoint Standalone Server Installation

Click the PowerPivot link for information on setting up PowerPivot for SharePoint as either a new installation or with an existing SharePoint server.

Upgrade Documentation

Click the Upgrade Documentation link to connect to online topics, including "Version and Edition Upgrades," which lists the supported paths.

Installation

The Installation page of the SQL Server Installation Center includes links to wizards that will start different types of installations.

New SQL Server Stand-Alone Installation or Add Features to an Existing Installation

Click the New SQL Server Stand-Alone Installation link to start the first-time install of SQL Server. Return to this link to add features to an existing installation.

New SQL Server Failover Cluster Installation

Use this link to install a single-node SQL Server 2008 R2 failover cluster.

Add Node To A SQL Server Failover Cluster

Use this link to add a second node to a single-node SQL Server failover cluster. This requires a second licensed copy of SQL Server and a second licensed copy of Windows Server 2008.

Upgrade from SQL Server 2000, SQL Server 2005 Or SQL Server 2008

Use this link to upgrade your existing version of SQL Server. Be sure to first check Upgrade Documentation on the Planning page and verify that your version of SQL Server is directly upgradable to SQL Server 2008 R2.

Search for Product Updates

Before installing SQL Server 2008, click the Search For Product Updates link to be sure that your Windows installation is up to date.

Maintenance

The Maintenance page links to wizards to update or repair your SQL Server installation.

Edition Upgrade

Click the Edition Upgrade link to start the process of changing your edition of SQL Server.

Repair

This link starts a repair wizard to fix a corrupt SQL Server 2008 R2 installation.

Remove Node From A SQL Server Failover Cluster

Click this link to remove an existing node from a failover cluster.

Tools

The Tools page of the SQL Server Installation Center includes three links, as described in the following sections.

System Configuration Checker

The System Configuration Checker examines the computer for possible installation problems. After it runs, select Show Details to see the rules and results. This links to the same tool as the System Configuration Checker link on the Planning page.

Installed SQL Server Features Discovery Report

When you're not sure just what SQL Server products are installed on the server, click this link to see a report. The report details any SQL Server 2000, SQL Server 2005, SQL Server 2008, and SQL Server 2008 R2 products and features that are present.

Upgrade Integration Services Packages

To upgrade SQL Server 2005 Integration Services Packages to the SQL Server 2008 R2 format, you can use this link, which is not activated until after SQL Server 2008 R2 is installed.

Resources

The Resources page of the SQL Server Installation Center, shown in Figure 25-5, includes multiple links to technical resources and other helpful websites.

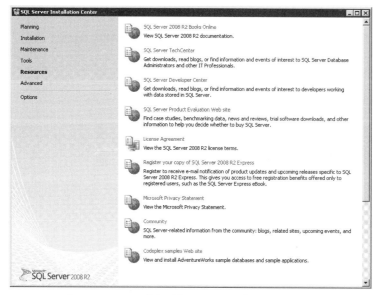

FIGURE 25-5 Resources page of the SQL Server Installation Center

Advanced

The Advanced page of the SQL Server Installation Center includes advanced installation options.

Install Based On Configuration File

Use this link to launch an installation using an existing configuration file.

Advanced Cluster Preparation

Click this link to launch a wizard for preparing a failover cluster installation.

Advanced Cluster Completion

This link starts a wizard that will complete a SQL Server 2008 R2 failover cluster from a list of cluster-prepared instances.

Image Preparation Of A Standalone Instance Of SQL Server

Use this link to launch a wizard that will prepare an imaged instance of SQL Server 2008 R2.

Image Completion Of A Standalone Instance Of SQL Server

Select this link to launch a wizard to configure a prepared imaged instance of SQL Server.

Options

The Options page of the SQL Server Installation Center shows processor-type options, but the option has already been determined by the operating system on the server where SQL Server will be installed. If the operating system is 32-bit, you can only install 32-bit SQL Server. If the operating system is 64-bit, you can only install 64-bit SQL Server.

Installing SQL Server (Part Two)

After you've reviewed all the relevant information in the previous sections and are at last ready to perform an initial installation of SQL Server, follow these steps:

1. On the Installation page of the SQL Server Installation Center, click the link for New Installation or Add Features To An Existing Installation. SQL Server 2008 Setup launches.

2. The Setup Support Rules are run. Click See Details to see the list of rules, as shown in Figure 25-6. Click OK if all rules show as Passed. Review any warnings to determine their relevance to your network. Correct the relevant warnings and all Failed rules before proceeding.

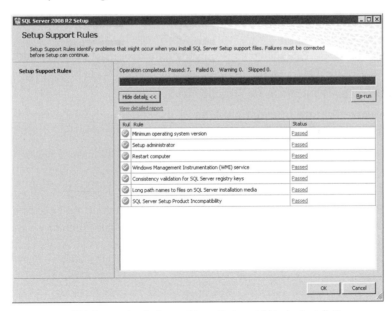

FIGURE 25-6 SQL Server checks for problems that could hinder installation

3. On the Product Key page, type the product key for SQL Server 2008 Standard Edition for Small Business. Click Next.

4. Read the license terms (shown in Figure 25-7), select the box to accept the license terms, and then click Next.

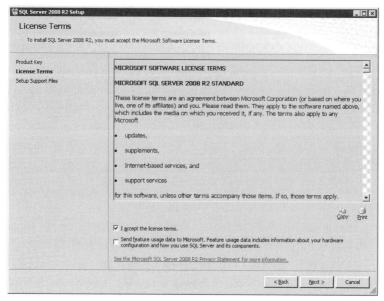

FIGURE 25-7 License terms for SQL Server 2008 R2

5. Click Install on the Setup Support Files, and the support files are installed.

6. Another set of Setup Support Rules run. Click See Details to see the list of rules. Click OK if all rules show as Passed. Review any warnings to determine their relevance to your network. Correct the relevant warnings and all Failed rules before proceeding.

7. On the Setup Role page, there are two options:

    • **SQL Server Feature Installation**   Choose this option and you can choose on the next page the features you want installed.

    • **All Features With Defaults**   This option will install all features of SQL Server 2008 R2 with default settings.

8. On the Feature Selection page, select the features to install. A description for each component group appears in the Description pane when you select it. See Table 25-1 for additional descriptions of the available features. Verify the location for shared features. Click Next.

TABLE 25-1 SQL Server available features

FEATURE	DESCRIPTION
Database Engine Services	The core service for storing and processing data.
SQL Server Replication	Replicates between and synchronizes two databases. It's unnecessary for a single database.
Full-Text Search	Allows full-text queries against plain, character-based data in SQL Server tables.
Analysis Services	Tools to create and administer online analytical processing (OLAP) and data-mining applications.
Reporting Services	Server and client tools to produce and manage reports.
Business Intelligence Development Studio	A development environment for Analysis Services, Reporting Services, and Integration Services solutions.
Client Tools Connectivity	Tools for client/server communication.
Integration Services	Graphical tools and programmable objects for moving, copying, and converting data.
Client Tools Backwards Compatibility	Tools for clients to access earlier versions of SQL Server.
Client Tools SDK	The software development tools for programming clients.
SQL Server Books Online	Core documentation for SQL Server.
Management Tools – Basic	Includes SQL Server Management Studio.
Management Tools – Complete	Adds SQL Server Management Studio support for Reporting Services, Analysis Services, and Integration Services.
SQL Client Connectivity SDK	Software development kit for client connectivity.
Microsoft Sync Framework	Platform to enable collaboration and offline synchronization for applications, services, and devices.

9. Still another set of Installation Rules run. Select Show Details to view the items that passed and failed. Click Next.

10. On the Instance Configuration page, specify whether to create a default instance or a named instance. If you plan to install a single instance of SQL Server on a database server, it should be a default instance. Verify the root directory for the instance, and click Next.

11. On the Disk Space Requirements page, review the available space and the amount of space required for the installation. Click Next.

> **NOTE** If the available space isn't sufficient, you can change the SQL Server features you want to install, change the installation directory to a drive with more space, or create more free space on the drive by moving other files.

12. On the Server Configuration page, assign login accounts to the various SQL Services. Click Help for the recommended procedures. Click Next.

 UNDER THE HOOD Service Accounts

SQL Server 2008 R2 requires several service accounts to run its various services. Choosing which account to use for a service account is always a tradeoff between simplicity and security. The simplest solution is to select the Local System account. You never need to worry about the password changing, and this account always has sufficient privileges. Unfortunately, running your SQL Server services under that account is not the best solution from a security standpoint. The Local System account is a powerful account, especially when it's running on your SBS server: if your security in SQL Server is breached, the entire network is compromised.

Using a regular user domain account is a possibility for the SQL Server service—it does not require any administrative privileges. But the SQL Server Agent process *does* require administrative privileges if your SQL Server environment uses CmdExec or ActiveScript jobs, or if you use the AutoRestart feature. If this is the case in your SQL Server environment, you should use separate service accounts for the SQL Server service and the SQL Server Agent.

Whatever domain accounts you use for SQL Server, you should use strong (long and complex) passwords. Also, when entering the domain name for a domain user account, you must use the NetBIOS name, not the DNS name. (In our environment, this means that the domain must be entered as "EXAMPLE" or "example", but not "example.local".)

13. The rest of the installation will configure the features selected in step 8. After you configure all these features and the Installation Configuration Rules are run (as seen in Figure 25-8), the Ready To Install page (shown in Figure 25-9) displays. Confirm that the installation tree is correct, and click Install.

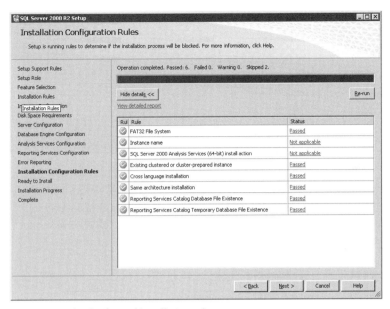

FIGURE 25-8 The final set of installation rules

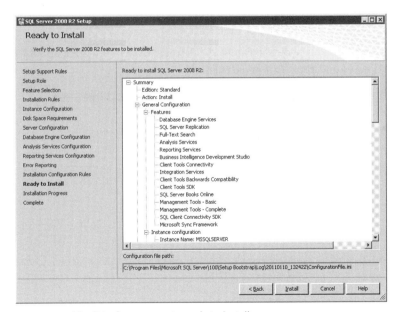

FIGURE 25-9 The list of components ready to install

14. The Installation Progress page follows the installation performance. (See Figure 25-10.)

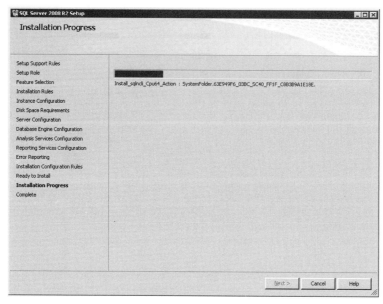

FIGURE 25-10 Installation progress is tracked

15. At the completion of installation, the Installation Progress page displays the features and their status (Success or Failure). Click Next.

16. On the Complete page (shown in Figure 25-11), review the information about your setup and notes that apply to your installation.

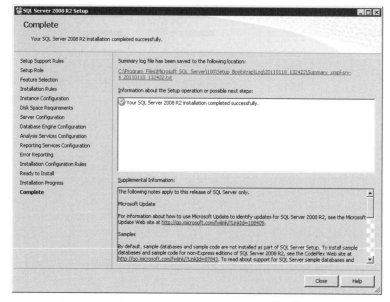

FIGURE 25-11 The Complete page showing the successful installation and any notes that apply.

17. Click the link at the top of the page to review an exceedingly detailed log file for the installation. This information can be very useful for any feature that failed installation. Click Close to finish.

When the installation is complete, select All Programs on the Start menu and then expand the Microsoft SQL Server entry. You can import an existing database and access the configuration tools you've installed.

 REAL WORLD **Putting SQL Server to Work**

For the most up-to-date SQL Server 2008 R2 documentation, select the links on the Resources page of the SQL Server Installation Center.

For help with setting up your database and maintaining it, select SQL Server Books Online from your Start menu. An extensive range of documentation on all aspects of SQL Server is available at this link.

Summary

In this chapter, we provided a brief look at how to plan the installation of SQL Server 2008 on your Windows SBS network and the steps needed to complete the installation. In the next chapter, we move on to adding and managing the very useful Remote Desktop Session Host.

## CHAPTER 26

Adding a Terminal Server

One of the potential uses for the second server that the Microsoft Windows Small Business Server (SBS) Premium Add-on includes is to configure it as a Terminal Server. Or, more properly, a Remote Desktop Session Host (RD Session Host). With the new RD Session Host features that are available in Windows Server 2008 R2, we think this is a very compelling option, and one that we've already implemented in our office.

> **NOTE** Throughout this chapter, we'll refer to *terminal server* (lowercase) when we want to talk about the general functionality but will use the formal new name, RD Session Host, when we're explicitly talking about enabling or configuring the role in Windows Server 2008 R2.

Adding a terminal server to SBS 2011 doesn't require purchasing the Premium Add-on—any copy of Windows Server 2008 or Windows Server 2008 R2 will do, though we strongly recommend Windows Server 2008 R2. The additional features and security in Windows Server 2008 R2 are compelling, especially those for a terminal server.

New Remote Desktop Services Features

Windows Server 2008 R2 Remote Desktop Services (RDS) is a significant update from the Terminal Services in Windows Server 2008 or Windows Server 2003. Not only has the name changed, but some significant new capabilities were added as well. The three major new features (when compared to Windows Server 2003) are Remote Desktop (RD) Gateway, RemoteApps, and RD Web Access. For most SBS environments, the first two of these are the most important. RD Gateway is used by the new Remote Web Access (RWA), and RemoteApps gives you the ability to use specific applications running on a terminal server as if they were local. RD Web Access is also useful, but rather than setting up a traditional web server to provide access to applications, we'll integrate them directly onto Companyweb, the SBS intranet. For more on that, see Chapter 23, "Customizing a SharePoint Site."

RD Gateway

The RD Gateway role service is not installed on the main SBS 2011 server, but the functionality is enabled to support RWA. In SBS 2003, Remote Web Workplace (RWW) acted as a proxy for the Remote Desktop Protocol, using port 4125 as the incoming port to connect remote users to clients in the SBS domain. This worked well and was the big application in SBS 2003. In fact, it was so successful that a lot of enterprise networks were envious of the technology.

Windows Server 2008 R2 uses RD Gateway to allow a similar functionality, but instead of using an RDP proxy across port 4125, RD Gateway tunnels traffic over HTTPS to help form a secure, encrypted connection between remote users on the Internet and the remote computers on which their productivity applications run, even if their use is located behind a Network Address Translation (NAT) Traversal–based router.

The SBS team chose to use the RD Gateway functionality of Windows Server 2008 R2 for Remote Web Access. Which allows us to do some really cool things with RWA, including adding links to applications that can be run directly from RWA across the Internet.

RemoteApps

RemoteApps was the single best feature added to Windows Server 2008, except for Hyper-V. But Hyper-V isn't exciting—it just makes our jobs easier. RemoteApps is actually exciting, and it gives us a way to give our users a better experience.

Terminal Services has always enabled us to allow users to run entire desktops as if they were local while actually using the power of the server. But RemoteApps takes this to a whole new level, allowing us to run just specific applications on the RemoteApp server and have them behave just as if they were local applications. This makes the entire process transparent to the user. The application runs on the server, using the server's memory, CPU, and resources, but it displays on the user's computer just as if it were running locally. It's uncanny how natural it feels. We use it here in our office all the time. Because we're constantly building and rebuilding new computers and virtual machines, it's a nuisance to try to have a single, predictable and accessible location for data files—especially when we have multiple domains here. But by enabling RemoteApps, we always have the same view of our environment.

Because RemoteApps lets you create .msi files for deployment, you can use Group Policy to deploy the remote applications. The applications can even be configured to take over the file association for a file type, just as if they were local applications—again making the user experience completely natural.

RD Web Access

RD Web Access provides a web-based front end that allows you to publish applications to a web page for easier user access. In SBS 2011, you can use RD Web Access to publish the application links directly in the SharePoint Companyweb site. We covered how to do this in Chapter 23.

Concepts

Remote Desktop Services is a new concept for many system administrators who expect systems to be essentially single-user. It brings true multiuser capability to Windows. Each user who connects to a Windows Server 2008 R2 server using Remote Desktop or a RemoteApp is actually using the resources of the server itself, not the particular workstation at which he or she is seated. The user's experience doesn't depend on the speed of the workstation—the user's workstation is actually sharing the processor, RAM, and hard disks of the server itself.

Each user gets his or her RDS session, and each session is completely isolated from other sessions on the same server. An errant program in one session can cause that session's user to have a problem, but other users are unaffected.

Each user who connects to a Windows Server 2008 R2 server using Remote Desktop is actually functioning as a terminal on that server. RDS supports a wide variety of computers as terminals—from diskless display stations running a version of Windows entirely in memory, with no hard disk at all, to legacy Windows desktop computers that are otherwise too underpowered for satisfactory use. Because the terminal is responsible solely for the console functions—that is, the keyboard, mouse, and actual display—the processing and RAM requirements for the terminal are minimal. All other functioning resides on and is part of the server, although the disks, printers, and serial ports of your local workstation can be connected to the remote session.

> **IMPORTANT** Versions of Windows prior to Windows XP SP3 can't install the latest version of the Remote Desktop Client software. All client workstations should be updated to Windows XP SP3 or later to take full advantage of the features of Windows Server 2008 R2 Remote Desktop Services, and to protect the security of the network.

Remote Access

RDS provides an ideal solution for the mobile user who needs to be able to run network-intensive or processor-intensive applications even over a dial-up connection. Because the local computer is responsible only for the actual console, the responsiveness and bandwidth requirements are substantially better compared to trying to run applications across a slow connection. The actual bandwidth used for Remote Desktop Services can be tuned by enabling or disabling certain graphics features to improve responsiveness over a slow connection.

Central Management

Because all applications in an RDS session are running on the server, management of sessions and applications is greatly simplified. Any changes to applications or settings need only be made once, on the server, and these changes are seen by all future RDS sessions.

In addition, RDS allows an administrator to view what is happening in a user's session, or even to directly control it. Help desk personnel can actually see exactly what the user is seeing without leaving their desks. If the user is configured accordingly, the Help desk person can share control of the session, walking the user through a difficult problem.

 REAL WORLD Requirements

The requirements for an RD Session Host (terminal server) depend on the number of users and the type of applications they run. Because each user will be executing his or her programs on the server itself, you need to determine exactly how your users work and what their real requirements are. Microsoft publishes a detailed white paper on capacity planning for an RD Session Host (which you can see at *http://www.microsoft.com/downloads/en/confirmation.aspx?displaylang=en& FamilyID=ca837962-4128-4680-b1c0-ad0985939063*) that has far more details than we can cover here and yet still manages to hedge its recommendations. And rightly so—capacity planning is subject to an enormous number of variables. So take the following as merely basic guidelines, and carefully consider how your environment affects these numbers.

> **IMPORTANT** Numbers in this sidebar are not intended to be definitive, but are a reflection of the authors' experience in real-world usage. System administrators and consultants should refer to the "RD Desktop Session Host Capacity Planning in Windows Server 2008 R2" white paper referenced above before making final recommendations.

RAM

Each session on the RD Session Host for a typical knowledge worker of Microsoft Office 2010—including Microsoft Word, Outlook, Excel, and PowerPoint— consumes roughly 70 Mb per session. If the available memory per user drops below this point, excessive paging can occur, causing an unacceptable user experience. Thus, a server or virtual machine running Windows Server 2008 R2 with 6 GB of RAM will easily support all the users you can have in an SBS environment.

CPU

Predicting exactly how much CPU power will be required per user is difficult because each user has a different mix of applications and expectations. A physical server with a single quad-core processor Windows Server 2008 R2 with sufficient RAM present to avoid swapping can realistically host somewhere between 100 and 150 users—in other words, more than an SBS network has to worry about. Even when that server is a virtual machine, the numbers are quite similar if the CPU supports Second Level Address Translation (SLAT). Without SLAT, the maximum number of users drops to roughly 50–70 users for a four-processor virtual machine—still enough to handle the vast majority of SBS environments.

One factor that affects the number of users per CPU core is the color depth used for each RDS session. Limiting the maximum color depth to 16-bits per pixel (bpp) significantly improves the capacity of the RD Session Host server. However, if your RD Session Host is supporting no more than 50 users, enabling Desktop Composition (Aero) and 32-bit color should not be an issue.

Network

A typical SBS network with 1 Gbps networking has more than sufficient network bandwidth to support as many Remote Desktop clients as necessary. If your network is limited to older 100 Mbps networking, you might end up with network bandwidth issues if your RDS users run graphics-intensive applications, even on an SBS-sized network. Remote users can tailor their RDP settings to limit bandwidth use over slow connections.

RemoteApps

The maximum number of RemoteApp users that a given server can support is actually slightly fewer than if the users were running full sessions with the same application mix. But the difference is small and is caused by higher CPU usage for RemoteApp scenarios.

Licensing

Remote Desktop Services use requires special licensing considerations. In addition to normal Client Access Licenses (CALs), which are covered by your SBS licensing, you also need to have an RDS CAL for each user or device that uses RDS functionality. Note that this includes RD Gateway or RD Web functionality beyond that included in Windows Small Business Server 2011 Standard. Unfortunately, RDS CALs are not included as part of either SBS or the Premium Add-on.

You'll need to install an RD Licensing server in the SBS 2011 network within 120 days of initially enabling the RD Session Host role, and you'll need to choose either per user or per device licensing mode for that RD Session Host server. The RD Licensing role service can be enabled on the same server as the RD Session Host role service. It should not be enabled on the main SBS server.

Installing the Remote Desktop Services Role

Installing the Remote Desktop Services role and its supporting role service should be one of the very first things you do on any server you plan to use as an RD Session Host. Important changes to how applications are installed happen automatically when you're in Application Mode on a Windows Server computer, and there can be problems if applications are installed before the server is converted to an application server. Our general preference is to run through the tasks on the Initial Configuration Tasks Wizard (ICTW), skipping only the Add Roles tasks, but joining the server to the domain, giving it a name, setting a fixed IP address, and installing the basic features we want on all servers. After that is done and all the required restarts have been completed, it's time to install the RD Session Host role. You'll also need to move the server from the SBSComputers OU to the SBSServers OU.

> **NOTE** If you've followed the installation steps in Chapter 24, "Installing the Second Server," and have already moved the server to the SBSServers OU, you can skip steps 1–5 in the following list of steps.

To install the Remote Desktop Services role, follow these steps:

1. On the SBS server, open the Active Directory Users And Computers console, shown in Figure 26-1, from the Administrative Tools menu, or by typing **dsa.msc** at a command prompt.

2. Navigate to the SBSComputers OU, as shown in Figure 26-1. Select the server that will be the RD Session Host server, and drag it to the SBSServers OU.

3. You'll be warned about moving objects in Active Directory, as shown in Figure 26-2. Click Yes to confirm you want to move the object.

4. Log on to the server that you want to add the RD Session Host role to.

5. Open a Windows PowerShell or command window as administrator.

6. Force a group policy update, as shown in Figure 26-3. This might cause Remote Desktop to be disabled, so you should avoid doing this from a Remote Desktop session. Alternately, you can simply reboot the server.

7. Log on to the server that you want to add the RD Session Host role to, and open the Server Manager console if it doesn't open automatically. (If the Initial Configuration And Tasks Wizard opens, you can close it and the Server Manager console will open automatically.)

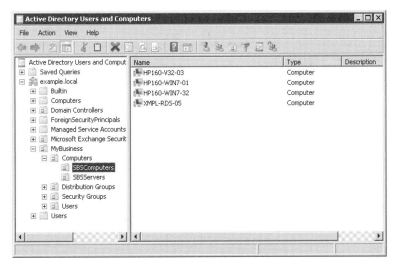

FIGURE 26-1 The Active Directory Users And Computers console

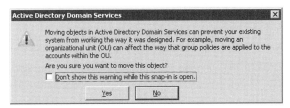

FIGURE 26-2 Moving the RD Session Host server object to the SBSServers OU

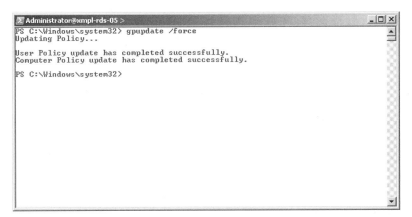

FIGURE 26-3 Forcing a Group Policy update after changing the server's organizational unit

8. In the left pane of the Server Manager console, select Roles, as shown in Figure 26-4.

FIGURE 26-4 The main Server Manager console, with Roles selected in the left (tree-view) pane

9. Select Add Roles from the action menu to open the Add Roles Wizard.

10. The Before You Begin page of the Add Roles Wizard contains some general information and recommended configuration settings. After you've seen this once and have read it, you can select the Skip This Page By Default check box. Once is quite enough.

11. Click Next to open the Select Server Roles page. Select Remote Desktop Services, as shown in Figure 26-5.

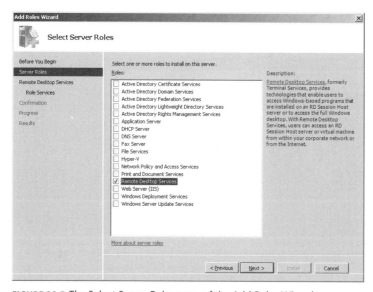

FIGURE 26-5 The Select Server Roles page of the Add Roles Wizard

12. Click Next to open the Remote Desktop Services page. Read the brief Introduction To Remote Desktop Services, and if you want more information on Remote Desktop Services roles and role services, click the Overview Of Remote Desktop Services link.

13. Click Next to open the Select Role Services page, as shown in Figure 26-6. Select at least the Remote Desktop Session Host role service.

NOTE You'll need to install an RD Licensing server in your SBS domain within 120 days of enabling Remote Desktop Services. This can be installed on any Windows Server 2008 R2 computer in the domain, and it can be installed at any point in that 120-day period.

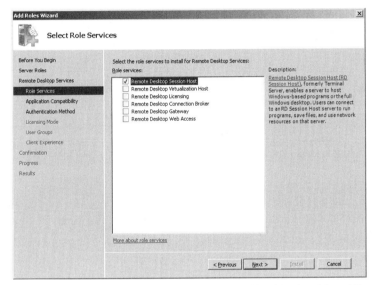

FIGURE 26-6 The Select Role Services page of the Add Roles Wizard for adding the Remote Desktop Services role

14. Click Next to open the Uninstall And Reinstall Applications For Compatibility page of the Add Roles Wizard, shown in Figure 26-7. This is a good reminder that applications that have already been installed should be uninstalled and reinstalled so that they are properly multiuser-aware.

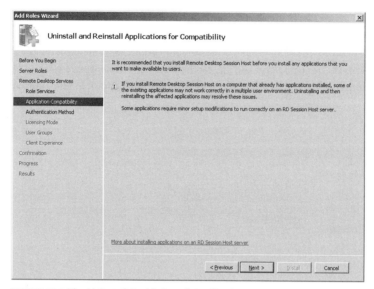

FIGURE 26-7 The Uninstall And Reinstall Applications For Compatibility page of the Add Roles Wizard

15. Click Next to open the Specify Authentication Method For Remote Desktop Session Host page, shown in Figure 26-8. There are two choices for authentication:

   - **Require Network Level Authentication**   Choose this if all your clients will be running at least Windows XP SP3 or Windows Vista. This option is more secure and should be used when possible.

   - **Do Not Require Network Level Authentication**   Choose this option if you have clients that can't be upgraded to at least Windows XP SP3. Clients will still require RDP 6 or later to use RemoteApps.

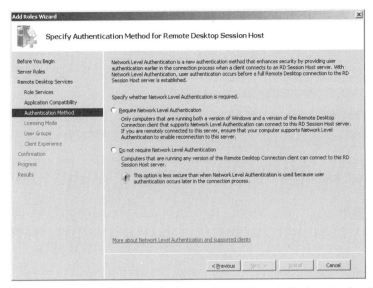

FIGURE 26-8 Setting the authentication level for the Remote Desktop Session Host

16. Click Next to open the Specify Licensing Mode page, shown in Figure 26-9. Here you can choose between per-device or per-user licensing, or you can delay the decision. In most cases, unless you've already bought your CALs, postpone this for now, until you've had a chance to decide how your users will actually use the terminal server. This will allow you to make the most cost-efficient choice for licensing.

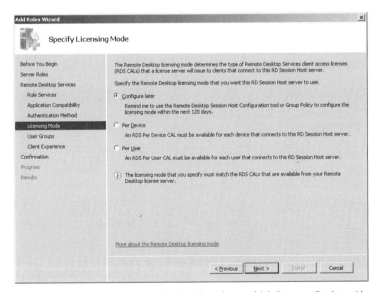

FIGURE 26-9 You can postpone the decision about which Remote Desktop Licensing mode to use.

17. Click Next to open the Select User Groups Allowed Access To This RD Session Host Server page, shown in Figure 26-10. The default is only Administrators, so you'll want to change that. We suggest creating a Security Group specifically to control Remote-Apps access, but you can also just give all users access or specify each individual user.

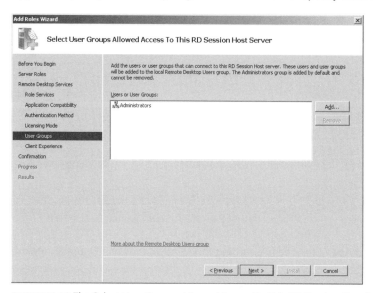

FIGURE 26-10 The Select User Groups Allowed Access To This RD Session Host Server page of the Add Roles Wizard

18. Click Add to specify additional users and groups that will be able to use the terminal server. To add the same group of users who are allowed access to Remote Web Access (RWA), enter **Windows SBS Remote Web Access Users** in the Select Users, Computers, Or Groups dialog box, as shown in Figure 26-11. Click Check Names to make sure you've typed the group name correctly, and then click OK to return to the Add Roles Wizard.

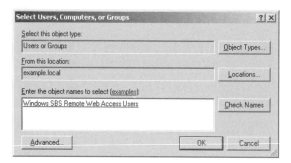

FIGURE 26-11 Selecting users and groups

19. Click Next to open the Configure Client Experience page shown in Figure 26-12. Here you can enable additional audio and display capabilities to provide the user with a richer experience. The choices are

- **Audio And Video Playback** Choose this to enable users to play audio and video from the RD Session Host to their desktop. This will automatically install the Desktop Experience feature on the RD Session Host.

- **Audio Recording Redirection** Select this to enable users to record audio on their client and have it available to the RD Session Host.

- **Desktop Composition (Provides The User Interface Elements Of Windows Aero)** Select this to enable full Aero glass to the RD Session Host client. This will automatically install the Desktop Experience feature on the RD Session Host.

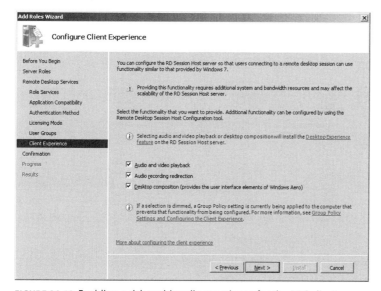

FIGURE 26-12 Enabling a rich multimedia experience for the RDS client

20. Click Next to open the confirmation page, and then click Install to begin the installation.

21. Before the installation is complete, you'll need to reboot the server. Click Close on the Installation Results page, and click Yes to begin the reboot.

22. When the server has restarted, log on with the same account as you used to add the Remote Desktop Services role. The Installation Results page will open and the installation will complete.

By default, there is no audio on a Windows Server 2008 R2 computer, and the default graphics level is set to a 16-bit maximum. You can improve this by adding the Windows Server 2008 Desktop Experience feature. This feature gives your client sessions the visual look and feel of Windows 7, as well as adding other programs that are normally part of Windows 7, including Windows Media Player.

If you enabled Desktop Composition and Audio And Video Playback during the installation of Remote Desktop Services, you're all set. But if you didn't, and now your users are asking for the full Windows 7 experience, you can improve the user experience by enabling 32-bit color and audio by following these steps:

1. Open the Server Manager console if it isn't already open.

2. Navigate to Roles and then Remote Desktop Services, and then select RD Session Host Configuration in the left pane of Server Manager.

3. Select RDP-Tcp in the center Connections pane, as shown in Figure 26-13.

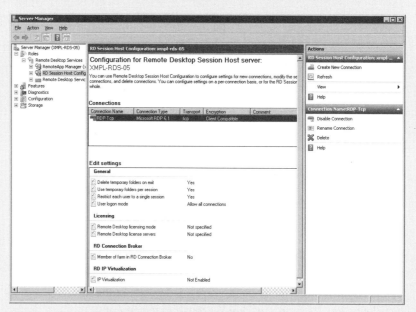

FIGURE 26-13 The RDP Configuration in Server Manager

4. Right-click the RDP-Tcp connection and select Properties to open the RDP-Tcp Properties dialog box.

5. Click the Client Settings tab, as shown in Figure 26-14.

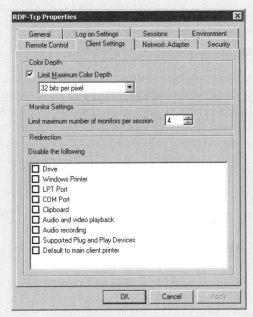

FIGURE 26-14 Setting RDP properties

6. Select a maximum color depth of 32 Bits Per Pixel from the Limit Maximum Color Depth drop-down list to enable 32-bit color.

7. Clear the check boxes for Audio And Video Playback and Audio Recording in the Disable The Following section.

8. Click OK to close the Properties dialog box. If there are current user sessions, you'll see the warning shown in Figure 26-15.

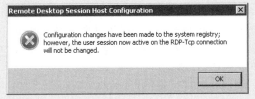

FIGURE 26-15 Warning when changing a configuration with open sessions

9. By default, the Audio service is manually started on Windows Server 2008 R2. You need to enable it before RDP clients will get audio.

10. Click Services on the Administrative Tools menu, and then scroll down to Windows Audio.

11. Right-click Windows Audio and select Properties, change the Startup Type to Automatic, and then click Start to start the service.

12. Click OK and then close the Services console.

Making these changes improves the overall user experience for end users but also increases the amount of resources used per connection. That's probably not a big issue in most SBS environments, and we think it's worthwhile. Adding the Desktop Experience doesn't, however, install the games that are normally included with Windows 7. This probably improves productivity, but we think there should at least be an option for them.

Configuring RD Licensing

Windows Server 2008 R2 requires that at least one Remote Desktop Licensing (RD Licensing) server be installed and running on any network that has an RD Session Host. If a license server is not installed within 120 days, all RD Session Host connections will be disabled. Remote Desktop Services requires a separate Windows Server 2008 R2 Remote Desktop Services CAL or Windows Server 2008 Terminal Service CAL for each user or device in addition to any Windows Server CALs you might need. The RD Licensing server does not enforce per-user licensing, but it does track usage in Active Directory against the installed per-user licenses. Per-device licenses are enforced by the RD Licensing server.

Installing Remote Desktop Licensing

In SBS, installing the RD Licensing role service on the same server that is running RD Session Host is the preferred choice, but you can also install it on the main SBS server, though it isn't recommended. If you're going to have more than a single RD Session Host, you can install it on any of the RD Session Host servers. To install RD Licensing on the computer running Remote Desktop Services, follow these steps:

1. Open Server Manager on the server running Remote Desktop Services if it isn't already open.

2. Select Roles, select Remote Desktop Services in the left pane, and then select Add Role Services from the action menu.

3. On the Select Role Services page, select Remote Desktop Licensing.

4. Click Next to open the Configure Discovery Scope For RD Licensing page, shown in Figure 26-16. Leave the Configure A Discovery Scope For This License Server box cleared.

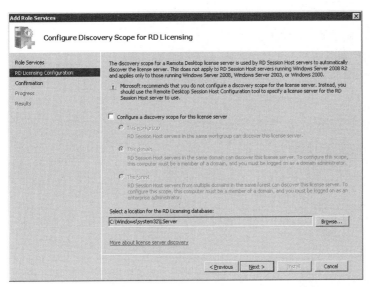

FIGURE 26-16 The RD Licensing Configuration page of the Add Role Services Wizard

5. Click Next to open the Confirm Installation Selections page. If everything looks correct, click Install to begin the installation.

6. Click Close when the installation completes.

After the RD Licensing role service is added, you need to activate the server before it will actually do anything. To activate the license server, follow these steps:

1. Open the RD Licensing Manager (licmgr.exe).

2. Select the RD Licensing server in the left pane, and select Activate Server from the Action menu.

3. The Activate Server Wizard opens. Click Next to open the Connection Method page shown in Figure 26-17.

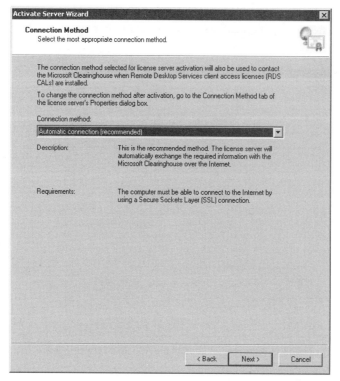

FIGURE 26-17 The Connection Method page of the Activate Server Wizard

4. Select a connection method from the drop-down list. The choices are Automatic Connection (Recommended), Web Browser, or Telephone. Automatic Connection requires an Internet connection from the server you are activating. Web Browser also requires an Internet connection, but it can be run from any workstation. Click Next.

5. If you've chosen Automatic Connection, the connection will be made, and then the first Company Information page is displayed, as shown in Figure 26-18. Fill in all the fields on this page—they are required. Click Next.

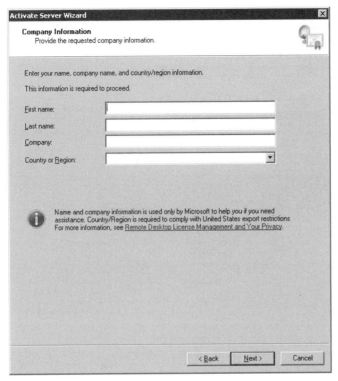

FIGURE 26-18 The required fields on the Company Information page of the Activate Server Wizard

6. The second page of company information is displayed. All information on this page is optional—fill it in only if you want to. Click Next, and if your connection is good, your server will activate and you'll be presented with the completion page. You can continue to add CALs by selecting the Start Install Licenses Wizard Now box.

7. Click Next until you get to the License Program page of the Activate Server Wizard, as shown in Figure 26-19.

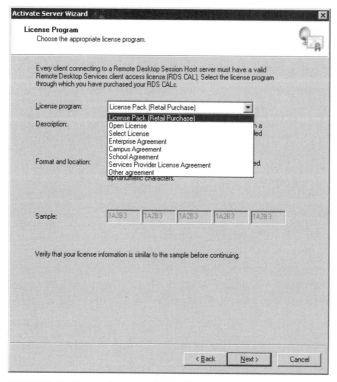

FIGURE 26-19 Choose the type of RDS CALs you've purchased

8. Select the type of license you're entering from the License Program drop-down list.

9. Click Next and fill in the license code. Click Next again, and the activation will complete.

> **NOTE** Additional steps are required for either web browser or telephone methods. If you need to reactivate your server and reinstall licenses, you'll be required to use the telephone method.

Assigning the Licensing Server and Licensing Mode

Prior to Windows Server 2008 R2, the recommended method for terminal servers to identify and connect to a licensing server was by discovery. This ended up being one of the most frequent causes of Customer Support Services (CSS) cases for Terminal Services, and with the introduction of Remote Desktop Services in Windows Server 2008 R2 the entire licensing server process has been significantly improved.

In Windows Server 2008 R2, the recommended method for assigning a license server is to explicitly assign one (or more) servers. This gets around many of the issues that the discovery process caused. To further improve the process, you can now move licenses from one server to another without having to call in to the Microsoft Clearinghouse, even if the server they are currently assigned to is offline. These changes should reduce the majority of the frustration and support calls that terminal server licensing caused.

The one source of licensing frustration that hasn't changed is that an RD Session Host must choose between per-user or per-device licenses and can't have both types enabled on the same server. This isn't a big deal in a larger enterprise where there are multiple RD Session Hosts, but on an SBS network, you'll need to make a decision about which type to use because most SBS networks will have at most a single RD Session Host.

To assign a specific licensing server for an RD Session Host and set the licensing mode for that server, follow these steps:

1. Open the Remote Desktop Session Host Configuration console (tsconfig.msc) if it isn't already open.

2. Double-click Remote Desktop Licensing Mode in the Licensing section of the center pane to open the Properties dialog box with the Licensing tab active, as shown in Figure 26-20.

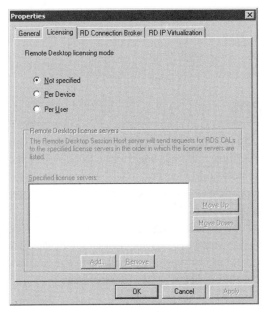

FIGURE 26-20 The RD Session Host Properties dialog box

3. Select Per Device or Per User, and then click Add to open the Add License Server dialog box shown in Figure 26-21.

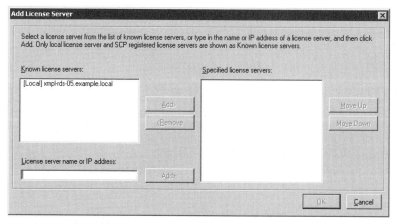

FIGURE 26-21 The Add License Server dialog box

4. Select the local RD Session Host in the left pane, and click Add to move it to the Specified License Servers pane. If you have a secondary license server (unlikely in an SBS environment), you can specify it here.

5. Click OK and then OK again to assign the licensing mode and server. (If you have open Remote Desktop sessions on the server, you'll see a warning that the changes won't affect the active sessions.)

Configuring RemoteApps

After you've installed the Remote Desktop Services role, along with the RD Session Host role service, you're ready to configure RemoteApps. If there is one thing in Windows Server 2008 R2 that we think is "cool," it has to be RemoteApps. Instead of having users connect to a remote terminal server, open a full desktop, and then run the applications they need, Remote-Apps allows users to run remote applications just as if they were running them locally, without opening up a desktop. The actual behavior is just like a regular application—when it needs to open an additional window, such as when you go to save a file, it automatically opens up a new window on your local workstation that has just the File Save dialog box in it. To the user, the application behaves just as it would if the application were running locally.

Applications can be published as .rdp files or as .msi files, allowing deployment through Group Policy. When installed with an .msi file, they can even be set to take over the default extension of the application on the user's workstation, enabling automatic launch.

RemoteApp Manager

The RemoteApp Manager console (remoteprograms.msc), shown in Figure 26-22, is used to manage remote applications. From here, you can define the various settings that control which applications are available, who can connect to them, and how they're distributed and published.

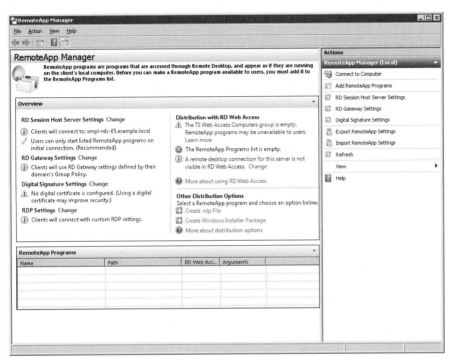

FIGURE 26-22 The RemoteApp Manager console

When you create a RemoteApp, you can set how it is distributed and available. You can create an .rdp file for it or a Windows Installer Package (.msi) file. Windows installer packages can be distributed using Group Policy and have additional options as compared to .rdp files.

To create a RemoteApp program, follow these steps:

1. Open the RemoteApp Manager if it isn't already open.

2. Click Add RemoteApp Programs in the Actions pane to open the RemoteApp Wizard.

3. Click Next to open the Choose Programs To Add To The RemoteApps Programs List page of the RemoteApp Wizard, as shown in Figure 26-23.

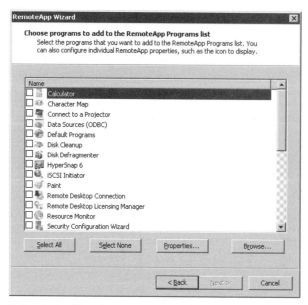

FIGURE 26-23 Choosing programs to make available through RemoteApps

4. Select one or more programs to add to the RemoteApps programs list. You can add any programs you see in the list, or use the Browse button to locate the program's executable.

5. To change the run properties of the application you are adding, select it from the list of programs and click Properties to open the Properties dialog box for the program, as shown in Figure 26-24 for our editor of choice, gVim.

6. Change any application-specific properties that you want to change.

7. Click the User Assignment tab to control which users have access to the RemoteApp program, as shown in Figure 26-25.

8. After you've made all your changes to User Assignment or application properties, click OK to close the Properties dialog box for the application.

9. Click Next and then click Finish to add the program to the list of available RemoteApps.

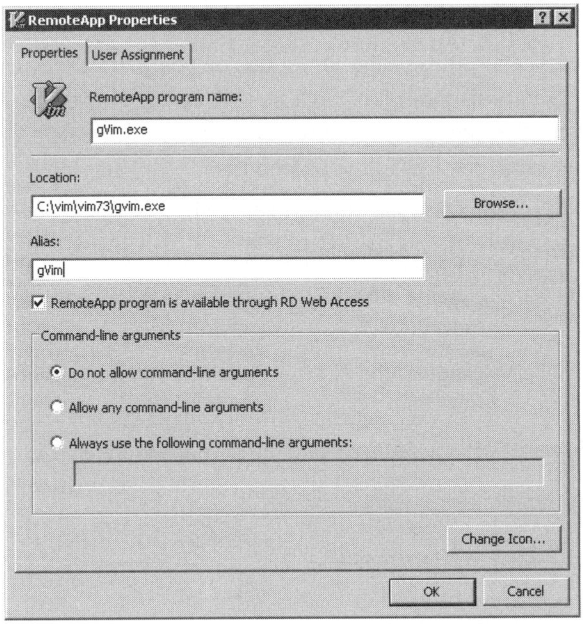

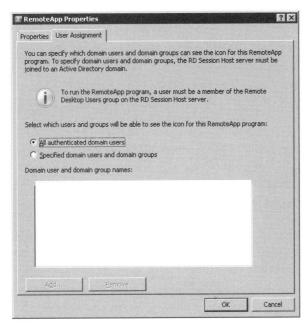

FIGURE 26-24 Setting the properties for a RemoteApp program

FIGURE 26-25 You can control which users or groups are allowed to use a RemoteApp program on the User Assignment tab

Deploying with .rdp and .msi files

You can easily deploy remote applications to specific computers on your network by creating .rdp or .msi files. Personally, we prefer using .msi files because they can be pushed out using Group Policy and you can control additional settings with them. Or you can create a file share to save the files to, and users can install the files to their computers.

To create a Windows Installer Package (.msi) file, follow these steps:

1. Open the RemoteApp Manager if it isn't already open.

2. Select the application you want to create a package for in the RemoteApp Programs pane.

3. Click Create Windows Installer Package in the Actions pane to open the RemoteApp Wizard.

4. Click Next to open the Specify Package Settings page, shown in Figure 26-26.

FIGURE 26-26 The Specify Package Settings page of the RemoteApp Wizard

5. Enter a location to save the package to. The default is C:\Program Files\Packaged Programs, but we think a shared folder makes more sense, so we create a RemoteApps folder on the RD Session Host and share that.

6. Change the RD Session Host or Certificate settings that need to be different for this application. There's really no need to change either in an SBS environment.

7. Click Change in the RD Gateway Settings section to open the Configure RD Gateway Settings dialog box shown in Figure 26-27. Set this to use the public DNS name of your SBS network if you expect to allow any connections from remote users.

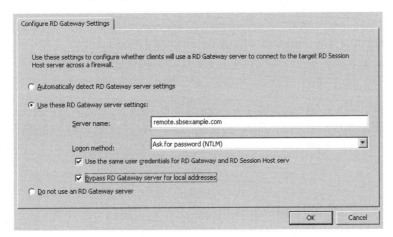

FIGURE 26-27 Configure RemoteApps to use an RD Gateway if you want remote users to have access to the application.

8. Click OK to return to the Specify Package Settings page, and then Next to open the Configure Distribution Package page shown in Figure 26-28.

FIGURE 26-28 The Configure Distribution Package page of the RemoteApp Wizard

9. The default is to add the program to the Start menu folder Remote Programs. If this folder doesn't already exist, it will be created as part of the installation. You can also choose to have the RemoteApp program automatically added to the user's desktop. And you can have the remote application take over all the client extensions it would normally take over for the user's computer. Do not choose to take over client extensions for applications that users will also have installed locally.

10. Click Next and then click Finish to create the Windows Installer Package.

> **NOTE** Creating an .rdp file for deployment follows similar steps but has fewer options. You can't have an RDP-deployed RemoteApp program take over the extensions on your local computer, for example.

 REAL WORLD   **RemoteApps Rock**

OK, you've probably figured out by now that we think the new RemoteApps capability is one of the best new things in Windows Server 2008 and now Windows Server 2008 R2. We think the RD Web Access is a nice touch when used through our Companyweb, and the new RD Gateway is used by Remote Web Workplace to enable Secure Sockets Layer (SSL) tunneling instead of using port 4125.

The best of the improvements in Remote Desktop Services, however, is RemoteApps. Now you can centralize all your critical applications onto an RD Session Host and deploy them directly to users with Group Policy. Because the applications can actually capture the extensions associated with the application and connect them to the remote program, the end user experience is almost completely transparent.

When Windows 2000 Server released and made Terminal Server Remote Administration mode available on every single server, we said that it was the reason to migrate to Windows 2000, and time has proven that feature to be absolutely indispensible. Well, we think two features in Windows Server 2008 R2 are just as important: Hyper-V and RemoteApps.

Adding a RemoteApp to Remote Web Workplace

One of the cool things you can do with the new RemoteApps capability is add an application directly to the RWA landing page. This allows a user working remotely to directly and securely access an application on the SBS network without having to log on to take a full Remote Desktop session.

The basic process is

- Create an .rdp file for the application.
- Save the .rdp file to the path where Remote Web Access resides on your SBS server.
- Create a new MIME type in Internet Information Services (IIS) for RDP.
- Add a link to the .rdp file to the RWA page using the SBS Console.

Let's go through the process to add a link to Microsoft Word 2010 to the RWA page. If you don't have Microsoft Office installed on your RD Session Host, you'll need to use a different program in these steps, but the result will be the same.

First, follow these steps on the terminal server to create an .rdp file for Microsoft Word 2010:

1. Open RemoteApp Manager if it isn't already open (remoteprograms.msc).

2. If you already have an entry in the RemoteApp Programs section for Microsoft Word 2010, skip to step 6. If not, select Add RemoteApp Programs from the Actions menu to open the RemoteApp Wizard.

3. Click Next to open the Choose Programs To Add To The RemoteApp Programs List page.

4. Scroll down and select Microsoft Word 2010 from the list, as shown in Figure 26-29.

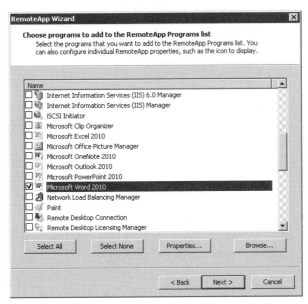

FIGURE 26-29 Selecting *Microsoft Word 2010* to add to the list of RemoteApps

5. Click Next and then click Finish to add *Microsoft Word 2010* to the list of RemoteApp programs.

6. Select *Microsoft Word 2010* in the list of RemoteApp Programs, and then click Create .RDP File in the Actions pane to open the RemoteApp Wizard.

7. Click Next to open the Specify Package Settings page of the RemoteApp Wizard.

8. Type in the UNC path to the Public share on your SBS server for the location to save, as shown in Figure 26-30.

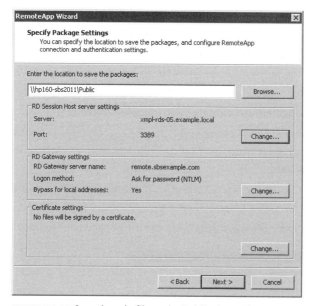

FIGURE 26-30 Save the .rdp file to the Public share of your SBS server

9. Verify that the RD Gateway Server Name is shown as the public DNS name of Remote Web Access. If it isn't, click Change and adjust as required.

10. Click Next and then click Finish to create the file.

Next, let's log on to the SBS server and move that .rdp file over to where we need it by following these steps:

1. Log on to the main SBS server with a Network Administrator account.

2. Open Windows Explorer, and navigate to \\localhost\public, as shown in Figure 26-31.

3. Highlight the WINWORD .rdp file, and copy it to the clipboard.

4. Navigate to the main directory for Remote Web Access. The default location is C:\ Program Files\Windows Small Business Server\Bin\WebApp\RemoteAccess. Paste the WINWORD .rdp file. You'll be prompted for permission because this is a protected folder.

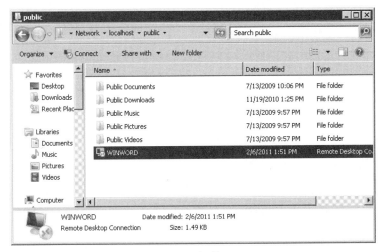

FIGURE 26-31 Locating the WINWORD .rdp file

Next, we need to create a new MIME type for the .rdp extension by following these steps:

1. Open the Internet Information Services (IIS) Manager from the Administrative Tools menu.

2. Highlight the server name in the left pane, navigate to Sites, then to Default Web Site, and finally to Remote. Click MIME Types in the center pane, as shown in Figure 26-32.

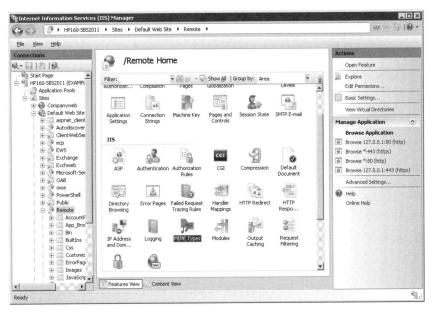

FIGURE 26-32 The IIS Manager console

3. Click Open Feature on the Actions menu to open the MIME Types in the center pane, as shown in Figure 26-33.

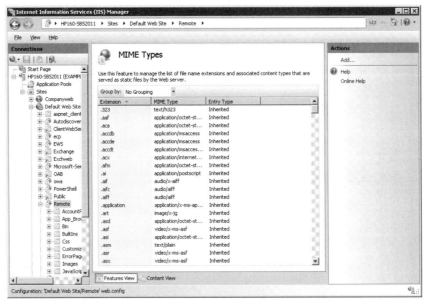

FIGURE 26-33 The MIME Types feature in the IIS Manager console

4. Click Add in the Actions pane to open the Add MIME Type dialog box. Type **.rdp** in the File Name Extension field, and type **application/x-remotedesktop** in the MIME Type field, as shown in Figure 26-34. Click OK.

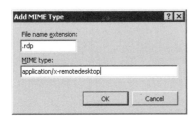

FIGURE 26-34 The Add MIME Type dialog box

5. Right-click the server name in the left pane and select Stop from the Actions menu.
6. Right-click the server name again and select Start.
7. Close the Internet Information Services (IIS) Manager console.

Finally, we need to add the Microsoft Word 2010 link to the RWA page by following these steps:

1. Open the Windows SBS Console if it isn't already open.

2. Click Shared Folders And Web Sites in the navigation pane, and then click the Web Sites tab as shown in Figure 26-35.

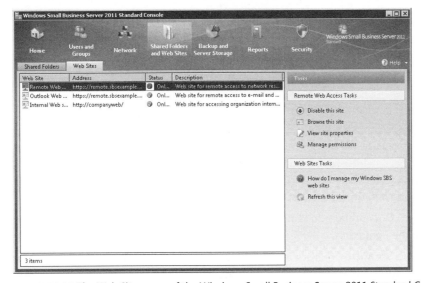

FIGURE 26-35 The Web Sites page of the Windows Small Business Server 2011 Standard Console

3. In the Remote Web Access Tasks section, click View Site Properties to open the Remote Web Access Properties dialog box as shown in Figure 26-36.

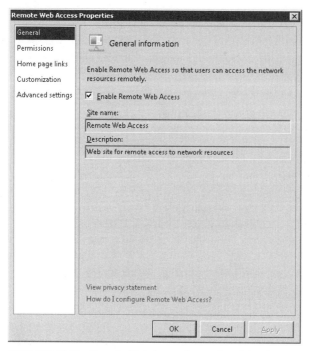

FIGURE 26-36 The Remote Web Access Properties dialog box

4. Click Home Page Links in the left pane, and then click Manage Links to open the Remote Web Access Link List Properties dialog box, shown in Figure 26-37.

5. Click Organization Links in the left pane to open the Manage Organization Links page in the right pane..

6. Type *Use Microsoft Word 2010* in the Link Description field, and then type the link to the .rdp file you added in the Link Address field, as shown in Figure 26-38. (This should be **https://remote.sbsexample.com/remote/winword.rdp**, where *sbsexample.com* is replaced by your DNS name.)

7. Click Add and then click OK twice to close the Remote Web Access Link List Properties dialog box and return to the Windows SBS Console.

8. Highlight Remote Web Access, click Disable This Site in the Tasks pane, and then click Enable This Site in the Tasks pane.

9. Log on to Remote Web Access, and you'll see the new link, as shown in Figure 26-39.

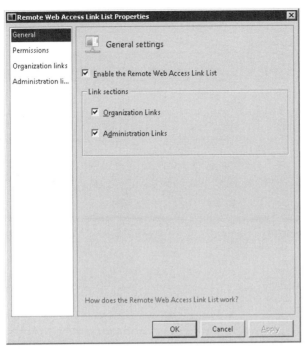

FIGURE 26-37 The Remote Web Access Link List Properties dialog box

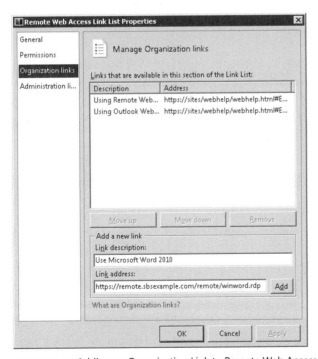

FIGURE 26-38 Adding an Organization Link to Remote Web Access

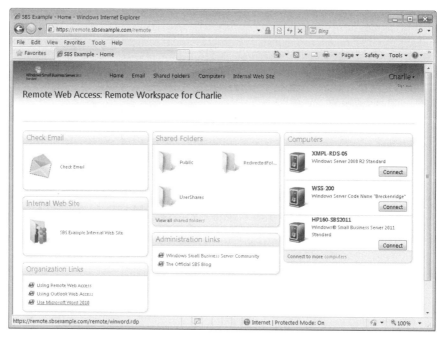

FIGURE 26-39 Remote Web Access showing the new link to Microsoft Word 2010

10. The first time you run this or any other RemoteApp, you'll have multiple prompts to provide credentials and confirm you really want to do this. You can save your selections so that you're not prompted again, if you choose.

Microsoft Word 2010 probably isn't the most important application that you'll want to be able to run remotely, but it provides a simple example for our purposes. Each business has a different application set that it needs to make available remotely, but any application that currently requires logging on to a remote desktop or using a virtual private network (VPN) connection is an obvious choice.

Summary

Windows Server 2008 R2 adds important new capabilities to Remote Desktop Services (formerly Terminal Services). When combined with the new second server that is part of the Premium Add-on, adding an RD Session Host to an SBS network is a natural fit, enabling additional application deployment options and giving the SBS administrator or consultant the tools to rationalize resources in the SBS domain. In this chapter, we covered the new features of Remote Desktop Services in Windows Server 2008 R2, the installation and configuration of the RD Session Host role service, and the implementation and deployment of RemoteApps.

In the next section, we move on to maintenance and troubleshooting of your SBS network, beginning with basic monitoring and fine-tuning of performance.

#### PART VI

Maintenance and Troubleshooting

## CHAPTER 27

Performance Monitoring

For a network to operate at its best, you must be able to recognize bottlenecks and take action to eliminate them. This chapter covers the system and network monitoring tools in Microsoft Windows Small Business Server (SBS) 2011 that enable you to detect problems and tune your system to its optimum performance level.

Performance Monitor encompasses simple tools that can help you track server loads, locate persistent errors, customize the data you want to collect in logs, define limits for alerts and automatic actions, generate reports, and view past performance data.

To open Performance Monitor, click Start, type **perfmon** in the Start Search box, and press Enter. Or you can select Performance Monitor from the Administrative Tools menu.

The initial view of Performance Monitor (shown in Figure 27-1) includes a brief overview as well as a system summary.

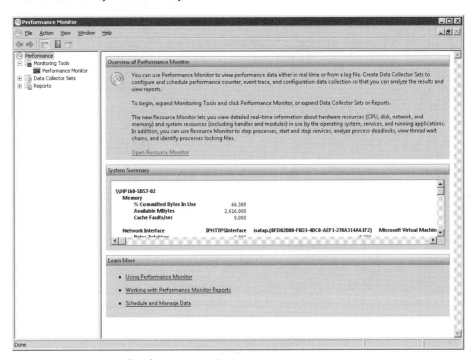

FIGURE 27-1 Initial view of Performance Monitor

Resource Monitor Overview

Click the Open Resource Monitor link in the Overview Of Performance Monitor section to access Resource Monitor, or click Start, type **resmon** in the Start Search box, and press Enter.

The Resource Monitor page, shown in Figure 27-2, shows four scrolling graphs for real-time monitoring of CPU, disk, network, and memory usage.

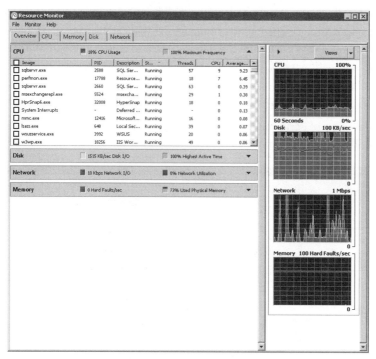

FIGURE 27-2 Resource Monitor page

The four sections next to the graphs contain details about each resource. Click the section to display the detail, as shown in Figure 27-3.

NOTE Click a row and the highlight will remain on that row, even when the application's position changes in the display.

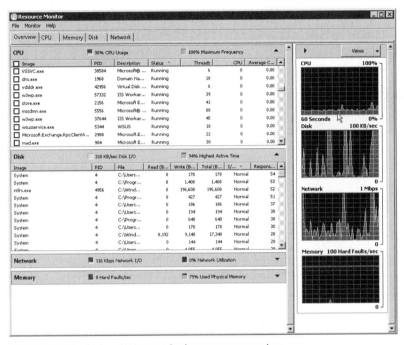

FIGURE 27-3 Displaying CPU usage in the resource overview

Click the column header in the detail view to sort by ascending order. Click a second time to sort in descending order.

On the CPU tab, you can see check boxes next to the Image header. Select the images that you are interested in investigating. An orange bar opens on each section showing what is being filtered, as shown in Figure 27-4. With filtering turned on, Resource Monitor now displays any associated modules or associated handles.

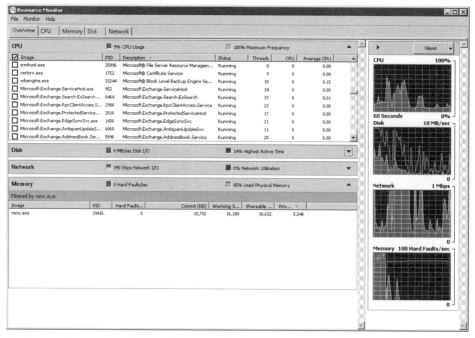

FIGURE 27-4 Resource Monitor with filtering enabled

Clear the check boxes to remove filtering.

The following list defines the headers in each Resource Monitor detail view:

- CPU Details
  - **Image**   The application using the CPU.
  - **PID**   The process identification for the application instance.
  - **Description**   The name of the application.
  - **Status**   Shows if the process is Running, Suspended, or Terminated. Right-click to change the status.
  - **Threads**   The number of active threads in this instance.
  - **CPU**   The number of currently active cycles for this instance.
  - **Average CPU**   The average CPU load over the past 60 seconds, expressed as a percentage of the total capacity of the CPU.
- Disk Details
  - **Image**   The application using the disk
  - **PID**   The process identification for the application instance
  - **File**   The file being read or written
  - **Read**   The speed (in bytes per second) at which the file was read in the last minute

- **Write**   The speed (in bytes per second) at which the file was written in the last minute
- **Total**   The average number of bytes per second read and written to the disk in the last minute
- **I/O Priority**   The priority of the IO task
- **Response Time**   The disk response time in milliseconds
■ Network Details
- **Image**   The application using the network resource.
- **PID**   The Process ID of the application instance.
- **Address**   The network address with which the local computer is exchanging information. This can be an IP address, computer name, or fully qualified domain name.
- **Send**   Amount of data (in bytes per second) sent in the last minute from the local computer to the network address.
- **Receive**   The amount of data (in bytes per second) that the application received in the last minute from the network address.
- **Total**   The total bandwidth (in bytes per second) of the data sent and received in the last minute.
■ Memory Details
- **Image**   The application using the memory resource
- **PID**   The Process ID of the application instance
- **Hard faults/min.**   The number of hard faults caused by the application instance in the last minute

> **NOTE**   A *hard fault* (also called a *page fault*) is not an error. It happens when a page at the address referenced is no longer in physical memory and has been swapped out or placed on a hard drive. However, an application that causes a high number of hard faults will be slow to respond because it constantly has to read from a hard drive rather than from memory.

- **Commit**   The amount of virtual memory (in kilobytes) reserved for the process
- **Working Set (KB)**   The amount of memory (in kilobytes) currently used by the application instance
- **Shareable (KB)**   The amount of the working set memory (in kilobytes) that might be available for other use
- **Private (KB)**   The amount of the working set memory (in kilobytes) that cannot be shared

Filtering Information from Resource Monitor

Resource Monitor produces a *lot* of data, so filtering out the unessential data is necessary if you're not to drown in a sea of graphs. To designate filters, start Resource Monitor and follow these steps:

1. Select a Resource Monitor tab. In the Image column, select the check box next to the name of each process you want to monitor. As you select a process, it's moved to the top of the column.

2. After selecting a process for filtering, the Associated Handles and Associated Modules tables on the CPU tab will contain data related to your selection.

3. Click another tab to view additional resource usage data for your selection. Tables that contain only filtered results have an orange information bar below the title bar of the table.

4. To stop filtering for a single process or service, clear its check box. To stop all filtering, clear the check box next to Image.

> **NOTE** If the process is not using any of the resources displayed on the current tab, the process name won't appear in the key table.

Troubleshooting Troublesome Applications

There can be many reasons for an application to appear nonresponsive—few of them obvious to the naked eye. Windows Resource Monitor allows you to view a process wait chain and to end processes that are preventing a program from functioning properly. In Resource Monitor, the entry for an unresponsive process appears in red.

> **IMPORTANT** Take care when using Resource Monitor to end a process. If an open program is dependent on the process, it will immediately close and unsaved data will be lost. Ending a system process can result in system instability and also cause data loss.

To examine a process, open Resource Monitor and click any tab. In the Image column, right-click the name of the process you want to analyze and select Analyze Wait Chain. (See Figure 27-5.)

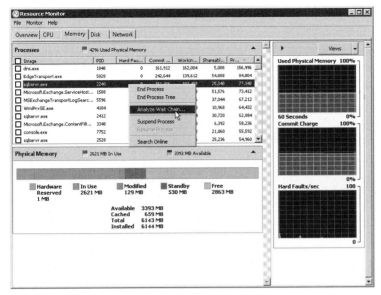

FIGURE 27-5 Checking for a process wait chain

If the process is running normally and is not waiting for any other processes, no wait chain information will be displayed.

If the process is waiting for another process, a tree organized by dependency on other processes will be displayed. To end one or more of the processes in the tree, select the check boxes next to the process names and click End Process.

Using Performance Monitor

Performance Monitor can help you visualize what is happening on your network and on individual computers. Like Resource Monitor, it displays events in real time but can also preserve data in logs for later viewing.

Insufficient memory or processing power can cause bottlenecks that severely limit performance. Unbalanced network loads and slow disk-access times can also prevent the network from operating optimally. Bottlenecks occur when one resource interferes with another resource's functioning. For example, if one application monopolizes the system processor to the exclusion of all other operations, there is a bottleneck at the processor.

Bottlenecks can occur in Windows subsystems or at any element of the network, for many reasons, including:

- Insufficient resources
- A program or client monopolizes a resource
- Failure of a program, service, or device

- Software incorrectly installed or configured
- Incorrect configuration of the system for the workload

Performance Monitor includes performance counters, event trace data, and configuration information, which can be viewed separately and can also be combined into data collector sets.

Performance counters are measurements of system state or activity. They can be included in the operating system or can be part of individual applications. Windows Performance Monitor requests the current value of performance counters at specified time intervals.

Event trace data is gathered from trace providers that are part of the operating system or of applications that report events. Information from several trace providers can be collected as a trace session.

Configuration information is collected from key values in the Windows registry. Performance Monitor can document the value of a registry key at a specific time into a log file.

Adding Performance Counters

Performance counters will show you the state of an application or a process in the operating system. You can display any number of counters on Performance Monitor. Simply right-click inside the Performance Monitor display and select Add Counters. This opens the Add Counters dialog box, as shown in Figure 27-6.

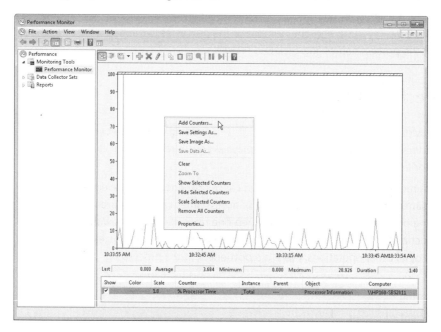

FIGURE 27-6 Viewing available counters

To add a counter to the Performance Monitor, follow these steps:

1. Select a computer from the drop-down list, or click Browse to find other computers.

2. Available counters are listed below the computer selection box. You can add all the counters in a group or click the plus sign to select individual counters.

> **NOTE** Select the Show Description check box in the lower left of the window for information on what the selected counters are actually counting.

3. When you click a group or an individual counter, the current instances display in the Instances Of Selected Object window. Select a particular instance or select All Instances. To search for a particular instance, type the process name in the drop-down box below the Instances Of Selected Object pane and click Search. If your search produces no returns, highlight another group to clear the search. The Search function is offered only if multiple instances are available.

4. Click Add to put the counter in the Added Counters list. Click OK when you're finished.

Changing the Performance Monitor Display

After you add multiple counters, the Performance Monitor screen can be difficult to decipher. To make the display more readable, follow these steps:

1. Right-click the Performance Monitor display and select Properties to open the Performance Monitor Properties dialog box as shown in Figure 27-7.

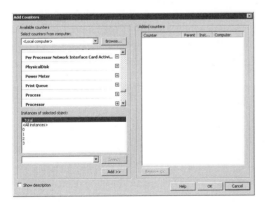

FIGURE 27-7 Changing how the Performance Monitor displays

2. Click the Data tab to select how you want the counters to display. Change the color, width, or style of the counter lines.

3. Change other display elements on the General, Graph, and Appearance tabs.

4. Click the Source tab to change the data source from Current Activity to a specified log file. For more information on using performance logs, see "Managing Collected Data" later in this chapter.

Saving the Performance Monitor Display

The current display of Performance Monitor can be saved as an image or as a web page.

To save the display as an image, follow these steps:

1. Right-click the Performance Monitor display and select Save Image As.

2. Select a location, and type in a name for the saved image. The image will se saved as a .gif file.

3. Click Save.

To save the Performance Monitor display as a web page, follow these steps:

1. Right-click the Performance Monitor display and select Save Settings As.

2. Select a location, and type in a name for the saved display. The display will be saved as an .html file.

3. Click Save.

Using Reliability Monitor

Reliability Monitor provides a System Stability Index that reflects whether unexpected problems are reducing system reliability. A graph of the Stability Index over time quickly identifies dates when problems began to occur. The accompanying System Stability Report presents details to help you locate and fix the root cause of reduced reliability. By looking at changes to the system (operating system updates or adding and removing software) along with failures (application, operating system, or hardware failures), you can develop a method for dealing with the problems.

To open Reliability Monitor, follow these steps:

1. Open Control Panel, and select Action Center.

2. Expand Maintenance and View Reliability History.

Click any item on the graph to view its details. Click events in the Action column for more details. Select either Days or Weeks to limit the report to specific time periods.

Viewing Reliability Monitor on a Remote Computer

Information about the location of Reliability Monitor files is stored in the registry. Therefore, remote registry access is required to open data on a remote computer. To enable the Remote Registry Service, complete the following steps:

1. On the computer where you want to access Reliability Monitor data, click Start, type **services.msc** in the Start Search box, and press Enter.

2. In the Services list, right-click Remote Registry and select Start, as shown in Figure 27-8.

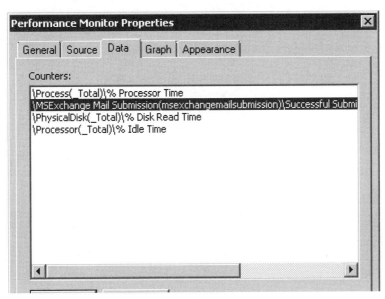

FIGURE 27-8 Starting the Remote Registry Service

Creating a Data Collector Set

Data collector sets are a method of monitoring and reporting wherein you can collect only information that's useful to you, and you can create individual data collector sets that can be viewed alone or combined with other data collector sets in Performance Monitor. Data collector sets can be configured to generate alerts when thresholds are reached, or you can associate them with scheduling rules to perform data collection at specific times.

Building a Data Collector Set from a Template

Performance Monitor includes several templates that concentrate on general system diagnosis information or collect performance data specific to server roles or applications. You can import templates created on other computers and export data collector sets that you create to use on other computers.

To create a data collector set from a template, follow these steps:

1. Click Start, type **perfmon** in the Start Search box, and then press Enter.

2. In the navigation pane, expand Data Collector Sets, right-click User Defined, point to New, and click Data Collector Set. The Create New Data Collector Set Wizard starts.

3. Enter a name for your data collector set. Select Create From A Template, and click Next.

4. From the Template Data Collector Set menu, select the template you want to use to create your data collector set. A description of the data collected appears as you highlight each template. (See Figure 27-9.)

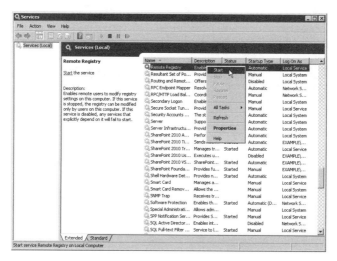

FIGURE 27-9 Highlight a template to read the description

5. The Root Directory contains data collected by the data collector set. If you want to store your data collector set data in a location other than the default, click Browse or type in the directory name.

6. Click Next to choose a custom location for the data collector set or to define more options. Click Finish to save the current settings and exit.

> **NOTE** If you type in a directory name, do not enter a backslash (\) at the end of the directory name.

7. Click Next to define a user for the data collector set to run as, or click Finish to save the current settings and exit.

8. When you click Next, you can configure the data collector set to run as a specific user. Click Change to enter the user name and password for a user other than the default listed, or click Finish to save the current settings and exit.

To start collecting data and storing it in the location specified in step 6, right-click the data collector set in the navigation pane and select Start.

To view the properties of the data collector set or make changes, right-click the data collector set you created in steps 1 through 8 and select Properties. For more information about the properties of the data collector set, see "Managing Collected Data" later in this chapter.

Importing Templates

Data collector set templates are stored as XML files, and you can import them directly from a local hard drive or from a network drive. To import a data collector set template, run the Create New Data Collector Set Wizard and click Browse when asked which template you'd like to use. Browse to the location of the XML file you want to use, select it, and click Open.

Exporting Templates

To export a data collector set for use on other computers, open Performance Monitor, expand Data Collector Sets, right-click the data collector set you want to export, and click Save Template. Select a directory in which to store the XML file, and click Save.

Creating a Data Collector Set from Performance Monitor

To use the counters in a Performance Monitor display to create a data collector set, follow these steps:

1. Start Performance Monitor, and add counters (as described in the "Adding Performance Counters" section earlier in this chapter) to create a custom view you want to save as a data collector set.

2. Right-click Performance Monitor in the navigation pane, point to New, and click Data Collector Set. The Create New Data Collector Set Wizard starts. The data collector set you create will contain all of the data collectors selected in the current Performance Monitor view.

3. Type in a name for the data collector set, and click Next.

4. The Root Directory will contain data collected by the data collector set. If you want to store your data collector set data in a location other than the default, click Browse to navigate to the location or type in the directory name.

NOTE If you type in a directory name, do not enter a backslash (\) at the end of the directory name.

5. After clicking Next, you can configure the data collector set to run as a specific user. Click Change to enter a user name and password.

6. Click Finish.

To start collecting data and storing it in the location specified in step 4, right-click the data collector set in the navigation pane and select Start.

Constructing a Data Collector Set Manually

You can create a customized data collector set made up of performance counters, configuration data, or data from trace providers. To make such a data collector set, follow these steps:

1. Open Windows Performance Monitor.

2. In the navigation pane, expand Data Collector Sets, right-click User Defined, point to New, and click Data Collector Set.

3. Type in a name for your data collector set. Select Create Manually, and click Next.

4. Select Create Data Logs. Select the check boxes next to the data collector types you want to use, which are described in the following list, and click Next:

   Performance Counter   Generates metric data about the system's performance.

   Event Trace Data   Provides information about activities and system events.

   System Configuration Information   Records the state of—and changes to—registry keys.

5. Depending on the data collector types you selected, you will be presented with dialog boxes to add data collectors to your data collector set:

   • Click Add to open the Add Counters dialog box. When you are finished adding performance counters, click OK. Then click Next to continue the configuration, or click Finish to exit and save the current configuration.

   • You can install event trace providers with the operating system or as part of a non-Microsoft application. Click Add to select from a list of available event trace providers, as shown in Figure 27-10. You can select multiple providers by holding down the Ctrl key and highlighting the providers you want. When you are finished adding event trace providers, Click OK and then click Next to continue the configuration, or click Finish to exit and save the current configuration.

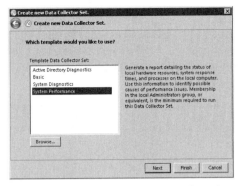

FIGURE 27-10 Selecting trace providers for a data collector set

6. To record system configuration data, type in the registry keys you want to track. You must know the exact key.

7. When you've finished adding registry keys, click Next to continue the configuration or click Finish to exit and save the current configuration.

8. The Root Directory will contain data collected by the data collector set. If you want to store your data collector set data in a location other than the default, click Browse to navigate to the location or type in the directory name.

> **NOTE** If you type in a directory name, do not enter a backslash (\) at the end of the directory name.

9. After clicking Next, you can configure the data collector set to run as a specific user. Click Change to type in the user name and password for a user other than the default listed.

10. Click Finish.

Creating a Data Collector Set to Monitor Performance Counters

Another type of data collector set that you can create monitors performance counters and sends out alerts when the counters exceed or fall below thresholds you set.

First create the data set, and then configure the alerts by following these steps:

1. Open Performance Monitor. In the navigation pane, expand Data Collector Sets, right-click User Defined, point to New, and click Data Collector Set.

2. Type in a name for your data collector set. Select Create Manually, and click Next.

3. Select the Performance Counter Alert option, and click Next.

4. Click Add to open the Add Counters dialog box. When you are finished adding counters, click OK.

5. Highlight the counter you'd like to monitor. From the Alert When drop-down list, choose whether to alert when the performance counter value is above or below the limit. In the Limit box, enter the threshold value.

6. When you've finished defining alerts, click Next to continue the configuration or click Finish to exit and save the current configuration.

7. After clicking Next, you can configure the data collector set to run as a specific user. Click Change to type in a user name and password.

Scheduling Data Collection

Data collection can be scheduled and log data managed using Data Collector Sets. You can store the reports after log data has been deleted so that you can still have performance statistics without storing masses of individual counter values.

To schedule when a data collector set starts, follow these steps:

1. After you create a data collector set, right-click the name of the data collector set in the navigation pane and select Properties.

2. Click the Schedule tab.

3. Click Add to create a start date, time, or day for data collection, as shown in Figure 27-11. If you are configuring a new data collector set, be sure that the start date is after the current date and time.

FIGURE 27-11 Scheduling a start date and time for a data collector set

4. If you don't want to collect new data after a specific date, select the Expiration Date check box and supply the date.

5. Click OK when finished.

To schedule when a data collector set stops, follow these steps:

1. After you create a data collector set, right-click the name of the data collector set in the navigation pane and select Properties.

2. Click the Stop Condition tab.

3. To stop collecting data after a specified time, select Overall Duration and choose the number and units of time.

4. In the Limits section, you can select When A Limit Is Reached, Restart The Data Collector Set to break the data collection into separate, more manageable logs:

    -   Select Duration to configure a time period for data collection to write to a single log file.

    -   Select Maximum Size to restart the data collector set or to stop collecting data when the log file reaches the limit.

5. If you have specified a value for Overall Duration, you can select Stop When All Data Collectors Have Finished so that all the counters can finish recording the most recent values before the entire data collector set is stopped.

6. Click OK.

Managing Collected Data

Data collector sets create log files and optional report files. Data Manager allows you to configure how log data, reports, and compressed data are stored for each data collector set.

To configure Data Manager for a data collector set, follow these steps:

1. Open Performance Monitor, expand Data Collector Sets, and expand User Defined.

2. Right-click the name of the data collector set that you want to configure and select Data Manager.

3. On the Data Manager tab, you can accept the default values or make changes according to your data retention policy. Table 27-1 describes each option.

- Select Minimum Free Disk or Maximum Folders, and previous data will be deleted when the limit is reached according to the Resource Policy you choose (either Delete Largest or Delete Oldest).
- Select Apply Policy Before The Data Collector Set Starts, and previous data will be deleted before the data collector set creates its next log file.
- Select Maximum Root Path Size, and previous data will be deleted when the root log folder size limit is reached.

4. Click the Actions tab. You can accept the default values or make changes. To make changes, use the Add, Edit, or Remove button. Table 27-2 describes each option.

5. Click OK to finish.

TABLE 27-1 Data Manager options

OPTION	DEFINITION
Minimum Free Disk	Amount of free disk space that must be available on the drive where log data is stored. When the limit is reached, previous data will be deleted based on your Resource Policy.
Maximum Folders	Number of subfolders allowed in the data directory. When the limit is reached, previous data will be deleted according to your Resource Policy.
Resource Policy	Specifies whether the largest or oldest log file or directory will be deleted when limits are reached.
Maximum Root Path Size	Maximum size of the data collector set data directory, including all subfolders. When selected, this maximum path size overrides the Minimum Free Disk and Maximum Folders limits. When the limit of the Maximum Root Path Size is reached, previous data will be deleted according to your Resource Policy.

TABLE 27-2 Actions properties

OPTION	DEFINITION
Age/Units	The age of the data file in days or weeks. If the value is set to zero, the age is not considered.
Folder Size	The size, in megabytes, of the log data folder. If the value is set to zero, the size is not considered.
Save, Create Or Delete A Cab File	Cabinet files are archives that are created from raw log data that can be extracted later.

OPTION	DEFINITION
Delete Data File	Raw data log created by the data collector set. To save disk space, the data log can be deleted after a cab file is created.
Delete Report File	Report file generated from the log data. Report files can be retained even after the log data has been deleted. Select this option to delete the report file.

Working with Data Log Files

When log files grow large, reports are generated more slowly. If you review your logs frequently, setting limits will automatically break up logs to make them easier to view. The relog command can divide long log files into more manageable segments, or you can use it to combine multiple log files.

The relog command has the following syntax. The parameters are detailed in the following sections:

```
Relog [filename [filename ...]] [-a] [-c Path [Path ...]] [-cf filename] [-f {bin
| csv | tsv | SQL}] [-t Value] [-o {outputfile | DSN!Counterlog}] [-b M/D/YYYY
[[HH:]MM:]SS] [-e M/D/YYYY [[HH:]MM:]SS] [-config {filename | i}] [-q]
<filename [filename ...]>
```

The <filename [filename ...]> parameter specifies the path name of an existing performance counter log. You can specify multiple input files.

The -a parameter appends output file instead of overwriting. This option does not apply to SQL format where the default is always to append.

The -c <Path [Path ...]> parameter specifies the performance counter path to log. To specify multiple counter paths, separate them with a space and enclose the counter paths in quotation marks (for example, "CounterPath1 CounterPath2").

The -cf <FileName> parameter specifies the path name of the text file that lists the performance counters to be included in a relog file. Use this option to list counter paths in an input file, one per line. The default setting is all counters in the original log file are relogged.

The -f {bin| csv| tsv| SQL} parameter specifies the path name of the output file format. The default format is bin. For a SQL database, the output file specifies the DSN!CounterLog. You can specify the database location by using the ODBC manager to configure the DSN (Database System Name).

The -t <value> parameter specifies sample intervals in "N" records. Includes every nth data point in the relog file. The default is every data point.

The -o {OutputFile | DSN!CounterLog} parameter specifies the path name of the output file or SQL database where the counters will be written.

The -b <M/D/YYYY HH:MM:SS[AM|PM]> parameter specifies begin time for copying first record from the input file. Date and time must be in this exact format: M/D/YYYY H:MM:SS.

The -e <M/D/YYYY HH:MM:SS[AM|PM]> parameter specifies end time for copying last record from the input file. Date and time must be in this exact format: M/D/YYYY HH:MM:SS.

The -config {FileName | i} parameter specifies the path name of the settings file that contains command-line parameters. Use -i in the configuration file as a placeholder for a list of input files that can be placed on the command line. On the command line, however, you do not need to use i. You can also use wildcards such as *.blg to specify many input filenames.

The -q parameter displays the performance counters and time ranges of log files specified in the input file.

The -y parameter bypasses prompting by answering "yes" to all questions.

The /? parameter displays help at the command prompt.

Viewing Reports

To help analyze collected data and identify trends, Performance Monitor generates reports from data collector sets.

To view a data collector set report, follow these steps:

1. Open Windows Performance Monitor.

2. Expand Reports, and click User Defined or System.

3. Select the data collector set that you want to view as a report. The report opens in the console pane, as shown in Figure 27-12.

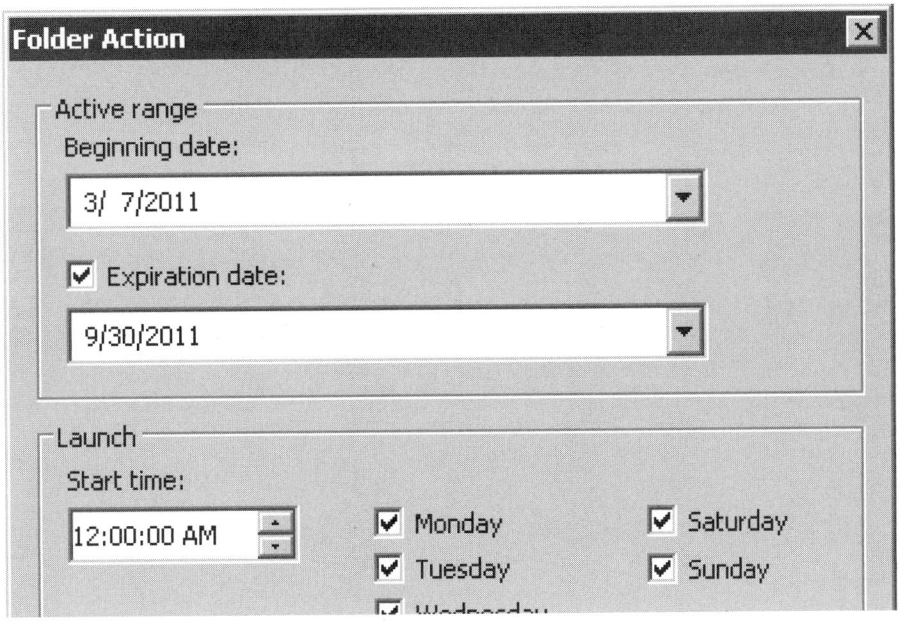

FIGURE 27-12 Viewing a data collector report

To create a new report for a data collector set, type **perfmon / report "Data_Collector_Set_name"** at a command prompt. Type **perfmon /report** without any other parameters to generate the System Diagnostics report.

Summary

In this chapter, we covered the available tools for keeping track of your network's health and performance. The next chapter offers strategies for protecting your network from potential disasters.

## CHAPTER 28

Disaster Planning

Smart SCUBA divers dive with a buddy and carry an alternate air source, even though they've trained extensively and checked their equipment thoroughly. Schools and businesses have fire drills even though the vast majority of buildings never burn down. System administrators are no different—we do verified backups and write up disaster recovery plans we hope never to use. But we do them because there are only two types of networks: those that have experienced disaster and those that haven't—yet.

Disaster can take many forms, from the self-inflicted pain of a user or administrator doing something really, really unwise to the uncontrollable, unpreventable results of a natural disaster such as a flood or an earthquake. In any case, your business will depend on how well you were prepared for the disaster, and how well you and your team respond to it and recoverfrom it.

This chapter covers emergency preparedness. It discusses creating a disaster recovery plan, with standardized procedures to follow in the event of a catastrophe. It also describes how to prepare for a disaster so that if (or when) one happens, you have the tools to recover. We'll also cover some of the specialized, and in some ways easier, recovery scenarios that virtualization uses.

Planning for Disaster

Some people seem to operate on the assumption that if they don't think about a disaster, one won't happen. This is similar to the idea that if you don't write a will, you'll never die—and just about as realistic. No business owner or system administrator should feel comfortable about their degree of preparedness without a clear disaster recovery plan that has been thoroughly tested. Even then, you should continually look for ways to improve the plan—it should only be your starting point.

A good disaster recovery plan is one that you are constantly examining, improving, updating, and testing. But understand your disaster plan's limitations: it isn't perfect, and even the best disaster recovery plan needs to be constantly examined and adjusted or it quickly gets out of date.

Planning for disaster or emergencies is not a single step, but an iterative, ongoing process. Systems are not mountains, but rivers, constantly moving and changing, and your disaster recovery plan needs to change as your environment changes. To put together a good disaster recovery plan—one you can bet your business on—you need to follow these steps:

1. Identify the risks.
2. Identify the resources.
3. Develop the responses.
4. Test the responses.
5. Iterate.

 REAL WORLD **Size Does Matter**

Disasters happen to businesses of all sizes and types. Small businesses are no more insulated from them than large businesses are, but generally they don't have the same levels of resources to respond to them and recover from them. A large, multinational corporation with an IT staff of several hundred worldwide certainly has more resources than a small accounting firm with an IT staff of one. As you work through the steps to build your disaster recovery plan, how you plan and implement it will vary depending on the size of your company and the resources available.

In the discussion of disaster planning that follows, many of the steps, and the actions associated with those steps, are quite formal and probably sound like a bit more than you can manage in your small business. And, in many cases, you're right—in a small business, one can often be substantially more informal. But do *not* make the mistake of ignoring something because it sounds too formal or involved. Rather, adjust the step and actions to fit within your smaller, but no less important, business. No matter how small your business, if it uses and depends on Microsoft Windows Small Business Server (SBS) 2011 Standard, you have valuable and business-critical assets on your server, so take the steps to protect them and your business before you have a disaster. You'll save money, time, and, most important, business reputation by being able to withstand and even grow in the face of disaster.

We've been through fires, earthquakes, crashed servers, and just plain egregious error, and we've learned the hard way that disaster recovery is something you can do a lot better if you've planned for it ahead of time. It's not sexy, and it's sometimes hard to sell to upper management, but it is worth the effort. If you're lucky, you'll never need to use all of your plans for worst-case scenarios, but if you do need them, you'll be really, *really* glad you have them.

Identifying the Risks

The first step in creating a disaster recovery plan is to identify the risks to your business and the costs associated with those risks. The risks vary from the simple deletion of a critical file to the total destruction of your place of business and its computers. To properly prepare for a disaster, you need to perform a realistic assessment of the risks, the potential costs and consequences of each disaster scenario, the likelihood of any given disaster scenario, and the resources available to address the risks. Risks that seemed vanishingly remote a few years ago are now part of our everyday lives.

This isn't a job for a single person. As with all the tasks associated with a disaster recovery plan, all concerned parties must participate. There are two important reasons for this: you want to make sure that you have commitment and buy-in from the parties concerned, and you also want to make sure you don't miss anything important.

No matter how carefully and thoroughly you try to identify the risks, you'll miss at least one. You can account for that missing risk by including an "unknown risk" item in your list. Treat it just like any other risk: identify the resources available to address it, and develop countermeasures to take should it occur. The difference with this risk, of course, is that your resources and countermeasures are somewhat more generic, and you can't really test your response to the risk, because you don't yet know what it is.

Start by trying to list all the possible ways that your network could fail. Solicit help from everyone with a stake in the process. The more people involved in the brainstorming, the more ideas you'll get, and the more prevention and recovery procedures you can develop and practice. Be careful at this stage in the process to not dismiss any idea or concern as trivial, unimportant, or unlikely.

Next, look at all the ways that some external event could affect your system. (The current buzz word for this is *threat modeling*, if you care.) The team of people responsible for identifying possible external problems is probably similar to a team looking at internal failures, but with some important differences. For example, if your business is housed in a large commercial office building, you'll want to involve that building's security and facilities groups even though they aren't employees of your business. They will not only have important input into the possible threats to the business, but also they'll also have information on the resources and preventative measures already in place.

The risk identification phase is really made up of two parts: identification and assessment. They are different tasks. During the identification portion of the phase, you need to identify every possible risk, no matter how remote or unlikely. No risk suggested should be regarded as silly—don't limit the suggestions in any way. You want to identify every possible risk that anyone can think of. Then, when you have as complete a list as you can create, move on to the assessment task. In the risk-assessment task, you will try to understand and quantify just how likely a particular risk is. If you're located in a flood plain, for example, you're much more likely to think flood insurance is a good investment.

NOTE Even in a very small business, where there might be only one person involved in disaster planning, it's a really good idea to get others involved somehow in at least the risk-identification task. Different people think up different scenarios and risk factors, and soliciting more and different viewpoints will improve the overall result of the process.

Identifying the Resources

After you've identified the risks to your network, you need to identify what the resources are to address those risks. These resources can be internal or external, people or systems, hardware or software.

When you're identifying the resources available to deal with a specific risk, be as complete as you can, but also be specific. Identifying everyone in the company as a resource to solve a crashed server might look good, but realistically only one or two people are likely to actually be able to rebuild the server. Make sure you identify those key people for each risk, as well as the more general secondary resources they have to call on, such as Microsoft Customer Support Services (CSS) and local Microsoft partners. For example, the primary resource available to recover a crashed server might consist of your hardware vendor to recover the failed hardware and your own IT person or primary system consultant to restore the software and database. General secondary resources could include Microsoft Support (*http://support.microsoft.com/oas/default.aspx?gprid=3208*), Microsoft Partners in your area, and the TechNet Forum for SBS (*http://social.technet.microsoft.com/Forums/en-US/smallbusinessserver/threads*).

An important step in identifying resources in your disaster recovery plan is to specify both the first-line responsibility and the back-end or supervisory responsibility. Make sure everyone knows who to go to when the problem is more than they can handle or when they need additional resources. Also, clearly define when they should escalate. The best disaster recovery plans include clear, unambiguous escalation policies. This takes the burden off individuals to decide when to notify someone and whom to notify, and it makes escalation simply part of the procedure.

Developing the Responses

An old but relevant adage comes to mind when discussing disaster recovery scenarios: When you're up to your elbows in alligators, it's difficult to remember that your original objective was to drain the swamp. This is another way of saying that people lose track of what's important when they are overloaded by too many problems that require immediate attention. To ensure that your swamp is drained and your network gets back online, you need to take those carefully researched risks and resources and develop a disaster recovery plan. There are two important parts of any good disaster recovery plan:

- Standard operating procedures (SOPs)
- Standard escalation procedures (SEPs)

Making sure these procedures are in place and clearly understood by everyone involved, before a disaster strikes, puts you in a far better position to recover gracefully and with a minimum of lost productivity and data.

Standard Operating Procedures

Emergencies bring out both the best and worst in people. If you're prepared for the emergency, you can be one of those who come out smelling like a rose, but if you're not prepared and let yourself get flustered or lose track of what you're trying to accomplish, you can make the whole situation worse than it needs to be.

It's just plain hard to stay calm and focused when you're in the middle of an emergency and there's a lot of extra stress being applied by everyone around you. Although no one is ever as prepared for a system emergency as they'd like to be, careful planning and preparation can give you an edge in recovering expeditiously and with a minimal loss of data. It's a lot easier to deal with the situation calmly when you know you've prepared for this problem and you have a well-organized, tested SOP to follow.

Because the very nature of emergencies is that you can't predict exactly which one is going to strike, you need to plan and prepare for as many possibilities as you can. The time to decide how to recover from a disaster is before the disaster happens, not in the middle of it when users are screaming and bosses are standing around looking serious and concerned. If you're lucky. (We seem to have been blessed by those who follow the more common adage, "When in trouble or in doubt, run in circles, scream and shout.").

Your risk-assessment phase involved identifying as many possible disaster scenarios and risks as you could; the resource-assessment phase identified the resources for those risks. Now you need to create SOPs for recovering the system from each of the scenarios. Having an SOP that details how to recover from a failed server makes that recovery a lot easier.

Reduce your stress and prevent mistakes by planning for disasters before they occur. Practice recovering from each of your disaster scenarios. Write down each of the steps, and work through questionable or unclear areas until you can identify exactly what it takes to recover from the problem. This is like a fire drill, and you should do it for the same reasons—not because a fire is inevitable, but because fires do happen, and the statistics demonstrate irrefutably that those who prepare for a fire and practice what to do in a fire are far more likely to survive the fire.

Even if you know you're the only resource the company has to recover from a disaster scenario, write down the basic steps to do it. You don't need to go into minute detail, but at the very least, outline the key steps. This might be something you do for real only once in your life, so don't count on being able to remember everything. Disasters, by their very nature, raise the overall stress level and cause people to forget important steps.

Your job as a system administrator is to prepare for disasters and practice what to do in those disasters—not because you expect the disaster, but because if you do have one, you want to be the hero, not the goat. After all, it isn't often that the system administrator or IT consultant gets to be a hero, so be ready when your time comes.

The first step in developing any SOP is to outline the overall steps you want to accomplish. Keep it general at this point—you're looking for the big picture here. Again, you want everyone to be involved in the process. What you're really trying to do is make sure you don't forget any critical steps, and that's much easier when you get the overall plan down first. There will be plenty of opportunity later to cover the specific details.

After you have a broad, high-level outline for a given procedure, the people you identified as the actual resources during the resource-assessment phase should start to fill in the blanks of the outline. You don't need every detail at this point, but you should get down to at least a level below the original outline. This will help you identify missing resources that are important to a timely resolution of the problem. Again, don't get too bogged down in the details at this point. You're not actually writing the SOP, just trying to make sure that you've identified all of its pieces.

When you feel confident that the outline is ready, get the larger group back together again. Go over the procedure and smooth out the rough edges, refining the outline and listening to make sure you haven't missed anything critical. When everyone agrees that the outline is complete, you're ready to add the final details to it.

The people who are responsible for each procedure should now work through all the details of the disaster recovery plan and document the steps thoroughly. They should keep in mind that the people who actually perform the recovery might not be who they expect. It's great to have an SOP for recovering from a failed router, but if the only person who understands the procedure is the IT person and she's on vacation in Bora Bora that week, your disaster recovery plan has a big hole in it.

When you create the documentation, write down everything. What seems obvious to you now, while you're devising the procedure, will not seem at all obvious in six months or a year when you suddenly have to follow it under stress.

 REAL WORLD **Multiple Copies, Multiple Locations**

It's tempting to centralize your SOPs into a single, easily accessible database. And you should do that, making sure everyone understands how to use it. But you'll also need to have alternative locations and formats for your procedures. Not only do you not want to keep the only copy in a single database, you also don't want to have only an electronic version—how accessible is the SOP for recovering a failed server going to be when the server has failed? Always maintain hard-copy versions as well. The one thing you don't want to do is create a single point of failure in your disaster recovery plan!

Every good server room should have a large binder, prominently visible and clearly identified, that contains all the SOPs. Each responsible person should also have one or more copies of at least the procedures he or she is either a resource for or likely to become a resource for. We like to keep copies of all our procedures in several places so that we can get at them no matter what the source of the emergency or where we happen to be when one of our pagers goes off.

Even if you're the only resource, keep multiple copies of your procedures and key phone numbers of external resources. Don't rely entirely on electronic storage, because even external electronic storage might be difficult to access if the disaster is major. But don't ignore electronic storage, either. Most of the time, it's the fastest and easiest to get to, and the most likely to be completely up to date.

After you have created the SOPs, your job has only begun. You need to keep them up to date and make sure that they don't become stale. It's no good having an SOP to recover your ISDN connection to the Internet when you ripped the ISDN line out three years ago and put in a DSL line with five times the bandwidth at half the cost.

You also need to make sure that all your copies of an SOP are updated. Electronic ones should probably be stored in a database or in a folder on SBS that is available offline. However, hard-copy documents are notoriously tricky to maintain. A good method is to make yet another SOP that details who updates what SOPs, how often that person updates it, and who gets fresh copies whenever a change is made. Then put a version control system into place and make sure everyone understands his or her role in the process. Build rewards into the system for timely and consistent updating of SOPs—if 10 or 20 percent of someone's bonus is dependent on keeping those SOPs up to date and distributed, you can be sure they'll be current at least as often as the review process.

Standard Escalation Procedures

No matter how carefully you've identified potential risks, and how detailed your procedures to recover from them are, you're still likely to have situations you didn't anticipate. An important part of any disaster recovery plan is a standardized escalation procedure. Not only should each individual SOP have its own procedure-specific SEP, but you should also have an overall escalation procedure that covers everything you haven't thought of—because it's certain you haven't thought of everything.

An escalation procedure has two functions—resource escalation and notification escalation. Both have the same purpose: to make sure that everyone who needs to know about the problem is up to date and involved as appropriate, and to keep the overall noise level down so that the work of resolving the problem can go forward as quickly as possible. The *resource escalation procedure* details the resources that are available to the people who are trying to recover from the current disaster so that these people don't have to try to guess who (or what) the appropriate resource might be when they run into something they can't handle or something doesn't go as planned. This procedure helps them stay calm and focused. They know that if they run into a problem, they aren't on their own, and they know exactly who to call when they do need help.

The *notification escalation procedure* details who is to be notified of serious problems. Even more important, it should provide specifics regarding *when* notification is to be made. If a particular print queue crashes but comes right back up, you might want to send a general message only to the users of that particular printer letting them know what happened. However, if your email has been down for more than half an hour, a lot of folks are going to be concerned. The SEP for email should detail who needs to be notified when the server is unavailable for longer than some specified amount of time, and it should probably detail what happens and who gets notified when it's still down some significant amount of time after that.

This notification has two purposes: to make sure that the necessary resources are made available as required, and to keep everyone informed and aware of the situation. If you let people know that you've had a server hardware failure and that the vendor has been called and will be onsite within an hour, you'll cut down the number of phone calls exponentially, freeing you to do whatever you need to do to ensure that you're ready when the vendor arrives.

Testing the Responses

A disaster recovery plan is nice to have, but it really isn't worth a whole lot until it has actually been tested. Needless to say, the time to test the plan is at your convenience and under controlled conditions, rather than in the midst of an actual disaster. It's a nuisance to discover that your detailed disaster recovery plan has a fatal flaw in it when you're testing it under controlled conditions. It's a bit more than a nuisance to discover it when every second counts.

You won't be able to test everything in your disaster recovery plans. Even most large organizations don't have the resources to create fully realistic simulated natural disasters and test their response to each of them under controlled conditions, and even fewer small businesses have those kinds of resources. Nevertheless, there are things you can do to test your response plans. The details of how you test them depend on your environment, but they should include as realistic a test as feasible and should, as much as possible, cover all aspects of the response plan. The other reason to test the disaster recovery plan is that it provides a valuable training ground. If you've identified primary and backup resources, as you should, chances are that the people you've identified as backup resources are not as skilled or knowledgeable in a particular area as the primary resource. Testing the procedures gives you a chance to train the backup resources at the same time.

You should also consider using the testing to cross-train people who are not necessarily in the primary response group. Not only will they get valuable training, but you'll also create a knowledgeable pool of people who might not be directly needed when the procedure has to be used for real, but who can act as key communicators with the rest of the community.

Iterating

When you finish a particular disaster recovery plan, you might think your job is done, but it's not. Standardizing a process is actually just the first step. You need to continually look for ways to improve it.

You should make a regular, scheduled practice of pulling out your disaster recovery plan with those responsible and making sure it's up to date. Use the occasion to actually look at it and see how you can improve on it. Take the opportunity to examine your environment. What's changed since you last looked at the plan? What equipment has been retired, and what has been added? What software is different? Are all the people on your notification and escalation lists still working at the company in the same roles? Are the phone numbers, including home phone numbers, up to date?

 REAL WORLD **Understand and Practice Kaizen**

*K*aizen is a Japanese word and concept that means "small, continuous, improvement." Its literal translation is, "Change (kai) to become good (zen)."

So, why bring a Japanese word and concept into a discussion about disaster recovery? Because a good disaster recovery plan is one that you are constantly Kaizening. When you really understand Kaizen, it becomes a way of life that you can use in many ways.

The first thing to understand about Kaizen is that you are not striving for major change or improvement. Small improvements are the goal. Don't try to fix or change everything all at once. Instead, focus on one area, and try to make it just a little bit better.

The second part of Kaizen is that it is continuous. You must constantly look for ways to improve and implement those improvements. Because each improvement is small and incremental, you can easily implement it and move on to the next one.

Kaizen is very much about teamwork. Good Kaizen balances the load on a team and finds ways to build the strengths of the team as a whole. If you practice Kaizen and continually look for small, incremental ways to improve your work, you will soon have a better and more enjoyable workplace. As a manager, if you find ways to encourage and reward those who practice Kaizen, your team and you will grow and prosper.

Another way to iterate your disaster recovery plan is to use every disaster as a learning experience. After the disaster or emergency is over, get everyone together as soon as possible to talk about what happened. Find out what they think worked and what didn't in the plan. What tools did you not have that would have made the job go quicker or better? Actively solic suggestions for how the process could be improved. Then make the changes and test them. You'll not only improve your responsiveness to this particular type of disaster, but you'll also improve your overall responsiveness by getting people involved in the process and enabling them to be part of the solution.

> **IMPORTANT** Do not use this post-disaster recovery discussion to assign blame or look for the cause of the disaster. This is about how to respond to, and recover from, a disaster better. And to do that, you need to learn from the experience so that you can do a better job planning for the next one. If everyone is trying to avoid blame, they won't have any energy for improving the process.

Preparing for a Disaster

As Ben Franklin was known to say, "Failure to prepare is preparing to fail." This is truer than ever with modern operating systems, and although SBS includes a number of exceptionally useful recovery modes and tools, you still need to prepare for potential problems. Some of these techniques are covered in detail in other chapters and are discussed here only briefly, whereas others are covered here at length.

Setting Up A Fault-Tolerant System

A fault-tolerant system is one that is prepared to continue operating in the event of key component failures. It's very useful for servers running critical applications. Here are a few of the many ways to ensure fault tolerance in a system:

- Use one or more RAID arrays for system and data storage, protecting you from hard-disk failure. If a hard disk in the array fails, only that disk needs to be replaced—and no data is lost. See Chapter 11, "Disk Management," for information about using RAID, both software and hardware, to provide fault tolerance for your disk subsystem.

- Use multiple disk array controllers to provide redundancy if a controller fails.

- Use an uninterruptible power supply (UPS) to allow the server to shut down gracefully in the event of a power failure.

- Use multiples of everything that is likely to fail, including power supplies and network cards.

- Keep key spares available to quickly recover by replacing a failed part. If you have only a single power supply and it fails, you'll be back online a *lot* faster if you swap out a failed power supply yourself and then call your hardware vendor for a replacement for the failed one.

Backups

We've got a whole chapter on backups—Chapter 16, "Configuring Backup"—but it's important to talk briefly about them here under disaster recovery because they're the backbone of any disaster recovery scenario. Having a backup of your critical system files is nice. Having backups of your data is nice. But having a tested backup of both of them is critical to a successful restore experience. By tested, we mean that you've actually restored the files in the backup and that you were able to read and use them.

Not every single backup will get tested for your ability to restore. That's not realistic, and there's no point even pretending it's going to happen. But you should have a regular schedule of testing backups to know you can restore from them. We like to do ours at least once a week. We pick a couple of key subdirectories and restore them to a temporary location on the server.

Image backups, such as those done by Windows Server Backup, pose additional testing issues. It's a really good idea to test full system restores to ensure that your recovery scenario for a full hardware failure is viable—especially if you intend to do restores to dissimilar hardware, which is something not directly contemplated by Windows Server 2008 R2 Backup. If you want to be able to do a restore to dissimilar hardware, you're probably going to need to use a third-party backup utility, such as Acronis True Image for Microsoft Windows Small Business Server (*http://www.acronis.com*) or StorageCraft ShadowProtect Server (*http://www.storagecraft.com*). Both of these products are designed to allow you to do backup and restore to dissimilar hardware, including physical to virtual (P2V).

Restoring from Backup

The process of restoring your SBS server from backup is something you should test and do before you find yourself in the middle of a disaster. And yes, we know, we're repeating ourselves. But it's really important. One last time and then we'll let it go: The only good backup is a fully tested backup. And the only reliable way to test a backup is to restore it.

When disaster strikes your SBS network and you have to restore an entire server, you'll need the following:

- Your backup.
- Hardware to restore the backup to. If you're using the native Windows Server 2008 R2 Backup that is part of SBS, it needs to be quite similar hardware to the server you're replacing.
- The original disk 1 from your SBS 2011 installation media, or another Windows Server 2008 R2 Standard DVD.
- Any drivers required for Windows Server 2008 R2 to "see" your hard disks, or your backup media. These should be on a USB key or other media that the target server can read.

After you have all the requirements together, you're ready to restore your server by following these steps:

1. Insert the first disk of the SBS 2011 installation media, and turn on the server.

2. If the BIOS needs to be changed to allow the DVD drive to be the first boot device, go into the server's BIOS and make the change, and then restart the server.

3. If prompted, press any key to boot from the DVD drive to bring up the initial localization page of the Windows Small Business Server 2011 Standard installation, as shown in Figure 28-1.

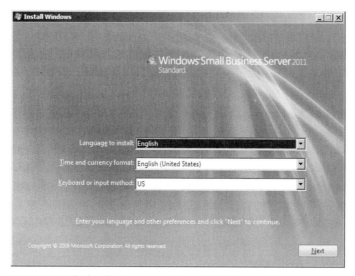

FIGURE 28-1 The localization page of the SBS 2011 installation

4. Set the localization options, and then click Next to open the Install Now page.

5. Click Repair Your Computer to open the System Recovery Options dialog box shown in Figure 28-2. If you're restoring to a bare system, no operating system is shown, as in the figure.

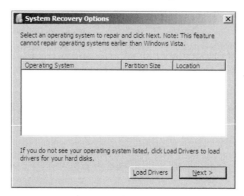

FIGURE 28-2 When restoring to a new server, no existing operating systems are present

6. Click Load Drivers if you need to load drivers for your hard disks, and follow the prompts to provide the necessary drivers.

7. Click Next to open the System Recovery Options dialog box shown in Figure 28-3.

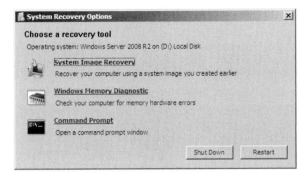

FIGURE 28-3 The System Recovery Options dialog box

8. Click System Image Recovery. Windows will search for attached backups and present the Select A System Image Backup page of the Re-Image Your Computer Wizard if it locates a backup, as shown in Figure 28-4. The most recent backup identified on the backup disk will be highlighted.

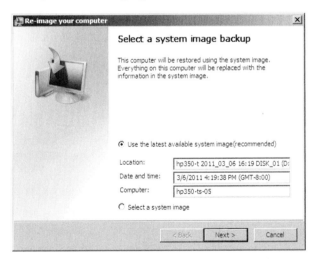

FIGURE 28-4 The most recent backup found is selected for restoration

NOTE If a backup isn't located, you will be offered an opportunity to attach a USB disk, or to point to the location of the backup.

9. Click Next to open the Choose Additional Restore Options page, shown in Figure 28-5. If your disks are identically sized and not yet partitioned, you won't have an option to format them and repartition.

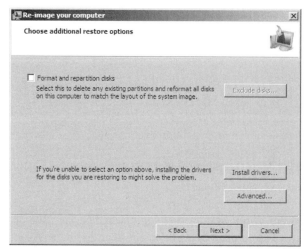

FIGURE 28-5 The Choose Additional Restore Options page of the Re-Image Your Computer Wizard

10. Select Format And Repartition Disks to completely remove any existing partitions and create new partitions that match those on the original server.

11. Click Exclude Disks to not reformat and repartition disks that you want to protect, as shown in Figure 28-6.

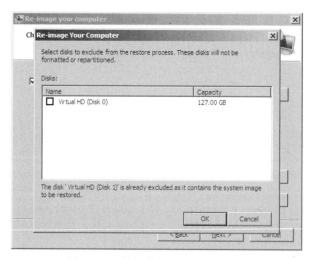

FIGURE 28-6 You can exclude disks to protect existing data

12. Click OK when you have selected disks to exclude, click Next to move to the confirmation page, and then click Finish.

13. Re-Image Your Computer requires a final confirmation before restoring, as shown in Figure 28-7. Select the confirmation check box, and click OK.

FIGURE 28-7 Final confirmation before formatting disks and restoring your computer

14. After the restore is complete, you'll be prompted to restart the server.

Virtualization and Disaster Planning

The core of disaster planning is the same whether you're running SBS virtualized or on physical hardware. The five steps described at the beginning of this chapter are almost exactly the same. But there are differences when dealing with virtualized SBS. The two biggest differences to address are

- No USB drive support inside the child partition
- Hardware independence

What do these differences mean for disaster planning? A few differences in the mechanics of backups and restores, primarily, with a possible change in the products used.

No USB Support

SBS 2011 is designed to back up to an attached USB hard disk, but Hyper-V doesn't support USB disks inside virtual machines (VMs). As discussed in Chapter 16, however, the native Windows Server Backup in Windows Server 2008 R2 supports additional backup target options, including remote shares and local hard disks. You can use these options without causing issues in the Windows SBS Console.

One important advantage to USB hard disks as a backup target is that you can remove a disk for off-site storage and attach another, something you can't do easily with a VM backup. A viable workaround, however, is to create a virtual hard disk on the USB hard disk and attach the VHD to the SCSI controller of SBS VM. The SCSI controller allows you to dynamically attach and unattach VHDs, and you can automate the entire process with Windows PowerShell.

Hardware Independence

The second difference with running SBS virtualized is all positive—hardware independence. Virtualization allows you to move VMs to different physical hardware almost transparently. Even when you haven't fully exported a VM, the rest is easy as long as you have copies of the VHD files—a bit of configuration of the virtualization settings, and then create the virtual networks. After SBS is up and running, you should rerun the Connect To The Internet Wizard and the Fix My Network Wizard to complete the restore.

This hardware independence gives you a lot of options as you plan for how you'll handle a disaster. Even if you don't immediately have an identical or even equivalent server available, most SBS networks could run in a somewhat reduced mode on a workstation class computer with 10–12 gigabytes (GB) of RAM and a quad-core processor. You wouldn't have the level of redundancy available as you would in a good server, and it's not a configuration we recommend using for any length of time, but it is more than adequate to get out of a disaster situation and get the business up and running.

Summary

Assume that a disaster will eventually occur, and plan accordingly. Create standardized recovery procedures, and keep them up to date. When there's a lot of turmoil, as always happens in the case of a major failure, people forget important steps and can make poor decisions. Standardized procedures provide a course of action without the need for on-the-spot decisions. If you've planned for a disaster and practiced what to do in the event of one, you'll be able to recover much more quickly than if you haven't. And recovering quickly in the event of a major disaster can be a significant competitive advantage.

Introduction to Networks

IF YOU'VE EVER MADE a phone call or used a bank ATM, you've already experienced using a network. After all, a *network* is simply a collection of computers and peripheral devices that can share files and other resources. The connection can be a cable, a telephone line, or even a wireless channel. The Internet itself is a network—a global network made up of all the computers, hardware, and peripherals connected to it.

Your bank's ATM consists of hardware and software connected to central computers that know, among other things, how much money you have in your account. When you call cross-country or just across town, telephone company software makes the connection from your phone to the phone you're calling through multiple switching devices. It's something we do every day, without thinking about the complicated processes behind the scenes.

Both the telephone networks and the ATM networks are maintained by technicians and engineers who plan, set up, and maintain all the software and hardware; however, the assumption underlying Microsoft Windows Small Business Server (SBS) is that there isn't anyone dedicated full time to maintaining the network and its operating system. Instead, Windows Small Business Server provides the Windows SBS Console —a unified administrative interface designed to meet the needs of small businesses and simplify your choices.

Servers

A *server* is a computer that provides services. It's really just that simple. The difficulty comes when people confuse the physical box that provides the service with the actual service. Any computer or device on a network can be a server for a particular service. A server doesn't even need to be a computer in the traditional sense. For example, you might have a print server that is nothing more complicated than a device connected to the network on one side and connected to a printer on the other. The device has a tiny little brain with just enough intelligence to understand when a particular network packet is intended for it and translate those packets into something that the printer can understand.

In Windows Small Business Server 2011 Standard, usually a single computer acts as the physical server box (though you can have secondary servers), but that box provides a variety of services to the network beyond the usual file and print services. These services meet your core business needs, including authentication and security, email and collaboration, an Internet connection, sharing, faxing, and even database services and a full-featured firewall in the Premium Add-on.

Clients

A *client* is anything on the network that avails itself of a server's services. Clients are usually the other computers on the network. The client computers typically print to network printers, read email, work on shared documents, connect to the Internet, and generally use services that aren't available on the client computer itself. Clients aren't usually as powerful as servers, but they're perfectly capable computers on their own.

Media Connecting Servers and Clients

Another portion of a network is the actual network media that connects the various servers and clients to each other. This media includes both the network cards that are part of the server or client and the physical wire (or wireless connection) between them and the various other components involved, such as hubs, routers, and switches. When all these media components work as they should, we pretty much forget about this portion of the network and take it for granted. But when a failure of one component of the network media occurs, we face troubleshooting and repairs that can be both frustrating and expensive—a good reason to buy only high-quality network components from vendors and dealers who support their products.

Features of the Windows Operating System

The Windows Server 2008 R2 operating system that underlies Windows Small Business Server is a proven, reliable, and secure operating system with the features to run a business of virtually any size. With SBS 2011, the operating system and server components have been specifically tuned to support from 5 to 75 users in a small business environment, with all the server functions residing on a single computer.

Some of the features that make Windows Server 2008 R2 ideal for a small business server include

- Easy installation that is almost fully automated in Windows Small Business Server
- A robust yet easy-to-administer security model using Active Directory
- The NTFS file system, which fully supports long file names, dynamic error recovery, shadow copies, user space limitations, and security
- Support for a broad range of hardware and software

Domains and Workgroups

Microsoft provides for two different networking models in its operating systems: workgroups and domains. Windows Small Business Server supports only the domain model of Microsoft networking, but it's worthwhile to go over why this decision makes sense, even in a very small business.

Do Workgroups Work?

Microsoft introduced the concept of the workgroup in 1992 with Windows for Workgroups. The *workgroup* is a logical grouping of several computers whose work or users are connected and who want to share their resources with each other. Usually, all the computers in a workgroup are equal, which is why such setups are referred to as *peer-to-peer networks*.

Workgroup networks are appealing because they're easy to set up and maintain. Individual users manage the sharing of their resources by determining what will be shared and who will have access. A user can allow other users to use a printer, a CD-ROM drive, an entire hard drive, or only certain files. The difficulty arises when it's necessary to give different levels of access to different users. Passwords can be used for this purpose in a limited way, but as the network gets larger, passwords proliferate, and the situation becomes increasingly complicated. Users who are required to have numerous passwords start using the same one over and over or choose passwords that are easy to remember and therefore easy to guess, and there is no way to enforce a minimum password quality level. If someone leaves the company to work for the company's biggest competitor, passwords have to be changed and everyone in the workgroup has to be notified of the new passwords. Security, such as it is, falls apart.

Another problem that occurs when a workgroup becomes too large is that users have difficulty locating the resources they need. The informal nature of workgroups also means that centralized administration or control is nonexistent. Everything has to be configured computer by computer. This lack of central administration and control, along with the limited security, makes the workgroup model a bad choice for all but the home network.

Defining Domains

To provide a secure and easy-to-manage environment that takes full advantage of Active Directory and the collaborative features of Microsoft Exchange 2010 and the other components of SBS, Microsoft made the decision to use a domain-based networking environment. Management is simplified and centralized on the server, reducing the complexity and security problems caused by having to manage users, resources, and passwords across multiple clients.

A *domain* is really just a type of workgroup that includes a server—but a server that manages and administers all of the users and computers in the network. It is a logical grouping of users who are connected by more than the cables between their computers. The goal of a domain is to let users share resources within the group and to make it easier for the group to work. However, the key difference is that Active Directory—and the server it runs on—manages, catalogs, and secures the users, groups, computers, and resources for the entire network, providing a single point of administration and control.

Additional Users

When adding a new user to the domain, you won't need to go around to each computer and enter all the information. As the administrator, you can simply connect to the server and add the new user, using the Windows SBS Console. You can create the user's mailbox, set up a home folder, add the user to security and distribution groups, configure his or her SharePoint access, set up disk quotas, and even configure a client computer—all with only a few clicks and the entering of the user name and password. The change will be immediately seen across the entire domain.

All users, including the newest, can get at their resources no matter which computer is being used. Permission to access resources is granted to individual users (or a group of users), not to individual computers. And when you need to restrict access to a sensitive document or directory, you need to log on to only a single workstation to make the change across the entire domain. You can easily and quickly grant or restrict access by individual user or by groups of users.

Access Control

In a workgroup, there are limitations on sharing your computer's resources with the rest of the workgroup. At the simplest level, you can either share the resource or not share it. Beyond that, you can require a password for a particular level of access to the resource. This enables only a very limited ability to control access to the resource, and virtually none if your computer is physically accessible to anyone but yourself.

Windows Small Business Server provides *discretionary access control*, which allows, for example, some users to create a document or make changes to an existing one while other users can only read the document and still other users can't even *see* it. You can set access for

- An individual file or files within a directory
- The entire directory

Windows Small Business Server lets you make selections as fine or as coarse as needed and makes the administration of security easy to manage.

Domain Components

An SBS domain has at least two main components and an optional third component:

- Domain controller
- Member server (optional)
- Workstations or clients

Let's take a look at these components.

Domain Controller

The main computer in the SBS domain is the *domain controller*. In many if not most SBS domains, the domain controller is the only server. It hosts Active Directory and all the components of SBS, as well as acting as the file and print server for the domain. All computers in the domain must authenticate to the domain controller, and all domain security is controlled by it.

Member Servers

In some larger SBS domains, additional Windows Server 2008 R2 computers might be in the domain. SBS 2011 includes a second server as part of the Premium Add-On. These computers can be used to spread some of the network's resource load around so that the domain controller doesn't carry the whole load, and the Premium Add-On includes SQL Server 2008 R2 Standard for Small Business, which can be installed on either the second serve, or the main SBS server.

Another reason you might have an additional member server in your SBS domain is to host Windows Remote Desktop Services. Remote Desktop Services allows you to use inexpensive, easily managed desktop computers and terminals whose only function is to run applications directly on the Remote Desktop (RD) Session Host computer. The RD Session Host provides the disk space and all the applications that the user has, while the terminal or computer of the user is merely a display and console (keyboard and mouse). Centralizing applications onto an RD Session Host can dramatically reduce costs and simplify administration in some scenarios. However, for security reasons, Remote Desktop Services cannot be run from the main SBS server, so if you use Remote Desktop Services, you'll need at least one additional server on your network.

Workstations or Clients

All the Windows clients of an SBS network must be running Windows XP SP3 or later, but in most networks they will be running Windows 7. If you have any workstations running earlier versions of Windows, they are no longer supported and should be upgraded. You can also have Mac and even UNIX or Linux clients, but their ability to integrate fully with the SBS network will be limited.

Windows clients must be running a business-class version of Windows. Specifically, Windows XP Professional, Windows XP Tablet PC Edition, Windows Vista Business, Windows Vista Enterprise, Windows Vista Ultimate, Windows 7 Professional, Windows 7 Enterprise, and Windows 7 Ultimate.

Automating Installation

YOU CAN ALMOST COMPLETELY automate the installation of Microsoft Windows Small Business Server (SBS) 2011 Standard. This is a definite change from Small Business Server 2003, where the level of automation was limited to the base operating system only. But with SBS 2011, you can use the SBS Answer File Generator (discussed in Chapter 5, "Installing Windows Small Business Server 2011," and Chapter 7, "Migrating to Windows Small Business Server 2011 Standard") to completely automate the SBS portion of the installation.

For automating the base Windows Server 2008 R2 installation, you need to use the Windows 7 Automated Installation Kit (AIK), which you can download from *http://www.microsoft.com/downloads/details.aspx?FamilyID=c7d4bc6d-15f3-4284-9123-679830d629f2&DisplayLang=en*.

For completely automating the install, you'll need a server running Windows Deployment Services, and your network card in the target server will need to support Preboot Execution Environment (PXE) boot. (This means that you'll need to use a Legacy Network Adapter if building SBS 2011 in a virtual environment because the high-speed synthetic NIC in Hyper-V doesn't support PXE.)

You'll use an unattend.xml file to define what is actually installed. The creation of this file and the details in it are covered at length in the Windows Automated Installation Kit documentation available at *http://www.microsoft.com/downloads/en/details.aspx?FamilyID=F1BAE135-4190-4D7C-B193-19123141EDAA*. But unless you're doing a lot of identical SBS installations, we really think this is overkill. The critical installation features and steps—the ones that take up your time—are already handled as part of the normal SBS installation in SBS 2011, and you can completely automate that process using the SBS Answer File Generator. The actual operating system installation is a matter of a few clicks.

After you've done that and selected the hard disk to install on, you're done. The installation will proceed automatically. If you've put your sbsanswerfile.xml where it can be found, the SBS portion of the installation will take over automatically and continue as soon as Windows Server 2008 R2 is installed.

Our overall opinion is that automating the installation beyond what the SBS Answer File Generator does is probably going to cost more time than it saves unless you're in a lab environment or a hosting environment where you are deploying at least dozens of SBS servers to make it worth the effort.

Where you can save time and effort, however, is automating the deployment of client computers. Using the Microsoft Deployment Toolkit (MDT) 2010 (*http://www.microsoft.com/ downloads/en/details.aspx?FamilyID=3BD8561F-77AC-4400-A0C1-FE871C461A89*), you can completely automate the deployment of new, ready-to-use Windows 7 workstations complete with applications, or automate the upgrade of existing Windows computers to Windows 7 and Microsoft Office 2010.

APPENDIX C

Additional Resources

BOOKS ARE GREAT. THEY'RE easy to use and very portable. We love books. They are, however, completely static and when you need information on the latest security threat or help with new applications, there's nothing like the Internet.

This appendix lists websites and blogs of use to Microsoft Windows Small Business Server (SBS) 2011 users and consultants. First we provide links to Microsoft resources, followed by websites and blogs maintained by other companies and knowledgeable individuals.

Microsoft Resources

http://blogs.technet.com/msrc — Microsoft Security Response Center

http://blogs.technet.com/sbs — Official SBS blog

http://blogs.technet.com/wsus — Latest information on Windows Server Update Services (WSUS)

http://blogs.technet.com/mu — Microsoft Update Product Team information

http://blogs.technet.com/sus — The WSUS Support Team blog

http://blogs.msdn.com/ie — IEBlog: The Windows Internet Explorer Weblog

http://www.microsoft.com/technet/security/advisory/RssFeed.aspx?securityadvisory — Microsoft TechNet Security TechCenter

http://feeds.feedburner.com/MicrosoftDownloadCenter — Microsoft Download Center

http://www.microsoft.com/mscorp/execmail — Microsoft Executive E-Mail: Insights from Microsoft executives about technology and public-policy issues important to computer users

http://blogs.msdn.com/MainFeed.aspx — Microsoft MSDN blogs

http://windowsteamblog.com — Windows Team blog

http://msexchangeteam.com — The Microsoft Exchange Team blog

http://blogs.msdn.com/sqlblog — Microsoft SQL Server Support Blog

Other Resources for SBS Users and Consultants

All the sites listed here have been found to be informative and useful. However, as with all Internet resources, you must use your judgment and think critically about what advice to follow.

http://msmvps.com/bradley—The SBS Diva. The first place we go for answers (and often the last).

http://www.eventid.net—Event details and general technical help.

http://feeds.feedburner.com/smbitprosposts—SMBITPro: Small and Medium Business (SMB) IT professionals.

http://blogs.msdn.com/aaron_margosis—Aaron Margosis' Web Log: The Non-Admin blog running with least privilege on the desktop.

http://msmvps.com/blogs/donna/rss.aspx—Donna's SecurityFlash: PC and Internet security blog.

http://blogs.iss.net/rss.php—Frequency X: Straight dope on the vulnerability du jour from IBM Internet Security Systems.

http://computer.forensikblog.de/en/atom.xml—Int for(ensic) blog: Notes on computer forensics, international edition.

http://msinfluentials.com/blogs/jesper/rss.aspx—Jesper's Blog by Jesper Johansson, the author of *Windows Server 2008 Security Resource Kit* (Microsoft Press, 2008).

http://www.smallbizserver.net—Frequently asked questions about SBS Server.

http://www.loglogic.com/blog—Everything about keeping and using security logs.

http://www.viruslist.com/en/rss/latestanalysis—All about Internet security.

http://msmvps.com/blogs/mainfeed.aspx—Blogs by current and former Microsoft Most Valuable Professionals.

http://sbs.seandaniel.com/rss.xml—Information about SBS and related technology.

http://www.symantec.com/content/en/us/enterprise/rss/securityresponse/srblogs.xml—Symantec Security Response blogs

http://smallbizthoughts.blogspot.com/feeds/posts/default?alt=rss—Small Biz Thoughts; intended primarily for small business consultants.

http://feeds.trendmicro.com/MalwareAdvisories—TrendMicro's Newest Malware Advisories.

http://www.smallbiztrends.com—Small Business Trends, an online publication for small business owners, entrepreneurs, and the people who interact with them.

http://blogs.msmvps.com/russel—Charlie's blog. Devoted to server issues in general, with a healthy dose of PowerShell thrown in.

http://social.technet.microsoft.com/wiki/contents/articles/windows-powershell-survival-guide.aspx—The Windows PowerShell Survival Guide.

Index

Symbols

$ (dollar sign) appended to shares, 235, 238
16-bit applications, not supported, 17
32-bit applications, support for, 16–17
32-bit architecture, 2
  for client computers, 17–18
  limited RAM access with, 2, 10–12
64-bit architecture, 2, 9–18
  32-bit application support with, 16–17
  for client computers, 17–18
  driver requirements for, 15
  hardware requirements for, 15
  increased RAM access with, 2, 10–12
  legacy software, potential problems with, 16–17
  registers with, 12
  security with, 13–14
  transitioning to, 9–10
  virtualization with, 14–15, 82
100BaseT (Fast Ethernet), 25, 26
500 account, 77, 139–142
802.1X standard (RADIUS authentication), 31, 34, 510
802.11a standard, 28
  for Internet connection, 24
  for network, 26
  range and interference issues, 32
802.11b standard, 27
  for Internet connection, 24
  for network, 26
  range and interference issues, 32
802.11g standard, 28
  for Internet connection, 24
  for network, 26
  range and interference issues, 32
802.11i standard (WPA2 encryption), 31, 43, 508–509, 510

802.11n standard, 28
  for Internet connection, 24
  for network, 26
  range and interference issues, 32

A

acceptable use policy, 307–308
access control, 755. *See also* permissions; security; shared resources
access point (AP), wireless, 31–33
  antennas for, 31
  authentication for, 31
  bridges and, 31
  built-in to firewall, 34
  built-in to router, 31
  channels for, 33
  interference of, 32
  placement of, 32–33
  range of, 32
  requirements for, 31
  security for, 31, 509
  supplementing wired network, 25
Access This Computer From The Network, logon right, 240
Account Operators domain local group, 210
accounts
  administrator accounts, 76, 77, 139–142
  computer accounts, 338
  POP3 email accounts, 474–478
  service accounts, SQL Server, 668
  Standard User domain accounts, 348–349
  user accounts
    adding, 217–221, 338, 754
    computer access, granting, 221
    migrating, 166–170

C

COM (Common Object Model), 16
Comexp.msc tool, 465
command line shortcuts, 465
Comma-Separated Values (CSV), storage reports
    in, 296
Common Object Model. *See* COM
company information, setting at installation, 75
Companyweb SharePoint site, 111, 597–598
  changing permissions for section of, 602–606
  migrating, 165
  RemoteApps links on, 613–624
  workspace, adding, 606–613
Compmgmt.msc tool, 465
Component Services Console, 465
COM ports, for VM (virtual machine), 102, 105
compression, 262
Computer Management Console, 465
computers. *See* client computers; servers
Configure E-mail and Internet Connectivity Wizard
    (CEICW), 495, 519, 543. *See also* FXMN (Fix My
    Network Wizard)
Configure Server Backup Wizard
  configuring server, 385–391
  requirements for, 383–384
conflict folder, DFS replication, 295
Connect Computer Wizard, 342–349
connectivity
  to Internet, 22–25, 182–184
  local, 495
    DHCP for, 496–503
    DNS for, 503–507
    Windows Firewall for, 511–519
    wireless, 508–510
  remote. *See* RDS (Remote Desktop Services); Remote-
    Apps; RWA (Remote Web Access); VPN (virtual
    private network)
  troubleshooting, with FMNW, 519–520, 542–546
consoles, command line shortcuts for, 465
constant voltage transformer. *See* CVT
contacts
  in Active Directory, enabling, 480–484
  adding, 484–486
  creating, 458–461
  OU (organizational unit) for, 459, 486
Contribute permission, SharePoint, 600–601
cost
  of NAS (Network Attached Storage), 248
  of OTP (one-time password), 353, 532

of printers, 315, 316–317
of RAID, 61
of WMS as alternative to Premium Add-on, 655
CPU cores, limits of, 11
CPU sockets, limits of, 11
CPUs (processors)
  client requirements for, 36
  Intel and AMD, compatibility between, 15
  monitoring, 712–714
  performance of, 6
  registers on, 12–13
  requirements for, 6, 7
  server requirements for, 35
  for VM (virtual machine), 101, 102–103
Create File file permission, 226
Create Folders file permission, 226, 227
critical updates, 363
CryptoCard OTP tokens, 42
Cryptographic Operators domain local group, 210
Cscript command, 327
CSV (Comma-Separated Values), storage reports in, 296
Customer Experience Improvement Program. *See* CEIP
Customer Feedback Options, 184
custom topology, 281
CVT (constant voltage transformer), 51, 52

D

data
  application data, recovering from backup, 404–406
  backing up. *See* backups
  in files and folders, recovering from backup, 401–404
  migrating to SBS 2011, 146–178
Database Engine Services, SQL Server, 667
data collector sets, 721–727
  creating from a template, 721–723
  creating from performance counters, 723–724
  creating manually, 724–725
  exporting templates for, 723
  importing templates for, 723
  log files from, 729–730
  managing data collected by, 727–730
  for monitoring performance counters, 725–726
  reports from, 730–731
  scheduling data collection for, 726–727
data execution bit. *See* DEP bit

E

G

O

W

X

About the Authors

Charlie Russel is an information technology consultant, specializing in combined Windows and UNIX networks. He is also a Microsoft Most Valuable Professional for Windows Server and Security. Together with Sharon Crawford, Charlie authored *Windows Server 2008 Administrator's Companion* and *Windows Small Business Server 2008 Administrator's Companion*. Charlie also coauthored the *Windows Essential Business Server 2008 Administrator's Companion*.

Sharon Crawford is a veteran writer of computer books. Together with Charlie Russel, Sharon authored *Windows Server 2008 Administrator's Companion* as well as the *Windows Small Business Server 2008 Administrator's Companion*.

What do you think of this book?

We want to hear from you!

To participate in a brief online survey, please visit:

microsoft.com/learning/booksurvey

Tell us how well this book meets your needs—what works effectively, and what we can do better. Your feedback will help us continually improve our books and learning resources for you.

Thank you in advance for your input!

Stay in touch!

To subscribe to the *Microsoft Press® Book Connection Newsletter*—for news on upcoming books, events, and special offers—please visit:

microsoft.com/learning/books/newsletter